The Omphalos
and the Cross

The Omphalos and the Cross

Pagans and Christians in Search of a Divine Center

by
Paul Ciholas

Mercer University Press   January 2003

ISBN 0-86554-783-1   MUP/P234

The Omphalos and the Cross.
Pagans and Christians in Search of a Divine Center.
   Copyright ©2003
   Mercer University Press USA
   All rights reserved
   Printed in the United States of America

Library of Congress Cataloging-in-Publication Data

Ciholas, Paul.
   The omphalos and the cross : pagans and Christians
in search of a divine center / by Paul Ciholas.
      p.   cm.
Includes bibliographical references (p. 479) and indexes.
   ISBN 0-86554-783-1 (pbk.)
   1. Christianity and other religions—Greek. 2. Greece—Religion.
3. Christianity and other religions—Roman. 4. Rome—Religion. 5. Church
history—Primitive and early church, ca. 30–600.   I. Title.
   BR128.G8   C49   2003
   261.2'2—dc21
                                                            2002151778
                                                               CIP

Contents

Collections of Works and Abbreviations

A major source for the literature of early Christianity is the thirty-eight-volume collection of writings from the first 800 years of the church routinely referred to as the Early Church Fathers. The collection is divided into three series: *The Ante-Nicene Fathers* and *The Nicene and Post-Nicene Fathers of the Christian Church* 1 and 2. These reference works are abbreviated as follows.

ANF *The Ante-Nicene Fathers.* Edited by Alexander Roberts, James Donaldson, et al. Photomechanical reprint in 10 volumes: Grand Rapids MI: Wm. B. Eerdmans Publishing Company.

NPNF-1 *The Nicene and Post-Nicene Fathers.* First series. Edited by Philip Schaff and Henry Wace. Photomechanical reprint (14 volumes): Grand Rapids MI: Wm. B. Eerdmans Publishing Company.

NPNF-2 *The Nicene and Post-Nicene Fathers.* Second series. Edited by Philip Schaff. Photomechanical reprint (14 volumes): Grand Rapids MI: Wm. B. Eerdmans Publishing Company.

ANF originally was published in 24 volumes by T.&T. Clark (Edinburgh, 1867–1872) as *Ante-Nicene Christian Library*. NPNF originally was published—14 volumes in each series—by the Christian Literature Company (Buffalo and New York, 1886–1889 and 1890–1900) and by Charles Scribner's Sons (New York, 1886–1900). "The Fathers," both ANF and NPNF, are readily available in the classic reprint [ANF] and original [NPNF] editions of Scribner's, the now-classic reprints by Eerdmans—cited herein—and now in the more recent photomechanical reprint by Hendrickson Publishers (Peabody MA, 1994).

Jacques Paul Migne's voluminous edition of *Patrologiae cursus completus*, comprising the *Patrologia Latina* (217 vols., 1844–1855) and the *Patrologia Graeca* (162 vols., 1857–1866) is now the best source for the original texts from which various translations were made.

Whenever possible, classical literature is quoted from the bilingual *Loeb Classical Library*, abbreviated as LCL.

LCL   *Loeb Classical Library*. Cambridge MA: Harvard University Press.

Biblical quotations are from the Revised Standard Version (1946, 1952, 1957) as it appears in the *Oxford Annotated Bible. Revised Standard Version*. New York: Oxford University Press, 1965.

Introduction

A recent archaeological trip through Greece and Israel provided the background for this study. I lingered in Delphi and Jerusalem, sites symbolic of two religious worlds that in historical times and for specific reasons claimed supremacy. Each of these sites boasts of having been a divine center with messages that shaped the religious and cultural outlook of their faithful.

In Greco-Roman times Delphi was known as the center of the world, the navel of the earth. A beautifully carved monument, a stone navel—the omphalos, graced the midpoint of Delphi's splendor to remind pilgrims of its importance. Mythological origins of the omphalos gravitated around the legend that two eagles released by Zeus from opposite ends of the world met at Delphi and marked the center of the cosmos.

For early Christians, divine purpose focused on the cross. Historical rather than legendary events were invoked as the support for the new movement. The church rose from the soil of a new faith grounded in the death and resurrection of its founder.

At its inception the church had no specific reason to concern itself with Delphic or Greco-Roman religion. But as Christianity developed into an institution that spread throughout the Roman Empire it had to define its existence as a legitimate contender to religious uniqueness and, eventually, religious dominion. The omphalos and the cross were not friendly rivals. To Tertullian's challenge, "What has Athens to do with Jerusalem?" one could substitute the question, "What has Delphi to do with Jerusalem?" or, later when Rome became a Christian center, "What has Delphi to do with Rome?" Mystery and ambiguity shroud both Jerusalem and Delphi. The church fathers grappled with these difficulties and sought to provide answers based on their notion of divine revelation. But Apollonian religion persisted long into the Christian era, and the pieces of the imponderable puzzle of human religious consciousness are numerous.

As we select the most obvious areas of influence in Delphic or Christian religion we discover that every new insight confronts us with greater perplexities leading to further quests. We rely on those who spoke, thought, and wrote down what they knew, what they felt, and what defined their search for the ultimate meaning of their devotion. We can choose to emphasize the spiritual and moral elements of the past that best mirror our feelings and discoveries, but no quest involving religious developments can be totally objective. And it should not be, for memory without intuition would lead to an amalgamation of facts deprived of meaning.

The road to Delphi winds upward through mountainous terrain. It is as if a majestic divine hand had carved it out of the southern approaches to Mount Parnassus before opening it up to the valley of the Pleistos River. We can imagine the earth splitting in a cosmic spasm to create this idyllic spot enchanted by the music of the Castalian Spring. The *Homeric Hymns to the Pythian Apollo* portray the young god as speeding swiftly toward the mountain ridge until he stopped under the snowy Parnassus to build there his glorious temple from which suppliants could receive his counsel.

The eagle-eyed view can now be frozen in time by aerial photography that accentuates the breathtaking beauty of the region. Yet the journey to Delphi is fraught with danger. A modern road makes it more accessible, but it is a hazardous road, and many have lost their lives in the ascent. The Greeks have a tradition of marking the spots along roads where people lost their lives with commemorative glass boxes. Those memorials are not lacking along the road to Delphi. We can meet the god only at a cost. Even today we wonder why so many people undertook such a perilous journey to receive an ambiguous answer to their quest.

I arrived in Delphi anxious but safe on the eve of my birthday. Little did I surmise that the greatest birthday gift one could ever be blessed with is to witness a sunrise over Delphi. The light of the morning sun enhanced the awesomeness of the excavated sites and monuments, falling upon a different world from that which had vanished with its glory. The sun has risen and set thousands of times, oblivious to the splendor and devastation of a sanctuary that has inspired countless visitors and caused the demise of the unwise. We can stand on the hills and look upon times thousands of years remote. The landscape can still stir our memory while forbidding us a true insight into the past. We can be overwhelmed by the legacy of the dead. I thought of Odysseus and his visit to the shades. He was fortunate to meet Agamemnon and Tiresias who warned him of impending perils. The world of the living becomes different, and I continue to hesitate among the stones. Is there still a voice left or a message to be deciphered? To what extent are we a part of a time that even memory cannot reconstruct? What did that distant past fashion that is so dear to us and that we try so hard to recover? Are we still included, in some archetypal way, in a message that has now been silent for so long? A sense of incompleteness overtakes the mind. The oracle has spoken in so many ways: absurd, senseless syllables and sublime wisdom. Heraclitus concluded that the Delphian Lord neither speaks nor hides but only gives signs. How many of those signs are still here to stir our quest?

At one point I decided to join an organized tour of the site. I was skeptical at the view of history through the eyes and words of guides, though some of them were excellent. That morning our guide chose to be philosophical rather than recite his lesson. He adopted a nostalgic mood centered on the alleged Heraclitean πάντα ῥεῖ. Lost indeed were many of the wonders, and no one knew exactly how they disappeared. A universal mind likes to hide from us that which would make our search easier. Heraclitus was correct again. Truth is only in the unexpected, and consequently very hard to find.

Delphi now seems empty. The great monuments and ornaments have no more permanence than the statues of Daedalus. Constantine finished the task of desecration by removing the splendid Delphic masterpieces to adorn his newly built Christian Constantinople. The little that remains here is jealously watched by vigilant guards who do not even allow you to capture it on film. What could be still stolen from such a depleted world? Is it that important to keep the place frozen in a static state, a ghost city emptied of actors and trampled only by tourists? Is it still possible to walk in the footsteps of the pilgrims of long ago and feel connected with them beyond the limits of time?

However much we now relegate Delphi to a lost era of religious intuition, the world of its dreams and oracles has not totally evaporated. There is a moving story told by the French archaeologists who excavated Delphi at the end of the nineteenth century. A woman had decided not to leave her little house on a site marked for excavation, which seriously hampered archaeological progress. One morning she announced that she would no longer oppose the project. Puzzled by this sudden change of heart, the archaeologists questioned her. She then told them of a dream she had just had in which a young boy was trapped beneath her house and crying to her, "Set me free!" She took it as a divine omen and relented. Thus was discovered the Charioteer, one of the finest bronze treasures of antiquity. Together with the original omphalos, they constitute the most prized possessions of the Delphi museum. It is as if the god watched over them to be preserved for all generations to follow.

The journey to Israel was not trouble-free, for ironically the City of Peace has had to live in the perpetual presence of war. From antiquity to this day neither peace nor unity have marked the life of Jerusalem. It was and remains an important site for several religions claiming it as the divine center of their legitimacy and permanence. But nothing is as persistent here as fear and frustration. The sun has risen and set here on many troubled souls. The events of the Old Testament were marked by religious failure and the hope of a messianic age that would resolve all conflicts. As much as Greco-Roman religion put the emphasis on the present, Judeo-Christian faith rests mostly on an eschatological future liberated from the ravages of time.

For centuries Jerusalem has pursued its own quest for transcendence, for the manifestation of its God who would make the sacred permanent. The hope for transcendence becomes a fact of life for a nation that has experienced the world as a painful place and that much too often has known the anguish of a threatened existence. Its hope resided in a continuous projection of its faith into a redemptive future. Eschatology distinguished Judeo-Christian religion from Delphic preoccupations, at least until the ancient sibyls assumed new prophetic functions.

I came to Jerusalem with the intention of verifying some research but soon found myself a pilgrim caught up in the aura of the city. Mystery, not knowledge, remains at the heart of life. Worship comes first; theological explanations later. The hope of transcendence and the experience of the sacred alone can assign some ultimate meaning to a flawed and tragic world. Now the sacred is engraved in stone, glass, and canvas, and immortalized in the souls of pilgrims who feel included in a divine eternal purpose.

Many places in and around Jerusalem convey divine presence. Geography becomes history. The hope for universality and for unity never died, even in troubled moments, and nostalgia for peace does not disappear with time. The voice of the Christian messiah has been eternalized among a people who considered him only a prophet. He did not spend much time in Jerusalem. He preferred the countryside. While in Jerusalem he spent his most important moments in the vicinity of the town, not in its center. He walked through the Garden of Gethsemane, and the place has never been the same since. From the Mount of Olives he could contemplate the holy city in all its splendor but could not avoid voicing its impending doom. It was on the Mount of Olives that he is supposed to have taught his disciples the prayer now repeated throughout the world. It is inscribed in thirty-five languages in the Pater Noster Chapel built there on a restful spot, a haven for all pilgrims.

Archaeology is directed to the rediscovery and preservation of original cultures and monuments. Yet in Israel, and especially in Jerusalem, old traditions remain more convincing than later religious developments. Christians have erected churches and monuments around sacred sites, but sometimes without preserving the simplicity and intensity of the gospel message. Crusaders, religious leaders, and political rulers wanted to reshape traditions according to their own views and not as a commitment to the sacred nature of the place. Yet the land of Israel is holy ground, the scene of many conflicts between God and his people, between divine purpose and human expectation. As a religious center Jerusalem is also the capital of memories now dispersed throughout the world. Unity becomes symbolic. There is no Delphic omphalos here as the navel of the earth. The physical as well as the spiritual center was decreed by God himself.

Jerusalem remains the scene of spiritual catharsis. One can walk from sacred place to sacred place almost endlessly, but the abundance of sanctuaries can also deprive them of their intended purpose. The material begins to dominate the spiritual. Monuments have a vernacular of their own, and we cannot always decipher their symbolic meaning. Jerusalem has suffered from an overdose of religious influences, each more concerned with its own perspectives than with an understanding of religious unity. Yet no human action or decision can alter its destiny as the cradle of three major religions.

In today's Jerusalem it is not obvious that God is one. The religious ideals of the past still dwell within the walls of old and new monuments of the city, and God often seems to remain silent in the midst of conflicts nowhere more evident than in the many attempts to grasp and hold on to traditions that have made Jerusalem a battleground for religious reinterpretations. Unity remains threatened by the coexistence of numerous factions of Christians, Jews, and Moslems in a religious world marked by distrust and unease.

For the church fathers Jerusalem and not Rome was the eternal city. Both places had to suffer periods of devastation mixed with moments of glory. But it remained the conviction of Christians that the vicissitudes of the present would not deprive Jerusalem of its eternal role.

In the first centuries of our era both pagans and Christians had to define their divine milieus more precisely, argue their importance and reason for being, and defend the centrality of their respective religious views. Two powerful symbols dominated the world of classical antiquity: the omphalos and the cross. One symbolized Apollonian religion. The other stood for the emerging force of Christianity. They clashed. They influenced each other. They became entwined. In the end the church-triumphant adopted ways that were partially indebted to a pagan heritage. The omphalos stood as a reminder of the Apollonian promise of well-being and prosperity for the Greco-Roman world. Early Christian apologists opposed that world forcefully at the beginning, less convincingly at the end. The cross, symbol of a new religion that had a slow beginning was ignored by the Romans until it became evident that it upset the religious equilibrium of the empire. Both Apollonian religion and Christianity had to find ways to reassure a threatened society of divine providence in the midst of perplexing events. Romans concluded that Christians, whom they viewed as superstitious atheists, had provoked an unacceptable political and social disequilibrium that compromised social peace and divine pleasure. Chaos could not be allowed to defeat order.

Despite persecutions and internal struggles, the cross eventually won out over the omphalos, but the coexistence of Apollonian oracular religion and the Gospel affirmation was viewed not only as the source of conflict, but also as the major reason for the calamities of the empire. It became imperative for the Roman emperors to assess the powers controlling the universe and to ensure that all obstacles to divine providence be removed. The choice of gods to whom to entrust the fate of the empire remained a burning question to resolve. It was a time of deep contradictions, of edicts superseding each other and often annihilating the purpose of preceding ones. Neither persecutions nor efforts at understanding appreciably changed well-entrenched positions. Fear often supplanted rationality in threatened circumstances. Violence aggravated catastrophic misunderstandings. Blame shifted from one camp to the other for the ills befalling the empire. Ritual religion proved insufficient, if not detrimental. In the end both Christians and pagans knew that religion stood in need of constant renewal, beyond the performance of specific rites. But it was not until the days of Cicero, and more particularly those of Plutarch that paganism became aware of the liabilities created by a lack of religious definition. Except for some recorded oracles that have been rescued from oblivion by historians, especially Herodotus, there were no pagan sacred writings and no specific Delphic doctrine. This was quite different from what Christianity had inherited from Hebrew scriptures and developed on its own. Yet there was a Delphic spirit that transcended the vulnerability of the shrine. There was an Apollonian view of life that survived the demise of paganism and inspired works of art and literature. There was in Delphic religion an essential spirit that refused to die and that shaped certain aspects of Christian religion. Thus the two distinctive cultures of paganism and Christianity were influencing each other well beyond foreseeable limits. Both made compromises, opposed each other, sometimes praised each other, reviewed their fundamental tenets, and, in the final analysis melted together, at least partially, into a new form of humanism which was to mark the subsequent development of history. For that very reason, even in a Christianized world, we should not dismiss the powerful role Apollonian religion played in the evolution of Christianity. Greek religion survived in human memory long after its decline and eventual death by infusing Christianity with its universal wisdom.

When forced into apologetic responses, the church fathers approached Greek oracles with the intent of discrediting them and proving their evil origin. The task of refutation proved more difficult than expected. Christian apologists appealed to classical literature as well as to their own scriptures to enhance their arguments. But there was no escaping the fact that Greek oracles predated the rise of Christianity by several centuries and had become a part of a global religious outlook. A revolution was shaping up, at first subdued, and then more vocal. Paganism and Christianity could no longer coexist in an empire in dire need of divine protection, yet neither could be totally excluded from a history shaping up the future of the known world. The result became a progressive and sometimes subtle "Christianization" of paganism and "paganization" of Christianity. Both were products of historical and religious traditions. It took the cosmopolitan nature of the Roman Empire to provide the stage for dramatic historical changes out of which the Christian church emerged triumphant.

Up to the time of Constantine it was with the fervor of the persecuted that Christians proclaimed the centrality of their message and faith. After Constantine it was the turn of pagans to come to the rescue of their declining religion. But all along, in tacit or more open ways and in spite of sporadic persecutions, a mutual assimilation of religious perspectives transformed both the pagan and Christian environment. In the final analysis it was as much by assimilation as by outright triumph that the post-Constantine church emerged as the prevailing world religion. Most church fathers, even if reluctantly, had to concede that they could not escape the influence of a Greco-Roman cultural background. Some went as far as to suggest that Christianity may have owed its triumph in part to Roman ways and culture.

This work shows how the religious climate of antiquity forced Christian writers to grapple with Apollonian religion and its hold over the citizens of the empire. Many church leaders tried to convince Christians that the welfare of all required that they be good citizens and that they respect Roman authority. Yet their faith compelled them to oppose what they would have liked to support. Faced with the dilemma of having to live in a world they could not accept, but without which they could not survive, early Christians had to reassess their place in civil life, their religious commitments, and their participation in a pagan-dominated cultural environment, without compromising their faith. In the end Christianity triumphed, but not without relinquishing a great deal of its original fervor to a pagan world that never totally accepted its death sentence. In a post-Constantine cultural and religious setting Christian theology was marked by a dialectical tension in which the spiritual could no longer be freed from the secular or the eternal from the temporal.

Early Christianity was a unique phenomenon with its own conceptual framework, its specific eschatology, and its special mode of argumentation often dictated by the nature of the supposed enemy they had to convert, if not conquer. It became necessary to prove that Christianity was not borrowing ready-made concepts to present its message. When Christians used Greek or Roman categories of thought it was after having adapted them to fit their purposes. Christianity kept its originality when explaining the validity of its new culture. Writings such as *The Epistle to Diognetus*, Tertullian's *Apologeticum*, Minucius Felix's *Octavius* already stressed the intellectual development of the church. Christianity was not a religion for barbarians, neither was it a negation of Roman civilization, but the logical end of Hellenism. Christians came to play the role of heirs of the Greco-Roman culture. They became the true representatives of the new world community.

Greek and Hellenistic philosophy had already postulated the existence of a divine cosmos (κόσμος) whose structure could be grasped by the principles of human reason. The Hebrews had their own notion of creation and divine providence which was refined as a consequence of the great exile to Babylonia. But their worldview was often limited to their religious and political surroundings and never reached the level of Greek intuition and science. Yet the church chose to vindicate the Hebrew legacy. The concept of piety and the worship of a monotheistic God were the defining attributes of Hebrew religion. But it was the Greeks who spoke of a universal logos that could unify all existing principles, scientific and religious. Unity, order, and harmony, however, were not yet to be, and conflicting views threatened both Christian and pagan philosophical and religious endeavors.

By maintaining that the world is the result of a creative act of the God they were proclaiming, Christians became responsible to ensure the stability of that world for as long as God would choose to let it exist. But church fathers failed to vindicate such a point of view, and Tertullian in particular attributed the well-being and permanence of the social and political order to Roman wisdom and ingenuity as much as to Christian proclamation. The debate persisted until the triumphant imperial church rendered it futile. But it also meant the death of a great deal of what the apostolic church had fought for. The transition from the apostolic church to the imperial church took place at the cost of spiritual changes which left the Christian message impoverished. Dogmatic debates too often replaced the fervor of faith.

The Roman Empire was a deeply religious world. The population felt that the gods were there to show their power in times of need, to help in marvellous ways, and to reveal inscrutable mysteries. The *Meditations* of Marcus Aurelius provide a persuasive reminder of the intensity of religious sentiment. Divine immanence was often taken for granted or fervently solicited in the performance of rituals. Many coins of the second and third centuries had engraved on them the motto, *providentia deorum*. Beyond what education, culture, and science could provide, Romans turned to their religion to cope with the routine business of life. From that point of view they were not very different from Christians. When philosophy and religion merged, the lines blurred even further. In the days of Constantine, it was with Christian fervor that Iamblichus could reassure a whole generation that their traditional religious beliefs were compatible with the principles of Platonic philosophy. In a way that was his revenge on Constantine.

Early Christians were convinced that God was placing in their hands creative forces which would ultimately transform the world around them. There was a new sense of a divine kairos. It became important to vindicate the continuity of God's purpose in spite of conflicts. Such a purpose, however, could no longer include religious practices challenging Christian beliefs. Apollo could not survive if Christ were to rule the new world.

From a Christian point of view it has become customary to label the Greco-Roman religion and Zeitgeist as paganism, a convenient designation for a segment of history not otherwise easily identifiable. Many eras received names they did not choose for themselves—Scholasticism, the Middle Ages, the Renaissance, the Enlightenment . . . —but the term Paganism extends well beyond a specific historical period, denoting more an attitude than a particular moment in history. The term *religio paganorum*, however, does not seem to have been used before 368 CE when it appeared in a law of the *Codex Theodosianus* (16.2.18) to refer to heathenism. Though no one can be sure that the term was used then for the first time, it nonetheless obtained wide currency after that.

The most logical derivation of the designation *pagan* is from the latin *paganus*: one who lives in a village, in the countryside, that is, a peasant. It came to mean the same as a heathen: one who lives on the heath, that is, away from civilization. Sometimes soldiers used the term *pagan* for civilians.

Neither the terms *christian* nor *pagan* have a clear origin. It was custom that finally gave them their meaning as convenient labels. Their usage proved more questionable when referring to cultural phenomena, especially to the literature of the epoch, often used and even admired by both sides, though perhaps for different reasons. It was to be expected that the followers of Christ would be called *Christians*. The term was used sporadically from the beginning. It appears only three times in the New Testament, twice in the Book of Acts and once in First Peter. Some of the church fathers devoted a great deal of effort to ensure the proper meaning and content of the term. By the time of Constantine the designation *Christian* was institutionalized, and its meaning debated mostly in the fight against heresies.

There will be no end to our endeavors to recreate the stage on which the early church played out its important role, and to capture the spirit that animated it. It is with a sense of awe and gratitude that I acknowledge the contributions of many scholars in this field. Time and space will not allow me to give more weight to some of their current perspectives, for I have chosen to emphasize primary sources both in patristic writings and Greco-Roman classical antiquity. I believe that through the eyes of the church fathers we can acquire a closer insight into their world. I am irresistibly drawn to the Christian giants in the early church. They embody a faith, a hope, a wisdom that the world has never known before or since. I like to listen to their voices and let myself be drafted into their struggles, their sacrifices, their inspiring wisdom, their faith in a universal God, and their resolute search for a divine center.

The Omphalos or the Cross? Or perhaps the Omphalos *and* the Cross? Seldom, if ever, have two worlds collided with such vehemence, only to realize that one could not survive without the other. Paganism was officially defeated through unrelenting legislation by Christian emperors. In many ways its spirit lives on in a universal religious consciousness that refuses to become the prerogative of a specific ideology. After Constantine, Christianity became the imperial religion and entered a new era of dogmatic definition, of institutional organization, of religious dominion. This triumph came at the cost of its apostolic fervor, at the cost of the legacy that martyrs had inscribed in the annals of the church with their own blood, at the cost of the hope that God would some day establish a kingdom that is not of this world. No one knew exactly what died and what was sublimated into different forms of religious and cultural practices. Whether on the side of paganism or Christianity there is a legacy that transcends dogmas, beliefs, rituals, and convictions, and compels us to pursue the search for a divine center.

Chapter 1

T͜he Elusive Divine Center

Nature is an infinite sphere, whereof the centre
is everywhere, the circumference nowhere.
—Pascal

From time immemorial, religious conflicts have disrupted societies and nations. Rituals commending worshipers to their divinities resulted from the conviction that the gods, though not free from trouble, could assert their rule through their undisputed authority. The credibility of the gods stood in direct proportion to their ability to subdue chaos into order. Very often the dominion of one divinity required the exclusion of others. The raising of new altars spelled doom for older ones. Religious practices were closely connected to cultural, political, and philosophical frameworks. Each system of belief evolved within a definite notion of sacredness that placed the gods beyond the vicissitudes of historical events, even as they were affected by them.

In the Greco-Roman world the multiplicity and heterogeneity of the gods created no serious disruption in religious outlook. Specific gods could solve specific problems even when in disagreement with each other. Homeric literature, for example, contains numerous instances of divine rivalries without threatening cultural unity. By contrast, the emerging Christian religion, finding its inspiration in Jewish religious history, rejected all notion of divine multiplicity and competition to proclaim the existence of one supreme God in the presence of whom all expressions of polytheism and henotheism became not only irrelevant but blasphemous.

Yet one phenomenon remained central for all religions. Their authority emanated from well-defined geographical and historical focal points from which their meaning and influence radiated to the world around them. Traditionally, mountains have been regarded as the dwelling places of the gods, as centers of the earth.[1]

In the first centuries CE two symbols, vying for the status of divine center, dominated the landscape of religious history, namely, the omphalos and the cross, the one losing progressively a great deal of its importance, the other providing the foundation for a new religion that eventually supplanted heathen practices. Both pagans and Christians found it imperative to anchor their beliefs and practices, to provide the stability necessary to ensure their place of prominence in the midst of uncertainties. But the proclaimed divine center refused to assume the place assigned to it, a fact perpetuating conflicts in the search for the finality every religion would like to claim.

The Omphalos and Apollonian Religion

Whatever meaning Greek society could attach to the mythological origins of the omphalos, it felt little inclined to refute the proposition that it defined the divine center of the world.[2] Delphi became the geographical hub of Greek religion and the repository of culture and oracular wisdom. Apollo's seat on the omphalos ensured the absolute character of his pronouncements. Plato believed that in matters of legislation the god seated on the omphalos delivered the final interpretation.[3] A detail from an amphora in the Naples Museum shows Apollo on the omphalos, holding the laurel in one hand and the lyre in the other, receiving pilgrims who had come to consult him, perhaps also including Orestes in search of purification and divine protection.[4] A fourth-century BCE coin, minted by the Amphictyonic Council, portrays Apollo enthroned on the splendidly

---

[1]Specific mountains became places of divine revelation for specific religions. See Mircea Eliade, *The Myth of the Eternal Return, or, Cosmos and History*, trans. Willard R. Trask (Princeton NJ: Princeton University Press, 1954) 12-14; Joseph Campbell, *The Masks of God: Primitive Mythology* (New York: Penguin, 1970) 148.

[2]For a history of the Omphalos myth and its position relative to the temple at Delphi see Sir James George Frazer, *Pausanias's Description of Greece*, 6 vols. (New York: Macmillan, 1913) 5:314-18.

[3]Plato, Rep 427BC.

[4]Jane Ellen Harrison, *Prolegomena to the Study of Greek Religion* (Cleveland: World Publishing Company, 1959) 319-20.

decorated omphalos. Other examples of Apollo on the omphalos are found in Greek tragedies, especially the *Ion* of Euripides. Says Hermes:

> Now to this Delphian land I come, where Phoebus
> Hath at earth's navel his prophetic seat,
> Revealing things that are and things to be.[5]

Nestled in an idyllic environment in the shadow of Mount Parnassus from which it derived a great deal of its inspiration, Delphi offered the Apollonian religion the tools it required to remold ancient religious perspectives into forceful new outlooks. The omphalos not only marked the mythical center of the earth but also served as the spiritual magnet attracting to it the numerous fragments of old religious practices to transform them into credible propositions. Delphi assumed the center from which was drawn the circle containing Greek culture, religion, and philosophy.

From a geographic site of importance, Delphi emerged into the religious hub of the Greek world, applying its wisdom to the colonization of faraway territories, infusing meaning and content into cults and religious practices in distant lands, inspiring poets, artists, and philosophers, and ensuring a modicum of political unity by divulging warning or reassuring oracles to warring factions. For a time, it secured the veneration of so many citizens of all walks of life that it was considered the most important place in the land. But the Greek mind, which had searched for an understanding of first principles in their relationship to reality, was destined to apply its critical powers to Delphic religion and expose serious flaws in organization and content. Apollo enjoyed the peak of his popularity in pre-Classical Greece. The omphalos kept a profound symbolic meaning in the Classical and Hellenistic periods, but progressively lost its appeal as the unifying element of Greek religion. Several developments robbed it of its uniqueness.

The rule of Apollo at Delphi followed several important events that left him scarred, though a strong master of his destiny. His prominence came at the expense of a former earth religion dominated by Ge and Themis, from whom he took over the omphalos and its symbolic meaning. He thus appeared as a second generation god who had to dispose of rival divinities. The ever present Python, original master of the

---

[5]5-7, trans. Arthur S. Way.

oracle, had to be destroyed by the hand of Apollo, who then trudged the land in search of purification until, according to Pausanias, it was granted to him by Karmanor.[6] The new Delphic God had finally become the master of its shrine. However, what, according to Pausanias,[7] stood as a white stone at the center of the earth evolved into a bone of contention. Erwin Rohde and Jane Harrison, contend that the omphalos was originally the stone of a tomb. Varro refers to a tradition according to which the omphalos was the tomb of the sacred serpent Python.[8] One could see in this allusion a double meaning: either that Apollo was fated to live in the perpetual presence of his former enemy, thus never becoming totally free from his past, or that the rule of Apollo on top of the omphalos prevented for ever the reappearance of Python on the religious scene. Throne of a new god of wisdom and knowledge, or monument to the now buried Python, guardian of former Earth's oracles, the omphalos was destined to lose its religious focus and mediate symbolic meaning rather than convincing proof of Apollo's undisputed rule at Delphi.

The presence of Dionysus at the shrine of Apollo proved even more disturbing. Dionysian religion was viewed in Delphic tradition as a congenial supplement to Apollonian elusiveness. Dionysus exercised full mastery at Delphi during the long absences of Apollo among the Hyperboreans. The navel of the earth no longer reflected religious unity. On many occasions Dionysus wandered out of Delphi bringing with him his own omphalos. At Eleusis we find him seated on it with his thyrsus in the company of Demeter and Kore.[9] Other religious sites, such as Claros, had their own omphalos. This suggested that the Greek religious center could be moved around to satisfy worshipers of divinities other than Apollo, or that Apollo himself could have different centers, modelled on the Delphic.

According to ancient traditions and modern speculations Dionysus was also buried under the omphalos. Statements to that effect from Philochoros led to the belief that the omphalos was the tomb of the dismembered Dionysus. Such a tradition has persisted in many fashions

---

[6]Pausanias, DescrGr 2.7.7; 30.3; 10.7.2.
[7]Ibid., 10.16.2.
[8]Varro, LingLat 7.17.
[9]Harrison, *Prolegomena*, 556-57.

throughout the centuries,[10] including in Tatian's assertion that "Omphalos is the burial place of Dionysus."[11] Erwin Rohde reluctantly concedes that some modern writers have put forth credible reasons to assume that Dionysus was buried under the omphalos.[12] But he strongly objects to the statement of Tatian, whom he considers an untrustworthy witness and a "careless pamphleteer."[13] He prefers to put the emphasis on the statement of Varro in whose writings we find a strong denial of the common belief that Delphi was the center of the earth, the omphalos being nothing more than one of the treasure houses performing the function of a tomb.[14]

Long before Varro, the assumption that the omphalos marked the center of the earth was challenged by Epimenides who, paradoxically, went to the Delphic oracle to test his doubts about it. He received an ambiguous answer, as was the case with most oracles, and, from the material he thought was contained in the Pythian declaration, composed two verses which remained both famous and unsettling for Delphic religion:

> There was no Omphalos, either in the centre of the earth or of the sea.
> If any there be, it is visible to the gods, not visible to mortals.[15]

The Fragments of Epimenides, including the one in the New Testament,[16] are often viewed with suspicion. According to Diels they were

---

[10]Ibid., 557.

[11]Tatian, OratGr 8 (ANF II) 68 (ὁ δὲ ὀμφαλός τάφος τοῦ Διονύσου).

[12]Erwin Rohde, *Psyche: The Cult of Souls and Belief in Immortality among the Greeks*, 2 vols., trans. W. B. Hillis (New York: Haper & Row, 1966) 1:iii n.32. Rohde contends that Dionysus was buried in the Adyton and cites Pausanias, DescrGr 10.24.5 as his support. But no such proof appears there or anywhere else in Pausanias. It is rather to Philochoros that we owe a mention that the tomb of Dionysus was beside the Golden Apollo, and thus it could be inferred that this was in the Adyton.

[13]Rohde, *Psyche*, 1:iii, 2 and n. 32.

[14]Varro, LingLat 7.17.

[15]Kathleen Freeman, *Ancilla to the Pre-Socratic Philosophers* (Cambridge MA: Harvard University Press, 1948) 10. The saying is also in Plutarch, DefOrac 409E (LCL. Mor V) 351. "Now do we know that there is no mid-centre of earth or of ocean; yet if there be, it is known to the gods, but is hidden from mortals." The Greek text reads: Οὔτε γὰρ ἦν γαίης μέσος ὀμφαλὸς οὐδὲ θαλάσσης· εἰ δέ τις ἔστι, θεοῖς δῆλος θνητοῖσι δ' ἄφαντος.

[16]Titus 1:12: "Cretans are always liars, evil beasts, lazy gluttons."

composed by other writers. But they were regarded by many Greeks as authoritative and intriguing. Plutarch was sufficiently disturbed by Epimenides' conclusions on the omphalos to compose a long refutation of them.[17]

The reputation of Epimenides as a divinely inspired prophet placed him in a strange relationship to Delphic religion. Due to Apollo's background, rites of purification assumed a prominent place in Delphic religion, as attested by the importance of the Castalian Spring rituals. But it was Epimenides who, after withdrawing to a sacred cave for fifty-seven years in search of visionary wisdom, was endowed with powers of purification as exemplified in the cleansing of Athens after a devastating plague reported in Diogenes Laertius and Plutarch.[18] On the advice of the Pythian priestess he purified the city by releasing black and white sheep, from the Areopagus and by building altars to unknown gods wherever the sheep collapsed. The tradition survived well into New Testament times.[19]

Plutarch suggested that the list of the seven sages established at Delphi was modified to include Epimenides instead of Periander. He bestowed on him the title of new Cures (Κούρητα νέον or Cretan priest of Zeus): "He was reputed to be a man beloved of the gods, and endowed with a mystical and heavenly sent wisdom in religious matters."[20] As a priest of Apollo, Plutarch must have wondered at the irony of an oracular wisdom that could establish the omphalos as the center of the earth, as well as a refutation of it by Epimenides, a prophet inspired by the same Delphic wisdom.

Hegel proposed a different interpretation of the meaning of the omphalos. The oracular end of Delphic religion was achieved through the very voice of the god—the ὀμφή, whence the name of the Delphic oracle was derived. According to Hegel this was "certainly more correct than that which would find in it the other meaning of the word, namely, the navel of the earth."[21] The use of ὀμφή in early Greek poetic literature could be understood as God's oracle itself. In Homeric epics ὀμφή

---

[17]Plutarch, DefOrac 409E-410B.

[18]Diogenes Laertius, Lives: Epim 2.109-10; Plutarch, Lives: Solon 12.

[19]Acts 17:23.

[20]Plutarch, Lives: Solon 12.4 (LCL I) 433; Plato, Laws 642D.

[21]Georg Wilhelm Friedrich Hegel, *On Tragedy*, ed. Anne Paolucci and Henry Paolucci (New York: Harper & Row, 1962) 336.

became the voice of God, the divine revelation amid human events.[22] In Theognis's *Elegies* (805–806) Kurnos received an oracle (ὀμφήν) from the Pythian priestess at Delphi. There is, however, no indication that any of the ancient authors have derived the name of omphalos from the Greek word ὄμφη. The myth of the omphalos, even after it lost its power of inspiration, remained indebted to the traditions that made it the navel of the earth, the center of oracular wisdom.

The Christian Idea of a Divine Center and the Cross

The Judeo-Christian tenet of divine election did not evolve into a coherent belief in a religious center. The promised land of Palestine was not the scene of some of the most important aspects of the revelation of God to His people. The patriarchs traced their ancestry to Mesopotamia. Hebrew monotheism developed in the context of Egyptian influences under Moses. The law was delivered at Mount Sinai, and the major theological outlooks of Hebrew religion found their support in the wilderness experience. The temple alone served as *the* focal point of Hebrew religion. Under those circumstances Hebrew religion lacked a sense of coherence. Until the great exile to Babylonia in the sixth century BCE the Hebrew nation, or what was left of it by then, chose to remain within the confines of a tribal understanding of its political and religious life.

Hebrew religion, however, could not establish its credibility without some conviction of its centrality in the scheme of cosmic events. Almost naturally the concept of "the land" acquired a specific status on the basis of divine choice. Though sporadically, the Old Testament refers to the elect people as dwelling at the center of the earth, in the divinely decreed "Tabbur" (טבור "highest part"; "center") which the Septuagint translates as the *omphalos* (ὀμφαλός) of the earth. Judges 9:37 mentions men coming down from the center of the land: ἀπὸ τοῦ ἐχόμενα ὀμφαλοῦ τῆς γῆς. Ezekiel 38:12 refers to the people as dwelling, literally, on top of the center of the world: ἐπὶ τὸν ὀμφαλὸν τῆς γῆς. Though the Hebrew prophets never thought of a mythic center of the world, and though some of them refuted the prominence of the temple, they nonetheless regarded Jerusalem as the place of divine revelation.

---

[22]Homer, Il 20.129; Od 3.215; 16.96.

From Hebrew religion and later Judaism, Christianity inherited a strong sense of continuity. For a time at least, Jerusalem played the role of a divinely appointed center. But its threatened position amid tragic events forced the religious community to regard it more and more as the heavenly ideal city possessing Platonic archetypes. The center would become even more operative in an eschatological future removed from the liabilities of temporality. The Christian community was urged to consider Jerusalem as the divine mother of all believers.[23] The heavenly Jerusalem stood at the center of history and will reappear on earth at the end of time to become the center of a redeemed creation.[24] In the meantime, and on a more practical level, the law was often regarded as the religious center of Judaism.

For Christians, the cross stood at the center of all events. The early Church did not concern itself with identifying the exact location of Golgotha, nor with establishing any kind of pilgrimage to it. It did not become a Delphi with an omphalos. Its symbolic meaning was derived from questionable traditions that the skull of Adam was buried there[25] and that it was the meeting place of all beginnings and ends within divine creation. At points, the fact that Christ shared the fate of criminals in the Roman empire cast serious doubt on the symbolic meaning of the cross. Most New Testament canonical writings portray the cross as the sine qua non condition of redemption.[26] Universal reconciliation could be achieved only through the power of the cross that alone brings to an end all the misguided forces astray in a world of ignorance.[27] In the New Testament truth became related to one's understanding of the meaning of the cross,

---

[23]Galatians 4:26.

[24]Hebrews 12:22; Revelation 3:12; 21:2; 21:10.

[25]According to an ancient pre-Christian tradition, first mentioned by Origen, the skull of Adam was supposed to be buried there: "I have received a tradition to the effect that the body of Adam, the first man, was buried upon the spot where Christ was crucified." Quoted in "Golgotha," *The International Standard Bible Encyclopaedia* 2:1275. Athanasius, Basil, and John Chrysostom also referred to such a tradition. Jerome suggested the name Golgotha arose from the fact that it was a place of common executions with unburied skulls lying around, though this would have violated Jewish ritual customs in Jerusalem.

[26]Matthew 16:24.

[27]Ephesians 2:6; Colossians 1:20; 1 Corinthians 2:8.

not according to prevalent modes of investigation, but through faith, a proposition which created as much grief as comfort to those left with the task of interpretation. Doubt must disappear.[28] The Christian community must accept three carefully designed propositions, namely, (1) that the event of the cross established a definite distinction between those who belong to the redeemed and those who, knowingly or unknowingly, constitute the camp of the enemies of God;[29] (2) that there could be no rational explanation of the cross which will remain a stumbling block, a cause of weakness and shame even Christ had to overcome and accept;[30] and (3) that, because of its fundamental absurdity outside of the realm of faith, the cross will remain the cause of persecutions.[31]

The early church fathers seldom presented a well-developed perspective on the meaning of the cross. Their apologetic activity revolved around four lines of debate, namely, that the event of the cross could not be understood by the heathen, that it did not need to be a cause of shame for Christians, that it reinforced the notion of God's universal rule, and that Romans were more guilty of worshiping crosses than Christians.

Caught in the grips of accusations of superstition, Christian writers focused their polemical responses to fit the charges. Justin exposed the spiritual inadequacy of pagans to grasp the symbolism of the cross. It surpassed their ability to understand it.[32] Minucius Felix rebuked those who accused Christians of worshiping a criminal and his cross, showing how far from the truth they had wandered in their comparison of Christ to lower individuals regarded as gods in other religions, especially in Egypt.[33] Many church fathers attempted to convince hesitant and wavering believers that though the crucifixion may appear as foolishness to many, it nonetheless remained the imperative condition of redemption.[34]

---

[28]First Corinthians 2:2.

[29]Galatians 2:20; 5:24; 6:14; 1 Corinthians 2:2; Philippians 3:18.

[30]Galatians 5:11. The theme is often pursued in early Christian martyrs. See for instance Ignatius, IgnEph 18; Hebrews 12:2; 2 Corinthians 13:4.

[31]Galatians 6:12.

[32]Justin Martyr, 1 Apol 55.

[33]Minucius Felix, Oct 29.

[34]Commodianus, Instr 36; Barn 11-12; Cyril, CatLect 13.3; Lactantius, Epit 51; DivInst 4.26 (ANF VII) 129. "Therefore in His suffering He stretched forth His hands and measured out the world, that even then He might show that a

Early Christians lacked the argumentative power to convince the more sophisticated pagan intellectuals that there was no contradiction between the event of the cross and the proclamation of redemption, a concept foreign to Greco-Roman culture. The realm of faith clashed with that of reason. Though one could adduce mutual absurdity for both pagan and Christian practices, Roman religion could claim a longer history, a greater level of acceptability, and the positive sanction of ruling authorities. "Being ashamed of the cross" became a proposition to be refuted for the sake of new converts unable to find logical explanations for their faith. The progress of Christianity depended on a kerygma that found no support in the prevalent religious and philosophical definitions. Thus we find in Christian writings exhortations directed at believers who betrayed their uneasiness in proclaiming the event of the cross or even in being ashamed of it.[35] After initial attempts at joining the new religion, many Christians reverted back to their pagan religious practices.

For Christians the cross defined God's universal rule. Though it represented a distinctive event at a specific time, it spanned all of religious history, including that of the Old Testament. The church fathers found it imperative to link Christianity with Hebrew and Jewish religion and to show that the cross was foretold in the Old Testament. Justin entered into a long dialogue with Trypho, who failed to be convinced by such an argument and pointed out that the crucifixion represented a curse according to Mosaic law and could not inaugurate the realm of salvation.[36]

Athanasius refuted the heathen scoffing at the cross by demonstrating how they failed to perceive that its power had filled the world and that through it God's knowledge was made manifest to all creation.[37] Gregory of Nyssa objected to the charge that Christians were ashamed of a crucified Lord and affirmed the role of the cross in establishing the final unity of all things. He refuted Eunomius's contention that the suffering on the cross brought a divergence in divine essence which would have

---

great multitude, collected together out of all languages and tribes, from the rising of the sun even to his setting, was about to come under His wings, and to receive on their foreheads that great and lofty sign [of the cross]."

[35]Cyril, CatLect 4.14; 13.3; Gregory of Nyssa, CEun 5.3.

[36]Justin Martyr, Trypho 86; 89 et passim.

[37]Athanasius, CGent 1.1.

meant a status of inferiority for Christ.[38] In Lactantius the power of the cross affected the whole world, including the demons of other religions, among them Apollo.[39] Socrates Scholasticus reported that Julian's orders to rebuild the Jewish temple were viewed by the church as being in violation of a prophecy of Christ. The project was abandoned when portents struck terror into the Jews, and crosses appeared on their garments, which they tried to rub and wash out in vain.[40]

The most elaborate argument of the church fathers against the charge that Christians worshiped the cross of a criminal consisted in exposing the fact that crosses represented a greater portion of Roman superstition than Christian worship. Tertullian and Minucius Felix denied that Christians ever worshiped the cross. Rather, it appeared on all Roman banners, on many trophies, and on numerous other objects of Roman religious devotion.[41] Denunciations of the reverence of crosses by Romans were fequent.[42]

The church fathers offered several explanations of this phenomenon. Justin contended that unwittingly the Romans have shown the power of the cross on their vexilla and what they symbolized. In that way they made the Christian symbol of the cross an expression of divine presence. For that reason it would be absurd for the Romans to persecute Christians.[43] Minucius Felix extended the argument to show that the sign of the cross had acquired a universal meaning and was sustained by natural reason either on the side of Roman practice or Christian worship.[44] Methodius offered a more daring, though more questionable explanation. The Christian cross became the weapon used in the fight against spirits, death. "Hence it is that our kings, perceiving that the figure of the cross is used for the dissipating of every evil, have made *vexillas* (*sic*), as they are called in the Latin language."[45]

---

[38]Gregory of Nyssa, CEun 5.3.

[39]Lactantius, DivInst 4.27.

[40]Socrates Scholasticus, HE 3.20.

[41]Tertullian, Apol 16; AdNat 1.12; Minucius Felix, Oct 29.

[42]Justin Martyr, 1 Apol 55; Jerome, Letter 107.2.

[43]Justin Martyr, 1 Apol 55.

[44]Minucius Felix, Oct 29.

[45]Methodius, Fragm (ANF VI) 399.

The vexillum, the official standard of the Roman army, because of its cruciform shape, lent itself to the analogy with the Christian cross. It may seem ironic that, after the conversion of Constantine, it was christianized to include the sign of the cross and the Chi-Rho to become the labarum carried to battle by pagans and Christians alike. The labarum remained at the center of numerous ecclesiastical, political, and military activities for many years.

The dream of Constantine during which the sign of the cross appeared to him and which determined his victory at the Milvian Bridge is well documented in Christian writings of the period.[46] No detail was spared in describing how the labarum came into existence and how, in the span of a few months in 312 and 313 the world turned upside down while the cross had entered the consciousness of much of the Roman empire.

It was, however, Queen Mother Helena who brought that segment of history to its conclusion by setting out to search for the real cross in Jerusalem. Historians of the time report that, having been led to identify the place of the crucifixion, she found there a mound with a temple to Venus on top of it. She ordered the statue of Venus destroyed and, under the rubbish, found the three crosses and the inscriptions of Pilate. After cleaning the place, she built there a magnificent church she called *New Jerusalem*. A special ritual helped identify the actual cross on which Christ was nailed, avoiding thus the danger of attributing to Christ the cross of one of the robbers.[47]

The sign of the cross influenced both pagans and Christians. Socrates reported that when the temple of Serapis was destroyed in Alexandria the hieroglyphics discovered there contained many signs in the form of the cross. Both pagans and Christians read into that discovery a special religious meaning.[48] A few decades later, Cyril could proclaim that "the whole world has since been filled with pieces of the wood of the cross."[49] That which had started as an object of shame now symbolized the glory

---

[46]Lactantius, DeMort 44; Socrates, HE 1.2; Sozomen, HE 1.3-4; Eusebius, VConst 1.30-31.

[47]Socrates, HE 1.17; Theodoret, HE 1.17; Sulpitius Severus, HistSacra 2.34; Sozomen, HE 2.1.

[48]Socrates, HE 5.17.

[49]Cyril, CatLect 4.10 (NPNF-2 VII) 21.

of the Christianized world. The church had finally accepted the fact that it was a Roman mode of execution (the crucifixion) that determined its major symbol (the cross).

The Omphalos and the Cross

The omphalos became the symbol of glory for Delphi. Through the oracle of Apollo, it radiated knowledge, wisdom, and virtue to generations of Greek citizens. But its influence faded. In the Classical period it progressively became an object of memory. Still its meaning persisted, no longer as the objective center of worship and inspiration, but in the manifold manifestations of Apollonian religion throughout Greece, Rome, and beyond. The symbol of the omphalos continued to mold the souls and minds of those in search of a central place in a threatened cosmos.

The cross marked a new beginning. But it took centuries for the church to vindicate its meaning to a world that considered it more of a curse than a reason for veneration. Its power resided in a message that greatly differed from Apollonian oracles. Both the omphalos and the cross were destined to move from a physical reality to the realm of religious intuition, reshaping the beliefs and practices of their followers. In both cases the center remained elusive, for it shifted with geographical, historical, and religious necessities.

At one point in particular the omphalos and the cross symbolized two different centers. The omphalos translated to the Greeks a cultural context fed by oracular knowledge and sagacity. Apollo remained the god of wisdom, influencing many Greek cultural and philosophical developments. In early Christianity, wisdom became the enemy of divine revelation, at least for Paul according to whom it would empty the cross of its meaning. The Gospel message could not be indebted to Greek wisdom which stood in an antagonistic relationship to faith.[50] But neither wisdom nor faith could exclude each other totally, and the long rivalry proved costly to both.

The omphalos, symbol of birth, gave rise to a religion at first vibrant, with a prophetic voice worthy of the Parnassus, with a Pythian wisdom ennobling the glory of a lively Delphi, and with a new god stirring the religious, poetic, and intellectual imagination of a nation at the apex of

---

[50]First Corinthians 1:17-18; 22-23.

its cultural activity. Yet its splendor was destined to fade with the fluctuations of a Delphic religion crossing from glory to obsolescence, to short-lived revival, and finally to death. The cross, symbol of death, appeared at first as a somber reminder of the inexorable destiny of men and women under the eternal judgment and decree of a God of justice. But it also proclaimed the way from death to rebirth with an appeal to a life that transcended the burdens of materiality and time. Faith rather than rational explanations defined the divine center. Neither the omphalos nor the cross totally obliterated the other in symbolic meaning, but mapped out, for pagans and Christians alike, the way toward a human intuition of the divine.

Chapter 2

The Legacy of Apollo

Give me my lyre and my curved bow;
I will declare to men the inflexible will of Zeus.
    —Apollo, *Homeric Hymns*

I am the eye with which the Universe
Beholds itself and knows itself divine.
    —Shelley, *Hymn of Apollo*

Apollonian oracular pronouncements dominated the religious scene of the Roman Empire and sometimes challenged the Christian message. For that reason Apollo was singled out as the target of patristic refutation. But apologetic writings of the period reflected the necessity to keep Christianity free of threatening tenets and practices more than well-reasoned argumentation. The intensity of the debate proved the difficulty of the task at hand. The archer god of the bow had to be opposed by forceful arrows capable of annihilating his influence. But the god of the lyre, who had enchanted generations of worshipers, proved impervious to theological argumentation. In the end the death of his religion came not through the persuasive wisdom of his foes, but through political decisions and decrees.

Apollonian Theogony

We possess an abundance of sources and commentaries on the relative position of Apollo in Greco-Roman history. But the religious landscape of that part of the ancient world lacks dogmatic or scriptural definition. Vast areas of controversy have persisted in the analysis of the role of the gods. The rise of Apollo to prominence and veneration was marked by events that remained the cause of serious disagreements among writers of the period.

Early church fathers accepted the thesis of Euhemerus (fourth century BC Greek mythographer) on the deification of heroes and on the birth of gods. Though the deification of heroes predated Euhemerism, Christian apologists chose it as one of the most powerful weapons in their arsenal against paganism. Many apologists were acquainted with Euhemerus's Ἱερὰ Ἀναγραφή (*Sacred History*), and considered it worthy of trust. Direct references to Euhemerus appeared in Lactantius. But while conceding some correctness to the views of Euhemeric poets, he also charged them with being more concerned with the beauty of their poetry than with truth.[1] When, for the sake of puzzled Christians, he undertook to explain historical and mythological traditions dealing with the birth of gods and religions, he invoked Euhemerus as the voice of wisdom enlightening a process of deification before poets pictured it in seductive terms.[2]

Church fathers discredited heathenism by exposing the ridiculous nature of its divinities, thereby sapping the intellectual, moral, and spiritual tenor of those worshiping them. Athanasius, disregarding the slim evidence for his suggestion, contended that all Greek gods and goddesses received their titles by a decree of Theseus before they could be venerated as legitimate divinities. This human source of religious sanction ensured inconsistency and madness which were shared even by philosophers as wise as Plato.[3]

Unlike the heroes of Greek tragedy who succumbed to one fatal flaw, Apollo's history revealed so many instances of hamartia that it should have proven deadly to his divinity. Commodianus drew up a list—from the birth of Apollo at Delos, to his intervention in the Trojan war as a subject to King Laomedon, to his misguided passion for Cassandra and Daphne, to his feeding the cattle of Admetus, to his unwitting killing of his friend Hyacinthus—which should suffice to prove that his worshipers were enticed into admiration for reasons alien to the essence of a divinity.[4] But the true defenders of Apollo placed him above temporary flaws. They endowed him with essential divine qualities which, in turn, gave form and content to human aspirations.

Apollo vindicated the principle that old religions must be revitalized by the emergence of young new gods, even when they disrupt sacred traditions. The beginnings of Apollonian religion remained a mystery.

---

[1]Lactantius, DivInst 1.11, 13; Epit 13.
[2]Lactantius, DivInst 1.13.
[3]Athanasius, CGent 10.
[4]Commodianus, Instr 11.

Athenagoras, pursuing a Euhemeristic argument, chose as his source the writings of Herodotus who, long before the time of Euhemerus, rejected the idea of the deification of gods. Herodotus invoked traditions which traced the origin of the gods to Egypt, making Apollo either the son of Osiris or the offspring of Isis and Dionysus.[5] Centuries later Diodorus Siculus perpetuated the legends of the beginnings of Apollo in Egypt where he received the laurel and where, under the instruction of his mother Isis, he perfected the art of medicine and divination. He left Egypt for Greece with the reputation that he could protect the human race from disaster through his oracles and healings.[6]

But it was Apollo's humble origin on the desolate island of Delos that captured the imagination of peoples who claimed him as their possession. Whether he exhibited purely Greek characteristics, or whether he came from Egypt, from Asia, from Crete, from Thessalia, or from any other place mattered very little, for all the attributes relating to his divinity found their integration in a Delphic religion which annihilated all the differences through the power of a prophetic Pythic voice.

The maze of roads on the map of Apollonian theogony leaves the traveler bewildered. Amid intrigues of love, jealousy, vengeance, and murder, one searches for the most plausible developments that could bring the god of light out of his dark mysteries and explain his victory as the undisputed Delphic oracular voice. As in the case of many heroes, prophets, and gods, the events surrounding his birth are shrouded in mystery. Clement of Alexandria mentioned a tradition according to which the first Apollo was the offspring of Hephaestus and Athena, a strange suggestion which would deprive the goddess of wisdom of her essential quality of virginity.[7] The most commonly accepted legends refer to Leto as the mother of Apollo and Artemis. Pursued by the furies of Python, Leto was refused hospitality in every land and on every shore until she found refuge on the island of Delos where she gave birth to her twins.[8]

---

[5]Athenagoras, Leg 28; Herodotus, Hist 2.50.

[6]Diodorus Siculus, Lib 1.25.7.

[7]Clement of Alexandria, Protr 2.

[8]There is of course no consensus on the birth of Apollo on Delos. According to Tacitus, Ann 3.61, the Ephesians revindicated that honor claiming that Apollo was not born on Delos but in the Ortygian grove at Ephesus. But the sacred nature of Delos is emphasized in antiquity. Thucydides, PelWar 3.104, reports

Before finding his way to Delphi, Apollo spent a long time among the Hyperboreans, on the mythical land of continuous sun and light, beyond the north wind, a mysterious region Sophocles placed at the end of the world, at the edge of night, stretching in all directions as the delightful garden of Phoebus.[9] The land of the Hyperboreans was free from troubles and sufferings afflicting the human race and kept Apollo renewed in his divine attributes during his annual visits there. He alone knew the way. The road leading to it could never be discovered by anyone else, either by land or sea.[10]

Even more mystifying were the various lists enumerating different Apollos, keeping the mystery of Apollo's divine essence beyond logical explanations. In his catalogue of divinities Cicero identified four Apollos, the first one born from Hephaestus and the guardian of Athens (avoiding a direct reference to the virgin Athena), the second one a Cretan Apollo, son of Corybas, the third one the son of Zeus and Leto who ruled at Delphi after his sojourn among the Hyperboreans, and a fourth one who settled down in Arcadia to become the lawgiver of its people.[11] The church fathers knew this list of Cicero. Arnobius mentioned the four Apollos without naming them.[12] Clement of Alexandria reproduced the list of Cicero, which he attributed to Aristotle, and extended it to contain two more Apollos, exclaiming, "How many Apollos are there?"[13]

Cicero established his lists of divinities to refute the theory that the gods existed only in thought, and not in reality. Clement turned the

---

specific rites of purification of the island on account of an oracle which he did not identify: "[T]he whole island was purified in the following way. All the tombs of those who had died in Delos were dug up, and it was proclaimed that in future no deaths or births were to be allowed in the island; those who were about to die or to give birth were to be carried across to Rhenea, which is so close to Delos that when Polycrates, the tyrant of Samos, and ruler over so many other islands, in the period of his naval supremacy, conquered Rhenea, he dedicated it to the Delian Apollo by binding it to Delos with a chain." See also 1.8.

[9]Marie Delcourt, *L'Oracle à Delphes* (Paris: Payot) 157.

[10]Pindar, TenthPythOde 29-30.

[11]Cicero, NatDeo 3.57.

[12]Arnobius, AdvGent 4.15.

[13]Clement of Alexandria, Protr 2 (ANF II) 179. See also Arnobius, AdvGent 4.17.

argument around to demonstrate that Greek gods were afflicted by human flaws, placing them lower than noble citizens. Eusebius used still another list based on traditions found in Diodorus which made Apollo share his divinity with four other gods: Osiris, Isis, Typhon, and Aphrodite.[14] The Egyptian genealogy of the gods was again evident. The confusion of Apollos resulted most likely from local traditions that had different stories attached to them.

Apollonian Apotheosis

Apollo's mastery of the Delphic oracle was achieved through the annihilation of former divinities, either by demonstrating their obsolescence or by destroying them. If Greek divinities were supposed to bring order out of chaos, they had to start the process within the council of the gods. By the time Apollo appeared at Delphi, Ge had already relinquished the oracle to her daughter Themis who shared the privilege with her sister Phoebe who, in turn, applied her name to the new young God, Phoebus. In Aeschylus the transition evolved smoothly. Apollo, now named Phoebus, became the fourth successor to the throne after the rule of Ge, Themis, and Phoebe. Zeus endowed the new god with intelligence and wisdom after bestowing on him the name of Loxias.[15]

Delphi appeared at first as a sanctuary with long-standing religious traditions and not obviously in need of the wisdom of Apollo. The legends preserved in the *Homeric Hymns to Apollo* portray him leaving Delos and wandering through many lands in search for the ideal location to establish his oracular temple. Having gone through Thessaly and Boeotia, he chose a grove in a place called Telphusa, inhabited by a nymph of the same name. After naively sharing his ambitions with Telphusa, Apollo achieved nothing but her anger at the thought of competition. Cunningly she described to him all the liabilities his temple would confront in her place and advised him to proceed to Delphi, convinced that Python there would destroy the new young god. The deceit proved convincing, and Apollo journeyed to Delphi where he entrusted the building of his temple to Trophonius and Agamedes.

---

[14]Eusebius, PraepEv 45d.
[15]Aeschylus, Eum 1-19.

The scheme of Telphusa rested on the belief that the Earth divinities of Delphi, guarded by the cruel Python, would reject Apollo and free the land of his unwelcomed confrontations. We find hints in that direction. Porphyry related that when Pythagoras came to Delphi, he engraved on the tomb of Apollo an elegy claiming that Apollo was the son of Silenus, that he was killed by Python, and that he was buried under the tripod.[16] There is hardly any way to reconcile this view of the fate of Apollo with the almost unanimous belief that he destroyed Python.

The fight between Apollo and Python at Delphi became so central to Pythian religion that the rest of the history of the oracular shrine depended on it. In the *Homeric Hymns to Apollo* Python is depicted as a cruel monster "wont to do great mischief to men upon earth."[17] The gory last moments of Python contrasted with the supernatural power of Apollo who boasted: "Now rot here upon the soil that feeds man. You at least shall live no more to be a fell bane to men who eat the fruit of the all-nourishing earth."[18]

Little insight is gained into the nature of the oracle, if it existed at all, when Python was protecting the tripod. Joseph Fontenrose has attempted to retrace the history of Delphi, as it may have been before the Greek legends were formulated. The myths surrounding the Delphic shrine may have had their source in the Canaanite religions of Baal and Mot, which then gave rise to the oldest Perseus myth. In the primordial manifestations of the Delphic combat myths, the antagonists were probably different

---

[16]Porphyre, *Vie de Pythagore* (Paris: Les Belles Lettres, 1982) 43. According to Minucius Felix, Oct 21.1, Euhemerus, in his listing of birthdays, countries, and places of sepulture of the gods, included the Delphian Apollo.

[17]Hesiod, HomHym 303 (LCL) 345. Other and older legends refer to several dragons as enemies of Apollo. According to some, Apollo first had a combat with a dragoness known as Delphyne, whence the name of Delphi was derived. The suggestion has also been made that at some point Python was confused with Typhon, the enemy of Zeus, and thus may have become a male dragon. But the most often accepted legends concur in supporting the traditional view focusing on the struggle between the she-dragon Python and Apollo. See especially C. Kerényi, *The Gods of the Greeks* (New York: Thames and Hudson, 1988) 135-39 and Joseph Fontenrose, *Python* (Berkeley: University of California Press, 1959) 13-22.

[18]Hesiod, HomHym 363-66 (LCL), 351.

from Apollo and Python, who were later renamed to fit the Greek legends. In that historical perspective Zeus was the counterpart of El.[19] The *Homeric Hymns to Apollo* throw no light on that past. They focused on establishing the mastery of Apollo at Delphi. This could be achieved only through a correct understanding of why the land of Pytho remembered those events and why the new god was called Pythian and the voice of his oracles came from the Pythia. As a final act of religious duty, Apollo gathered the bones of Python into a caldron, deposited them in his temple, and instituted funeral games in her memory, known as Pythian games.[20] Having secured his victory at Delphi, Apollo returned to Telphusa to punish her for her deceit by choking her streams with rocks. He then built an altar where men could pray to the new Telphusian Apollo.[21]

Plutarch deplored the emphasis placed on the stories of the struggle between Apollo and Python for, in his view, they threatened the sacred character of the most venerated sanctuary of Greece. The myth of Python had to be preserved as the original archetype of chaos which had to be subdued before divine rule could be established in the world. Plutarch did not question the wisdom of the ancients who recorded the evil power of Python and her ability to make desolate and unapproachable the oracle at Delphi. But he also made it clear that "it was the desolation that attracted the creature rather than that the creature caused the desolation."[22] As for the struggle between Apollo and Python, his reaction bordered on anger when he reflected on the misconceptions that had penetrated so deeply into religious perceptions that they affected all levels of philosophical and artistic representations:

---

[19]Fontenrose, *Python*, 139. One is reminded here of the biblical Leviathan, the symbol of chaos opposing divine order, and the need for God to keep him under control so that his creation would not fall back into chaos. Job 41:1; Psalms 74:14; 104:26; Isaiah 27:1. In the Perseus myth, Perseus was able, with the help of Pluto, Hermes, and Athena, to defeat the intentions of the Medusa and to cut off her head. He then saved Andromeda whom he found chained to a rock as the result of divine punishment.

[20]Hyginus, Myths 140.

[21]Fontenrose, *Python*. 366.

[22]Plutarch, DefOrac 414B (LCL. Mor V) 373.

But the greatest error in regard to the truth is that of the theologians of Delphi who think that the god once had a battle here with a serpent for the possession of the oracle, and they permit poets and prose writers to tell of this in their competitions in the theatres, whereby they bear specific testimony against the most sacred of the rites that they perform.[23]

The rule of Apollo at Delphi could not become reality without securing the mastery of the tripod possessed by Themis after it was relinquished to her by her mother Ge. In a lengthy choral tribute to Loxias, Euripides recounted the steps which led Apollo to Delphi and the mysterious struggle which ensued for the right to be seated on the tripod. The first attempt of Apollo to drive Themis from her sacred position gave rise to a revolt of the telluric powers, sending forth dreams of cosmic evils to visit the cities of men amid the darkness of the night. To avenge Themis, Ge waged war on Apollo who, after his defeat, fled to the throne of Zeus and begged him to put an end to the rivalry. By divine decree, power was restored to Apollo, who was then entrusted with the sole prerogative of proclaiming the will of the gods to suppliants from every city in Greece.[24]

Mythical aetiology of the tripod led to many divergent suggestions. In the context of the legends which gave victory to Python over Apollo, the burial place of the beloved god received the name of tripod as a consequence of praises sung at the funeral by the three virgin daughters of Triopas.[25] A more fantastic history of the tripod appeared in Diogenes Laertius. The tripod was part of a catch of fish purchased by young Ionians from the Milesians. A dispute arose as to whether the Ionians or the Milesians should keep the tripod. The question was referred to the oracle at Delphi whence came the answer: "Who shall possess the tripod? Thus replies Apollo: Whosoever is the most wise." All agreed that it should be given to Thales, who gave it to another wise man, and yet another one, until it finally came to Solon, who knew that the god alone was wise. Thus the tripod was sent to Delphi.[26]

---

[23]Ibid., 417F (LCL. Mor V) 393-95.

[24]Euripides, IphTaur 1235-83.

[25]Porphyre, *Vie de Pythagore*, 43; Fontenrose, *Python*, 86.

[26]Diogenes Laertius. Lives: Thales 29 (LCL I) 29; Ulrich Wilckens, Σοφία, TDNT 7:469, relates the story of the tripod to the seven wise men: "The . . .

Thucydides gave a different account of the presence of the tripod at Delphi: "There was the case of the tripod in Delphi, dedicated by the Hellenes as the firstfruits of the Persian spoils, on which Pausanias, entirely on his own responsibility, had thought fit to have inscribed the following couplet:

Leader of Hellenes in war, victorious over the Persians,
Pausanias to the god Phoebus erected the trophy.

As for this couplet, the Spartans had immediately had it erased, and had inscribed by name all the cities who had joined in defeating the Persians and who were making the dedication."[27] The suggestion that Delphi operated as an oracular shrine under the prophetic mastery of Apollo before a tripod existed there finds very little support in the most commonly accepted traditions and legends.

The importance of the tripod in Greek religion was everywhere evident, especially in epic literature. It grew into a saying dear to poets. They often referred to that which was true (ἀληθής) as being synonymous with that which came from the tripod (ἀπὸ τρίποδος).[28] At times, the clash between wisdom and prophecy developed into a contest which challenged the relevance of the tripod. Heracles especially was known for his disagreements with the Delphic god, who had let himself be distracted from his mission by shameful and impious questions propounded by ignorant people.[29] On those occasions he wrestled the tripod away from Apollo.

The sophistry which had invaded Delphi often led to misguided oracular responses. To correct such a problem, Heracles, who had himself acquired venerable prophetic qualities, would carry off the tripod by force, leaving the god of divination at a loss.[30] A major confrontation

---

tripod which came forth from the sea with the inscr. ΤΩΙ ΣΟΦΩΤΑΤΩΙ, was handed round from one to the other, finally dedicated by the seventh (or all of them) to Apollo as the supreme sage, and brought to Delphi."

[27]Thucydides, PelWar 1.132.

[28]Pierre Amandry, *La Mantique apollonienne à Delphes: Essai sur le fonctionnement de l'Oracle* (Paris: Boccard, 1950) 140. Oracles were sometimes referred to as ὡς ἐκ τρίποδος.

[29]Plutarch, DefOrac 413AB.

[30]Plutarch, DeE 387D. See also Cicero, NatDeo 3.42.

between Heracles and Apollo took place when Heracles awoke from the crime he had committed by murdering Iphitus. Heracles came to Delphi for an oracle which would show him the way to be purified, but Apollo refused to give him an answer through the Pythia. Angry Heracles again wrestled the tripod away from Apollo with the intention of setting up his own oracle. The conflict was settled when Zeus ordered Heracles to restore the tripod while ordering Apollo to give him the oracular response.[31] This, however, did not assuage Apollo, who wreaked disaster on the Pheneates a thousand years after Heracles was said to have brought the tripod of prophecy to Pheneüs. Plutarch, one of the greatest defenders of the Delphic shrine at which he was a priest, rebuked Apollo for a vengeance he found absurd on the part of a venerated god of wisdom.[32]

The process of deification of Apollo never liberated itself from struggle and ungodlike failings. Everywhere he went, his cult had imposed itself on earlier religious practices whose gods he superseded. In the end he prevailed. Apollo's wisdom, however, remained threatened by his impulsiveness, and his benevolence by his misguided quest for revenge. His good qualities outnumbered his negative traits, and, like Proteus, he could blend into various contexts. Elusiveness took many forms. The Greeks could see in Apollo many diverse manifestations of the divine. At times he was the Delian god, at other times the Pythian or the Clarian. His name was Apollo, but he could also put the stress on different attributes when known as Loxias or Phoebus. In the final analysis, Delphi became the focal point of all divergent interpretations, and the oracular god was praised more for his wisdom than questioned for his indefinable nature.

Dionysian Challenge

Zeus favored Apollo's dominion at Delphi. But religious practices often tend to be shattered into fragments. Coherence in religious perspectives remains as puzzling as the attempts of Monists to reduce everything to a primal principle. "The world is full of gods!" exclaimed Thales as he was groping to discover the fundamental unity of all things. In the same

---

[31]Hyginus, Myths 32; Apollodorus, Lib 2.6.2.3.
[32]Plutarch, SeraNum 557C.

way that the human mind proved incapable of bringing order out of chaos, the oracles of the gods failed to speak with clarity and persuade their worshipers of any ultimate unity. Even under the brilliance of its new oracular god, the land of Pytho was visited by the ghosts of dethroned gods, goddesses, and slain dragons, and by the memories of telluric and chthonic voices which were never totally silenced. Python still rested in the shadow of the tripod, and without Ge and Themis, Apollo would not have had his sanctuary at Delphi. He may have learned the art of divination from Isis or Pan, but it was at Delphi that he could usurp the oracular genius which predated his coming. In the end only two prophetic voices persisted in Delphi, that of Apollo and that of Dionysus, giving shape and form to traditions which portrayed the two gods in need of each other, though they were destined to remain in conflict with each other.

The beginning of the cult of Dionysus at Delphi is less well documented than that of Apollo. The relationship between the two gods remained perplexing. Plutarch stated that Dionysus's share of veneration was no less than that of Apollo.[33] But Heraclitus identified Dionysus with Hades, giving thus a positive sanction to forms of conduct which would otherwise be regarded as shameless.[34] The correlation between the forces of the underworld and the realm of rationality proved perplexing. Plutarch considered Dionysus as performing the same functions for the Greeks as Osiris did for the Egyptians.[35] Indeed, Delphic religion included rites similar to those of Osiris, such as the dismemberment and the death of the god Dionysus and his resurrection and rebirth as a child.[36]

The advent of Dionysus at Delphi remained the object of conflicting points of view. Aeschylus seemed to infer a pre-Apollonian cult of Dionysus there.[37] His ubiquitous presence on Parnassus, in the company of nymphs, was assumed by playwrights.[38] No one could pinpoint the historical moment at which Dionysus appeared on Parnassus. But he must have ruled there long enough to establish traditions which could not be

---

[33]Plutarch, DeE 388E.
[34]Freeman, *Ancilla*, fragm 15.
[35]Plutarch, IsOsir 362B; 364DF.
[36]Harrison, *Prolegomena*, 439.
[37]Aeschylus, Eum 24.
[38]Euripides, IphTaur 1243.

uprooted by the coming of Apollo to Delphi. The most persuasive argument for the presence of Dionysus at the shrine before the coming of Apollo relates to the inspiration and ecstasy of the Pythia, a phenomenon identifiable more with Bacchic religion than Apollonian rationality.[39] But early evidence concerning Delphic religion did not favor the contention of Dionysus having preceded Apollo there. The *Homeric Hymns to Apollo* were silent on both the Pythia and Dionysus. We possess no strong indication that there was a Dionysian oracle influencing the Apollonian. The conditions under which Apollo and Dionysus may have cooperated remain obscure and may rest more on historical accidents than on conclusive textual evidence.

Two major lines of thought can be identified in terms of an Apollonian-Dionysian relationship at Delphi, either in the way of cooperation or in the way of rivalry. Plutarch's assertion of Dionysus's importance in Delphic religion has found echoes in the writings of numerous scholars, and many accepted the suggestion that both Apollo and Dionysus felt quite at home in the land of Pytho. In spite of Zeus's preference for Apollo, he may have decreed that his destiny would be linked with that of Dionysus. According to a tradition preserved in Eusebius, Zeus himself delivered the limbs of Dionysus to be buried by Apollo, who did not disobey the master, but carried the body of Dionysus to Parnassus and deposited it there.[40] The Bacchic God who was delicate in body, eminently beautiful, and successful in his amorous pleasures would perpetuate his presence through his death as much as he did through his life. Plutarch simply stated the fact that "the people of Delphi believed that the remains of Dionysus rest with them close beside the oracle; and the Holy Ones offer a secret sacrifice in the shrine of Apollo whenever the devotees of Dionysus wake the God of the Mystic Baskets."[41]

Nothing in the evidence available indicates that Apollo and Dionysus exercised their cult concurrently in Delphi. Plutarch worked out a formula based on the cycles of transformations according to which Apollo ruled for nine months in Delphi, time during which the paean was used for sacrifices. But when winter came, the dithyrambs would be awakened and

---

[39]Henri Jeanmaire, *Dionysos: Histoire du culte de Bacchus* (Paris: Payot, 1978) 187-98.

[40]Eusebius, PraepEv 65b.

[41]Plutarch, IsOsir 365A (LCL. Mor V) 87.

used in the invocation of the gods, while the paean would be put to rest.[42] No overlapping of the two was allowed. The intimation that Dionysus could exercise his divine rule only during the three winter months made him appear as a divinity of death, which contradicted his essential nature as a god of exuberance, of harvest and vintage. Or was he simply to be considered the chthonic god of the underworld symbolizing an aspect of the divinity not present in Apollo? On the other hand, it was necessary to avoid the appearance that Apollo abdicated his role at Delphi during the three winter months. Thus the myth of the magical land of the Hyperboreans was invented to satisfy the idea of a dual rule at Delphi.

Equally heated is the debate trying to establish that Dionysus had no particular sphere of influence at Delphi. Kurt Latte and Martin Nilsson reject any idea of Dionysus's participation in the oracle.[43] For them he was an inferior divinity without prophetic gift, and, during the three months he spent at Delphi, the oracle remained silent. Latte views the idea of a Dionysian influence at Delphi as a result of the romantic bent of the philosophy of Nietzsche. He argues that when Rohde suggested that the new religion of Dionysus affected the cult of Apollo by introducing into it the ecstatic element, he was simply betraying his close friendship with Nietzsche rather than providing acceptable evidence.

The nature of the relationship between Apollo and Dionysus cannot be resolved on the basis of theological and philosophical speculations. No evidence is conclusive either way, though it strongly favors Apollo. Attempts to assign specific roles to Greek divinities encounter too many obstacles. Obscurity surrounds their origin, and the high level of anthropomorphism connected with them reveals more about the Greek psyche than about theological coherence. Apollo answered the need for rationality and wisdom. But the Dionysian cult was an invitation to a life of immediacy and intensity which counterbalanced the Apollonian need to tame the irrational in life. What each owed to the other remains relative. In the Mysteries of Phlya and Myrrhinus in Attica we find the mention of an Apollo known as Dionysodotus (Dionysos-given—

---

[42]Plutarch, DeE 389C.

[43]Kurt Latte, "The Coming of the Pythia," *Harvard Theological Review* 33 (1940): 9-18; Martin P. Nilsson, *A History of Greek Religion*, trans. F. J. Fieden (Oxford: Clarendon Press, 1949) passim.

Ἀπόλλωνος Διονυσοδότου), suggesting that Apollo was a gift of Dionysus.[44] On the other hand, Dionysus, buried near the tripod and the omphalos, or as some contend under the omphalos itself, remained present under the rule of Apollo, as if he had become the chthonic counterpart of the beloved son of Zeus.

In a duality of principles, sometimes emerging at the edge of metaphysical dualism, the Greeks had learned to consider life in its contradictory aspects, in a balance of forces either threatening or taming each other. Religion did not escape the influence of that duality, and the Greeks did not exclude one side of the religious impulse in favor of the other. Apollo as the god of light, beauty, reason, and eventually moderation could coexist with the god of revelry and ecstasy. Whether or not Apollonian religion could tame Dionysian excesses, it remained a fact that the ecstasy of the Pythia owed something to the influence of Dionysus. The creative energy and enthusiasm of the Dionysian cult was recognized by the Greeks as an important part of spiritual life, but never to the extent that it did not stand in need of correction by the wisdom and rationality of Apollo. In the end one may conceive of Apollo as the superior of the two. Plutarch placed the debate on the level of artistic expression:

> Apollo the artists represent in paintings and sculpture as ever ageless and young, but Dionysus they depict in many guises and forms; and they attribute to Apollo in general a uniformity, orderliness, and unadulterated seriousness, but to Dionysus a certain variability combined with playfulness, wantonness, seriousness, and frenzy.[45]

Dionysian orgies and ecstatic manifestations swept Greece from very early times, giving full sway to uncontrollable practices in conflict with rationality, wisdom, and moderation. Apollonian religion played the role of a taming force, though it could not eliminate the Dionysian element altogether. After Dionysian religion was freed from what was regarded as dangerous in it, it could assume a respectable place in state cult.

The church fathers were not positively inclined toward Dionysian rites, although, if they had applied a critical eye to it, they may have dis-

---

[44]Pausanias, DescrGr 1.31.4. See also Walter Burkert, *Greek Religion*, trans. John Raffan (Cambridge MA: Harvard University Press, 1985) 224.

[45]Plutarch, DeE 389B (LCL. Mor V) 223-25.

covered Bacchic influences in images such as the branch and the vine in
John 15. Much more obvious was the Dionysian context in the conduct
of Christians at Corinth, a conduct which led Paul to despair and resignation. But on moral as well as on spiritual grounds, the church fathers had
to oppose a god of debauchery. Eusebius was the least virulent among
patristic writers, often reflecting on the meaning of Dionysus within
Greek religion in a casual, sometimes neutral way. He gathered information from heathen and Christian writers to compile his *Praeparatio
evangelica*. In it we are reminded that the Greeks confused the names of
Dionysus and Osiris, that the orgiastic rites of Dionysus came from
Egypt, that men worshiped Dionysus especially for his discovery of beer
and wine (as they worshiped Demeter for her discovery of wheat as
food), that the Bacchanals were celebrated with frenzy, that Apollo had
to perform the burial rites for Dionysus (having been killed by the Titans
after Athena stole his heart and received the name Pallas from the
pulsation of that heart), that the mysteries of Dionysus were repulsive,
especially in their requirement of human sacrifices.[46]

The *Apology* of Aristides assumed without explanation that everything
in the cult of Dionysus stood in sharp contrast to Christian teaching. His
divine presumptions crumbled under the blows of his misconduct. He
proved powerless to come to his own rescue in the event of his death.[47]
But this specific argument appeared strange in the light of the fact that
Christ did not attempt to save himself from his death on the cross.

Justin was concerned about the implications of a god who, like
Christ, dies and rises, and about the gift of prophecy and divination
which may have been regarded by some as the source of inspiration for
figures of the Old Testament. The solution for Justin was to cast all the
statements about Greek gods into the mode of fables invented by the
devil to mislead the seekers of truth.[48]

In his discourse on the superiority and exclusivity of the Christian
God, Lactantius reviewed the life and death of Greek divinities and con-

---

[46]Eusebius, PraepEv 27cd; 47cd; 53bd; 62c; 64d; 65b; 120d; 155d; 157d;
163a; 233d. In Crat 406C Plato derived the name of Dionysus as the giver
(διδούς) of wine (οἶνος).

[47]Aristides, Apol 10.

[48]Justin Martyr, Trypho 69.

cluded that Dionysus was neither worse nor better than the rest of them. All suffered from the same disgrace.[49]

Athanasius suggested a wider sphere of influence for Dionysus, who was worshiped also by Indians. But he remained the perfect example of excess in drunkenness which contrasted with the Christian teaching of temperance.[50]

Christian apologists did not establish theological or philosophical differences between Greek gods, who were considered evil en masse. In the case of moral pollution, Dionysus was singled out as the most detrimental to the spiritual welfare of society in general. His role was considered doubly troubling, as his death did not eliminate moral corruption, but reaffirmed it in his rebirth from the thigh of Zeus.[51] He happened to be just on a slightly lower level than Athena, who issued directly from Zeus's head.

Under the rule of Julian, a revival of Dionysian practices swept throughout the empire. As an act of revenge against Christians, Dionysian cult symbols were introduced into newly erected churches. Bacchic revelers, often accompanied by devotees of Demeter and by Jews, came out of their hiding places to which they were confined during the reign of pious emperors and filled the forum. It was not until the advent of Theodosius that such excesses were abolished.[52]

The destinies of Apollo and Dionysus, at first linked together by the Delphic power of religious persuasion, followed different avenues of influence. Apollo remained the master of oracles, well into the Christian era, up to the days of Theodosius. His rival was remembered more for the various festivals known as the *Dionysia* and for his role as the source of the tragic sense of life which inspired the Greek playwrights. In that particular respect the legacy of Dionysus may be viewed as greater than that of Apollo. In a strange way Arnobius suggested that the identification of Dionysus with Apollo, as representing some of the same elements of Greek religion, namely, both being considered the sun, actually destroyed the divinity of both.[53]

---

[49]Lactantius, Epit 8.
[50]Athanasius, CGent 9.4.12; 24.2.
[51]Arnobius, AdvGent 4.22. See also 5.19, 28.
[52]Theodoret, HE 3.3; 4.21; 5.20.
[53]Arnobius, AdvGent 3.33.

Miasma and Catharsis

In a world driven by a moira that neither gods nor mortals can escape, the threat of pollution dictates the parameters of religious practices. However divergent religions may seem to be in their definitions and outlooks, they must provide a remedy to a universal miasma and alleviate the fear that personal and collective destinies can be destroyed by divine vengeance, at times rational, at other times aimlessly wandering in the flow of blind cosmic forces propelled by their own sense of justice. When the gods themselves deviate from the path of purity and virtue, when they resort to acts contrary to their essential nature, the need for catharsis assumes a sense of urgency. As Empedocles remarked,

> There is an oracle of Necessity, an ancient decree of the gods, eternal, sealed fast with broad oaths, that when one of the divine spirits whose portion is long life sinfully stains his own limbs with bloodshed, and following Hate has sworn a false oath—these must wander for thrice ten thousand seasons far from the company of the blessed, being born throughout the period into all kinds of mortal shapes, which exchange one hard way of life for another.[54]

While the gods wander, fugitives from heaven, worshipers search for the best forms of purification. When the gods acknowledge their powerlessness, mortals must bear the weight of their afflictions. As Zeus sat upon Olympus in the company of other gods, meditating on the death of Aegisthus and Clytemnestra, he mused on how mortals take the gods to task and blame them for all their afflictions, while forgetting their own failings.[55] Aeschylus had Orestes proclaim that the word of Apollo is of great power and will be fulfilled. His voice, urgent, insistent, drove Orestes to dare the greatest of perils, chilling his heart's hot blood with terrors, should he fail to exact fit vengeance from those who killed his father. The god's command was to shed blood for blood.[56] When justice claims its due, the *lex talionis* sanctions the laws of vengeance and ensures that the price of hamartia is death.

---

[54]Empedocles, Kath 115. In Freeman, *Ancilla*, 65.
[55]Homer, Od 1.32-34.
[56]Aeschylus, Choeph 269-96.

The powers of primordial chaos were operative through the presence of Python on Parnassus. In ancient mythologies the cunning of the serpent predated the wisdom of human beings, and in many cases their existence. As for Apollo, it remained an ineluctable fact that Python was before him, ruling on Parnassus with full divine attributes, delivering oracular responses,[57] and representing elements contrary to divine nature. Apollo and Python symbolized the conflict of two realms of cosmic powers which could not both prevail. The struggle began in an archetypal past before any human consciousness of it. Python's furies pursuing Leto could not be forgotten, and the outcome of the struggle had to come swiftly. In one of the legends, Apollo destroyed Python by his arrows at the age of four days.[58]

We are here confronted with a complex conception of archetypal guilt, of the inevitable reality of a preexistent miasma, of angry divine behavior which ensures a mad discord of the elements into which mortals have only a limited insight. At one point Saint Paul suggested that Christ was not crucified by men as such, but by heavenly powers and principalities marked by wickedness and intent on perpetuating chaos on earth.[59]

Beyond the historical awareness of miasma and hamartia, religion had to define a process of atonement which could restore peace and reconciliation. The *Homeric Hymns to Apollo* provided no insight into a universal miasma and the need for catharsis. The question was first raised in earnest in Hesiod's *Theogony* and *Works and Days*. In Aeschylus it developed into an intensive analysis of the complexity and the gravity underscoring the tenuous links between the pervasiveness of miasma and the need for catharsis, almost in spite and beyond the gods involved. By necessity Delphi had to assume a leading role in ritual purification required for atoning bloodshed. The chthonic character of the gods precluded any easy solution. Mortals and gods remained in a precarious relationship within which the divinity appeared envious and troublesome (φθονερόν τε καὶ ταραχῶδες).[60]

With the destruction of Python by Apollo the emphasis fell not so much on the violence of the act as on the fact that blood was shed. For

---

[57]Hyginus, Myths 140.
[58]Ibid.
[59]Ephesians 6:12; 1 Corinthians 2:6-8.
[60]Herodotus, Hist 1.32.

every blood spilled, earth clamors for revenge.[61] Leto was avenged, and the death of Python meant that the furies she unleashed came to their end. One could read into Apollo's action a divine decision to free the realm of mortals from destructive powers and to replace a vengeful divinity with a benevolent one. But even the gods cannot escape an inexorable destiny so well known to Orestes, namely, that a murder requires another murder, according to a blind law which feeds an infernal machine grinding to its bitter end. For his murder Apollo had to accept his punishment. To atone for the death of Python, he was exiled for nine years in Thessaly before he obtained the necessary purification to rule at Delphi free of stain. A rather obscure festival was reenacted every ninth year at Delphi to symbolize the return of Apollo and to prove that his sanctuary had become the legitimate center of purification whence all priests received their empowerment to perform cleansing rites at other Apollonian shrines. The same applied to special interpreters (*exegetai*) who replaced the priests in large cities such as Athens and who could negotiate relief in the case of epidemics or civil discords.

The idea of divine defilement presented the most serious challenge to the credibility of the gods and their efficacy in solving human afflictions. Plutarch rebuked Delphic theologians who accepted and actually divulged the legends according to which Apollo, after slaying Python, had to flee to the end of Greece in search of purification in order to placate the spirits. Such tenets not only destroyed the sanctity of Delphi, but proved ridiculous.[62] Long before Plutarch, however, Aeschylus undertook a more systematic analysis of the tragic disruption of universal order which afflicts both gods and mortals. The charges of the Eumenides that Apollo defiled justice and his own altar by condoning the matricide of Orestes were met by the angry response of the god who ordered them out of his sanctuary. Later the Chorus warned Apollo that, because of his patronizing blood-guilty Orestes, his oracle will cease to be *hagnos* and will be delivered from a polluted shrine.[63]

The fear of defilement blurs the path of human destiny. Troubled Orestes accepted Apollo's pronouncement of purification and the god's paradoxical acknowledgement that he, and not Orestes, was to be blamed

---

[61]Aeschylus Choeph 66-70; Genesis 4:10.
[62]Plutarch, DefOrac 418B.
[63]Aeschylus, Eum 149-62; 715-18.

for the murder. But was the murder justified? Apollo had to provide the answer which determined the outcome of the trial of his suppliant.[64] When Athena was invoked to settle the dispute, she pointed out that the matter was too grave for anyone to decide, and certainly was fraught with perils and complexities. The Furies upheld the need for justice and could not be faulted for pursuing Orestes even after he was proclaimed pure by Apollo. Thus the judgment had to come from a jury, which was equally divided on the issue, with the deciding vote in favor of Orestes being cast by Athena herself. Even the goddess of wisdom had to extend the concept of justice to include wise citizens.[65] The furies of the gods were resolved by human decisions, though still under divine decree and influence. Neither Delphi nor Apollo emerged victorious in the case of Orestes, and one is left to wonder why Aeschylus developed the story to its bitter end, and with what intention.

Suppliants coming to Apollo to be delivered from defilement could approach his sanctuary only after performing the proper rites and sacrifices. Once purified, the decree was irrevocable.[66] The oracular god who acquired the title of *catharsios* could prescribe purification for individuals and cities in the grip of personal guilt or of scourges such as plagues. The Pythian god could keep evil away in his function as *apotropaios*, and as the *Catharsios* he could proclaim purity. Progressively Delphi assumed the role of center of purification, and Apollo was regarded as the teacher of respect for human life.

A murder was especially offensive if committed on premises dedicated to the gods, as exemplified in an event that took place at Sybaris. Its population had an argument with a harp player, a protégé of the Muses, who was killed after he sought protection at the altar of Hera. As a result plagues struck the city, and the Sybarites went to Delphi in search of an oracle. The Pythia rebuked them angrily: "Forth from my tripods! Still your murderous hands drip gore and bar you from my marble portals. No oracle I give you."[67]

---

[64]Ibid., 276-85; 576-82; 609-13.

[65]Ibid., 470-89.

[66]Plato, Laws 865AC.

[67]Martin P. Nilsson, *Greek Piety*, Trans. Herbert Jennings Rose (Oxford: Clarendon Press, 1948) 43. See also T. Dempsey, *The Delphic Oracle: Its Early History Influence and Fall* (New York: Benjamin Blom, 1972) 144. For a similar

Many considered Delphi as the center of purification under the rule of its god of catharsis and healing. There are, however, dissenting voices. Robert Parker, for instance, concedes to Apollo the function of cleansing and healing. But when it comes to murder purification, the evidence shows that the altar of Zeus was the only place for absolution. Apollo's oracle was certainly consulted in cases of murder, and he may have become an authority on it. But neither he nor his priests could perform that which was the prerogative of Zeus alone.[68]

Much more interesting was the story of the relationship of Apollo to Admetus. The myth is recounted by many ancient writers in many different ways with different points of emphasis. In essence it starts with Asclepius, who is said to have restored life to either Glaucus or Hippolytus.[69] It angered Zeus, who struck Asclepius with his thunderbolt. Since Apollo could not exact revenge from Zeus for the death of his son, he proceeded to destroy the Cyclops who had fashioned the deadly thunderbolt. As a punishment, Apollo was given in servitude to Admetus, king of Thessaly.[70] Euripides was sufficiently impressed by the story to develop it into a tragedy, *Alcestis*, in which he portrayed Apollo as a willing servant in the house of a just and hospitable man. Praises for Admetus abounded in Euripides. On account of his extraordinary qualities, Apollo attempted to secure from the Fates a favor for Admetus whereby at the time of his death they would accept the substitution of someone else. The person who volunteered as a ransom was Alcestis, wife of Admetus. When the time came for her to depart from this world,

---

story see Eusebius, PraepEv 228c.

[68]Robert Parker, *Miasma: Pollution and Purification in Early Greek Religion* (Oxford: Clarendon Press, 1983) 139.

[69]Plato strongly objected to the way tragedians and Pindar handled the story of Asclepius: "In disregard of our principles the tragedians and Pindar affirm that Asclepius, though he was the son of Apollo, was bribed by gold to heal a man already at the point of death, and that for this cause he was struck by the lightning. But we in accordance with the aforesaid principles refuse to believe both statements, but if he was the son of a god he was not avaricious, we will insist, and if he was greedy of gain he was not the son of a god." Rep 408BC (LCL IV) 281.

[70]Hyginus, Myths 49; Diodorus Siculus, Lib 6.8; Eusebius, PraepEv 57ab.

Apollo pleaded with Death to release Alcestis, who was finally rescued by Heracles before she could be buried.

Apollo's servitude to Admetus was meant to atone for bloodshed. A god destroying his son was not new in Greek mythology, and, for that matter, is not absent from the Christian religion. The mode of punishment, though common among Greek gods and heroes, was surprising. In many ways Admetus was endowed with characteristics superior to those of the god condemned to serve him, a fact Apollo recognized and to which he responded with kindness and wise advice. A legend circulating in ancient Greece preserved a precept of Apollo to Admetus: "Live as though you must die tomorrow, and yet as though you had fifty years before you."[71]

Church fathers refer to the legend of Admetus and Apollo to reinforce their argument of the inferiority of Greek gods and to deny them the attributes of power and benevolence. The impotence of the gods, their inability to avert tragic situations such as the death of Asclepius, their submission to mortals from whom they cannot free themselves and to whom they have to pay the price for their punishment were special subjects of attacks.[72] It is difficult to identify the sources Christian apologists used in referring to the story of Admetus. Most of them mention it without comment. Athenagoras showed a definite knowledge of Euripides' *Alcestis*. The more contemporary writings of Diodorus were well known at the time, but the church fathers probably could not agree with his portrayal of Admetus as a man dear to the gods because of his righteousness and piety that brought him respect. The idea of a god made the servant of humankind in order to bring atonement and purification was certainly not foreign to Christian theology, but the church fathers preferred to ignore the possible parallel.

---

[71]Ulrich von Wilamowitz-Moellendorff, *Greek Historical Writing and Apollo* (Chicago: Ares, 1979) 41.

[72]Arnobius, AdvGent 4.25; Cyprian, Treat 6.2; Clement of Alexandria, Protr 2; Athenagoras, Leg 21. Athenagoras also quotes a passage from a lost play of Aeschylus in which the playwright reproaches Apollo for being a false prophet: "And I believed Apollo's mouth divine was full of truth, as well as prophet's art. . . . The very one who sings while at the feast, the one who said these things, alas! is he who slew my son." Leg 21 (ANF II) 139.

The favors of the gods were usually secured through sacrifices. In the *Republic* Plato referred to the performance of private sacrifices (419A, 362C); but in the *Laws* (909DE) he explicitly stated that they were forbidden. They had to be performed by priests in a public place. Arnobius derided all sacrifices as absurd acts benefitting neither worshipers nor gods:

> But, I ask, where is there room for honour among the gods, or what greater exaltation is found to be given to them by piling up sacrifices? Do they become more venerable, more powerful, when cattle are sacrificed *to them?* is there anything added to them from this? or do they begin to be more *truly* gods, their divinity being increased? And yet I consider it almost an insult, nay, an insult altogether, when it is said that a god is honoured by a man, and exalted by the offering of some gift.[73]

Unfortunately, Arnobius remained silent on the meaning of sacrifices in the Old Testament.

The existence of an imposing sacrificial system is well attested in Hebrew religion, especially in the Levitical code. In that specific area, Yahwistic religion allowed customs alien to its essence but deeply rooted in contemporary practices:

> When meantime Moses, that faithful and wise steward, perceived that the vice of sacrificing to idols had been deeply ingrained into the people from their association with the Egyptians, and that the root of this evil could not be extracted from them, he allowed them indeed to sacrifice, but permitted it to be done only to God, that by any means he might cut off one half of the deeply ingrained evil, leaving the other half to be corrected by another, and at a future time. . . .[74]

Christian apologists refuted the meaning of sacrifices on several grounds. Their uselessness could be demonstrated on a rational level, and even the heathen poets made fun of them.[75] The gods were in no need of them. Some Old Testament prophets advocated the substitution of a

---

[73]Arnobius, AdvGent 7.14 (ANF VI) 523.

[74]Pseudo-Clementine Literature, Recogn 1.36 (ANF VIII) 87. The future time referred to is the era of the messiah. See also 1.39 for the time at which sacrifices stop and are replaced by baptism.

[75]Clement of Alexandria, Strom 7.6.

spiritual dimension for ritual duty.[76] Sacrifices were instituted because of the sins of the people and not because of any intrinsic value. They were never performed for God's sake, because he could not be disturbed or angered by the mistakes of his people.[77] The blood spilled on altars did not remove the miasma.[78] Contrary to heathen divinities, the Christian God, because of his purity, could not be soothed or assuaged by offerings of any kind.[79]

To the charges of impiety levelled against Christians because they did not sacrifice to pagan gods, the church fathers responded not by invoking the Scriptures but by quoting heathen writers. After exposing the pettiness of pagan divinities who exact sacrifices through fear, Arnobius contended that no such situation could arise with the Christian God to whom no shrines or temples were built. He then appealed to the writings of Varro in support of his contentions:

> What, then, some one will say, do you think that no sacrifices at all should be offered? To answer you not with our own, but with your Varro's opinion—none. Why so? Because, he says, the true gods neither wish nor demand these; while those which are made of copper, earthenware, gypsum, or marble, care much less for these things, for they have no feeling; and you are not blamed if you do not offer them, nor do you win favour if you do.[80]

Along the same lines of thought, Lactantius quoted Seneca to prove that there are no pure offerings to God:

> Will you think of God as great and placid, and a friend to be reverenced with gentle majesty, and always at hand? not to be worshipped with the

---

[76]Isaiah 1:11; Hosea 6:6; Clement of Alexandria, Strom 7.6; Barn 2.4-5; Athenagoras, Leg 13; Tertullian, AdvMarc 2.22.

[77]Justin Martyr, Trypho 22; Irenaeus, AdvHaer 4.17.1; Psalms 51.

[78]Lactantius, DivInst 6.1.

[79]Athenagoras, Leg 13; Pseudo-Clementine Literature, ClemHom 3.45. The absurdity of Jewish sacrifices to God became a leitmotif in patristic literature. *The Epistle to Diognetus* considers them as misguided as all heathen sacrifices. 3.5.

[80]Arnobius, AdvGent 7.1 (ANF VI) 518. There has been a good deal of controversy about Arnobius's statement that Christians did not have any temples, ibid., 6.1-3.

immolation of victims and with much blood—for what pleasure arises from the slaughter of innocent animals?—but with a pure mind and with a good and honourable purpose. Temples are not to be built to Him with stones piled up on high; He is to be consecrated by each man in his own breast.[81]

Early Christian writers have on occasion considered the death of martyrs as a special sacrifice to their God and as extending spiritual benefits to others. In martyrdom the powers of evil suffered defeat.[82] The death of the faithful mirrored the supreme sacrifice of their Lord. The early church found itself in a paradoxical situation when it had to provide theological tenets according to which the elimination of all sacrifices required the supreme one in the person of the Messiah, identified as the sacrificial lamb, and without the shedding of whose blood there could be no redemption.[83]

Much more perplexing and disturbing was the reported practice of human sacrifices in Greek religion. Plutarch regarded them not as acts performed to satisfy the gods, but as soothing and appeasing rites for the averting of evil spirits. Then he observed that

> Nor is it credible that the gods demanded or welcomed the human sacrifices of ancient days, nor would kings and generals have endured giving over their children and submitting them to the preparatory rites and cutting their throats to no purpose save that they felt they were propitiating and offering satisfaction to the wrath and sullen temper of some harsh and implacable avenging deities. . . . [84]

The testimony to human sacrifices was, however, far too extensive to be overlooked. The *De abstinentia* of Porphyry included a brief listing of those performed among Mediterranean peoples. Hyginus recounted how, after Poseidon and Apollo had built the wall around Troy, Laomedon

---

[81]Lactantius, DivInst 6.25 (ANF VII) 192.

[82]Origen, CJohn 6.36; Tertullian, Scorp 7-8.

[83]Hebrews 9:22.

[84]Plutarch, DefOrac 417CD (LCL. Mor V) 391. The indignation of Lactantius at the thought of parents sacrificing their children surpassed that of Plutarch: "To think that men were so barbarous, so savage, that they gave the name of sacrifice to the slaughter of their own children, that is, to a deed foul, and to be held in detestation by the human race." DivInst 1.21 (ANF VII) 35.

vowed that he would sacrifice to them, an oath he failed to fulfill to the satisfaction of the gods. A plague in the form of a huge monster followed, and the king sent to Apollo for advice. The god angrily replied that the plague will cease once Trojan maidens were bound and offered to the monster. Many died until Heracles killed the creature.[85]

Dionysius of Halicarnassus elaborated on the story of the Pelasgians who were afflicted by all kinds of calamities. When they asked the oracle what god they had offended, they were reminded of their failure to sacrifice human offsprings. Were they to do so, the oracle would be satisfied.[86] Eusebius, who knew the writings of Dionysius and quoted them extensively, refuted this story, not on account of its inaccuracy, for he had great respect for the writer, but to show the grip bloodthirsty demons had on the consciousness of people in ancient days. Eusebius then quoted fragments of Porphyry, which have been preserved only in his writings, to show that sacrifices were always performed in violation of natural reason. When Apollo required human sacrifices, it was not as a god of purification, but as an evil demon that he did so. Then Eusebius added: "But should any one say that the custom of human sacrifice is not wicked, but most rightly practiced by the men of old, he must at once condemn all of the present day, because none worship after the manner of their fathers."[87] In a more generalized attack on human sacrifices, Clement of Alexandria denounced the cruelty of the gods who delighted

---

[85]Hyginus, Myths 89.

[86]Dionysius of Halicarnassus, RomAnt 1.23.1-24.2.

[87]Eusebius, PraepEv 169a; 186. See also 158c-160d; 168b-169a. Eusebius quotes Porphyry; "The best sacrifice to the gods is a pure mind and a soul free from passions." Ibid., 152d. Porphyry's contention that Apollo acted as an evil demon in the case of sacrifices represents a theme extensively developed in Marcel Detienne, *Apollon le couteau à la main: Une approche expérimentale du polythéisme grec* (Paris: Gallimard, 1998). Apollo is described there as an impure god, exiled from heaven, and full of troublesome passions which require countless sacrifices, useless pouring of blood, and numerous altars dedicated to his misguided thirst for revenge. In other words, Apollo is a god in love with the knife, a kind of religious butcher who disregards the sanctity of life and secures the friendship of criminals and murderers. In his book, Detienne exposes meticulously the instances of Apollonian cruelty to conclude that the major force underlying his behavior was the love of murder.

in the murder of human beings and rebuked the misguided expectations of mortals who wished to secure good omens through such atrocities. As an example, among many, he referred to Aristomenes who slew three hundred human beings in order to secure good favors from Zeus.[88]

As a contrast to the repulsive custom of human sacrifices, Clement of Rome alluded to the noble self-sacrifices of heathen kings and rulers who, in obedience to oracles, gave themselves up to death in order to rescue their subjects through their own blood.[89] This is the closest example of redeeming self-sacrifices among heathen that could find a parallel in the death of Christ.

The practices of human sacrifices among Mediterranean peoples of antiquity also entered into Hebrew religion.[90] The most often mentioned event concerned Jephthah's immolation of his own daughter as the result of a fateful oath to Yahweh. Unless we relegate the story to the realm of myth, we are confronted here with a religious act more in tune with old Canaanite cult than with Yahwistic religion as expressed later by the prophets. Referring to that unfortunate event, Origen tried to mitigate the demands of a cruel God with the mystery that surrounds him: "The story suggests that the being must be a very cruel one to whom such sacrifices are offered for the salvation of men; and we require some breadth of mind and some ability to solve the difficulties raised against Providence, to be able to account for such things and to see that they are mysteries and exceed our human nature."[91]

In pre-Mosaic times human sacrifices were common among Canaanite tribes. After the Hebrews settled in those lands, the practice crept into their sacrificial ritual. No clear development on human sacrifices emerges from the Old Testament, but it seems to be first mentioned as an established practice in Judah under king Ahaz and in Israel under king Hoshea.[92] But it could be read back into Mosaic times.[93] It was probably

---

[88]Clement of Alexandria, Protr 3.

[89]Clement, First Corinthians 55.

[90]For a more complete statement on human sacrifices among the Israelites, see Charles F. Burney, *The Book of Judges* (London: Rivington, 1918) 329-31.

[91]Origen, CJohn 6.36 (ANF X) 377.

[92]Second Kings 16:3; 17:17.

[93]Exodus 22:29b. The manner of "sacrifice" is not discussed, and Exodus 34:20 seems to infer that an animal could be substituted for the firstborn.

under the idolatrous reign of Manasseh that the sacrifice of children reached its peak.[94]

Human sacrifices in the Old Testament were often connected with a divinity named Molech, having its major sanctuary in the Valley of Hinnom, near Jerusalem. References to human sacrifices to Molech abound in the Old Testament.[95] Solomon built a High Place to Molech.[96] But there is also a severe denunciation of those sacrifices.[97] Occasionally we encounter the paradoxical suggestion that Yahweh wilfully misled people into offering their firstborn in sacrifice so it might horrify them and lead them back to faith. Such sacrifices have also been mentioned as a means to receive forgiveness for sin.[98] But nowhere is there any direct evidence that Yahweh demanded such sacrifices. They were considered as an idolatrous aberration resisted by Mosaic law and prophetic proclamation.

In the festival of the Thargelia we have the best insight into a relationship between human sacrifices and the cult of Apollo. The Thargelia, so named because it took place on the sixth and seventh of Thargelion[99] (unless we accept the contention that it was the festival that gave the name to the month), was the principal festival of Apollo in Athens. Pisistratus was believed to have built a temple to Apollo for that purpose. Somewhat in the mode of a harvest festival, it involved a procession and an offering of the firstfruits. A central component of the Thargelia was the expulsion of two *pharmakoi*, two men beaten and chased through the streets by people who threw stones at them, believing that it was the only way to obtain purification from an overwhelming miasma that had afflicted them.

There is good reason to believe that Apollo was venerated as the "averter of evil," but it is not certain that he was symbolically identified

---

[94]Second Kings 21:6.

[95]Leviticus 18:21; 20:2-5; 2 Kings 23:10; Jeremiah 32:35; cf. Psalms 106:37; Isaiah 57:5, 9; and Jeremiah 7:31.

[96]First Kings 11:7.

[97]Deuteronomy 18:10; 12:31; Leviticus 18:21; 20:2-5; Jeremiah 19:5.

[98]Micah 6:7.

[99]Thargelion is the eleventh month of the Athenian year, corresponding to the last three weeks of May plus the first week of June. Thargelion 6-7 corresponds to May 16-17.

with the *pharmakoi*. Human sacrifices in the Thargelia were meant to free the community of its sins, but, as Lewis Richard Farnell pointed out: "It is singular how little Apollo is heard of in the account of this part of the Thargelia."[100]

The Thargelia may have played a central role in identifying the φαρμακός with one who is sacrificed as an atonement for others, as a scapegoat. Biblical literature never used the term φαρμακός as scapegoat, but always in the other sense of magician or sorcerer.[101] In the same context φαρμακεία referred to sorcery and magic.[102] In the Septuagint the words φαρμακεία, φαρμακός, φάρμακον are always used in the sense of sorcery and magic.[103] In the rare instance where the idea of a scapegoat is intended, the Septuagint uses the term ἀποπομπαῖος, referring to goats, not human beings.[104]

Apollo's Ascension to Wisdom

As early as the sixth century BCE, close to the heart of the oracle at Delphi, Pindar sat on an iron chair especially consecrated to his poetic power and composed songs of praises to Apollo.[105] His eloge of his beloved god was unsurpassed in his own day:

Secret, O Phoebus! are the keys of wise Persuasion, that unlock the shrine of love. . . . For thou, who canst not lawfully breathe a lie, hast been tempted by thy pleasant mood to dissemble in thy words. . . . thou who knowest the end supreme of all things, and all the ways that lead thereto, the number of the leaves that the earth putteth forth in spring, the number of the sands that, in the sea and the rivers, are driven before

---

[100]Lewis Richard Farnell, *The Cults of the Greek Cities*, 5 vols. (Oxford: Clarendon Press, 1907) 2:281-82. Other scholars point to a more defined connection between the Thargelia and the cult of Apollo. Among them, Delcourt, *L'Oracle*, 165.

[101]Revelation 21:8; 22:15.

[102]Galatians 5:20; Revelation 18:23.

[103]Exodus 7:11, 22; 9:11; 22:18; Deuteronomy 18:10; 2 Kings 9:22; Isaiah 47:9, 12; Daniel 2:2; Micah 5:12.

[104]Only at Leviticus 16:8, 10.

[105]Pausanias, DescrGr 10.24.5.

the waves and the rushing winds, and that which is to be, and whence it is to come—all this thou clearly seest.[106]

Poetic verve found its equal in philosophical assertions that Apollo's statements ought to be regarded as certain and unalterable, as containing no deception, and as being propositions to be grasped not through perception but through thinking.[107]

The rise to prominence of the Delphic sanctuary was achieved by a slow but consistent process of transformation and purification. Through the power of transcendence, misdeeds of gods and mortals could be relegated to the past. Generations of worshipers could be convinced that there existed a source of thought and truth related to a divine presence that sees and knows all and to which Greek people of good will could turn to for reassurance and guidance. The Delphic God of light alone remained beneficent to the whole human race by dispensing a wisdom not available anywhere else. That wisdom could temper the old furies of the gods with understanding and rationality. To appeal to the Greek citizenry, the Delphic oracle had to show respect for religious traditions and practices of diverse origin and nature and remold them into a coherent perspective on all aspects of life. This could be achieved only through the belief in a god whose knowledge of the human condition surpassed the claims of previous divinities. Apollo's oracle became all-inclusive and often regarded as a Delphic doctrine—*eine delphische Lehre*, to use Otto Kern's designation.[108]

In the ancient world, the success or demise of divinities fluctuated with the political, social, and moral conditions of society. When the internal strength and resilience of a people collapsed, the vacuum created made room for new prophetic voices promising more stable and civilizing elements capable of subduing conflicts, doubts, and sometimes despair. With time the new Delphic god overcame the image of the killer of monsters, of a passionate lover incapable of controlling his urges, of a vengeful ruler seeking superiority through revenge. Perhaps the greatest transformation to take place in Greek religious life consisted in reshaping

---

[106]Pindar, PythOdes 9.40-49. (LCL) 277.

[107]Cicero, TuscDisp 1.17; Plutarch, SeraNum 566C; PythOr 400D.

[108]Jean Defradas, *Les Thèmes de la propogande delphique* (Paris: Les Belles Lettres, 1972) 11-12.

a god like the primal Apollo into a divinity that could mediate dignity, peace, and equanimity.

Apollonian worship rose to its position of distinction through its ability to bring together mythological insights and the intellectual power of a people who could combine mystery with knowledge and belief with rationality. The elusiveness of Apollo reinforced his inscrutability. The interpretation of his intentions required intelligence. Heraclitus's short summary of the Delphic oracle remained an example of aphoristic incisiveness: "The Lord whose prophetic seat is at Delphi neither speaks nor conceals, but gives a sign."[109]

As Apollonian religion evolved from legends to more rational perspectives, it had its critics and supporters. Euripides never failed to expose the nefarious interferences of Apollo in human affairs. His aim was to show how rationality can win over divine whim. Plato was more consistent in his support of the Delphic god and reprimanded poets, especially Aeschylus, for diminishing the authority of the gods, and that of Apollo in particular, by connecting them to stories he found unacceptable.[110] But no greater friend has Apollo ever had than Plutarch who, in spite of some occasional misgivings about the Delphic oracle, considered Apollo as *the* god and liked to quote the venerable Pindar: "And towards mortal men he hath been judged the most gentle."[111] Poetic and mantic wisdom was backed at Delphi by the proximity of a temple to Athena discovered in recent archaeological excavations.

The god who won the reverence of his nation also inspired profound fear in his suppliants. In her indignation at the injustice of Apollo, Cassandra played on the etymology of the name of the god, clearly expressing his destructive side, for indeed the name Apollo could be

---

[109]Self-translation of DK B 93: ὁ ἄναξ, οὗ τὸ μαντεῖόν ἐστι τὸ ἐν Δελφοῖς, οὔτε λέγει οὔτε κρύπτει ἀλλὰ σημαίνει.

[110]Plato, Rep 383BC. Plato was especially disturbed by the way Aeschylus handled the story of Thetis, which put Apollo in a terrible light.

[111]Plutarch, DefOrac 413C (LCL. Mor V) 369; DeE 394B; Martin P. Nilsson, *Greek Folk Religion* (Philadelphia: University of Pennsylvania Press, 1940) 106 would disagree with Plutarch. He points out that Apollo did not satisfy the requests of people in areas of practical life. He cared only for his cult, and not for people.

derived from the Greek ἀπόλλυμι, a derivation Aeschylus chose to emphasize:

"Απολλον "Απολλον
ἀγυιᾶτ', ἀπόλλων ἐμός
ἀπώλεσας γὰρ οὐ μόλις τὸ δεύτερον.
Apollo, Apollo,
God of the Ways, my destroyer!
For thou hast destroyed me—and utterly—this second time.[112]

For having refused his advances, Apollo placed a curse on Cassandra whereby she would be endowed with prophetic powers, but nobody would believe her, making her an object of derision during the Trojan war. Having suffered the first time because of her rejection of Apollo, she now had to die for having granted to Agamemnon what she had refused to the god.

Mindful of such dreadful interpretations and the disastrous consequences for Apollo's cult, Plato undertook, in his etymologies of the *Cratylus*, to clarify the score. He bestowed four positive qualities on Apollo: music, prophecy, medicine, and archery. Then he emphasized the beneficial attributes of a god who purifies and washes away (ἀπολούων) and delivers (ἀπολύων) from evils. But he knew that people would keep fearing the name Apollo by thinking that it has some terrible meaning. Thus he elaborated on the significance of the name and the ways in which it could be presented as more reassuring. He suggested that the second lambda was inserted because, without it, the name sounded of disaster (ἀπολῶ, ἀπόλωλα . . .). Even so the suspicion did not disappear on the part of those who misunderstood the name and thought that it denoted some kind of ruin.[113] Centuries later such fears were still common, as suggested by Plutarch who could not condone the attitude of those who did not think reasonably about the gods, especially Apollo, and who trembled and dreaded them.[114]

The preferred etymology of the name Apollo, at least among philosophers, was ἀ-πόλλων = not the many = the one, the eternal god. According to Plutarch, "He is Apollo, that is to say, denying the Many

---

[112]Aeschylus, Agam 1080-83 (LCL II) 90-91.
[113]Plato, Crat 404C-406A.
[114]Plutarch, Superst 170B.

and abjuring multiplicity; he is Ieius, as being One and One alone; and Phoebus, as is well known, is a name that the men of old used to give to everything pure and undefiled."[115] Even Clement of Alexandria was willing to concede that the name Apollo could be interpreted mystically by "privation of many" (ἀπολλοί), meaning the one God.[116]

The universality of Apollo was not established on the basis of his numerous names which could identify him with all aspects of life. Rather it rested on an abstraction which defied final interpretation. In the same way Moses learned that the awesomeness of his God was contained in a short, mysterious statement: Yahweh (I am who I am), Plutarch connected Apollo with the enigmatic E engraved on the portal of the Delphic temple, the essence of a god reduced to a letter, itself a contraction from εἶ (you are). Plutarch understood the E as the supreme affirmation of human aspiration in the presence of the eternal god. We are now far removed from the Apollo who had to fight his way to recognition and resort to acts of violence contrary to divine essence. The god of Plutarch underwent a long process of purification in the intellectual as well as the religious landscape of Greek thought. That god was no less a philosopher than a prophet, "thus creating in the soul a craving that leads onward to the truth, as is clear in many other ways, but particularly in the dedication of the E."[117]

As the all-knowing and all-seeing divinity Apollo could be equated with the sun as the supreme god of light. Such an analogy has been so ancient and so widespread that it has become impossible to establish its origin or its actual content. The association of Apollo with light made his oracles all-illuminating, though their content often remained ambiguous and sometimes even misleading. The lucent god kept his appeal in spite or perhaps because of the mystery surrounding his cult. Augustus built a magnificent temple to him on the Palatine Hill. Atop it he placed a golden chariot containing Apollo as the sun. In Plutarch's view, we are not even justified in referring to two different divinities when we speak of Apollo and the sun. They are one, and those who perceive that fundamental truth are the most happy and worthy of special honor.[118]

---

[115]Plutarch, DeE 393C (LCL. Mor V) 247; 394A.

[116]Clement of Alexandria, Strom 1.24.

[117]Plutarch, DeE 384F-385B (LCL. Mor V) 201.

[118]Plutarch, PythOr 400D; DeE 393D. Eusebius has taken the opposite view,

The benevolent nature of Apollo was often attributed to his relationship to the Muses and his occasional dwelling with them on Mount
Helicon. A painting by Claude Gellée (Claude Lorrain) in the Boston
Museum portrays Apollo with the Muses on the lawn in front of their
temple, playing the lyre and perfectly at ease on the mountain of
inspiration. Apollo as leader (*hegetes*) of the Muses was also called
Musegetes.[119] The god who combined inspiration and philosophy came
the closest to vindicate what Plato called universal "ideas." Delphi was
not only the seat of the oracle but also the visible expression of what the
Muses intended to communicate to mortals. They were always welcomed
there. The consecration of the artistic life of Apollo remained essential for
Greek religion. In that sense the Apollo cult exercised its purifying and
edifying influence on society, both on the collective level and within the
context of individual conscience. The leader of the Muses could ensure
that civilization included the components which gave it dignity and
permanence, and that the higher order would win over the lower in the
search for immortality.

> In this sense, also, the Muses are goddesses, and Apollo is leader of the
> Muses, and poetry as a whole is laudatory of the gods. And by the same
> course of reasoning they also attribute to music the upbuilding of
> morals, believing that everything which tends to correct the mind is
> close to the gods.[120]

Plato attributed to Apollo and the Muses the origin of all education,
as well as the sense of rhythm and harmony indispensable to a healthy
soul.[121] Eusebius, quoting Porphyry, acknowledged Apollo as the leader
of the Muses, with the Muses exercising a powerful influence on him:

> Ye Nymphs and Naiads with the Muses join
> To set Apollo free; and then in songs
> Exalt the praises of the archer god.[122]

PraepEv 125d-126a.
[119]Diodorus Siculus, Lib 1.18.4.
[120]Strabo, Geog 10.3.10 (LCL V) 95.
[121]Plato, Laws 654A; 672D.
[122]Eusebius, PraepEv 196a.

On a more practical level Apollo and his son Asclepius, were worshiped as the gods of healing, a function any divinity aspiring to supremacy had to exercise to the fullest extent. Healing became a central trait of Apollo worship. The god who could avert evil also had to ensure the physical well-being of his followers. The eternity of the divinity had to translate itself into benefits for mortals who were burdened by the liabilities of physical being. Sickness was viewed as the result of demonic interference with human life. To exorcise it required supernatural means available only from the heavens. Early in the process Apollo appropriated for himself the art of healing as part of his divine wisdom. When poets like Pindar sang the praises of the Delphic god, it was quite often as a recognition that he alone had revealed to his followers the art of averting and healing disease. Though there is no direct evidence that medical science owes anything to Apollo's cult, it remains a fact that the field of therapeutic science was and remains dominated by religious outlooks. Cicero lamented the fact that human beings were willing to attribute to the gods the discovery of the art of healing in the hope of maintaining the physical body in good condition, while investing much less ingenuity in taking care of the things of the soul.[123]

According to some traditions, Apollo and Asclepius learned the art of healing from the Centaur Chiron, a fact that led Justin to question the divinity of gods who had to learn their art from men.[124] But no one was likely to question the origin of a divine beneficence so essential to life. Already in the fifth century BCE the healing power of Apollo had become known beyond the limits of Greece. A temple to him was erected in Rome as the result of the end of a plague. Many sanctuaries were dedicated to Asclepius who shared Apollo's gift and could provide relief for those afflicted with physical ailments. In Delphi, however, only Apollo could mediate healing, and Asclepius stayed in his shadow.

One of the most memorable oracular responses of the Pythia was delivered to Chaerephon, who came to Delphi to inquire about the wisdom of Socrates. We do not know at what point in the life of Socrates the oracle was consulted on this specific question. But it was probably at a time when he had already acquired a great deal of notoriety and had

---

[123]Cicero, TuscDisp 3.1.
[124]Justin Martyr, SoleGov 6.

created a high level of enthusiasm among his friends and disciples. It is fair to assume that he was already well known at Delphi. The episode was revealed by Socrates himself during his trial as he addressed the judges and the court:

> For of my wisdom—if it is wisdom at all—and of its nature, I will offer you the god of Delphi as a witness. You know Chaerephon, I fancy. He was my comrade from a youth and the comrade of your democratic party, and shared in the recent exile and came back with you. And you know the kind of man Chaerephon was, how impetuous in whatever he undertook. Well, once he went to Delphi and made so bold as to ask the oracle this question; and, gentlemen, don't make a disturbance at what I say; for he asked if there were anyone wiser than I. Now the Pythia replied that there was no one wiser. And about these things his brother here will bear you witness, since Chaerephon is dead.[125]

Xenophon elaborated on the Delphian response by qualifying it: "Once on a time when Chaerephon made inquiry at the Delphic oracle concerning me, in the presence of many people Apollo answered that no man was more free than I am, or more just, or more prudent."[126] It is unlikely that Socrates would have used Xenophon's version in his defense. One even wonders why he brought up that question at all, if not to repudiate the charges of atheism levelled at him by his accusers. Socrates interpreted the event, generalizing its meaning and applying it to all wisdom seekers:

> But the fact is, gentlemen, it is likely that the god is really wise and by his oracle means this: "human wisdom is of little or no value." And it appears that he does not really say this of Socrates, but merely uses my name, and makes me an example, as if he were to say: "This one of you, O human beings, is wisest, who, like Socrates, recognises that he is in truth of no account in respect to wisdom."[127]

The compliment of Apollo to Socrates marked a definite connection between philosophy and religion and the emergence of Apollo as a judge of philosophical wisdom. Was Socrates really in need of Apollo's support, or was the Delphic oracle seeking for a channel of communica-

---

[125]Plato, Apol 21A (LCL I) 81.
[126]Xenophon, Apol 14 (LCL IV) 651.
[127]Plato, Apol 23AB (LCL I) 87.

tion as perfect and powerful as Socrates? Who better than Socrates could attribute validity to religious propositions that much too often were relegated to the realm of the absurd? Did not Apollo know how irrelevant and meaningless some of the requests of his suppliants were? Is it possible that, as Martha Nussbaum suggested, Apollo, the god revered by Pythagoras, looked down at the plight of the human race he did not want to perish, and chose his most resourceful messenger, Socrates, to reveal to them the marvelous gift which would convey the right knowledge and the right enjoyment?[128]

Whatever the case, we find in Socrates a paradox in his denunciation of the vulgar religious practices of the masses, while praising his personal relationship to Apollo. If philosophy was the prerogative of the few, so perhaps was right religion. On several occasions Socrates referred to his special divine sign (εἰωθὸς σημεῖον) which kept him from pursuing a wrong course of action.[129] When the god commanded him to do specific things as disclosed to him through oracles and dreams, was it not to Apollo that he referred?[130] And was he not returning the compliment to Apollo when he asserted that he shall obey the god rather than men?[131] The relationship of Socrates to Apollo became more profound as he approached death, comparing his prophetic gifts to Apollo's birds, the swans:

> I do not believe they sing for grief, nor do the swans; but since they are Apollo's birds, I believe they have prophetic vision, and because they have foreknowledge of the blessings in the other world they sing and rejoice on that day more than ever before. And I think that I am myself a fellow servant of the swans, and am consecrated to the same god and have received from our master a gift of prophecy no whit inferior to theirs, and that I go out from life with as little sorrow as they.[132]

Tertullian elaborated on the relationship of Apollo to Socrates in a way complimentary to neither. He reproached Apollo for declaring the

---

[128]Martha Nussbaum, *The Fragility of Goodness* (Cambridge: Cambridge University Press, 1986) 118.

[129]Plato, Apol 40C; Phaedr 242BC; Euthyd 272E.

[130]Plato, Apol 33C.

[131]Ibid., 29D.

[132]Plato, Phaedo 85AB (LCL I) 295.

wisest the very man who was denying the existence of his race. In that specific instance Apollo was revealing flaws which belied his claims to divinity. Tertullian's purpose was to show that Christian faith does not suffer from such contradictions and that it is superior to the oracle of Apollo as well as to the inconsistencies of Socrates, who condemned the gods of the vulgar while offering a cock to one of them.[133]

Origen referred to a tradition according to which Socrates was chosen as the wisest from among three candidates: "Sophocles is wise, and Euripides is wiser, but wiser than all men is Socrates." The designation "wise" for Socrates in such a context was of no great account for Origen, who considered tragic poets as deserving very little credit: "It is poor praise of Socrates to say that he [Apollo] prefers him to men who for a paltry reward compete upon the stage, and who by their representations excite the spectators at one time to tears and grief, and at another to unseemly laughter."[134]

Justin connected the oracle of Apollo that made Socrates the wisest with Socrates' own confession that he knew nothing. His acknowledgment of ignorance was taken seriously by Justin to prove that philosophers did not possess true knowledge and could not know of heavenly things, whatever the oracle decreed. Even the wise could not penetrate divine mysteries while pursuing the truth. Justin could not attribute much validity to the Delphic oracle, but he praised Socrates for attributing to God alone the things that are hidden from mortals. Thus Socratic ignorance was not a feigned attitude, and the oracle may have been right, but for the wrong reasons.[135]

Apollonian wisdom at Delphi culminated in the maxims inscribed on the walls of the temple: γνῶθι σαυτόν καὶ μηδὲν ἄγαν (Know thyself, and nothing in excess). Their exact origin cannot be determined, but, according to Plato, we owe them to the seven wise men known for their memorable sayings:

> They assembled together and dedicated these as the first fruits of their lore to Apollo in his Delphic temple, inscribing there those maxims which are on every tongue—"Know thyself" and "Nothing overmuch."

---

[133] Tertullian, AdNat 1.4; DeAnim 1.
[134] Origen, CCel 7.6 (ANF IV) 613.
[135] Justin Martyr, CohGent 36.

To what intent do I say this? To show how the ancient philosophy had this style of laconic brevity.[136]

What the history of the saying was before Plato can only be conjectured. We find in Heraclitus a surmise that he had given some thought to the maxim and had tried to link it with his own view of philosophy. In one short statement, not sufficiently developed to give us a clear insight into its meaning, Heraclitus said: "Ἐδιζησάμην ἐμεωυτόν" ("I search my self." Or "I have sought for myself.")[137] Whether or not Heraclitus had in mind the Delphic temple, he already voiced a strong preoccupation with the intent of the inscription by the seven wise men.

Cicero attributed the maxim directly to the divinity, for he regarded it as "too lofty for it to be thought to have emanated from a human being, and it was therefore ascribed to a god."[138] He intended to show how the Pythian Apollo meant for us to relate to the wisdom of self-knowledge by properly estimating the powers of body and mind and by following the path that would give us the greatest share of enjoyment of those powers.

That which was supposed to encapsulate the essential knowledge of self and god was open to so many interpretations that even oracular pronouncements could not reconcile. Few aphorisms have generated more debate, more inquiries, and more explanations than the Delphic maxims, perhaps for the very reason that their brevity is a tribute to their depth. Divine exhortation can be as ambiguous as human language, and pilgrims to the shrine of Apollo were not meant to leave his sanctuary fully satisfied with either themselves or the counsel of the god they encountered. Seldom did oracles provide final solutions to human dilemmas. They were pointers indicating the direction in which the search had to be oriented, and that required the participation of intelligence and perseverance.

Divine ambiguity did not preclude practical advice. Juvenal proposed that the maxim "Know thyself" did indeed come to us from the skies, that it should be imprinted in the heart and stored in the memory, but that the greatest benefit of such a precept came in practical situations such as the

---

[136]Plato, Prot 343B (LCL II) 197. So also in Pausanias, DescrGr 10.24.1 (LCL IV) 507: "These sages then came to Delphi and dedicated to Apollo the celebrated maxims, 'Know thyself' and 'Nothing in excess.' "

[137]Heraclitus, Fragm. 80. In *On the Universe*. (LCL) 494.

[138]Cicero, DeFin 5.44 (LCL XVII) 443.

choice of a wife or the desire to serve in the senate.[139] In Stoic philosophy the maxim "know thyself" could not be separated from the postulate that nature administers the universe. Personal wisdom could be derived only from universal principles of reasonable conduct. The Delphic precept, far from being superfluous, reinforced the need to pay attention to all forms of behavior, especially in relationship to a larger context where human actions and decisions influenced the unity and harmony of the world of which we are a part.[140] In that sense Delphic sagacity was not the result of specific sixth-century BCE philosophical activity but reflected current ideas on a variety of issues which had forever pertained to the human race. Even when related to contemporary questions, the oracle functioned as a sounding board that could amplify on religious conceptions that have perplexed men and women of all generations. The search for the new is only a rediscovery of the old in another form, a way to bring the mind to a proper appreciation of the moment.

As with all forms of wisdom, the inquirer is faced with human inadequacy. Pessimism cannot be totally excluded from the search for moral and intellectual progress. Ethical and moral reflections accentuate the gap between mortals and the gods. Worship requires a distance without which the honor of the gods would be compromised, a problem the Greeks often confronted without being able to offer credible explanations. In the case of the Delphic Apollo one could almost hear the warning given to the wise:

> Know that you are a human being in the presence of your god, fully aware of your position in relationship to that which is eternal and immortal. At the same time know that the god can bestow upon you intelligence, wisdom, and knowledge, and that you can enter a process leading to serenity and spiritual perfection, as you move from one conflict to another until you learn how to hear and interpret the oracle in a way acceptable to both the god and you.

The identification of the Delphic precept with the seven sages testified to the unity of wisdom and to its divine source. In the absence of a body of scriptures containing the final word of the divinity, the Delphic maxims came the closest to a holy text, positing the right relationship to

---

[139]Juvenal, Sat 11.27-30.
[140]Epictetus, Fragm 1.

religion. In the same way the E at Delphi could be taken to represent the assertion of the eternal Being, truthful and free from deception, the "know thyself" reminded the worshiper of his or her threatened position in front of the god:

> But this much may be said: it appears that as a sort of antithesis to "Thou art" stands the admonition "Know thyself," and then again it seems, in a manner, to be in accord therewith, for the one is an utterance addressed in awe and reverence to the god as existent through all eternity, the other is a reminder to mortal man of his own nature and the weaknesses that beset him.[141]

Divine wisdom does not always find a proper response in the human quest, and the Delphic precept may not have been meant to be the object of reflection for everybody. Not all pilgrims to Apollo's sanctuary personalized the meaning of the precepts. Socrates pointed out that, though troubled by religious questions, Euthydemus went to Delphi without paying sufficient attention to the inscriptions.[142] The correlation between the two maxims "know thyself" and "nothing in excess" often led people to conclude that temperance equalled self-knowledge. In Plato we find the surprising suggestion that the seven wise men fell into error by disconnecting the two, thinking that to the advice "know thyself" they had to add the practical injunction of temperance, not realizing that the two were indeed the same.[143]

The Socratic quest, which was rooted in a constant examination of life, found in the Delphic wisdom the incentive to probe deeper and deeper into the goals of ideal philosophy. As the horizon retreats while we attempt to reach it, so Socrates discovered that a knowledge of the self represented a program of life beyond human reach: "But I have no leisure for them at all; and the reason, my friend, is this: I am not yet able, as the Delphic inscription has it, to know myself; so it seems to me ridiculous, when I do not yet know that, to investigate irrelevant things."[144]

The process of internalization of the Delphic "know thyself" became essential to Cicero's perspective on the nature of the soul. Apollo's

---

[141]Plutarch, DeE 394C (LCL. Mor V) 253.
[142]Xenophon, Mem 4.24.
[143]Plato, Charm 164D-165B.
[144]Plato, Phaedr 229E (LCL I) 421-23.

maxim should be viewed in the light of the proposition that "the soul sees by means of the soul alone." Thus we should not be misled by any other practical interpretation of the saying. "To the soul occupied night and day in these meditations there comes the knowledge enjoined by the god at Delphi, that the mind should know its own self and feel its union with the divine mind, the source of the fullness of joy unquenchable."[145]

The god who journeyed the long road leading to his position as counselor of the human race knew of the dangers and the anxieties along the way, and his advice came as much from experience as from divine status. At Delphi, his beginnings and all the aberrations of his impulsive and vengeful personality were relegated to that distant past when even the gods had to share in the chaos preceding order. Now he ruled supreme, and his worshipers saw in him the final appeal to a life of reason, harmony, and wisdom. His voice pierced through time and history, filling his oracle with the kind of advice and sagacity which brought the plights of human beings close to solutions, yet removed in mystery beyond grasp.

---

[145]Cicero, TuscDisp 5.70 (LCL XVIII) 497; 1.52. The position of Cicero may be further supported by an apophthegm attributed by Diogenes Laertius to Pittacus and which was allegedly part of the Delphic inscriptions. It read, καιρὸν γνῶθι, know your opportunity, know the right season. Lives: Pittacus 79 (LCL I) 81.

Chapter 3

The Prophet and the Pythia

The prophetess at Delphi and the priestess at Dodona
when they have been mad conferred many splendid benefits
upon Greece both in private and public affairs,
but few or none when they have been in their right mind.
—Socrates

The best of seers is he who guesses well.
—Euripides

In a somewhat melancholic mood Plato dismissed human affairs as not being worthy of serious consideration. Yet he knew that necessity compels us to be in earnest about earthly life which is not totally despised by God, though men and women remain playthings of the divinity.[1] The search for a realm of absolute rationality within which all phenomena would find a logical explanation was not a part of the Greco-Roman way of thinking. Their world was full of threatening forces capable of disrupting personal well-being and collective security, sometimes well beyond the remedies provided by philosophical speculation or religious practice. They had to discern the workings of a divine will, often mysterious and obscure, that might bring affliction to those caught in the grips of a universal moira. Pagans and Christians alike sought to penetrate the inscrutability of divine decrees by appealing to priests, prophets, and saints able to mediate the kind of revelation that eluded intelligence and rationality.

"We do not rule the gods with our authority, nor do we know anything of the divine with our knowledge, and by the same reasoning, they likewise, being gods, are not our masters and have no knowledge of human affairs."[2] This astonishing Platonic assessment of divine transcen-

---

[1] Plato, Laws 803BC.
[2] Plato, Parm 134E (LCL IV) 227-29.

dence, which he put in the mouth of Parmenides, would suggest a radical separation between divinities and mortals. God's perfection, to remain unstained, forbids his contact with the material world of which we are a part. Divine mystery, however, could be penetrated by divination that, in one form or another, had always existed but had escaped conscious reasoning. Communion with the gods, from whom their intentions toward mortals could be deduced, belonged to the realm of dream and frenzy, emerging at the edge of religious impulses rather than controlled behavior. Prophets and prophetesses knew of the dichotomies and conflicts separating them from their suppliants or, as in the case of the Old Testament, from their nation.

In the Greco-Roman world religious practices evolved within a metaphysical dualism which assigned the proper place to gods and their subjects. A certain analogy between the divine and human minds was assumed. Without those important points of contact all religious systems would have collapsed by the sheer presence of mutual ignorance. Thus everybody was believed to be endowed with an embryonic gift of divination that found its seat in the soul. "How prophetic the soul is, my friend!" exclaimed Socrates as his conscience reminded him of religious obligations he had to perform in order to avoid the displeasure of the gods.[3]

As long as the soul resides within the body it cannot fully develop and utilize its prophetic function. According to Cicero inspiration can overtake the soul only when it acquires the skill of being alone with itself:

> Therefore the human soul has an inherent power of presaging or of foreknowing infused into it from without, and made a part of it by the will of God. If that power is abnormally developed, it is called "frenzy" or "inspiration," which occurs when the soul withdraws itself from the body and is violently stimulated by a divine impulse."[4]

The Sources of Divination

Contrary to Hebrew religion that linked all forms of prophetic inspiration with its monotheistic God, the Greco-Roman world assigned to divi-

---

[3]Plato, Phaedr 242C (LCL I) 459.
[4]Cicero, DeDiv 1.66 (LCL XX) 297.

nation many different sources, making it difficult to bring them together into a coherent system. In religious traditions that have spanned generations of worshipers, the divinity itself remained the source of inspiration, ensuring the trustworthiness of all spiritual quests. The gods dispensed divination as a means to secure their place of honor among mortals.

In a now-lost treatise, *Concerning Divination*, Posidonius of Rhodes identified two kinds of divination. The first was *artificial* divination that required specific skills in interpreting the signs sent by the gods. This gave rise to a group of religious leaders capable of discerning the meaning of the omens, auguries, and other specifics pertaining to ritual and mantic religion. The other was *natural* divination in which case the divine message was made clear directly to the mind of the prophet, and no specific art of interpretation was needed. Posidonius also suggested that we may not be able to discover the vital principle of divination until, to its divine source, we add the role of fate and nature as indispensable components of religious life. Fate, however, placed on the path of divination the greatest obstacle. It absolutized divine foreknowledge, deprived inquirers of freedom, and rendered prophetic insights powerless, for they would be limited to the prediction of what was bound to happen. But even within fate some of the outcomes could be deduced from experience: floods resulted from heavy rains, political events from human decisions, healings from the physician's art. . . .

Religious masters exercised their predictive skills and sharpened the art of conjecture, though it often led to mistakes. In a universe filled with the intelligence of the divine mind human quests eluded rational explanations. The Stoics made every soul a spark of the universal one and considered divination a search for the connection with one's divine origin. In such a context Chrysippus defined divination as "the power to see, understand, and explain premonitory signs given to men by the gods. Its duty . . . is to know in advance the disposition of the gods towards men, the manner in which that disposition is shown and by what means the gods may be propitiated and their threatened ills averted."[5]

Divination did not always find a favorable reception among critics of religion. Some of them put aside the idea of divine revelation altogether and appealed to human understanding to elucidate the mysteries of the

---

[5]Ibid., 2.130 (LCL XX) 517.

unknown. As early as the sixth century BCE Xenophanes wrote: "Truly the gods have not revealed to mortals all things from the beginning; but mortals by long seeking discover what is better."[6] So also Dio Cassius expressed skepticism about the claim that specific events could be foretold by divination: "For what does prophesying mean, if a thing is going to occur in any case, and if there can be no averting of it either by human skill or by divine providence? Let each man, then, look at these matters in whatsoever way he pleases."[7]

In the case of Delphic religion the Pythia was filled with prophetic insights through a power arising from the depths of the earth and filling her with the spirit of the divinity, or of lesser gods and demons. By the time of Plutarch, both theories were accepted, though the notion of vapors arising from a chasm has been refuted as a Hellenistic invention.[8] For many ancient Greeks the Pythian frenzy had to be supplemented by a more rational explanation of the phenomenon. While not denying the impact of the chasm theory, many suggested that the oracle also contained the wisdom of the Muses who could impart measure and harmony to Pythic pronouncements.

Few critics of the oracles dismissed outright the notion of the inspiration of the Pythia, and even accepted with reservation the beliefs connected with the chasm, the tripod, and the vapors. The Delphic intelligentsia had already promoted all of it to the level of acceptable traditions. With the passage of time even frenzy and enthusiasm at Delphi were sufficiently "officialized" to fit the mold of the Greek mind. Through ritual practices the phenomenon of divination was placed within a more understandable context.

The purification at the Castalian Spring initiated the prophetess into oracular wisdom. The belief that inspiration was the result of drinking at the sacred fountain was adopted by Greeks and survived in Christian writings, especially those of Clement of Alexandria and Eusebius.[9] Frazer mentions a less-well-known ritual of inspiration related to a temple of Apollo at Argos, where a lamb was sacrificed at regular intervals. A

---

[6]Freeman, *Ancilla*, Fragm 18, 22.

[7]Dio Cassius, RomHist 15.57.22 (LCL II) 135.

[8]A contention voiced first by Wilamowitz. See E. R. Dodds, *The Greeks and the Irrational* (Berkeley: University of California Press, 1951) 73.

[9]Clement of Alexandria, Protr 2; Eusebius, PraepEv 61d.

woman, bound by vows of chastity, tasted the blood, became inspired, and prophesied.[10]

The Blessings of Madness

"The greatest of blessings come to us through madness, when it is sent as a gift of the gods."[11] Inspiration stood in conflict with rationality and rested on two central concepts: ecstasy (to be outside oneself, to stand outside one's own being) and enthusiasm (to be in the god or to be filled with the god). Plato suggested that the gods did not enter the rational part of the mind, that they did not compete with the power of intelligence, preferring to disclose their intentions in divination and dreams. The purpose of the mind was to recollect the content of inspiration and to ponder the things that came to us in those dreams.[12] Speaking of the rhapsodes who could compose only what the Muse stirred in them, Socrates explained why God took away their minds and used them as his ministers and seers in order that those who heard them might know that they were listening to God himself.[13] As for soothsayers and diviners, they uttered many true things when inspired, but had no knowledge of anything they said.[14]

The ravings of the Pythia while in ecstasy did not contain the kind of advice that would be readily understandable to her suppliants. For that reason a well-developed cultic usage emerged. It ensured that the pronouncements of the Pythia were collected, clarified, and if necessary supplemented. Delphic priests and prophets transformed them into valid

---

[10]Sir James George Frazer, *The Golden Bough: A Study in Magic and Religion* (New York: Macmillan, 1922) 109.

[11]Plato, Phaedr 244A (LCL I) 465.

[12]Plato, Tim 71E. Tertullian, DeAnim 47 (ANF III) 226, placed a great deal of emphasis on the fact that knowledge comes from dreams: "It was, indeed by an inspiration from God that Nebuchadnezzar dreamt his dreams; and almost the greater part of mankind get their knowledge of God from dreams." The way in which the dreams of Nebuchadnezzar are reported in Dan 2 could be viewed as the prototype of other dreams of great political leaders to whom God revealed himself, as for example the dream of Constantine at the Milvian bridge. But we should also note that for Tertullian, many dreams came from demons.

[13]Plato, Ion 534C.

[14]Plato, Meno 99C.

oracles. Plato, though attributing a great deal of validity to frenzy and inspiration, nonetheless pointed out that those who found themselves in such states were not capable of interpreting their own words. Then he added:

> Wherefore also it is customary to set the tribe of prophets to pass judgment upon these inspired divinations; and they, indeed, themselves are named "diviners" by certain who are wholly ignorant of the truth that they are not diviners but interpreters of the mysterious voice and apparition, for whom the most fitting name would be "prophets of things divined."[15]

This came close to the distinction Saint Paul established between those who spoke in tongues and were of no use to the community and those who were endowed with the gift of prophecy and could edify the church.[16]

Plato divided divine madness into four distinct categories: the prophetic madness was inspired by Apollo, the mystic madness by Dionysus, the poetic by the muses, and that of love by Aphrodite and Eros.[17] This classification has been questioned by Rohde who attributed prophetic madness to Dionysus, and not to Apollo. According to him, prophetic madness was unknown in Greece before the coming of Dionysus to whom Pythic ecstasy should be attributed rather than to Apollo.[18] At Delphi, however, the distinction between Apollonian and Dionysian influences may not have been central to worshipers. Ecstatic inspiration owed no particular debt to any precise religious system. Its influence, though it may have been rooted in a specific cult, assumed its own modus operandi, often determined by the political and psychological moods of society. When the Pythia was *entheos*, full of the god, every worshiper could attribute his or her name of choice to that god, often not analyzing the question to any extent. Divination was interpreted *post eventum* when philosophical and theological explanations attempted to

---

[15]Plato, Tim 72AB (LCL IX) 187-89.

[16]First Corinthians 14:1-5.

[17]Plato, Phaedr 265B.

[18]Rohde, *Psyche*, IX.3. See also Dodds, *Greeks and the Irrational*, 68. Plato, Laws 672B also offers the interesting suggestion that Bacchic ecstasy was due to the fact that Hera, the stepmother of Dionysus, stole his mind.

bring rationality to that which did not fit into it. We could regard Apollo's vaticinations as inventions of theologians or philosophers. But, in the final analysis, he was the god revered through his Pythia on account of oracles that could deliver society from its threats, doubts, and fears, while providing a certain measure of harmony in the midst of madness. In fact excavations at Delphi do not support the existence of a chasm under the adyton nor of a pneuma emanating from it. The validity of the oracle could not be linked to that kind of physical reality. Cultic practices tended toward integration at a time when mantic inspiration was crossing over to traditional religion.

Again we owe to Plato a crucial clarification on the connection between madness and prophecy, which for him could be only one and the same thing. In a key passage he elaborated on the unfortunate semantic problem that separated madness from prophecy in the most unnatural fashion. The Greeks should have known of only one term: μανική (madness). Those who felt uncomfortable with the meaning of the term as applied to prophecy took the liberty of inserting a τ, thus reading the word as it is now known to us: μαντική (prophecy).[19] Socrates held μαντική as superior to what human beings considered sanity. This was the kind of madness that anyone who came to the door of the Muses should have possessed in order to meet with success. Only the truly wise accepted the paradoxical proposition that madness, when sent by the gods, created the greatest happiness.[20]

Biblical Prophecy

Biblical literature does not have a well-developed notion of inspiration.[21] Yet the prophetic movement considered it the heart of divine revelation. The awesome nature of a God whose name was not to be formed or spoken by human lips filled his creation with his numinous presence in front of which no one could survive. To a cultic obedience

---

[19]Plato, Phaedr 244C.

[20]Ibid., 245A.

[21]The Hebrew term נְשָׁמָה n'shamah (breath) is used in the sense of inspiration only in Job 32:8. The Greek word θεόπνευστος (inspired) is a hapax legomenon in the New Testament (2 Timothy 3:16) and does not refer to a person but to Holy Scriptures.

derived from laws and commandments was added the mysterious status of a people chosen to radiate the universal creative power, though they were reluctant to extend their religious vision beyond the borders of their land. It was in such a context that classical prophets arose, spoke, and often failed in their poorly defined roles as representatives of God.

One searches in vain in the Holy Scriptures for a definition of who and what prophets were. At times they spoke before God, as the term would imply. At other times they spoke for God, or in the name of God. Later still their function involved predicting the future. But none of those elements were really distinguishable, for the prophet was taken into the mysteries of the divine being that in reality knew of no past, present, or future. History and eschatology fused together into an eternal present containing simultaneously judgment and redemption, punishment and forgiveness, justice and grace. Prophets carried within themselves the awesome "knowledge of God," creating a sense of holiness as in the case of Isaiah, or a sense of social justice as in the case of Amos, or a sense of despair as in the case of Jeremiah. The prophet who received the Word could also be crushed by it, for no human situation could be recreated into a congenial home for the divine oracle. It was not in a moment of ecstasy but as the result of a lucid analytical understanding of his existential situation that Jeremiah exclaimed: "Cursed be the day on which I was born! / The day when my mother bore me, let it not be blessed!"[22] and this almost in the same breath as his statement of indignation against God:

> O LORD, thou hast deceived me,
>   and I was deceived;
> thou art stronger than I,
>   and thou hast prevailed.
> I have become a laughingstock all the day;
>   every one mocks me.[23]

---

[22]Jeremiah 20:14 (see also Job 3). The reluctance of Jeremiah to proclaim his message found an echo in the story related by Plutarch, DefOrac 438AC in regard to the Pythia who, in a specific instance, refused to serve while inspired and possessed, and paid for it by the loss of her life.

[23]Jeremiah 20:7.

Prophetic preaching generated endless conflict with popular faith, or the lack of it. Prophets stood alone in their knowledge of impending divine irruptions on the human scene, a fact seldom perceived by their contemporaries. The divine imperative was so inaccessible to the people that it often burdened prophets to the extent that they wished not for the closeness of God but for his distance that would be more beneficial and less threatening than his presence. Cultic performance mitigated some aspects of divine anger, but the prophet knew that it could not mediate God's dynamic power and awesomeness.

Who, then, were biblical prophets, and did they share any qualities with their Greco-Roman counterparts? As in the case of Delphic religion, the Hebrew nation had some prophets tied to specific sanctuaries, interpreting divine will to the faithful of the region. There were also raving bands of ecstatics, some of whom were possessed by madness.[24] They more likely assumed a role similar to that of Delphic Pythias. They spoke under the influence of ecstasy and possession. They were known in Canaan long before the Hebrews settled there.

The distinction between μάντις and προφήτης did not appear to affect the office of prophet in the Old Testament. According to Aeschylus, Apollo was both. As μάντις he possessed the power of divination. As προφήτης he interpreted the will of Zeus to men, being simultaneously god and prophet, Διὸς προφήτης.[25] One might see here a parallel with Christ who, in some instances, was considered a prophet,[26] while he also was *the* Word of God among his people.

Biblical prophets manifested two mutually exclusive characteristics. On the one hand their temperament was fiercely individualistic, and their whole being was involved in the act of prophesying and in the formulation of oracles. They often combined the charismatic qualities of poet, preacher, teacher, moralist, statesman, and social critic. On the other hand they were conscious of being mere instruments of divine purpose. In that sense they formulated no personal theory or idea of God. Yet they tried to explain that which was not always clear to them and took responsibili-

---

[24]Cf. 2 Kings 9:11.

[25]Aeschylus, Eum 18-19.

[26]Matthew 21:46; Luke 9:8; John 9:17. But see also John 7:52 according to which Jesus could not be regarded as a prophet.

ty for the correct delivery of the oracle.[27] Their message depended on the hypostatic nature of a divine Word in conflict with human outlook but unalterable in purpose.[28] The relationship to that Word established the legitimacy of the prophet as distinct from ecstatic seers who had to be eliminated on account of their corruption.[29] The fear of false prophets remained real and difficult to solve.

Philo, who claimed to possess some prophetic ability, undertook to define the frame within which prophecy was acceptable and commendable. In many cases possession and madness were considered the result of the weakening of the mind and had a negative impact on life. Exceptions had to be made for true prophets whose minds had to be evicted to make room for the divine spirit, until all returned again to normal.[30] While serving as the home for the divine spirit, the prophet lost his own identity: "Nothing of what he [the prophet] says will be his own, for he that is truly under the control of divine inspiration has no power of apprehension when he speaks but serves as the channel for the insistent words of Another's prompting. For prophets are the interpreters of God, Who makes full use of their organs of speech to set forth what He wills."[31] But the prophet was also privileged to partake of divine knowledge. For him nothing was hidden. The spiritual light gave him an insight into that which was not understandable on a rational level.[32]

Hebrew prophetic proclamation defined the circle within which divine mysteries were contained in images, visions, riddles, metaphors, and threats of condemnation and chastisement. Its riddles often exceeded those of Apollonian oracles, for they were part, especially in Ezekiel, of a new eschatological and universal apprehension of divine teleology. The wheels within wheels had too many different centers to produce a coherent vision of unity and harmony within historical vicissitudes.

New Testament writers took over the notion of divine inspiration in its broad and general meaning. Epimenides was called a prophet.[33] The

---

[27]Jeremiah 6:27.
[28]Isaiah 55:8-11.
[29]Zechariah 13:2.
[30]Philo, QuisRer 264-65. See also 249-50.
[31]Philo, SpecLeg 1.65 (LCL VII) 137. See also QuisRer 259, 266.
[32]Philo, SpecLeg 4.192.
[33]Titus 1:12.

spirit of divination was referred to only once[34] in the context of a slave girl pursuing Paul and exalting the qualities of the apostles, until Paul put an end to it by exorcising her spirit. It would be tempting to see in this episode the survival of a Pythian form of possession.

Prophetic activity in the New Testament was regarded as one of many charismatic gifts. The church possessed prophetic insights which ensured order in belief and practice. The fact that prophecy was related to revelation did not exclude the participation of human wisdom in keeping that revelation from deteriorating into unacceptable forms.[35] In the earlier days of the Christian church, when it was still considered a sect of Judaism, we find references to organized groups of prophets moving about the land, and sometimes their names were mentioned.[36] With the emergence of an institutionalized Christian church the old function of prophet disappeared. It was replaced by theological investigations and conciliar pronouncements.

The church fathers generally accepted the prevalent views on prophets and prophecy. Justin referred to different kinds of prophecy, the only valid ones coming from prophets who were moved by the divine word in them. But that divine word was connected with Christ, and the Jews, who did not recognize Christ as the Messiah, failed to understand their own prophets.[37] The gifts of prophecy did not stop with Christ. They were transferred to the Christians.[38] Irenaeus fought those who sought to damage the reputation of prophets. He refuted the argument of Basilides that because there are different names for God in the Old Testament, prophets spoke under the influence of different gods. Even more pointed was his rejection of the notion proposed by some critics of the church that the prophecies of the Old Testament were uttered not under the authority of the spirit of God, but from the demiurge itself, thus reducing prophecy to the level of demons rather than of God.[39]

For Origen, the Jewish prophets were the only ones enlightened by the spirit of God and were the first ones to enjoy the benefits of

---

[34]Acts 16:16.
[35]First Corinthians 14:26-33.
[36]Acts 11:27-28; 13:1; 15:32; 21:10.
[37]Justin Martyr, 1 Apol 36.
[38]Justin Martyr, Trypho 82.
[39]Irenaeus, AdvHaer 2.25.3; 4.35.1-2.

inspiration. For him the Pythia was inspired by the kind of demons that Christians now have the power to cast out. He criticized Apollo for choosing a woman Pythia while disregarding the higher class of men who would have been better interpreters of his message, provided that they would have accepted to lower themselves to that kind of inspiration and religious rituals.[40]

T̲ẖe Pyt̲ẖia an∂ Her Go∂

When Apollo allowed his oracle to be dependent on the Pythia, he introduced into Delphic religion a reassuring voice mortals could relate to even when they did not totally understand it. The mythological origins of the Pythia and her role at Apollo's shrine are shrouded in mystery. Many believed she perpetuated the divine presence that marked the rule of Ge and that she was inspired through the emanation of a telluric pneuma arising from the depths of the open earth to disclose the hidden secrets of her mysterious world. Diodorus suggested that, in the early pre-Apollonian stages, many eager pilgrims came to the chasm and met their death by disappearing into it. To minimize such risks a tripod was built over the chasm and became the seat from which the oracle was delivered. At first the god chose as his Pythia a young virgin in her state of innocence until the days when Echecrates fell enamored with her, abducted her, and raped her. Because of that incident Delphians decided to entrust the oracle to a woman of at least fifty.[41]

By the time of Plutarch the list of credentials for the Pythia was well established and, to say the least, was quite surprising:

> Even so the maiden who now serves the god here was born of as lawful and honourable wedlock as anyone, and her life has been in all respect proper; but, having been brought up in the home of poor peasants, she brings nothing with her as the result of technical skill or of any other expertness or faculty, as she goes down into the shrine. On the contrary, just as Xenophon believes that a bride should have seen as little and heard as little as possible before she proceeds to her husband's house,

---

[40]Origen, CCel 7.4-6. It is interesting to note the insistence of Origen on the superiority of men in performing divinely appointed offices and on the decadence of religious institutions resorting to women.

[41]Diodorus Siculus, Lib 16.26.6. Such a tradition may have been known to Aeschylus, Eum 38.

so this girl, inexperienced and uninformed about practically everything, a pure, virgin soul, becomes the associate of the god.[42]

The humble origin of the instrument chosen to reveal the god's word and purpose added credibility to Apollo's intent to communicate divine mysteries to worshipers trapped within human limitations. At points the humble origin of Jesus was emphasized with the same intent. Humble ancestry, however, did not mean lack of nobility or character. The prophetic priestess was known to be beyond reproach, and when she found herself at the service of her god she cared for nothing but fulfilling her duties, oblivious to praise or blame on the part of her suppliants.[43]

There was no universal agreement on the status of the Pythia. Those who spoke of her mentioned her blameless life and her strict adherence to stated requirements. We find references to the fact that she was not always a maiden, that she could have been a wife and mother but that, while fulfilling her appointment, she was not allowed to live with her husband, perhaps because she was considered in Delphic myth to be the bride of Apollo.

The selection process of the Pythia was nowhere described in detail, and speculations abound. Her psychological state and fitness for the office may have been determined by those who selected her, and occasionally we have reports of abuses on her part. Secular and Christian writers reported instances when the Pythia succumbed to the lure of bribes, letting herself be influenced to deliver oracles suitable to the requests of those who approached her.[44]

---

[42]Plutarch, PythOr 405CD (LCL. Mor V) 319-21. We find a different assessment in Plato: "There were certain priests and priestesses who have studied so as to be able to give a reasoned account of their ministry." Meno 81A (LCL II) 301.

[43]Plutarch, DefOrac 408CD.

[44]Diodorus Siculus, Lib 14.13.3 mentions several attempts to bribe the prophetess to lead her to deliver suitable oracles. See also Thucydides, PelWar 5.16; Cicero, DeDiv 2.118. Dio Cassius, RomHist 62.14.2-3 (LCL VIII) 161 reported an incident in which Nero paid, in vain, a large sum of money to the Pythia in order to obtain self-fulfilling oracles: "This same emperor gave 400,000 sesterces to the Pythia for uttering some oracles that suited him; this money Galba recovered. But from Apollo, on the other hand, whether from vexation at the god for making some unpleasant predictions to him or because he was merely

Christian writers adduced as the most serious charge against the Delphic oracle the fashion in which the Pythia became the receptacle of Apollo's spirit. They referred to the dubious traditions according to which the god entered the Pythia through her private parts as she was astride on the tripod, a fact that would not fail to horrify the faithful in the early church. The reports of such occurrences were carefully crafted to emphasize the obscenity of the most venerated Greco-Roman religion as well as the moral and spiritual deficiency of those who considered oracles emanating from such a source as divine truths. For Origen Apollo exhibited his profane and impure nature by choosing to manifest himself through such a channel, debasing not only his divine status, but also the character of the Pythia. Origen insisted on the superiority of the divine spirit revealed in Christ whose material being in no way diminished the wonder of God's presence in him through the spirit.[45]

John Chrysostom went far beyond Origen in his attacks on pagan mantic practices. In order to prove not only the superiority but also the absolute divine essence of Christian revelation, he had to lower pagan expressions of divination to the level of the obscene and the ridiculous, not to say the horrifying:

> This same Pythoness then is said, being a female, to sit at times upon the tripod of Apollo astride, and thus the evil spirit ascending from beneath and entering the lower part of her body, fills the woman with madness, and she with dishevelled hair begins to play the bacchanal and to foam at the mouth, and thus being in a frenzy to utter the words of her madness. I know that you are ashamed and blush when you hear these things: but they glory both in the disgrace and in the madness which I have described.[46]

---

crazy, he took away the territory of Cirrha and gave it to the soldiers. He also abolished the oracle, after slaying some people and throwing them into the fissure from which the sacred vapours arose." Origen, CCel 8.46 contrasted the vulnerability of the Pythia, when she let herself be influenced, with the admirable faithfulness of biblical prophets. To make matters worse Apollo chose, on purpose, a Pythia so deficient in credentials as to ensure catastrophe for his oracles.

[45]Origen, CCel 3.25; 7.3.
[46]John Chrysostom, HFirstCor 29.2 (NPNF-1 XII) 170.

Christian apologists sharpened their antipagan polemic by pushing to its extreme the objectionable bodily relationship between the Pythia and her god. On the whole, however, they found very little support among classical authors. Divine possession and inspiration were linked to spiritual phenomena, and the Pythia had to conform to the strict requirements of virginity or chastity, at least while in the service of her god.

The extent to which the prophetess spoke the words of Apollo depended on an understanding of the spiritual union between the Pythia and her god. Was the god in need of a human voice to make his will known to mortals? Celsus accused Christians of error in their belief that God would make use of the voice of Jesus to achieve his purpose of persuasion. To that Origen retorted that the Greeks never denied Apollo his divinity while he made use of the voice of the Pythia or other prophetesses.[47] Plutarch was not willing to concede a total identification of the voice of the Pythia with the divine message. The prevailing understanding of inspiration whereby the god entered the Pythia and spoke through her, using her mouth and voice as instruments, was never totally rejected. But it had to be qualified in ways proper to maintain both divine perfection and human participation.

Lamprias took the most negative approach to commonly held beliefs in inspiration and considered it foolish and childish to portray the god as some kind of ventriloquist who, after having entered the bodies of his prophets would use their voices as his instruments. For if the god would allow himself to be entangled in men's needs, he would thereby forfeit his greatness and preeminence.[48] To such an argument we find two alternatives in Plutarch. First he had Sarapion put forward the idea that the voice of the Pythia was not directly that of the god, nor were the utterances as such, nor the dictation or the meter, but that the god put in her mind only visions and created a light in her soul that led to her inspiration. It would have thus been inappropriate to expect a perfect consistency in the Pythia's responses. Divine inspiration affected different parts of her soul in various ways so that she fluctuated in temperament and could not escape the liabilities of changing moods.[49] The other possi-

---

[47]Origen, CCel 1.70.
[48]Plutarch, DefOrac 414E.
[49]Plutarch, PythOr 397C; DefOrac 437D.

bility was voiced by Heracleon, that the gods were not in charge of the oracles because they must be free of earthly concerns, but the demigods, ministers of Apollo, were responsible for them.[50] But Ammonius, the teacher of Plutarch, would not readily concede that the cause of inspiration and prophecy could be removed from the god himself.[51]

The inspiration of the Pythia transcended her temporal service to the god, somewhat like the sibyl, who sang of herself that even after death she will not cease from prophesying as her spirit moves through the air.[52] Arnobius elaborated on the presence of God in his representatives while his own being was not affected by such an identification. If the sibyl or the Pythia, or the prophet were cut down by robbers while prophesying, the god in them would not die by that fact. The works of Pythagoras did not lose their meaning when he was unjustly condemned and burned. The words of Socrates are still with us as those of a true martyr. Nor could Christians conceive that God died when Christ was nailed on the cross,[53] speculations which served as the foundation for docetic tenets. There were benefits of inspiration even when they came from divine beings who were not immune to death and whose works may have been threatened by oblivion. The gods, however, were believed to be everlasting, and those who shared a relationship with them carried some of that immortality in their own beings. Aeschylus summarized it by stating that the works of the gods may die, but not the gods themselves.

The Pythia and the Prophet

Both the Pythia and the biblical prophet assumed the role of reassuring voices or of bearers of prophecies of impending disaster. Hebrew prophets were the masters and authors of their own oracles, often in advance of the morality of their age. It is less certain that the Pythia crafted her oracles, but rather relied on Delphic prophets to formulate the content of her visions. As early as the sixth century BCE the field was wide open in Greece for chresmologues, collectors and peddlers of oracles who devised their own versions of oracular pronouncements made to order for their clients. Even at Delphi the priesthood managed to sap

---

[50]Plutarch, DefOrac 418E.

[51]Ibid., 413E.

[52]Plutarch, PythOr 398D.

[53]Arnobius, AdvGent 1.40, 62; 2.36.

the authority of the Pythia by putting together judicious interpretations mixed with ambiguities, coincidences, and sometimes luck to keep the visitors to the shrine satisfied.

Christian apologists, who made every effort to portray Delphic oracles and Pythic pronouncements as concealed deceptions, had to admit that the phenomenon had been sufficiently powerful to represent for Greek worshipers what the Hebrew prophets came to mean for Christianity. They cast Delphic religion into a theological mode that made it inferior to their faith. They prevailed by assigning to the Pythia a death surrounded by obscenity and impurity, while praising the biblical prophets for their virtue. Yet "the Greeks believed in their Oracle, not because they were superstitious fools, but because they could not do without believing in it. And when the importance of Delphi declined, as it did in Hellenistic times, the main reason was not, I suspect, that men had grown (as Cicero thought) more sceptical, but rather that other forms of religious reassurance were now available."[54] Later Athanasius sang the hymn of victory over oracles that had been prominent and held in repute by so many: "Now, since Christ has begun to be preached everywhere, their madness also has ceased and there is none among them to divine any more."[55] The prophet displaced the Pythia, and Christ dethroned Apollo in a long struggle that knew of many centers displacing each other while contending for the allegiance of worshipers in search for the best forms of reassurance in a world full of threatening forces.

---

[54]Dodds, *Greeks and the Irrational*, 75.
[55]Athanasius, DeIncarn 47.1 (NPNF-2 IV) 62.

Chapter 4

The Rise and Fall
of the Delphic Oracle

The Oracles are dumm,
No voice or hideous humm
  Runs through the archèd roof in words deceiving.
Apollo from his shrine
Can no more divine,
  With hollow shriek the steep of Delphos leaving.
  —Milton, *On the Morning of Christ's Nativity,* st. 19

The end of life lies in achieving communion with the divine, thought Pythagoras, whose well-known saying that "human beings are at their best when they approach the gods" appeared in theological treatises either with approval or rebuttal. If there be any connection between divine expectation and human compliance, the decrees of the gods must be translated to mortals in understandable terms. The appeal of Apollonian religion rested on oracular pronouncements disclosing and reordering a mysterious world beyond rational analysis.

We do not know how the Delphic oracle rose to its position of prominence in secular and religious matters during the archaic period. It would appear that Apollonian priests were able to assess the currents of the time, adapt to them, and establish a link between religious aspirations and the wisdom of the age. The oracle progressively widened its perspective until it could propose solutions to requests ranging from ecstatic divination, to practical concerns of civic and political life, to the legislation of human behavior.

The wisdom of the seven sages kept the Delphic oracle within the bounds of harmony and balance, avoiding the excess of both legalism and chaotic mysticism, though neither could be totally excluded. To the dismay of Plutarch the oracle had been visited by people lacking respect for the god and presenting irreverent petitions hardly conducive to cogent responses. But Delphi also attracted statesmen, philosophers, artists, and, most of all, suppliants whose personal and collective lives fell into the throes of natural or social devastation. To them Apollo could mediate the reassurance rooted in ancestral traditions through carefully crafted oracles, impugning neither the status of the gods nor the liabilities of visitors to the shrine.

The strength of Delphi did not reside in the intrinsic value of its oracles, which sometimes bordered on the absurd, but in its ability to convince the ancient world of its universal influence. To a divine moira capable of destroying gods, demons, and men, Apollo added reason and wisdom. If the Delphic sanctuary was to remain at the center of the religious world, the god who ruled there had to be the omniscient minister of all events, past, present, and future. Divine decrees to be credible had to appear to intelligent citizens as being good and just.

The prestige of philosophy and poetry ensured that Apollonian religion would not deteriorate to the level of the inane. Delphi may not always have been conscious of its unique mission, and one should not attribute to its religious role an importance it did not assume. Critics of the oracle could not ignore two propositions Greek philosophers have tried to elucidate, namely, that the soul contains God-given elements ensuring the proper link to the divine, and that the body blinds the soul's vocation and makes oracles the more necessary in an attempt to recover a knowledge of divine purpose.

Many personalities of the Greco-Roman world praised the Delphic oracles. Socrates, Cicero, and Plutarch held Apollonian religion in very high esteem. In obedience to an Apollonian response the great rhetorician Dio Chrysostom wandered through many lands disguised as a beggar until he reached what he believed to be the end of the earth.

Delphic religion never attempted to annihilate the natural qualities of suppliants. Reason (λόγος) helped achieve harmony of purpose. Plutarch urged those who came to the oracle to think devoutly and speak reverently, though he knew that the majority would act absurdly. Divine reverence remained beyond the grasp of those who failed to pay respect to the gods.[1]

---

[1]Plutarch, IsOsir 378CD. In his works on Delphic religion Plutarch often refers to the Platonic tenet that the pure cannot mingle with the impure. Consequently the god cannot be blamed for the religious failures which are due to the

Delphic priesthood progressively liberated itself from obscure beginnings to emerge into a position of authority in religious matters, giving advice in troubling situations such as plagues, floods, droughts, or any misfortunes requiring the placation of the gods. Even when democratic assemblies could decide on their private affairs, the advice and confirmation of the Delphic oracle added a layer of legitimacy, making their decisions more final. Though the oracle never achieved or aspired to secular success, it left a definite imprint on Greco-Roman private and public life for well over a millennium. This was especially true in the areas of framing laws, in the making and undoing of kings and kingdoms, in deciding the outcome of wars, and in shaping the destinies of individuals and nations.

Much too often, however, oracles proved detrimental to rational action. The credulity of suppliants prevented them from taking into consideration the deceiving ability of chresmologues. In his assessment of decisions made during the Peloponnesian war, Thucydides suggested that oracles never had a beneficial influence since everybody listened to them according to personal expectation. In times of distress people resorted to inadequate oracles, giving rise to false hopes that precipitated the demise of those who entertained them.[2] For the sake of expediency

---

contamination of the human medium.

[2]Thucydides' skepticism of oracles and religion in general is well documented. When the Spartans consulted the Delphic oracle to know whether it was wise for them to go to war, Apollo "replied that if they fought with all their might, victory would be theirs, and that he himself would be on their side, whether they invoked him or not" (PelWar 1.118). Hence the futility of religion. Often the oracle offered no enlightenment whatsoever (1.126). Prophecies were of no help (2.8). Prophets seemed to be everywhere, seducing leaders of all parties to listen to them (2.21). In times of tragedy religion should have brought relief. Yet it was then that it appeared the most useless: "Equally useless were prayers made in the temples, consultation of oracles, and so forth; indeed, in the end people were so overcome by their sufferings that they paid no further attention to such things" (2.47). During the plague of 430 CE temples became mortuaries, as religion found itself in a total state of collapse: "The temples . . . were full of the dead bodies of people who had died inside them. For the catastrophe was so overwhelming that men, not knowing what would happen next to them, became indifferent to every rule of religion or of law" (2.52). In the same breath Thucydides added: "As for the gods, it seemed to be the same thing

the Delphic oracle often refrained from denouncing the moral corruption of the society it served. It lacked the insight of biblical prophecy and gospel morality. Eusebius conceded that all oracles may have been inspired by the Supreme God through his universal providence, but he made a clear distinction between the oracles of biblical prophets, which he regarded as superior, and the practices of pagan religions.[3]

The Nature of the Oracle

Oracles provide the best source of information on Delphic religion and the prominence of the Apollonian cult. We possess, however, no collections of oracles and no corpus of authoritative writings emanating from Delphi itself. No original records, if they existed at all, survived. The oral tradition preserved stories and legends which may have originated with priests, prophets, or even with guides to the sanctuary. Some oracular responses such as the ones delivered in the case of Oedipus or Croesus show the kind of insight and depth which could not be attributed to unskilled prophets. Pythic statements circulated for a long time before reaching their final legendary meaning. Prophecy turned to poetry, then to popular wisdom and religious traditions supporting the cultus of a nation.

Our information on Delphic oracles comes from poets, playwrights, philosophers, historians, and church fathers. Several collections are now available in a reconstructed form, the most complete ones being those of Herbert William Parke and D. E. W. Wormell, organized in nine specific periods,[4] and Joseph Fontenrose who attempted a systematic classification of the responses under the headings of *historical, quasi-historical*, and *legendary*.[5] Herodotus built his notion of history around oracular

---

whether one worshipped them or not, when one saw the good and the bad dying indiscriminately" (2.53). If one is still to believe that gods do send whatever comes to us, then one must endure it with resignation and fight with courage (2.64).

[3]Eusebius, DemEv 5.202d-203c.

[4]Herbert William Parke and D. E. W. Wormell, *The Delphic Oracle*, 2 vols. (Oxford: Basil Blackwell, 1954) 2:1-138.

[5]Joseph Fontenrose, *The Delphic Oracle: Its Responses and Operation with a Catalogue of Responses* (Berkeley: University of California Press, 1978) 244-427.

responses. But he was accused by Plutarch and others of diminishing their historical value through inconsistency and even by altering the record in order to fit the moral lessons he wanted to teach.

In its early stages the oracle was regarded by the Greeks as reflecting spiritual strength, which it progressively lost. Socrates believed that the ancients were better and lived nearer the gods, and that they handed down superior traditions concerning divine knowledge.[6] By the time of Plato, reflections on religion had already shifted to a more analytical phase, and the suspicion of negligence of older traditions often led to charges of impiety. The old prophets and their teaching vanished from memory. Oracles still ensured continuity in religion. But their importance receded in favor of more rational explanations. At times they were rejected as feigned responses, or as being invented altogether. Such was the charge of Minucius Felix, a Christian disciple of Cicero:

> Ennius invented the replies of the Pythian Apollo concerning Pyrrhus, although Apollo had already ceased to make verses; and that cautious and ambiguous oracle of his failed just at the time when men began to be at once more cultivated and less credulous. And Demosthenes, because he knew that the answers were feigned, complained that the Pythia *philippized*. But sometimes, it is true, even auspices of oracles have touched the truth.[7]

In the days when the oracle had great prestige, some forgeries were produced and peddled as authentic responses.

Until the Hellenistic period, Apollo was linked to a strong sense of teleology. The solemn consent of the divinity became necessary to secure authority and permanence for popular as well as philosophical reflections on life. In reality, Delphic theologians did not concern themselves with universal truth in the way the Babylonians or the Hebrews had. For many visitors to the Delphic shrine, especially for those with immediate needs, the role of the god was limited to answering requests. Thus truth was fashioned out of questions and responses based on the necessities of the moment.

Oracles circulating around the country did not lend themselves to the creation of a logical theological system. One could even question the

---

[6]Plato, Phil 16C-17A.
[7]Minucius Felix, Oct 26 (ANF IV) 189. See also Cicero, DeDiv 2.116.

motives of Delphic priests in their careful avoidance of issues not directly related to the praises of the sanctuary and its god. Scholars such as Defradas have suggested that Delphic religion was a carefully designed and carried out enterprise of propaganda meant to glorify a god who would return a favor by delivering oracles protecting the interests of those who formulated the requests.[8] This may have been especially true in the areas of the founding of cities, legislation, and especially politics where, as in the case of the Persian War, the Delphic oracle was accused of compromise in its attempt at diplomacy.

"God has ordained" (ἀνεῖλεν ὁ θεός) was used as a stamp of authority. Often it was not even the result of a speech by the Pythia, but simply of a sign of the hand she gave, meaning that the god had agreed to the request with no need for elaboration. Plutarch distinguished between two categories of difficulties the oracles were called upon to solve. There were two kinds of ἀπορία: the ἀπορία περὶ τὸν βίον, the kind of problem connected with life itself. To those problems Apollo could provide an easy response. But to the ἀπορία περὶ τὸν λόγον, the problem connected with the power to reason, there was no simple solution. All Apollo could do was to create in the soul a craving that would lead to the truth.[9]

Plutarch warned against the dangers of interpreting the god's will in the absence of clear prophetic pronouncements. According to him, some ministers of Apollo lost their lives at the hands of evil men, a fact that did not diminish the determination of the oracle to persist in the proclamation of what it considered the truth.[10] Plutarch may have referred not only to the fate of some of Apollo's prophets but also to men like Socrates who were the victims of proponents of a popular religion within which there was no longer any room for higher levels of divine disclosure. Did not Christ feel the need to hide from the people, and even from his disciples, certain truths which could not be comprehended at the moment? The oracle had to commend itself to the Greek people. It could not mold popular opinion beyond the acceptable. Thus, the Delphic priesthood exercised caution in answering controversial requests by issuing ambiguous responses.

---

[8]Defradas, Thèmes.
[9]Plutarch, DeE 384F.
[10]Plutarch, PythOr 407DE.

Critics of Delphic religion aimed their weapons at the nature of the oracles, especially the language in which they were delivered. Epicureans considered Pythic verses unworthy of the leader of the Muses and rejected practically all the forms in which the prophetess expressed the supposed wishes of Apollo. The general assumption that the soul must be properly equipped to understand the oracle led to a condemnation of the form in which the Pythia delivered the utterances of Apollo. In response to Celsus, who criticized Christians for not placing any value on the oracle of the Pythian priestess, Origen replied:

> In regard to the oracles here enumerated, we reply that it would be possible for us to gather from the writings of Aristotle and the Peripatetic school not a few things to overthrow the authority of the Pythian and the other oracles. From Epicurus also, and his followers, we could quote passages to show that even among the Greeks themselves there were some who utterly discredited the oracles which were recognised and admired throughout the whole of Greece. But let it be granted that the responses delivered by the Pythian and other oracles were not the utterances of false men who pretended to a divine inspiration; and let us see if, after all, we cannot convince any sincere inquirers that there is no necessity to attribute these oracular responses to any divinities.[11]

In his *De pythiae oraculis*, Plutarch undertook a systematic *apologia* of the unimpeachability of Delphic religion. With adversaries of the stature of Aristotelians and Epicureans, the task demanded more than partisan argumentation and required the depth of analysis which Plutarch alone was able to provide in the ancient world. There was no denial of the barrenness and cheapness of many oracles, as pointed out by Diogenianus, who observed that the leader of the Muses did not take interest in the elegance of diction and was probably inferior to Hesiod and Homer. Sarapion, himself a poet, reluctantly agreed to the argument, reinforced by Boëthus, that the oracles were carelessly wrought. To that Sarapion chose as the most plausible explanation the error of suppliants who considered that only pleasant things were fair and lovely, not realizing that human beings are often the victims of ailing ears and eyes.[12] Aristotle was brought back to the stand to declare that Homer alone could

---

[11]Origen, CCel 7.3 (ANF IV) 611.
[12]Plutarch, PythOr 396C-397A.

be dignified with greatness in poetry, thus challenging Apollo's superiority on account of his being filled with the divine spirit.[13] Pindar, who often sang the praises of Apollo from his iron seat at Delphi, was also made to confess that he was puzzled by the obvious neglect in the presentation of the oracle, urging to seek for the causes of such an abnormal fact.[14] But none of this would have justified doing away with the oracle, since the Muses were still the guardians of the prophetic art.[15] Later Eusebius exposed the paradoxical stance of the Greeks who revered their ancestral traditions while disparaging the oracles. Aristotelians, Cynics, and Epicureans poured ridicule on the oracles instead of being struck by their wonders.[16]

Plutarch adopted three major lines of debate in defense of the oracle. The first one consisted in disconnecting the will of the god from the medium through which he communicated it. The inferior quality of oracles was due to the fact that Apollo was not directly the author of them. He supplied the original incitement, but the prophetess took over and formulated the responses in accordance with her natural faculties. In either written or oral oracles the god was not responsible for the handwriting, the diction, the voice, or the meter, but only for the visions he created.[17] The perfect divine design could be contaminated by the nature of the medium, especially when that medium was a mortal body or soul unable to keep quiet and free from restlessness.[18]

In his second argument Plutarch contended that there was a purposeful attempt to simplify the oracle in order to make it understandable. That required eliminating strange words, circumlocutions, and vagueness: "The introduction of clearness was attended also by a revolution in belief, which underwent a change along with everything else."[19] This attempt,

---

[13]Ibid., 398A.

[14]Ibid., 403A.

[15]Ibid., 402D.

[16]Eusebius, PraepEv 139bc.

[17]Plutarch, PythOr 397BC. Plutarch also pointed out that when people have the priests read the omens of the birds, they do not expect a rational discourse, while they insist that the voice and language of the prophetess be precise and logical.

[18]Plutarch, PythOr 404CE.

[19]Ibid., 407A (LCL. Mor V) 329.

however, also came under attack by those who would complain whatever the case: "Just as in those days there were people who complained of the obliquity and vagueness of the oracles, so to-day there are people who make an unwarranted indictment against their extreme simplicity. Such an attitude of mind is altogether puerile and silly."[20]

The third argument of Plutarch had to do with the nature of poetry itself. It was not the meter or the diction which were at stake. Some oracles were still delivered in meter,[21] whereas in ancient times some were delivered in prose and others in poetry.[22] But poetry could be used, or misused, to distort the oracles at the hands of skilled versifiers: "Moreover there was the oft-repeated tale that certain men with a gift for poetry were wont to sit about close by the shrine waiting to catch the words spoken, and then weaving about them a fabric of extempore hexameters or other verses or rhythms as 'containers,' so to speak, for the oracles."[23] Because of the charlatanry of wandering soothsayers, who had developed the poetic art for dishonorable ends, poetry had lost all standing with truth at the tripod.[24]

In the speech of Sarapion we find what could be considered Plutarch's intention for the whole work:

> For we must not show hostility towards the god, nor do away with his providence and divine powers together with his prophetic gifts; but we must seek for explanations of such matters as seem to stand in the way, and not relinquish the reverent faith of our fathers.[25]

Throughout his works on Delphi Plutarch presented the same plea, that we should never disregard or speak ill of the benefits of the oracles because they came from providence and were not due to chance and accident.

---

[20]Ibid., 409C (LCL. Mor V) 343-45.
[21]Ibid., 403F.
[22]Ibid., 404AB.
[23]Ibid., 407B (LCL. Mor V) 331.
[24]Ibid., 407C.
[25]Ibid., 402E (LCL. Mor V) 305.

Divine Ambiguity

"In searching out the truth be ready for the unexpected, for it is difficult to find and puzzling when you find it,"[26] were the words of warning of Heraclitus who added: "To God, all things are beautiful, good and just; but men have assumed some things to be unjust, others just."[27] Divination and prophetic art, being removed from the sphere of rationality, led either to a more profound sense of divine mystery or to a rejection of all mantic explanations. When subjected to critical analysis, many Delphic oracles failed to give adequate responses to those believed to have legitimate requests. Ambiguity permeated the religious quest for the very reason that divine and human spheres of activity had no absolute points of contact. Perfect harmony between divine will and human expectation would render religion useless and oracles unnecessary. Fontenrose warned against our misinterpretation of religious ambiguity, which he conceded was an article of Delphic belief. But the concept, he claimed, was wholly modern, and Delphi had no such reputation in the past.[28]

Double entendre in oracular pronouncements lost its appeal with the rise of critical inquiry. Plutarch rejected the call of Euripides for clear prophecy that should be delivered by Apollo alone. To expect absolute consistency in divine intentions was to misunderstand the perennial fluctuation in human affairs, which even the divinity could not resolve: "Therefore anyone is very foolish who, now that conditions have become different, complains and makes unwarranted indictment if the god feels that he must no longer help us in the same way, but in a different way."[29]

A great deal of the ambiguity surrounding the Delphic oracle revolved around the extent to which the god himself was involved in the responses. Once the assumption was made that the gods had no definite connections to human affairs but delegated the task of solving problems to either demons or pythias, the terrain was ripe for misunderstandings.

---

[26]Heraclitus, Fragm 19, trans. Guy Davenport, *Herakleitos and Diogenes* (San Fransisco: Grey Fox Press, 1976) 14.

[27]Freeman, *Ancilla*, Fragm 102.31.

[28]Fontenrose, *Delphic Oracle*, 236-39.

[29]Plutarch, PythOr 407EF (LCL. Mor V) 335. Note in this instance the difficulty Apollo had to resolve in his attempt to hide the truth from despots and enemies.

The gods were free from error and blameless while mortals groped for the proper interpretation of divine signs. The religious landscape was filled with puzzled suppliants and catastrophic decisions. The story of Oedipus, as told by Sophocles, revealed the deep-seated conflicts pitting human beings against ambiguous Delphic decrees. The warnings of Apollo to Laius that he should not beget a son who would destroy him went unheeded, either for lack of clarity or through sheer defiance of the god.[30] What appeared clear to the god as a sign of inexorable destiny could not penetrate the realm of mortals little intent on letting their routines be disrupted by divine whim. Yet the premonition was strong enough to eliminate from the family circle that which might bring its demise. Oedipus's pursuit of the truth turned out to be the cause of his destruction, after having spent almost all of his life in total ignorance of his origins and family status. Horror and ambiguity coexisted to the end as Jocasta derided the oracle of Phoebus, or rather of his ministers, probably out of terror that it might, after all, be true. Oedipus was driven to penetrate the fatal workings of the oracle. Creon became the most unfortunate of messengers. Tiresias, the blind prophet, alone could see clearly the implications of a fate in which both gods and mortals played the role of powerless spectators.

Troubled by the inscrutability of Apollo's revenge on Cassandra, Aeschylus had the chorus declare that the oracles of Delphi are delivered in good Greek, but hard to understand.[31] The Heraclitean Delphic god who neither spoke nor concealed, but gave signs, must have also known that human reason would prove inadequate to understand warnings contained in his oracular communications. Zosimus reports at least one instance when a well-known philosopher, Hilarius of Phrygia, was killed "on the grounds that he had interpreted all too clearly a certain ambiguous oracle."[32]

One of the most famous Delphic oracles concerned the person of Croesus. Under the pen of Herodotus, it came to us as a well-developed tragedy. Whatever the case, the wisdom of Solon could not dissuade Croesus from pursuing goals of self-destruction by hoping to achieve a

---

[30]Euripides, PhoenMaid 18-20. Oenomaus used the oracle to prove the deceit of Apollo and the absurdity of the prophecy. Eusebius, PraepEv 258ad.

[31]Aeschylus, Agam 1254-55.

[32]Zosimus, HistNova 4.15.

fame he did not merit and that he hoped to secure through generous liberalities made to Apollo's shrine at Delphi. As a result, he came face to face with the ambiguity of an oracular promise that would end at the exact opposite of what could be read in it. It enlightened the vulnerability of any relationship between gods and mortals. Divine will could prove costly to unsuspecting devotees, especially when they failed to detect the ways in which gods become playful with their worshipers' expectations. The prophecy that Croesus would destroy a great empire came true when he brought his own to a sorrowful end.

The story of Croesus, however, should be read from the point of view of its end as he expiated his misplaced ambitions through tragic events sent to him and his family by angry portents. In the end Herodotus tried to convince his readers that the wisdom of Solon was not lost on Croesus and that Apollo could be made into a merciful god, both of those elements contributing to rescue Croesus from the pyre after a bewildered Cyrus became convinced of his greatness. But it was too late for his servants to put out the fire on their own. Through a spectacular miracle, Apollo, on a clear and sunny day, gathered a storm which extinguished the pyre and saved Croesus. The story of Croesus in Herodotus was further immortalized in Aristotle's *Ethics* and placed in a negative light in Eusebius who emphasized Apollo's deceit as unworthy of a divinity who, through an ambiguous oracle, misled Croesus to undertake a wrong course of action and at the end be saved from it.[33]

In some instances the ambiguity of the oracle was the result of the predisposition within human beings to achieve ends contrary to ethical requirements. Diogenes Laertius reported that when Diogenes of Sinope went to Delphi to inquire of Apollo whether he should alter the currency and to issue false coins in the city of Sinope, he understood that the god gave him permission to proceed with his plan. But he misinterpreted the oracular response which was referring not to the coinage of Sinope but to the political "currency" in great need of change. It was only when in exile, after disgracing his family, that he realized that the Delphic response was indeed an enigma. By playing on the Greek word which could mean either "currency" or "custom," the oracle, in a subtle way,

---

[33]Eusebius, PraepEv 211c-212b.

encouraged him to direct his efforts at changing the conventional customs of his native land.[34]

Sometimes it was the human request that was presented to the god with intentional ambiguity. When Xenophon was on the point of joining the army of Cyrus in Asia, he conferred with Socrates about the proposed journey. Seeing the potential dangers in such a move, Socrates advised him to consult the oracle at Delphi in order to ascertain the propriety of such an endeavor. But when Xenophon approached the god, he had already made up his mind to undertake the journey, and simply asked Apollo to which god he should sacrifice in order to meet with success. Apollo complied with his request. When Xenophon came back from Delphi, he reported the response of the oracle to Socrates who found fault with him for having, so to speak, forced the god's hand instead of letting him decide on the validity of the journey itself. Socrates, however, counseled Xenophon not to question the response he got from Delphi.[35]

Divine ambiguity would prove meaningless if not for the power of inquiry it released within the human mind. The importance of the oracle did not always consist in providing a solution to difficult dilemmas, but in stirring questioners to discover within themselves the hidden forces and qualities that could elevate life to new levels of intellectual and moral activity. Such was the case with the altar at Delos. The story went that when Delians were beset with devastating troubles, they implored Plato to solve for them a problem which was part of a strange oracle urging them to double the volume of their altar, which itself was a cube. The suggestion to make a cube twice the volume of another cube required a knowledge of geometry that the Delians did not possess. The oracle, which sounded simple enough to inquirers unaware of the difficulties involved, promised an end to their troubles, should they be successful in fulfilling its requirement. Having tried on their own to solve the riddle, they doubled the size of all sides, thus producing a cube *eight* times the volume of the original one. It was then that they called on Plato, whose knowledge of geometry was equated with divine attributes. But he

---

[34]Diogenes Laertius, Lives 6.20-21; Parke and Wormell, *Delphic Oracle*, 1:406.

[35]Xenophon, Anab 3.1, 5-7.

derided them for their ignorance and their neglect of education, and bade them to engage again in the study of geometry.[36]

The intent of the oracle was to persuade the Delians that political and social difficulties could be solved only within a larger context, including the study of geometry and philosophy, for there could be no conflict between the life of reason and the will of the gods:

> That the god is a most logical reasoner the great majority of his oracles show clearly; for surely it is the function of the same person both to solve and to invent ambiguities. Moreover, as Plato said, when an oracle was given that they should double the size of the altar at Delos (a task requiring the highest skill in geometry), it was not this that the god was enjoining, but he was urging the Greeks to study geometry. And so, in the same way, when the god gives out ambiguous oracles, he is promoting and organizing logical reasoning as indispensable for those who are to apprehend his meaning aright.[37]

Divine solicitude which put an end to human troubles by granting death as the supreme reward of the gods could also be viewed as ambiguous. The fate of Cleobis and Biton was sufficiently stirring to allow them a place within the Delphic sanctuary in the form of statues carved by Polymedes. Today, in their slightly mutilated form, the two kouroi grace the Museum at Delphi. Sons of Hera's priestess at Argos, they harnessed themselves to the chariot (which should have been pulled by oxen that did not show up) to drive their mother to the temple to perform her religious duties. Stirred by their devotion, the priestess-mother entreated the goddess to bestow on them the best gift available to mortals. Their reward was to fall asleep in the temple, never to wake again.

A similar destiny awaited Trophonius and Agamedes, the legendary builders of Apollo's temple at Delphi. When they approached the god to collect their wages, his oracle told them to live merrily and indulge in every pleasure for six days. On the seventh day they were found dead in their beds. These two episodes attest to an early Delphic belief in the immortality of the soul and the rewards of peace after death for those who deserve them.[38]

---

[36]Plutarch, GenioSocr 579BC.

[37]Plutarch, DeE 386EF (LCL. Mor V) 211.

[38]Cicero, TuscDisp 1.113-14. Cicero followed a different tradition placing the

The church fathers, especially Eusebius, tended to regard the oracles not only as ambiguous, but as deceptive, playing on the emotions of people whose discriminating ability in matters of religion did not reach very high:

> For the poems and the compositions of the oracles, he would say, are fictions of men not without natural ability but extremely well furnished for deception, and are composed in an equivocal and ambiguous sense, and adapted, not without ingenuity, to either of the cases expected from the event: and the marvels which deceive the multitude by certain prodigies are dependent on natural causes.[39]

Even educated Greek citizens were taken by the poetry of the oracles, not being aware of the exaggerations and the pretense to inspiration.[40] Oracles that were considered free from ambiguity belonged to the realm of conjecture rather than knowledge, and even so they failed so often in their predictions as to cast doubt on the authority of the oracles in general.[41] Demons were blamed for the deceit in the oracles. There was no attempt to vindicate Apollo, just a further indictment of his carelessness in letting the oracle be delivered by inferior spirits. Eusebius was not willing to concede to Porphyry the Neoplatonic mystic way of salvation shrouded in divine mystery: "These things I beg you to conceal as the most unutterable of secrets, for even the gods did not make a revelation concerning them openly, but by enigmas."[42]

Divine and Human Law in Delphic Perspective

In many lands of antiquity the purpose of religion was to bring all aspects of life under divine authority. The gods were regarded as the authors of bodies of laws. Such was the case for the Code of Hammurabi and the Hebrew Decalogue. Plato opened his massive work on the *Laws* by raising the pertinent but complex question: "To whom do you ascribe the authorship of your legal arrangements, Strangers? To a god or to some man?" The expected answer came as no surprise. For Plato, human

---

death of Trophonius and Agamedes on the third day and not the seventh.

[39]Eusebius, PraepEv 131c.

[40]Ibid., 132d.

[41]Ibid., 133ab.

[42]Ibid., 144c.

law without divine sanction would have been reduced to a futile pursuit doomed to failure.

Most lawmakers of Greco-Roman antiquity felt compelled to claim divine inspiration by seeking the approval of oracles, especially those pronounced at Delphi. In some instances they not only received divine approbation but had bestowed on them special qualities they shared with the gods. According to Herodotus, such was the case of Lycurgus, a most distinguished Spartan, who, having decided to seek the support of the oracle at Delphi, was greeted by the Pythia with the words: "I know not whether to declare you human or divine—Yet I incline to believe, Lycurgus, that you are a god."[43]

The origin of Lycurgus's constitution remained a source of debate. Plutarch attributed its authorship to the Delphic oracle: "The Pythian priestess addressed him as 'beloved of the gods, and rather god than man,' and said that the god had granted his prayer for good laws, and promised him a constitution which should be the best in the world."[44] In the *De divinatione* Cicero acknowledged the tradition that Lycurgus established his laws by authority of the Delphic oracle and that the religious foundation of his constitution was so unassailable that when Lysander wanted to repeal it he had to abandon his project on account of the uproar of the people who felt that Apollo would be betrayed. But when writing the *De natura deorum*, he questioned the divine element in the laws: "I will never allow that Sparta received the Lacedaemonian rule of life from Apollo rather than from Lycurgus."[45]

Clement of Alexandria chose not to refute the connection between Apollo and the laws of Lycurgus, who had learned the art of lawmaking from Delphi: "Plato, and Aristotle, and Ephorus write that Lycurgus was trained in legislation by going constantly to Apollo at Delphi."[46] The purpose of Clement, however, remained apologetic. He was not concerned with a vindication of Apollo or Lycurgus. His goal was to show the superiority of the Mosaic law, a fact that Greek legislators and philosophers should have discovered, had they been pursuing the truth of the

---

[43]Herodotus, Hist 1.65.65.
[44]Plutarch, Lives: Lycurgus 5.3 (LCL I) 217-19.
[45]Cicero, DeDiv 1.96; NatDeo 3.91 (LCL XIX) 377.
[46]Clement of Alexandria, Strom 1.26 (ANF II) 339.

matter. Eusebius preserved a longer, and somewhat different, version of the response of the Pythia to Lycurgus than the one in Herodotus:

> To my rich shrine thou com'st, Lycurgus, dear
> To Zeus and all who in Olympus dwell:
> Whether to hail thee god or mortal man
> Doubts my prophetic soul, yet hope prevails
> To welcome thee as god. To seek good laws,
> Lycurgus, thou art come; such will I give.[47]

The role of Delphi in giving the laws was clear. Yet Eusebius, in a rather witty way, detailed Oenomaus's exegesis of the oracle with which he found so many faults that he concluded: "I suppose that this Lycurgus never had a nurse, nor even sat in a company of old men, from whom, as well as from her, he might have heard nobler and wiser lessons than these."[48]

No definite connection between religion and political and civic life in ancient Greece can be inferred from the documents we possess. Religious beliefs and practices were too diverse to be precisely described. Said Protagoras: "About the gods, I am not able to know whether they exist or do not exist, nor what they are like in form; for the factors preventing knowledge are many: the obscurity of the subject, and the shortness of human life."[49] We do not have a global view of Delphic religion. It was constructed of fragments, often contradictory in their content and intent. But in the area of legislation the role of Delphi appeared more certain. Plato and Socrates reinforced the conviction that no nation or colony could last if not rooted in laws originating with Apollo. Constitutions had to supersede mythological perspectives and create a worldview based on moral and religious authority clearly expressed in codes of laws. The readiness of the Greeks to place religious life under the discretion of Delphic pronouncements was a powerful witness to the moral and spiritual prestige of Apollo.[50]

---

[47]Eusebius, PraepEv 222c.

[48]Ibid., 223c.

[49]Freeman, *Ancilla*, Fragm 4.126

[50]Olivier Reverdin, *La Religion de la cité platonicienne* (Paris: E. de Boccard, 1945) 92, writes: "L'abandon de toute la vie religieuse de la cité à la discrétion de Delphes est infiniment plus remarquable. Il témoigne de l'immense

When Plato undertook to formulate the best conditions of life for his ideal commonwealth, he appealed to the oracle to guide every lawgiver.[51] Though there is no evidence that Plato ever went to Delphi in order to consult the oracle, he was credited with a thorough analysis of Pythic pronouncements in the area of legislation. In his days the Athenian court responsible to sanction the laws and enforce their observance was known as "That at the Delphinium" (τὸ ἐπὶ Δελφινίῳ).[52] Because of its constant presence in the laws of the state, Delphic religion asserted its universality among the Greek people, and, to a certain extent, partook of the immortality of the classical age. But there were also competing oracles not clearly associated with Apollonian religion, such as the Chaldaean ones.

Oracular Religion and Chaldaean Oracles

Sometime during the second century CE a corpus of oracles surfaced in religious and philosophical circles and soon became known under the name of *Chaldaean Oracles*.[53] Its destiny fluctuated between oblivion, intense interest, revival, and sometimes sheer disdain. Recent research on the subject has tried to elucidate almost insoluble mysteries surrounding the existence of those oracles and their place in history. Among still unresolved problems are the origin and intent of the oracles, their influence on Neoplatonic theurgy, the assessment of their meaning by Neoplatonic philosophers, their relationship to Porphyry's work *Of the Philosophy to Be Derived from Oracles* (περὶ τῆς ἐκ λογίων φιλοσοφίας, most often referred to as ἐκ λογίων φιλοσοφίας), the trustworthiness of Eusebius's analysis of Porphyry's text, the possible connection of those oracles to Apollonian religion, and the historical stance of the church on the question of theurgy.

---

prestige moral et spirituel dont jouissait le sanctuaire."

[51]The most important instances where Plato connects his laws with the Delphic oracle are: Rep 427AC; 469A; 540C; Laws 738BC; 759CD; 828A; 856E; 865BD; Epin 988A. See also Xenophon, Mem 4.3.16.

[52]Dempsey, *Delphic Oracle*, 105.

[53]For a bilingual (Greek and French) edition of the *Chaldaean Oracles*, see Édouard des Places, *Oracles chaldaïques: avec un choix de commentaires ancients* (Paris: Les Belles Lettres, 1971).

A short but informative study of theurgy appears in Dodds[54] who, following Joseph Bidez's suggestion, considers Julianus as the probable first theurgist, if not the inventor of the name. Chaldaean doctrines were connected with Julianus who claimed to have received the oracles directly from the gods. But the origin of those oracles remains debatable, and there exists no certain way to place them within a precise historical framework. They were alternatively considered as frauds, forgeries, or compilations by authors dissatisfied with the religion of the day. Though their style was often bizarre and their content obscure, they were sometimes related to the Neoplatonic system of philosophy, a fact which may have rescued them from instant oblivion. Whether or not they were at the center of the new theurgy, and whether or not they influenced the Neoplatonic view of religion, it remains difficult to ascertain their real impact. Evidence points to Plotinus's opposition to theurgical practices, though the article "Theurgie" in Pauly-Wissowa's *Realencyclopädie der classischen Altertumswissenschaft* considers him a theurgist. Christianity's assessment of theurgy remained ambiguous. The medieval church opposed theurgical practices, but they were revived, albeit briefly, during the Renaissance.

Three major areas of contention dominated the attempt to define the importance of *Chaldaean Oracles*: the role of Porphyry in the collection of the oracles, the attacks of Eusebius and Augustine on Porphyry, and the possibility that the oracles may have originated from within Apollonian religion. At about the time those oracles were coming into existence, Justin was invoking similar ones to testify to Moses' connection with Chaldaean wisdom:

> For when one inquired at your oracle—it is your own story—what religious men had at any time happened to live, you say that the oracle answered thus: "Only the Chaldaeans have obtained wisdom, and the Hebrews, who worship God Himself, the self-begotten King."
>
> Since, therefore, you think that the truth can be learned from your oracles, when you read the histories and what has been written regarding the life of Moses by those who do not belong to our religion, and when you know that Moses and the rest of the prophets were descended from the race of the Chaldaeans and Hebrews, do not think

---

[54]Dodds, *Greeks and the Irrational*, 283-99.

that anything incredible has taken place if a man sprung from a godly line, and who lived worthily of the godliness of his fathers, was chosen by God to be honoured with this great gift and to be set forth as the first of all the prophets.[55]

A similar approach appeared in the writings of Justin's contemporary, Tatian.[56] One would be tempted to see in these references a connection with the *Chaldaean Oracles*. But the evidence remains inconclusive and based on speculations that, so far, have not generated a great deal of scholarly interest.

A study of the work of Porphyry does not usually include an emphasis on his *Of the Philosophy to Be Derived from Oracles*, a collection he brought together in his young years while afflicted "with an incurable weakness for oracles." His work was dismissed by many critics as the result of youthful excess, and Porphyry disavowed some of it himself later in his life when he wrote another important work, *Fifteen Books against the Christians* (Κατὰ Χριστιανῶν). In his *Vie de Porphyre* Bidez described Porphyry and his work as an amalgamation of all sorts of qualities and faults, going from critical insight to naivete, from enthusiasm to opportunism, from science to childish reasoning, a mind which accepted everything and succumbed to vulgarity and absurdity, yet an intriguing personality no one has yet been able to analyze properly.[57] Recent scholarship felt the need to rescue Porphyry from Bidez's estimation of him as a mere shadow of Plotinus.[58]

Two texts of the early church contain invaluable information on the work of Porphyry: Eusebius' *Praeparatio evangelica* and Augustine's *De civitate Dei*. Eusebius quoted extensively from Porphyry's *Of the Philosophy to Be Derived from Oracles*, and without his contribution the work may not have been known to us. Part of it is in Eusebius alone. Most

---

[55]Justin Martyr, CohGent 11 (ANF I) 278.

[56]Tatian, OratGr 36. On the mysterious learning of the Chaldaeans see Arnobius, AdvGent 1.5 and 4.13.

[57]Joseph Bidez, *Vie de Porphyre le philosophe néo-platonicien aves les fragments des traités ΠΕΡΙ ΑΓΑΛΜΑΤΩΝ et DE REGRESSU ANIMAE* (Hildesheim: Georg Olms Verlagsbuchhandlung, 1964) ii.

[58]John J. O'Meara, *Porphyry's Philosophy from Oracles in Eusebius's Praeparatio Evangelica and Augustine's Dialogues of Cassiciacum* (Paris: Etudes Augustiniennes, 1969) 121.

scholars accept that the *Chaldaean Oracles* served as the major source for the work of Porphyry. It remains to be determined, however, to what extent it was known in the early church and on what basis the selection of quotations was made. To answer those questions more pertinently we may have to turn to John O'Meara's works on Eusebius and Augustine. There O'Meara has focused on proving that the work of Porphyry mentioned in Augustine's *De civitate Dei* (10.29, 32) under the title *De regressu animae* is in reality part of the same work as *Of the Philosophy to Be Derived from Oracles*: "It is concluded that the *de regressu animae* and the *Philosophy from Oracles are separate titles referring to the same work whose formal title was Philosophy from Oracles.*"[59]

The fate of the *Chaldaean Oracles* proves difficult to determine. Interest in the work persisted among Neoplatonists. In the fifth century Proclus produced a commentary on it, which may have been known until the fourteenth century.[60] Beyond that point Eusebius' *Praeparatio evangelica* served as the principal source for our link to the original work of Porphyry. Since Eusebius's purpose was to demonstrate the wickedness and deceit of oracles in general, we find in him a hostile witness who selected the parts of Porphyry's collection which best suited his apologetic intentions. He did not adequately represent Porphyry's attempt to reinterpret ancient philosophy in the light of divine oracles, whatever their source. In Eusebius we have a second hand interpretation. Moreover, as

---

[59]John J. O'Meara, *Porphyry's Philosophy from Oracles in Augustine* (Paris: Etudes Augustiniennes, 1959) 1. *De regressu animae* as a title for a work of Porphyry is known only from Augustine, CivDei 10.32. See the remarks of O'Meara taken from Bidez, *Vie de Porphyre*, 7-8: "Sauf quelques allusions et des répétitions peu importantes, tous les emprunts faits par Augustin au *De regressu* se trouvent dans le livre X de la *Cité de Dieu*. . . . Indépendamment d'Augustin, Arnobe est le seul écrivain chez qui l'on découvre peut-être des doctrines du *De regressu*." On the purpose of Augustine in introducing the debate, O'Meara, *Porphyry's Philosophy from Oracles in Augustine*, 2-3, refers to the position of Pierre Courcelle, *Les lettres grecques en occident*, 168: "Son grand effort apologétique dans la *Cité de Dieu* consiste, si je ne me trompe, à méditer sur le processus de sa propre conversion pour acheminer les disciples de Porphyre vers le christianisme."

[60]Dodds, *Greeks and the Irrational*, 289. There are also recent collections of Chadaeans oracles. See especially Édouard des Places, *Oracles Chaldaïques*.

a novice in the field, Porphyry summarized the oracles for his specific purpose before they became common knowledge among Neoplatonic philosophers. For Porphyry, the purification of the soul, a crucial tenet of Neoplatonic philosophy, could be reached only through philosophical contemplation, a goal that could not be achieved through the promises made in Chaldaean mysteries.[61] From a Neoplatonic point of view, *Chaldaean Oracles* were destined to play a role inferior to that of philosophical illumination, especially as it came from Plato and Plotinus. Thus we may ask to what extent Porphyry was influential in translating into Christian literature important ideas of Plotinus which may have given the church an intellectual and spiritual advantage over dying paganism.

In the *Praeparatio evangelica* the writings of Porphyry were directly connected with the oracles of Apollo: "He therefore, in the book which he entitled *Of the Philosophy to Be Derived from Oracles*, made a collection of the oracles of Apollo and the other gods and good demons."[62] There are indeed instances where Porphyry connected Apollo with Neoplatonic theurgy.[63] But Eusebius portrayed Porphyry as an author whose writings contained numerous contradictions and who felt the need to attest the truthfulness of his intentions:

> For I myself call the gods to witness, that I have neither added any-thing, nor taken away from the meaning of the responses, except when I have corrected an erroneous phrase, or made a change for greater clearness, or completed the meter when defective, or struck out anything that did not conduce to the purpose; so that I preserved the sense of

---

[61]Pierre Hadot, *Porphyre et Victorinus*, 2 vols. (Paris: Etudes Augustiniennes, 1968) 1:108: "Pour Porphyre, la purification apportée par les mystères chal-daïques ne pouvait remplacer la purification que donne la contemplation philoso-phique. Elle n'avait de valeur que pour les non-philosophes."

[62]Eusebius, PraepEv 143a.

[63]Bidez, *Vie de Porphyre*, 17. " 'Arrive vite pour me sauver—cesse ces colloques, éteins ces lumières—par un effort vigoureux de tes mains, arrache le tissu qui enveloppe mes membres—fais taire ces voix qui sortent des profon-deurs—débarasse-moi de mes couronnes—efface ces lignes magiques, que je puisse m'en aller.' C'est un dieu qui parle ainsi dans la *Philosophie des Oracles*; c'est Apollon lui-même, qu'un sortilège a fait prisonnier. Et en effet, le traité nous donne tout un système de théurgie à l'usage des prêtres des mystères païens."

what was spoken untouched, guarding against the impiety of such changes, rather than against the avenging justice that follows from the sacrilege.[64]

Porphyry's collection of oracles was directed against Christians, a fact which led Eusebius to assign to him a malicious intent in compiling the Pythian responses.[65] The falsification of the oracles was acknowledged by Porphyry and blamed on the gods who could not avoid it as they were themselves the victims of the surrounding atmosphere.[66] That being the case, no credibility could be attached to oracles in general: "Is there not now an end to all doubt in your judgment, that there was nothing divine at all in the responses of the gods? For how could the divine ever speak falsely, being in nature most truthful, since surely the divine is truthful?"[67] Porphyry especially must be rejected as not having been able to perceive the deceit of the gods:

> By these and the like quotations this noble philosopher of the Greeks, this admirable theologian, this initiate in secret mysteries, exhibits *The Philosophy to Be Derived from Oracles* as containing secret oracles of the gods, while openly proclaiming the plots laid against men by their wicked and truly daemoniacal power. For what benefit to human life can there be from these evil arts of sorcery?[68]

In order to vindicate the superiority of Hebrew religion over Greek philosophy, Eusebius again called Porphyry to task and made him acknowledge the errors of the Greeks:

> Also in the work which he entitled *Of the Philosophy Derived from Oracles* he expressly acknowledges that the Greeks have been in error, and call his own god as a witness, saying that even Apollo had proclaimed this by oracles, and had testified to the discovery of the truth by the Barbarians rather than by the Greeks, and moreover had even mentioned the Hebrews in the testimony which he bore. . . . This is the statement of the philosopher, or rather of his god. Is it right then after this to blame us, because forsooth we forsook the Greeks who had gone

---

[64]Eusebius, PraepEv 143d.
[65]Ibid., 234c.
[66]Ibid., 241c.
[67]Ibid., 242a.
[68]Ibid., 203ab.

astray and chose the doctrines of the Hebrews, who had received such testimony for comprehension of the truth?[69]

Eusebius related that the oracles of Apollo were closely connected with the collection of Porphyry to extoll the wisdom of the Hebrews: "But Porphyry, in the first book of his *Philosophy from Oracles*, introduces his own god as himself bearing witness to the wisdom of the Hebrew race as well as of the other nations renowned for intelligence." He then quoted an oracle of Apollo in support of his contention:

Only Chaldees and Hebrews wisdom found
In the pure worship of a self-born God.[70]

In Augustine's evaluation of Porphyry's oracles the argument is extended to include prophecies concerning Christ, and both Apollo and Hecate were scrutinized for the meaning of their pronouncements.[71] The argument started with a strong indictment of Christianity by Apollo who could see no possibility of purification for those who have once been polluted by the impiety of the Christian religion. All things being equal, when Apollo had to voice an opinion on the validity of non-Greek religions, he had to conclude that Jews rather than Christians worshiped the right God. Augustine tried to point out the fallacies and biases propounded in Apollonian oracles leading to the conclusion that Christ was put to death by right-minded and just people and that he deserved to die. This specific oracle appeared so bizarre that Augustine suggested that it had been invented by Porphyry himself. At the same time, the claim of the superiority of the Jewish religion enhanced Augustine's argument that Apollo might have grasped some fundamental truth about the universality of the God of creation without perceiving the implication of such divine illumination. Porphyry came to recognize that the God of the Hebrews was so great that all other deities were afraid before him.

As a young philosopher influenced by Chaldaean wisdom and mysteries, Porphyry still had some favorable remarks to make about

---

[69]Ibid., 741d -742a.

[70]Ibid., 412d-413c. There is a hint to that saying in a corrupt passage of OracSib 3.218-21. See Milton S. Terry, *The Sibylline Oracles* (New York: AMS Press, 1973) 267-70. In Porphyry's *Philosophy from Oracles* it is never stated from which sanctuary of Apollo the responses were delivered.

[71]Augustine, CivDei 19.23.

Christ, but not about Christians. Those of the gods who spoke ill of Christ did so in their sleep, but had to change their assessment when awake. Here Augustine quoted Porphyry:

> "What we are going to say will certainly take some by surprise. For the gods have declared that Christ was very pious, and has become immortal, and that they cherish his memory: that the Christians, however, are polluted, contaminated, and involved in error. And many other things," he says, "do the gods say against the Christians."[72]

The Apollonian oracle was corroborated by a similar one from Hecate:

> Of this very pious man, then, Hecate said that the soul, like the souls of other good men, was after death dowered with immortality, and that the Christians through ignorance worship it. And to those who ask why he was condemned to die, the oracle of the goddess replied, The body, indeed, is always exposed to torments, but the souls of the pious abide in heaven.[73]

Augustine saw no comfort to be derived from either Apollo's or Hecate's misguided praise of Christ. Both oracles were meant to prevent people from becoming Christians, and both deserved condemnation for not grasping the redeeming purpose of Christ, or, even worse, for making him a misleading religious figure.

If we agree with most of recent scholarship in maintaining that the *Chaldaean Oracles* served as the major source for Porphyry's *Of the Philosophy to Be Derived from Oracles*, and if we accept the contention of O'Meara that the *Philosophy from Oracles* is the same work as the *De regressu animae*, and if we can lend any credence to the assertion of Eusebius that *Of the Philosophy to Be Derived from Oracles* was basically a collection of Apollonian oracles, then we would have a direct link between the *Chaldaean Oracles* and those of Apollo. This would not totally explain the intellectual Neoplatonic detour through theurgy. But it would introduce us to an oracular religion fundamentally different from its original Delphic expression and preoccupied with the need to assess the place of the Hebrews, of Jewish religion, of Christ, and of his followers in the context of Roman religion. Neither Eusebius nor

---

[72]Ibid., 19.23 (NPNF-1 II) 416.
[73]Ibid.

Augustine could accept the praises directed at the Hebrews or at Christ without questioning the reasons why Christians were repudiated in all of the oracles, be they from Apollo or Hecate. The oracles that praised Christ while condemning and despising Christians had to be rejected by the church.

Porphyry's views changed radically between the writing of the *Philosophy from Oracles* and *Against the Christians*. Yet he provided an important explanation of the need for the purification of the soul, a theme that progressively entered Christian consciousness. The longest quotations of Porphyry in Eusebius relate to sacrifices and their place in purification, an element which had dominated Apollonian religion. But the oracles suffered at the hands of demons who acted poorly on behalf of gods and who were forced to invoke fate as the reason for their failures.[74] In such a context it became more understandable that Porphyry would have promoted the use of theurgy to remedy the errors of demons, a position he may have kept even after becoming a pupil of Plotinus.

The place and role of the *Chaldaean Oracles* will be further debated, and their relationship to Apollonian oracles will continue to be perplexing. Their influence was destined to be short-lived in the first centuries CE as the church entered a period of profound changes during the reigns of Constantine and Theodosius. In his discussion of the subject, Augustine may have been incited more by a desire to analyze Neoplatonism than by a genuine need to penetrate the meaning of dying oracles.

Apollonian Oracles in Christian Perspective

To some extent oracular religion provided a parallel to the body of Scriptures the early church was in the process of adopting. Oracular wisdom influenced a great deal of civic and political life and forced Christians to formulate specific responses when confronted with a challenge they could no longer ignore. As early as the second century, Christian apologetic literature directed its weapons against what it considered evil spirits dominating the Roman religious scene. Pagan oracles began to reflect on Christianity and its troubling presence within a religious world that would otherwise not have known serious conflicts. The battle of words, and at some points the open war between two

---

[74]Eusebius, PraepEv 242d.

religious approaches aspiring to supremacy, intensified the need for rational, philosophical, and spiritual definitions and explanations. Christians knew that they were hindered in their missionary endeavors by deeply rooted pagan traditions that had survived the threatening forces of history. On the other hand paganism could no longer ignore the missionary zeal of the church and the appeal of a God proclaimed as the universal creator and redeemer.

The paradoxical nature of pagan oracles puzzled Eusebius, who had to acknowledge the philosophical and intellectual mastery of some Apollonian pronouncements while having to prove their deceit and irrelevance.[75] By the time the church became a visible force in the empire, two contradictory tenets supported the religious edifice of the Romans: the demonic origin of the oracles, and their power to keep people and cities together.

In the first instance we find that Roman religion could not extricate itself from the growing emphasis placed on the demonic, on the agents communicating the will of the gods to mortals, on their questionable divine qualities. The church fathers identified those demons with evil spirits. They chose to ignore the positive role demons assumed in ancient philosophy, especially in Plato and later in Plutarch. Christian apologists contended that from the hierarchy of gods and demons arose a great deal of the ambiguity plaguing oracular responses. Having relinquished their powers to demons, gods could remain blameless within their realm of perfection, outside of complaints their worshipers could level at them in times of sorrow. But those gods also lost their appeal and authority. Oracles proceeding from inferior divinities could easily be exposed as frauds or forgeries when compared to biblical prophecy and revelation.

References to heathen gods as being demons abound in patristic writings. It was an easy way to discredit pagan religion and the oracles on which it was built. A representative approach is found in Eusebius:

> But in fact this whole discussion of ours is summed up in two chief points, that those who have been supposed in each city to give oracular responses are not gods, and that they are not even good daemons, but are on the contrary a class of jugglers, cheats, and deceivers, who for

---

[75]Ibid., 130a-131c.

the destruction and perversion of true religion have put forward, besides all other delusion among mankind, especially this delusion about Fate.[76]

In the second instance, especially in the Antonine age, oracles possessed the persuasive power to hold together people and cities, to generate collective perspectives on questions of religion as well as civic life. In those instances oracles played a much deeper role than passing fancies of remote gods. Apollo dominated the Roman religious scene, and Christian apologists were conscious of that reality when they undertook a systematic refutation of oracular wisdom and truthfulness. The old Apollo of Delphi whom they tried to relegate to a corner of Greek religious aberration proved to be far more than a dead adversary they could disdain and ridicule, an art they had developed as much through religious fervor as through the necessity to keep Christianity free from pagan influences. Some Christian writers such as Origen chose not to display a total skepticism about pagan oracles. But, by the time of Eusebius, apologists had become quite bold in their attacks on oracular religion and on the demons connected with it.

In the introduction to his *Historia ecclesiastica* Sozomen credited some Greeks with a higher prophetic insight than was present among Hebrews. Some oracles appeared in forms that were apprehended only by Greeks of superior education. They were privileged to participate in the divine revelation concerning the coming of Christ, and sometimes to a greater degree than those among the Jews who misread their own literature. Divine foreknowledge made it possible for strangers to be the repositories of the prophetic enlightenment in its universal aspect. But on the level of actual events, most oracles proved very unreliable, for people read into them their personal wishes. Such, for instance, was the case

---

[76]Ibid., 295d. Eusebius seems to leave the door open for the existence of "good" demons. The Romans never regarded demons as enemies of the human race or as destroyers of religion. Plutarch, DefOrac 414F-415A (LCL. Mor V) 377-79 stressed the positive function of demons or demigods: "They put the case well who say that Plato . . . has relieved philosophers of many great perplexities; but, as it seems to me, those persons have resolved more and greater perplexities who have set the race of demigods midway between gods and men, and have discovered a force to draw together, in a way, and to unite our common fellowship." On that point see also Peter Brown, *The Making of Late Antiquity* (Cambridge MA: Harvard University Press, 1978) 20.

with Licinius in his dispute with Constantine. Through oracles and sacrifices he convinced himself of an impending victory which was not meant to be.[77]

A stratagem to unmask the deception of oracles consisted in introducing into the debate a Greek philosopher as a witness against the religion of his people. Such was the ploy of Eusebius who quoted extensively from the writings of Oenomaus of Gedara, a philosopher espousing the propositions of the old Cynic school and exposing oracles as being willful deceptions aimed at a credulous populace. Eusebius prefaced the long sections of Oenomaus he used for his apologetic purpose by saying: "So listen again to him who entitled his own writing, 'The Detection of Impostors,' and note with what a fine vigorous spirit he corrects the error of the multitude, and indeed of Apollo himself, by what he writes. . . . "[78] The carefully chosen sections portray Zeus and Apollo as useless and misleading divinities sharing the same fate as mortals in the world of necessity: "Cease therefore from thy wrath, O Zeus, the lord of famine: for that which has been destined will be, and that is what thy chain has been appointed to do: and we are nothing compared to it. And thou too cease, Apollo, from uttering vain oracles: for just that which will be, will be, even though thou keep silence."[79]

The church fathers liked to adduce the vicissitudes of Apollo's temples, especially the one in Delphi, as proof of the fallacy and unreliability of the oracles. In the ancient world religious sanctuaries, centers of wealth on account of the sumptuous gifts offered to the gods, were often the targets of pirates and sea robbers who, after plundering their goods, often set them on fire. On other occasions they had been destroyed by lightening or other natural catastrophes. Thus the question arose as to why Apollo could neither predict those calamities nor be of any help while they were occurring. Following Varro's remark that it would be an endless task to enumerate the countless shrines that were destroyed by natural disasters or by robbery and arson, Arnobius questioned the divine qualities of Apollo, who had to settle for being a powerless witness to his own misfortunes.[80]

---

[77]Sozomen, HE 1.7.
[78]Eusebius, PraepEv 254d.
[79]Ibid., 260c. For Oenomaus's evaluation of Apollo's oracle, see also 213c.
[80]Arnobius, AdvGent 6.23. See also Clement of Alexandria, Protr 4. Temple

Similar indictments of Apollo abound in Eusebius, who not only questioned the ability of the gods, but derided human efforts to secure help by prayers and sacrifices from divinities so unable to help themselves in times of need. Eusebius appealed to the writings of Porphyry in support of his contention that the fraud and magic of oracles could not stand the test of divine beneficence when the temples of the gods were destined to fall at the hands of evil men or natural forces. If the gods cannot escape their own fate, what chance was there for human beings to circumvent their destiny?[81] Gregory of Nazianzus and Jerome extended the argument to challenge the very essence of the oracle built on Delphic trickery and never able to foretell anything accurately, good or bad.[82]

Christian apologists stressed the vulnerability of Greco-Roman religion that made itself dependent on the existence of the material abodes of the gods, rather than on an intrinsic spiritual power. For the faithful in the church, God must be worshiped in spirit alone, apart from a specific connection with a sacred temple. Apollonian religion could not have expressed itself within such a context. But apologetic invectives against Apollo not being able to protect his temple were sorely one-sided in view of the fact that Yahweh did not do any better during the successive destructions of the temple in Jerusalem, for a long time considered his dwelling place.

The evaluation of Apollonian oracles by the standards of biblical prophecy yielded unusual and unexpected results which never coalesced into a unified outlook. Some apologists wondered why Delphic religion failed to establish the kind of universality which would have included a foreknowledge of the coming of Christ and of the work of his disciples:

---

robbing was attributed by Plato, Laws 854AB (LCL XI) 201 to an evil desire which was neither of human nor divine origin, but was the result of unexpiated sin: "By way of argument and admonition one might address in the following terms the man whom an evil desire urges by day and wakes up at night, driving him to rob some sacred objects: My good man, the evil force that now moves you and prompts you to go temple-robbing is neither of human origin nor of divine, but it is some impulse bred of old in men from ancient wrongs unexpiated, which courses round wreaking ruin; and it you must guard against with all your strength."

[81]Eusebius, PraepEv 134d-135b; 238c-239d; 241b.
[82]Gregory of Nazianzus, Holylights 39.5.

"Why could they never predict anything concerning Christ and His apostles?"[83] Yet if we maintain the correlation between the *Chaldaean Oracles* and Apollonian religion, the preoccupation with the person of Christ was certainly not absent, and not always presented in a hostile manner. A text of Lactantius probably translated into latin by Augustine and used in an expanded version in the *De civitate Dei* (19.23) in connection with his analysis of Porphyry's *Philosophy from Oracles*, has the Milesian Apollo, who was asked whether Jesus was man or God, declare that Christ "was mortal as to His body, being wise with wondrous works; but being taken with arms under Chaldean judges, with nails and the cross He endured a bitter end."[84] Lactantius analyzed the statement of Apollo, showing how it could deceive people ignorant of the mystery of the truth and how a denial of the divinity of Christ seemed to be implied in his statement. But Lactantius also concluded that the statement of Apollo was in fact no greater mistake than that of the Jews who held the same position, though instructed by their scriptures to believe differently. The recognition of the wisdom of Jesus went as far as the oracle of Apollo could allow without being forced to resort to trickery.

According to Sozomen it should have been possible to deduce the future events concerning Christ from the prophecies of the Sibyl and other oracles.[85] By his time, in a christianized empire, the antagonism between Christianity and paganism had considerably receded. The new age had finally proved all oracles to be on the side of Christ:

> These promises, having been long ago laid up in divine oracles, have now shone forth upon our own age through the teaching of our Saviour Jesus Christ; so that the knowledge of God among all nations, which was both proclaimed of old and looked for by those who were not ignorant of these matters, is duly preached to us by the Word. . . .[86]

More than two centuries earlier, under totally different circumstances, Origen had already declared that Old Testament prophecies would always surpass Apollonian oracles: "These, and a multitude of others, prophesy-

---

[83]Remark of Jerome on Isaiah 41:22. Quoted in (NPNF-2 VII) 353.
[84]Lactantius, DivInst 4.13 (ANF VII) 112.
[85]Sozomen, HE 1.1.
[86]Eusebius, PraepEv 3d.

ing on behalf of God, foretold events relating to Jesus Christ. We therefore for this reason set at nought the oracles of the Pythian priestess."[87]

In the first centuries CE the persecution of Christians was sometimes
blamed on oracles. But the correlation between the cult of Apollo and the
persecutions cannot be precisely determined. Pagan religion was
becoming increasingly conscious of the threats generated by the presence
of Christians. As early as the end of the first century, under Nero and
Domitian, the first recognized Roman emperors involved in decrees of
persecution, Apollonian religion may have played an indirect role in those
decisions. Under Domitian especially, around the year 84, the temple of
Apollo at Delphi underwent extensive renovation as a deliberate sign of
the revival of his religion, an event which coincided with the persecution
of Christians. There is, however, no indication that specific oracles were
involved in those developments. Much later, in the dying days of
paganism, Christian writers intimated that oracles may have been used as
excuses for actions against Christians, even if not in the context of
specific persecutions. Augustine referred to demons and their oracles
trying to estimate how long Christianity would survive and how it could
be brought to an end.[88]

Lactantius, who wrote a treatise on the fate of the persecutors, *De
mortibus persecutorum*, related at length how Galerius and Diocletian
reached the decision to initiate persecutions against Christians, first at the
instigation of the mother of Galerius, then through Galerius's own conviction that this was the right course of action. At first, Diocletian was much
more restrained and even opposed such a drastic solution. Uncertain of
what should be done, he decided to consult the oracle of Apollo.[89] The
expected response never came, and Eusebius took it upon himself to tell
us why:

> About that time it is said that Apollo spoke from a deep and gloomy
> cavern, and through the medium of no human voice, and declared that
> *the righteous men* on earth were a bar to his speaking the truth, and
> accordingly that the oracles from the tripod were fallacious. Hence it

---

[87] Origen, CCel 7. 7 (ANF IV) 613.
[88] Augustine, CivDei 18.53
[89] Lactantius, DeMort 11-13.

was that he suffered his tresses to droop in token of grief, and mourned the evils which the loss of the oracular spirit would entail on mankind.[90]

The narrative went on to show how pagan priests identified the righteous men as being the Christians. In the same context it was reported that Diocletian and Galerius attended a sacrifice ceremony to ascertain the omens of the gods. But the priests searched the entrails without any success. After repeating the ceremony several times, the chief augur concluded that the gods would remain silent on account of the presence in the neighborhood of Christians who had crossed themselves to exorcise demons. Diocletian was finally convinced that Christians should be exterminated, and the great persecution began, probably in the context of the festival of the Terminalia, in February 303.[91] We may doubt the accuracy of Eusebius's reports or the authenticity of the sacrifice ceremony. They do, however, fit the general pattern of the Diocletian era. The events surrounding that period marked the beginning of the decline of Apollonian official religion.

The Decline of the Oracle

"While the god gives many fair things to mankind, he gives nothing imperishable."[92] Such were the words of Plutarch who, writing in the second century CE, looked back at the glorious Delphi of the past that left behind a rich heritage to be engraved in human memory. But it could no longer claim a great deal of prestige. The intellectual and religious world which brought it to its apex had vanished from the center of influence. Plutarch officiated as a priest of Apollo at Delphi for more than twenty years, bringing to the sanctuary the remnants of what was still known of the Academy of Plato. But the god of wisdom and light could no longer find among his people the reverence which had marked several centuries of the search for a divine presence in the midst of human chaos. To the best of our knowledge, never before and never after, was there at Delphi

---

[90]Eusebius, VConst 50 (NPNF-2 I) 512.

[91]Lactantius, DeMort 12 identifies the date of the festival of the god Terminus as the seventh of the Kalends of March (February 23). Playing on words, it was chosen, he suggested, in preference to all other dates to terminate, as it were, the Christian religion.

[92]Plutarch, DefOrac 414D (LCL. Mor V) 375-77.

a priest of the intellectual and philosophical stature of Plutarch. He gave us both a passionate and rational view of the vicissitudes of a sanctuary and its god, and a perspective on the vulnerability of divine participation in human affairs.

Delphic scholars have pondered the fate of the oracle, its periods of glory, as well as the stages of its decline and eventual disappearance.[93] Delphi owed its noble destiny to its close connection with Greek civilization when it was at its best and when Greek culture had ensured its immortality through the brilliance of its literature and intellectual life. Its decline seemed to be closely tied to the deterioration of the Greek *polis*, a phenomenon which became obvious after Alexander's conquests, and which culminated in the Roman period. The sacred shrine of Apollo could not disconnect its destiny from the fluctuations of a world in the grips of expansion, wars, calamities, and successes shaping a new society going from the empyrean to the absurd in its attempt to understand and define itself in the midst of constantly threatening forces.

In the postclassical, Hellenistic, and Roman periods the Delphic oracle fought, sometimes in vain, to maintain its appeal and authority. But, in spite of the veneration the oracle had enjoyed in the past, it could not survive the onslaught of Cynicism or Epicureanism, as well as the waves of critical questioning by a people who had become less credulous. A historical perspective on the oracle revealed that it did not, in fact, generate profound insights into religious and spiritual questions, but that it owed its success to the power of imagination of a very creative people. Apollo was a product of the Greek mind, and the oracle the medium through which people could make Apollo an efficient presence in their affairs. For a long time, until the Hellenistic period, Apollo enjoyed a reputation which was far more than the oracles could reveal. But when the oracles failed, when ecstasy no longer moved the Pythia, when the voices of the Parnassus were replaced by critical inquiry, Apollo became a distant, though nostalgic, god who was made to concede, from his own pronouncements, that his rule had come to an end.

In the first century BCE when the oracle was at a very low ebb, or sometimes nonexistent, Cicero came to its defense, not on account of its intrinsic worth, but as a testimony to the spirit of Greek and ancient

---

[93]For a summary of the different stages of the decline of the Delphic oracle, see Dempsey, *Delphic Oracle*, 164-81.

peoples. Cicero found no fault with the numerous oracles collected by Chrysippus. He recommended them to his readers with the following comment:

> I will urge only this much, however, in defense: the oracle at Delphi never would have been so much frequented, so famous, and so crowded with offerings from peoples and kings of every land, if all ages had not tested the truth of its prophecies. For a long time now that has not been the case. Therefore, as at present its glory has waned because it is no longer noted for the truth of its prophecies, so formerly it would not have enjoyed so exalted a reputation if it had not been trustworthy in the highest degree.[94]

Whatever the explanation of the decadence of Delphi, to deny that the oracle there issued genuine prophecies for many hundreds of years would be to distort the entire record of history, a proposition Cicero would not allow. At the same time no acceptable explanation of the demise of the oracles could be formulated, mostly because they came to be regarded with high contempt. Delphic apologists liked to point out that the spirit which inspired the Pythia progressively dissolved with the passage of time until it evaporated into nothingness, to which Cicero retorted:

> But what length of time could destroy a divine power? And what is as divine as a subterranean exhalation that inspires the soul with power to foresee the future—a power such that it not only sees things a long time before they happen, but actually foretells them in rhythmic verse? When did the virtue disappear? Was it after men began to be less credulous?[95]

It had become evident to Cicero that Delphic religion which had exercised its dominion over so many people for so long was now relegated to such a small corner of influence that it had no further place of honor in the universal essence of religion. It would, however, be an error to dismiss the powerful role it played in infusing wisdom and authority into the portion of Greek religion which was destined to survive in human memory long after its decadence and eventual death.

In his *De defectu oraculorum* Plutarch reproduced a conversation between scholars of the day reflecting on the decline of prophetic religion

---

[94]Cicero, DeDiv 1.37-38 (LCL XX) 267-69.
[95]Ibid., 2.117 (LCl XX) 503.

at Delphi. When religion fails to fulfill the aspirations and expectations of the people, it enters an analytical phase in which philosophers and theologians are expected to provide satisfactory interpretations of phenomena which were supposed to be obvious. The line of argumentation seemed simple, as it had to answer one fundamental question: How could divine influence, which was so great in the past, be now evanescent to the point of suffering silence or even total desolation?[96] Delphic decline ushered in an age of anxiety characterized by the feeling that the death of the oracle would compel citizens to seek comfort in alien religions. Christianity was never mentioned in Plutarch, and obviously represented no threat to his conception of religion. Juvenal, a contemporary of Plutarch, feared that the silence which had come upon the sanctuary of Apollo had turned his worshipers away from his religion to Chaldaean wisdom and the promises of astrologers.[97] Whether or not Juvenal knew of the *Chaldaean Oracles* which were in the process of being collected, he already sensed the popular shift toward the kind of revelation contained in them.

Fearful that three thousand years of Delphic tradition might come to an end because of a growing contempt for the oracles, Plutarch appealed to his contemporaries to renew their commitment to the intrinsic mystery that surrounds divine revelation and that is not always open to rational understanding. In his day popular confidence in the oracle had disappeared, and he found himself fighting against religious desolation, the product of unfortunate confusion and irreverence.[98]

Plutarch undertook to review the major arguments adduced for the decline of the oracle. There were five reasons proposed: The wickedness of the people, the decline in population, the fact that oracles had been entrusted to demons and demigods, the changes willed by the gods and nature, and the unavoidable remoteness of the gods.

Long before Plutarch, Hesiod predicted a time when the gods would gather up their oracles and, on account of human wickedness, abandon

---

[96]Plutarch, DefOrac 411E-412A.

[97]Juvenal, Sat 6.553-64.

[98]Plutarch, PythOr 408D. It would be very difficult to prove that the Delphic oracle had been in existence for three thousand years by the time of Plutarch. We have no specific insight into such an affirmation which could not be supported by any historical data.

mortals to their grievous troubles, leaving them totally powerless against all evils.[99] The fear of a universal miasma generating the kind of wickedness which would force the gods to desert the earth permeated much of the religious thinking of the ancient world and determined an important aspect of the Judeo-Christian kerygma. In Plutarch's case, the argument of the Cynic Didymus, that the silence of the god had to be explained by the wickedness of human beings, had to be rejected as impious because it denied divine providence which could not be made dependent on human unworthiness. Thus the answer to the obsolescence of the oracle must have its source somewhere else: "Come, sit down again and make a 'Pythian truce' with evil, which you are wont to chastise with words every day, and join us in seeking some other reason for what is spoken of as the obsolescence of oracles; but keep the god benign and provoke him not to wrath."[100]

Starting with the assumption that prophecy has its origin in the god and that no power could destroy it, the philosopher Ammonius refused to connect the obsolescence of the oracle to any cause that would degrade divine being. As a logical explanation for the decline of the oracle he pointed to a gradual depopulation of Greece, the result of wars and discords. It was thus not surprising that in the past two or even three priestesses were needed to deliver the responses, whereas at the present time one was fully sufficient to meet all the needs.[101]

---

[99]Hesiod, Works, 199-201.

[100]Plutarch, DefOrac 413D (LCL. Mor V) 371. By "Pythian Truce" Plutarch probably means the sacred truce observed throughout the Greek world for the duration of the Pythian games.

[101]Ibid., 414AC. In Plutarch, PythOr 408BC (LCL. Mor V) 337 there is a more surprising argument adduced for the decline of the oracle. It concerns not the turmoils and ills of Greece, but its well-being and prosperity. The oracle is no longer consulted because there is no need to solve problems: "For my part, I am well content with the settled conditions prevailing at present, and I find them very welcome, and the questions which men now put to the god are concerned with these conditions. There is, in fact, profound peace and tranquility; war has ceased, there are no wanderings of peoples, no civil strifes, no despotisms, nor other maladies and ills in Greece requiring many unusual remedial forces. Where there is nothing complicated or secret or terrible."

Following Aristotle's concept of motion and change, Plutarch applied the principle to the guardians of the oracle: "Plainly the same sober opinion is to be held regarding the spirits that inspire prophecy; the power that they possess is not everlasting and ageless, but is subject to changes."[102] Plutarch's view on the origin of the oracle remained ambiguous, as it was attributed either directly to the god or to his ministers, prompting some critics to conclude that some oracles were not inspired. He also conceded that the god does not conduct ceremonies and does not honor them with his presence. Those matters were committed to the god's servants, clerks, and demigods.[103] A most serious problem arose when those demigods were proven to be bad ones, the product of philosophical speculations rather than religious conviction, assuming and performing a role threatening the authority of Apollonian religion.[104] When, in their instability, the guardian spirits decided to wander around, the prophetic shrines and the oracles to which they were assigned suffered from their defection until they decided to return.[105]

While the earth itself was believed to be everlasting and imperishable, the powers associated with it suffered change, dislocation, and possible destruction.[106] Change affected even the immutability of the god, and at some points proceeded from his providence:

> In fact, the Deity is not averse to changes, but has a very great joy therein, to judge, if need be, by the alternations and cycles in the heavens among the bodies that are visible there. Infinity is altogether senseless and unreasoning, and nowhere admits a god, but in all relations it brings into action the concept of change and accident.[107]

But the question remained: If the oracles were of divine origin, could it also be that their decadence and disappearance were equally willed by the gods?

The argument of Ammonius that the god creates and abolishes prophetic shrines was refuted on the basis that it was nature, and not the

---

[102]Plutarch, DefOrac, 434B (LCL. Mor V) 479.
[103]Ibid., 417A.
[104]Ibid., 419A.
[105]Ibid., 418CD.
[106]Ibid., 433EF.
[107]Ibid., 426D (LCL. Mor V) 439.

god, which brought destruction and desintegration, a process in which the god does not participate.[108] If indeed the god chose remoteness from human affairs, and if the prophetic powers were managed by his demigods, then the obsolescence of the oracles could be attributed to the fluctuating circumstances on earth rather than to any teleological divine purpose.

The church fathers referred to the disappearance of the oracles as the result of the coming of Christ. Writing about a century after Plutarch, Clement of Alexandria already assumed the total silence of Castalia.[109] Eusebius, somewhat in an anachronistic way, had the Greeks proclaim the demise of their religion in the context of the preaching of the Gospel:

> Hear therefore how Greeks themselves confess that their oracles have failed, and never so failed from the beginning until after the times when the doctrine of salvation in the Gospel caused the knowledge of the one God, the Sovereign and Creator of the universe, to dawn like light upon all mankind.[110]

In other instances, sometimes quoting Plutarch extensively, Eusebius attributed the death of the oracle to the work of Christ who exorcized all demons, including the ones responsible for the oracles.[111]

The emperor Julian attempted to revive the oracle, but without great success. Fontenrose thought that, in some limited way, it functioned up to the time when Theodosius's edict, in 391, ordered all oracles closed and all divination forbidden.[112] Theodoret mentioned Julian's desperate attempts to obtain responses from diverse Apollonian shrines to secure victory in his military enterprises.[113] But in one of his invectives against Julian, Gregory of Nazianzus considered the oracle already dead:

---

[108]Ibid., 414D.

[109]Clement of Alexandria, Protr 2.

[110]Eusebius, PraepEv 178cd.

[111]Ibid., 207d-208a; DemEv 204a.

[112]Fontenrose, *Delphic Oracle*, 265. The last great poet of heathenism, Claudian, assumed that the oracle had been silent even before the edicts of Theodosius. A pagan at heart, though nominally a Christian, Claudian witnessed the rapid changes under Theodosius, some of which are reflected in his eloquent poetry.

[113]Theodoret, HE 3.16.

No more does the *Oak* speak; no more does the *Cauldron* give oracles; no more is the Pythia filled with I know what, save lies and nonsense. Again the Castalian Fount has been silenced and is silent, and becomes no longer an oracular stream, but an object of ridicule; again a voiceless statue is Apollo.[114]

Whatever the fate of the oracle up to the time of Theodosius's edict, its actual demise was generally placed under the reign of Julian who, having sent Oribasius to inquire for him from the oracle at Delphi, received the disturbing response: "Tell the king the fair-wrought hall has fallen to the ground. No longer has Phoebus a hut, nor a prophetic laurel, nor a spring that speaks. The water of speech even is quenched." In this specific legend, in a final cry of despair, through one of his imaginative priests, Apollo sealed his fate forever by composing his own epitaph.

---

[114]Gregory of Nazianzus, Orat 5.32. In Charles William King, *Julian the Emperor* (London: George Bell and Sons, 1888) 111-12.

Chapter 5

The Sibyl and Sybylline Oracles

There is madness in the Sibyl's voice, her words are gloomy, ugly, and rough, but they are true for a thousand years, because a god speaks through her. —Heraclitus

The prophetic Sybilline outlook lasted for more than a millennium, from about 600 BCE to shortly after 400 CE and influenced four different religious perspectives: the Greek, the Roman, the Jewish, and the Christian. Sybilline oracles developed into a persuasive phenomenon without a definite central authority and never gelled into a coherent religious tradition. Prophetic voices arose in the ancient world before the Sibyl emerged into focus. In a period that corresponded to the Greek archaic age, Hebrew Yahwism refined its monotheistic worship as the result of the proclamation of the Old Testament prophets. All of them warned of impending disasters as the penalty for wrong religious beliefs and practices. Meanwhile, at different stages of their history, the Greeks heard the soothsayings of seers such as Tiresias and Calchas, and began to regard the Pythia as the voice of Apollo. But it was the Sibyl, with her prophetic power of divination, who was destined to dominate the religious scene at a time when worlds in conflict provided the necessary material to formulate visions of doom and to prescribe new rituals. With the rise of Sibyls, oracular pronouncements evolved into broad eschatological interpretations of cultural, political, natural, and cosmic phenomena.

The earliest written reference to the Sibyl came from the *Fragments* attributed to Heraclitus. Up to the time of Plutarch, we find references to both male and female prophetic figures, Bakides and Sibyls, roaming through the countryside predicting events to come. Their fate and influence fluctuated with the political fortunes and the philosophical alertness of society. Their activities transcended specific connections with official sanctuaries, though Sibyls usually claimed inspiration from

Apollo. The importance of Bakides never matched that of Sibyls.[1] They arose and vanished without leaving behind a record of their sayings. Thus they played no important role in the Roman period. As for the Sibyls, the pattern on which their oracles were fashioned remains obscure. It has been suggested that Cassandra served as a model: "The prototype of the Sibyls, who occur in both epic and dramatic poetry, was the strange figure of the young Trojan woman, Cassandra, the daughter of Priam and beloved of Apollo."[2]

The origin and number of Sibyls cannot be determined. Clement of Alexandria quoted an obscure, and now lost, work on oracles penned by an astronomer and disciple of Plato, Heraclides of Pontus. In that work two Sibyls of the ancient world gained prominence. The first was Artemis who prophesied in Phrygia before making her way to Delphi. Far from being inspired by Apollo, she is made, in this instance, to proclaim her rage at her twin brother and to persuade his followers that it was she, and not the Delphian god, that could read the mind of Zeus and reveal its

---

[1]Bakides received their name from the legendary Bakis who came from Eleon and was known as the Boeotian Bakis who claimed to have been inspired by the Nymphs. Then came the Attic and Locrian Bakides, until the designation *Bakides* became a title for male prophets who assumed a role similar to that of Sibyls.

[2]Robert Flacelière, *Greek Oracles*, trans. Douglas Garman (New York: W. W. Norton, 1965) 27. It is noteworthy that some ancient authors did not establish precise distinctions between different types of prophetic personalities. Cicero, DeDiv 1.34, placed on the same level Bakis of Boeotia, Epimenides of Crete, and the Sibyl of Erythrae. "Bacis and Sibyl" were regarded as the same prophetic voice by Plato in the Theag 124D. Many scholars, however, view the work as spurious. Plutarch, PythOr 399A (LCL. Mor V) 285 had the Sibyl and Bakis share the same liabilities in some of their prophetic limitations: "These prophets of the type of Sibyl and Bacis [bakides] toss forth and scatter into the gulf of time, as into the ocean depths with no chart to guide them, words and phrases at haphazard, which deal with events and occurrences of all sorts; and although some come to pass for them as the result of chance, what is said at the present time is equally a lie, even if later it becomes true in the event that such a thing does happen." Sometimes the Bakides were called the sons of Apollo.

The model of Cassandra for the Sibyl must have been in Ovid's mind when he had the Cumaean Sibyl tell Aeneas: "I am no goddess, nor do thou deem any mortal worthy of the honour of the sacred incense. But, lest you mistake in ignorance, eternal, endless life was offered me, had my virgin modesty consented to Phoebus's love." Ovid, Met 14.130-33 (LCL II) 309.

secrets to mortals. The other was the Erythraean Sibyl, Herophile, long regarded as the oldest. To that list, Clement added two more Sibyls, the Egyptian and the Italian, who played a dominant role in Roman religion.[3]

By the time of Varro, at least ten Sibyls had been identified, and their nature and function were partially defined on the basis of a semantic meaning derived from the Aeolitic dialect in which the gods were referred to as *Sioi*, not *Theoi*, and the counsel they gave as *bule*, and not *boule*. Thus came the name *Siobule* which translated into the common title *Sibyl*. The listing of Varro included the following Sibyls: Persian, Libyan, Delphian, Cimmerian, Erythraean, Samian, Cumaean, Hellespontian, Phrygian, and Tiburtine. Lactantius reproduced this enumeration from Varro's now lost voluminous work *Antiquitates rerum humanarum et divinarum* with ample commentary on some of the Sibyls listed and a surprisingly generous eloge of an author he considered a great man of learning.[4] For both Varro and Lactantius the Delphic priestess served as a model for all Sibyls. Such was not the case for other Greek and Roman

---

[3]Clement of Alexandria, Strom 1.21. The three lines quoted by Clement were probably only the beginning of a much longer oracle intended to discredit Apollo. The source of the oracle is not known, but one can surmise that the church fathers would have willingly used it for apologetic purposes. The respect for the Sibyl was often matched by a rejection of Apollo who was considered by most Christian writers as a demon.

[4]Lactantius, DivInst 1.6. It has been suggested that some of the Sibyls listed by Varro and Lactantius may be fictional: "As the earliest extant reference to Sibylla is dated about 500 BCE, these oracles are shown to be originally a product of the archaic period. If one tries to be more precise in defining the context of their origin, one is driven back on conjecture. The earliest Sibyls of later scholarship, such as the Persian and the Libyan, can easily be rejected as fictions. The Delphic does not seem to be founded on a genuine primitive tradition." Herbert William Parke, *Sibyls and Sibylline Prophecy in Classical Antiquity* (London: Routledge, 1988) 51. Thus it remains difficult to ascertain to what extant there really was a Sibylline tradition. "It is probably incorrect to speak of a 'Sibylline tradition' in antiquity. As was also the case with works attributed to the inspiration of Orpheus, the oracles attributed to sibyls are too varied in content, and beliefs about the lives of sibyls are too confused." D. S. Potter, *Prophecy and History in the Crisis of the Roman Empire: A Historical Commentary on the Thirteenth Sibylline Oracle* (Oxford: Clarendon Press, 1990) 102. Potter believes, however, that we may gather some valuable insights into how the oracles were read in view of the expectations of audiences.

writers. Strabo declared Erythrae as the native city of Sibylla, who was the only one known until the time of Alexander when Athenaïs, another inspired Sibyl from the same city, appeared on the scene with a similar gift of prophecy.[5] More than two centuries after Varro, Pausanias reduced the list of Sibyls to four, the oldest of all a Lybian one, daughter of Zeus and Lamia (daughter of Poseidon). She was followed by Herophile, who also called herself Artemis, Apollo's sister, born before the Trojan war in the region of the red-earthed Marpessos in the Troad. She traveled extensively, having spent most of her life in Samos, but also visited Colophonian, Claros, Delos, and Delphi where she sang on the rock. Her epitaph summarized her importance:

> I Sibylla, Phoibos's wise woman
> am hidden under a stone monument:
> I was a speaking virgin but voiceless
> in this manacle by the strength of fate.
> I lie close to the nymphs and to Hermes:
> I have not lost my sovereignty.

Pausanias then listed a third Sibyl, Demo, the Cumaean, whose remains were kept in an urn in the temple of Apollo. The fourth Sibyl was known as the Palestinian Sabbe.[6] She described herself in the now recollected corpus of the *Sibylline Oracles* as the daughter-in-law of Noah.[7]

---

[5]Strabo, Geog 14.34.

[6]Pausanias, *Guide to Greece*, 2 vols., trans. Peter Levi (London: Penguin Books, 1971) 1:10.12.1-6. The epitaph of the Sibyl is in 10.12.2. Pausanias's effort at all-inclusiveness in his portrayal of the Sibyl remained unconvincing: "Toute l'histoire de la Sibylle delphique et des autres Sibylles contée par Pausanias trahit un laborieux et infructueux effort de syncrétisme." Amandry, *Mantique*, 237. Judged by extant sources of known authors, Pausanias was the last pagan writer who felt compelled to clarify the murky waters in the area of Sibylline activity and to suggest a list of Sibyls as they may have existed in the ancient world.

[7]OracSib 3.823-29. As a reply to accusations that men will say that she was born of Circe and Gnostos and that she was mad, the Sibyl answered:

> For when the world was deluged with a flood
> Of waters, and one man of good repute
> Alone was left and in a wooden house
> Sailed o'er the waters with the beasts and birds,

By the fourth century BCE it had become evident that more than one Sibyl was known to the Greek world. Neither Homer, nor Hesiod, nor Herodotus mentioned any by name. Aristophanes (in whose writings we find the first written reference to a Sibyl on the Greek mainland) and Plato seemed to have known of only one Sibyl.[8]

The origin and ancestry of the Sibyl remained mysterious. One searches in vain for a unifying thread that would define the vocation of inspired women who were considered descendents of an original Sibyl until they received their particular names connected with their places of origin. The qualifications required for prophetic inspiration varied from place to place according to interpretations of diverse chresmologues. The ways in which the Sibyls were spoken of ranged from purely demonic beings to Plutarch's suggestion that they were trained in the company of the Muses on Mount Helicon and that their voice will be heard in the eons following their departure from the realm of the living.[9]

The Pythia, the Sibyl, and the Sibyllini Libri

Apollo figures prominently as the source of inspiration for both the Pythia and the Sibyl. Yet it would be impossible to conclude that Apollonian divination and Sibylline prophecy always agreed. Only in the case of the Pythia could one establish a total dependence of the prophetess on her god who fully possessed her as his instrument and voice. Sibyls emerged and spoke in a much larger context, and often projected an independent understanding of the status of the world. But no specific sibylline tradition could be formulated from their oracles. Some sibyls were connected with specific sanctuaries. Others wandered through the world with vaticinations not directly related to contemporary religious outlooks.

In order that the world might be refilled,
I was his son's bride and was of his race
To whom the first things happened, and the last
Were all made known; and thus from mine own mouth
Let all these truthful things remain declared.
Terry, *The Sibylline Oracles* III.1023-31.
[8]Aristophanes, Peace 1095; 1116; Plato, Phaedr 244B; Theag 124D.
[9]Plutarch, PythOr 398CD.

Most Christian apologists ridiculed the Pythia and the oracle of her god. But some of them took a different approach to Sibylline oracles they considered as inspired as their Scriptures before the notion of canonicity, fully accepted only in the fourth century, put definite limits on authoritative writings. Pythian oracles never appealed to the church fathers because they came from a god they considered an evil demon. Apollonian oracular responses confined the Pythia to specific situations defined by the questioners who came to her shrine. The ambiguity of her responses as well as the content of her advice were often a rebuke to the god of wisdom who claimed to possess her. The Sibyl, on the other hand, was deemed by many Christian apologists as possessing spiritual insights similar to those of biblical prophets, interpreting with divine wisdom the state of the known world. Christians could see in the eschatological pronouncements of the Sibyl a confirmation of their message.

The Sibyl could achieve what the Pythia never intended, namely, bringing together divergent religious outlooks through prophetic visions and oracles dealing with the nature of the world, its destiny, and the place of mortals within it. The legendary origin of the Sibylline oracles or the possibility of wholesale forgeries did not create major obstacles to their acceptance in the Greco-Roman world, including the Judaic and the Christian segments of it.

Collections of Sibylline oracles circulated already around the time of Solon under the editorship of more or less competent chresmologues. Any attempt at retracing the history of the *Sibyllini libri* proves difficult and inconclusive. Except for a few excerpts subject to conjecture, the original text of the Sibylline oracles vanished in the turmoil of centuries of political and civil upheavals and with the devastation of natural catastrophes. Later quotations threw very little light on what the original text might have been. Religious orientations of centers such as Erythrae or Cumae suffered distortions at the hands of collectors and interpreters from places like Alexandria and Rome. Hellenized Jews turned the collections into prophetic literature spanning their history and vision of the future. Christian apologists preferred not to apply to those books the same critical eye they had directed against heathenism in so many other instances.

The earliest collection of Sibylline oracles consisted of nine books which were offered by the Sibyl to Tarquinius Priscus for the sum of three hundred philippics. The king considered that excessive and sheer madness on the part of the woman. He refused to purchase them. The

Sibyl, in the sight of the king, burnt three of the books and demanded the same price for the remaining six. Again the king refused, and three more books were destroyed. Out of desperation, the king bought the three left over for the original price.[10] The fate of the oracular books was not immediately clear. According to Dio Cassius, the Cumaean Sibyl died shortly after the incident with Tarquinius, casting a veil of uncertainty around the future of her prophecies and of those who were appointed to keep them. The public was not allowed access to the oracles, since they were a closely guarded secret of the senate for consultation in times of distress. In fact if one of the keepers broke the vow of secrecy and revealed some of the content to friends, he was punished by death.[11]

Extant sources suggest that the books were kept in a stone chest underground in the temple of Jupiter Capitolinus. At first they were entrusted to two patrician officials who could release them to a body of priests selected by the senate to consult them on specific matters. Later, around the middle of the fourth century BCE the board of guardians was expanded to ten: the *Decemviri Sacris Faciundis* also known as *Decemviri Sacrorum*. They were elected for life. Five were selected from among patricians, and five from among plebeians. By the first century

---

[10]Lactantius, DivInst 1.6. Since lactantius's comment comes within the enumeration of Varro's list of Sibyls, it can be presumed that the story was related by Varro himself.

[11]Dio Cassius, RomHist (Zonaras) 2.7.11. (LCL I) 73-77. We find there an oracle of the Sibyl to Tarquin with the following scholia: "The Sibyl about whom Lycophron is now speaking was the Cumaean, who died in the time of Tarquin the Proud, leaving behind three or nine of her prophetic books. Of these the Romans bought either one or three, since her servant had destroyed the rest by fire because they would not give her as much gold as she asked. This they later did, and bought either one that was left, or else three, and gave them to Marcus Acilius to keep. But because he lent them to be copied, they put him to death by enclosing him alive in the skin of an ox; and for the book or books they dug a hole in the midst of the forum and buried them along with a chest."

On the tradition that ten men should be chosen by the state to interpret the Sibylline verses, see Cicero, DeDiv 1.4; Livy, 22.57.4. On the suggestion that nobody should be allowed to read the Sibylline Books without the permission of the senate, see Cicero, DeDiv 2.112 (LCL XX) 497: "Therefore let us keep the Sibyl under lock and key so that in accordance with the ordinances of our forefathers her books may not even be read without permission of the senate and may be more effective in banishing rather than encouraging superstitious ideas."

BCE, under Sulla, the number was expanded to fifteen: the *Quindecimviri Sacris Faciundis*. Appointment to that board represented a very high honor. Though names of those who served were usually not recorded, we know from Tacitus that he was appointed to that function.[12]

The fate of the "Sibylline Books" also called *Fata Sibyllina*[13] or *Libri Fatales*[14] suffered serious setbacks. The temple of Jupiter Capitolinus was destroyed by fire in 83 BCE, and the Sibylline books housed there perished. A few years later the senate decided to rebuild the collection. This was achieved through three especially appointed officials, the *Triumviri*, who in all probability were selected from among the *Quindecimviri*. Sayings purported to be Sibylline were collected from many places, especially Erythrae. But the question of authenticity could never be resolved. Far too many books were circulating in Rome under the guise of Sibylline oracles, a fact which placed the senate in the intolerable situation of not being able to control their content and privacy. At the beginning of imperial Rome, Augustus tried to remedy the situation by instituting a series of religious reforms which secured again a place of honor for the Sibylline books.[15]

On many occasions Sibylline oracles continued to be consulted by the senate. When, in 363 under the reign of Julian, the temple of Apollo on the Palatine was reduced to ashes by fire, the Sibylline books were rescued as if by miracle. Their final fate was sealed at the beginning of the fifth century when, in a Christianized empire no longer in need of them, zealous Stilicho allegedly destroyed them.[16] The original content of the *Libri Sibyllini* may never be known again. Except for a few fragments considered to have belonged to the pagan collections and which are still included in more recent textual reconstructions, the original text is almost entirely missing. Insufficient or prejudiced evidence does not allow for

---

[12]Tacitus, Ann 11.11. On plebeians serving as members of the ten appointed to interpret the Sibylline oracles, see also Livy 10.8.2.

[13]Cicero, InCat 3.9 (*ex fatis Sibyllinis*).

[14]Livy, 22.57.6 (*ex fatalibus libris*).

[15]Suetonius, Ceasars: Augustus 31.

[16]Our knowledge of this episode comes mostly from the Roman poet Rutilius Claudius Namatianus who, contrary to some historians who thought that Stilicho was attempting to restore the Julian failed revival of heathenism, considered him the most uncompromising adversary of paganism.

a credible restoration of it. Attempts at rebuilding a corpus of Sibylline oracles began as early as the sixth century. In the last three centuries a number of collections have tried to incorporate the results of ongoing scholarship. The most recent editions are divided into fourteen books, some more complete than others, but with no definite certainty about the original text. At this time we have a far better insight into additions, alterations, and occasional forgeries which constitute the legacy from the Jewish and Christian eras.

The Sibylline Books in Roman History

The history of the Republic and the Roman Empire can be summarized as the quest for world dominion amid persisting threats and conflicts. Traditional religious practices as expressed on the local and family levels provided practically no insight into world catastrophes and natural disasters. Omens and portents could be interpreted within their own spheres but did little to understand a worldview constantly reshaped by forces beyond human control. Thus came into prominence a body of oracular literature which transcended the popular conceptions of the gods. While claiming inspiration, the Sibyl often spoke of eschatological events beyond the conventional purview of the divinity. The *Libri Fatales* cast the Sibyls into the roles of ancient Fates who could penetrate the inscrutability of a universal moira beyond the control of the gods themselves.

When chaos threatened to engulf nations and individuals in catastrophic calamities, and when the natural order was disrupted beyond remedy, Romans turned to Sibylline books for counsel and advise. They deferred to prophecy that which could not be resolved by conventional wisdom: the fate of cities and kingdoms, the ravages of war, the devastation of famine and pestilence, the unpredictability and savagery of natural phenomena such as floods, volcanic eruptions, and earthquakes. In most such instances the Pythia remained silent, and popular religion was of no avail. The Sibylline books alone could be interpreted by the *Decemviri* and the *Quindecimviri* to reveal the cause and end of divine and natural discontent and explain the unalterable decrees of destiny. The consultation of oracles acquired a compelling importance when the fate of Rome itself was in the balance and when disasters concerning its future could not be explained away. In those instances the authentification of oracles created divisive tensions which even the *Quindecimviri* could not always resolve. The question often revolved around the presence of acrostics in the oracles, a fact which, with the passage of time, came to be accepted as a sign of authenticity.

In the Republic Sibylline books were consulted for a wide range of circumstances. Popular religion was supplemented by vows and expiations prescribed by Sibylline oracles and designed to alleviate anxiety concerning the fulfillment of religious obligations.[17] There are numerous examples of the senate's recourse to the sacred books and to the interpretations of the *Decemviri*.[18] In some instances new rituals were spawned or existing ones altered.[19] In the case of natural disasters and unexplainable phenomena, such as showers of stones, an effort was made to combine the predictions of the Sibyl with sacrifices offered to the Pythian Apollo.[20]

The Sibylline books did not always provide the expected confirmation of the senate's wishes. In 54 BCE, the senators were convinced that a series of calamities were due to the treason of Gabinius. The senate condemned him to death in abstentia, only to find out that a Sibylline oracle prevented them from carrying out such a decree. Gabinius was spared until tried again on new charges.[21] Often the Sibyl simply chose to remain silent.[22]

The search for clues to strange phenomena opened up new avenues of inspiration. When, in the days of Mark Antony, soldiers were destroyed by storms, and owls and wolves invaded cities, when unexpected sun eclipses darkened the Republic, when a thunderbolt damaged the scepter of Jupiter, and when animals brought forth creatures outside their species, the Sibylline oracles were made known with the result that some men became inspired and uttered prophecies.[23]

Cicero cited numerous instances of the use of Sibylline oracles to reflect on diverse episodes in the life of the Republic or to explain unimaginable, natural phenomena.[24] He knew how those oracles could be

---

[17]Livy, 21.62.11.
[18]Ibid., 22.9.8; 40.19.4; 37.2; 45.5; 41.21.11; 38.45.3.
[19]Ibid., 36.37.4.
[20]Ibid., 5.13.5; 29.10.4-6.
[21]Dio Cassius, RomHist 39.59.1; 61.4.
[22]Ibid., 43.24.4.
[23]Ibid., 41.14.2-4.
[24]Cicero, DeDiv 1.97-98. Among the phenomena related by Cicero were

manipulated at the hands of interpreters who could create a maze of obscurity around the prophecies so that the same verses could be adapted to different situations at different times. The Sibyl herself, when composing acrostics, was certainly not under the influence of frenzy and inspiration, but in the state of concentrated thought, thus bringing into question the validity of prophecy in general.[25]

The role of Sibylline oracles in matters of religious and civil justice was not always clear and could end in tragic requirements. When, in the age of the Metelli three vestal virgins were brought to trial for having violated their vows, the pontiffs acquitted them. Fearing the consequences of such a decision, the people requested that the virgins be tried by a secular court. There their condemnation was secured, but unrest did not subside. The Sibylline books were consulted. The interpreters concluded that, to appease divine anger, two Greeks and two Gauls should be buried alive. This enormity was still possible before the senate expressly forbade human sacrifices sixteen years later.[26] Still it turned out to be a useless sacrifice, for divine displeasure was thought to have manifested itself in a fire which devastated much of the city in 111 BCE.

The transition from the Republic to imperial Rome was marked by religious reforms, some of which involved the Sibylline books. Displeased with the current state of the oracles, Augustus decreed that all

---

those caused by known natural disasters. But to those he added such unbelievable occurrences as the appearance of two suns and two moons, the weeping of the statue of Apollo and that of Victory, the water being changed into blood in the river Atratus (we do not know what Cicero referred to, a river by that name not being known), showers of stone, blood, milk. . . .

[25]Ibid., 2.110-12.

[26]Livy, 22.57.6 (LCL V) 385-87, reports a similar incident which had happened more than a century earlier when two vestal virgins were convicted of unchastity, a fact which brought pollution to the land. When the Sibylline Books were consulted, they required the same kind of sacrifice which had by then become a tradition to which Livy strongly objected: "In the meantime, by the direction of the Books of Fate, some unusual sacrifices were offered; amongst others a Gaulish man and woman and a Greek man and woman were buried alive in the Cattle Market, in a place walled in with stone, which even before this time had been defiled with human victims, a sacrifice wholly alien to the Roman spirit."

A scholium to the text points out that for Livy the sacrifice prescribed by the Greek Sibylline Books, was a Greek and not a Roman rite. The earlier instance referred to in the text was in 228 BCE (Zonaras 8.19).

prophetic works in existence, Greek or Latin, regardless of authorship, should be collected for review. He then burned two thousand of them, keeping only what could be positively identified as Sibylline books, and even among those he made a choice. The oracles selected were then placed in two gilded cases under the pedestal of the Palatine Apollo. After completing that task, Augustus proceeded with other religious reforms, reviving some of the ancient rites that had fallen in disuse, and showing particular interest in the College of Vestal Virgins.[27]

Little insight is gained on the frequency of the use of Sybilline oracles by the senate at the beginning of the empire. When, under Tiberius, the waters of the Tiber flooded part of Rome with considerable loss of property and life, Asinius Gallus attempted to revive the practice of consulting the Sibylline books in times of distress. Tiberius, though superstitious himself, voiced his opposition to the proposal and suggested that a better approach to averting a flood resided in engineering wisdom. He appointed Ateius Capito (who had interpreted the Sibylline books for Augustus) and Lucius Arruntius to see to that matter.[28] Some time later a motion was made in the senate to consider a request by Caninius Gallus (one of the *Quimdecimviri*) that an alleged book by the Sibyl be added to the official collection. Tiberius sent a letter of reproach to Quintilianus, the tribune of the people, who presented the matter. He scolded Gallus for not having sufficiently investigated the authenticity of the book in question and for having introduced the request at a time when the senate was poorly attended, a move which cast doubt on his competence. Citing the decree of Augustus as well as the regulations which guided the search for new oracles after a fire destroyed the capitol, Tiberius opposed the

---

[27]Suetonius, Caesars: Augustus 31. Dio, RomHist 54.17.2, referred to a decree of Augustus according to which the Sibylline verses which, with time, had been confused with other prophecies should be copied off only by priests so that no one else would happen to have an opportunity to read them. This decree of Augustus, however, would suggest that not all of the Sibylline Books were a monopoly of the state and that some may have circulated openly. The punishment by death of those who disobeyed the Roman law forbidding the reading of the Sibylline oracles was still well attested in the days of Justin Martyr, 1 Apol 44.

[28]Tacitus, Ann 1.76.

request of Gallus to include the new book into the Sibylline corpus but agreed to let the College of the Fifteen scrutinize its content.[29]

A much more troublesome situation arose when the Roman people became disturbed by an oracle believed to have originated with the Sibyl and which predicted the end of Rome: "When thrice three hundred revolving years have run their course, civil strife upon Rome destruction shall bring." Though the oracle, even if true, could not have applied to Tiberius's age, he denounced those verses as spurious and weeded them out of the collected prophecies, rejecting some as worthless and retaining others as genuine.[30]

The Sibylline books were again opened and consulted under Nero who tried to find in them instructions that would appease waves of popular discontent. At points he enjoyed the reputation of being the new Roman Apollo, acclaimed by the masses in the numerous religious processions as the divine presence itself:

Hail, Olympian Victor! Hail, Pythian Victor! Augustus! Augustus! Hail Nero, our Hercules! Hail Nero, our Apollo! The only Victor of the Grand Tour, the only one from the beginning of time! Augustus! Augustus! O, Divine Voice! Blessed are they that hear thee![31]

Quite different were the sentiments of the people after the fire in Rome when the multitudes began to suspect Nero as perpetrator, this in spite of his accusation of the Christians. While in the process of clearing up the burnt section of Rome and building his grandiose new palace, the *Aurea Domus*, Nero could not ignore the resentment of a substantial portion of the citizenry. Sibylline books were opened more often, prayers were offered to numerous gods, sacred banquets and nightly vigils were celebrated. Tacitus remarked:

All human efforts, all the lavish gifts of the emperor, and the propitiation of the gods, did not banish the sinister belief that the conflagration was the result of an order. Consequently, to get rid of the report, Nero fastened the guilt and inflicted the most exquisite tortures on a class hated for their abominations, called Christians by the populace.[32]

---

[29]Ibid., 6.12.
[30]Dio Cassius, RomHist 57.18.5 (LCL VII) 161.
[31]Ibid., 62.20.5 (LCL VIII) 169-71.
[32]Tacitus, Ann 15.44.

The Sibylline prophecy on the destruction of Rome surfaced again, this time more forcefully:

> And they were disturbed above all by recalling the oracle which once in the time of Tiberius had been on everybody's lips. It ran thus: "Thrice three hundred years having run their course of fulfillment, Rome by the strife of her people shall perish."[33]

Nero was successful in convincing the people that such verses did not exist. But the stratagem turned against him when the people turned to another oracle which they considered an authentic Sibylline saying: "Last of the sons of Aeneas, a mother-slayer shall govern," to which Dio added: "And so it proved, whether this verse was actually spoken beforehand by some divine prophecy, or the populace was now for the first time inspired, in view of the present situation, to utter it."[34]

The preoccupation of the Romans with their destiny as a world power took on a sense of urgency under Nero. The empire could not last forever. Its destiny would meet its own nemesis. The fear that the Sibyl may have been right persisted in the consciousness of perceptive citizens for several centuries, well into the days of Constantine. To internal strife would be added the fear that the East would overpower the West, a theme Lactantius did not fail to exploit.[35] As proof, the Sibyl was summoned again to predict the inexorable end Rome would suffer: "Nevertheless the Sibyls openly say that Rome is doomed to perish, and that indeed by the

---

[33]Dio Cassius, RomHist 62.18.3-4 (LCL VIII) 117.

[34]Ibid., 62.18.4-5 (LCL VIII) 117. Lactantius, DeMort 2 (ANF VII) 302, reflected on the belief that Nero was still alive after believed dead and chose to apply to him the following Sibylline verses: "The fugitive, who slew his own mother, being to come from the uttermost boundaries of the earth."

[35]Lactantius, DivInst 7.15 (ANF VII) 212: "And—my mind dreads to relate it, but I will relate it, because it is about to happen—the cause of this desolation and confusion will be this; because the Roman name, by which the world is now ruled, will be taken away from the earth, and the government return to Asia; and the East will again bear rule, and the West be reduced to servitude. Nor ought it to appear wonderful to any one, if a kingdom founded with such vastness, and so long increased by so many and such men, and in short strengthened by such great resources, shall nevertheless at some time fall."

judgment of God, because it held His name in hatred; and being the enemy of righteousness, it destroyed the people who kept the truth."[36]

The Sibylline prophecies edged closer to their realization after the suicide of Nero. Civil strife threatened the stability of the empire. To the critical eye of Tacitus, who was well trained in the art of interpretation of the oracles, the reign of Nero never ceased to appear in its mysterious dual aspect of greatness and failure, of artistic sensitivity and cruel barbarity. Though Tacitus would not have given credence to the predicted cycles foretelling the hegemony of the East and the doom of Rome, he nonetheless wrote:

> I am entering on the history of a period rich in disasters, frightful in its wars, torn by civil strife, and even in peace full of horrors. . . . There was success in the East, and disaster in the West. . . . The armies of Parthia were all but set in motion by the cheat of a counterfeit Nero.[37]

It was believed, or perhaps feared, that Nero might return to save or to haunt the empire. Many people could not make up their minds as to whether they should consider him dead or still alive.[38] Suetonius reported

---

[36]Ibid., 7.15 (ANF VII) 213. In the struggle of Christianity against heathenism, mostly in times of persecutions, the hatred against Rome and the prediction of its downfall were attributed to the Sibyl:

There shall come to thee sometime from above
A heavenly stroke deserved, O haughty Rome.
And thou shalt be the first to bend thy neck
And be rased to the ground, and thee shall fire
Destructive utterly consume, cast down
Upon thy pavements, and thy wealth shall perish,
And wolves and foxes dwell in thy foundations.
And then shalt thou be wholly desolate,
As if not born. OracSib 8.35-42.

Terry, *The Sibylline Oracles* 47-55).

[37]Tacitus, Hist 1.2.420. Later editions of the Sibylline oracles supported this view:

And then strife
Awakened of war shall come to the West,
Shall also come the fugitive of Rome. . . .

OracSib 4.135-37 (Terry, *The Sibylline Oracles*, 176-78).

[38]Tacitus, Hist 2.8.

that, even after his death, Nero's edicts continued to circulate. Many claimed that he was still alive and would come back to destroy his enemies.[39]

Though Sibylline oracles progressively lost some of their power of persuasion, they surfaced at intervals in the political life of the empire to settle questions which appeared to require divine intervention. As Hadrian was contemplating his ascension to power after having tried to secure Trajan's favors which were not always willingly granted, he found his ambitions confirmed in a Virgilian oracle. But people around him preferred to believe that the prophecy came to him directly from the Sibylline verses, which constituted a far greater basis of authority.[40]

The belief in the power of the Sibylline oracles to avert evil remained evident in times of natural disasters. In Gordian's reign an earthquake severe enough to swallow entire cities and their inhabitants compelled Romans to offer vast sacrifices throughout the known world. But it was only when the Sibylline books were consulted and everything required by them fulfilled, that the evil was finally stayed.[41] A similar catastrophe, combined with other calamities was reported to have happened under the two Gallieni, in the consulship of Gallienus and Fausianus. The Sibylline books commanded special sacrifices to Jupiter Salutaris after thousands of men died of the pestilence which followed the earthquake.[42]

The fear of foreign invasion often determined the nature of religious ceremonies. When Aurelian blundered in his military tactics, allowing the Marcomanni to inflict disaster on the empire, the Sibylline books were again consulted, but not early enough to avoid some of the calamities. Once the proper ceremonies and sacrifices were dutifully taken care of, Aurelian supposedly defeated the enemy. But not all senators were convinced that they should defer to prophecy for the destiny of the empire. A debate arose, and long speeches were offered, most of them praising the benefits that the Books of Fate had bestowed upon Rome every time they have been scrutinized and obeyed. Others objected to a questionable obedience to prescribed rituals, praising the ability of Aurelian himself

---

[39]Suetonius, Ceasars: Nero 57.
[40]ScriptHistAug: Hadrian 2.8. The Virgilian oracle can be found in the Aen 6.808-12.
[41]ScriptHistAug: The Three Gordians 26.1-2.
[42]Ibid., The Two Gallieni 5.2-5.

both in matters of military genius and in religious competence. The decree of the senate was in favor of the books, and they performed with great pomp what the interpreters advised. Due to unexpected delays, which some had interpreted as a cause for additional harm to the emperor, a letter from Aurelian was presented to the senate. It read:

> I marvel, revered Fathers, that you have hesitated for so long a time to open the Sibylline books, just as though you were consulting in a gathering of Christians [*Christianorum ecclesia*] and not in the temple of all the gods. Come, therefore, and by means of the purity of the pontiffs and the sacred ceremonies bring aid to your prince who is harassed by the plight of the commonwealth. Let the books be consulted; let all that should be done be performed; whatever expenses are needful, whatever captives of any race, whatever princely animals, I will not refuse, but will offer them gladly, for it is not an unseemly thing to win victories by the aid of the gods. It was with this that our ancestors brought many wars to an end and with this that they began them. Whatever costs there may be I have ordered to be paid by the prefect of the treasury, to whom I have sent a letter. You have, moreover, under your own control the money-chest of the state, which I find more full than were my desire.[43]

We may have in this instance one of the last eloquent and urgent pleas for the consultation of Sibylline oracles as a means to ensure the safety of Rome. The challenge of the Christian movement is veiled in the derogatory remark which insinuates a conflicting approach to religious questions, contrasting the *Christianorum ecclesia* to the body of pontiffs. The open discord on the validity of Sibylline books within the senate reflected the uneasiness with which some senators viewed the destiny of the empire. Judicious political and military decisions were at last regarded openly as more beneficial than the promises of superstition, however legitimate. Even after the books had been consulted and all rites performed, Aurelian suffered such a devastating defeat near Placentia that it almost wrecked the empire. Again a final victory, though less than spectacular, was attributed to the intervention of the Sibyl, a claim which was

---

[43]Ibid., The Deified Aurelian 20.4-8 (LCL III) 233.

received with little enthusiasm among the senators. In his violent mood, Aurelian killed some senators of noble birth on the most trivial charges.[44]

In the case of Probus, Sibylline books were credited with the fore-sight to predict the choice of an emperor long before his time. Since Probus was regarded as a good emperor who, had he lived long enough, would have freed the world of all barbarians, many believed that he had always been part of the Sibyl's vision of the future.[45]

At the dawn of the Christian empire Sibylline oracles were invoked by pagans and Christians alike. But, by that time, besides the official collection housed on the Palatine, Christianized versions of the prophecies had infiltrated most of the segments of the early church. The ultimate test came at the Milvian Bridge. There the confrontation between Constantine and Maxentius was regarded as the most crucial turning point in the history of the empire and of the church. Superstitious Maxentius, who would not even leave Rome on account of premonitions which planted fear into all of his actions and decisions, had also become convinced of the nefarious results of a long siege. Having spanned a temporary bridge across the Tiber he could position his troops for battle. But at the same time Constantine, urged by a dream to place the chi-rho sign on the shields of his soldiers, gained firm confidence in the superiority of the God of the Christians. Socrates elaborated on this episode, mainly by introducing another vision of Constantine before the final confrontation at the Milvian Bridge. At dusk the emperor saw a pillar of light in the heavens, in the form of a cross, on which were inscribed the words *In hoc signo vinces* ("By this sign conquer"). On the next night Christ appeared to him and directed him to prepare a standard on the pattern of what he had seen, an oracle promptly obeyed by Constantine who saw it as the assurance of his victory against Maxentius.[46]

Lactantius compared the two camps, showing how political and military circumstances turned against Maxentius who, in a desperate move ordered the Sibylline books to be consulted. An obscure and ambiguous prophecy was discovered: "On the same day the enemy of the Romans should perish." Misled by what he thought was a sign pointing to his victory, Maxentius went head on to his defeat: "The hand of the

---

[44]Ibid., 21.1-7.
[45]Ibid., Tacitus 16.6.
[46]Socrates, HE 1.2.

Lord prevailed, and the forces of Maxentius were routed. He fled towards the broken bridge; but the multitude pressing on him, he was driven headlong into the Tiber."[47] Eusebius compared the episode to the drowning of the forces of pharaoh in the sea when the Hebrew nation freed itself from Egyptian servitude. By implication, Constantine was the new Moses leading his empire to the promised land.[48]

The so-called Battle of the Milvian Bridge could be construed as a conflict between dying paganism and victorious Christianity, as well as the point at which pagan Sibylline prophecies met their death. But Maxentius was cast in the role of the villain in order to enhance Constantine's image as the benevolent Christian emperor. The beginning of the reign of Maxentius had been marked by leniency toward Christians and by the abrogation of persecutions. Even Eusebius had to allow him that much credit.[49] The need to portray Constantine as the divinely elected emperor compelled Christians to establish the contrast with Maxentius.

Sibylline books were not consulted again until the brief rule of Julian, sometimes with a strange twist. During the trials for treason Julian confiscated the property of Artemius and condemned him to death. The reason given was that, under Constantine, as the commander of the troops in Egypt, he used his position to destroy the idols there.[50] It is reported that during the trial he appealed to the emperor by the evidence of pagan prophecies contained in the Sibylline books.[51] Should this have been actually the case, we would have here the ironic situation in which the

---

[47]Lactantius, DeMort 44 (ANF VII) 318. On the way Maxentius put his trust in the arts of sorcery and did not go beyond the limits of the city. See Eusebius, HE 9.9.3.

[48]Eusebius, HE 9.9.5; VConst 1.38.

[49]Eusebius, HE 8.14.1 (NPNF-2 I) 336: "Maxentius his [Maximianus's] son, who obtained the government at Rome, at first feigned our faith, in complaisance and flattery toward the Roman people. On this account he commanded his subjects to cease persecuting the Christians, pretending to religion that he might appear merciful and mild beyond his predecessors. But [Eusebius continued with emphasis] he did not prove in his deeds to be such a person as was hoped, but ran into all wickedness and abstained from no impurity or licentiousness, committing adulteries and indulging in all kinds of corruption. . . . "

[50]Theodoret, HE 3.14.

[51]Parke, *Sibyls*, 166.

last appeal to the pagan prophecies before their destruction by Stilicho would have been made by someone attempting to prove that the Christian dominion of the empire was willed by the Roman gods. We can only surmise how Julian would have reacted to such audacity.

Sibylline Oracles in Jewish Religion

The historical and philosophical developments that followed the death of Alexander the Great altered the Jewish understanding of religion. In the Diaspora the Jews translated nationalistic beliefs and practices into universally acceptable theological propositions in two distinct ways. First, it was not until about the end of the third century BCE that Judaism recognized the validity of biblical prophets who, until then, were regarded as iconoclasts within the Hebrew tradition. Challenged by the new waves of cultural transformation, Jews found it necessary to supplement the teaching of the Torah with a philosophical and theological analysis of their religion. Such an opportunity lay latent in the voice of the prophets who were transformed from heretics to be persecuted into heroes of the faith. Second, Diaspora Judaism recast existing pagan prophecies into missionary tools capable of meeting the challenges of the new cosmopolitan cultural atmosphere. Judaism found itself in the position of being the sole religion sufficiently all-inclusive to deal with past, present, and future phenomena. Communities of Hellenized Jews served as the platform for the composition of new apocalyptic predictions in the more congenial context of Greek culture.

From the second century BCE to the end of the third century CE a large body of pseudepigraphical literature came into existence to reinforce the Jewish belief in the primacy of its religion as the force reshaping the destiny of the world. Among the most notorious compositions were the *Testaments of the Twelve Patriarchs*, the *Book of Jubilees*, the *Book of Enoch*, the *Psalms of Solomon*, the *Assumption of Moses*, the *Ascension of Isaiah*, and the *Fourth Book of Ezra*. Though there exists no definite consensus of authorship, place, and date of composition, it is generally assumed that such literature began to flourish in Alexandria in the days of the Ptolemies. The *Zeitgeist* also encouraged the propagation of Sibylline oracles, attributed to pagan prophetesses, but heavily reworked to fit Jewish perspectives. The third book of the Sibylline oracles could be placed together with other apologetic works such as the *Letter of Aristeas*, the *Book of Wisdom*, the *Book of Esther*, and the pseudo-

Justinian *Cohortatio ad Graecos*, all of them directed against the Greeks of the time.

The new Sibylline oracles did little to alleviate tensions with the peoples among whom the Jews were destined to live. In the Greco-Roman world, Jewish claims to universalism were interpreted as hostility towards the rest of the human race. The demeanor of the Jews was regarded as *odium generis humani* ("hatred of the human race"), a characterization Christians later inherited. Ironically, all of this stood in sharp contrast to the mission the Jews thought they had received from God, namely, to be the true philosophers, the genuine light to the nations, the voice of wisdom in a world of chaos. The Jewish conviction that the world could not find redemption outside of its faith fueled the fires of enmity between Jews and heathen. Sibylline visions turned nationalistic again:

> And every land shall be filled up with thee,
> and every sea; and everyone shall be
> Offended with thy customs.[52]

The alleged existence of a Palestinian Sibyl, Sabbe, mentioned in Pausanias's list, facilitated the production of new prophetic texts and oracles meant to convey divine expectations from a Jewish point of view. What at first appeared as a genuine attempt to recommend Jewish religion to the Hellenized world turned out to be too limited to be effective. Jewish chronographers adopted a rather narrow perspective while attempting to establish the antiquity of their status as the chosen people of God. By utilizing edited pagan prophecies they could place on the lips of the Sibyl the testimony regarding the prominence of the Jewish God, the hegemony of the Jewish race, the eventual conversion of the Gentiles, and the fulfillment of the promised messianic age. The Sibyl could thus be cast into the role of the repository of God's eternal decrees,[53] well

---

[52]OracSib 3.271-73. (Terry, *The Sibylline Oracles*, 333-35).

[53]The end of book 3 of the Sibylline Oracles is concerned with the identification of the Sibyl and her specific prophetic function:

> For he showed me what happened formerly
> To my ancestors; what things were the first
> Those God made known to me; and in my mind
> Did God put all things to be afterwards,

ahead of the prophetic wisdom of former Hebrew women prophetesses such as Deborah and Huldah.[54]

The reasons the Jews chose to imitate a pagan Sibyl cannot be totally explained. The Hebrew prophetic voice had already vindicated a lofty monotheism. Their Scriptures were available to the Greeks in the form of the Septuagint, one of the jewels of the Alexandrian library. Even pagan writers who found fault with Jewish misguided ambitions acknowledged the persuasive force of their religion and the superiority of their worship. Augustine has Seneca say of the Jews, as if by divine providence: "When, meanwhile, the customs of that most accursed nation have gained such strength that they have been now received in all lands, the conquered have given laws to the conquerors." Then he assessed Jewish religion with the surprising conclusion: "Those, however, know the cause of their rites, whilst the greater part of the people know not why they perform theirs."[55]

The use of Sibylline prophecies among Jewish writers is, to say the least, very limited. Philo, who was the greatest exponent of Jewish religion from a Hellenistic point of view, did not honor the Sibylline oracles with any attention, though he has sometimes been suspected of knowing them.[56] By the time of Josephus at least part of the Sibylline corpus was known in its Jewish version. We find in Josephus's writings one lone mention of the Sibyl in reference to a specific prophecy regarding the Tower of Babel.[57]

The Jewish collections of Sibylline oracles have often been criticized for their poor literary quality and for the lack of organization which afflicted most of the collectors and peddlers of oracles in the ancient world. Prophecies were often gathered by persons little trained in the art and insufficiently sensitive to the deeper meaning of the statements. The

---

That I might prophesy of things to come,
And things that were, and tell them unto men.
OracSib 3.818-24. (Terry, *The Sibylline Oracles*, 1017-23).

[54]Judges 4:4-5; 2 Kings 22:14-20.

[55]Augustine, CivDei 6.11 (NPNF-1 II) 120-21.

[56]In a note on Philo's DePraem 87 Heinemann, *Bildung*, suspected that Philo drew the picture of the Beast-peace from the "Wise Sayings" (*Weissagungen*) of the Sibylline Oracles (3.788). See Appendices in LCL VIII, 456.

[57]Josephus, Ant 1.4.3. The reference is to OracSib 3.97-104.

most important segment of the oracles which formed what is now known as book III appears as an amalgamation of prophecies "composed in a traditionally wild, chaotic, and obscure style in which the sequence of thought and subject must be followed across intervening sections, and the events referred to are rarely identifiable beyond dispute."[58]

In his analysis of the Jewish Sibylline Oracles Joseph Klausner accepted the perspective of what he called "Schürer's well-conceived expression," namely, that those oracles are *Jüdische Propaganda unter heidnischer Maske* ("Jewish propaganda under a pagan mask").[59] The Greek influence is everywhere evident, but it is felt more in the general tone of the oracles than in their content. From that point of view they differ greatly from other original Palestinian Jewish literary compositions.[60] According to Klausner the element of Jewish propaganda, especially in book III, was

> exceedingly shrewd, penetrating, and clever. . . . In all these excellencies of the Jewish Sibyl lies the secret of the influence of this Sibyl even upon pagans of high position. . . . Thus it is not to be wondered at, that these oracles had such a great influence upon the best of the pagans. Except for the Hellenistic Jewish author of the third Sibylline book, no Jewish apocalyptist reached the twin heights of Jewish nationalism and universalism as they had already been reached by Isaiah, First and Second. Thus Isaiah became "a light to the Gentiles" by means of an Alexandrian Jew, who styled himself [herself?] "Assyro-Babylonian Sibyl" and "daughter-in-law of Noah."[61]

Jewish Sibylline oracles are only a part of the incomplete collection we now possess. Books III, IV, and V are of definite Jewish authorship.

---

[58]P. M. Fraser, *Ptolemaic Alexandria* (London/New York: Oxford, 1972) 1:711. Quoted from John R. Bartlett, *Jews in the Hellenistic World: Josephus, Aristeas, the Sibylline Oracles, Eupolemus* (Cambridge: Cambridge University Press, 1985) 37. Frazer, *Golden Bough*, 404, dismissed contemptuously the Sibylline Books as a "Convenient farrago of nonsense."

[59]Joseph Klausner, *The Messianic Idea in Israel: From Its Beginning to the Completion of the Mishnah*, trans. W. F. Stinespring (New York: Macmillan, 1955) 370.

[60]Joseph Klausner, *From Jesus to Paul*, trans. W. F. Stinespring (New York: Macmillan, 1944) 178.

[61]Ibid., 161-63.

Other books contain a great deal of Christian interpolations, and many of the quotations of early church apologists are not even a part of traditional collections. But the Jewish corpus of oracles was sufficiently well selected to serve as an apologetic tool emphasizing the philosophical and theological nature of the prophecies without connecting them with the ritualistic and ceremonial requirements of Hebrew religion. It is in such a context that they were used by Christians who expanded the collection in order to enhance the apologetic presentation of their religion to the pagan world.

Sibylline Oracles in Early Christianity

By the second century CE extant collections of Jewish Sibylline oracles had been heavily edited by Christians, to the point that it became difficult to identify what was Jewish and what was Christian. Original pagan material which escaped Christianization is now scarce.[62] New Sibylline books appeared (especially those now known as books VI–VIII) with a decidedly Christian content, including new elements such as a hymn to Christ and a discussion of the nature of the Messiah. New collections of Sibylline oracles came from Jews and Christians. They had no common ground with the Sibylline books consulted by the senate. No direct claim arose from Jews or Christians that their collections were identical to those in the possession of the official Roman government. But it served their apologetic purpose to appeal to books by the same name and claiming the same divine origin. Nobody seriously questioned the fact that Christian Sibylline oracles, like those of the Jews, might have originated in spurious interpolations or even forgeries.

By the middle of the second century the Christian Sibyl had entered the prophetic mode to such an extent that Hermas could no longer distinguish her from the church:

> Now a revelation was given to me, my brethren, while I slept, by a young man of comely appearance, who said to me, "Who do you think that old woman is from whom you received the book?" And I said, "The Sibyl." "You are in a mistake," says he; "It is not the Sibyl." "Who is it then?" say I. And he said, "It is the church." And I said to

---

[62]An example of such verses is found in OracSib 3.108-60 (Terry, *The Sibylline Oracles*, 130-95).

him, "Why then is she an old woman?" "Because," said he, "she was created first of all. On this account she is old, and for her sake was the world made."[63]

As the vision continued, we learn that the Sibyl had not yet finished her work and that she needed to add some words to her book. After doing so, it was Hermas's duty to compose two books from what he received and to give one to Clement and one to Grapte. Clement was responsible to make his book known throughout the world.[64]

The authority of the Christian Sibyl was questioned by opponents of the church, especially Celsus who coined a word to designate those who put their trust in the Sibylline prophecies. He called them Sibyllists (σιβυλλιστάς). According to Celsus, the stories invoked as a proof of Christ's divinity do not measure up to the divine attributes of former Greek heroes such as Hercules, Asclepius, Orpheus, or even Epictetus. But even more to the point, Celsus argued that, since Christians were willing to acknowledge the authority of the Sibyl, she, and not Christ, should have been proclaimed a child of God. If Christians felt the necessity to introduce new material into the Sibylline books, it was not to the life of Christ that they should have turned. By doing so they have interpolated into the oracles "many impious things, and set up as a God one who ended a most infamous life by a most miserable death." The Old Testament would have provided less objectionable models such as Jonah

---

[63]*Pastor of Hermas*, second vision 4 (ANF II) 12.

[64]Grapte was presumably a deaconess, and the book she received seemed to have less importance, giving her specific instructions on how to deal with orphans and widows. We do not know for certain who Clement was. The text assumes a clear knowledge of the person, and some have identified him with the renowned bishop of Rome, the author of 1 Clement, who may have also been connected with the imperial Flavian family through Titus Flavius Clemens. But the chronology does not favor such an identification, the *Pastor of Hermas* having been written much later than 1 Clem.

Of interest also is how this early in the process the voice of the church was connected, if not confused, with that of the Sibyl. It was the prophetic voice of the Sibyl which prefigured the future of the church, and possibly also its stability and power: "Like the Sibyl, the church is the prophetic voice of society, the predictor of the future, the one that defines a Christian's role in society." Douglas R. Edwards, *Religion and Power: Pagans, Jews, and Christians in the Greek East* (New York: Oxford University Press, 1996) 141.

in the whale's belly or Daniel delivered from the wild beasts. Origen challenged the attackers of Christianity to produce older copies of the oracles without those interpolations, a proposition he knew would remain impossible.[65]

Among the extant works of Origen only the *Contra Celsum* contains references to the Sibyl, and they all reflect a polemical reply to the charges levelled by Celsus against the church. But nowhere did Origen appeal directly to the Sibyl or her oracles in support of his apologetic work. It is thus difficult to assess his perspective on the new body of literature so revered by some other church fathers. Eusebius, who studied under the Origenist scholar Pamphilus, adopted a similar approach. But this time the reply was to Jewish and Christian writers. In his voluminous *Praeparatio evangelica* he referred to four episodes where the Sibyl appeared, namely, in Josephus, Tatian, and Clement of Alexandria.[66] Eusebius's *Historia ecclesiastica* does not mention either the Sibyl or any Christian usage of her oracles. In the *Vita Constantini*, Eusebius simply reports the views of Constantine on the Erythraean Sibyl and her alleged prophecies about Christ.[67]

The earliest extensive quotations of Sibylline oracles among the church fathers appeared in Justin, who may have been influential in setting the tone for the reverence accorded to prophecies not directly related to the Old Testament. The question of authenticity revolved not so much around the nature of the Sibylline oracles as around the credibility of Justin and his reports.[68] For him, the same divine agency inspired the prophecies of the Old Testament, those of the Sibyl, and those of Hystaspes, a legendary anti-Roman Persian king who was believed to have composed prophetic books regarding Chaldaean mysteries. A clue to Justin's relationship to the Sibylline oracles may be

---

[65]Origen, CCel 5.61; 7.53, 56 (ANF IV) 632-33.

[66]Eusebius, PraepEv 416d (Josephus); 495c (Tatian); 678cd and 681d (Clement of Alexandria).

[67]Eusebius, OratSanct 18-19.

[68]Justin has not always been regarded as a trustworthy witness and judge of events in the early days of the Christian movement, and this despite his unquestionably good intentions. Said Renan, *Eglise Chrétienne*. In *Oeuvres Complètes* (Paris: Calmann-Lévy, 1879) 606: "Justin était un esprit faible, mais c'était un noble et de bon coeur."

found in a rather obscure passage directed against those who would forbid the reading of such literature:

> But by the agency of the devils, death has been decreed against those who would read the books of Hystaspes, or of the Sibyl, or of the prophets, that through fear they may prevent men who read them from receiving the knowledge of the good, and may retain them in slavery to themselves; which, however, they could not always effect. For not only do we fearlessly read them, but, as you see, bring them for your inspection, knowing that their contents will be pleasing to all. And if we persuade even a few, our gain will be very great; for, as good husband-men, we shall receive the reward from the Master.[69]

In such a limited and enigmatic context, the decree mentioned cannot be precisely identified. If it refers to a Roman law, the devils being the governing senators, we would have here nothing but the traditional position that the Sibylline books were the property of the senate and should never be made known to the people. But the text refers not only to the Sibylline oracles but also to Hystaspes and Old Testament prophecies, which would have hardly been of concern to the official governing body. Another possible, but still not convincing, suggestion has been proposed by W. H. C. Frend. He regards the decree mentioned as an attempt to set limits to Jewish propaganda and proselytism. All three works mentioned were part of Jewish literary weapons against the attackers of Judaism. Forbidding their reading would be an effective attack on Jews.[70] But if there was a strong dislike of the Jews by Justin, it certainly did not lead to a praise of the imperial government. Jews and Christians shared the same antipathy toward the Roman government, a position deserving of notice in an age that produced Marcion.

Justin found many analogies between the prophecies of the Sibyl and Hystaspes and the teaching of Greek philosophy. He contended that though they started from different premises, Stoics and Plato agreed with

---

[69]Justin Martyr, 1 Apol 44 (ANF I) 178.

[70]W. H. C. Frend, *Martyrdom and Persecution in the Early Church: A Study of a Conflict from the Maccabees to Donatus* (Garden City NY: Doubleday, 1967) 174-75.

oracular perspectives on the nature of God and his decrees concerning the destiny of the world.[71]

Two chapters of the *Cohortatio* (16 and 37) are entirely devoted to the Sibyl, and in this case she is no longer identified with any other prophets. This has made the question of authorship difficult to resolve. Most scholars refer to it as a pseudo-Justinian document, written somewhat later, perhaps into the fourth century. In chapter 16 the author invoked the credentials of Plato and Aristophanes as a proof of the Sibyl's authority and trustworthiness in matters of monotheism. Then he quoted the Sibyl:

> There is one only unbegotten God,
> Omnipotent, invisible, most high. . . .
> But we have strayed away from the Immortal's ways,
> And worship with a dull and senseless mind
> Idols, the workmanship of our own hands,
> And images and figures of dead men. . . .
> Blessed shall be those men upon the earth
> Who shall love the great God before all else. . . .

Chapter 37 represents the longest statement on the Sibyl as the Christians came to know her. Her pronouncements were as inspired as those of other prophets, though her origin remained shrouded in mystery. We learn that she was of Babylonian extraction, the daughter of a certain Berosus, who wrote the Chaldaean history. In a way which no longer could be determined, she came to Cumae. On a visit to that place the author was introduced to the large basilica, home of the Sibyl, which he described with wonder and admiration. Then again the writings of Plato were invoked in support of the Sibyl's inspiration, which far exceeded the sayings of the poets. Unfortunately, those who wrote down her prophecies were illiterate persons who much too often distorted and compromised the integrity of the meters. After her death her remains were preserved in a coffer made of brass. Her influence persisted, though the writer of the *Cohortatio* could not help but call on Plato again to warn that the inspiration of the Sibyl happened while she was in a state of frenzy and that she could not remember, while in her right mind, what her prophecies really meant. At this point she may have been confused with the

---

[71]Justin Martyr, 1 Apol 20.

Pythia who was a mere medium at the disposal of Apollo. But such was not the case for the Sibyl, inspired by the monotheistic God and not Apollo. Even in a state of frenzy she kept her prophetic insight. Due to the importance of such early patristic testimony to the Sibyl, the text of chapter 37 is reproduced in appendix 1.

Tatian, a contemporary of Justin, did not allow the Sibyl any place of importance in his apologetic work. We find in his writings just a casual reference to her, as she was listed with dozens of other heroes, gods, and poets as being of a more recent origin than Moses. The purpose was to show that no divine prophetic wisdom could predate Moses in the heathen world. The Sibyl was no exception.[72]

Theophilus, writing just a few years after Justin, quoted the Sibyl extensively. He used her to ridicule the conceptions of the gods among heathen and to support the Christian notion of monotheism. He cited the verses of the Sibyl to deride the kind of anthropomorphic view of the gods which would render them meaningless.[73] Speaking of prophets he remarked: "And there was not one or two, but many, at various times and seasons among the Hebrews; and also among the Greeks there was the Sibyl; and they all have spoken things consistent and harmonious with each other. . . . "[74] The history of the human race after the flood, the catastrophic results of the story of the Tower of Babel, as well as the wrath to come upon the world were all predicted in the Sibyl whom Theophilus quoted in detail.[75] A whole chapter was devoted to quotations of the Sibyl.[76] The passages are reproduced without explanation, leading us to assume that they were known to his audience.

Since Lactantius quoted from the fragments in Theophilus as well as from Book III of the Sibylline oracles, it has been sometimes conjectured that what we have in Theophilus was in fact an introduction to book III

---

[72]Tatian, OratGr 51.
[73]Theophilus, AdAut 2.3 (ANF II) 94:
For if the gods beget, and each remains
Immortal, then the race of gods must be
More numerous than mortals, and the throng
So great that mortals find no room to stand.
[74]Ibid., 2.9 (ANF II) 97.
[75]Ibid., 2.31.
[76]Ibid., 2.36.

as it circulated before it was officially compiled in its present form.[77] In the final analysis, what appeared important to Theophilus was not the chronological sequence of prophets, Sibyls, and poets, but the fact that they all agreed on the eschatological destiny of the world and the rule of divine providence: "The Sibyl, then, and the other prophets, yea, and the poets and philosophers, have clearly taught both concerning righteousness, and judgment, and punishment; and also concerning providence. . . ."[78]

In 177 Athenagoras wrote his *Legatio pro christianis* in which he referred to the same Sibyl Plato mentioned to explain why divinity had sometimes been ascribed to human beings. He also alluded to a segment of the Sibylline oracles which is part of the rare excerpts that have survived from the original pagan material:

> It was the generation then the tenth,
> Of men endow'd with speech, since forth the flood
> Had burst upon the men of former times,
> And Kronos, Japetus, and Titan reigned,
> Whom men, of Ouranos and Gaïa
> Proclaimed the noblest sons, and named them so,
> Because of men endowed with gift of speech
> They were the first.[79]

---

[77]Robert H. Pfeiffer, *History of New Testament Times* (New York: Harper & Row, 1949) 227. A similar position is expressed by Parke, *Sibyls*, 161. The prophecies of Theophilus attributed to the Sibyls are much too long to be quoted here, but worth reading in the context of book III of the Sibylline oracles.

[78]Theophilus, AdAut 2.38 (ANF II) 110.

[79]Athenagoras, Leg 30 (ANF II) 145. See OracSib 3.108-13.

A text of Phlegon, meant to be a tribute to the longevity of the Erythrean Sibyl, is considered to be a rare, if not unique, Sibylline oracle predating the fire of the temple of Jupiter Capitolinus. It has a better claim to being a part of the original pagan material as used officially by the Roman senate. In it we find an enlightening comment on the relationship between the Sibyl and Apollo. The text has been preserved in F. Jacoby's *Die Fragmente der griechischen Historiker* (257 fragm 37). I quote it here in summary fashion:

> But why indeed all-sorrowful do I sing divine oracles about other people's suffering, holding to my fated madness? Why do I taste its painful sting, retaining my grievous old age into the tenth century . . . ? Then, envious of my prophetic gift, the son of famous Leto, filling his destructive heart with passion, will loose my spirit, chained in its miserable body, when he will

Athenagoras was probably the first Christian apologist to have known at least book III of the collection of Jewish and Christian oracles as they have now come to us through the centuries. How the original pagan material remained part of the oracles is not clear. But we have here two important turning points in the latter part of the second century: The consolidation of Jewish and Christian perspectives on the oracles and the progressive Sibylline surrender of outworn paganism.

Tertullian quoted the same passage to show that Greek divinities were human. Though he was willing to consider the Sibyl as the *veri vera vates* ("true prophetess of truth"), he rebuked those who misused her status for the wrong purposes: "That Sibyl, I mean, who was the true prophetess of truth, from whom you borrow their title for the priests of your demons."[80] Tertullian pointed out the inconsistencies and absurdities of Greek gods, absurdities from which even the Sibyl could not be totally rescued.

Clement often referred to the Sibyl with great respect, considering her superior to Greek gods, heroes, poets, and philosophers with the same aura of antiquity as Moses.[81] She was invoked not only for her prophetic insight, but also as an authority in ethical conduct.[82] By her counsel and wisdom she brought reassurance to those who had been the victims of the terrifying and threatening misconduct of the gods.[83] In his function as a teacher, Clement adopted the Sibyl's world view which was also shared

---

have shot through my frame with a flesh-piercing arrow. Then straightway, my spirit, having flown through the air, sends to the ears of mortals audible omens. . . . My body will lie shamefully unburied on mother earth. No mortal will cover it with earth or hide it in a tomb. . . . And birds in their feathered robes, if they taste my flesh, will give true prophecy to mortals.

I use the text as given by D. S. Potter in *Prophets and Emperors: Human and Divine Authority from Augustus to Theodosius* (Cambridge MA: Harvard University Press, 1994) 71. It is also quoted in Parker, *Sibyls*, 115.

[80]Tertullian, AdNat 2.12 (ANF III) 142.

[81]Clement of Alexandria, Strom 1.21 (ANF II) 325: "We have also demonstrated Moses to be more ancient, not only than those called poets and wise men among the Greeks, but than the most of their deities. Nor he alone, but the Sibyl also is more ancient than Orpheus."

[82]Clement of Alexandria, Paed 3.3.

[83]Clement of Alexandria, Protr 2.

by Heraclitus.[84] If God's majesty and dominion were already apparent among the Greeks of wisdom, it was as the result of their contact with the Hebrew Sibyl. Such, according to Clement, was the case of Xenophon, who would have shared his convictions about the universal God, had he not been afraid to suffer the fate of Socrates.[85]

The connection between prophetic message and salvation prompted Clement to give the Sibyl a place of prominence based on her majestic description of monotheism. She was introduced as the one who, through the simplicity of her song and her perfect accord with divine inspiration, could distinguish between truth and error and between light and darkness: "Let the Sibyl prophetess, then, be the first to sing to us the song of salvation."[86] The Greek origin of the Sibyl did not present an obstacle for Clement who considered philosophy as a gift of God to the Greeks, and not in conflict with Christian preaching. To stress his point he appealed to the Κήρυγμα Πέτρου and Paul's challenge to the Greeks who possessed excellence:

> Take also the Hellenic books, read the Sibyl, how it is shown that God is one, and how the future is indicated. And taking Hystaspes, read, and you will find much more luminously and distinctly the Son of God described, and how many kings shall draw up their forces against Christ, hating Him and those who bear His name, and His faithful ones, and His patience, and His coming.[87]

Canonical and pseudo-Pauline writings provide no insight into the context of Clement's quotations. Even when addressing pagans of the

---

[84]Ibid., 4 (ANF II) 186: "But if you attend not to the prophetess, hear at least your own philosopher, the Ephesian Heraclitus. . . . "

[85]Ibid., 6 (ANF II) 192: "Whence, then, does the son of Gryllus [Xenophon] learn his wisdom? Is it not manifestly from the prophetess of the Hebrews [the Sibyl], who prophesies in the following style. . . . "

[86]Ibid., 8 (ANF II) 194. In this passage prophetic scriptures and Sibylline oracles seem to be placed on the same level of inspiration. Her proclamation of the One supreme God took place in a context including both Hebrew piety and Greek conceptions of the gods: "Know, and lay up wisdom in your hearts: There is one God, who sends rains, and winds, and earthquakes, thunderbolts, famines, plagues, and dismal sorrows, and snows and ice. But why detail particulars? He reigns over heaven, He rules earth, He truly is."

[87]Clement of Alexandria, Strom 6.5 (ANF II) 490.

Hellenized world, it is difficult to imagine Paul encouraging the reading of the Sibyl and Hystaspes to find there revelations about Christ. The traditions from which Clement drew his knowledge of Paul did not survive in the church. But Clement felt the need to have the apostle to the gentiles give his support to a prophetic voice that had progressively reshaped the perspective of the church and to endow it with a universal appeal for a pagan audience.

In any attempt to determine the extent to which Sibylline oracles influenced the course of church apologetic activity we are especially indebted to Lactantius whose writings contain one of the fullest accounts of Sibylline prophecies and their history. He was sometimes criticized for believing in the antiquity of the Sibylline prophetic literature without questioning the fact that most of it came from Jewish and Christian authors who were more concerned about their apologetic needs than with the history of the oracles.

Lactantius's credulity was already part of a tradition, as many church fathers before him saw no specific obstacle in using the Sibyl as a witness to the events of Christ and Christianity. But no consensus existed on that question in the early church. Those who quoted the Sibyl did it with approbation. Some, as Irenaeus, never used that prophetic literature for any purpose. Others, like Origen, showed a knowledge of the Sibylline corpus and were ready to engage in polemical arguments without using the content of it for any Christian theological support. Why, then, did Lactantius refer to so much of it so late in the process? He may have been naive and misguided, or he may have known that here was a formidable weapon for vindicating the Christian truth from a pagan point of view. His ability to wrench from the Sibyl a consistent testimony in favor of Christianity probably justified, in his opinion, an equally consistent use of it.

Lactantius divided the Sibylline oracles into two groups: those accessible to the public and the restricted version of the Cumaean Sibyl concealed by the Romans and inspected only by the *Quindecimviri*.

> But because it is related by most learned men that there have been many Sibyls, the testimony of one may not be sufficient to confirm the truth, as we propose to do. The volumes, indeed, of the Cumaean Sibyl, in which are written the fates of the Romans are kept secret; but the

writings of all the others are, for the most part, not prohibited from being in common use.[88]

The prophecies were used without specific attribution of authorship, though the Erythraean Sibyl received very special mention in Lactantius and was regarded as the most prolific and the most worthy of attention. Her importance came from the fact that it was to her that the Romans, under the leadership of Gaius (Caius) Curio, turned for the reconstitution of the collection of Sibylline Books after the original ones were destroyed in 83 BCE.

The ultimate purpose of Lactantius, however, was not to dwell on the history of the Sibyls or their books. He assumed that each of them produced her own collection. No detail was given on that account, and, except for the Cumaean collection, they were all regarded as the same general prophetic voice. He emphasized the portions of the Sibylline teachings which corroborated the Christian belief in "One God, who is alone, most mighty, uncreated." With the conviction of faith, Lactantius elaborated on Sibylline prophecies which, he thought, vindicated the Christian concept of God.[89]

Having set the specific tone for an agreement between Christian theology and Sibylline perspective, Lactantius referred to the Sibyl in numerous instances. We do not find in his writings the long and elaborate Sibylline quotations as they appeared in Justin and Theophilus. Rather he selected a multitude of short, almost aphoristic, sayings which he used throughout the *Divinae institutiones* whenever he found in them a congenial support for his theological exposition. Of all the church fathers who quoted the Sibylline prophecies he seems to be the best informed on the subject, giving the impression of having studied it carefully in both Greek and Christian contexts. He accepted the long and complex explanations of the Euhemeristic theories on the rise of the gods and concluded that: "The truth of this history [Euhemeristic] is taught by the Erythtraean Sibyl, who speaks almost the same things, with a few discrepancies, which do not affect the subject matter itself."[90] At the same

---

[88]Lactantius, IraDei 23 (ANF VII) 278. We find here a confirmation that, as late as the fourth century, the traditions about the secrecy of the Sibylline books were still in force.

[89]Lactantius, DivInst 1.6.

[90]Ibid., 1.14 (ANF VII) 26. The Sibylline support for that history is found in

time the Sibyl rebuked the Greeks who elevated the gods to a position beyond what was becoming to them.[91]

The circumstances in which the Sibylline sayings appeared in Lactantius varied greatly and were used to corroborate numerous arguments. The Sibylline Books were credited with being the source of miracles.[92] They were invoked in support of the segment of Platonic philosophy which agreed with Christian teaching.[93] They assigned the place of man within divine creation and in relationship to the rest of divine decisions.[94] The Erythraean Sibyl, especially, put the emphasis on the true worshipers and said: "But they who honour the true God inherit everlasting life, themselves inhabiting together paradise, the beautiful garden, for ever."[95] Those who fell into the errors of astrology and magic divination were warned by her of the consequences.[96]

Lactantius put the emphasis on the way the Sibyl predicted the coming of Christ and his work here on earth. Several Sibyls have joined their voices to the declaration of Trismegistus in proclaiming the coming of a Son of the most High God. Again primary importance was accorded to the Erythraean Sibyl. But another Sibyl, not identified by Lactantius, also prophesied the Son of God, the one who should be known as God himself.[97] It was also the Sibyl who, in accordance with Old Testament Prophets, foretold the great miracles of Christ. Here, however, even Lactantius had to acknowledge that the words of the Sibyls resembled the

---

the present collection 3.110-57. (Terry, *The Sibylline Oracles*, 132-86).

[91]Ibid., 1.15 (ANF VII) 27: "And thus from admiration of them [the gods] they [the Greeks] first undertook their sacred rites, and handed them down to all nations. On account of this vanity the Sibyl thus rebukes them:

"Why trustest thou, O Greece, to princely men?
Why to the dead dost offer empty gifts?
Thou offerest to idols; this error who suggested,
That thou shouldst leave the presence of the mighty God,
And make these offerings?"

[92]Ibid., 2.8.
[93]Ibid., 2.11.
[94]Ibid., 2.12.
[95]Ibid., 2.13 (ANF VII) 62.
[96]Ibid., 2.17.
[97]Ibid., 4.6.

language of biblical writings much too closely and felt the need to answer critics who asserted that those poems were not of the Sibyls but were composed by unscrupulous Christian writers. Lactantius protested, not very convincingly, that those who read Cicero and Varro, and other ancient writers referring to the Erythraean and other Sibyls would have found those examples there, but with a distinct difference. Those authors who lived before the Christian era could not have understood the sayings of the Sibyls, and most likely regarded the prophecies concerning Christ as mad ravings. The Erythraean Sibyl predicted that many people would consider her mad and deceitful until the time when her sayings would prove to be true: "They will say that the Sibyl is mad, and deceitful: but when all things shall come to pass, then ye will remember me; and no one will any longer say that I, the prophetess of the great God, am mad."[98]

Lactantius asserted that the Sibyl, more than anybody else, predicted that the Son of God would destroy the Jewish law and fulfill it in respect to his own mission, that the last judgment will assume an inescapable finality, and that the passion and resurrection of Christ had been decreed from before the foundation of the world.[99]

Though the most important information on Lactantius's use of Sibylline oracles is found in the *Divinae institutiones*, there are other works in which he elaborated on his views of the prophetess. In the *De ira Dei* he introduced the readers to a more complete description of the process which destroyed the Sibylline Books in the fire of the Capitol and the attempts to rebuild the collection. It was in that context that the Erythraean Sibyl not only rose to prominence, but also was made known to the world for her verses respecting the supreme God and Maker of the world, who shows both his providence and anger in acts of creation and

---

[98]Ibid., 4.15 (ANF VII) 116. At points the Erythraean Sibyl was portrayed in Christian writings as foretelling the future against her will: "Why, O Lord, dost thou compel me still to foretell the future, and not rather remove me from this earth to await the blessed day of thy coming?" Eusebius, OratSanct 21 (NPNF-2 I) 577.

[99]The passages in Lactantius are too numerous to list and the quotes of the Sibyl amount to hundreds of lines. But see especially DivInst 4.17-19; 7.13, 16, 18, 19, 20, 24.

destruction.[100] The ways in which Lactantius brings the Sibyl to witness against the evils of Roman history in his work *De mortibus persecutorum* were already mentioned.

Arnobius, a contemporary of Lactantius, mentioned the Sibyl but never referred to her prophecies. Both were deeply concerned with the preservation of orthodoxy but chose different ways to approach the task. From about the same period we find a statement in the *Constitutions of the Holy Apostles* testifying to the prevalent view that Gentiles can learn from the Sibyl that which they disbelieve in the Christian Scriptures, the one being equal to the other: "But if the Gentiles laugh at us, and disbelieve our Scriptures, let at least their own prophetess Sibylla oblige them to believe, who says thus to them in express words. . . . "[101]

Lactantius witnessed changes almost beyond human imagination. He was appointed by Diocletian to the post of professor of Latin rhetoric at Nicomedia, only to witness the great persecution which compelled him to flee to his native Africa. Some of the things he wrote were addressed to the church as a minority, but remained a driving force in imperial Christianity which was born only a few short years later. His writings profoundly influenced Constantine's conception of Christianity.

Lactantius was chosen by Constantine to become the tutor of his son Crispus. The respect for Sibylline oracles so prominent in Lactantius was soon shared by Constantine. Two chapters of his *Oratio ad sanctum coetum* were devoted to an exposition of the role of the Sibyl and her prophecy of the coming of Christ.[102] The event represented a unique phenomenon, for even a Christian emperor who would have decided to consult the Sibylline Books would have turned to those kept by the Senate and not to a Christianized version of them. The appeal to the Sibyl as a Christian witness on the part of a Roman emperor marked a revolutionary stance never used before or after.

The position of Constantine on Sibylline prophecies was far from clear. As in the case of Lactantius, the emphasis was placed on the Erythraean Sibyl as the most trustworthy in predicting Christian events. In a Christianized world pagans were still opposed to Christian doctrines.

---

[100]Lactantius, IraDei 22-23.
[101]*Constitutions of the Holy Apostles* 5.7 (ANF VII) 440.
[102]Eusebius, OratSanct 18-19.

An appeal to the Scriptures alone would prove insufficient to persuade an assembly of men who came from a long tradition of opposing the Christian movement. The Sibylline testimony would more readily convince those who accepted her prophecies concerning the fate of the empire.

As a context for his oration, Constantine gave an elaborate, and somewhat difficult to prove, history of the Erythraean Sibyl. She lived in the sixth generation after the flood. As a priestess of Apollo she guarded his sacred tripod and shared a life of folly void of anything good and noble. But on one occasion, having entered the sanctuary of her vain superstition, she became inspired and prophesied the advent of Christ in the form of an acrostic with the initial letters of the verses being: Jesus Christ, Son of God, Savior, Cross. Having quoted the whole poem to the assembly, Constantine concluded: "It is evident that the virgin uttered these verses under the influence of Divine inspiration. And I cannot but esteem her blessed, whom the Saviour thus selected to unfold his gracious purpose towards us."[103]

Having failed to persuade the assembly, Constantine engaged in self-defense and refuted the arguments of those who considered the verses he just quoted as forgeries composed after the death of Christ for less than laudable apologetic purposes. Like Lactantius, he had heard the charge often repeated and convincingly adduced. Having exhausted his Christian logic about the subject, he turned to the writings of Cicero which he twisted to fit his purpose. The claims that Cicero was acquainted with the poem, that he translated it into Latin, and that he incorporated it into his work do not find any credible support. Cicero does mention the fact that in Sibylline Books "each prophecy is embellished with an acrostic," but he does not quote any specific example. Furthermore, the use of acrostics is not a proof of inspiration, but quite the contrary: "Such a work comes from a writer who is not frenzied, who is painstaking, not crazy."[104]

---

[103]Ibid., 18 (NPNF-2 I) 575. The poem is reproduced in chap. 18 and is based on a loose translation of the Sibylline Oracles starting at 8.217. Other translations have been suggested, including the one of Augustine, to be quoted later in this work. The NPNF offers still another translation produced at the beginning of the eighteenth century and inspired by the *Dies irae*.

[104]Cicero, DeDiv 2.112 (LCL XX) 497.

The address of Constantine lacked credibility. He left himself open to the charge of forgery or ignorance while speaking of the Sibyl. His verve did not match the wisdom of Lactantius, and his information, or lack of it, seriously diminished the impact of the effect intended. If we trust Eusebius, one fact remains indisputable, namely, that an emperor chose to proclaim, on a Good Friday, that the Sibyl possessed divine wisdom and inspiration and predicted the coming of the Son of God. For that reason, she should be trusted as the voice of God Himself.

With Constantine, the Sibylline prophecy, at least that of the Erythraean Sibyl, reached its apogee and started the decline toward its death. The Council of Nicaea changed Christian apologetics forever. The church had to defend itself against heresies, and the major weapon became dogmatic theology in the form of councilor pronouncements endowed with cold logic and no longer indebted to any form of prophecy. Sibylline oracles, or for that matter biblical prophecy, had no further contribution to make. The Sibyl survived in literary and artistic consciousness while Christianity invented and reinvented its own dogmas to define its place in the world.

In the post-Constantine Roman empire Christian references to the Sibyl greatly diminished. With a more radical shift from the Greek language to the Latin, fewer and fewer Greek works were read. The Sibylline books played less and less of a role. This is apparent in the writings of Augustine where we search in vain for a consistent perspective on the Sibyl. He read Lactantius, and much of his knowledge of the Sibylline tradition comes from the *Divinae institutiones*. But Augustine never felt the same admiration for the Sibyl, considering her either as a mouthpiece of God or placing her together with the Greek demons to be rejected. On the whole, the Sibyl received little credit in his works. At times she was used as a witness against paganism.

Augustine was acquainted with the Roman tradition of consulting the Sibylline Books in times of hardship. But he was also aware of the growing trend among the Roman intelligentsia to blame natural and civil calamities on the presence of Christians in the empire. Augustine argued that in those times of hardship the pagan gods were of no avail, and the reading of Sibylline Books an indication of their questionable character, a conclusion he derived from Cicero's statement that, at best, those

oracles were conjectures lacking any persuasive worth.[105] At times one
could detect a veiled attack on the Sibyl in the general tone Augustine
had adopted when speaking of pagan gods whose influence had, by then,
deserted the Romans.[106]

In his dialogue with the Manichaean Faustus, Augustine was forced
to answer the charge that the church owes more to the Sibyl and other
Greek prophecies than to the Hebrews. The argument of Faustus was
summarized thus: "Again, I say, the Christian church, which consists of
more Gentiles than of Jews, can owe nothing to Hebrew witnesses. If, as
is said, any prophecies of Christ are to be found in the Sibyl, or in
Hermes, called Trismegistus, or Orpheus, or any heathen poet, they might
aid the faith of those who, like us, are converts from heathenism to
Christianity. But the testimony of the Hebrews is useless to us before
conversion, for then we cannot believe them; and superfluous after, for
we believe without them."[107]

Augustine exposed the fallacies in Faustus' arguments, including the
ambiguities involved in them. No specific perspective on the Sibyl can
be derived from the exchange. Contrary to former church fathers who had
a specific view of the Sibyl, here she is grouped together with many other
Greek religious figures so as to make her specific influence unidentifi-
able. Augustine does admit, though without great conviction, that the
Sibyl may have correctly foreseen and predicted the coming of the Son
of God. But he qualified the statement by pointing out that, contrary to
Hebrew prophets, she spoke about God against her will, not being able
to help it and not knowing what she was saying. Her testimony to the
true God was invalidated by the very fact that, while she was speaking

---

[105]Augustine, CivDei 3.17.

[106]Augustine, ConsEv 1.50 (NPNF-1 VI) 98-99: "Where are their gods?
Where are the vaticinations of their fanatics, and the divinations of their prophets
[*pythonum*]? Where are the auguries, or the auspices, or the soothsayings, or the
oracles of demons? Why is it that, out of the ancient books which constitute the
records of this type of religion, nothing in the form either of admonition or of
prediction is advanced to oppose the Christian faith, or to controvert the truth of
those prophets of ours, who have now come to be so well understood among all
nations?"

[107]Augustine, CFaust 13.1 (NPNF-1 IV) 199-200.

of the Son of God, she, at the same time, taught the people around her to worship idols and demons.[108]

The most important statement on the Sibyl appears in the *De civitate Dei* 18.23 and shows a heavy dependence on Lactantius. The Erythraean Sibyl is given prominence, though she is not always distinguishable from the Cumaean. The Sibylline prophecies concerning Christ were quite impressive. Unfortunately Augustine confessed that he had read them in a Latin translation so poor and so misleading that rejection was unavoidable. It was only after the right interpreters, especially the proconsul Flaccianus, produced a Greek manuscript, that the prophecies of the Erythraean Sibyl became clear and worthy of attention. The specific passage forming the acrostic built on the letters of the Greek Ἰησοῦς Χρειστός Θεοῦ υἱὸς σωτήρ was singled out from Sibylline Oracles book VIII, 217-50, to form the following poem.

I	Judgment shall moisten the earth with the sweat of its standard,
H	Ever enduring, behold the King shall come through the ages,
Σ	Sent to be here in the flesh, and Judge at the last of the world.
O	O God, the believing and faithless alike shall behold Thee
Υ	Uplifted with saints, when at last the ages are ended.
Σ	Seated before Him are souls in the flesh for His judgment.

X	Hid in thick vapors, the while desolate lieth the earth,
P	Rejected by men are the idols and long hidden treasures;
E	Earth is consumed by the fire, and it searcheth the ocean and heaven;
I	Issuing forth, it destroyeth the terrible portals of hell.
Σ	Saints in their body and soul freedom and light shall inherit;
T	Those who are guilty shall burn in fire and brimstone for ever.
O	Occult actions revealing, each one shall publish his secrets;
Σ	Secrets of every man's heart shall reveal in the light.

Θ	Then shall be weeping and wailing, yea, and gnashing of teeth;
E	Eclipsed is the sun, and silenced the stars in their chorus.
O	Over and gone is the splendor of moonlight, melted the heaven.
Υ	Uplifted by Him are the valleys, and cast down the mountains.

---

[108]Ibid., 13.15.

Υ Utterly gone among men are distinctions of lofty and lowly.
Ι Into the plains rush the hills, the skies and oceans are mingled.
Ο Oh, what an end of all things! earth broken in pieces shall perish;
Σ Swelling together at once shall the waters and flames flow in rivers.

Σ Sounding the archangel's trumpet shall peal down from heaven,
Ω Over the wicked who groan in their guilt and their manifold sorrows.
Τ Trembling, the earth shall be opened, revealing chaos and hell.
Η Every king before God shall stand in that day to be judged.
Ρ Rivers of fire and brimstone shall fall from the heavens.

What followed was an explanation of how the acrostic was devised, since the Latin does not always have corresponding letters to the Greek, and since the formula was preserved to make the cube of three, which is twenty seven. At the same time the first letter of each Greek word when put together preserved the traditional symbol of the Christians, that is, "fish" = ἰχθύς. In this specific case Augustine concluded that the Sibyl was indeed worthy of being reckoned among those who belong to the city of God. He then explained why he adopted a different use of the Sibyl than Lactantius who used the Sibylline prophecies bit by bit in his exposition. Here Augustine summarized Lactantius in a continuous quotation of the Sibyl, uninterrupted by comments, mentioning the fact that the Erythraean Sibyl was, in the mind of some writers, as early as the Trojan war.

Various translations of the Sibylline acrostic have been proposed. Some followed the one given by Constantine on the letters of the words *Jesus Christ, Son of God, Saviour, Cross*, or the alternate *Jesus Christ, Son of God, the Saviour, the Cross*. Interpretive attempts sometimes connected the acrostic with the *Dies irae*.[109]

Long after the edicts of Theodosius and the writings of Augustine, the church historian Sozomen tried to put a perspective on the meaning of the Sibyl from both a Greek and Christian point of view. In his introduction to the *Historia ecclesiastica* he described the sources he used in order to arrive at the truth. Concerning the testimony of the Sibyl he reflected on two astonishing phenomena, namely, that the Hebrews failed

---

[109]For examples of different versions of the Sibylline acrostic see NPNF-2 I, 574-75 and Terry, *The Sibylline Oracles*, 274-77.

to turn to Christianity as they would have been expected to, and that the Greeks persisted in their unbelief. Divine foreknowledge alone could enlighten a process within which both biblical prophets and strangers were to play a role in testifying to the agreement of future events.[110] The only other reference to the Sibyl in Sozomen appeared in the context of Helena's journey to Jerusalem in search of the original cross and how the prophetess had predicted that Christ would die on it: "Oh most blessed tree, on which our Lord was hung."[111] It was assumed that because of the Sibylline prophecies, even the adversaries of Christianity could not deny the truth of the matter.

The prestige of the Sibyl among Christians may be due to Virgil whose poetry is often quoted by the church fathers, sometimes with admiration. More than any other statement concerning her, book 6 of the *Aeneid* has immortalized the Cumaean Sibyl as she responded to a fervent appeal of Aeneas for her to guide him to his father Anchises in the lower world at the cave of Avernus. In this *katabasis* the Sibyl became the incarnation of fate and of the destiny of Rome. She proved to be more than the mouthpiece of Apollo as she became the guided conscience of Aeneas. She spoke with the god's voice, but also with her own, fulfilling the role of both prophetess and mentor, always reminding the hero of the courage required.[112] The *Divinae institutiones* of Lactantius contain so many references to book 6 of the *Aeneid* that it could be considered a guide in the search for the knowledge of God and proper Christian conduct.[113]

---

[110]Sozomen, HE 1.1 (NPNF-2 II) 239-40:

When I consider this matter it seems reasonably remarkable to me, that the Hebrews did not anticipate, and, before the rest of men, immediately turn to Christianity; for though the Sibyl and some oracles announced beforehand the future of events concerning Christ we are not on this account to attribute unbelief to all the Greeks. For there were few, who, appearing superior in education, could understand such prophecies, which were, for the most part, in verse, and were declared with more recondite words to the people. Therefore in my judgment, it was the result of the heavenly preknowledge, for the sake of the agreement of future events, that the coming facts were to be made known, not only by his own prophets, but in part also by strangers.

[111]Ibid., 2.1 (NPNF-2 II) 259. The quote comes from OracSib 6.26.

[112]Virgil, Aen 6.261.

[113]As an example of Lactantius's praise of Virgil (known in the ancient world

It is to the *Fourth Eclogue* that Christians turned most often to proclaim it as a masterpiece of pagan prophecy fulfilled in Christianity. The poem was often considered an oracle of the Sibyl, and Christians after the time of Constantine and Augustine regarded it as a prophecy of the coming of the Messiah. It remains, however, very difficult to identify a precise purpose of Virgil in writing it. It was composed as a tribute to his patron, Pollio, and may have been intended as nothing more than a poem of praise, possibly even a playful one. Many critics suggest that the poem was written for the birth of Marcellus whose untimely death was lamented by Virgil in the *Aeneid* (6.860-86). But no amount of exegesis allows a clear picture of what the miraculous child represents. We are more confident in assuming that the poem expressed an intense yearning for a new age of prosperity.

In Constantine the *Fourth Eclogue* played a role similar to that of the Sibyl herself and was an integral part of his *Oratio ad sanctum coetum*. But he took so many liberties with the text that it became as much his prophecy as that of Virgil.[114] It could be argued that Virgil put the

---

as Maro) one could adduce the following statement:

> Maro was the first of our poets to approach the truth, who thus speaks respecting the highest God, whom he calls Mind and Spirit:
> "Know first, the heaven, the earth, the main,
> The moon's pale orb, the starry train,
> Are nourished by a Soul,
> A spirit, whose celestial flame
> Glows in each member of the frame,
> And stirs the mighty whole."

DivInst 1.5 (ANF VII) 14.

[114]See for instance Constantine's quotation of Virgil in OratSanct 19 (NPNF-2 I) 575:

> Behold! the circling years new blessings bring:
> The virgin comes, with her long-desired king.

which is supposed to be a translation of:

> *magnus ab integro saeclorum nascitur ordo.*
> *iam redit et Virgo, redeunt Saturnia regna.* Ecl 4.5-6.

A connection has sometimes been established between Virgil and Constantine's conversion: "But, if a more splendid, and indeed specious, interpretation of the fourth eclogue contributed to the conversion of the first Christian emperor, Virgil may deserve to be ranked among the most successful missionaries of the gospel." Edward Gibbon, *The History of the Decline and Fall of the Roman*

emphasis on the Sibylline oracles because Pollio had shown a great deal of interest in Herod and Judaism. Much later, Dante promoted the idea of a "Christian" Virgil when he made him his guide through the *Inferno*. For whatever reason, Christians, through the Middle Ages, had no difficulty in accepting the *Fourth Eclogue* as a pagan prophecy serving the eschatological beliefs of the church. In the *Dies irae* the Sibyl was linked with David:

> Dies irae, dies illa,
> Solvet saeclum in favilla,
> Teste David cum Sibylla.[115]

In the Middle Ages and early Renaissance Sibyls shared the dubious distinction of being the authors of the oracles circulating under their names. The church paid little attention to their prophecies, but they were rescued from oblivion by the genius of great sculptors such as Nicola and Giovanni Pisano, Quercia, Donatello, and Ghiberti. In all of those artists, however, the "Sibyls are only resonances without a convincing physical existence."[116]

The greatest honor paid the Sibyls came from Michelangelo who included five of them in his Sistine Chapel ceiling where they shared with seven biblical prophets the eternity of the prophetic voice piercing through a world of conflicts, doubt, judgment, faith, and hope.[117] There they acquired not only the reward of memory but a new status meant to ensure their apotheosis: "Michelangelo's *Prophets* and *Sibyls* are supernatural beings in the strength of their corporal existence and in the

---

Empire, 5 vols. (repr.: Philadelphia: Henry T. Coates, 1845ff.; orig., 1776–1788) 2:178-79.

[115]See the translation of T. W. Irons, *English Hymnal*, 351:
> Day of wrath and doom impending,
> David's word with Sibyl's blending,
> Heaven and earth in ashes ending.

Most translators omit the reference to David and the Sibyl.

[116]Charles De Tolnay, *The Sistine Ceiling* (Princeton: Princeton University Press, 1949) 46.

[117]The five sibyls were the first ones in the list of Varro: the Erythraean, the Cumaean, the Delphic, the Libyan, and the Persian. The seven prophets were Ezekiel, Jeremiah, Isaiah, Daniel, Zechariah, Joel, and Jonah.

superiority of their intellectual life. It is a *spiritualis ignis* which illuminates the total existence, physical and spiritual, of these seers who, enlightened, are inwardly reborn. It is a *renovatio*, brought about by the contemplation of truth."[118]

When Michelangelo altered his original plan to paint twelve apostles into a series of prophets and Sibyls, he not only widened the religious historical scope but also surrendered the prophetic voice to both male and female figures. The prophets, however, were to dominate the Sibyls in the realm of inspiration: "The series of the Prophets is a continuous crescendo of visionary faculties which moves in the direction of the altar; whereas the Sibyls, alternating with the seers, show a gradual decrescendo of inspiration."[119] The crescendo ascribed to the emergence and dominance of Hebrew prophecy along with the decrescendo ascribed to the Sibyls' roles in antiquity illustrate both their syncretistic interdependence and the ultimate vindication of the Judeo-Christian religious outlook. Even in the company of biblical prophets, with whom they shared the divinely appointed mission of freeing human beings from the prisons of intellectual and spiritual limitations, the Sibyls kept their ambiguous and mysterious nature, proclaiming a world view and maintaining a prophetic perspective as elusive as ever, never matching the veneration of canonical Hebrew Prophets, yet remaining a part of a religious consciousness which cannot fully contain them while it cannot be complete without them.

---

[118]De Tolnay, *Sistine Ceiling*, 46.
[119]Ibid., 47.

Chapter 6

The Rise of Christianity

*Let intellectual and spiritual culture progress, and the human mind
expand, as much as it will; beyond the grandeur and moral elevation
of Christianity, as it sparkles and shines in the Gospels, the human
mind will not advance. —Goethe*

The evolution of Christianity to the position of a world religion was
marked by three important developments.

1. The appearance of Christ in Galilee and Judea, the events and
words which defined his ministry, as well as the conviction of his
disciples that he was the promised messiah, altered the eschatological
outlook of a small part of Judaism. Soon after the death of Christ his
followers became a new Jewish sect claiming the resurrected Lord as its
leader and as the fulfiller of Old Testament predictions. Yet Christianity
evolved very slowly. It was not until about half a century after the
crucifixion of Christ that it took definite steps to sever its connections
with Judaism and to vindicate its claim to religious uniqueness. Christianity owed its allegiance to Christ alone.

The disconnection of Christianity from Judaism was not achieved by
a conscious repudiation of a long religious history which remained the
cradle of its emergence. Christ was the product and culmination of the
Jewish prophetic proclamation. Even Marcion and the overwhelming
appeal of Gnosticism could not convince the church to free itself from
Old Testament religion. Rather, a large segment of Christianity believed
that its adherents were the rightful heirs to the promised kingdom and the
true descendents of Abraham.[1] The church was viewed as the New Israel.

---

[1]For an example of how some early church writers reinterpreted the Old
Testament to prove that the Christians and not the Jews are the the true heirs of
the covenant, see Barn 13. On the whole, *The Epistle of Barnabas* rejects a
Judaic conception of the Old Testament and favors a symbolic interpretation

2. Christianity grew on Roman-Hellenistic soil and could not ignore the strong affinities it had with Greek culture. The church fathers waged an uneasy battle which lasted for about three centuries, either condemning or praising the religious insights of Greek poets, playwrights, and philosophers, especially Socrates and Plato. In many instances Christianity availed itself of noble and persuasive Greek philosophical tenets while protesting any claim that they influenced its message, beholden only to divine revelation and not to human wisdom. Thus, whatever Greek influence the early church felt comfortable with could be adopted only after it was proven inferior to biblical teaching.

3. Though some church fathers conceded the worth and nobility of many Greek insights and philosophical formulations, in matters of religious practice Christianity rejected heathenism in the name of a monotheistic belief which allowed no compromise and no divided loyalties. Greco-Roman religion, regardless of its background, persuasiveness, or universal appeal was the target of strong patristic refutations. The cult of Apollo was often singled out for attack, for it was viewed as the most enticing pagan promise of divine providence in the midst of misfortunes and historical threats. Apollonian religion was often regarded as a credible contender for the loyalties of hearts and minds which would have espoused Christianity if not for the reassurance they gathered from oracular pronouncements. The official victory of Christ over Apollo was to change the world in ways which have forever baffled the most rudimentary laws of historical necessity.

No clear picture of the church during the first centuries of its existence emerges out of the writings of that period. At best those writings witness to the struggle of a movement convinced of its divine mission while unable to generate agreement, consensus, and harmony as to its implementation. Apologetic treatises tend toward polemical stances narrowly focused. The church concerned itself with theological definitions not always conducive to promote its growth and welfare. For a long time it did not even envisage its long-range organization, and even less the future of the society surrounding it. Early Christians expected the imminent return of their Lord and the irrevocable end to all aspects of human history. It was not until the second century that the coexistence of

---

rather than a literal reading of Old Testament law. The Old Testament must be understood in a way that never contradicts the teaching of Jesus.

church and society became a matter for serious reflection and for a revision of the original belief in the Parousia.[2]

As the church formulated theological explanations of its status in a world it felt compelled to condemn, it also had to propose reasons for its divinely ordained presence in it. It became important for the church to assert that, as the visible body of a heavenly Lord, it was in no fashion a form of Hellenism or Judaism. Thus the necessity to reinterpret history, to finalize the messianic expectation, and to place divine revelation beyond any further alteration. Christians claimed to possess the final stamp of divine approval. Salvation consisted in convincing the pagan world that Christianity alone was the repository of God's redemptive purpose.

Tᶀe Olᶌ anᶌ tᶀe New in Joᶀn tᶀe Baptist

The age of the great Hebrew prophets had been over for almost four centuries when the message of John the Baptist rekindled the hope that history was moving toward its final stage according to a divine purpose that had been frustrated by political uncertainties and religious discouragement. God would finally vindicate his suffering people through redemption. Tribulations were to lead to victory, and repentance to divine blessings.

The proclamation of John the Baptist in the wilderness seemed to provide a focal point for a nation in search of divine intervention. The background of John's life and preaching, however, remains a mystery. The possibility that he was related to the Essene community has long appealed to New Testament scholars.[3] The discovery of the Dead Sea Scrolls fueled the contention that he shared with the Qumran community

---

[2]A shift in the reinterpretation of the Parousia is found in Justin Martyr, 2 Apol 7 (ANF I) 190, who believed that the destruction of the world was delayed by God for the sake of the Christians: "Wherefore God delays causing the confusion and destruction of the whole world, by which the wicked angels and demons and men shall cease to exist, because of the seed of the Christians, who know that they are the cause of preservation in nature."

[3]The contention that John was related to the Essenes predates the discovery of the Dead Sea Scrolls and was already well established in the nineteenth century. See especially David Frederick Strauss, *The Life of Jesus Critically Examined*, ed. Peter C. Hodgson and trans. George Eliot (Philadelphia: Fortress Press, 1972) 214.

the conviction that Jewish society was corrupt and unable to remedy the situation through traditional religious performance. When he appeared on the banks of the Jordan, however, he only partially represented Essene messianic expectations, though his baptism was often linked with the Dead Sea Scrolls community's bath of purification. But to portray John as a representative of that group alone would be to deny him his originality.[4]

If the presence of John meant the beginning of the messianic age, it could equally mean that he was the Messiah. John never claimed the title for himself. But neither did Jesus, at least not publicly. There is, nonetheless, sufficient evidence, both canonical and extracanonical, that John was at times acclaimed as the Messiah. Whether he intended to create a community for his followers is questionable. But that there was such a community in rivalry with the Christian church is an attested fact. When Paul came to Ephesus, on a missionary journey, he had been preceded by Apollos who "knew only the baptism of John" and who was described as being instructed in the way of the Lord and "spoke and taught accurately the things concerning Jesus."[5]

New Testament sources on John the Baptist betray the difficulty the early church encountered in its attempt to eradicate the idea that he was the Messiah and not the forerunner of Jesus. In their overreaction against John in favor of Jesus, the Evangelists introduced polemical elements into the debate which vindicated the uniqueness of Jesus but also opened the way for an ultimate separation of Judaism and Christianity, John the Baptist representing the old eon, and Christ the new one.

Traces of an old tradition which once related messianic attributes to John are present in the Synoptic Gospels. Those traditions originated in Baptist circles and underwent a process of Christianization before infiltrating the New Testament records. The so-called "Baptist document"

---

[4]Many New Testament scholars oppose the idea that John had any decisively important connection with the Qumran or any other community when he reemerged into history. John A. T. Robinson, "The Baptism of John and the Qumran Community," *Twelve New Testament Studies*, Studies in Biblical Theology 34 (London: SCM Press, 1962) 13, wrote: "Whatever he may have received from his association, if there was one, with Qumran, he remoulded into something quite distinctive and independent."

[5]Acts 18:24-26.

in Luke 1 represents a recension in which the author left sufficient pointers to an original tribute to John.[6]

The importance of John in the Synoptic Gospels is related to the messianic nature of his baptism and to the fact that Jesus chose to submit to it. But from a Christian point of view the baptism of John lost most of its significance to become secondary to the baptism the Messiah would offer. The question that baptism was not part of Jesus' ministry was never raised. The early church saw in John's baptism the source of Christian baptism.

It is difficult, however, to see how John, with his definite convictions, with his sense of messianic mission, and endowed with an authority that his nation understood as being divine, could have discredited his own baptism to the point of invalidating it in view of a further baptism with which he himself would no longer be associated. Those who came to him, partially representing the religious elite of the nation, could hardly have felt it appropriate to submit themselves to an interim baptism. To accept to be called broods of vipers, degenerate children of Abraham, and to be willing to partake of a new baptism, the Jews must have seen in John more than a voice crying in the wilderness. For them John's baptism was messianic. He was already performing messianic functions. His movement had become, as well as that of Jesus, a messianic movement.[7]

This has raised the very difficult question of the relationship between John and Jesus. In 1928 Maurice Goguel published a volume dedicated solely to that problem, *Au seuil de l'évangile, Jean-Baptiste*. His goal was to prove that Jesus started his ministry as a disciple of John the Baptist until a confrontation on the question of purification (baptism) resulted in an inevitable separation.

Goguel rejected the Synoptic Gospels' position that would limit the contact between John and Jesus to the event of baptism. He found ample support in the Gospel of John to develop his argument of a common

---

[6]Attempts to transform the *Benedictus* into a hymn to Jesus have met with failure. Thus it may be inferred that Luke entertained the possibility that John exhibited messianic qualities, a fact he later repudiated in the Gospel.

[7]See the strong emphasis on this question in Rudolf Bultmann, *Jesus and the Word*, trans. Louise Pettibone Smith and Erminie Huntress Lantero (New York: Scribners, 1958) 25: "*Both movements, that of John and that of Jesus, were Messianic*" (italics in the text).

ministry between Jesus and John during which their work rested on the same eschatological outlook, was expressed with the same conviction, and sanctioned with the same symbol, baptism. During that formative period in the life of Jesus, John would have dominated his thought until Jesus became convinced that John's message did not adequately represent God's offer of the kingdom of God. Ensuing events led to disagreements and finally to a separation. That idea is shared by many other New Testament scholars.[8]

The most persuasive arguments in favor of Jesus having been a disciple of John are derived from the third chapter of the Gospel of John. The debate on the relationship of Jesus to John is reopened there after Jesus had already been involved in his own ministry. This contradicts the view expressed in the Synoptic Gospels. Both baptized with the same baptism. When it became known that Jesus was making more disciples than John, the situation became more intense and the score was corrected in chapter 4. The separation was inevitable, though friendly. Jesus continued to speak of John with gratitude and warmth, but also in an enigmatic way, proclaiming John as the greatest person ever to appear on earth while conceding him no place at all in the kingdom he was proclaiming.[9]

The separation of Jesus from John is difficult to assess. In view of John's question from prison, there was no final break. Jesus never convinced John of his messiaship. On the other hand, if John saw in Jesus the Messiah, which is highly debatable, he never acknowledged himself as a follower of Jesus.

It became a primary concern for the early church to prove that the coming of Jesus brought John's work and influence to an end. At the same time it appeared impossible to eradicate the belief that Jesus was regarded as John the Baptist *redivivus*. It meant, at least within some

---

[8]C. H. Dodd, *Historical Tradition in the Fourth Gospel* (Cambridge: Cambridge University Press, 1963) 273-75; Alfred Firmin Loisy, *The Origins of the New Testament*. trans. L. P. Jacks (New York: Collier Books, 1962) 288; Charles H. H. Scobie, *John the Baptist* (Philadelphia: Fortress Press, 1964) 154; Walter Wink, *John the Baptist in the Gospel Tradition* (Cambridge: Cambridge University Press, 1968) 88. Others are opposed to such a notion. See especially Charles Guignebert, *Jesus*, trans. S. H. Hooke (New York: University Books, 1956) 163.

[9]Matthew 11:11.

Palestinian groups, that John was still present among his people in a risen form. The awesome presence of John was not stopped by his death. Herod saw in Jesus the new leader of the Baptist movement.[10] It remained a puzzle for the disciples who, when confronted with the problem of identifying Jesus, suggested as the first answer that he was John the Baptist.[11] They still expected Jesus to fulfill the hopes proclaimed by John but cut short by his imprisonment and brutal death. It could be done only through the belief that the risen John was at work in Jesus. On occasion the disciples pressured Jesus to give them a teaching similar to that of John the Baptist.[12]

It is surprising that the early church did not eliminate from its records such controversial material, a fact which testifies to the place of honor John had among Christians. One has, however, to view the interpolations in the first chapter of the Gospel of John as the work of an unskilled editor, mostly when John is made to agree to the inferiority of his work when compared to that of Christ.

The relationship of Jesus to John presented itself to the Christian church as a web of complex interrelationships which did not proffer a simple solution. Both created movements, had disciples, and influenced each other. But there was one undeniable fact: the movement of John came first. Jesus was related to that movement as a follower of John, and, for many, the movement of Jesus appeared as an offshoot of the Baptist community. Such a position proved intolerable for the early church. Yet both Jesus and John had appeared with the same message, suffered the same fate in their brutal deaths, left their disciples to further their work, and finally were conceived as present among their people through their resurrection. But they could not be both acclaimed as Messiah, though Judaism would have allowed such a belief.[13] Why then did the early church put all the emphasis on Jesus and not on John? Evidently because it believed him to be the Messiah and established him as such far beyond

---

[10]Mark 6:14-16; Matthew 14:1-2; Luke 9:9.

[11]Mark 8:28; Matthew 16:14; Luke 9:19.

[12]Luke 11:1. According to Luke this instance represents the way the Lord's Prayer came into existence.

[13]We could adduce the belief of the Dead Sea Scroll community that, after the first Messiah, a son of David, will have finished his work of liberation, he would be followed by a priestly Messiah, who would be a descendent of Aaron.

the limits of Judaism in the Hellenistic world. In the end Judaism failed to see in either John or Jesus more than products of their times. Their violent deaths were not even deplored.

In a dark room of the isolated fortress of Machaerus John died a senseless death, without trial, at the hand of an incompetent ruler. He was remembered as a good moral and spiritual man. No one could properly estimate his place in the divine redemptive purpose. In spite of a momentary surge of success, history remembers him only as a voice crying in the wilderness and, except for a few excerpts which survive in the biblical records, his words were lost in the very wilderness in which they were pronounced. Jesus began to see in John's fate a prototype of his own.

Tђe Coming of tђe Messiaђ

From the Maccabean revolt to the uprising of bar-Kochba under Hadrian the nation of Israel witnessed the rise and fall of numerous messiahs in a succession of historical events marked by sporadic successes and tragic failures. Many people lost their lives. Countless others fled their land in a self-imposed exile known as the great Diaspora. Judaism suffered the annihilation of major long-standing symbols of religious life, especially the temple of Jerusalem. All of this could be read back into Old Testament prophetic literature and reinforced the conviction that the time of divine intervention through the Messiah was at hand.

At its inception, Christianity did not appear with clear characteristics and definite marks of uniqueness. By the time of the composition of the Gospels in the latter part of the first century, the early church had finally resolved the uneasy relationship of Jesus to John the Baptist, and, unlike in the case of Apollo and Dionysus, was not willing to allow for the coexistence of multiple or even rival realms of religious loyalties. Christ was proclaimed as the absolute divine presence in the world. But the old could not cross over to the new without a radical transformation. The coming of Christ gave rise to the greatest religious reformation ever known to humankind and split the known world into old and new eons.

The nativity narratives in Matthew and Luke bestow upon Jesus special divine attributes which set him apart as the Messiah. Legends surrounding the birth of individuals destined to assume more than human stature abounded in both Jewish and heathen history. In the same way Mary gave birth to Jesus in the stable because there was no room for her in the inn, pregnant Leto was refused hospitality in every land until she found refuge on the desolate island of Delos where she gave birth to Apollo.

The church fathers, who espoused the scriptural tenet of the virgin birth, were nonetheless aware of the intractable problems connected with it, especially in reference to the heathen world whose culture and religion contained similar legends. Tertullian elaborated on the divinity of Christ by explaining the nature of his virgin birth: "This ray of God, then, as it was always foretold in ancient times, descending into a certain virgin, and made flesh in her womb, is in His birth God and man united. The flesh formed by the Spirit is nourished, grows up to manhood, speaks, teaches, works, and is the Christ."[14] But then he pointed out to his readers that they were fully knowledgeable about such tales, though the case of Christ is very special: "Receive meanwhile this fable, if you choose to call it so—it is like some of your own—while we go on to show how Christ's claims are proved."[15]

Jerome gives a short list of alleged virgin births in the heathen world, with special attention to the case of Plato. He knew the legends which had been written down by Diogenes Laertius who, in his *Life of Plato*,

---

[14]Tertullian, Apol 21 (ANF III) 34-35.

[15]Ibid., 21 (ANF I) 35. The image of a miraculous conception as the result of a ray of light was used by Herodotus and Plutarch in reference to the sacred bull Apis, the image of Osiris, worshiped as a god by the Egyptians: "The Egyptian belief is that a flash of light descends upon the cow from heaven, and this causes her to receive Apis." Herodotus, Hist 3.29. And: "The Apis, they say, is the animate image of Osiris, and he comes into being when a fructifying light thrusts forth from the moon and falls upon a cow in her breeding season." Plutarch, IsOsir 368C (LCL. Mor V) 105.

Pierre de Labriolle, *La Réaction païenne: Etude sur la polémique anti-chrétienne du Ier au IVe siècle* (Paris: Artisan du Livre, 1948) 118-19, mentions legends in which vestiges of pagan beliefs in the virgin birth and the resurrection are predominant: "Des vestiges de légendes païennes restent discernables au fond de plusieurs de leurs croyances: l'affirmation que le Christ serait né d'une vierge visitiée par l'Esprit Saint rappelle les fables de Danaé, de Mélanippe, d'Augé et d'Antiope; l'épisode de la résurrection fait songer à l'histoire d'Aristée de Proconnèse, qui, d'après Pindare et Hérodote, fut ravi par la mort aux yeux des hommes, puis se fit voir en divers points de l'univers, à des intervalles fort éloignés, comme un annonciateur des volontés divines."

alluded to the story of Ariston and Perictione, parents of Plato, who could trace their ancestry to Solon and all the way back to Poseidon. Diogenes Laertius accepted the legend according to which when Perictione was still very young, Ariston failed to thrust his love on her. At the urging of Apollo, who appeared to him in a dream, Ariston respected the virginity of Perictione until Plato was born.[16] Jerome reports the legend, but offers a different explanation of the role of Apollo: "Anaxelides in the second book of his philosophy, relates that Perictione, the mother of Plato, was violated by an apparition of Apollo, and they agree in thinking that the prince of wisdom was born of a virgin."[17]

Some church fathers attempted to answer critics of Christianity who regarded the story of the virgin birth with suspicion or as a fable which lacked dignity and persuasiveness. Justin tried in vain to convince Trypho that some of the Old Testament prophecies concerning the virgin birth applied to Christ.[18] Irenaeus referred to the doctrines of Cerinthus, who appealed to Egyptian wisdom to prove that Jesus was not born of a virgin, but was the son of Mary and Joseph as the result of normal human generation. Yet, in spite of that he was "more righteous, prudent, and wise than other men."[19] One of the most derogatory story about Jesus was voiced by Celsus in a supposed dialogue with a Jew. Mary was declared adulterous, rejected by her husband, wandering into Egypt where she gave birth to Jesus, who grew up there and acquired special wisdom and miraculous power. He then returned to his people to proclaim himself a god born of a virgin.[20]

Beliefs in the virgin birth of Jesus evolved relatively late in the apostolic age. Whether or not they were known to Paul, he never referred to such tenets, nor did the other writers of the New Testament except for Matthew and Luke. The meaning of the coming of Christ, as well as the

---

[16]Diogenes Laertius, Lives: Plato 3.1-2.

[17]Jerome, AdvJov 1.42 (NPNF-2 VI) 380-81. Anaxelides was the source for Diogenes Laertius Lives: Plato 3.2. But Jerome reports the story in a slightly different manner, though preserving a high respect for Plato (*sapientiae principem non aliter arbitrantur, nisi de partu virginis editum*).

[18]Justin Martyr, Trypho 68.

[19]Irenaeus, AdvHaer 1.26.1 (ANF I) 351-52.

[20]Origen, CCel 1.28.

formulation of Christian theology in the early stages of the church were not affected in any significant way by the doctrine of the virgin birth.

As new religions progress toward stages of maturity, their faithful have to grapple with the obscurities surrounding their birth. Christianity was not spared the difficult task of giving an account of its origins and of explaining its faith which could not be reconciled with the prevalent modes of religious thinking and practice, be they Jewish or heathen. Though rejected or ignored by most of the Jewish nation, the Christ of the Pentecost remained a Jewish messiah. It took some time for the disciples and the new community they formed to come to grips with the fact that the promised kingdom could not have resulted solely from the preaching and teaching of their master, however much they now believed him to be the Messiah. Their newly acquired faith rested on the event of the resurrection, a unique phenomenon within God's redemptive purpose which led the disciples to contemplate everything through this new experience and not through a careful remembrance of the words and deeds of their master they so often failed to understand. From the beginning the Christ of faith and the Jesus of history merged in a new religious consciousness. The unity of faith proclaimed by the church rested on spiritual conviction rather than on rational discourse.

By the time the Gospel writers attempted to give final shape to oral traditions concerning the life and work of Christ, the early church had already flourished on Hellenistic soil and its major missionary, Paul, had already suffered martyrdom. For more than half a century Gentile churches kept a close connection with Judaism of which they often considered themselves a spiritual part. But they did not seem to have been concerned with the details of the historical Jesus. Very little was heard in that regard from the writings of Paul whose theology was centered on the death and resurrection of Christ as the sole supports for Christian faith.[21]

---

[21]Paul's silence about episodes in the life and work of Jesus remain without credible answers. There are no references in his writings to parables, miracles, or teaching summaries such as the Sermon on the Mount. Yet all of that remained part of the oral tradition up to the time of the writing of the Gospels. The alleged Jerusalem conference of Acts 15 may provide some insight on how the early church coped with theological and practical differences and why Paul and his colleagues distanced themselves more and more from the traditions of the

For the last two centuries, since Reimarus, modern historical theology has followed countless *Holzwege* in an attempt to extricate the real Jesus from the faith of the church. The *Lives of Jesus* movement up to the turn of the twentieth century was brilliantly summarized by Albert Schweitzer in his masterpiece *The Quest of the Historical Jesus* with the conclusion that all endeavors in that field must remain unsatisfactory and inconclusive. Since then myriads of other books have appeared on the subject with no more success. Hidden somewhere in the depths of divine mystery are all the secrets God has chosen not to reveal to the human mind. They consist of all the things essential to universal redemption but which can find no permanent place within historical circumstances. Redemption rests on faith, not knowledge, certainly not rational knowledge. In that area records preserved by the early church would baffle any historian with the likely result of conceding inevitable ignorance.

Some important questions, however, will continue to occupy the center of Gospel research. The coming of the Messiah requires a transformation of the religious community which proves impossible to achieve. Messianic groups, such as the Dead Sea Scrolls community withdrew from the world in order to enhance their eventual participation in the eschatological kingdom. The prophetic voice, however respected and revered, or however despised and rejected, does not seem to find a congenial home in traditional cultic expressions. A Messiah who could be understood by all would cease to be the divine representative, for he would be reduced to unacceptable human dimensions. The religious community would bestow on him all the marks of its expectations rather than to discover in him the compelling elements leading to a metanoia. For that reason John the Baptist failed, and the kingdom did not arrive with Jesus, at least not in the way popular religion thought of it. The very notion of Messiah has remained shadowy through the years, the promised Messiah being made to assume diverse functions, from a national liberator, to a benevolent king, to a universal ruler, to the one securing a proper end to human history.

Thus we shall continue to probe into the scanty historical data at our disposal and wonder why Jesus the Nazarene vanished from the memory of the early church to be acclaimed as the glorified Christ, appearing

---

original disciples.

either as the exalted Son of God or as the suffering Son of Man, as the one who, though disclosing the eternal will of God, also kept his messianic status secret.[22] The early church felt more inclined to rest its faith on the spiritual blessings derived from the death and resurrection of its Lord than on an accurate knowledge of what by then had already become the object of far too many legends, canonical and apocryphal. At the same time the disputes over the human or divine nature of Christ had given rise to Christian sects and movements claiming exclusive possession of the truth, and later divided the theological world through debates and pronouncements of councils.

Christianity never was in possession of a clear understanding of its existence. There was no tripod from which oracular pronouncements received their authority, no elaborate Delphi as the residence of the supreme god. Save at the very beginning, the temple of Jerusalem played a minimal role in the development of Christianity. Dogmatic theology, as a means to secure consensus among faithful, did not arise until the Council of Nicaea in 325, too late to regain control of so many different ways to look at the meaning and mission of Christianity, a fact which ensured perpetual disagreement and continuous fragmentation. No one knows exactly what Christianity owes to the primitive church, and what primitive Christianity owes to Christ. It has become a question of faith, not historical certainty. Whether Jesus was a typical Jew who came to his people and confined his ministry to his nation, or whether he was a representative of humankind, unbound by geographical and cultural limits, or whether he was none of what we attribute to him, may never be determined. Nor do we know for certain that we possess his ipsissima verba, but rather what the early church has done with them. That dispute too will last forever and fuel the principles of redaction and form criticism, small marvels of modern textual criticism.

In its search for a divine center primitive Christianity gave a new meaning to the concept of universality, far beyond geographical and historical definitions as they had existed in heathen religion, especially

---

[22]The term "Messianic secret" was coined by Wilhelm Wrede at the turn of the twentieth century with the publication of his work *Das Messiasgeheimnis in den Evangelien. Zugleich ein Beitrag zum Verständnis des Markusevangeliums* (Göttingen, 1901). ET: *The Messianic Secret*, trans. J. C. G. Greig (Greenwood SC: Attic Press, 1971).

that of Apollo. The will of God did not radiate from religious centers such as Delphi or Dodona, but from the hearts of the believers. Jesus was known and proclaimed as he lived, through his spirit, in the new religious consciousness of early Christians. It is from that perspective that they understood his life and preaching and that they considered themselves the spiritual leaven slowly transforming the world according to the predictions of their redeemer. For a long time they remained the invisible kingdom in a powerful empire. Hope resided more in the return of the Messiah to vindicate his people than on what he was in his earthly appearance before his death and resurrection. There was a tacit, and sometimes open, belief that if the Jews as a nation had accepted the call to repentance, the death and resurrection of Christ would not have been necessary, perhaps even absurd.

Early Christians obeyed the command of their Lord to forsake the old and enter a new mode of life which rested on the promises of the coming kingdom and on the need to reshape the immediate context within which redemption could be achieved at any cost. Hence the unbelievable willingness of Christians to die as martyrs. The Lord of the early Christians remained mysterious. Had they been able to view Christ from a more historical and rational perspective, they would have avoided many conflicts by keeping their faith and religious beliefs within the bounds of heathen and Jewish religious and cultural syncretism. The church fathers were left with the task of explaining why, in the context of the new faith, the world Christians shared with Jews and Gentiles had to be viewed in a different perspective.

By the time the Gospels were written, Christianity had become an independent movement. In his missionary activity Paul had already emphasized the need to view the church's relationship to Judaism in the context of the redemptive work of Christ. His purpose was to liberate Christianity from a realm of law and justice, replaced by grace and faith. When Matthew wrote his Gospel, some thirty years after the main letters of Paul, he appealed to the Christian community to treasure its Jewish legacy. But the relationship of the church to the Old Testament remained rocky, especially in the days of Gnosticism and Marcion. It survived after heavy allegorization by the church fathers and especially by the School of Alexandria which derived many of its exegetical principles from the great Jewish philosopher Philo.

Gospel writing focused as much on giving the early church the tools and knowledge it needed in its apologetic activity as on an account of what the life of Christ may have been. By the end of the first century Paul's theology dominated the Christian scene, and little was remembered of the original disciples. Yet surviving traditions were written down for the edification of the church. They also provided some important historical information.

The Teaching of Jesus

All four Gospel writers confirm that, except for rare instances, Jesus spent his ministry within the geographical confines of his nation and that his message was intended for his people alone.[23] No specific notion of universalism permeates his teaching, and, though the Gospels mention the heathen, no reference is made to the gods of the Romans. Jesus did not intend to invalidate the religious history or prophetic voice of the Jews as the chosen people. Neither polytheism nor syncretism of any kind were part of his reflections, nor did the disciples question him on such matters. There was a tacit conviction that the Jewish religion was the only one approved by God and that no debate was necessary to vindicate such a proposition.

---

[23]This point is strongly emphasized by Adolf Harnack, *The Mission and Expansion of Christianity in the First Three Centuries* (New York: Harper & Brothers, 1961) 36:

> He [Jesus] preached only to the Jews. Not a syllable shows that he detached this message from its national soil, or set aside the traditional religion as of no value. . . . Rather he took his stand upon the soil of Jewish rights, i.e., of the piety maintained by Pharisaism. But he showed that while the Pharisees preserved what was good in religion, they were perverting it none the less, and that the perversion amounted to the most heinous of sins.

Depending on one's view on the nation of Israel at the time of Jesus, there may be room for disagreement. The Gospel of John (chap. 4) speaks of a ministry of Jesus in Samaria. The excursion of Jesus to Caesarea Philippi may also be viewed as a conscious departure from a typically Jewish region. Yet it is there that Jesus chose to reveal to the disciples who were with him that he was the Messiah, a fact he enjoined them not to share with the rest his followers, much less the nation as a whole (Matthew 16:13-20; Mark 8:27-30).

From the traditions at its disposal, the early church rebuilt a Jesus different from what he was as the divine prophet and Messiah. Since the disciples so often misunderstood Jesus while they were with him, one would expect that the traditions linked with them would not be totally free from misconceptions. Adolf Harnack spoke of two different Gospels, the Gospel as Jesus proclaimed it (*Evangelium Christi*), and the Gospel as it became known in the early church (*Evangelium de Christo*), a Gospel which went far beyond the remembered words of Jesus to emphasize the fulfillment of redemption. It is doubtful, however, that early Christians would have been aware of such a distinction, much less that they would have consciously maintained it.

Progressively it was the teaching of Christ that enlightened his death and resurrection. Masterpieces of religious literature such as the Sermon on the Mount were destined for immortality, whatever the conditions under which they were spoken, remembered, and written down.[24] It was not the amount of teaching which, by Greco-Roman standards, was rather minimal, but its intensity and depth which stirred the faith of Christians. It generated a level of enthusiasm and dedication which played a major role in establishing Christianity as an irresistible power destined to alter the history of a large segment of the religious world.

When trying to convey the essence of the teaching of Jesus, the Synoptic Gospels placed the emphasis on parables as the most appropriate way to enlighten the crowds. Matthew and Mark insist that Jesus never addressed the multitudes without resorting to parables.[25] But they reject the view that parables can be easily understood by listeners unprepared to penetrate their mysterious meaning. Parables designed to elucidate difficult sayings about the kingdom were presented in an oracular form so ambiguous that even the disciples often failed to perceive the intended purpose.

---

[24]Augustine wrote a long exposition of the Sermon on the Mount in two books and started his explanation with these words: "If any one will piously and soberly consider the sermon which our Lord Jesus Christ spoke on the mount, as we read it in the Gospel according to Matthew, I think that he will find in it, so far as regards the highest morals, a perfect standard of the Christian life." SermDom 1.1 (NPNF-1 VI) 3.

[25]Matthew 13:34; Mark 4:34.

Mysteries which have remained hidden since the origin of the world gave the parables their sense of universality. At this point Matthew quoted Psalm 78:2:

I will open my mouth in parables,
I will utter what has been hidden
    since the foundation of the world.[26]

As with the sages of old in the Semitic world, Jesus liked to speak in ways sufficiently unclear to stir the mental and spiritual resources of his hearers. He expected them to seek for new dimensions of life not evident on the level of everyday existence. The parables were meant not only to explain a new perspective on life, but to channel the power of conviction into the hearts and minds of men and women in search of divine compassion and providence. Ambiguities persisted and stressed the necessity for divine illumination.

Not all New Testament writers adopted the position of the Synoptic Gospels. The author of the Gospel of John never mentions the parables. For him the mysteries of creation are disclosed in the Logos, the divine power through which the universe came into existence, the light dissipating the darkness of ignorance and sin, the incarnate word bringing together the old and the new and endowing everything with everlasting meaning.[27] Such a perspective was already present in Paul, who spoke of Christ as predating creation as we know it and holding it together in his eternal being.[28]

The assumption that parables can translate in simple images difficult propositions about divine intentions is contradicted by Mark and Luke in statements that seem to stand in opposition to the general purpose of the message. Implied is that Christ used the parables to ensure that those outside "may indeed see but not perceive, and may indeed hear but not understand; lest they should turn again, and be forgiven"[29] Matthew has

---

[26]Matthew 13:35.

[27]John 1:1-18.

[28]Colossians 1:15-17: "He is the image of the invisible God, the firstborn of all creation; for in him all things were created, in heaven and on earth, visible and invisible. . . . All things were created through him and for him. He is before all things, and in him all things hold together."

[29]Mark 4:12; Luke 8:10.

given us a more complete insight into the ways in which Jesus interpreted his ministry in the light of prophetic discouragement and into the intentions of Jesus to keep the crowds in ignorance:

> "This is why I speak to them in parables, because seeing they do not see, and hearing they do not hear, nor do they understand. With them is indeed fulfilled the prophecy of Isaiah which says:
>   'You shall indeed hear but never understand,
>   and you shall indeed see but never perceive.
>   For this people's heart has grown dull,
>   and their ears are heavy of hearing,
>   and their eyes they have closed,
>   lest they should perceive with their eyes,
>   and hear with their ears,
>   and understand with their heart,
>   and turn for me to heal them.'
> But blessed are your eyes, for they see, and your ears, for they hear. Truly, I say to you, many prophets and righteous men longed to see what you see, and did not see it, and to hear what you hear, and did not hear it."[30]

The uncompromising nature of the kingdom Christ was announcing stood in contrast to traditional notions of Messianic expectations. The parables dealt not only with redemption but also with judgment, especially with the judgment of those who will succumb to the process of hardening their hearts to the point of staying "outside." There may have been a fear on the part of Jesus that the parable was destined to failure for lack of spiritual power to grasp its meaning, or if there were no heart ready to open up to divine revelation contained in it. Thus the disturbing context or, as in the case of Matthew, the discouraging anticipation of the lack of understanding among those who where confronted with the truth hidden in the images supporting the parable: "For to him who has will more be given, and he will have abundance; but from him who has not, even what he has will be taken away."[31] The parables established the dividing line between those who understand and are part of the kingdom, and those deprived of knowledge and condemned to remain in obscurity. At points the harshness of Jesus was quite

---

[30]Matthew 13:13-17.
[31]Matthew 13:12.

surprising, as when he gave the following advice to his disciples: "Do not give dogs what is holy; and do not throw your pearls before swine."[32]

If the parables were meant to contain the universal language of creation, they also cast profound truths into hopeless ambiguities. Without special divine revelation they would remain obscure for everybody. The key which opens the door of understanding was granted to the disciples, as to a small remnant distinct from the multitudes: "To you it has been given to know the secrets of the kingdom of heaven, but to them it has not been given."[33] That which was the source of understanding was also the cause of obscurity. Even with the key of the secret, the road was long and painful for the disciples, who were rebuked for their slow progress: "Do you not understand this parable? How then will you understand all the parables?"[34] On some occasions we find the disciples asking for clarification, only to be met with Christ's disbelief of their ignorance.[35] There is also the suggestion that to help the disciples achieve comprehension, Jesus taught them privately.[36]

At points the terminology used in the Gospels to distinguish between those who understand and those who do not came close to esoteric mysteries known to the Greco-Roman world. The term μυστήριον, as it was used first in the Septuagint and then in the New Testament, evoked a process of initiation related to mystery cults, especially when secrets were disclosed to those taking part in specific rites, as in the case of the initiation of priests. Failure to enlighten the new initiates also meant failure of the process itself. We find in Jesus a rebuke of the religious leaders which would support such a contention: "Woe to you lawyers! for you have taken away the key of knowledge; you did not enter yourselves, and you hindered those who were entering."[37] References to mysteries and secrets as the prerogatives of those who were the recipients of divine revelation were common in apocalyptic literature and in Sibylline oracles.

By the time of Jesus, elements of mystery religions had already influenced some segments of Judaism. In his allegorical interpretations,

---

[32]Matthew 7:6. The statement appears only in Matthew.
[33]Matthew 13:11; Mark 4:11; Luke 8:9.
[34]Mark 4:13.
[35]Matthew 13:36; 15:15-16; Mark 7:17-18.
[36]Mark 4:34.
[37]Luke 11:52.

Philo deplored the pagan inability to acknowledge that the supreme God can take possession of the human being and make the soul the receptacle of his mysteries. There is a wisdom unknown to those deprived of the key of understanding. Wrote Philo:

> These thoughts, ye initiated, whose ears are purified, receive into your souls as holy mysteries indeed and babble not of them to any of the profane. Rather as stewards guard the treasure in your own keeping, not where gold and silver, substances corruptible, are stored, but where lies that most beautiful of all possessions, the knowledge of the Cause and of virtue. . . . I myself was initiated under Moses the God-beloved into his greater mysteries. . . .[38]

We find in such a statement an interesting combination which could apply to Jesus' comment on the mysterious content of his parables as well as to his teaching in the Sermon on the Mount.

The interpretation of parables remained a cause of debate for the church fathers, especially when answering critics of Christianity. In a refutation of Marcion's ideas, Tertullian proposed that "on the subject of *parables,* let it suffice that it has been once for all shown that this kind of language [*eloquii*] was with equal distinctness promised by the creator."[39] Aware of the difficulties created by the sayings of Jesus, that those who shall hear shall nonetheless not understand, Tertullian made clear the correlation between what Christ was saying and the will of the creator: "Not as if Christ, actuated with a diverse spirit, permitted a hearing which the Creator had refused. . . . For they wilfully refused to hear, although they had ears. He, however, was teaching them that it was the ears of the heart which were necessary."[40]

For Tertullian it was essential to penetrate the deeper meaning of the parables. It was not a drachma that a woman lost, nor the straying of a ewe, nor even the return of a prodigal son, that were important, but the discovery of the nature of God. We must persevere in searching out what Christ meant in the parables until we discover the way to achieve forgiveness of sins and to find satisfaction in his kingdom.[41]

---

[38]Philo, DeCher 48-49 (LCL II) 37.
[39]Tertullian, AdvMarc 4.19 (ANF III) 376.
[40]Ibid., 4.19 (ANF III) 377.
[41]Tertullian, DePoen 8.

As to the principles of interpretation applying to the parables, Tertullian warned against the ease with which their meaning could be distorted:

> We, however, who do not make the parables the sources whence we devise our subject-matters, but the subject-matters the sources whence we interpret the parables, do not labor hard, either, to twist all things (into shape) in the exposition, while we take care to avoid all contradictions.[42]

After praising his own intrepretation of the parables, he spoke against any departure from the essence of the subjects under consideration, unless we apply the parable to give meaning to martyrdom:

> In short, if it were lawful to transfer the parables to other ends (than they were originally intended for), it would be rather to *martyrdom* that we would direct the hope drawn from those now in question." Even then extreme caution has to be applied, for "we prefer, if it must be so, to be *less* wise *in* the Scriptures, than to be wise *against* them. We are as much bound to keep the *sense* of the Lord as His *precept.*[43]

Irenaeus suggested that the interpretation of the parables would pose no serious difficulty for a sound mind devoted to piety and the love of truth. Scriptures, he contended, are free from ambiguities. "And therefore the parables ought not to be adapted to ambiguous expressions. For, if this be not done, both he who explains them will do so without danger, and the parables will receive a like interpretation from all."[44] As far as they refer to God, parables contain the whole truth, and, according to Irenaeus, we should never seek to discover in them the answers to our own inclinations.

John Chrysostom advised against a literal reading of the parables: "And, as I am always saying, the parables must not be explained throughout word for word, since many absurdities will follow."[45] We should always remember that the parables of Jesus demand virtue in our works rather than supposed correctness in interpretation: "For concerning

---

[42]Tertullian, DePud 9 (ANF IV) 82.
[43]Ibid., 9 (ANF IV) 84.
[44]Irenaeus, AdvHaer 2.27.1 (ANF I) 398.
[45]John Chrysostom, HMatt 47 (NPNF-1 X) 292.

doctrines He [Jesus] discourses seldom, for neither doth the subject need labor, but of life often or rather everywhere, for the war about this is continual, wherefore also is the labor."[46]

The Miracles of the Kingdom

The saying of Goethe, *Das Wunder ist des Glaubens liebstes Kind* ("The dearest child of faith is miracle," *Faust*, 766), applies to biblical history, and to some extent also to paganism. Signs and wonders marked the great moments of redemption in the Old Testament. The future of the people depended on the power of God made available to them to overcome whatever threatened the fulfillment of divine purpose. The world was full of miracle workers competing for supremacy. Moses had to outdo the wisdom and art of Egyptian magicians to prove that divine finality, of which he was the instrument, could no longer be equated with traditional religious claims to power. In the days of Jesus the religious world expected miracles as signs of divine will. Without his miracles, the ministry of Jesus would have been severely limited, and the Gospels would have lost some of their persuasive power.

All four evangelists refrain from attributing miracles to John the Baptist, though he was sometimes regarded as the source of power by which Jesus performed his wonders.[47] The variety and nature of Gospel miracles do not allow for definitions and summary statements. Four words are used to refer to the miraculous activity of Jesus: σημεῖον or sign (especially in John), δύναμις or power (especially in the Synoptic Gospels), ἔργον or work, and occasionally τέρας or wonder (associated with σημεῖον as a way to refer to the miraculous work of God among his people through signs and wonders).

The majority of miracles reported in Gospel narratives emphasize compassion on the part of Jesus.[48] As part of the messianic proclamation, they mediate mercy to a degree not known before. Matthew has the crowd marvel and exclaim: "Never was anything like this seen in

---

[46]Ibid., 64 (NPNF-1 X) 395.

[47]Matthew 14:1-2. On one occasion at least, when the chief priests and elders questioned the source of Jesus' authority, he connected it with the baptism of John, though he did not make it dependent on it.

[48]Matthew 15:32; 20:34; Luke 7:13.

Israel."[49] The healing of the possessed and the sick, the feeding of the multitudes, all belong to the merciful and compassionate work of Christ. They may be regarded as Jesus' way to present his credentials as the appointed Messiah sent by God.

Healing miracles were often performed with a sense of urgency. Many of them are reported to have taken place on the sabbath, contrary to Mosaic and levitical proscriptions.[50] In those instances religious leaders, especially the Pharisees, sought to destroy Jesus in order to preserve the sanctity of their rituals, which Jesus considered superseded by a higher law of love and mercy. In certain cases healing miracles were performed on an individual basis, requiring the faith of those who sought the cures. In other instances the Gospels report healings on almost a mass level.[51] Occasionally Jesus disregarded the fact that his mission should have been limited to the house of Israel, and, on the basis of faith on the part of outsiders, extended his healing wonders to those who did not belong to his people, as in the case of the Canaanite woman, whose faith surpassed that of traditionally religious Jews.[52]

Miracles which were intended to modify or overrule natural phenomena generated a great deal of debate, for natural laws could be viewed as immutable divine decrees. Yet the disciples did not hesitate to beg Jesus to calm storms and rescue them from the furies of the elements.[53] Sometimes common and simple processes of nature were turned into poetic or spiritual lessons, as in the case of the cursing of the barren fig tree, a metaphor illuminating the proper relationship of human beings to God.[54]

---

[49]Matthew 9:33.

[50]Matthew 12:9-14; Mark 3:1-6; John 5:9-18.

[51]Matthew 14:34-36; 19:2.

[52]Matthew 15:21-28.

[53]Matthew 8:23-27; 14:22-33. The idea that natural laws can be overruled by faith, as in the case of Peter attempting to walk on water, serves more as a warning against the lack of faith than an encouragement to prevail on God to alter the behavior of nature.

[54]Matthew 21:18-22. The narrative of the cursing of the fig tree reveals an interesting development in the Synoptic Gospels. Matthew's text appears in its simplest form. It omits a statement made by Mark (11:13)—"For it was not the season for figs"—thus avoiding to portray Jesus as unreasonable in his expectations of nature. In Luke (13:6-9) the narrative becomes a parable showing

In the Gospel of John the element of power in the miraculous no longer dominated the activity of Jesus. His works were pointers to a transcendent reality contained in the creative Logos. They were signs of divine presence and did not always convey a deep spiritual meaning. The changing of water into wine at the wedding at Cana in chapter 2 stood in contrast to the depth of teaching in chapter 1. But there was a crescendo of meaning in the signs of Jesus and how they revealed his glory. The feeding of the multitudes conveyed the same compassionate concern as in the Synoptic Gospels, but it soon evolved into the notion of sacrificial meal, and from there into a profound teaching on eternal life.[55] The healing of the blind also went far beyond an act of kindness to an individual into a reflection on universal blindness and divine light attempting to overcome it.[56] The climax came in the resurrection of Lazarus and the disclosure of the divine purpose of redemption through death and resurrection.[57]

The most vivid description of miracles is connected with the casting out of demons, especially as related in the Gospel of Mark. Matthew and Luke toned down the extreme level of conflict with demons and departed from the emphasis on exorcism in Mark, who brought the intensity of the struggle almost beyond human endurance.[58] All three Synoptic Gospels report that the disciples were unable to cast out demons, which brought a rebuke from Christ.[59] The world of demons was considered a kingdom of its own, impenetrable by human wisdom or even religious ritual. It could not be assailed from the outside. Hence, the conclusion of the

---

a frustrated gardener who had a fig tree planted in his vineyard but was unable to collect any fruit after a three-year wait. He ordered the tree cut down. But the vinedresser begged for more time to correct the situation by taking special care of the tree, which was thus saved, at least for another year.

[55] John 6:1-59.

[56] John 9:1-41.

[57] John 12:1-26.

[58] Mark 5:1-20; Matthew 8:28-34; Luke 8:26-39. Matthew and Luke left out the vivid descriptions of Mark 5:4-5: "[F]or he had often been bound with fetters and chains, but the chains he wrenched apart, and the fetters he broke in pieces; and no one had the strength to subdue him. Night and day among the tombs and on the mountains he was always crying out, and bruising himself with stones."

[59] Mark 9:14-19; Matthew 17:14-24; Luke 9:37-43.

Pharisees that Jesus cast out demons by the prince of demons.[60] Such a suggestion elicited on the part of Jesus a response that proved the absurdity of the statement and the victory of the kingdom of God over that of Satan. For, if Satan is divided against himself, the end of his dominion could not be far off.[61] The notion persisted among the Jews, long after the New Testament era, that the casting out of demons by Jesus was the result of magic, an art which, according to the Talmud, he brought with him from Egypt.[62] A spurious passage in Josephus also attributes wonderful works to Christ.[63]

Miracles in the Gospels are presented so as to minimize a misunderstanding of their purpose. On many occasions Jesus refused to perform them, especially when it would have enhanced his status as the Messiah apart from a knowledge of his true mission. The temptation story, for instance, put the emphasis on obedience to God rather than proof of power.[64] The miracles which could strengthen faith could also mislead people and cloud their understanding of the real purpose of the messianic age. Hence, the refusal of Jesus to perform them.[65] By the end of his life, miracles were expected from Jesus. When he was sent to Herod by Pilate, Herod was less concerned with the right judgment of the case than with the hope that Jesus would perform a miracle.[66] While Jesus was dying on the cross, witnesses to his agony still hoped that he would stun the world by saving himself from his fate, so that all could believe in him.[67]

Miracles did not always achieve the purpose intended. Jesus had to acknowledge a sense of futility in his attempt to place them in the right perspective. They failed to disclose God, and might have been more effective in the past than during his ministry. He bemoaned the fact that if the same wonders had been performed in Tyre and Sidon, they would have repented. Thus the present age will bring judgment upon itself for not having been able to see in the works of Christ God at work among

---

[60]Matthew 9:34.
[61]Matthew 12:22-30; Luke 11:14-20.
[62]H. van der Loos, *The Miracles of Jesus* (Leiden: E. J. Brill, 1968) 140.
[63]Josephus, Ant 18.3.3.
[64]Matthew 4:1-11.
[65]Matthew 12:38-42; 16:4.
[66]Luke 23:8.
[67]Matthew 27:42.

his people.[68] On other occasions, Jesus had to perform his miracles in the midst of people who ridiculed them.[69] Healing miracles, especially, exposed the failure of conventional wisdom and of official medical art.[70]

The authority to perform miracles was bestowed on the disciples by Jesus himself.[71] But they often failed to utilize that power successfully.[72] Healings on the part of the disciples continued well into the apostolic era, including the power to bring people back to life.[73] In the *Constitutions of the Holy Apostles* we find an explanation of the reasons why the power to work miracles was extended to the disciples:

> These gifts were first bestowed on us the apostles when we were about to preach the Gospel to every creature, and afterwards were of necessity afforded to those who had by our means believed; not for the advantage of those who perform them, but for the conviction of the unbelievers, that those whom the word did not persuade, the power of signs might put to shame: for signs are not for us who believe, but for the unbelievers, both for the Jews and Gentiles.[74]

References to Christians performing miracles, including the casting out of demons, are numerous in patristic literature.[75] The greatest difficulty, however, resided in interpreting the statement of Christ: "He who believes in me will also do the works that I do; and greater works than these he will do, because I go to the Father." Augustine devoted a tractate of his commentary on the Gospel of John to that question without totally clarifying the problems connected with the fact that no one could be greater than Christ or perform greater works.[76]

In the Gentile world the church fathers had to defend Christ against the charge of sorcery or magic:

---

[68]Matthew 11:20-24.

[69]Mark 5:40.

[70]Mark 5:25-26.

[71]Luke 9:1-2.

[72]Matthew 17:16.

[73]The Book of Acts especially contains many healing miracles on the part of the disciples, including the resurrection of Eutychus by Paul. The New Testament Apocrypha refer to many more such events.

[74]*Constitutions of the Holy Apostles* 8.1 (ANF VII) 479.

[75]Justin Martyr, 2 Apol 6; Irenaeus, AdvHaer 2.32.4; Eusebius, HE 5.7.

[76]John 14:12; Augustine, JoanEv, Tractate 72.

The spring of living water which gushed forth from God in the land destitute from the knowledge of God, namely the land of the Gentiles, was this Christ, who also appeared in your nation, and healed those who were maimed, and deaf, and lame in body from their birth, causing them to leap, to hear, and to see, by His word. And having raised the dead, and causing them to live, by His deeds He compelled the men who lived at that time to recognize Him. But though they saw such works, they asserted it was magical art. For they dared to call Him a magician, and a deceiver of the people.[77]

Origen came to the defense of Christians who performed miracles and refuted those who accused Christ of sorcery.[78] Celsus had maintained that Jesus wrought all of his miracles by resorting to magic.[79] Like Origen, Arnobius turned his apologetic verve towards his opponents who labeled Jesus as a magician without examining the evidence.[80]

The miracles of Jesus were often compared with magical powers of Jewish and heathen wonder workers. Josephus attributed to Solomon the art of expelling demons, an art practiced by other Jews, especially a certain Eleazar who released people from their demoniacal spirits in the presence of the emperor Vespasian.[81]

Much more disturbing was the reverence accorded to Simon Magus who, like Christ, was worshiped as a god, even by the Romans:

There was a Samaritan, Simon, a native of the village called Gitto, who in the reign of Claudius Caesar, and in your royal city of Rome, did mighty acts of magic, by virtue of the art of the devils operating in him. He was considered a god, and as a god was honoured by you with a statue, which statue was erected on the Tiber river, between the two

---

[77]Justin Martyr, Trypho 69 (ANF I) 233. Throughout patristic literature we find references to critics of Christianity who refer to the work of Jesus as the product of magical arts. Sometimes the same judgment is passed on the disciples. Augustine mentioned an obscure Greek oracle which proclaimed Christ innocent of magic but made Peter responsible for enchantment and works of magic. CivDei 18.53.

[78]Origen, CCel 1.6.

[79]Ibid., 2.14, 16, 48, 49.

[80]Arnobius, AdvGent 1.43.

[81]Josephus, Ant 8.2.5.

bridges, and bore this inscription, in the language of Rome: "Simoni deo sancto," "To Simon the holy god." And almost all the Samaritans, and a few even of other nations, worship him, and acknowledge him as the first god.[82]

Irenaeus acknowledged Simon Magus's renown but exposed the evil intent of his magical practices meant to lead astray those who believed in them. For those who were acquainted with the miracles of Christ, the limitations of Simon's deeds were evident, and their preposterous nature obvious:

> For they can neither confer sight on the blind, nor hearing on the deaf, nor chase away all sorts of demons—[none, indeed], except those that are sent into others by themselves, if they can even do so much as this. Nor can they cure the weak, or the lame, or the paralytic, or those who are distressed in any other part of the body, as often been done in regard to bodily infirmity. Nor can they furnish effective remedies for those external accidents which may occur. And so far are they from being able to raise the dead, as the Lord raised them, and the apostles did by means of prayer. . . .[83]

Irenaeus expounded at length on how the doctrines and practices of Simon were derived from Jewish sources and from the world of Greek and Roman gods. He refuted Simon's claim to divine power and challenged his dismissal of the miracles of the disciples as sheer magic.[84]

The success of Simon Magus was portrayed in Origen as a compromise with the religious mood of the day. The disciples of Simon were

---

[82]Justin Martyr, 1 Apol 26 (ANF I) 171. The same point is stated again and amplified in section 56. A great deal of debate persists as to the accuracy of Justin's report. But it was not refuted in his own day by other writers, and since his apology was addressed to the Romans, we could have expected some negative reaction had the statement been a pure forgery. It is interesting that Eusebius, HE 2.13, quoted the same passage from 1 Apol 26 with the intention of showing how Simon became the enemy of Christ, mostly among the Romans. At the same time he had been the greatest antagonist of the disciples, especially Peter in Rome, HE 2.14.

[83]Irenaeus, AdvHaer 2.31.2 (ANF I) 407. See also 32.4 and the reply of Irenaeus to those who maintain that the miracles of Jesus were performed only in appearance and not in reality.

[84]Ibid., 1.23.1-4.

encouraged to prefer idolatry to death, which the Christians suffered for their belief. Thus Simonians were never exposed to persecutions.[85]

Apocryphal literature often referred to Simon Magus as the enemy of Peter, who resisted him, as the great magicians resisted Moses in Egypt. In the *Recognitions of Clement*, Niceta, a disciple of Peter, questioned him on the correlation between the signs of Simon and those of Christ: "But if he sins who believes those who do signs, how shall it appear that he also does not sin who has believed our Lord for His signs and works of power?" Peter answered Niceta by exposing how mysterious is the truth of God, buried deep in the earth, with mountains heaped on it, "and it may be found by those only who are able to dig down into the depths."[86] The conclusion was that the signs of Simon have no validity, while the miracles of Christ are of the good kind because they show divine compassion.[87] The same argument was repeated in the *Clementine Homilies.*[88]

In the pagan world, the veneration of Asclepius presented the greatest challenge to Christian miracles. His claims to healings were often compared to those of the Christians. His popularity was almost universal, with numerous religious centers dedicated to him. His major temple was at Epidaurus, attracting there, somehow in the fashion of Lourdes, many citizens in search of cures for their ailments. Christianity could not ignore the phenomenon, for Asclepius was regarded as a god for the same reasons which Christians applied to Christ. The emperor Julian believed that Asclepius represented an attractive alternative to the savior of the Christians, a fact which did not escape the attention of the church.

Already in the days of Plato it was common to invoke Asclepius as the god of healing, and Socrates is reported to have had his last thought for him.[89] Plato considered him far superior to poets, for he was a true physician, and his art was real, as opposed to that of the poets, who were only imitators of reality.[90] Cicero declared him a distinguished benefactor

---

[85]Origen, CCel 6.11.
[86]Pseudo-Clementine Literature, Recogn 3.56-58 (ANF VIII) 129.
[87]Ibid., 3.60.
[88]Ibid., ClemHom 2.34.
[89]Plato, Phaedo 118A.
[90]Plato, Rep 599C.

of the human race,[91] worthy of worship.[92] But he would ascribe to Hippocrates rather than to Asclepius the power to bestow health on the sick.[93]

The miracles of Asclepius were sometimes the subject of ridicule or even scorn.[94] Some mighty acts of Jesus also suffered the same fate. In some instances people sought the help of Asclepius because of the failure of conventional medicine. This was not unlike what happened in the days of Christ. The Synoptic Gospels report the case of "a woman who had had a flow of blood for twelve years, and who had suffered much under many physicians, and had spent all that she had, and was no better but rather grew worse."[95] We find a similar account in the experience of Aristides, "who had consulted various doctors to no avail and who had finally had recourse to the temple of Aesculapius at Pergamum."[96]

The early church did not systematically refute the healing power of Asclepius, though the majority of church fathers pointed out the limits of his miracles when compared to those of Christ. The only instance recorded where Asclepius brought back to life a human being, Hippolytus, also produced his death caused by the anger of Zeus. On account of such punishment, Justin imagined Asclepius as having ascended to heaven.[97] Justin established an analogy between the works of Asclepius and those of Christ, with the intent, of course, of proving Christ superior to Asclepius.[98] Without denying the impact of the miracles of Asclepius

---

[91]Cicero, NatDeo 2.62.

[92]Ibid., 3.39.

[93]Ibid., 3.91.

[94]Van der Loss, *Miracles*, 122.

[95]Mark 5:25-26.

[96]Van der Loos, *Miracles*, 121. See also Aristides, Apol 10 (ANF X) 271: "They also bring forward Asklepios as a god who is a doctor and prepares drugs and compounds plasters for the sake of a living."

[97]Justin Martyr, 1 Apol 21. Later, Ambrose, DeVirg 3.2 contrasted the power ascribed to Asclepius with his inability to escape his own death when struck by lightning. The argument loses some its relevance when we remember that Christ suffered death, though he had the power to prevent it.

[98]Justin Martyr, 1 Apol 22 (ANF I) 170: "And in that we say that He [Jesus] made whole the lame, the paralytic, and those born blind, we seem to say what is very similar to the deeds said to have been done by Æsculapius."

on both Greeks and Barbarians, Origen exposed the contradictions in the argumentation of Celsus, who required Christians to accept such stories, while labeling those who believe in the miracles of Christ as a set of "silly" individuals.[99]

In response to those who ridiculed the Christians for worshiping a savior who died on a cross, Arnobius reminded the heathen he was trying to persuade, that they did not hesitate to make Asclepius the discoverer of medicines and the guardian protector of health, even after he suffered death as the result of divine anger.[100] He ridiculed Asclepius as an evil serpent: "That Æsculapius, whom you extol, an excellent, a venerable god, the giver of health, the averter, preventer, destroyer of sickness, is contained within the form and outline of a serpent, crawling along the earth as worms are wont to do. . . . "[101] Arnobius pursued the argument, attacking Asclepius for his lack of divine power in helping plague-stricken Rome, though he was worshiped by the people as a great god.[102] On this point we find a different assessment in Lactantius: "It is equally wonderful, that during the prevalence of a pestilence, Æsculapius, being called from Epidaurus, is said to have released the city of Rome from the long-continued plague."[103]

Christian apologists often referred to the miracles of Jesus, especially to his healings. They were considered persuasive propositions in the proclamation of the Gospel to pagans. As a proof of the power and uniqueness of Gospel miracles some church fathers put forth the claim that those who were raised from the dead by Christ during his earthly ministry were still alive centuries after, up to the time of Eusebius.[104] Origen asserted that miracles were not only powerful symbols of a divine truth, but that they also confirmed the works of Christ as predicted long ago by the prophets.[105]

---

[99]Origen, CCel 3.24.

[100]Arnobius, AdvGent 1.41.

[101]Ibid., 7.44 (ANF VI) 536.

[102]Ibid., 7.47.

[103]Lactantius, DivInst 2.8. (ANF VII) 51.

[104]Irenaeus, AdvHaer 2.32.4; Eusebius, HE 4.3.2.

[105]Origen, CCel 2.48-52. In the same way Lactantius proves that the miracles of Jesus did not owe anything to magic for the very reason that they were already planned in the history of revelation as disclosed in the Old Testament,

For most apologists, miracles such as the virgin birth of Christ,
should not be reduced to the processes of reasoning. Gregory of Nyssa
suggested that we should not investigate the reasons for such mysteries.

> For though we believe, as we do, that all the corporeal and intellectual
> creation derives its subsistence from the incorporeal and uncreated
> Being, yet the *whence* and the *how*, these we do not make a matter for
> examination along with our faith in the thing itself.[106]

The debate as to whether the miracles of Jesus changed the laws of nature
was of special concern to Augustine. He knew the position of Cicero on
portents:

> Nothing can happen without a cause; nothing actually happens that
> cannot happen; if that has happened which could have happened, then
> it should not be considered a portent; therefore there are no such things
> as portents. Now if a thing is to be considered a portent because it is
> seldom seen, then a wise man is a portent.[107]

Taking Varro as a reliable source in matters of interpretation,
Augustine pursued the debate on the correlation between portent and law
of nature:

> So Great an author as Varro would certainly not have called this a
> portent had it not seemed to be contrary to nature. For we say that all
> portents are contrary to nature; but they are not so. For how is that
> contrary to nature which happens by the will of God, since the will of
> so mighty a Creator is certainly the nature of each created thing? A
> portent, therefore, happens not contrary to nature, but contrary to what
> we know as nature.[108]

But it could be contended that God has the power to change the order of
nature if he so desires. For Augustine the miracles performed by Christ
are divine works, and they allow the human mind to apprehend God from
the things that are seen. But the real wonder for him is the governance of
the world by the Logos, a miracle far greater than the feeding of the
multitude. The purpose of the miracle is to discover Christ, the true

---

especially the Prophets, DivInst 5.3.
    [106]Gregory of Nyssa, GrCat 11 (NPNF-2 V) 486.
    [107]Cicero, DeDiv 2.61 (LCL XX) 439.
    [108]Augustine, CivDei 21.8 (NPNF-1 II) 459.

Logos, through it.[109] Heathen have been induced to worship their gods by means of miraculous works, or, in the absence of such power, they have asserted that the gods did not care for human affairs.[110] But it was Augustine's conviction that the church might be more laudable without the miracles. Some Christians among his contemporaries had a nostalgia for the days of Jesus and his wondrous works, forgetting that Christ preferred those who do not see, yet believe.[111]

The Death of the Redeemer

When Paul wrote to the Christians at Corinth: "For I decided to know nothing among you except Jesus Christ and him crucified,"[112] he established the conviction in the early church that the death of Christ conveyed the promise of redemption more powerfully than his earthly life. In the Jewish world, with which Christianity kept strong connections for a long time after the death of Christ, such a proposition was destined to raise serious questions of scriptural interpretation. The Deuteronomic curse pronounced on anyone who hangs on a tree could not be taken lightly.[113] Paul did not deny that it applied to Christ. It was, according to him, a necessary part of salvation.[114]

---

[109]Augustine, JoanEv, Tractate 24.1-2.

[110]Augustine, CivDei 10.18. Miracles played an essential role in both paganism and Christianity. They may have constituted one of the strongest points of analogy between the two. When Gibbon identified five historical causes for the triumph of Christianity in the Roman empire, he placed the miraculous powers of the church as the third cause. Perhaps it was also one of the most difficult to refute, though Gibbon invested a great deal of ingenuity in contesting the truth of alleged miracles.

[111]Augustine, SermDom 38.2.

[112]First Corinthians 2:2.

[113]Deuteronomy 21:22-23: "And if a man has committed a crime punishable by death and he is put to death, and you hang him on a tree, his body shall not remain all night upon the tree, but you shall bury him the same day, for a hanged man is accursed of God."

[114]Galatians 3:13: "Christ redeemed us from the curse of the law, having become a curse for us—for it is written: Cursed be every one who hangs on a tree."

In his *Dialogue with Trypho* Justin offered the most extensive refutation of a Jewish interpretation of the curse. To understand why Christ had to be placed under it, it was important to remember that the whole human race was under a perpetual curse in respect to the Mosaic law: "For it is written in the law of Moses, 'Cursed is every one that continueth not in all things that are written in the book of the law to do them.' And no one has accurately done all, nor will you [Trypho] venture to deny this."[115] According to Justin, by rejecting Christ and by persecuting Christians, the Jews perpetuated the curse and failed to grasp the universality of redemption.

The church fathers accepted Paul's idea that Christ had to suffer the indignity of the cross in order to redeem us from the burden of the law, a position which could not find favor with the Jews.[116] In the same way Justin had to answer the logical arguments of Trypho, Tertullian had to counter the way in which Marcion exposed the absurdity of the Christian understanding of the cross.[117] Sozomen felt confident with the assertion that the death of Christ was predicted by the prophets, and even by pagans and the sibyl:

These things, indeed, were formerly known to the sacred prophets, and predicted by them, and at length, when it seemed to God that they should be manifested, were confirmed by wonderful works. Nor does this appear so marvelous when it is remembered that, even among the Pagans, it was confessed that the Sibyl had predicted that thus it should be,—"Oh most blessed tree, on which our Lord was hung." Our most zealous adversaries cannot deny the truth of this fact, and it is hence evident that a pre-manifestation was made of the wood of the cross, and of the adoration (σέβας) it received.[118]

The heathen were well acquainted with the idea of a dying and rising god, such as Adonis in Phoenicia, Tammuz in Babylonia, Osiris in Egypt, and especially the Phrygian Attis of the Romans. The dying and rising of

[115]Justin Martyr, Trypho 94-96 (ANF I) 246-47. See also Deuteronomy 27:26.
[116]See for example Irenaeus, AdvHaer 3.18.3; Tertullian, AdvJud 10; AdvMarc 3.18; AdvPrax 29; DePat 8; DeFuga 12.
[117]Tertullian, AdvMarc 5.3.
[118]Sozomen, HE 2.1 (NPNF-2 II) 259. See also OracSib 6.25-26 (Terry, *The Sibylline Oracles*, 33-34).

Osiris, as reported by Plutarch, is reminiscent of the story of Christ. Osiris dies on the seventeenth of Athyr and resurrects on the nineteenth.[119] Even more striking is the Roman ritual surrounding the death of Attis which happens on the 22nd of March, with his coming back to life on the 25th.[120] The analogies between the death and resurrection of Christ with heathen belief were sometimes pointed out by church fathers:

> And when we say also that the Word, who is the first-birth [firstborn] of God, was produced without sexual union, and that He, Jesus Christ, our Teacher, was crucified and died, and rose again, and ascended into heaven, we propound nothing different from what you believe regarding those whom you esteem sons of Jupiter.[121]

In such a context of Jewish and heathen perspectives on dying and rising, the early church sought to finalize the death of Christ and his resurrection as the only tenets of universal redemption. The cross continued to be an instrument of curse for both Jews and Romans. Romans persisted in using it to torture those condemned to death. Many Christians had come to wish that redemption could be mediated to the world without such a heavy emphasis on the cross, and church fathers had to protest that, apart from the cross, no redemption was possible. In fact in the very early church the emphasis was on the redemptive death of Christ, apart from direct allusions to the cross, which is not mentioned in the original preaching of Peter, or, for that matter, in the whole book of Acts.[122] The emphasis on the cross as the instrument of redemption

---

[119]Plutarch, IsOsir 356D; 366DF.

[120]Johannes Weiss, *Earliest Christianity: A History of the Period A.D. 30-150*, 2 vols., trans. the faculty of Seabury-Western Theological Seminary (New York: Harper Tortchbooks, 1959) 1:95.

[121]Justin Martyr, 1 Apol 21 (ANF I) 170.

[122]It is not always possible to determine at what point the cross becomes central to the realm of redemption in the New Testament. There can indeed be no Christianity without the centrality of the cross. In the very early church the cross may not have played as important a role as often claimed. Oscar Cullmann, in *The State in the New Testament* (New York: Scribners, 1956) 7, suggested that "In the New Testament the cross has not yet become a religious symbol: it is a Roman sign of the most shameful death to modern sensibilities—the gallows." The difficulties connected with establishing the centrality of the cross have been dealt with in chap. 1 of this work.

came primarily with Paul, and with him indelibly entered the theology of Christianity. It was no longer the death of Christ, but his death *on the cross* which determined the realm of redemption, leading from the most ignoble death to the most glorious resurrection.

Attempts were sometimes made to circumvent what appeared to be the absurdity of the death of Christ on the cross. Irenaeus referred to the teachings of the Gnostic Basilides who contended that Christ, being pure mind ($\nu o \tilde{u} \varsigma$), could not have suffered death:

> But the father without birth and without name, perceiving that they would be destroyed, sent his own first-begotten Nous (he it is who is called Christ) to bestow deliverance on them that believe in him, from the power of those who made the world. He appeared, then, on earth as a man, to the nations of these powers, and wrought miracles. Wherefore he did not himself suffer death, but Simon, a certain man of Cyrene, being compelled, bore the cross in his stead; so that this latter being transfigured by him, that he might be thought to be Jesus, was crucified, through ignorance and error, while Jesus himself received the form of Simon, and, standing by, laughed at them.[123]

Several months into his ministry Jesus saw his work come to an end. He was given a chance to prove himself the Messiah. He refused. To the bewilderment of his disciples he was nailed to a cross. He restored nothing, at least not in the way his followers expected a messiah to act. As he was contemplating his unexpected death, perhaps as a disillusioned man who considered his ministry to have ended in failure, one conclusion impressed itself deeply on him: that the time of fulfillment was not yet and that, in his historical condition, he had appeared only as the forerunner of his own future work: "You will see the Son of man seated at the right hand of Power, and coming on the clouds of heaven."[124] Thus the early church was faced with the task of proving—paradoxically—that its faith rested on the dialectical tension created by the conviction that the Messiah had already come and yet was still coming. The early church had

---

[123]Irenaeus, AdvHaer 1.24. 4 (ANF I) 349. Basilides was a Gnostic who believed the world was created by fallen angels, and that Christ came to deliver the believers from their power. Like Marcion, he believed that the leader of those fallen angels was the God of the Jews.

[124]Matthew 26:64; Mark 14:62.

to include this element of mystery which, ever since, placed Christ above theological definitions: "He comes to us as One unknown, without a name, as of old, by the lake-side, He came to those who knew Him not. He speaks to us the same words: 'Follow thou me!' and sets us to the tasks which He has to fulfil for our time. He commands. And to those who obey Him, whether they be wise or simple, He will reveal Himself in the toils, the conflicts, the sufferings which they shall pass through in His fellowship, and, as an ineffable mystery, they shall learn in their own experience Who He is."[125]

The Disciples in the Post-Resurrection Era

Messianic movements that rose and fell into oblivion failed to ensure their permanence for lack of leaders to perpetuate the teaching and work of their masters. Such was not the case with Christ. His disciples were able to overcome incredible obstacles and maintain the conviction that their teacher was the one sent by God to establish his kingdom on earth. Luke preserved a speech of Gamaliel delivered to the council of priests, in which he mentioned several messianic movements of the day having suffered tragic ends. In referring to the Christ's disciples he agreed with the priests that the new movement may also fail, in which case they would not have to concern themselves with it. But if the new community of the disciples has the sanction of God, it will not only last, but the priests may find themselves in the awkward position of opposing God.[126]

It took some time for the disciples to come to grips with the meaning of the death and resurrection of Christ. They were not prepared for such developments. In view of that, Christ ordered them to stay put in Jerusalem until the reception of the Spirit.[127] They had been warned by Christ on the eve of his death that they would be scattered and lost without his leadership.[128] The transition from followers of Christ during his ministry to proclaimers of a risen Lord required more than an act of faith. Most of what they remembered was of no avail, for all appeared

---

[125] Albert Schweitzer, *The Quest of the Historical Jesus: A Critical Study of Its Progress from Reimarus to Wrede*, trans. William Montgomery (repr.: New York: Macmillan, 1968; orig. ET, 1910) 403.

[126] Acts 5:33-42.

[127] Acts 1:4.

[128] Mark 14:27.

now in a new light. Peter took the leadership and established the foundation of the new apostolic preaching, defining it in specific terms in his Pentecost address.[129] As time elapsed, further refinements of the message took place until it gelled into a more or less coherent perspective shared by all. Christianity owed its definition not only to what was remembered of the sayings of Jesus, but also to the direction given to it by the first generation of disciples.

Gospel records were collected after the original disciples had given their movement a definite direction. Paradoxically, the future of Christianity rested less on their legacy than on newcomers, especially Paul who eclipsed the disciples and was instrumental in universalizing their memory and work. No great enthusiasm, however, was shown by Paul toward the original disciples, especially Peter. When the Gospel writers composed their works they relied on traditions which did not seem to be known to Paul and which preserved a great deal of what the disciples experienced while in the company of Jesus. But by the time of the writing of the Gospels, the evangelists were mostly concerned with the specific needs of the church and with establishing a foundation for their apologetic work. Hence the doubts that have persisted regarding the accuracy of their portrayal of the person of Jesus.

The early church accepted the traditions preserved in the New Testament records, especially in Matthew, that Jesus intended for Peter to be the leader of the new movement and to have the key to its future:

> I tell you, you are Peter, and on this rock I will build my church, and the powers of death shall not prevail against it. I will give you the keys of the kingdom of heaven, and whatever you bind on earth shall be bound in heaven, and whatever you loose on earth shall be loosed in heaven.[130]

To that tradition we find an exception in the *Gospel of Thomas* where James and not Peter is chosen as the leader of the flock:

> The disciples said to Jesus, "We know that you will depart from us, who is to be our leader?" Jesus said to them, "Wherever you are, you

---

[129]Acts 2.

[130]Matthew 16:18-19. In John 20:23 the same power is extended to all the disciples and not only to Peter.

are to go to James the righteous, for whose sake heaven and earth came into being."[131]

The church fathers followed a long and difficult road toward consensus and agreement on the records at their disposal, canonical or apocryphal. By the time of Augustine it was the authority of the church which made the Scriptures the official guidance in faith and practice: "For my part, I should not believe the gospel except as moved by the authority of the catholic church."[132] No such claim can be easily identified in writings predating those of Augustine.

Stephen and His Contributions to the Early church

The rift between Hebrews and Hellenists reported by Luke in Acts 6 has generated numerous and difficult debates, and the conflict probably goes much deeper than suggested in the text. The role played by Stephen, the acknowledged leader of the Hellenists, is of primary importance for an understanding of the emerging early church. For the first time in the account of the trial and death of Stephen, we encounter in a precise manner the serious problems of the relationship between the new community and Judaism. Stephen advocated a new way of worshiping God, a way not familiar to traditional Judaism and not always consonant with the beliefs of the disciples of Christ.

The mystifying personality of Stephen remains a puzzle for New Testament scholars, who have alternatively considered him as a Christian martyr, as a Samaritan Christian with unorthodox religious views, or as a reformer who propounded radical interpretations of messianic prophecies.

Some biblical scholars have attempted to connect Stephen with Samaritan religion. Johannes Munck, for instance, pointed to a tradition claiming that Stephen was a Samaritan.[133] It has been long recognized from the speech in Acts 7 that Stephen quoted from a Samaritan Pentateuch, extolling Abraham and somehow downgrading Moses, whose

---

[131]*The Gospel of Thomas*, logion 12, *The Nag Hammadi Library*, ed. James M. Robinson (San Francisco: Harper & Row, 1978) 127.

[132]Augustine, CEpistMan 5 (NPNF-1 IV) 131.

[133]Johannes Munck, "Stephen's Samaritan Background," *The Acts of the Apostles*, Anchor Bible 31 (Garden City NY: Doubleday, 1967) 285.

mighty works and deeds came from the fact that he was instructed in the wisdom of the Egyptians. The charges that he spoke against Moses, against the law, and against the temple could have been perceived as emanating from a Samaritan perspective he was trying to introduce into Judaism. The situation remained very complex, and certainly was not clarified by Luke.

The Gospel of John offers better insight into a troublesome episode. After the separation of Jesus from John the Baptist, some have contended that John the Baptist pursued his ministry in Samaria for some time:

> We can now see in fact that a ministry by John in Samaria makes extremely good sense. . . . The separation between John and Jesus necessitated that one or other of them should move away. The decision, however it was arrived at, apparently was that Jesus should remain in Judaea, while John moved north to Samaria.[134]

Such a view may conflict with the report in John 4, that it was Jesus who moved through Samaria and was acclaimed there as the Messiah. The saying of John 4:38—"others have labored, and you have entered into their labor"—is placed in the middle of the testimony of the Samaritan woman through whom the Samaritans of the place see in Jesus the one sent by God. Any interpretation of who is meant by the "others" remains in the area of speculation. They may have been some of the disciples of John or some of the Hellenists who had found their way to Samaria.

Though Stephen had a definite Christological perspective based on the Son of Man theology, his martyrdom was not the result of his belief in Christ but the outcome of the way in which he treated Jewish history by pointing out that all the great moments of divine revelation happened outside the promised land and that the claims of Jews to specific divine favor could not rest on their exclusive notion of them. Stephen's Christological insight was more refined than that of the traditional Jewish-messianic leaders. He was the first one to grasp and assert that the office and significance of Jesus were to be understood in terms of global religious history, a fact that later became one of the pillars of Paul's theology. Attempts to place Stephen within a definite group have all failed. He simply did not fit any mold adopted by the religious communities of the day.

---

[134]Scobie, *John the Baptist*, 173-74.

An even more compelling suggestion is offered by Marcel Simon that the college of the seven Hellenists in Acts 6 already existed before the conflict between Hellenists and Hebrews arose and that it may well go back to a pre-Christian movement in Jerusalem.[135] In that case Stephen would no longer stand as an isolated figure but represent a whole movement. After the death of Stephen that movement disintegrated and was absorbed into the Antiochene and Hellenistic developments of Christianity.

The information provided in Acts 6 and 7 proves insufficient to embark on a definite reconstruction of what the movement of Stephen may have been. Some of the traditions are even under suspicion. We may, however, propose several reasons why a Stephanian group of disciples temporarily changed the course of the development of the early church. (1) Whatever the reliability of the sources in Acts, there is hardly any argument that a group of Hellenists representing definite anti-Jewish trends was opposed to a Petrine group claiming apostolic authority. (2) Though it has become increasingly difficult to identify the origin of the Hellenists in Acts, their lasting impact was felt throughout the missionary world of Paul's activity. (3) It is difficult to assess the course Christianity might have taken had Stephen's premature death not intervened and eliminated the possibility for him to play the role Paul assumed later. (4) One could reasonably contend that the Hellenists, under the leadership of Stephen, had a long-standing history in their attempt to reform Judaism and produce a Jewish Hellenism open to the message of Jesus. (5) The group of Hellenists referred to in Acts may well have included followers of Jesus during his earthly ministry with the possibility that Stephen himself had contacts with Jesus. (6) Finally, this group of Hellenists may have understood elements of the message of Christ hidden to traditionally Jewish disciples.

The narrative in Acts 8 reveals three important developments connected with the death of Stephen. (1) That a severe persecution arose against the church in Jerusalem, but the persecution did not affect the apostles. No one could easily explain such a phenomenon where the attacks against a movement spares its leaders. The most likely explanation

---

[135]Marcel Simon, *St. Stephen and the Hellenists in the Primitive Church* (London: Longmans, Green, 1958) 8.

is that the persecution affected only the Hellenistic part of the church, the circle of the disciples of Stephen, and that the traditionally Hebrew Christians, followers of Peter, did not feel any urgency to come to the defense of their Hellenistic brethren. (2) Those who were scattered around by the persecution went out to preach the word. Philip, a disciple of Stephen, went to Samaria where the multitudes accepted what he was saying and witnessed his many miracles. Others went as far as Phoenicia, Cyprus, and especially Antioch. In all of those places, according to Luke, they preached only to Jews.[136] (3) Paul consented to the death of Stephen and became even more ferocious in his persecution of Christians. In this context it may be taken to mean any one who sympathized with Stephen's Samaritan views, which Paul detested. We are thus introduced to Paul who will occupy the center of the rest of the Book of Acts.

The Rise of Paul to Supremacy in Christianity

Less than three decades after his death, Paul was immortalized as the greatest apostle of Christianity. The church's decision to consider the *Corpus Paulinum* as an inspired body of Scriptures represented the final step in the long journey of Christianity toward independence. Long before the Gospels were selected and made an official part of the New Testament canon at the end of the second century, Paul's religious teaching reigned almost supreme in the theological formulations of the early church.

The dominance of Paul in emergent Christianity remains a mystery. Seldom have historical events played as decisive a role in the transformation of the life and thought of an individual. His religious genius, which he claimed as a gift of God, allowed him to rise to a position of leadership, often at the expense of other apostles and religious leaders.

Paul was not, as often thought, the founder of Christianity. But it was to him that the early church owed its theological orientation and its ability to express Christian beliefs in the frame of universal truths. With him was born Christian doctrine, a phenomenon which allowed the rapid growth of a movement that had remained limited and almost provincial until then. Under his leadership the preaching of the Gospel could move

---

[136]Acts 11:19.

west, and the church could secure a place of importance in the political empire.

Yet Hellenistic Christianity existed before Paul's missionary journeys. Antioch had already developed along Hellenistic-Jewish lines before he appeared there at the request of Barnabas. As pointed out by Harnack, "Of the four centers of Christianity during the first century—Jerusalem, Antioch, Ephesus, and Rome—one alone was the work of Paul, and even Ephesus did not remain as loyal to its founder as might have been expected."[137] Concerning the church of Rome, whose origin cannot be determined, Irenaeus stated that it was "founded and organized at Rome by the most glorious apostles, Peter and Paul."[138]

Thus by the end of the second century a strange kind of Christian universalism was dominant in the church's perspective on its past. Paul had played a fundamental role in the development of "Gentile Christianity," though he was not the first missionary to the Gentiles. The New Testament records show him closely connected to the synagogues of the places he visited. He put the emphasis on the vindication of the New Israel which had by then been identified with the church. History proved that Paul stood at an important turning point and that "he tore the Gospel from its Jewish soil and rooted it in the soil of humanity."[139]

The relationship of Paul to the Jerusalem community has remained a subject of debate throughout the history of Christianity. Luke was unsuccessful in minimizing the antagonism between Paul and the original disciples, a negative element in Paul's missionary work which often led to a self-imposed isolationism. The extent of Paul's contact with the Jerusalem culture cannot be firmly established. Paul's speech in Acts 22, inferring that he was raised at the feet of Gamaliel, was meant to emphasize his Jewish-Hellenistic background. But even if he learned from Gamaliel, he must have regarded such an episode as unimportant since it was not included in the list of credentials given in some of his epistles.

From the biblical record we gather that Paul was seldom in agreement with the original disciples, and through direct or indirect attacks on them eroded their leadership until the group in Jerusalem was reduced to a secondary position and faded out for lack of spiritual support. The

---

[137]Harnack, *Mission and Expansion*, 77.
[138]Irenaeus, AdvHaer 3.3.2 (ANF I) 415.
[139]Harnack, *Mission and Expansion*, 57.

Jerusalem conference reported in Acts 15, if there indeed was such a conference, gave Paul the stamp of approval for the spreading of his brand of Christianity which salvaged from the historical Jesus only the events surrounding his death and resurrection.

From his undisputed leadership in the first chapters of the Book of Acts, Peter is portrayed by Luke as the uncertain and anxious soul of Acts 10, innerly torn apart by the revelation of the universality of Jesus' message which he failed to perceive.

The animosity between Peter and Paul surfaced in an outburst of Pauline self-righteousness in his letter to the Galatians.[140] This episode seems to have brought Peter's influence in Jerusalem to an end. No longer was the church to be built on Peter, the rock who, lacking some of the insights into the challenges of the time, was eclipsed by Paul and thrown into oblivion by later New Testament writers. Paul was reluctant to consider the knowledge and experience of other apostles as relevant for his message.[141] The conflict between Peter and Paul as reported in Galatians 2 presented an intransigent Paul little prepared to forgive what he considered inconsistencies in Peter's attitude. Not much is known of what happened to Peter after that incident, and even less about its immediate impact on the church. Some church fathers portrayed Paul as being in full agreement with other apostles on theological and practical questions. They proposed explanations of the censure of Peter by Paul.[142] The apostle who boasted to be endowed with the gift of being everything to everybody did not extend that favor to others.

The revitalization of Jerusalem Christianity under the leadership of James, who succeeded Peter, was far from pleasing to Paul. The hand of fellowship began to slacken. As time passed, Paul's missionary decisions

---

[140]Galatians 2:11-15.

[141]See especially Galatians 1-2.

[142]Such an attempt is found in Tertullian, AdvMarc 5.3. Cyprian, Epist 70.3 credits Peter with a conciliatory spirit in his disputes with Paul. Though he could have invoked his authority given him by Christ, Peter preferred not to claim any special privilege and seek the voice of reason when in disagreement with Paul. In Eusebius, HE 2.25.8, we find the more perplexing suggestion that Peter and Paul collaborated together in Rome and Corinth and that they suffered martyrdom at the same time: κατὰ τὸν αὐτὸν καιρόν.

were made independently of any consultation with the group in Jerusalem and, after his disagreement with Barnabas, of the church in Antioch.

The strong personality of James, however, dominated Palestinian Jewish Christianity and could not be eradicated, a fact which provoked within Paul a sense of guilt when he felt too radically alienated from what, historically speaking, was bound to remain the mother church. The leaders of the Jerusalem community often adopted a cold stance in relationship to Paul, and sometimes were openly hostile.

The Book of Acts reflects Luke's preoccupation to keep Jerusalem at the center of the Christian development and the legitimate birthplace of the church. Paul did not consider Jerusalem or any other place as the starting point of a Christian movement. The continuity between the old and the new needed no other expression than the death and resurrection of Christ. Paul knew that to obey the wishes of the Jerusalem group would have brought disaster for him as well as for his missionary endeavors. His religion may have demanded a Jerusalem-centered approach, but his understanding of the task he had to perform kept him at odds with the original disciples. It may have been Luke's purpose, as claimed by Burton Scott Easton, to portray Paul as inferior to the Twelve and subordinated to them.[143] Such a concession to the Twelve is certainly not present in Paul's own writings.

Luke and Paul leave their readers with the impression that Paul's dissociation from Jerusalem haunted him profoundly in spite of his protest to the contrary. The story of the last journey of Paul to Jerusalem amidst highly emotional pronouncements and a full knowledge of the dangers involved shows a degree of remorse in his attitude toward the saints of that city. But Jerusalem never became the center of the new Pauline churches. Christians in the early church kept their love for Jerusalem but, through Paul, they also knew themselves emancipated from the Jewish traditionalism it stood for.

Paul understood Judaism through the categories of thought of the Hellenized world to which he related his message. Whether raised in Hellenistic Tarsus or in Jerusalem, he was acquainted with the Hellenistic religious ideas of his day, often shared by the Jews of the Diaspora. His

---

[143]B. S. Easton, "The Purpose of Acts," *Theology*, occasional papers 6 (London, 1936) 19.

language was Greek. His style was often syncretistic even when he tried to vindicate the uniqueness of Christianity.

In spite of the Lukan tradition that the term "Christian" is of Antiochene origin and predates the coming of Paul there, it never appears in the writings of Paul. Yet he must have known that the term was widely used if we trust the reports of luke, especially when Agrippa protested that Paul might be persuasive enough to make him a Christian.[144] Samuel Sandmel points out that Paul, though commonly called a Christian, would have vehemently denied such a title to affirm his Jewishness.[145]

The difficulty in establishing Paul's relationship to Judaism arises from an equally perplexing task, that of defining Judaism in the first century. The variety of first-century expressions of Jewish religion as found in representatives such as John the Baptist, Jesus, Paul, Philo, Josephus, the apocalypses, and all the events that led to the finalization of the Old Testament canon at Jamnia, would frustrate any attempt at harmonizing such a system to the liking of everyone. Claude Montefiore opposes Palestinian Judaism to that of the Diaspora. For him Paul was so essentially related to the Diaspora that he shows an appalling lack of familiarity with Palestinian Judaism. To compound the difficulty, Judaism at the time of Paul could not even be adequately described since the great bulk of rabbinical literature was written much later.[146] The real thrust of

---

[144]The term "Christian" appears three times in the New Testament. In Acts 11:26 Luke gives us the origin of the term as it was used for the first time in Antioch to refer to the disciples. In Acts 26:28 it was used by Agrippa, who considered Paul a Christian. By the time 1 Peter was written, it had become a common designation for the faithful: "[I]f one suffers as a Christian, let him not be ashamed, but under that name let him glorify God" (1 Peter 4:16).

[145]Samuel Sandmel, *The Genius of Paul: A Study in History* (New York: Schocken Books, 1970) 21.

[146]Claude G. Montefiore, *Judaism and St. Paul: Two Essays* (New York: E. P. Dutton, 1915) 14. It might be interesting to speculate on what would have happened to Judaism had not Christianity come into existence. Paul Johnson, *A History of Christianity* (New York: Atheneum, 1976) 12-13, thinks that Judaism may have well become the world religion:

> Was there a real possibility that Judaism might become the world religion in an age which longed for one? Or, to put it another way, if Christianity had not intervened, capitalized on many of the advantages of Judaism, and

Montefiore's argument is that, since Paul's knowledge of Rabbinical Judaism is so limited, his attacks are of no value "as regards that particular religion."[147] Quite different is the assessment of Judaism by Sandmel, who regards it as a unified system from which both Paul and Philo drew their basic religious presuppositions: "Philo and Paul have in common that each sees in his Judaism the answer for which all Greeks, pagans and Jews, were universally searching."[148]

Whatever disagreement there was between Paul and Judaism, it came more from the nature of his missionary work than from a well thought-out theological position. In the final analysis Paul's theology was not pro- or anti-Jewish. But he was leading the new Christian movement away from Judaism and paving the way for the final separation from it. From a Christian point of view Judaism was defeated by the very weapons which Paul took from the arsenal of the Pharisaic religion of which he was an integral part and which he never totally outgrew.[149]

The role of Paul in the Hellenization of Christianity continues to be debated. The process did not start with him. It was already present in the embryonic missionary endeavors of the group in Jerusalem. Paul's knowledge of the Greek language and his acquaintance with mystery religions is not sufficient proof that he tried to model his faith and kerygma on the notions prevalent in those religions. The Hellenization of Christianity was not a logical or even conscious outcome of the proclamation of the early church. It was a subtle, slow process which drifted into

---

taken over its proselytizing role, might Judaism have continued to spread until it captured the empire?

[147]Montefiore, *Judaism and St. Paul*, 21.

[148]Sandmel, *The Genius of Paul*, 24.

[149]Klausner, *From Jesus to Paul*, 466, sees Paul's teaching as essentially Jewish:

There is nothing in the teaching of Paul . . . that did not come to him from authentic Judaism. For all the theories and hypotheses that Paul drew his opinions *directly* from the Greek philosophical literature or the mystery religions of his time have no sufficient foundation. But it *is* a fact that most of the elements in his teaching which came from Judaism received unconsciously at his hands a *non-Jewish coloring* from the influence of the Hellenistc-Jewish and pagan atmosphere with which Paul of Tarsus was surrounded during nearly all of his life.

Christian ritual and theology in the post-Pauline churches and lasted for centuries.

It is hard to determine to what extent, if at all, Paul was trained in the Greek way of knowledge. His younger Alexandrian contemporary Philo, with whose writings he may have been familiar, was by far his superior in formulating for the Hellenized Jews a philosophy which would not only preserve the uniqueness of God's revelation, but exalt it through the medium of Greek culture. Finding himself, like Philo, at the meeting point of Jewish and Greek cultures, Paul assimilated elements from both without a firm psychological or intellectual commitment to either.

Paul's understanding of Greek culture was not very deep.[150] He remained impervious to Greek spiritualism mostly on the issue of immortality. Adolf Deissmann places him among the unliterary and lower class of men of his day.[151] In fact Paul shows little knowledge of Greek masters. The quotations of Epimenides and Aratus attributed to him are found in the Book of Acts or in the Pastoral Epistles.[152] No such quotation appears in the body of his letters accepted as authentic. One exception might be 1 Corinthians 15:33: "Bad company ruins good morals" which came from Menander's comedy *Thais* and was known as a popular proverb.

The author of the Book of Acts portrays Paul as a skillful debater with the Greeks. But it has been established that most of the speeches in that book are the free compositions of Luke. This is especially true of the Areopagus address where nothing of Paul's basic kerygma appears, where the person of Christ, whose name is not even mentioned, is relegated to a secondary role, and where the major scriptural authorities for the debate are Greek poets. This is one of the most un-Pauline passages which

---

[150]Maurice Goguel, *Les premiers temps de l'Eglise* (Neuchatel: Delachaux et Niestlé, 1949) 90.

[151]Adolf Deissmann, *Paul: A Study in Social and Religious History*, trans. William E. Wilson (New York: Harper & Brothers, 1957) 48: "It appears to me to be certain, that Paul of Tarsus, although his native city was a seat of Greek higher education, was not one of the literary upper classes, but came from the unliterary lower classes and remained one of them." This approach becomes a leitmotiv in Deissmann, who portrays Paul as having no intellectual or philosophical influence in his own time, but was nonetheless a religious genius.

[152]Acts 17:28; Titus 1:12.

nonetheless throws an interesting light on the second generation Christian's attempts to harmonize Paul's teaching with the inevitable Hellenization of the Christian movement.

Paul's silence on the historical Jesus raised serious questions. He has sometimes been accused of introducing a "Christianity without Christ." Such accusations came mostly from Jewish scholars, in particular Sandmel: "Jesus as Jesus meant nothing to Paul. It was God revealed in Christ Jesus who meant something to Paul. Many of the nineteenth-century commentators read into Paul their own all-consuming interests in Jesus—and Paul simply had no such preoccupation."[153]

The slogan "back to Jesus and away from Paul" inspired many scholars of the last two centuries. One of the most respected philosophers of modern times, Alfred North Whitehead, had this to say about Paul:

> Alexandria provided the intellectual framework for Christian theology, and the man who, I suppose, did more than anybody else to distort and subvert Christ's teaching was Paul. I wonder what the other disciples thought of him—if they thought anything. Probably they did not understand what he was up to, and it may well be doubted whether he did himself. It would be impossible to imagine anything more un-Christlike than Christian theology. Christ probably couldn't have understood it.[154]

Others such as Albert Schweitzer have seen in Paul the universal center of the preaching of Jesus: "Paul is so great that his authority has no need to be imposed upon anyone. All honest, accurate, and living thought about Jesus inevitably finds in him its center."[155]

The debate on the role of Paul in Christianity in relationship to that of Jesus does not proffer any simple solution. It cannot be viewed apart from the fact that Christianity was displaced from its Palestinian soil to Gentile nations. In such a situation it is quite possible not only that the message of Paul eclipsed that of Jesus, but it is also conceivable that the sources we now have for the life of Jesus came from Paulinized circles,

---

[153]Sandmel, *The Genius of Paul*, 212.

[154]Alfred North Whitehead, *Dialogues of Alfred North Whitehead as Recorded by Lucien Price* (Boston: Little, Brown and Co., 1954) 307.

[155]Albert Schweitzer, *The Mysticism of Paul the Apostle* (New York: Henry Holt & Co., 1931) 395.

which would place an accurate account of the message of Jesus out of reach.

The historical events of the first centuries vindicated Paul's approach to Christianity and proved him the greatest apostle of the Gentile world. Paulinism determined the destiny of the church in matters of faith and practice. The question was no longer whether it was Jewish or Hellenistic, or a synthesis of the two. Paul appeared to the church of the first centuries as a man chosen by God to surpass the wisdom of the Greeks, of the prophets, and even of the disciples.

In the Middle Ages, with the progressive revival of Peter in the Catholic Church, Paul lost more and more of his position of eminence. The Protestant tradition, starting with the Reformers and culminating in Karl Barth, made Paul again the center of Christian theology.

Chapter 7

The Early Church
and Greek Philosophy

The divine is not expressible, so the initiate is forbidden to speak of it to anyone who has not been fortunate enough to have beheld it himself.
—Plotinus

Excluding the Platonists from their commentaries, present-day theologians strangle the beauty of revelation.
—Erasmus

The major aspects of Christian theology were formulated in a Gentile world. The shift away from its birthplace compelled the early church to adopt a dual position in regard to its apologetic rhetoric. The event of Christ had to keep its absolute status. The formulation of Christian theology, however, required a terminology not always available in the language of the Jewish world at the time of Jesus. Christianity was in need of a new philosophical form, and it was derived from a culture at first alien to it.

Greek was the language of a large segment of early Christianity, and in many instances the Greek conceptual framework shaped Christian tenets. The Septuagint had already served as the basic repository for translating possibilities. Hellenistic ways of thinking influenced some Christian theological beliefs. For instance, in regard to the immortality of the soul, we owe more to Platonic philosophy than to New Testament writings, where resurrection, not immortality, dominates the eschatological outlook.

Patristic Reactions to Platonic Thought

Religious ideas of Greek philosophers, especially those of Plato, became the object of extensive scrutiny by early church writers. Patristic debates endeavored to minimize the debt of Christianity to Platonic philosophy and Socratic wisdom. Critics of Christianity forced the church fathers to answer charges that they borrowed from heathen wisdom many of their tenets. Patristic literature, however, betrays a lack of unity in its reply to heathenism. It either waged war on philosophy as an enemy of Christianity or praised Greek philosophers as the forerunners of the Christian system.

Tatian and Tertullian adopted an antagonistic stance. Tatian's *Oratio ad Graecos* waged war against Greek culture in an almost fanatical way. The purpose was to show that Christian faith had its roots in Mosaic religion and bypassed Platonic or any other "barbarian" wisdom. Not even Socrates could receive praise for his sacrifice in the name of truth.

Tertullian brought more credibility to his system by showing a greater awareness of Platonic tenets. But he asserted that Christians had no choice but to reject Greek philosophy as the source of heresy.[1] Christian faith was not to be interpreted by means of Greek wisdom: "What indeed has Athens to do with Jerusalem? What concord is there between the Academy and the church? . . . Away with all attempts to produce a mottled Christianity of Stoic, Platonic, and dialectic composition!"[2]

Quite different was the approach of Justin Martyr in whose writings we find genuine attempts to harmonize Christianity and Platonism. He knew the available works of Plato and was a Platonist before his conversion. Through his doctrine of the Logos he defined a unifying principle at work among Greeks and Christians alike: "For not only among the Greeks did Reason (Logos) prevail to condemn these things through Socrates, but also among the Barbarians were they condemned by Reason (or the Word, the Logos) Himself, who took shape, and became man, and was called Jesus Christ."[3] Justin went as far as to conclude that Jesus was partially known to Socrates through the Logos.[4]

---

[1]Tertullian, Apol 46.

[2]Tertullian, PraescrHaer 7 (ANF III) 246.

[3]Justin Martyr, 1 Apol 5 (ANF I) 164.

[4]Justin Martyr, 2 Apol 10. On another occasion, 1 Apol 46 (ANF I) 178, Justin spoke of both Socrates and Heraclitus as being Christians on account of their being under the guidance of the Logos: "He is the Word of whom every race of men were partakers; and those who lived reasonably [μετὰ λόγου] are Christians, even though they have been thought atheists; as among the Greeks, Socrates and Heraclitus, and men like them." Roland Minnerath, *Les Chrétiens*

But the coming of Christ determined the limits within which Plato and Socrates were acceptable as shadowy anticipations of the parousia of the Logos among men.[5]

Origen and Clement of Alexandria gave Platonism an intellectual and spiritual status often equal to that of New Testament writers. The works of Plato (especially the *Republic*, the *Laws*, and *Phaedo*) are often quoted by Clement. In matters of justice and religion he offered the suggestion that philosophy played the role of divine revelation for the Greeks. It enabled them to live in righteousness and maintain a high level of piety. Philosophy was a divine gift to the Greeks functioning as a schoolmaster to bring the enlightened Hellenistic mind to Christ in the same way the Hebrew law was supposed to serve as a pointer to the coming of the messiah.[6] One had to discriminate, however, between philosophy as a gift from heaven and philosophy as a corrupting force. The choice of Clement was simple. The true and reliable philosophy is that of Socrates spoken in Plato.[7]

Like Justin, Clement stressed the universal inspiration distributed by the same God among all people devoted to intellectual activity. The same Logos operated in all philosophers: "Well done Plato! Thou has touched on the truth. But do not flag. Undertake with me the inquiry respecting the Good. For into all men whatever, especially those who are occupied with intellectual pursuits, a divine effluence has been instilled."[8]

---

et le monde (Paris: Gabalda, 1973) 22, suggests that, in their determination to please a pagan audience, second-century apologists did not pay much attention to the person of Jesus: "Pour eux, il est avant tout le Verbe ou Logos de Dieu. Par le biais du Logos, ils espéraient parler un langage commun avec les Hellènes de toute religion et de toute philosophie."

[5]Justin Martyr, Trypho 2.

[6]Clement of Alexandria, Strom 1.5. Clement, Strom 5.5 (ANF II) 451 spoke of the love Greeks had for the true, the beautiful, and the good as of a light which was kindled by Hellenic men of wisdom but which could not shine in full till the coming of the Messiah: "Whence the Hellenic philosophy is like the torch of wick which men kindle, artificially stealing the light from the sun. But on the proclamation of the Word [λόγος] all that holy light shone forth."

[7]Ibid., 1.19.

[8]Clement of Alexandria, Protr 6 (ANF II) 191.

To Origen rightly belonged the title of first Christian theologian. With him the new faith could finally rest on a firm theological foundation. But that foundation was Platonic and liable to throw the church into philosophical confusion. Origen's fate shifted from that of saint to heretic depending on the level of Platonism the early church was willing to accept. He was known, however, to resist the contention that Christianity was a misunderstood and distorted Platonism.[9]

Under the influence of the Cappadocians the church reached a vision of Christian civilization. The epoch-making treatise of Saint Basil—*Ad adolescentes, de legendis libris gentilium* (*Address to Young Men on Reading Greek Literature*)—became a classic of Western culture. In this short work dealing with the education of the young, Basil made a plea not to overlook the advantages to be derived from pagan literature.

It was with Gregory of Nyssa that philosophy became subordinated to the theological needs of the church. The principle of *philosophia ancilla theologiae* slowly took root in Christian thinking and dominated the medieval conviction that theology was the queen of all sciences. Gregory's attempt to free himself from Platonic influences was necessary to prove that Christianity was not dependent on a foreign or heathen way of thinking. But his discourse remained thoroughly Platonic.

Augustine more or less closed the circle of Platonizing church fathers, although in his day Platonism was already identified with Neoplatonism. Plato's influence on Christianity is discussed in books 8 and 10 of Augustine's *De civitate Dei*. There Plato was considered one of the greatest minds of antiquity, superior to many gods. He is also given a great deal of credit in the formulation of a viable Christian philosophy. The task of Augustine was to vindicate the greatness of Plato while proclaiming him inferior to biblical prophets and apostles.[10]

The debt of Christianity to the Platonic system was reluctantly conceded by Augustine who, nonetheless, praised Plato for having perfected philosophy by combining contemplation and action. Speaking of Platonists he concluded: "We prefer these to all other philosophers and confess that they approach nearest to us."[11] The major task was, of course, to make Plato agree with Christianity and not vice versa: "All

---

[9]Origen, CCel 5.65.
[10]Augustine, CivDei 2.14.
[11]Ibid., 8.9 (NPNF-1 II) 150.

philosophers, then, who have these thoughts concerning God, whether Platonists or others, agree with us."[12]

The uneasiness with which Augustine treats the systems of Plato, Plotinus, and Porphyry, especially in book 10 of the *De civitate Dei*, shows the difficulty of his apologetic goal to prove that Platonism and Neoplatonism, while they present themselves as genuine rivals of Christian theology, cannot lead to a proper worship of God as revealed in Christ.

Tertullian attempted to establish a unity between a Christian background and Platonic philosophy by emphasizing the dependence of Plato on Old Testament prophets: "What poet or sophist has not drunk at the fountain of the prophets? Thence, accordingly, the philosophers watered their arid minds, so that it is the things they have from us which bring us into comparison with them."[13]

Ambrose of Milan adduced dubious records according to which Plato traveled through Egypt at the time when Jeremiah was there, and that he shaped his philosophy on what he heard from the prophet. Augustine would have liked to keep the idea alive but had to acknowledge an egregious miscalculation of dates.[14]

When considering the *Timaeus*, Augustine concluded that it could not have been written unless Plato knew the Mosaic teachings about creation.[15] Clement had already emphasized that Plato imitated Moses in framing laws: "Whence, O Plato, is that hint of the truth which thou givest? . . . But for the laws that are consistent with truth, and your sentiments respecting God, you are indebted to the Hebrews."[16] Clement also quoted the Pythagorean philosopher Numenius: "What is Plato but Moses speaking in Attic Greek?"[17]

To make Plato agree with Christian theology became a necessity for apologists who could no longer conceive of a universal monotheism

---

[12]Ibid., 8.10 (NPNF-1 II) 151.

[13]Tertullian, Apol 47 (ANF III) 51-52.

[14]Augustine, DoctChr 2.28.43. (See also the corrective in *Retractations* 2.4.) In CivDei 8.11 a corrective to the dates still remains wrong and shows a discrepancy of about one century.

[15]Augustine, CivDei 8.11.

[16]Clement of Alexandria, Protr 6 (ANF II) 191-92.

[17]Clement of Alexandria, Strom 1.22 (ANF II) 334-35.

which would exclude all of Platonic tenets and Socratic insights. The idea that Jesus himself was instructed by the writings of Plato had gained some acceptability in the days of Ambrose, who wrote several books to refute the contention. The books of Ambrose dealing with that question are unfortunately lost.[18]

Plato stands at the beginning of a great mystical tradition which left its mark on the early church and was in evidence among the Neoplatonists and the medieval scholastic theologians, a fact that allowed Etienne Gilson to speak of a medieval "Christian Socratism."[19] Greek religion evolved from a collective piety into a mystical claim of personal religion (a fact totally unthinkable in Socrates' Athens). Even philosophy was viewed as having its origin in contemplation. Early church fathers, in their attempt to deny their dependence on Greek philosophy, often revealed their debt to a legacy they could not willingly accept, but could not totally reject without diminishing the spiritual and intellectual strength of Christianity.

Celsus's Platonistic Logic

Celsus opens the tradition of an intellectual refutation of Christianity through logical, scholarly, and polemical written works. In that regard he was followed by Porphyry and Julian. Celsus exposed the absurdity of the church's insistence on a faith that did not require any justification. That, he claimed, was contrary to anything a well-educated citizen could accept.

The most important work of Celsus, Ἀληθὴς Λόγος (*The True Word* or *The True Discourse*), is known to us only in part as quotations appearing in Origen's *Contra Celsum*. There is widespread consensus that Origen, himself a trained Platonist who studied under Ammonius Saccas in Alexandria, has preserved the work of Celsus in its essential original state. We shall never know, however, how much of it was lost.

The intent of Celsus, however polemical it may appear to us under the pen of Origen, was also highly apologetic. He wrote at the end of the reign of Marcus Aurelius, around 178. His reasons for denouncing

---

[18]Our major source on these questions comes from Augustine, DoctChr 2.28.43, and especially Letter, 31.8.

[19]Etienne Gilson, *The Spirit of Mediaeval Philosophy*, trans. A. H. C. Downes (New York: Scribners, 1940) 213.

Christianity were rooted in his conviction that it was the cause of radical shifts that led to a degradation of the empire's status and strength. He argued that Christians had become a menace to the achievements of the Romans and that they were subverting traditional culture. It had already become fashionable in those days to blame Christians for the ills of the empire.

Celsus endeavored to persuade renegade Romans that they were bringing disaster upon themselves by neglecting the old religion and by contributing to the inroads made by the church. Christians, by rejecting the Roman gods, espoused a barbarous superstition and sapped civilization at its roots.

Yet it was to Christians that Celsus directed his appeal to return to the religion of their ancestors and to venerate their gods in order to save the empire from disintegration and collapse. Even Origen agreed that obedience to the emperor must be defined in such a way that it does not incur the charge of disloyalty, while preserving Christian integrity.[20]

Parke sees in the work of Celsus the greatest challenge the church fathers had encountered, mostly in their attempt to curb the influence of Apollonian oracular centers, many of which had already suffered their death, whether or not Christians could take credit or blame for it:

> About AD 180 when Celsus produced the first comprehensive attack on Christianity from the philosophic standpoint in a book called *The True Word*, he based one of his major arguments in defence of the pagan gods on the genuineness of their oracular revelations. This threw down a challenge to the Christian apologists which they eagerly took up. Clement of Alexandria writing about the end of the century could contemptuously treat the oracle-centers as already defunct, and scornfully reject the evidence of their responses. It was no doubt true that Dodona had ceased to function and Delphi may have virtually stopped again after its temporary revival under Hadrian, but Claros was undoubtedly still in operation, though its activity may already have begun to decline and the same was true of Didyma.[21]

---

[20]Origen, CCel 8.67.

[21]Herbert William Parke, *Greek Oracles* (London: Hutchinson University Library, 1967) 144. Of note is this comment of Labriolle, *Réaction païenne*, 112: "Le *Logos Alethès* (tel était le titre de l'ouvrage de Celse) offre la première enquête approfondie dont le christianisme a été l'objet, du côté païen, et les

Origen's refutation of Celsus proceeded methodically along apologetic lines already well defined among church fathers. His speech was decidedly Christian, yet his way of thinking and arguing betrayed an intellectual sagacity indebted to Greek philosophy. It was a sort of love-hate relationship which leaves the reader wondering who won or lost the arguments.[22] Origen carved for himself a very special place in the church by analyzing and interpreting the new religion on the basis of first principles, especially in the *De principiis*, a traditionally Greek approach to philosophical investigation. This, if we trust the reports of Eusebius, also earned him the charge made by Porphyry that he introduced Greek ideas into foreign fables and that in doing so he succeeded in transforming a barbarous religion into a respectable intellectual and philosophical movement.

Celsus accused the new Christian religion of being a concoction of philosophical tenets turned into absurdities, making a mockery of the heathen virtues they stole and shamelessly reworked to fit their malicious purposes. In his reply, Origen put the emphasis on showing that the God proclaimed by Celsus was a cold being, deprived of love and care, and governing the world through disincarnated laws totally foreign to Christian theology. He refuted every argument of Celsus, leading the reader to feel that no common ground could ever be established between his ideas and those of Christianity. But Celsus was far too intelligent to succumb to tactics that had been employed before in attacks against Christians.[23]

---

polémistes ultérieurs s'en inspireront sans y ajouter grand chose."

[22]Labriolle, *Réaction païenne*, 151, puts it this way: "Origène déteste Celse parce qu'il se sent très loin de lui; il le déteste plus encore peut-être parce qu'il se sent très près de lui et qu'il ne peut méconnaître qu'il est lié à ce pamphlétaire sans pitié par une parenté intellectuelle plus profonde encore que leurs dissentiments de doctrine et de tempérament."

[23]Harnack, *Mission and Expansion*, 502, offers the following assessment: "Our first impression is that Celsus had not a single good word to say for Christianity. He reoccupies the position taken by its opponents in the second century; only, he is too fair and noble an adversary to repeat their abominable charges. To him Christianity . . . appears to have been nothing but an absurd and sorry tragedy from its birth down to his own day."

At points he introduced an argument for the universality of the divinity on the basis of religious practices that were common to many people.[24]

To Celsus's charges that Christianity was based on absurd and subversive beliefs and practices, Origen responded that many noble Greeks had espoused the Christian principles and that so-called heresies originated in sincere literary pursuits and were not the result of strife. Contrary to Celsus's accusations, there was an earnest desire on the part of literate citizens to become acquainted with the doctrines of Christianity.[25]

Christianity and Neoplatonic Philosophy

Because of its religious orientation, Neoplatonism has often been viewed as a means to rescue declining systems of belief. We could assign its origin to Philo, who was the first one to show that the categories of thought underlying Greek rationalism were indispensable tools to interpret Jewish Scriptures. The influence of Philo on primitive Christianity remains a topic of debate among scholars. Though often great admirers of his learning, Christian apologists seldom refer explicitly to his works even when clearly aware of them.[26] Philo, however, tried painstakingly to

---

[24]Origen, CCel 5.41 (ANF IV) 561. "And I think," continues Celsus, "that it makes no difference whether you call the highest being Zeus, or Zen, or Adonai, or Sabaoth, or Ammoun like the Egyptians, or Pappaeus like the Scythians. Nor would they be deemed at all holier than others in this respect, that they observe the rite of circumcision, for this was done by the Egyptians and Colchians before them."

[25]Ibid., 3.12 (ANF IV) 469. "So, then, seeing Christianity appeared an object of veneration to men, not to the more servile class alone, as Celsus supposes, but to many among the Greeks who were devoted to literary pursuits, there necessarily originated heresies,—not at all, however, as the result of faction and strife, but through the earnest desire of many literary men to become acquainted with the doctrines of Christianity."

[26]Clement of Alexandria mentions Philo's allegorical method. Strom 1.5, 23. Origen thought that Celsus knew of the works of Philo, though he may not have read them. CCel 4.51. Origen also encouraged the reading of Philo. CCel 6.21. Eusebius had direct quotes of Philo. PraepEv 322d-323d, 533a-534b. Eusebius, HE 2.17-18, undertook a listing of the works of Philo and referred to the tradition that when Philo traveled to Rome as a legate of his nation to Gaius [Caius] he met Peter there. It is hard to agree with Eusebius that Peter influenced the writings of Philo. We do, however, find hints in that direction in Jerome, Lives

unite the perfect philosophy of Plato with the divinely inspired Scriptures of the Hebrews. But all of his efforts failed to provide a convincing case for Platonism. One could speculate that he was regarded with suspicion by the orthodox segment of Palestinian Judaism because of his Hellenistic allegorical approach to the Scriptures. Some church fathers felt uneasy with his Jewish outlook which, from a Christian perspective, caused him to err. Such was the position of Augustine who considered Philo (a recognized rival of Plato in eloquence) as having gone astray in a maze of ingenious but inferior speculations. Philo failed to produce a convincing system of interpretation because it was not based on a knowledge of Christ.[27]

It was in the third century of the Christian era that the genius of Plotinus, nourished partially by the teaching of his master Ammonius Saccas, could transform the Platonic philosophy into a syncretistic religious superstructure. Very little is known of the actual ideas of Ammonius Saccas, though he has often been credited with the founding of Neoplatonism. His disciples were sworn to secrecy, and it is still debated whether Plotinus, his main student, remained faithful to his master.

Ammonius was brought up a Christian and later was converted to paganism, especially to heathen philosophy. His message was simple and in the mode of Gospel teaching: Give your wealth to those in need and turn to contemplation. He left no writings. There is, however, a claim put forth by Jerome that Ammonius was a distinguished philosopher of Alexandria and that he composed two works attesting to his genius: *On the Harmony of Moses and Jesus* and the *Gospel Canons*, works which

---

11 (NPNF-2 III) 365: "They say that under Caius [Gaius] Caligula he [Philo] ventured to Rome, whither he had been sent as legate of his nation, and that when a second time he had come to Claudius, he spoke in the same city with the apostle Peter and enjoyed his friendship, and for this reason also adorned the adherents of Mark, Peter's disciple at Alexandria, with his praises." Some scholars have taken very seriously the accounts of Eusebius that Peter came to Rome as early as 42 under Claudius, and that he influenced the life of the Christian church there long before Paul's visit to that city. See especially Roland Minnerath, *De Jérusalem à Rome: Pierre et l'unité de l'église apostolique* (Paris: Beauchesne, 1994) 136-37.

[27]CFaust 12.39.

Eusebius of Caesarea later followed. Jerome rejected the statement of Porphyry that Ammonius became a heathen again after being a Christian, and contended that Ammonius remained a Christian to the very end of his life.[28]

Neoplatonism became the dominant philosophy of the Greco-Roman world in a historical period E. R. Dodds called "The Age of Anxiety," shared equally by pagans and Christians. Most of its proponents came from the upper class of citizens, from the intellectual elite of society. But they also dealt with popular beliefs and practices which they attempted to explain in the context of a metaphysical spiritual reality. It helped paganism to hold on to the beliefs in polytheism as much as it reinforced the Christian belief in one God. Philosophy became a religious commitment:

> The idea of conversion to philosophy is particularly applicable in the case of Neoplatonism, one branch of which formed the basis for a pagan dogmatic theology, and a doctrine of salvation often in bitter opposition to Christianity. . . . In this sense Neoplatonism proceeds in the opposite way to Patristic exegesis, which is theoretically obligated to deny the truth of philosophy if it cannot be made to harmonize with scripture.[29]

Both Christian and heathen religious perspectives, however different and antagonistic they may have appeared on many levels, could find in Neoplatonism a support indispensable for their credibility and permanence. Perhaps for the last time in the long history of philosophical investigation, important metaphysical questions were restated in defense of both pagan and Christian positions.

With Plotinus, Neoplatonism reached its apogee and also the beginning of its decline. Writers praising his genius are numerous and include Christians, especially Augustine: "Plotinus, whose memory is quite recent, enjoys the reputation of having understood Plato better than any other of his disciples."[30] Augustine acknowledged his agreement with Plotinus and

---

[28]Jerome and Gennadius, Lives 55.

[29]Jay Bregman, *Synesius of Cyrene: Philosopher-Bishop* (Berkeley: University of California Press, 1982) 38-39.

[30]Augustine, CivDei 9, 10 (NPNF-1 II) 171.

other Neoplatonists.[31] He agreed with those who, long after him, still contended that the religious side of Plato's thought was not revealed in its full power till the time of Plotinus. Alfaric tried to vindicate the idea that, for Augustine, Christ was the Plato of the masses, and then concluded that, "if Plato came to life with Plotinus, Plotinus in turn came to life in Augustine."[32]

The writings of Plotinus were preserved and rearranged by his disciple Porphyry who organized them in six groups of nine treatises each (thus called the *Enneads*, "groups/sets of nine"). The *Enneads* offer an analytical interpretation of Plotinus's main religious ideas revolving around three primal hypostases: the One, the Intelligence, and the Soul. To understand one's place in the universe the soul must rise to the pure level of contemplation.[33] In Plotinus this level of contemplation transcended even Christian ideas of it. It became important for Christianity to place Plotinus within the proper mystical experience and accord him the credit he deserved, as Augustine did. With Plotinus the knowledge of the One is reached only in ecstasy, and the content of the divine vision becomes incommunicable. In an age of anxiety he was able to show a way out of despair, and the solution resided in the discovery of a salvation that no longer rested on knowledge alone. The dictum of Plotinus "to soar above knowledge" seemed to deny the Greek foundation on which his system rested. But, in the final analysis, he could not help but place the emphasis on the great final struggle which awaits every soul.

Plotinus, who represents the apex and the end of Greek philosophy, gave a new orientation to Christianity. He made Platonism almost indispensable for its survival as well as for its historic strength. What became known to the church in way of Greek philosophy after the third century was a Platonism as revised by Plotinus, a compromise which brought together Christian ideas of revelation and neo-Pythagorean views of life. This, according to Eduard Zeller, was philosophical suicide: "Neoplatonism with its need of revelation instead of independent

---

[31]Ibid., 10.2.

[32]Alfaric, *L'Évolution intellectuelle de St. Augustin*. Quoted in Charles N. Cochrane, *Christianity and Classical Culture: A Study of Thought and Action from Augustus to Augustine* (Oxford: Oxford University Press, 1940) 376.

[33]Plotinus, Enn 5.1,2. *The Essential Plotinus*, trans. Elmer O,Brien (New York: Mentor Books, 1964) 92.

investigation carried to its end the development begun in neo-Pythagore-anism and the Greek-Jewish philosophy and thus completed the suicide of philosophy."[34]

The historical mission of Neoplatonism cannot, however, be over-looked in the important phases of the Christianization of the West. It provided a rational foundation for theology as used by Augustine in the formulation of a Christian system of thought that was to prove the greatest until the Middle Ages. The contention that Augustine made Neoplatonism an integral part of the Christian doctrine need not be readily accepted. But that Neoplatonism gave Christianity a victory over contending systems such as Mithraism is more convincing. What profited Christianity in times of turmoil and conflict may have been what Harnack called a wave of Hellenization.

The strength of the philosophy of Plotinus may well be in the fact that it is not totally communicable. His disciples wondered about his teaching on God and the extent to which his soul had reached the full knowledge of the divinity. When he died in the year 270 a group of his students went to Delphi to consult the oracle about the destiny of his soul.[35] This would attest to the commitment his followers had for Apollonian religion.

With Porphyry, disciple, amanuensis, and successor of Plotinus, the investigating mood shifted radically, at least insofar as it concerned the critique of Christianity. Two of his major works can be reconstructed from quotations found in the writings of his critics. The first one, *Of the Philosophy to Be Derived from Oracles*, appears to be the result of a youthful Porphyry trying to evaluate the place of Christianity in the context of the wisdom derived from oracles. We shall not repeat here what was already said on that question in chapter 4. The second work—

---

[34]Eduard Zeller, *Outlines of the History of Greek Philosophy* (Cleveland: World Publishing Company, 1955) 312. We find a different perspective in Léon Robin, *Greek Thought and the Origin of the Scientific Spirit*, trans. M. R. Dobie (London: Alfred Knopf, 1928) 376: "Except for violent popular reactions, such as that to which the learned Hypatia, the daughter of the mathematician Theon, fell victim in Alexandria in 415, triumphant Christianity tended not so much to fight Neo-Platonism as to absorb it and to feed its own theology with it."

[35]Robin Lane Fox, *Pagans and Christians* (New York: Harper & Row, 1986) 187.

Against the Christians (κατά χριστιανῶν or συσκεύη καθ' ἡμῶν, as referred to by Eusebius who has chosen to put the accent on the notion of intrigue)—is a more direct denunciation of Christianity.

The question of sources remains puzzling. We have a fair insight into the kind of writings Porphyry produced against the Christians, but we cannot rely on their accuracy or authenticity. Many quotations have come from Eusebius, who most likely had the works of Porphyry when he wrote his *Praeparatio evangelica* and his *Demonstratio evangelica*. But his quotations lack precision and are mostly used for polemical ends. Most of them refer to Porphyry's work on oracles.[36] For the rest of the quotations we depend mostly on the *Apocriticus* of Macarius Magnes: "Fully half of the fragments which allegedly make up the book [*Against the Christians*] come from the *Apocritus* [*sic*] of Macarius Magnes with no sure evidence that they actually derive from Porphyry."[37]

Judging from his works, one would reconstruct a rather complex portrait of Porphyry. He seems to have dealt with everything and nothing in ways that often appear contradictory. Bidez has tried to summarize such a picture, while acknowledging the impossibility of the task.[38] We find a similar divergence of opinion about Porphyry in Augustine. In one

---

[36]The only quotations in Eusebius that could be ascribed to *Against the Christians* are in PraepEv 31a; 179d; 485b.

[37]Robert L. Wilken, "Pagan Criticism of Christianity: Greek Religion and Christian Faith," in *Early Christian Literature and the Classical Intellectual Tradition* (Paris: Editions Beauchesne, 1979) 118. It is not the purpose of this work to review and explain the fragments of Porphyry's *Against the Christians* as they have come to us. The *Apocriticus* of Macarius Magnes remains our major source. For a modern collection with ample notes and comments, see the work of R. Joseph Hoffmann, *Porphyry's "Against the Christians": The Literary Remains* (Amherst: Prometheus Books, 1994).

[38]Bidez, *Vie de Porphyre*, ii: "Esprit critique et naïveté, enthousiasme sincère et habile opportunisme, science solide et érudition puérile; curiosité d'un Hellène avide de savoir et de comprendre, abérrations d'un occultiste; libre allure d'une pensée qui discute et raisonne, docilité d'un croyant prêt à accepter toutes les révélations; apostolat moral très élevé, accointances compromettantes, vulgarisation lucide et facile, compilations, absurdités même, il semble qu'il y a de tout dans l'oeuvre de Porphyre; et personne n'a encore essayé ni de cataloguer et de décrire chacun de ces éléments disparates, ni de dire comment ils ont pu se rencontrer."

place he called Porphyry "the most learned of the philosophers, though the bitterest enemy of the Christians,"[39] while in another place in the same work he referred to a mystery "unintelligible to Porphyry's Pride."[40] Then he goes on to expose the impiety of Porphyry as one of the worst known to him.[41]

Most scholars would place the writing of *Against the Christians* in the latter part of the third century, probably around 270. As noted above, by that time it had become fashionable to blame Christians for the ills of the empire and for the failure of civilization. The church fathers, especially Arnobius and Lactantius, replied to such accusations. Porphyry's main purpose was to convince intelligent religious-minded pagans that the Christian doctrine was deficient, though he must have known that his verbal assaults would remain limited in their effectiveness. As in the works of his predecessors, especially Celsus, the line of argumentation in Porphyry remained philosophical and apologetic in essence. He was careful not to attack Christ or the disciples directly but to expose the lack of social and intellectual responsibility of Christians whom he considered dangerous revolutionaries. This was his way to produce a credible apology of paganism, while maintaining that Christ was a most pious person.

The writings of Porphyry marked a new approach that surprised many Christians. As a pagan philosopher he sought to vindicate the traditional religion of the empire. But he gave Jesus such high praise that it almost appeared as a contradiction. It was not Christ who was the enemy of civilization, but the Christians who rejected the traditions educated people had accepted in so many different places. It is quite conceivable, as Harnack pointed out, that Porphyry "*was quite at one with the Christian philosophy of religion, and was perfectly conscious of this unity.*"[42]

---

[39] Augustine, CivDei 19.22 (NPNF-1 II) 415.

[40] Ibid., 10.24 (NPNF-1 II) 195.

[41] Ibid., 10.27.

[42] Harnack, *Mission and Expansion*, 508. Harnack considers the attack of Porphyry against Christianity as the most thoroughgoing ever to take place, and then remarks: "It earned for its author the titles of πάντων δυσμενέστατος καὶ πολεμώτατος (most malicious and hostile of all)." Then he suggests that "the controversy between the philosophy of religion and Christianity lies today in the very position in which Porphyry placed it" (505).

Porphyry's praise of Christ as well as his attitude toward Christianity may have greatly changed between the writing of *Of the Philosophy to Be Derived from Oracles* and *Against the Christians*. In the meantime he may have had to abandon one of his dreams, namely, the integration of Christianity into the culture of the Greco-Roman world. He may have come to realize that the very nature of Christianity was the major obstacle to such a synthesis. In the words of Giuseppe Ricciotti:

> Porphyry, however, never achieved what he had set out to do—to bring Christians and pagans into one religion which would show a united front against the barbarian menace. With all his philosophical acumen Porphyry failed to realize that such a fusion was absurd and that the new wine would not go into the old bottles.[43]

Christianity was able to elevate its conception of salvation to a higher degree than what Porphyry's philosophy or Neoplatonism as a whole could provide. Porphyry was persuasive in his refutation of Christian notions of creation, incarnation, and resurrection. But his logical reasoning in those areas was insufficient to displace a theology of redemption the church had been able to bring to the level of absolute certainty. Hadot questioned the fact that there might have been any kind of credible "system" in Porphyry's philosophy.[44]

Whether or not we can assign any consistency to Porphyry's work, it can be read on two different levels, and very often the church fathers, especially Augustine, made that distinction. The first level is that of *Of the Philosophy to Be Derived from Oracles*. It influenced Neoplatonism, and its impact can be detected in the thought of Iamblichus and Damascius, mostly in their search for a definition of the divinity. The problems Porphyry raised were never solved within Neoplatonism. But from that time on, oracular religion could no longer be regarded as disconnected

---

[43]Giuseppe Ricciotti, *The Age of Martyrs: Christianity from Diocletian to Constantine*, trans. Anthony Bull (New York: Barnes and Noble, 1992) 26.

[44]Hadot, *Porphyre et Victorinus*, 1:87: "On peut mettre en doute qu'il y ait eu un "système" de Porphyre. Les 'variations' de Porphyre étaient bien connues déjà dans l'antiquité. Même lorsqu'il traite un sujet identique, par exemple la philosophie de la religion, il peut avoir les attitudes les plus diverses, depuis la bonne volonté crédule qui transparaît dans la *Philosophie des Oracles* jusqu'au scepticisme inquiet de la *Lettre à Anébon*."

from the teachings of his master Plotinus. After the death of Porphyry, Christians turned their weapons against the polytheistic ideas propounded in his writings. *Of the Philosophy to Be Derived from Oracles* provided a fertile ground for Eusebius to expose not only the inadequacies of argumentation but also the numerous contradictions on which it was based.

Quite different was the second level and the reaction of the church to *Against the Christians* in which Porphyry was relatively successful in exposing the superstitious nature of Christianity. The work was based on rationalism as it had crossed over from Greek philosophy. Porphyry was not alone in his appeal to that rationalism. Many Christians availed themselves of that weapon used mostly by Gnostics and writers of Hermetic Literature. In some instances it was the only way to solve philosophical problems. Pagans objected to the Christian use of heathen philosophy to attack non-Christian modes of though:

> Perhaps the account of the last great persecution [that of Diocletian] seemed too favorable to the persecutor in the sight of zealous Christians, and they found it easier to maim the work [the history of Zosimus] than to refute it, just as contemporary pagans mutilated Cicero's book *On the Nature of the Gods*, to prevent Christians from finding in them weapons for their polemic against polytheism.[45]

Many Christians, who never showed hostility toward the Neoplatonism of Plotinus, arose against Porphyry. The fields were different, the weapons used often the same. Among the most important Christian writers against Porphyry were Eusebius.[46] Methodius,[47] Apollinarius, who is credited with thirty books entitled *Against Porphyry*,[48] and Rufinus.[49]

---

[45]Jakob Burckhardt, *The Age of Constantine the Great*, trans. Moses Hadas (Berkeley: University of California Press, 1983) 55.

[46]Eusebius, PraepEv passim.

[47]Methodius, Fragm. In ANF VI. 382. Jerome and Gennadius, Lives 83.

[48]Jerome and Gennadius, Lives 104.

[49]Rufinus, Apol 2.12 (NPNF-2 III) 466-67. The attack of Rufinus was especially directed at Jews who chose Barabbas over against Jesus, a fact that would have been applauded by Porphyry: "And I should like to know what Porphyry, that friend of yours who wrote his blasphemous books against our religion, taught you? . . . From Porphyry you gained the art of speaking evil of

The works of Porphyry, especially *Against the Christians*, were the object of official repudiation in the Christian empire, starting with Constantine, who prohibited that kind of attack on Christianity. He ordered all the copies of *Against the Christians* to be burned, with the death penalty against those who would disobey the order.[50] In 448 Theodosius II signed an order according to which the works of Porphyry were not allowed to exist in the empire.[51] In a Christianized empire the threat of Porphyry lost its impact. Yet it was necessary to curb its influence through imperial decrees.

Christians, to strike at those who live in virginity and continence, at our deacons and presbyters, and to defame in your published writings, every order and degree of Christians."

[50]Socrates, HE 1.9 (NPNF-2 II) 14: "Wherefore as Porphyry, that enemy of piety, for having composed licentious treatises against religion, found a suitable recompense, and such as thenceforth branded him with infamy, overwhelming him with deserved reproach, his impious writings having also been destroyed. . . . "

[51]*Codex Justinianus* 1.1.3. See W. H. C. Frend, *The Early Church* (Philadelphia: J. B. Lippincott, 1966) 240.

Chapter 8

Christians and Pagans in Their Roman Environment

In our neighborhood, there are so many divinities, that it is easier to meet a god than it is to find a man.
—Petronius, *Satyricon* 17.2

Ἁπλῶς δ' εἰπεῖν, ὅπερ ἐστὶν σώματι ψυχή, τοῦτ' εἰσὶν ἐν κόσμῳ Χριστιανοί. (*Simply stated, what the soul is in the body, that are Christians in the world.*)
—*Epistle to Diognetus* VI.1

Nations of the ancient Mediterranean world, especially Roman society, could boast of strong and influential religious traditions. For Cicero, Rome was the most religious of all nations, a claim which reflected a lack of knowledge of Jewish history and customs. Yet Cicero writes:

> Moreover if we care to compare our national characteristics with those of foreign peoples, we shall find that, while in all other respects we are only the equals or even the inferiors of others, yet in the sense of religion, that is, in reverence for the gods, we are far superior.[1]

---

[1]Cicero, NatDeo 2.8 (LCL XIX) 131. This contention is further developed in HarResp 19 (LCL XI) 341:

> However good be our conceit of ourselves, conscript fathers, we have excelled neither Spain in population, nor Gaul in vigour, nor Carthage in versatility, nor Greece in art, nor indeed Italy and Latium itself in the innate sensibility characteristic of this land and its peoples; but in piety, in devotion to religion, and in that special wisdom which consists in the recognition of the truth that the world is swayed and directed by divine disposal, we have excelled every race and and every nation.

Not all Roman writers shared Cicero's perspective on the religious character of their society. Ovid attributed the multiplicity of the gods not to the fundamental

There was no consensus on the nature of religion or on the meaning of life in a cosmos that lent itself more to astrological and metaphysical speculations than to reflective piety. Platonic idealism now belonged to a distant past. The search for pure *forms* remained threatened by events that compelled the Romans to alter their notion of a perfect cosmos of order and harmony. Yet there persisted the tacit Platonic dream that all natural laws reason can discover and implement owe their existence to divine principles. Even before Plato, Heraclitus proposed that one divine law nourishes all human laws. The principle remained attractive to both pagans and Christians in their search for a divine center. From the Epicureans the Romans had learned that gods exist only as the result of people's belief in them. No divinity, however, could be burdened by the particulars of human life, or by the requirements of the universe. There was no room in an Epicurean worldview for any kind of divine providence. From the Stoics the Roman elite espoused the tenet that the essence of the universe is none else than the essence of God. The entire cosmos is controlled by God, and in the final analysis, is God. The true Stoic believed that there was within the divine cosmos peace and joy that human beings could discover through the power of reason. It was thus expected that there would be a diversity of opinions concerning the gods and that an explanation of their existence would affect social and personal lives in various ways.

---

piety of people but to expediency: "It is expedient there should be gods, and as it is expedient let us deem that gods exist" (*Expedit esse deos, et, ut expedit, esse putemus*). ArsAmat 1.637 (LCL II. 1) 57. But it was Cicero who grasped the originality of Roman religious thought and the way it bound men and gods together in contractual and legal fashions: "Piety is justice towards the gods [*Est enim pietas iustitia adversum deos*]; but how can any claims of justice exist between us and them, if god and man have nothing in common? Holiness is the science of divine worship; but I fail to see why the gods should be worshipped if we neither have received nor hope to receive benefit from them." Cicero, NatDeo 1.116 (LCL XIX) 113. Polybius, Hist 3.112. 8-9 (LCL II) 279, had already mentioned how indiscriminate Romans were in surrounding themselves with oracles, sacrifices, signs, and prodigies: "For in seasons of danger the Romans are much given to propitiating both gods and men, and there is nothing at such times in rites of the kind that they regard as unbecoming or beneath their dignity."

Roman religion was indebted to its Greek and Hellenistic background. Yet it evolved into many practices at odds with the traditions from which they sprang. Romans took over Greek religion in its more practical aspects but did not continue the philosophical and metaphysical debates about its purpose. In no sense was there a spiritual life dispensed by the divinity. Much too often poets and playwrights exposed the inadequacy of local and national gods, dishonoring them in public. Such negative portrayals of the gods did not escape the eye of the church fathers. Tertullian established a catalogue of absurdities attributed to pagan divinities and concluded, "I am not sure but your gods have more reason to complain of you than of Christians."[2]

A deep sense of destiny and fate permeated the Greco-Roman psyche. To the ordinary mortal the gods meant little. To philosophers they remained the subject of endless debates. Patristic authors chose to analyze and tear apart those debates which they considered as lacking in religious intuition and in which there was no room for faith, grace, or redemption. But it remains doubtful that Christian apologists would have had the intellectual weapons to oppose Roman religion if not for what they learned, often without acknowledging it, from Greek ways of thinking.

Religion without transcendence defined the Greek outlook. The cosmos operated according to its own laws, unrelated to any divine participation. Universality in religion would have required a perspective on monotheism, a concept foreign to ancient Mediterranean religions, except for the Jews who made it a powerful tenet of their faith. Thus the cosmos of the Greeks had no relationship to any religious history. Roman religion chose not to alter such a position. It took the rise of Christianity to revolutionize the concept of divine providence by linking it to divine creation.

In the early church the dialogue between paganism and Christianity led to increasing conflicts. It became doubtful that any common ground between the two could be salvaged. It seemed as though the one could survive only by the defeat of the other. The rhetoric often turned violent. Yet Gaston Boissier suggested that we ought to view Roman religion from two different vantage points defined by two different historical periods. Up to the reign of Commodus and more particularly Septimius Severus, Roman paganism evolved on the basis of its own internal

---

[2]Tertullian, Apol 15 (ANF III) 30.

principles. But beyond that period it sought to reform itself on the model of the Christian religion which threatened it and which it opposed. The influence of the one on the other became inevitable, and Roman paganism could no longer remain unaffected by the inroads of Christianity.[3]

Brief Estimate of Roman Religion

In his *Octavius*, Minucius Felix developed the argument that the goal of all nations, in the worship of their gods, has been to secure the dominion over the world. The more divinities worshiped, the better the chances of success. This, according to him, was what motivated worship among Romans. In their victories over other peoples they adopted their gods. That which appeared a legitimate source of greatness to the Romans was denounced by Minucius Felix:

> For to adore what you have taken by force, is to consecrate sacrilege, not divinities. As often, therefore, as the Romans triumphed, so often they were polluted; and as many trophies as they gained from the nations, so many spoils did they take from the gods. Therefore the Romans were not so great because they were religious, but because they were sacrilegious with impunity.[4]

This is of course a polemical view of religion, correct to the extent that it rests on observed facts, but wrong by its incompleteness.

The catalogue of gods worshiped by Romans on the personal, family, and corporate levels is endless. Yet the search for consistency, continuity, and stability remained the preoccupation of Roman historians and poets.

---

[3]In the introduction to his work *La Religion romaine d'Auguste aux Antonins*, 2 vols. (Paris: Hachette, 1892) 1:viii-x, Gaston Boissier writes:
> L'histoire du paganisme romain, depuis Auguste jusqu'à ses derniers moments, me paraît se diviser en deux périodes distinctes, celle où il se développe lui-même, d'après son principe et sa nature, et celle où il essaye de se réformer sur le modèle de la religion qui le menace et qu'il combat. . . . A partir du règne de Commode, et surtout de celui de Septime-Sévère, les rapports entre les deux cultes sont évidents; ils rayonnent, pour ainsi dire, l'un sur l'autre. Une période nouvelle commence alors pour la religion romaine pendant laquelle, volontairement ou non, elle subit l'action du Christianisme.

[4]Minucius Felix, Oct 25 (ANF IV) 188.

The syncretistic nature of Roman religion had to be qualified. Suetonius reports that "Augustus showed great respect towards all ancient and long-established foreign rites, but despised the rest."[5] We find an admonition in Dio Cassius against any venture to alter Roman religion:

> Those who attempt to distort our religion with strange rites you should abhor and punish not merely for the sake of the gods (since if a man despises these he will not pay honor to any other being), but because such men, by bringing in new divinities in the place of old, persuade many to adopt foreign practices, from which spring up conspiracies, factions and cabals, which are far from profitable to a monarchy. Do not therefore permit anybody to be an atheist or a sorcerer.[6]

Several centuries before Dio Cassius wrote, Epicurus had already voiced numerous warnings concerning the beliefs in the gods, mostly as they appeared in the practices of the masses of people who were fully satisfied with false opinions but seldom reached the level of philosophical concepts.[7] On this particular point Cicero provided a different perspective by suggesting that the existence of God rests on a universal consensus of all peoples.[8]

Already in the second century BCE Polybius tried to account for the rapid and dramatic rise of the Romans to supremacy. The key to that

---

[5]Suetonius, Caesars: Augustus 93, 104.

[6]Dio Cassius, RomHist 52.36.1-2 (LCL VI) 173-75. It seems that Roman religion was protected from the kind of abuse referred to by Dio Cassius. Tertullian, Apol 5 (ANF III) 21 refers to old Roman laws regulating the introduction of new divinities: "To say a word about the origin of laws of the kind to which we now refer, there was an old decree that no god should be consecrated by the emperor till first approved by the senate."

[7]Diogenes Laertius. *Epicurus, Letter to Monoeceus* 10.124 (LCL II) 651: "For the utterances of the multitude about the gods are not true preconceptions but false assumptions."

[8]Cicero, DeLeg 1.24-25 (LCL XVI) 323-25:
Therefore among all the varieties of living beings, there is no creature except man which has any knowledge of God, and among men themselves there is no race either so highly civilized or so savage as not to know that it must believe in a god, even if it does not know in what sort of god it ought to believe. Thus, it is clear that man recognizes God because, in a way, he remembers and recognizes the source from which he sprang.

success, he claimed, rested on the strength of a constitution based on religion and on a specific conception of the gods.

> But the quality in which the Roman commonwealth [πολίτευμα] is most distinctly superior [to all other known constitutions] is in my opinion the nature of their religious convictions. I believe that it is the very thing which among other peoples is an object of reproach, I mean superstition, which maintains the cohesion of the Roman State.[9]

But Roman religious practices had to be kept within proper limits. The law of the land dictated the way and the manner in which gods were to be worshiped, and the same law could be used to punish those who trespassed its injunctions. Going beyond accepted definitions was regarded as *superstitio*, literally the act of standing above the accepted norm. Romans developed a strong dislike of *superstitio* which they connected with impiety.

A reflection on the gods can never be disconnected from the nature of those worshiping them. Romans tended to show a stern preoccupation with religion, a preoccupation which developed from their constant confrontation with political and social misery and a strong foreboding of potential dangers. Fear dominated their lives more often than hope. The accuracy of religious practices became a necessity in the search for security.[10] But that security was not to be found in outward religious practices, a danger Cicero exposed:

> Piety however, like the rest of the virtues, cannot exist in mere outward show and pretence; and, with piety, reverence and religion must likewise disappear. And when these are gone, life soon becomes a

---

[9]Polybius, Hist 6.56.6-7 (LCL III) 395. See also Anders Bjørn Drachman, *Atheism in Antiquity*, trans. Ingeborg Andersen (Copenhagen: Gyldendal, 1922) 90.

[10]See especially the statement of Boissier, *Religion romaine*, 1:2:
Ces peuples [Italiens et Romains] étaient en général graves, sensés, prudents, fort préoccupés des misères de la vie présente et des dangers de l'avenir. Comme ils étaient plus naturellement portés vers la crainte que vers l'espérance, s'ils respectaient beaucoup leurs dieux, ils les redoutaient encore davantage, et le culte qu'ils leur rendaient consistait surtout en supplications timides et en expiations rigoureuses. Leur imagination manquait d'abondance et d'éclat.

welter of disorder and confusion; and in all probability the disappearance of piety towards the gods will entail the disappearance of loyalty and social union among men as well, and of justice itself, the queen of all the virtues.[11]

The goal of religion was to diminish, as far as possible, all reasons for unrest and social agitation. Consequently Romans never developed a high level of religious criticism as it has existed in Greece. Philosophical attacks propounded by writers such as Seneca were directed at the people as much as at the gods. In many instances peace with the gods excluded analytical reflection and revolved around a cold ritual that lacked appeal and credibility.

Stoic tenets have often been considered the most serious rivals of the early church's doctrines. Some beliefs common to Stoicism and Christianity led many church historians to see a close connection between the two. In the case of Seneca, for instance, the church was willing to consider him one of its own. This may be due to the power and eloquence with which Seneca translated the Stoic concept of providence (πρόνοια) into his more personal conception of the universe as the great community which binds together gods and men (*urbs Dis hominibusque communis*). There is a fellowship with God within which human beings are no longer mere spectators but cocreators of a new order conforming to divine will. Here Seneca seems to be indebted to Cicero, who in the *Laws* (1.23) speaks of the universe "as one commonwealth of which both gods and men are members" (*ut iam universus hic mundus sit una civitas communis deorum atque hominum existimanda*).

About a century and a half after the death of Seneca we find in patristic literature references to him as someone who indirectly belonged to the Christian way. Tertullian spoke of him as a philosopher "whom we so often find on our side."[12] Two centuries later the tradition persisted, and Jerome called him "Our Seneca."[13]

---

[11]Cicero, NatDeo 1.3-4 (LCL XIX) 7.

[12]Tertullian, DeAnim 20. (*Seneca saepe noster*) (ANF III) 200.

[13]Jerome, AdvJov 1.49 (NPNF-2 VI) 385: "Aristotle and Plutarch and our seneca [*noster Seneca*] have written treatises on matrimony." The attempts to make Seneca a Christian have persisted throughout the history of the church with some works openly proclaiming such a fact, as for example Schellemberch's book *Seneca Christianus*. Referred to in Amédée Fleury, *Saint Paul et Sénèque:*

In Lactantius we find a mixture of admiration and skepticism concerning Seneca: "How often, also, does Annæus Seneca, who was the keenest Stoic of the Romans, follow up with deserved praise the supreme Deity!"[14] He also quoted Seneca with approval.[15] On occasion, however, Lactantius also pointed out that Seneca shared the errors of other philosophers.[16]

Seneca was credited with having indirectly helped the Christian movement by waging war against the beliefs of his contemporaries. In that specific area Augustine attributed to him more insight and more influence than one could find in Varro, a concession Augustine did not make lightly. He then described Seneca's attack on pagan fallacies in religion.[17] That attack, however, was mitigated by what citizens owed the state in civic duty. It led to compromises which cast some shadow on the determination of Seneca to reject traditional religious practices: "Whence, with respect to these sacred rites of the civil theology, Seneca preferred, as the best course to be followed by a wise man, to feign respect for them in act, but to have no real regard for them at heart."[18] Then Augustine mentioned how Seneca summarized the best course of action in regard to a perspective on religion: "All this ignoble crowd of gods, which the superstition of ages has amassed, we ought . . . to adore in such a way as to remember all the while that its worship belongs rather to custom than to reality."[19] It is evident that Augustine knew the works of Seneca and that he used them in theological argumentation.[20]

Recherches sur les rapports du philosophe avec l'apôtre, 2 vols. (Paris: Librairie Philosophique de Ladrange, 1853) 1:2-3.

[14]Lactantius, DivInst 1.5 (ANF VII) 15. (*Annaeus Seneca qui ex Romanis vel acerrimus Stoicus fuit, quam saepe summum Deum merita laude prosequitur.*)

[15]Ibid. 2.4.

[16]Ibid. 3.15.

[17]Augustine, CivDei 6.10.

[18]Ibid. (NPNF-1 II) 120.

[19]Ibid.

[20]Ibid., 5.8. (NPNF-1 II) 89. Augustine then quotes a long passage of Seneca's Ep 107 to show how Seneca speaks of fate in terms of the supreme divinity. The passage is interesting because it reveals a great deal of affinity with the Christian way of thinking:

Father supreme, Thou ruler of the lofty heavens,
Lead me where'er it is Thy pleasure; I will give

There is some evidence that Seneca was invoked as an authority in church councilor meetings and in Christian festivals:

> In one Ecclesiastical Council at least, held at Tours in the year 567, his authority is quoted with a deference generally accorded only to fathers of the Church. And even to the present day in the marionette plays of his native Spain St Seneca takes his place by the side of St Peter and St Paul in the representations of our Lord's passion.[21]

A prompt obedience, making no delay,
Lo! here I am. Promptly I come to do Thy sovereign will;
If Thy command shall thwart my inclination, I will still
Follow Thee groaning, and the work assigned,
With all the suffering of a mind repugnant,
Will perform, being evil; which, had I been good,
I should have undertaken and performed, though hard,
With virtuous cheerfulness.
The Fates do lead the man that follows willing;
But the man that is unwilling, him they drag.

[21]J. B. Lightfoot, *Saint Paul's Epistle to the Philippians*, rev. ed. (repr.: Grand Rapids: Zondervan, 1967) 270. This information comes mostly from the work of Amédée Fleury, *Saint Paul et Sénèque*, 1:14 where we find the following comments:

> Cependant une singularité qui équivaut presque à une déclaration d'adoption de Sénèque parmi les fidèles, c'est la mention de son nom dans les décisions des conciles. Comme pour servir de corollaire à l'opinion des Pères qui rangent le philosophe au nombre des leurs, le quatorzième canon du deuxième concile de Tours invoque sa parole à l'instar d'un verset de la Bible ou du Nouveau-Testament. . . .

Elsewhere (1:289) he writes:

> On se rappelle que l'Espagne est le pays de Sénèque et de sa famille. Par suite, aux yeux d'une dévotion un peu superstitieuse, il est vrai, mais assez répandue, sa mémoire s'y est maintenue jusqu'à nos jours en honneur, presque à l'égal de celle des saints ou des bienheureux, auxquels il est assimilé.

Then he adds in a note:

> En Espagne, les montreurs de *marionnettes...* ne manquent guère, dans leurs représentations de la *Passion*, de faire intervenir Sénèque, ou même *saint Séneque*, qui tient ordinairement compagnie aux apôtres saint Pierre et saint Paul.

By the time of Jerome most of the traditions concerning Seneca had been finalized. The most intriguing development centered around the belief that Paul and Seneca exchanged a copious body of correspondence and that the early church had knowledge of it. The authenticity of the supposed letters exchanged has been seriously doubted. They are most often attributed to an unskilled forger who could imitate neither Seneca nor Paul and who betrayed flagrant errors in style and chronology. Yet, without denying or affirming the genuineness of the letters, Jerome was willing to confer on Seneca the title of saint.[22] Speculations of all kinds continued to grow around the notion that, as early as Paul, Christianity would have had as powerful a Roman ally. Eventually the idea was put forth that Seneca was a disciple of Paul.[23]

Much closer to Christian thinking than Seneca was the Roman Stoic philosopher Epictetus. Yet patristic literature almost totally ignored him in spite of his stirring perspectives on wisdom, suffering, and divine communion. No religious *Zeitgeist* of the period, either pagan or Christian, would be accurately estimated without his contributions. His religious outlook was simple and direct: "I am a free man and a friend of

---

[22]Jerome and Gennadius, Lives 12 (NPNF-2 III) 365. It is worth reproducing the text unique in patristic literature:

> Lucius Annæus Seneca of Cordova, disciple of the Stoic Sotion and uncle of Lucan the Poet, was a man of most continent life, whom I should not place in the category of saints were it not that those *Epistles of Paul to Seneca and Seneca to Paul,* which are read by many, provoke me. In these, written when he was tutor of Nero and the most powerful man of that time, he says that he would like to hold such a place among his countrymen as Paul held among Christians. He was put to death by Nero two years before Peter and Paul were crowned with martyrdom.

[23]Fleury, *Saint Paul et Sénèque,* wrote his work to promote such an idea. But the fallacies in argumentation were so numerous that it necessitated a serious refutation. Such a refutation came in the work of Charles Aubertin, *Etude critique sur les rapports supposés entre Sénèque et Saint Paul* published in Paris in 1857 and reissued under the title *Etudes sur les rapports entre le philosophe et l'apôtre* (Paris: Didier, 1972). Other works try to clarify the relationship of Paul to Seneca. See for example Jan Nicolaas Sevenster, *Paul and Seneca* (Leiden: E. J. Brill, 1961).

God."[24] His consoling and comforting philosophy was derived from a sincere belief in divine presence in the midst of human affairs. His words sometimes echoed the message of the gospel: "Wherefore, when you close your door and make darkness within [your room], remember never to say that you are alone, for you are not alone; nay, God is within, and your own genius is within."[25]

Divine essence, claimed Epictetus, is distributed in human lives through the presence of the logos: "But you are a being of primary importance; you are a fragment of God; You have within you a part of Him. Why, then, are you ignorant of your own kinship? Why do you not know the source from which you have sprung?"[26] Human misery is rooted in our ignorance of divine intention and in our inability to estimate the purpose of life: "God has brought man into the world to be a spectator of Himself and of His works, and not merely a spectator, but also an interpreter."[27] The presence of God in us should awaken us to the dangers of leading a life which does not conform to the morality revealed to us through the logos: "When God Himself is present within you, seeing and hearing everything, are you not ashamed to be thinking and doing such things as these, O insensible of your own nature, and object of God's wrath?"[28]

Divine providence for the universe creates the only reality no one can escape: "Now the philosophers say that the first thing we must learn is this: That there is a God, and that He provides for the universe, and that it is impossible for a man to conceal from Him, not merely his actions,

---

[24]Epictetus, Disc 4.3.9 (LCL II) 311. On that basis Epictetus can claim to obey God of his own free will. It is probably in the context of this passage that we got the famous epigram:

Slave, poor as Irus, halting as I trod,
I, Epictetus, was the friend of God.

This epigram has been regarded as the best summary of Epictetus's life. As a former slave, permanently injured in his weak body, he kept a vision of divine universality made real by the indwelling of sparks of the logos in every human being.

[25]Ibid., 1.14.13-14 (LCL I) 105.
[26]Ibid., 2.8.11-12 (LCL I) 261.
[27]Ibid., 1.6.19 (LCL I) 45.
[28]Ibid., 2.8.14 (LCL I) 263.

but even his purposes and his thoughts."[29] Conversely, God's presence in us allows us to draw from our own being the good for our lives.[30]

At points the words of Epictetus resemble the call to faith among Christians: "But to have God as our maker, and father, and guardian,— shall this not suffice to deliver us from griefs and fears?"[31] Divine leadership should be accepted in trust and simplicity: "We ought to go to God as a guide, making use of Him as we make use of our eyes; we do not call upon them to show us such-and-such things by preference, but we accept the impressions of precisely such things as they reveal to us."[32] Confidence in God leads to full dependence and communion with him: "Use me henceforth for whatever Thou wilt; I am of one mind with Thee; I am Thine; I crave exception from nothing that seems good in Thy sight; where Thou wilt, lead me."[33]

Equally important in Epictetus was the life of reason, the acknowledgement that the presence of the logos in us makes us rational (λογικός). It is that kind of rational life that elevates us to communion with God: "I am a rational [λογικός] being, therefore I must be singing hymns of praise to God. This is my task; I do it, and will not desert this post, as long as it may be given me to fill it; and I exhort you to join me in this same song."[34]

It is not known to what extent Epictetus knew the Christian movement or was interested in analyzing it. In his essay *Of Freedom from Fear* he compared the habits of the Galilaeans (whom we could justifiably identify with Christians) which he considers as madness to the power of reason through which God made all things in the universe. If Epictetus knew anything about Christians, he was not willing to give them much credit.[35]

---

[29]Ibid., 2.14.11 (LCL I) 309.

[30]Ibid., 1.29.5.

[31]Ibid., 1.9.7 (LCL I) 65. Some of the remarks of Epictetus in the context of this saying suggest a similarity with some of the teaching of Jesus in the Sermon on the Mount.

[32]Ibid., 2.7.11 (LCL I) 257.

[33]Ibid., 2.16.42 (LCL I) 335.

[34]Ibid., 1.16.21 (LCL I) 113.

[35]Ibid., 4.7.6.

Marcus Aurelius more or less closes the circle of Stoic philosophers. A paradoxical emperor amid troubling circumstances, he tried to vindicate the noble precepts of the teachings of Zeno while besieged by events intent on negating honor and dignity. His meditations, which often read as the product of a serene mind, were composed amid the clutter of arms in the tumult of a military camp. The Stoic apatheia and ataraxia were allowed a place of prominence only in his thought, not his actions. Yet it is from those meditations that we are able to penetrate the soul of a pagan leader whom Christians would have liked to have on their side. Perhaps the most appropriate summary of his life is contained in two of his verses:

> Whatever wind blows from the gods on high
> We must endure, and labor without tears.[36]

His *Meditations* are a philosophic diary written to himself, reflecting on what he learned from his father and from the gods. From his father he learned to be free from superstitious fear of the gods and never to count on any favors from men.[37] From the gods he learned the meaning of beneficence and providence in all circumstances.[38] With Epictetus and other Stoic philosophers he shared the notion that fragments of the divinity have been given to everyone as a guide. This is the intelligence and the reason in everyone.[39] On that basis, whatever the circumstances, divine guidance does not fail: "If the gods made plans for me and for what should happen to me, they made the right plans, for it is not easy even to conceive of a god counseling ill. . . . If they did not make plans for me in particular, yet they certainly planned the general good, and as incidental consequences of this I should love and welcome what happens to me."[40] This attitude should lead to equanimity and peace: "The gods must not be blamed, for they do no wrong whether voluntary or involuntary. Nor should men be blamed, for they do no wrong that is not involuntary. So you must blame no one"[41]

---

[36]Marcus Aurelius, Med 7.51.
[37]Ibid., 1.16.
[38]Ibid., 1.17; 2.3.
[39]Ibid., 5.27.
[40]Ibid., 6.44.
[41]Ibid., 12.12.

The most paradoxical aspect of Marcus Aurelius's tenure as emperor was his persecution of Christians. He proclaimed that "rational beings are born for the sake of each other, that tolerance is a part of righteousness."[42] Even in the case of evil men, he claimed, the gods cooperate with them to achieve good things.[43] He believed that, in the order of the universe, intelligent creatures should never injure one another.[44] Why then the persecution of Christians and a pronounced spirit of intolerance towards them?

The philosophy of Marcus Aurelius could not stand the test of events surrounding him. His quest led him to the most pertinent question: "What is the essential nature of the universe and what is my own essential nature? How is the one related to the other, being so small a part of so great a Whole?"[45] Could this be the reason why Marcus Aurelius had such an aversion for Christians whom he considered intent on destroying the harmony of the whole by their fanatic separation from what he thought should have contributed to the unity of nature? He thought that by emphasizing their particular perspectives on life, Christians made too powerful a statement against the harmony of the whole.

Marcus Aurelius considered Christian actions contrary to what benefits society, a position dear to him: "When I act, I relate my action to the benefiting of mankind; when something happens to me I accept it and relate it to the gods and to the common source in which all events are interrelated."[46]

The only direct reference to Christians in the extant writings of Marcus Aurelius is in book 11.3 of the *Meditations*. It is a rejection of Christians' attitudes to martyrdom: "What an admirable soul is that which is ready and willing, if the time has come to be released from the body. . . . This readiness must be the result of a specific decision; not, as with the Christians, of obstinate opposition, but of a reasoned and dignified decision, and without dramatics if it is to convince anyone else." For

---

[42]Ibid., 4.3. See also 9. 1.

[43]Ibid., 9.11.

[44]Ibid., 9.1: "Wrongdoing is impious, for the nature of the Whole has fashioned rational creatures for each other's sake, so that they should benefit each other as they deserve but never injure one another."

[45]Ibid., 2.9.

[46]Ibid., 8.23.

Marcus Aurelius Christianity was a religion of emotions, not of reason. He must have been profoundly disappointed by the results of the martyrdom he inflicted on Christians and by his inability to convince them of the need for a rational control of emotions. Yet on further reflection he may have discovered that Christians often welcomed death for reasons not so greatly different from a Stoic stance.

Patristic literature has not dealt extensively with the specific actions of Marcus Aurelius, though Athenagoras's *Legatio pro christianis* was addressed to him and to his son Commodus. We also learn from Eusebius that Bishop Melito addressed a book to him, the content of which we do not know. Yet several church fathers, especially Tertullian and Eusebius, reported a perplexing story which cast Marcus Aurelius in a totally different light. During a German campaign Roman soldiers were the victims of a severe drought and were dying of thirst. A few Christians who happened to be part of the Roman legion prayed for rain, which was granted, and saved the situation. It was considered a miracle by both Christians and pagans and convinced Marcus Aurelius of the power of Christian religion.[47] According to Tertullian, a document detailing the miracle was sent to the Roman Senate.[48]

Tertullian used the episode to question the way Roman law was applied after the event in respect to Christians. Though he does not mention it, Tertullian must have been in possession of the alleged letter that Marcus Aurelius sent to the Senate, in which he elaborated on the fact that Christians were the cause of his victory. The letter is reproduced at the end of the *First Apology* of Justin. The document is spurious. But it contains interesting information on the battle. It also describes the way Christians were treated after the alleged miracle and how their accusers were to be punished.

The perplexity increases as we consider the dates of those events. Justin died as a martyr during the early years of the reign of Marcus Aurelius, probably in 165. The forged letter would have had to be composed so early in Marcus Aurelius's tenure that it seems almost impossible. The epistle, if it appeared before the death of Justin, would

---

[47]Eusebius, HE 5.5.1-7. See also Tertullian, AdScap 4 and his contention that, in that particular case, pagans may have borne witness to the true God while giving him the name of Jupiter.

[48]Tertullian, Apol 5.

be in flagrant contradiction with his martyrdom. For the content of the letter see appendix 2, below.

There is no consensus on Marcus Aurelius's impact on Christianity, and no one can fully understand his paradoxical reaction to Christians. Stewart Perowne summarized his legacy as follows:

> Of all the Roman emperors, Marcus Aurelius is the most pathetic and paradoxical. In him, posterity has chosen to see all that is best in the "pagan" character—although the very word was unknown when he lived. In him is fixed all that is highest, in "the high Roman fashion"; and yet it was Marcus who was to be the harbinger of Rome's dissolution, he, the one and only philosopher king to adorn a throne, was to demonstrate how vain is philosophy, how transient a throne.[49]

In his conclusion to his history of the period which ended with the reign of Marcus Aurelius, Dio Cassius stated: "For our history now descends from a kingdom of gold to one of iron and rust, as affairs did for the Romans of that day."[50]

With the death of Marcus Aurelius in 180 the Antonine empire came to an end. It was considered a time of inner tranquility and good government. In matters of religion during the Antonine period, Gibbon gives the following summary:

> The policy of the emperors and the senate, so far as it concerned religion, was happily seconded by the reflections of the enlightened, and by the habits of the superstitious, part of their subjects. The various modes of worship, which prevailed in the Roman world, were all considered by the people as equally true; by the philosopher, as equally false; and by the magistrate, as equally useful. And thus toleration produced not only mutual indulgence, but even religious concord.[51]

There were some exceptions to that for the Christians, mostly under the rule of Marcus Aurelius.

By the time of Augustine Christian attacks on pagan religion had become less focused, more tolerant, and sometimes inconclusive. Book 6 of the *De civitate Dei* was almost totally devoted to an analysis of Varro's

---

[49]Stewart Perowne, *Caesars and Saints: The Rise of the Christian State* (New York: Barnes and Noble, 1962) 33.

[50]Dio Cassius, RomHist 72.36.4 (LCL IX) 69.

[51]Gibbon, *History* 1:73-74.

position on the gods. In it Augustine compared Varro to Cicero and invoked such authorities as Tully (Cicero) and Terentian in support of
Varro's reputation as "the most learned man . . . a man universally informed."[52] Augustine seems to extol the accuracy and completeness of the
works of Varro: "Who has investigated those things more carefully than
Marcus Varro? Who has discovered them more learnedly? Who has considered them more attentively? Who has distinguished them more acute-
ly? Who has written about them more diligently and more fully?"[53] It is
from Varro more than from any other author of antiquity that Christians
could derive their argumentation against paganism. He offered cogent and
thoughtful criticism of the nature of the gods whose worship might perish
"not by an assault by enemies, but by the negligence of the citizens."[54]

Augustine believed that Varro might have served the cause of pagan
theology through his silence more than through his writings that were
often viewed as an attack on popular worship. Augustine crafted his
response to the works of Varro along the lines of Varro's classification
of the three branches of theology as fabulous, natural, and civil. Such an
approach had already been adopted by Tertullian in his book 2 of *Ad
nationes* which he devoted in great part to a debate on the theology of
Varro.[55] Though Tertullian conceded to Varro the title of "serviceable
guide for us," his attacks on him were more forceful than those of
Augustine. At any rate, it would be difficult to deny the influence of
Varro on the cultural and religious perspectives of the early church.

Varro, and to a great extent also Cicero, forced some church fathers
to prove that Christianity was superior to civic religion. In its prophetic

---

[52]Augustine, CivDei 6.2 (NPNF-1 II) 110.
[53]Ibid., 6.2 (NPNF-1 II) 110.
[54]Ibid., 6.2 (NPNF-1 II) 111.
[55]Tertullian, AdNat 2.1 (ANF III) 129.

For he in his [Varro's] treatise *Concerning Divine Things*, collected out of
ancient digests, has shown himself a serviceable guide for us. Now, if I
inquire of him who were the subtle inventors of the gods, he points to either
the philosophers, the peoples, or the poets. For he has made a threefold
distinction in classifying the gods: one being the *physical* class, of which the
philosophers treat; another the *mythic* class, which is the constant burden of
the poets; the third, the *gentile* class, which the nations have adopted each
one for itself.

view of redemption the early church had to take the position that it is religion which reshapes history. For the pagans, history defined religion. Varro concluded that the truth of religion, which is civic in nature, should be defined by a certain elite, and not the people as a whole: "One of his convictions was precisely that there are truths which should remain unknown to the ordinary man and there are falsehoods which should be spread among the mob as truths. Civic religion was ultimately not a matter of truth but of civic cohesion: the Romans owed their empire to their own piety."[56] Such a perspective, could certainly not be shared by Christians.

Christian Faith in Search of a Home in the Roman Empire

Roman religion, and paganism as a whole, could flourish only as long as the aristocracy gave it its full support. When some members of the nobility in the empire turned toward the church, the equilibrium of paganism was threatened and, according to some church fathers, entered its final decline. Though some of the shrines of pagan gods imposed rigorous ordinances on their worshipers, sometimes more demanding that the requirements of Christianity, enthusiasm failed. On some occasions pagans acknowledged that they have been unable to stop the decline of their worship, and even blamed themselves for the success of Christianity. In his criticism of paganism Arnobius wrote:

> These are your ideas, these are your sentiments, impiously conceived, and more impiously believed. Nay, rather, to speak out more truly, the augurs, the dream interpreters, the soothsayers, the prophets, and the priestlings, ever vain, have devised these fables; for they, fearing that their own arts be brought to nought, and that they may extort but scanty contributions from the devotees, now few and infrequent, whenever they have found you to be willing that their craft should come into disrepute, cry aloud, The gods are neglected, and in the temples there is now a very thin attendance. Former ceremonies are exposed to derision, and the time-honoured rites of institutions once sacred have sunk before the superstitions of new religions. Justly is the human race afflicted by so

---

[56]Arnoldo Momigliano, *On Pagans, Jews, and Christians* (Middletown CT: Wesleyan University Press, 1987) 63.

many pressing calamities, justly it is racked by the hardships of so many toils.[57]

The role of Christianity in the progressive decline of paganism cannot be firmly established. Historical circumstances allowed and often required different responses on the part of the church. The more educated Christians chose the route of argumentation. But both pagan and Christian literature emphasized the fact that, at its inception, the Christian movement was composed of mostly uneducated people. It lacked an intellectual and aristocratic basis the pagans enjoyed. This led critics of Christianity such as Celsus to level charges of misconduct against zealous church members.

Origen refuted Celsus's arguments that the church had among its members ignorant and lawless people. According to Celsus some Christians boasted that they could go up to a statue of Jupiter or Apollo, revile it, and not fear any vengeance on their part. Origen pointed out that Celsus failed to take into consideration the fact that informed Christians would know the biblical injunctions: "Thou shalt not revile the gods," or "Bless, and curse not." Consequently Christians could neither speak nor act in the way Celsus described their behavior.[58]

A great number of Christians in the early church had no clear commitment to a strong faith or to a cogent doctrine. Tertullian wrote a stinging short piece against them in his *Scorpiace*. In it he described some Christians as the victims of all kinds of moods and doctrines, veering about with the wind and conforming to its moods.[59] Under duress or persecutions many reverted back to pagan practices. Eusebius reported a series of events in Alexandria which happened during the reign of

---

[57]Arnobius, AdvGent 1.24 (ANF VI) 418-19.

[58]Origen, CCel 8.38 (ANF IV) 653. The quotation "Thou shalt not revile the gods" refers to Exodus 22:28. But Origen does not follow the Hebrew text, but the Septuagint, which reads: Θεοὺς οὐ κακολογήσεις. His two other biblical references could hardly be understood as pertaining to pagan gods. The one refers to Romans 12:14: "Bless those who persecute you; bless and do not curse them." The other comes from 1 Corinthians 6:9-10: "Do you not know that the unrighteous will not inherit the kingdom of God? Do not be deceived; neither the immoral, nor idolaters, nor adulterers, nor homosexuals, nor thieves, nor the greedy, nor drunkards, nor revilers, nor robbers will inherit the kingdom of God."

[59]Tertullian, Scorp 1.

Decius and his decree of persecution against the Christians. After giving us stirring examples of faithful Christians who chose to die rather than abdicate, he described how some others, jeered by the crowds, were afraid either to sacrifice to the pagan gods or to die. Then he stated, "But some advanced to the altars more readily, declaring boldly that they had never been christians."[60]

A rescript against Christians which Maximinus had engraved on the pillar of Tyre contained an eloquent praise of pagan gods and a long description of all the benefits that the recovery of pagan faith had brought. These included bumper crops and many other material advantages. The rescript was also circulated in many portions of the empire with the expectation that many Christians would revert to paganism.[61]

By the third century Cyprian lamented the inevitable tendency of Christians to adopt pagan ways of life. Especially in periods of success the faith of some church goers easily adapted to the advantages of civil life and benefits. The concept of nominal Christians arose as their enthusiasm for martyrdom diminished. In times of prosperity many Christians felt it unnecessary to cut themselves off from wealth and positions of leadership. In some cases bishops took secular government positions and even became land owners. Cyprian saw it all as a relapse, as a betrayal of the blood of the martyrs and as a cause for deep sorrow.[62] Paganism remained a force to be reckoned with as it moved from success to failure, and back to success, a journey through historical events the church could not avoid either.

By the end of the second century the designation "third race" (*genus tertium* for those who spoke Latin, and τρίτον γένος for those who spoke Greek) for Christians was well known and sometimes accepted by church fathers themselves. Whatever Christians drew from Greek philosophy and culture and however great a debt they owed to Judaism, they were willing to identify with neither, though some admitted that they were a new race formed out of both.[63] Greeks and Romans were associated together as the

---

[60]Eusebius, HE 6.41.10-12 (NPNF-2 I) 284.

[61]Ibid., 9.7.1-16.

[62]Cyprian, DeLaps, especially 5 and 6. Origen voiced similar concerns in his scholia on Genesis.

[63]It is not easy to trace the development of the concept of a "third race" or the way it was used by pagans and Christians. The roots of the designation may

first race, having in common their national and sometimes foreign gods. On the basis of their exclusiveness and strong monotheistic worship, the Jews constituted the second race. The Christians, who could agree with neither and often showed contempt for both, formed the third race.

It appears, however, that the term *genus tertium* was often used by the heathen as a derogatory designation for Christians. In his *Scorpiace* Tertullian challenged the heretics to visualize a heaven free from persecutions. Then he added: "Will you plant there both synagogues of the Jews—fountains of persecution—before which the apostles endured the scourge, and heathen assemblages with their own circus, forsooth, where they readily join in the cry, Death to the third race?" (Or more literally, how long shall we suffer the third race = *Usque quo genus tertium*).[64] In his *Apology* (8 and 42) he protested the classification of Christians as being different from other human beings. They were not monsters, as sometimes adduced. They shared with all of humanity the same needs for food, clothes, and daily necessities. Tertullian was surprised by the designation *genus tertium* and would certainly not have used it himself as a sign of Christian uniqueness.

In his work *Ad nationes* Tertullian expressed his anger against those who considered Christianity a third race:

> We are indeed said to be the "third race" of men. What, a dog-faced race? . . . Take care, however, lest those whom you call the third race should obtain the first rank, since there is no nation indeed which is not Christian. Whatever nation, therefore, was the first, is nevertheless Christian now. It is ridiculous folly which makes you say we are the latest race, and then specifically call us the third. . . . Now, if they who

---

go back as early as the *Apology of Aristides* (Syriac version, 16). (ANF X) 278 where we read: "And verily, this is a new people, and there is something divine (lit: a divine admixture) in the midst of them." Clement of Alexandria, Strom 6.5 connects the idea with the apocryphal *Kerugma Petri* and the assumption that the same god who gave the law to the Jews also favored the Greeks with philosophy. But both are now gathered into a third race of the saved people who have accepted the faith. See also OracSib 1.383-84: βλαστὸς νέος ἀνθήσειεν ἐξ ἐθνῶν. Quoted in Wilhelm Bousset, *Kyrios Christos. A History of the Belief in Christ from the Beginnings of Christianity to Irenaeus*, trans. John E. Steely (Nashville: Abingdon Press, 1970) 367.

[64]Tertullian, Scorp 10 (ANF III) 643.

belong to the third race are so monstrous, what must they be supposed
to be who preceded them in the first and the second place?[65]

Long before Tertullian, Gentile Christianity had ceased to be
obviously connected to judaism, though patristic literature all along
stressed the exegesis of the Old Testament. The church also denied that
many of its beliefs resembled Hellenistic tenets. From that point of view
the designation "third race" provided a classification both pagans and
Christians could define according to their own wishes and intentions. For
the heathen who were committed to the vision of the *orbis Romanus* and
to the fundamental unity of humankind, the concept of a "third race" had
to be limited to questions of religion. Even the church fathers agreed with
that, pointing out that in all other aspects it would have been difficult to
categorize Christians as different from the rest of the people. But the
orbis Romanus presupposed unity in religion as well. Consequently the
position Christians adopted in their beliefs had to be rejected as detrimental to the welfare of the empire. As a movement claiming a permanent
role within the empire, Christianity was viewed as a kind of antireligion,
as the negation of all that brought together the traditions of the land, as
a threat to a divinely willed order that alone could maintain the harmony
of all things. Christianity represented an aberration on both the philosophical and religious levels.

Up to the end of the first century, in spite of sporadic persecutions,
the heathen world did not offer an organized criticism of Christianity. In
fact it is surprising to realize how little was known about the movement,
either on the part of Roman writers or Jewish Hellenistic philosophers
and historians. There are no references to Christ in Philo. Except for a
spurious text, which does not appear in all of the versions, Josephus
chose silence about Christ and the new sect. When Pliny the Elder wrote
his section on Palestine, about a generation after the death of Christ, he
mentioned neither Jesus nor the early church. Roman critics voiced a
wholesale rejection of the church as a superstition to be eradicated for the
sake of the unity of the empire.

Under the pen of some Roman writers of the end of the first century
and the beginning of the second, Christianity came under verbal attacks
which left a lasting impact. Pliny the Younger refers to it as a "depraved

---

[65]Tertullian, AdNat 1.8 (ANF III) 116-17.

and excessive superstition."[66] Suetonius mentions that under Nero "Punishments were also inflicted on the Christians, a sect professing a new and mischievous religious belief."[67] Tacitus chose even stronger words to describe Christians. After the fire in Rome, he reported that Nero blamed the Christians for it. Though Tacitus could no longer ignore the almost universal feeling that Nero was wrong and that he committed the deed himself, nonetheless he seemed to agree with the general aversion for Christianity:

> But all human efforts, all the lavish gifts of the emperor, and the propitiation of the gods, did not banish the sinister belief that the conflagration [the fire in Rome] was the result of an order [that of Nero]. Consequently, to get rid of the report, Nero fastened the guilt and inflicted the most exquisite tortures on a class hated for their abominations, called Christians by the populace. Christus, from whom the name had its origin, suffered the extreme penalty during the reign of Tiberius at the hands of one of our procurators, Pontius Pilatus, and a most mischievous superstition [*exitiabilis superstitio*], thus checked for the moment, again broke out, not only in Judæa, the first source of the evil, but even in Rome, where all things hideous and shameful [*per flagitia invisos*] from every part of the world find their centre and become popular. Accordingly, an arrest was first made of all who pleaded guilty; then, upon their information, an immense multitude was convicted, not so much of the crime of firing the city, as of hatred against mankind [*odium generis humani*].[68]

The gloomy and austere atmosphere within which Christianity evolved appeared unacceptable even to the most pessimistic of Romans. The withdrawal of Christians from the common business and pleasures of life and their proclamation of impending calamities ended up influencing pagans, and sometimes making them fearful of the dangers

---

[66]Pliny the Younger, *Letters* 10.96 (LCL II) 405. In his letter to trajan, Pliny complains that after he had done all he can to extract the truth from Christians he was unsuccessful: "But I could discover nothing more than depraved and excessive superstition" (*Sed nihil aliud inveni, quam superstitionem pravam, immodicam*) (405).

[67]Suetonius, Caesars: Nero 16. According to Suetonius, Christianity is a *superstitio nova et malefica*.

[68]Tacitus, Ann 15.44, 380.

the new sect was predicting. Pliny thought that their obscure conduct was deserving of punishment. If we trust Origen, Celsus's attacks on Christianity were replete with accusations that Christians formed unlawful associations marked by secrecy and obscurity, preventing their members from taking part in the normal activities of their contemporary society.

Tertullian's two treatises *Ad nationes* refuted such charges, as did the *Octavius* of Minicius Felix where we find a long catalogue of accusations against Christians, including the one that "their vain and senseless superstition [*vana et demens superstitio*] glories in crimes."[69] The treatise is an informative and enlightening argument between the heathen Caecilius and the Christian Octavius during the reign of Marcus Aurelius.

In the latter part of the second century accusations against Christians reached a new low, often based on an interpretation of their rites, such as the eucharist. Wrote Athenagoras:

> Three things are alleged against us: atheism, Thyestean feasts, Œdipodean intercourse. But if these charges are true, spare no class: proceed at once against our crimes; destroy us root and branch, with our wives and children, if any Christian is found to live like the brutes. And yet even the brutes do not touch the flesh of their own kind.[70]

The determination of Christians to keep themselves free from contamination with polytheism became more and more difficult to realize. Pagans did not understand the obstinacy of Christians, and Christians regarded polytheism as the major source of troubles in the empire. To the accusation that Christians do not worship the gods of the land and do not offer sacrifices to the emperor, Tertullian replied:

---

[69]Minucius Felix, Oct 9 (ANF IV) 177.

[70]Athenagoras, Leg 3 (ANF II) 130. The heathen parallel between the Eucharist and the Thyestean feast was especially abhorred by the Christians. When Thyestes ate his own children, he was not aware of what he was doing. This did not avert the curse of Atreus. Those in the church who remembered the impact of the curse as it was portrayed in Greek playwrights had good reason to object to the charges levelled at Christians. The charge of atheism against Christians was frequent and meant to please the crowds. Such is the argument of Justin Martyr, 2 Apol 3, against Crescens who labelled Christians as atheists and impious, while knowing nothing of the teachings of Christ.

So we are accused of sacrilege and treason. This is the chief ground of charge against us—nay, it is the sum total of our offending. . . . And punishment even were due to Christians, if it were made plain that those to whom they refused all worship were indeed divine.[71]

After a long exposition of Christian virtues and rites, Tertullian offered his challenge: "Give the congregation of the Christians its due, and hold it unlawful, if it is like assemblies of the illicit sort: by all means let it be condemned, if any complaint can be validly laid against it, such as lies against secret factions."[72]

On the strength of the information gathered from apocryphal writings, some church fathers claimed that, from the beginning, Christianity had a high level of appeal among Roman officials. Tertullian, who was well acquainted with Roman law, has Tiberius propose to the Senate that Jesus be regarded as a legitimate god. The Senate rejected the proposal.[73] Eusebius elaborated on the story, taking the account of Tertullian as trustworthy. But he pointed out that the rejection by the Senate did not change Tiberius's mind. He continued to proclaim Christ's divinity and threatened the accusers of Christians with death.[74]

The alleged action of Tiberius was prompted by a supposed report of Pilate after the condemnation of Christ. Again we find in Tertullian the puzzling suggestion that Pilate became a Christian, and that emperors were on the verge of doing the same: "All these things Pilate did to Christ; and now in fact a Christian in his own convictions, he sent word of Him to the reigning Cæsar, who was at the time Tiberius. Yes, and the Cæsars too would have believed on Christ, if either the Cæsars had not been necessary for the world, or if Christians could have been Cæsars."[75]

An extensive apocryphal literature developed around the report of Pilate, either blaming him for his actions, or making him a Christian

---

[71]Tertullian, Apol 10 (ANF III) 26.

[72]Ibid., 39 (ANF III) 47.

[73]Ibid., 5.

[74]Eusebius, HE 2.2.1-6. It has been pointed out that, if the accounts of Tiberius's position were correct, subsequent imperial actions, including Trajan's rescript could not be explained.

[75]Tertullian. Apol 21 (ANF III) 35.

saint.[76] According to Eusebius the first version of the *Acta Pilati* was a forged document full of blasphemies against Christ and his people. It was widely circulated in the empire.[77] Christians produced a new version of the *Acta Pilati* as it is known to us from the apocryphal *Gospel of Nicodemus*.

The pagan version of the *Acta Pilati* remained in circulation for a long time. As late as the beginning of the fourth century the emperor Maximin Daia made use of them to reinforce his vigorous denunciation of Christianity. He posted them in public places together with alleged confessions of renegade Christian women who had taken part in incestuous orgies.[78]

Christians had to follow an arduous road to overcome the assaults of pagan intelligentsia. The strength of the church was not yet in its traditions which were insufficiently established. At different times and in most parts of the empire Christians failed to reach any level of social acceptability. Yet in many instances there was an irresistible appeal in what the church was proclaiming, a vital force which paganism could not offer or verbalize.

Christians were offering a message of liberation and hope based on a concept of redemption and resurrection. It appealed to working people, to slaves, and to all of those who felt threatened within the Roman hierarchy. The promise of eternal happiness had its expected effect on converts from all levels of Roman society. This marked the beginning of a Christian dominance over paganism. It was formulated in the form of a dream in Tertullian: "We want to serve no longer, our wish is to reign soon."[79]

---

[76]Pilate and his wife Procla, on the basis of her dream reported in the Gospel of Matthew, were considered martyrs and saints of some segment of the church. The Eastern Church celebrates a beatified Procla on October 27. The Coptic Church still honors Procla and Pilate on June 25.

[77]Eusebius, HE 9.5.1-2.

[78]Arnold Hugh Martin Jones, *The Later Roman Empire 284–602: A Social, Economic and Administrative Survey*, 2 vols. (Norman: University of Oklahoma Press, 1964) 1:73.

[79]Tertullian, DeOrat 5. Quoted in Harnack, *Mission and Expansion*, 92.

Christian Refutations of Paganism

Most Christian writers regarded the pagan world as evil. There was an indiscriminate rejection of pagan observances, especially rites connected with astrology and divination, oracles, and orgiastic mysteries. As an example, Tatian's *Oratio ad Graecos* consisted of an unrelenting denunciation of paganism and the demons which created it. He spoke of the "trickeries of frenzied demons" (12). After giving us catalogue after catalogue of what the demons are capable of, he called on the pagans to repudiate them and follow the true God (19). No comparison could be made between those demons and the true God: "It is not allowable even to compare our notion of God with those who are wallowing in matter and mud" (21).

Yet early church apologists were more concerned about defending their faith than about engaging in a systematic demolition of paganism. In his *Legatio pro christianis* Athenagoras offered a careful and thorough investigation of all symbolic meanings devised by heathen philosophers in regard to their gods. He conceded that pagan religion had its attractive and reasonable supporters and could be considered as well equipped. But it was misplaced and lacked divine guidance: "Just as if any one should put the ship he sailed in in the place of the steersman. But as the ship, although equipped with everything, is of no use if it have not a steersman, so neither are the elements, though arranged in perfect order, of any service apart from the providence of God. For the ship will not sail of itself; and the elements without their Framer will not move."[80]

Apologetic arguments tended to reassure new converts more than to convince pagans of their errors. The transition from paganism to Christianity was often fraught with subtle dangers not clear to the new recruits. It was important to stress that demons formerly worshiped no longer had any hold or power over those who had accepted the Christian faith. They were now protected by God, and no longer the victims of injuries they had suffered before being initiated into the mystery of truth.

Lactantius called the demons (often identified with the major pagan gods such as Jupiter, Apollo, Asclepius . . .) "enemies and harassers of men" and compared them to wicked angels. They most often deceived

---

[80]Athenagoras, Leg 22 (ANF II) 140.

through oracles which many people could not distinguish from the truth.
Lactantius adduced three major reasons for the rejection of pagan demon-
gods:

> In the first place, because those images which are worshipped are repre-
> sentations of men who are dead. . . . In the second place, that the sacred
> images themselves, to which most senseless men do service, are desti-
> tute of all perception. . . . In the third place, because the spirits which
> preside over religious rites themselves, being condemned and cast off
> by God, wallow over the earth.[81]

A general condemnation of what the young had learned from pagan
mythology had already been pronounced by Justin: "We proceed to
demonstrate that they [the myths] have been uttered by the influence of
the wicked demons, to deceive and lead astray the human race."[82]

Tertullian undertook to explain why it was not appropriate for
Christians to submit to the rites of pagan religion. Christians were
accused of treason when they refused to comply with Roman religious
rites. But Tertullian denied Roman gods any real existence, making their
worship senseless: "Enough has been said in these remarks to confute the
charge of treason against your religion; for we cannot be held to do harm
to that which has no existence. When we are called therefore to sacrifice,
we resolutely refuse, relying on the knowledge we possess."[83]

Tertullian was aware of the difficulty of proving that heathen gods
cannot lay any claim to divinity, and that the stories surrounding them
must be regarded as unacceptable. He knew of the possible counter-
arguments of pagans, and he wished to preempt their strikes. Christian
religion could be regarded as having its own fables: "But at once will you
say, Who is this Christ with his fables? is he an ordinary man? is he a
sorcerer? was his body stolen by his disciples from its tomb? is he now
in the realms below? or is he not rather up in the heavens.?"[84] Such
questions and challenges lingered in the minds of new converts. They
would be unexpected on the part of pagans who would not have taken

---

[81]Lactantius, DivInst 2.18 (ANF VII) 67. The debate over demons begins at
2.16.

[82]Justin Martyr, 1 Apol 54 (ANF I) 181.

[83]Tertullian, Apol 27 (ANF III) 40-41.

[84]Ibid., 23 (ANF III) 38.

that much pain to study the details of the Christian religion. That which was a question of faith for Christians had to be exposed and explained in terms the Romans could understand.

Tertullian's appeal was for tolerance rather than theological disputes. The Christian worship of the true God should not give offense to the Romans and force them to exclude church members from social rights and privileges. In his work *Ad nationes* (2.17) he challenged the notion that the Romans rose to the mastery of the world as a result of their devotion to the gods. History plainly exhibits the weakness of those gods. The God of the Christians alone directs all of history to its fulfillment.

Debates devised to posit Christian superiority persisted throughout the first centuries of our era. The universality and eternity of God were adduced as a proof that monotheism alone was a legitimate religious perspective. Since the world existed before the pagan gods appeared on the scene, it seemed easy and logical to refute their claim to power or originality. The cosmos reflects God's presence and providence, and pagan gods were simply out of the competition. Some Christian apologists were willing to concede that heathen philosophers may have already developed a universal concept of the divinity, which transcended the traditions and rites of the populace. They found a more appealing view of the divinity in writers such as Plato, Cicero, or Seneca.

Among Christian apologists who were willing to give them some credit for their understanding of religion we find Clement of Alexandria, Origen, and to some extent Augustine. At one point Arnobius focussed the debate along the lines of natural events:

Does Apollo give you rain? Does Mercury send you water from heaven? Has Æsculapius, Hercules, or Diana devised the plan of showers and of storms? And how can this be, when you give forth that they were born on earth, and that at a fixed period they received vital perceptions? For if the world preceded them in the long lapse of time, and if before they were born nature already experienced rains and storms, those who were born later have no right of rain-giving, nor can they mix themselves up with those methods which they found to be in operation here, and to be derived from a greater Author.[85]

---

[85]Arnobius, AdvGent 1.30 (ANF VI) 421. The appeal of the cult of Apollo was a special focus of Arnobius's refutation: "Is Apollo, whether called Delian or Clarian, Didymean, Philesian, or Pythian, to be reckoned divine, who either

A century after the Christianization of the empire, paganism was still alive, having not succumbed to the predicted sudden death. Augustine wrote about the ways heathen beliefs and practices had a checkered history in the master plan of God. Death with dignity is all that paganism could now hope for. In the *De civitate Dei* Augustine offered one of the last patristic interpretations of the demise of Roman gods. In fact they never ruled anywhere in any way. He credited Plato and the Platonists with the idea that gods could not mingle with men, for that would produce their defilement. To maintain their purity, the gods resorted to demons to communicate with men. Hence the unavoidable collapse of pagan religion which was based on divine beings unable to protect themselves from contamination, while being capable of assuming the role of intermediaries between gods and men.

The argument appears plausible on the surface but may also reveal that Augustine did not treat Plato in a fair way. In Plato the true intermediary between God and man is Love. In a conversation with the mysterious Diotima, Socrates asked her to define Love, which she described as: "A great spirit, Socrates: for the whole of the spiritual is between divine and mortal . . . interpreting and transporting human things to the gods and divine things to men . . . being midway between, it makes each to supplement the other, so that the whole is combined in one. . . . God with man does not mingle."[86]

Augustine took the debate to a level not adopted by earlier church fathers. He refrained, however, from making a parallel with Christ, who also assumed the role of intermediary between God and men to fulfil that which would have remained impossible otherwise, including the redemption of the world. Sayings of Christ such as "No one comes to the Father, but by me" may imply that there is no final communication between God and man but by the intermediary of a savior.[87]

In the final analysis the contention for religious dominion in the Roman empire defined three different areas of the fourth century: the age

---

knows not the Supreme Ruler, or who is not aware that He is entreated by us in daily prayers?" AdvGent 1.26 (ANF VI) 419.

[86]Plato, Symp 202DE (LCL III) 179. For the discussion of gods and demons in Augustine, see CivDei 9.16-18.

[87]John 14:6.

of Constantine, the age of Julian, and that of Theodosius. Paganism and Christianity were redefined in ways dictated by radical shifts that no historical necessity could have predicted.

The Age of Constantine

Some events disrupt history beyond the foreseeable. Constantine's victory at the Milvian Bridge changed the destiny of the Roman empire and that of the church. The implications still echo throughout the world. They involved much more than the conversion of an individual, if indeed there was a conversion.

Our information on the religious life of Constantine comes mostly from the Latin writings of Lactantius and the Greek accounts of Eusebius. They serve as the major source of our estimate of Constantine's conversion from paganism to Christianity. Both Lactantius and Eusebius lived through political changes for which they may not have been prepared. History appeared to them in a different light, away from the gloomy predictions of the church to a vision of a Christianized world favored by God. When the great leviathan becomes a redeemer, all interpretations shift into new modes. The question of accuracy in the reports has remained a battleground replete with affirmations and accusations of all kinds. As early as the fifth century the Christian writer Socrates produced an ecclesiastical history of his own. In his introduction he states the exaggerations and omissions of Eusebius's reports on Constantine as the major reason for his endeavor.

By the time of Constantine, Christianity, though far from being a dominant presence in the empire, had progressively established itself as a relatively stable entity. It came out of persecutions stronger and more anchored in its beliefs and doctrines. It had successfully resisted and corrected a process of internal disintegration by refuting the positions of many sects threatening its unity. The church had produced apologists of the caliber of Origen, who could refute the anti-Christian arguments of Celsus. Even Porphyry's works *Against the Christians* had not achieved their predicted goal. Yet the church was by no means a homogenous body, with many theological battles, especially Arianism, still to come and to challenge Constantine's new views on religion.

Thus there was the search for a more precise definition of the Christian movement. Its history, though young, was already unclear. The unity of Christendom was still elusive. The new concepts of orthodoxy and heresy fluctuated according to the persuasion of some leaders. The views on ecclesiastical authority shifted from groups to groups. Some representatives of the church such as Origen were alternatively considered heroes of the faith or heretics. The same remained true in a Constantine and post-Constantine era, as in the case of Athanasius. Christian heresies continued to dominate the scene, often confused for the true faith. Augustine was a Manichaean for several years before concluding that it was not the true Christian way.

Constantine forged his own opinion of heresy, mostly in the wake of Arianism which plagued his tenure as emperor and which was only partially defeated in the Council of Nicaea in 325. Sozomen reported how Constantine enacted laws against all heresies. But he wrongly concluded that on the strength of the laws of Constantine almost all the heresies disappeared.[88]

The relationship of Constantine to Christianity may have begun in his young years. His father Constantius had to feign compliance with paganism, but also showed understanding and even some favor toward Christians: "Constantius, on the other hand, lest he should have seemed to dissent from the injunctions of his superiors, permitted the demolition of churches,—mere walls, and capable of being built up again,—but he preserved entire that true temple of God, which is the human body."[89] In this comment Lactantius showed the ambivalent posture of Constantius, giving him credit for his judicious decisions which prevented bodily harm to people in the church. Eusebius, probably less trustworthy in this area, suggested that Constantius was already a Christian at heart. He expelled from his palace those who were willing to sacrifice to pagan gods, while retaining Christians. Then Eusebius added this surprising comment: "Accordingly, during the whole course of his quiet and peaceful reign, he dedicated his entire household, his children, his wife, and domestic attendants, to the One Supreme God: so that the company assembled within the walls of his palace differed in no respect from a church of God."[90] On

---

[88]Sozomen, HE 2.32.

[89]Lactantius, DeMort 15 (ANF VII) 306.

[90]Eusebius VConst 1.17 (NPNF-2 I) 487. See also 1.16. The reference to "the One Supreme God" (τὸν ἐπέκεινα τῶν ὅλων θεόν) does not systematically mean the Christian God. There are sufficient allusions from his contemporaries that Constantius remained a polytheist. It has also been remarked that Constan-

the basis of such testimonies, it might be inferred that, from a very young age, Constantine lived in an atmosphere favorable to Christians, a contention bound to raise more questions than provide answers.

There is far greater evidence that both Constantius and Constantine remained well anchored in their pagan ways, though finding in Christianity an attractive alternative. As emperor, Constantine was also the *Pontifex Maximus*, the protector of the state religion, especially the cult of Apollo, referred to as his personal god (*Apollo tuus*). Several years before his alleged conversion he was present at Didyma when Apollo impressed on him that Christians were interfering with his ability to deliver oracles.[91] In Latin panegyrics praising Constantine we find allusions to his spiritual union with Apollo, often expressed in ecstatic visions. During a journey which took him through Massilia in the year 310 the emperor insisted on making a pilgrimage to "the fairest temple in the whole world," that is, the temple of Apollo Grannus at Grand. There Constantine could contemplate Apollo in the company of the goddess of Victory, bestowing on him four laurel crowns, each symbolizing thirty years of success and the promise of a long and joyful life. In that vision Constantine found

---

tine's choice of the Christian God was more political than religious in nature. In fact, Christianity did not really propound a strict unity of God and was quite satisfied with the doctrine of the trinity, reinforced in the Council of Nicaea:

> Constantine had perceived monotheism as an appropriate creed for an autocrat who aspired to rule the whole world. But the particular monotheism he espoused, Christianity, was as careless about the unity of God, Whom it defined as a Trinity, as Constantine himself was about that of his empire when he divided it among his three sons and his half-nephew Dalmatius.

Garth Fowden, *Empire to Commonwealth: Consequences of Monotheism in Late Antiquity* (Princeton: Princeton University Press, 1993) 106. In the accounts of Eusebius, VConst 1.1, Dalmatius is no longer mentioned. The empire is divided among Constantine's children. Eusebius does not refer to their names or number.

[91]It is probably about that incident that Eusebius wrote: "About that time it is said that Apollo spoke from a deep and gloomy cavern, and through the medium of no human voice, and declared that *the righteous men* [Christians] on earth were a bar to his speaking the truth, and accordingly that the oracles from the tripod were fallacious." VConst 2.50 (NPNF-2 I) 512.

himself identified with Apollo as a world ruler whose advent poets and oracles foretold.[92]

Constantine's devotion to Apollo need not mean his acquiescence of paganism as a whole. It would be a task indeed to try to provide any definition of paganism in the later Roman empire. It lacked coherence. In its own way it became a very syncretistic system which progressively rested on an amalgamation of cults, practices, and beliefs gathered from the whole known world over which emperors ruled. There was no deliberate attempt to organize or formulate a coherent system of beliefs. There was scarcely a well-trained professional priesthood and no definite religious texts that could be compared to the Bible of the Christians. Cultic practices varied from place to place and from institution to institution.

There was no safe or convincing way for Constantine to free himself from paganism as a whole. Even in its state of disorganization, paganism pervaded the structure and operation of the empire to an extent that did not allow its eradication without doing serious violence to centuries of traditions. Public and social life reflected a deep commitment to religion, even in the absence of a persuasive philosophical and theological formulation. Whatever definition one could entertain of *superstitio*, it became evident that all attempts at eliminating traditions such as burning incense on the Altar of Victory by the senators was met with insoluble conflicts.

Debates over Constantine's conversion to Christianity will continue without any foreseeable conclusion. Christian accounts in Eusebius and Lactantius failed to provide a convincing historical context acceptable to

---

[92]Edouard Galletier, *Panegyrici Latini. Panégyriques Latins. Texte établi et traduit par Édouard Galletier* (Paris: Les Belles Lettres, 1949–1952). The French translation reads: "Tu as vu le dieu et tu t'es reconnu sous les traits de celui à qui les chants divins des poètes ont prédit qu'était destiné l'empire du monde entier. J'estime que ce règne est maintenant arrivé puisque, empereur, tu es, comme lui, jeune, épanoui, secourable et admirablement beau!" PanLat 7.21.72. See also the comment offered by Timothy D. Barnes, *Constantine and Eusebius* (Cambridge MA: Harvard University Press, 1981) 36: "It is not necessary to believe that Constantine ever saw such a vision." One could also note that the coins minted after the conversion of Constantine still bear the figures and attributes of pagan gods, especially Jupiter, Apollo, Hercules, and Mars. See Gibbon, *History* 2:161.

all. Constantine's motives remain mysterious. The combination of political and religious necessities may have led him to adopt a stance which would satisfy his faith while not destroying the traditions of the empire. He wanted to secure the support of the church and may even have surmised that Christianity might win over paganism. But it is also evident that by 312 the church had not yet acquired a political status worth courting by an emperor.

The religious beliefs of Constantine in the first years of his reign before he embraced the Christian faith were nowhere clearly stated. The shift from polytheism to Christian monotheism may not have been sudden. For some time Constantine kept his Apollonian religion together with his new commitment to Christianity. Apollo was identified with the sun and often considered a manifestation of *Sol Invictus*, the true Helios, the Unconquered Sun. The Sun was celebrated as the unfailing guide of Constantine. There may have been a political as well as a religious move in Constantine's attempt to disassociate himself from the other gods, a position he could ill afford to make obvious in his role as the protector of the religion of the state.

The Arch of Constantine was erected in Rome to commemorate his triumph of 312. It did not place any emphasis on the new religion of Constantine. The victory was not attributed to Christ, as might have been expected. It did not give credit to Jupiter either. Rather, prominent in the foreground is the Sun god Apollo as the protector of the army and the emperor. On the arch we find an equivocal inscription which attributes the victory to "the instigation of the divinity" (*instinctu divinitatis*). Both pagans and Christians could read such an inscription in their favor.

Whatever interpretation one could attach to the decisions of Constantine, they represented the first systematic attack on some forms of paganism. Soon his mother Helena joined the church and became a fervent promoter of the Christian cause. Constantine himself could foresee disastrous clashes with paganism, and perhaps he was not altogether eager to sever all of his relationships with it. From Eusebius we learn that he resisted baptism to the very end of his life.[93] But as the years went by, it

---

[93]Eusebius, VConst 4.61 (NPNF-2 I) 556: "Being at length convinced that his life was drawing to a close, he felt the time was come at which he should seek purification from sins of his past career, firmly believing that whatever errors he had committed as a mortal man, his soul would be purified from them through

was unavoidable for Constantine to adopt a more global and comprehensive religious policy favoring Christianity. His destruction of paganism, however, was not of the fanatic type. The glory of what was paganism continued to be visible and to adorn the new city of Constantinople. Statues of Muses from Mount Helicon decorated the new senate chambers. Treasures from Dodona, Delphi, and other places, including statues of the gods, especially Zeus and Apollo, also graced the hippodrome and the palace itself. Eusebius saw in such a move the destruction of the idols.[94] Few accept such an interpretation. Constantine the Christian was not Constantine the iconoclast. He must have felt at home in an environment which kept the glory and the treasures of his former religion. It has been suggested, however, that by uprooting all the religious treasures from their sanctuary, Constantine made sure that he deprived them of their religious meaning.[95] But none of this brought an end to paganism, which was deprived of its externals, but not yet of its sanctuaries and rituals. The process of demolition lasted through the reign of Theodosius.

After 312 Constantine found himself in the dual role of protector of both Christianity and the *Pax Romana* which included the vestiges of paganism. The question of his personal beliefs has never been settled. The information has come to us mostly through Christian apologists with the exaggerations and distortions one would expect. There were no evident advantages for Constantine in declaring himself in favor of Christianity, unless the episode at the Milvian Bridge meant more to him than evident from his subsequent decisions. Christians were still a minority in the empire, at least from a statistical point of view. Thus we must deal with

---

the efficacy . . . of baptism." On the question of the baptism and death of Constantine, see also Sozomen, HE 2.34.

[94]Eusebius, VConst 3.54.

[95]Barnes, *Constantine and Eusebius*, 247: "Constantinople was adorned by cult objects displayed in a context which deprived them of their original religious significance." Zosimus, HistNova 2.31 gave us a quite different interpretation. After recounting in a matter of fact all the spoils of the Greek religious world that Constantine brought to his new city, including the tripod of the Delphic Apollo with the image of the god on it, Zosimus emphasized the fact that most people believed that Constantine failed to recognize the value of divine objects and treated them despitefully.

the problematic question: What did Constantine see in Christianity that might be useful to him and to the empire? Did the Christ who appeared to him in a vision require the systematic demolition of paganism?

In the nineteenth century Jacob Burckhardt wrote an epoch-making book on the times of Constantine, casting serious doubt on the records compiled by Eusebius and concluding that, to the end of his life, the emperor was in the grip of superstition for the sake of the pagan population of the empire. But Moses Hadas, in his introduction to the book, points out that Burckhardt used sources which date from the time of Julian and Theodosius rather than from the days of Constantine. This may explain the strong anti-Christian bias as well as an unwarranted attack on Lactantius and, more specially, Eusebius.[96]

Whatever the nature of any apologetic work, it is never totally free of bias. Yet in broad lines some truths are inescapable and supported by historical evidence. Lactantius reported the first imperial decision of Constantine: "Constantine Augustus, having assumed the government, made it his first care to restore the Christians to the exercise of their worship and to their God; and so began his administration by reinstating the holy religion."[97] But Constantine also desired that total peace be the supreme rule in the church. Writing to Miltiades (Melchiades), bishop of Rome, he voiced his concern about some schisms in the African church and said: "For it does not escape your diligence that I have such reverence for the legitimate Catholic church that I do not wish you to leave schism or division in any place."[98]

The most important document of the era was the 313 Edict of Milan, issued jointly by Licinius and Constantine and preserved in its Latin form by Lactantius, and in its Greek form by Eusebius.[99] The document suggested a peaceful compromise between the views of Licinius and Constantine's new religious beliefs. It was to be promulgated by province rulers. In both editions the question of religious tolerance played an essential role. The texts of Lactantius and Eusebius are reproduced in appendix 3.

---

[96]Burckhardt, *The Age of Constantine.*
[97]Lactantius, DeMort 24 (ANF VII) 311.
[98]Eusebius, HE 10.5.20 (NPNF-2 I) 381.
[99]Lactantius, DeMort 48; Eusebius, HE 10.5.1-14.

All edicts remain subject to interpretation. The edict of Milan was no exception. It was viewed by apologists as a vindication of Christianity with a prescribed tolerance for the vestiges of paganism which they secretly believed was already a discredited cause. Tolerance does not mean support. It may be the product of political expediency. Absolute tolerance never existed, and to ask Christians to tolerate paganism almost seemed to be a contradiction in terms. Constantine knew that and acted accordingly. Eusebius praised him for promoting Christians to offices of government and for forbidding the Gentiles who had such positions to continue to offer their sacrifices. No new statues or images were to be erected to the gods. Eventually the triumph of the Christian God required that all pagan divination and sacrifices be eliminated. Instead, all efforts were to be directed to building new churches.[100] The Edict of Milan corrected some of the evils Christians had suffered under Diocletian's reign. They could now recover lost lands, homes, and churches, and even secure necessary revenues for the progress of their work.

Part of the reign of Constantine could have been called the war of the temples, those he built, and those he ordered destroyed. Sozomen offered lavish praise for Constantine's unfailing zeal to erect new Christian temples in every place and especially in cities of importance.[101] Theodoret quoted an alleged letter of Constantine in which he urged Bishop Eusebius:

> Exert yourself, therefore, diligently in the reparation of the churches under your own jurisdiction, and admonish the principal bishops, priests, and deacons of other places to engage zealously in the same work; in order that all the churches which still exist may be repaired or enlarged, and that new ones may be built wherever they are required.[102]

Then he told the story of how Helena built the holy church in Jerusalem.

On the other hand we have in Eusebius a long list of temples demolished by Constantine and his troops throughout the empire under his jurisdiction. In the list we find such renowned temples as the one of

---

[100]Eusebius, VConst 2.45-46.
[101]Sozomen, HE 2.3.
[102]Theodoret, HE 1.14 (NPNF-2 III) 53. See also Socrates, HE 1.18.

Asclepius at Aegae, the temple of Venus at Heliopolis, and others in places like Phoenicia.[103]

On the battlefield Constantine had to face the fact that his army was composed mostly of pagans, and actually remained so to the end of his reign. Through the pledge of obedience to their emperor, pagan soldiers accepted whatever they felt would lead them to victory. Because of his dream before the Milvian Bridge episode, Constantine had already ordered the Chi-Rho to be placed on the new labarum, the new imperial standard, as a sign of divine protection and guidance.[104] Eusebius reported how Licinius made the connection between the new standard bearing the cross and Constantine's numerous victories. For that reason "he admonished his soldiers never to direct their attack against this standard, nor even incautiously to allow their eyes to rest upon it; assuring them that it possessed a terrible power, and was especially hostile to him; so that they would do well carefully to avoid any collision with it."[105]

The sign of the cross on the labarum was not the only change Constantine brought to his army. He also commanded that his troops, including pagan soldiers, pray regularly: "With regard to those who were as yet ignorant of divine truth, he provided by a second statute that they should appear on each Lord's day on an open plain near the city, and there, at a given signal, offer to God with one accord a prayer which they had previously learnt."[106]

---

[103]Eusebius, VConst 3.54-58.

[104]Lactantius, DeMort 44. For a description of the labarum see Eusebius, VConst 1.31; Socrates, HE 1.2.

[105]Eusebius, VitConst 2.16 (NPNF-2 I), 504. This is a surprising position on the part of Licinius who had been involved in severe punishment against Christians, forbidding some of their meetings, banishing them, confiscating their properties, dismissing from military service those who would refuse to sacrifice to pagan gods, and many other forms of persecution. See 1.51-56.

[106]Ibid., 4.19 (NPNF-2 I) 545. In 4.20 Eusebius gives us the text of the prayer that soldiers were instructed to offer to God on Sundays:

> We acknowledge thee the only God: we own thee, as our King, and implore thy succor. By thy favor have we gotten the victory: through thee are we mightier than our enemies. We render thanks for thy past benefits, and trust thee for future blessings. Together we pray to thee, and beseech thee long to preserve to us, safe and triumphant, our emperor Constantine and his

Records from the period are far from clear. The picture we gather from Christian writers is quite different from the one we collect from the writings of Libanius, a master of rhetoric who, though he was a close friend of Julian the Apostate and openly anti-Christian, had several Christian students, including John Chrysostom. In his *Pro templis* he maintained that Constantine had not changed anything in the pagan practices of the day. Even more astounding are the writings of the fifth-century historian Zosimus, who managed to tell the story of Constantine without mentioning Christianity as an institution of the empire.[107]

---

pious sons.

[107]Zosimus, HistNova. The picture Zosimus gives us of Constantine reflects a strong pagan reaction to the changes which took place in the empire during the reign of the emperor. There is a tacit acknowledgement of the influence of Christianity but no direct mention of the role of Constantine in the radical transformation of the religious scene. Zosimus has undertaken, mostly in book II, to depict Constantine as a corrupt, incompetent, and dangerous ruler. He gives him absolutely no credit for the years of stable government and for his role in the changes in civilian life and the fine arts. His extensive descriptions of the evils of Constantine portray an emperor more akin to the picture we find in Julian, but bears no resemblance to the Constantine praised by Eusebius.

The first mention of anything related to Christians appears in the context of the family murders committed by Constantine in a visit to Rome. Shortly after he had bestowed on his son Crispus the rank of Caesar he put him to death on the suspicion that he had become too intimate with his stepmother Fausta. In order to cleanse his own household of what he perceived to be impiety, he then proceeded to eliminate his wife Fausta by putting her in a bath of boiling water until she died. There is no way to verify the accuracy of the mode of death of Fausta. But the two murders created a strong rebuke on the part of Helena and plunged Rome into a scandal. Constantine sought purification from his evil deeds but could receive none from the pagan priests who claimed that there was nothing capable of cleansing such abomination. He then heard from a Spaniard that the doctrine of the Christians could wash away any crime. Thus began the religious downfall of Constantine to the dismay of the people and the senate. (2.29.71-72.)

On several occasions Zosimus mentions Christian churches, but almost exclusively as a refuge for those fleeing persecution or prosecution and seeking a place of safety. There is a tacit recognition in Zosimus that churches had acquired a sanctity which rulers could not violate. (5.8, 18-19, 29, 34, 45.)

Constantine opened a new era in the realm of relationships between politics and religion, church and state. He was often torn between political expediency and the need to balance Christian and pagan forces in such a way as not to threaten the stability of the society over which he felt providence had placed him. His commitment to Christianity did not always mean his rejection of paganism, in spite of decrees which may argue for the contrary. He had to play political games, waging war on institutions of paganism whenever the circumstances dictated it, but not beyond the acceptable. Constantine's decisions about religious practices were not free of compromise and, in some instances, he had to tolerate moral and spiritual conditions which did not agree with his beliefs.

As emperor and *Pontifex Maximus*, Constantine had to associate with prominent pagans and share their friendship. Less tolerant Christians may have seen that as a cause for concern. But Constantine knew that in any search for unity tolerance must dominate and persecutions kept to a minimum. He knew the agony of leadership in a world where diversity had often erupted into deadly confrontations.

Scholars disagree in their assessment of the reign of Constantine. It was to be expected due to the nature of the sources preserved. Jacob Burckhardt offered a vitriolic attack on Eusebius, blaming him for our false view of Constantine:

> Constantine's historical memory has suffered the greatest misfortune conceivable. That pagan writers must be hostile to him is obvious and would do him no damage in the eyes of posterity. But he has fallen into the hands of the most objectionable of all eulogists, who has utterly falsified his likeness. The man is Eusebius of Caesarea and the book his *Life of Constantine*. The man who with all his faults was always significant and always powerful is here presented in the guise of a sanctimonious devotee; in points of fact his numerous misdeeds are amply documented in a number of passages. Eusebius's equivocal praise is basically insincere.[108]

Johnson pointed out the megalomania of Constantine, not only in his life, but also in his death: "His coffin and tomb, in fact, were placed in the centre, with monuments to six apostles on each side, making him the

---

[108]Burckhardt, *Age of Constantine*, 260-61.

thirteenth and chief; and he contrived to die on Whitsunday." Then he adds:

> How could the Christian church, apparently quite willingly, accommodate this weird megalomaniac in its theocratic system? Was there a conscious bargain? Which side benefited most from this unseemly marriage between church and state? Or, to put it another way, did the empire surrender to Christianity, or did Christianity prostitute itself the the empire?[109]

Arnold Hugh Martin Jones, a foremost scholar on the history of the Roman empire, does not have many kind words for Constantine either, denying that he deserves such titles as "great" or "saint" which have been bestowed on him. His temper, his lack of firmness of purpose, and even his spiritual leadership are not altogether praiseworthy. There is a title, however, that he deserves: "To the other title which the Orthodox Church has bestowed upon him, 'The Peer of the Apostles,' he has a better claim, for his career profoundly influenced the history of the church and the future of Christianity."[110]

At the death of Constantine neither the omphalos nor the cross could claim victory nor were they placed in a position to have to acknowledge defeat. Christian apologists continued to wage war on paganism during the reign of the sons of Constantine, Constantius and Constans. The most outspoken Christian writer of the era, Firmicus Maternus, wrote a scathing attack on paganism, *The Error of the Pagan Religions* (*De errore profanarum religionum*). Maternus was annoyed by the policies of tolerance of Constantine and hoped to convince the new emperors of the necessity for more drastic measures. It had some effect, as Constantius issued an edict in 341 ordering the end of superstition and of sacrifices. It is unclear, however, to what extent the sons of Constantine were willing to depart from the policies of their father. The concept of tolerance was as elusive as that of authority. Quite often the antipagan laws had to be enforced by pagan administrators, ensuring the lack of result and the hesitation to pursue those who failed to uphold the law to the letter.

---

[109]Johnson, *History*, 69.

[110]Arnold Hugh Martin Jones, *Constantine and the Conversion of Europe* (Baltimore: Pelican, 1972) 233.

Firmicus Maternus showed his inclination toward fanaticism rather than rational discourse:

> These practices [paganism] must be eradicated, Most Holy Emperors [Constantius and Constans], utterly eradicated and abolished. All must be set aright by the severest laws of your edicts, so that the ruinous error of this delusion may no longer besmirch the Roman world, so that the wickedness of this pestilential usage may no longer wax strong.[111]

For all practical purposes paganism was not eradicated. It produced one its strongest defenders in the person of the emperor Julian, who was spared because of his youth in a massacre ordered by Constantius, though his father and other members of the family perished.[112]

The Age of Julian

The short reign of Julian revealed the vulnerability of the Christian movement and the deep entrenchment of pagan philosophy and religion. Julian symbolized in his own person the turmoil of the times. He received a Christian education while turning his attention to Greek classics. But he did not reveal openly his commitment to pagan religion, which he fully intended to reinstitute, until he became emperor. He would have rather pursued his studies at Athens, but fate put him in charge of the empire.[113]

The first part of Julian's education took place during his forced six-year exile at Marcellum under a tutor called Mardonius. It was strictly Christian. After his release from exile, which he shared with his brother Gallus, Julian returned to Constantinople. When his attempts at classical training were discovered, he was forced by Constantius to another kind of exile at Nicomedia. He stayed there until the death of his guardian, Bishop Eusebius. It may even be contended that in his young years he

---

[111]Firmicus Maternus, *The Error of the Pagan Religions* (New York: Newman Press, 1970) 77-78.

[112]We have a firsthand account by Julian of the brutality of Constantius against his own family. In Ath 270CD, he reflects on his blood relationship to Constantius, on how Constantius put most of the family to death without trial, which included Julian's father, and on how Julian himself was spared but sent to exile with one of his brothers.

[113]In Them 260B, Julian tells us why he would have preferred Athens to all the pomp of his office.

was a devoted Christian. Later in life he demonstrated a thorough knowledge of the biblical text and of patristic literature. But all efforts at keeping him around Christian tutors and away from pagan teachers only increased Julian's impatience and strong desire to develop his own approach to life. Hence the difficulty in eliminating some contradictory information about him and his religious background.

In spite of attempts from his entourage to keep him away from pagan influences during his young years, he procured himself the orations of Libanius, and admired them. He began rejecting his Christian upbringing when he became a disciple of Greek literature and philosophy.

Yet Julian's admiration for Neoplatonic paganism was kept officially secret before his ascension to the throne, though it was evident to many in the empire. To avoid Constantius's displeasure Julian affected an outward compliance with Christian practices, a facade he shed as soon as it was safe for him to do so.[114] We learn from his letter 47, written to the Alexandrians in 362 that, at that time, he had already ceased to be a Christian for twelve years. Ammianus Marcellinus elaborated on the situation and on how Julian was forced to feign compliance with the Christian religion while abhorring it.[115]

---

[114]Ammianus Marcellinus, though not a Christian himself and though he shows a lack of acquaintance with the church's traditions, describes at length the appointment of Julian by Constantius II. After a long speech he concluded: "Let this young man of quiet strength, whose temperate behavior is rather to be imitated than proclaimed, rise to receive this honour conferred upon him by God's favour. . . . Therefore with the immediate favour of the God of Heaven I will invest him with the imperial robes." ResGest 15.8.9-10 (LCL I) 169. But as soon as Julian accepted the rule of Gaul, when he reached the city of Vienne, he was already heard declaring that he would repair the temples of the gods. ResGest 15.8.22.

[115]An example of the dual approach to religion on the part of Julian is given by Ammianus Marcellinus. The episode takes place in Vienne: "In order to win the favour of all men and have opposition from none, he pretended to be an adherent of the Christian religion, from which he had long since secretly revolted; and making a few men sharers in his secret, he was given up to soothsaying and auguries, and to other practices which the worshippers of the pagan gods have always followed." ResGest 21.2.4 (LCL II) 99-101. He then commented on the fact that Julian went to the Christian church for the festival of Epiphany and acted as if he were a Christian.

Libanius, a close friend of Julian, explained the dual attitude of the emperor as necessary prudence in a volatile world. In the first months of his reign Julian still sought the support of Christians for reason of expediency. But he soon became vocal against them as being the ungodly. At that point his verve and intellectual inflexibility were matched only by his strong and deliberate asceticism.

Julian's rejection of Christianity was motivated by his conviction that the Sun God alone should be the object of worship. This was made manifest in his long *Hymn to King Helios*, and in his adoration of Mithra where he found the best expression of a pure cult to his intellectual Sun God.[116]

The initiation of Julian into Mithraic mysteries did not diminish his devotion to Apollo whom he regarded as the equal of Mithra:

And Apollo himself also we called to witness to our statements, since it is certainly likely that he knows better than we about his own nature. For he too abides with Helios and is his colleague by reason of the singleness of his thoughts and the stability of his substance and the consistency of his activity.[117]

Apollonian oracles continued to spread in the empire.[118] But the younger religion of Mithra was bound to dominate: "If after this I should say that we also worship Mithras and celebrate games in honour of Helios every four years, I shall be speaking of customs that are somewhat recent."[119]

Julian's opposition to Christianity lacked clarity and cogency. He must have seen in that religion more than misguided practices or supersti-

---

[116]It would be far too complex and time consuming to give a summary of Mithraism. It was a powerful cult, often considered a dangerous rival of Christianity, but about which we have but very few records. Seldom has a religion become so attractive and so successful without a definite organization and a precise orientation. Ernest Renan believed that it is a sheer historical accident that determined whether Christianity or Mithraism would dominate the religious scene. For a concise introduction to the mysteries of Mithraism see the work of David Ulansey, *The Origins of the Mithraic Mysteries: Cosmology and Salvation in the Ancient World* (Oxford: Oxford University Press, 1989).

[117]Julian, HymnHel 143D-144A (LCL I) 391-93.

[118]Ibid., 152D.

[119]Ibid., 155A (LCL I) 425.

tious beliefs to be eradicated. After all, he earned for himself the title of apostate, and history remembers him as such. His attempt to reinstate paganism has often been seen as much more than a conflict between different religious tenets. The battle transcended social and political necessities. For Julian it was a question of the mind and the heart.[120]

The personality of Julian is far too complex, and his religious loyalties far too perplexing to draw a definite picture of his feelings and ambitions. Nor can we understand fully his relationship to Christianity, a relationship that was marked by both tolerance and profound aversion. He found in Jewish religion and customs an unexpected ally, which he transformed into a weapon against Christians, whom he called Galilaeans.

There is no logical explanation for Julian's choice of the Jewish religion as an exemplary ritual system. By the fourth century both Christianity and Judaism had developed a skillful relationship to Roman authorities. Their quest for recognition, and sometimes for power, was not annihilated by oppositions and persecutions. The Christian movement had already produced such legal minds as Tertullian. Judaism had often enjoyed a privileged status in the empire. Julian may have become concerned that Christian domination was enhanced by anti-Jewish legislation decreed by some of his predecessors. He may have calculated that an intellectual and verbal attack on Christians would strengthen the Jewish position and make it more acceptable to pagans in his overall purpose.

We may find a clue to Julian's assessment of Judaism in his own words:

> The Jews agree with the Gentiles, except that they believe in only one God. That is indeed peculiar to them and strange to us; since all the rest we have in a manner in common with them—temples, sanctuaries,

---

[120]Ernest Renan estimated the situation in the following statement:

Si le rétablissement du paganisme ne devait servir qu'à relever les grossières superstitions dont on voit cet empereur sans cesse préoccupé, on ne comprend guère qu'un homme de tant d'esprit se soit donné pour d'aussi plates follies le mauvais nom d'apostat.

Nouvelles études d'histoire religieuse. Quoted in Labriolle, *Réaction païenne,* 391.

altars, purifications, and certain precepts. For as to these we differ from one another either not at all or in trivial matters.[121]

Julian's assertion that Jews agree with the Gentiles may strike us as a curious inference hard to support historically. Even more surprising are the ways in which he elevated Jews to models of religious reform. When he appointed Theodorus to revitalize the pagan temples in Asia he encouraged him to make the Jews the models to be followed by pagans. This was the surest defense against the "disease of the Galilaeans."[122] It might also be conjectured, as Wayne Meeks and Robert Wilken have, that the interest of friend and mentor Libanius in the Jewish cause in Antioch may have influenced Julian in his praise of Judaism.[123]

Julian's reliance on some kind of alliance between Jews and Gentiles against Christians was not as unprecedented as it seemed. It may have belonged to the Neoplatonic tradition which constituted the backbone of his education.[124] Some scholars have even suggested that Julian's move

---

[121]Julian, CGal 306B (LCL III) 407. There is little doubt that Julian's treatise *Contra Galilaeos* represents his major attack on Christianity. But the original text was lost, and we do not really know exactly what it contained. The text as we have it now comes from the quotations by Cyril of Alexandria which were included in his refutation of Julian. It is from those quotations of Cyril that Neumann reconstructed a great portion of the text which we now find in the *Loeb Classical Library*. More details are given in Wilmer C. Wright's introduction to Julian's *Contra Galilaeos* in LCL III, 313-17. We know from Cyril's own admission that he omitted many of Julian's invectives against Christ, so as to avoid disturbing Christians uselessly. But without the quotations of Cyril very little of the present work of Julian would be known. We must, however, read it with the caveat that we are dealing with the reports of a hostile witness and apologist. Scholars may find a special interest in the the bilingual (Greek and Latin) edition of J. P. Migne's *Patrologia Graeca* which includes the works of Cyril of Alexandria (vols. 68–77).

[122]Julian, Theod 453D-454B. At the end of the letter, though, he accuses the Jews of folly for not recognizing other gods.

[123]Wayne A. Meeks and Robert L. Wilken, *Jews and Christians in Antioch in the First Four Centuries of the Common Era* (Missoula MT: Scholars Press, 1978) 28. The authors have also reproduced the nine letters of Libanius dealing with the Jewish question, 59-66.

[124]Joseph Vogt, *Kaiser Julian und das Judentum: Studien zum Weltanschauungskampf der Spätantike* (Leipzig: J. C. Hinrichs, 1939) as mentioned in Meeks

to Antioch rested in part on the assumption that the large Jewish community there would prove of a great support to him.[125] Whatever the case, he considered both Jews and pagans as the proper vindicators of long-standing religious traditions, rites, and ceremonies, all of which were threatened by the Galilaeans. The concept of *religio licita* had shifted again.

Julian's love for sacrifices led him to seek the support of the Jewish religion which could boast of the best organized ritual system. As a disciple of Neoplatonic philosophy Julian was aware of what Iamblichus suggested in his *De mysteriis*, namely that without the proper sacrifices the gods would not accept any form of worship, and all prayers would remain incomplete and, therefore, useless. But Julian could not have ignored the fact that Jewish religion, as it was expressed in the synagogue, no longer rested on sacrifices. Not only had the prophetic voice of old seriously undermined the Jewish concept of ritual religion, but sacrifices had totally disappeared in the diaspora, and for that matter even in Jerusalem after the fall and destruction of the temple in 70. Hence the obsession of Julian with the rebuilding of the Jewish temple, the only way to reinstitute Jewish sacrifices.

The writings of Julian, whether accepted as authentic or rejected as forgeries, do not allow us to explain his admiration of the Jews, nor to summarize his position in any definite form. He may deserve our indulgence for having composed some of those works in a hasty way and in the clatter of arms on a military front. In one of his most vehement writings, *Against the Galilaeans*, he entered into long, and sometimes diffuse, theological debates on how the human race has been able to formulate a notion of the divinity, not as a result of specific teachings but on the basis of natural intuition. He then attempted to play the role of scholar himself by engaging in a lengthy comparison between Moses and Plato. His goal, however, was simple. Christians have been unable to understand the teachings of either and consequently have missed their chance to be a part of an acceptable historical development. They even proved to be enemies of it.[126]

---

and Wilken, *Jews and Christians*, 28.

[125]Glanville Downey, *A History of Antioch in Syria*, as referred to in Meeks and Wilken, *Jews and Christians*, 28.

[126]Julian, CGal 43AB.

Much more surprising were Julian's strange explanations of Old Testament events twisted theologically and historically to fit his purpose. Moses remained his most important Hebrew personality, though he did not properly address the validity of other religions:

> Moses says that the creator of the universe chose out the Hebrew nation, that to that nation alone did he pay heed and cared for it, and he gives him charge of it alone. But how and by what sort of gods the other nations are governed he has said not a word,—unless indeed one should concede that he did assign to them the sun and the moon.[127]

He may have had in mind Deuteronomy 4:19:

> And beware lest you lift up your eyes to heaven, and when you see the sun and the moon and the stars, all the host of heaven, you be drawn away and worship them and serve them, things which the LORD your God has allotted to all the peoples under the whole heaven.

Julian was aware of the vicissitudes of Jewish history and the fate that Jerusalem had to endure throughout history. Perhaps he could prove greater than the Jewish leaders of the past and restore the temple of Jerusalem in honor of the god whose name has been associated with it.[128]

It is difficult to sort out the intentions of Julian from the apocryphal writings attributed to him. His letter 51 addressed to the community of the Jews has especially come under attack and is regarded by most scholars as a forgery. In it we find this exhortation to the Jews:

> This you ought to do, in order that, when I have successfully concluded the war with Persia, I may rebuild by my own efforts the sacred city of Jerusalem, which for so many years you have longed to see inhabited, and may bring settlers there, and, together with you, may glorify the Most High God therein.[129]

Church historians Socrates, Sozomen, and Theodoret elaborated on the tragic events which have marked Julian's attempt to rebuild the temple. They used the same sources or have depended on each other for their information. They cast Julian in the role of an evil person intent on

---

[127]Ibid., 99E (LCL III) 341
[128]Julian, Priest 295C (LCL II) 313.
[129]Julian, Jews 398A (LCL III) 181.

destroying the truth of Christianity. As divine punishments, omens, and portents of destruction have accompanied the efforts at rebuilding the temple of Jerusalem.

A summary of responses on the part of Christian historians reveals the following: Julian was remiss in not noticing that, despite his aversion for Christians, the church rested on an Old Testament foundation. Yet it was in his design to entreat the Jews to pray for him and the empire, and thereby make the Jews automatic enemies of Christianity. The Jews were pleased with the project of rebuilding the temple of Jerusalem at the expense of the empire. Pagans who were not necessarily well disposed towards Jews nonetheless helped them in the enterprise. A warning against the project came from Cyril, the bishop of Jerusalem. He invoked the prophecy of Christ that it was God's intention that the temple be destroyed and that no stone should remain upon another stone. He saw in that prophecy a finality that Julian should have respected. As soon as construction began, gales, storms, and tempests blew everything apart. Violent earthquakes finished the demolition and crushed workers to death. Crosses appeared on the clothes of those involved in the project. Even after Julian received news of all those catastrophes, he remained unrepentant and, like pharaoh, hardened his heart. Many Jews and pagans, however, recognized the true God and were spared further demise.[130]

A more sober and more trustworthy account is given in Ammianus Marcellinus. According to him the purpose of Julian in rebuilding the Jerusalem temple was to connect the memory of his reign with one of the most splendid monuments of all times. Marcellinus then recounted the story of the project:

> [Julian] had entrusted the speedy performance of this work to Alypius of Antioch, who had once been vice-prefect of Britain. But, though this Alypius pushed the work on with vigor, aided by the governor of the province, terrifying balls of flame kept bursting forth near the foundations of the temple, and made the place inaccessible to the workmen, some of whom were burned to death; and since in this way the elements persistently repelled them, the enterprise halted.[131]

---

[130]Socrates, HE 3.20; Sozomen, HE 5.22; Theodoret, HE 3.15.
[131]Ammianus Marcellinus, ResGest 23.1.3 (LCL II) 311.

Julian's praise of the Jews was at points mitigated by a voice of reason. Once he succeeded in enlisting them as enemies of Christianity, he was less willing to grant them a special place in God's universal design: "Furthermore observe from what follows that God did not take thought for the Hebrews alone, but though he cared for all nations, he bestowed on the Hebrews nothing considerable or of great value, whereas on us he bestowed gifts far higher and surpassing theirs."[132] His Hellenistic and Neoplatonic training led him to the conclusion that the right perception of the universe came from Greek philosophy, unmatched by any other culture, not even that of the Hebrews.[133] Thus we are confronted with another great paradox of Julian's. After securing the favors of the Jews he showed a strong anti-Hebrew inclination.

Christian historians who denounced Julian's relationship to the Jews abstained from direct attacks on Judaism. Later, Chrysostom wrote one of the most virulent anti-Jewish diatribe: *Homilia adversus judeos*.[134] Similar invectives against the Jews came from the pen of Ambrose.

Julian's religious orientation may be attributed to the turmoil and restlessness of his younger years. It may also be attributed to the fact that the kind of Christianity he was exposed to in the surroundings of Constantius was a distorted system he intended to make conform to his desires:

> The plain and simple religion of the Christians he obscured by a dotard's superstition, and by subtle and involved discussions about dogma, rather than by seriously trying to make them agree, he aroused many controversies; and as these spread more and more, he fed them with contentious words.[135]

---

[132]Julian, CGal 176AB (LCL III) 367.

[133]133. Ibid., 178AB.

[134]The *Homilia adversus judeos* (1 and 8) has been reproduced from the *Patrologia Graeca* in Meeks and Wilken, *Jews and Christians*, 85-126. In it John Chrysostom has proven himself to live up to the judgment of him by Marcel Simon as "le maître de l'imprécation anti-juive." Speaking of the synagogue he says: "For it is not simply a gathering place for thieves and hucksters, but also of demons; indeed, not only the synagogue, but the souls of Jews are also the dwelling places of demons." Meeks and Wilken, *Jews and Christians*, 92.

[135]Ammianus Marcellinus, ResGest 21.16.18 (LCL II) 183-85.

As emperor, Julian was expected to set up residence in Constantinople, the new capital city of the empire, sumptuously decorated and everywhere reflecting the new religion which had Constantine as its greatest defender. Though paganism was not totally absent from Constantinople, and though Constantine himself brought in many pagan masterpieces of art, including a statue of Apollo he placed in the center of town, Julian did not wish to be constantly reminded of the triumph of Christianity. Furthermore, he could not find there the temples and altars that would have allowed him to revive the old ceremonies of paganism. Constantinople was just not the right place for someone intent on reviving paganism. Nor did he wish to go back to Rome or even Milan where he had stayed for some time. His training in Greek philosophy and literature dictated otherwise. For better or for worse he chose Antioch, a city which brought him honor and disgrace.

From a strategic point of view Antioch was a perfect choice for the military expeditions against Persia. But Julian received no warm welcome there by the ruling authorities. Sometimes he had to submit to insults and a lack of support in times of need. Instead of resorting to imperial powers which would have allowed him to punish the city, Julian chose to answer by writing his *Misopogon*. It was a satire on his own habits and then a virulent one on the city of Antioch, sometimes witty, and sometimes angry, but never really cruel. Ammianus Marcellinus, who was with Julian in Gaul, gives us some details on the reasons why Julian wrote the *Misopogon*, exposing the faults of the people of Antioch beyond what was necessary.[136] Julian had taken seriously the advice of his most trusted

---

[136]Ibid., 22.14.1-3. See in particular the less than flattering description of Julian:

> For he was ridiculed as a Cercops, as a dwarf, spreading his narrow shoulders and displaying a billy goat's beard, taking mighty strides as if he were the brother of Otus and Ephialtes, whose height Homer describes as enormous. He was also called by many a slaughterer instead of high priest, in jesting allusion to his many offerings.

ResGest 22.14.3 (LCL II) 273-75.

Socrates connected the *Misopogon* (Beard-hater) to the ridicule the Antiochans made of his beard which was very long and ugly, saying "that it ought to be cut off and manufactured into ropes." He also suggested that the *Misopogon* left "an indelible stigma upon that city and its inhabitants." HE 3.17

confidant Oribasius that a true philosopher should be able to hide his anger from the public.

Christianity had a long history in Antioch. It pleased Julian, however, that the local church was going through a process of disintegration, of theological fights, and vengeful reprisals. It all culminated in a synod during which Eustathius was deposed amid a raging controversy over Sabellianism. Other heresies whose outcome failed to be decided at Nicaea also found their way to Antioch. Socrates, Sozomen, and Theodoret left behind copious records of those disputes and their detrimental results.[137]

Julian's determination to reorganize paganism remained to a large extent in the realm of a pious wish. All his efforts gravitated around two major goals: Vindicate the superiority of pagan, and mostly Greek, philosophy, and discredit Christianity, not through persecution, but by arguing its barbarity. According to him paganism was better equipped than Christianity to unite together the different human races and their respective gods. He developed his philosophy mostly in *Against the Galilaeans*.[138]

Specific events in the life of Julian have reinforced his conviction that he was under the protection of the gods. When he and his brother Gallus were set free from exile at Marcellum, Gallus was made caesar but soon after that was murdered. Julian attributed his better fate to the providence of the gods: "As for me, the gods by means of philosophy caused me to remain untouched by it and unharmed."[139] In response to divine favors, Julian trained himself to invoke the Muses, the gods, and especially Apollo, in such a way as to utter only what is pleasing to the gods and what should be believed about them by all the people.[140] But his gratitude goes primarily to King Helios who renews his power and determination. It is through the power of the god that he was able to compose *Hymn to*

(NPNF-2 II) 88.

[137]Socrates, HE 1.23; 3.6; Sozomen, HE 2.19; 4.28; 5.13; Theodoret, HE 1.21.

[138]Julian, CGal 115D; HymnHel 131C. See also 133B and 151AB and Fowden, *Empire to Commonwealth*, 52.

[139]Julian, Ath 271D-272A (LCL II) 251.

[140]Julian, HymnHel 132A.

King Helios in just three nights.[141] In that hymn we are brought closer to
a notion of henotheism and even monotheism than we could expect from
a die-hard polytheist such as Julian: "Helios the most mighty god,
proceeding from itself and in all things like unto himself."[142] We come
to the best hint of a qualified notion of monotheism when he speaks of
King Helios: "For the distribution of his rays over the whole universe,
and the unifying power of his light, prove him to be the master workman
who gives an individual existence to everything that is created."[143] Helios
as the eternal One stands at the center of Julian's "theology" with the
exception perhaps that Apollo, who is also the sun god, shares in the
oneness.[144]

As a disciple of Neoplatonic philosophy and as a religious enthusiast,
Julian often showed a mystical inclination in his religious statements. His
religion was close to what is described in Salutius Secundus's treatise *On
the Gods and the World*, a work that has often been considered as one of
the most authoritative statements on pagan practices. It was a short work
discussing briefly the major points of pagan religion in a Platonic fashion,
and trying to offer an efficient weapon against Christianity. Julian, who
elevated Salutius Secundus to the position of prefect and then consul, had
a great admiration for him and dedicated to him his *Hymn to King Helios*.
But to understand the work of Salutius, a certain grounding in Neoplatonic philosophy was necessary. It could appeal only to the educated,
and Julian remained aware of the fact that religious reforms based on
intellectual propositions usually do not reach the masses.

Ammianus Marcellinus portrays Julian as a person obsessed by omens
and portents and as being superstitious rather than truly religious.[145] His
commitment to the art of divination was limited to what fitted his
purposes. For the same reason he rejected a great deal of the ancient
myths when they were not properly interpreted.[146] When the advice of

---

[141]Ibid., 158A; 157B.
[142]Ibid., 132D (LCL I) 359.
[143]Ibid., 141AB (LCL I) 383-85.
[144]Ibid., 144C.
[145]Ammianus Marcellinus, ResGest 25.4.17.
[146]Julian, CGal 75B-94A.

soothsayers was contrary to his plan, in his abrupt manner, he dismissed it. He also liked to be known as an ascetic free from sexual passion.[147]

Julian was not a great philosopher. His writings, often contradictory and reflecting the turmoils of his times, lacked the depth and the insight of other philosophical treatises of his century. Yet he never tired of connecting his religion with philosophical arguments. He claimed that through the agency of fire, the gods bestow on us reason and mind. Therefore we must seek, in a Platonic fashion, to make ourselves like the divinity, even when we feel that the goal is unachievable. Our pursuit of virtue alone can keep us from evil. In obedience to the Pythian god, the Delphic maxim *know thyself* must remain our major focus of attention.[148]

At times we find in Julian a sincere desire to live up to the Platonic ideal of the philosopher-king. According to him that quality was lacking in Constantine, whom he portrayed as misled by the promises of a gospel that offered murderers, adulterers, seducers, and all other kind of sacreligious people forgiveness for their misdeeds. This was abhorrent to Julian. He preferred to think of himself as a protégé of Mithra, who granted him knowledge from the beginning.[149] But his relentless efforts to restore paganism were dictated by much more than family and political conflicts which disrupted his life as a young man. He kept an authentic fascination for Greek culture which was linked in his mind with the old religion. Yet he was not sufficiently aware of the gap which existed between his conception of Greek culture and what the Athens of Pericles or Plato really was. He often revealed his inability to disconnect himself from a Hellenistic syncretism he believed to be original Greek philosophy.

Julian was obsessed by sacrifices to the point of being regarded as a slaughterer rather than a faithful of the gods. Ammianus Marcellinus speaks critically of the orgies Julian regarded as religious acts:

He drenched the altars with the blood of an excessive number of victims, sometimes offering up a hundred oxen at once, with countless

---

[147]Ammianus Marcellinus, ResGest 25.2.8; 4.2.

[148]Some of the major ideas connecting religion and philosophy in Julian's perspective are found in his oration, *To the Uneducated Cynics*.

[149]Julian, Caes 336AC. Attacks on the work of Jesus reappear elsewhere in the writings of Julian. They almost sound Nietzschean.

flocks of various other animals, and with white birds hunted out by land and sea; to such a degree that almost every day his soldiers, who gorged themselves on the abundance of meat, living boorishly and corrupted by their eagerness for drink, were carried through the squares to their lodgings on the shoulders of passers-by from the public temples, where they indulged in banquets that deserved punishment rather than indulgence.[150]

Julian's ardent wish to overwhelm the population with his new devotion to paganism often worked against his purpose. He failed to apply his power and his genius to promote a religious reform that would have given paganism what it had lacked all along and what the Christians possessed from the beginning, namely fundamental theological principles, clearly defined moral precepts, and a credible ecclesiastical discipline. None of his sacrificial extravaganzas could solve that problem. Under those circumstances, his reforms were doomed.

Julian's relationship to Christians lacked consistency. Sozomen portrays him as acting prudently against the Christians so he would not be considered tyrannical. He removed the sign of the cross which had appeared on the labarum since the time of Constantine and replaced it with the old standard of the Roman army.[151] This proved to be one of his better moves since the Roman army was still more pagan than Christian and since the religion of Mithra appealed mostly to soldiers.

Those who refused to abjure Christianity were excluded by law from serving in the praetorian guards and could not hold any office at court. They were not allowed to become governors of provinces under the pretext that they would refuse to use the sword against offenders deserving of capital punishment.[152] In his letter To Atarbius Julian stated that god-fearing pagans must be preferred to Christians. As often as possible pagan behavior was rewarded while Christians were denied any place of honor.

Yet Julian was careful not to persecute Christians. He went as far as to forbid persecution: "I affirm by the gods that I do not wish the Galilaeans to be either put to death or unjustly beaten, or to suffer any other injury."[153] He showed kindness to Christians exiled during the reign

---

[150]Ammianus Marcellinus, ResGest 22.12.6 (LCL II) 267.
[151]Sozomen, HE 5.17.
[152]Socrates, HE 3.13.
[153]Julian, Atarb 376C (LCL III) 123.

of Constantius by restoring their properties which had been confiscated by law. That kindness was, however, offset by more subtle mistreatments of Christians.[154] One example is how he treated Athanasius upon his return from exile. He did not allow him to stay in Alexandria where he could have rallied Christians into a kind of unity which would not have served Julian's purpose.

Julian was particular in his choice of friendship with Christians. He showed special affection for Basil who, together with Gregory, was a fellow student of Julian at Athens. He wrote him a letter (26) in which he praised him as one "whose words bring tidings of gold." Though Julian was aware of the gap in thinking between the two, he nonetheless was intent on keeping the friendship: "But we, though we refute and criticize one another with appropriate frankness, whenever it is necessary, love one another as much as the most devoted friends."[155] In the same letter Julian invites Basil to come to his court at the state's expense. But most Christian writers have been far less inclined to grant Julian any credit for religious tolerance. Gregory of Nazianzus, Socrates, and Sozomen have all documented some form of persecution against Christians.

The role of religion in the affairs of the state was also a point of special concern to Julian. We find some fundamental instructions in a fragment of his *Letter to a Priest*. The sacred laws of the gods cannot be transgressed, and all governors should exercise great care in their implementation. Ritual purity alone can ensure that the symbols of the gods are not polluted. Philanthropy must be exercised to the highest degree possible, for it brings numerous blessings. It may imply the sharing of money. Julian was evidently disturbed by the efficiency with which Christians have been able to implement philanthropic acts. He saw in that a menace to his religious reform: "For when it came about that the poor were neglected and overlooked by the priests, then I think the impious Galilaeans observed this fact and devoted themselves to philanthropy" (305 C).

---

[154]Sozomen, HE 5.5.

[155]There is no convincing reason to dismiss letter 26 to Basil (LCL III) 81-83 as spurious. There is another letter of Julian to Basil (81) which is so full of inconsistencies that it is regarded by most scholars as a Christian forgery. But it may have, unfortunately, influenced the Christian historian Sozomen.

Julian was a prolific writer convinced of the power of his own words. But he did not prove himself a master of public controversy and often did not express his objections to Christians in any focused fashion. He believed himself to be endowed with the intellectual ability to expose the fallacies of his opponents and to convince his friends of his correctness. To the end he hoped that people would come to see his views as unassailable and return to the true religion of paganism. *Against the Galilaeans* was to serve as his masterpiece of debate with Christianity. It delivered much less than expected. It failed in its attempt to prove that Christianity had to offer nothing but wickedness, that it could not claim any credible relationship to Judaism, much less to the lofty philosophy of the Greeks, and that most Christians were not even following the teachings of the apostles.

There were numerous treatises from pagans attacking Christianity, and some were more powerful than the writings of Julian. Among them we could mention the works of Celsus and Porphyry. They proved to be of concern to the church, to a much greater extent than the short-lived efforts of Julian.[156]

When it became evident to Julian that Christians would not be changed through his persuasiveness, he resorted to more malicious tactics. He thought, with good reason, that while Christians were attempting to destroy each other trough their doctrinal debates, he might have a better chance at restoring paganism. Ammianus Marcellinus elaborated on one of the ruses of Julian. After the emperor felt it safe to decree the restoration of pagan temples and sacrifices, Ammianus said:

> And in order to add to the effectiveness of these ordinances, he sum-
> moned to the palace the bishops of the Christians, who were of conflict-
> ing opinions, and the people, who were also at variance, and politely

---

[156]Wilmer C. Wright in his introduction to *Contra Galilaeos* gives a summary of how different writers, Christian and pagan, assessed the writings of Julian. Then he adds: "At any rate the Council of Ephesus, in a decree dated 431, sentenced Porphyry's books to be burned, but did not mention Julian's; and again in a law of Theodosius II, in 448, Julian was ignored while Porphyry was condemned. When in 529 Justinian decreed that anti-Christian books were to be burned, Porphyry alone was named, though probably Julian was meant to be included." CGal (LCL III) 316. Among Christian writers Gregory of Nazianzus and Cyril, bishop of Alexandria, produced the best-known responses to Julian.

advise them to lay aside their differences, and each fearlessly and without opposition to observe his own beliefs. On this he took a firm stand, to the end that, as this freedom increased their dissension, he might afterwards have no fear of a united populace, knowing as he did from experience that no wild beasts are such enemies to mankind as are most of the Christians in their deadly hatred of one another.[157]

The conflict between Julian and the Christians in Antioch reached its peak in the events surrounding the fate of the remains of the martyr Saint Babylas. The story is told by many Christian writers.[158] Babylas had been a bishop of Antioch and died as a martyr during the persecutions under Decius. When Gallus, the brother of Julian, became caesar he was dismayed at the corruption of Daphne, a rich suburb of Antioch which served as the religious center of Apollonian religion and was reputed for its pagan rites and luxurious pleasures.[159] To counteract the dismal reputation of Daphne, Gallus, a defender of the Christian cause, decided to transfer the bones of Babylas and bury them near the temple of Apollo. He was convinced that such action would bring more austerity and decency to the place. But it was not meant to last long. His short and troublesome rule at Antioch contributed to his trial by Constantius and to his death.

Soon after Gallus's death, Julian decided to make Antioch his capital city and the staging area for his Persian campaigns. He tried without success to consult the oracle of Apollo at Daphne. After a long silence and as the result of many entreaties and sacrifices, Apollo voiced the reason for his silence. His shrine was polluted by the proximity of the remains of Babylas. A purification was in order and could not be attained until the remains of Babylas were removed. Without delay Julian ordered the Christians to comply with his request, and the bones of Babylas were taken to Antioch.

What was supposed to remain a simple imperial decree developed into a huge procession by Christians who followed the coffin of their saint. As the popularity of Babylas grew, so did the problems of Julian.

---

[157]Ammianus Marcellinus, Resgest 22.5.3-4 (LCL II) 203.

[158]See especially Socrates, HE 3.18; Sozomen, HE 5.19; Theodoret, HE 3.6; John Chrysostom, HomIgnBab.

[159]For a fuller description of Daphne and its history which brought it fame see especially Sozomen, HE 5.19.

The Christian procession not only burst into the singing of their psalms and hymns, but also into shouts against the demon Apollo. No sooner was the coffin of Babylas removed that fire destroyed the magnificent temple of Apollo, bringing to an end the oracular activity and leaving Julian in one of the worst quandaries. John Chrysostom related that the emperor was so struck by fear that he did not even order the rebuilding of the temple of Apollo, fearing that the next victim of divine wrath would be Julian himself. Thus the mutilated shell of the temple of Apollo became a symbol of Christian triumph.

The anger of Julian, however, was out of bounds in spite of the advice of his counselors not to give Christians more reasons to celebrate their triumph. But he, and many others, were convinced that the burning of the temple of Apollo was the act of Christians who sought revenge for the edict concerning Babylas. He ordered the leaders of the choral procession to be arrested. He confiscated the holy vessels and treasures of the Christians and ordered the great church Constantine had built there to be closed.[160] Antioch began to look different, all claiming injury, and all protesting some form of religious persecution. The status of the citizenry at that time had never been clear. Libanius considered it as almost totally pagan, while, according to John Chrysostom, it was almost wholly Christian.

Ammianus Marcellinus recorded the event of the burning of the temple of Apollo and Julian's reaction to it. His descriptions may have served as a source for later Christian writers. Without directly exonerating Christians, he suggested an accidental cause of the fire.[161] Julian's own reaction showed some inconsistencies. His anger was directed not only to his contemporary citizens, but also to all of those who, since the days of Constantine, had seen to it that the shrine of Apollo would be rendered useless. In his satire against the people of Antioch, the *Misopogon*, he castigated the citizens for having allowed Constantius to build a Christian church right in Apollo's grove in Daphne. Many of the altars were overturned and pagan religion so shaken that Julian concluded: "Now, in my opinion, even before that fire the god had forsaken the temple, for when I first entered it his holy image gave me a sign thereof."[162] Julian

---

[160]Theodoret, HE 3.8.
[161]Ammianus Marcellinus, ResGest 22.13.1-5.
[162]Julian, Misop 361C (LCL II) 487.

needed no reminder of the fact that the diminishing number of oracles and the eventual silence of the shrine were considered a triumph of Christianity. The progressive elimination of pagan shrines in the Constantine and post-Constantine era did not silence Apollo, but the future of his oracle was already in serious doubt.

Julian was unsuccessful in reviving the oracle. His stay in Antioch was too brief and his death on the Persian front too untimely. To some extent the other oracles still functioned and, according to Theodoret, Julian had been able to receive directives for his Persian campaigns from Delphi, Delos, and Dodona, though we are not sure that he visited those places.[163] Christian writers were left with the task of sorting out the nature of the events. They liked to picture an emperor in search of revenge. When he could not be satisfied with pinning the arson on Christians, he turned his anger toward the officiating pagan priest he suspected of connivance with the infidels. Though subjected to torture, he could not name the culprits, and Julian continued to accuse him of dereliction of duty.[164]

The zeal with which Julian wanted to restore paganism was not shared by many wise people of his day. His behavior in Antioch contributed to the failure of his reforms. But he never wavered from his devotion to his gods, mostly Mithra and Apollo. He pleaded for sincerity of worship, free from flattery and pretense, however much his own practices led him to be obsessed with rituals and ceremonies beyond what his entourage could accept. No one really knows what course history might have taken, had he been successful in restoring paganism and rebuilding Jerusalem and its temple, two ideal goals which may have brought more conflicts than satisfaction.

There was as much controversy and mystery about Julian's Death as there had been about his life. He died at Maranga on June 26, 363 in a campaign against the Persians that was ill-conceived from the beginning. His close friend Ammianus Marcellinus, who had followed him throughout Gaul and knew the military strategies of the emperor, reflected on how Julian could not be persuaded to listen to the voice of wisdom. All omens agreed that Julian should not undertake the campaign. After he had

---

[163]Theodoret, HE 3.16.

[164]For a fuller description of the story of Babylas and its consequences see Samuel N. C. Lieu, ed., *The Emperor Julian: Panegyric and Polemic* (Liverpool: Liverpool University Press, 1986) 44-87.

ordered the Sibylline books to be consulted in Rome, the answer came that he must not move and go to battle.[165] Even those who supported him up to that time had basically reached two conclusions, namely that Julian had lost the favor of the gods and that they could no longer be an integral part of his megalomania.

Christian writers exposed the folly of Julian in his Persian campaign. Theodoret emphasized the major strategic blunders, including the wilful destruction of the boats after his troops landed, so they could not turn back. He then burned the major bridge not to allow any retreat. He also failed to provide food for his troops or even to request supplies from Rome. But most of all, he failed to notice that he had received the wrong oracles and that his gods, including his cherished Apollo, were of no use to him and led him to his demise.[166] Following the reports of Ammianus Marcellinus, Socrates also commented on the imprudence of Julian in failing to wear his protective gear.[167] But it is in Ammianus Marcellinus that we find a long narration on the courage and the folly of Julian in that war.[168]

The circumstances surrounding the death of Julian have never been elucidated. No one really knows who shot the arrow that killed him. Ammianus Marcellinus reported that after having been wounded he tried again to enter the battle, but to no avail. On having heard that he was in Phrygia, he was willing to accept his death, for a dream had warned him that he would die there.[169] Speculations abounded as to the killer of Julian. Christian historians suggested all possible scenarios, ranging from foe, to friend, to angel, to demon.[170] But all agreed that it was the will of God. Sozomen gave a long version of the events at the battle front and quoted Libanius to prove that Julian fell at the hand of a Christian. He then pointed out that this was the outcome of divine will to prevent Julian from carrying out his threat of greater persecution after the war against Persia.[171]

---

[165]Ammianus Marcellinus, ResGest 23.1.7.
[166]Theodoret, HE 3.20.
[167]Socrates, HE 3.21.
[168]Ammianus Marcellinus, ResGest 25.3.1-14.
[169]Ibid., 25.3.9.
[170]Socrates, HE 3.21; Sozomen, HE 4.1; Theodoret, HE 3.20.
[171]Sozomen, HE 6.2.

Though mortally wounded, Julian found the strength to deliver a long speech to his entourage. It is reported in Ammianus Marcellinus, and most certainly is as much the oration of the writer as that of the emperor. In essence Julian reiterated that he was not aware of any grave misdeed, that in all situations, whether in exile or as emperor, he conducted himself with moderation, always bowing to higher powers which determine our fate. Consequently he conducted himself as a just ruler. He wanted to die as a true philosopher, knowing the end of things and begging his friends not to mourn him.[172] On another occasion he tried to comfort those who were saddened by his fate, reminding them that heaven can sometimes dispense death as the reward for great virtues. He may have had in mind the way the gods rewarded Cleobis and Biton or Agamedes and Trophonius.[173]

Theodoret was the first known writer to report the alleged final words of Julian: "It is related that when Julian had received the wound, he filled his hand with blood, flung it into the air and cried, 'Thou hast won, O Galilean'."[174] The saying has been mostly regarded as apocryphal, but stirred the imagination of many Christians wishing for the kind of vindication that would come from such a concession on the part of Julian.

The funeral oration for Julian was delivered by Libanius. It was in the form of a carefully worded biography of his great friend, stressing his frugality, asceticism, restraint, and mostly his tireless capacity for work. It was different in tone from the panegyric delivered some months before by Claudius Mamertinus on the occasion of his being chosen as consul by Julian. They both offered invaluable information on the tenure of the emperor. Christian writers, however, found the praises of Julian highly partisan and offered their own assessment. Among them, Socrates was the

---

[172]Ammianus Marcellinus, ResGest 25.3.15-20.

[173]Ibid., 25.3.15.

[174]Theodoret, HE 3.20 (NPNF-2 III) 106. The saying has been remembered in its Greek and latin form: Γαλιλαῖε νενίκησας and *Visisti Galilaee*. Swinburne, in his *Hymn to Proserpine*, wrote of Julian's alleged memorable words: "Thou has conquered, O pale Galilean; the world has grown grey from thy breath." Montaigne discussed the alleged saying of Julian in some detail in his essay *Of Liberty of Conscience*, but has also concluded that the silence of trustworthy and reliable ancient writers such as Ammianus Marcellinus makes the authenticity of the saying quite questionable.

fairest to Julian. He felt compelled, however, to write a rebuttal of Libanius's funeral oration to refute the assertion that Julian had successfully proven the ridicule of Christian Scriptures.[175] The most prolific Christian writers who denounced Julian were Ephrem the Syrian and Gregory of Nazianzus.

The poetic works of Ephrem were well know in the early church and, at least according to Jerome, were often read alongside the Scriptures. He praised the divine protection by God of his city Nisibis in his *Carmina Nisibena*. But his sharpest verve was turned against Julian in his *Hymni contra Julianum* written to prove the errors of Julian and the providence of God in the death of the emperor.[176]

The best-known Christian critic of Julian was Gregory of Nazianzus. As much as Libanius was the best defender of Julian, Gregory became his worst literary enemy. As a schoolmate of Julian in Athens, he watched the emperor step by step and never failed to analyze and criticize his words and actions. For Gregory, Julian was a traitor, a Nebuchadnezzar *redivivus* consumed by an anti-Christian rage.[177] On many occasions Gregory denounced the tactics of Julian in his ability to veil persecution and to appeal to persuasion while doing evil and resorting to tyranny. But Gregory's invectives often lacked honor and dignity when he allowed himself to mix spiritual insights with an attack on Julian's physical disability. Socrates quoted an excerpt of Gregory's fifth oration:

> For it seemed to me that no good was portended by a neck seldom steady, the frequent shrugging of shoulders, an eye scowling and always in motion, together with a frenzied aspect; a gait irregular and tottering, a nose breathing only contempt and insult . . . ; immoderate and very

---

[175]Socrates, HE 3.22-23.

[176]For a detailed analysis of the *Hymni contra Julianum*, see Lieu, *The Emperor Julian*, 90-134. Lieu has given us a translation of the Hymns. Another source of information for Ephrem is in NPNF-2 XIII, 115-341.

[177]Gregory of Nazianzus, *The Last Farewell* 3, which is reproduced in NPNF-2 VII, 386. In his fifth oration known as *Second Invective against Julian the Emperor*, Gregory tries to attribute to Julian other Old Testament names: "Is it more proper to call him Jeroboam or Ahab, those most wicked of the Israelites; or Pharaoh the Egyptian, or Nebuchadnezzar the Assyrian; or combining all together shall we name him one and the same?" *Second Invective* 3.87. (See n. 179.)

loud laughter . . . ; speech with hesitancy and interrupted by his breathing. . . . Why need I enter into minute particulars?[178]

Gregory's most pointed attacks on Julian were in his fourth and fifth orations.[179] Those invectives, though written after the death of Julian, did not contain an analysis of the emperor's writings. They were an *apologia* for the Christian movement that was temporarily threatened by the revival of paganism. The Vituperations of Gregory against Julian also turned out to be a severe indictment of most of the great personalities of Greece, such as Solon, Socrates, Plato, Xenocrates, Diogenes, Epicurus . . . who were viewed as destroyers of human qualities.[180]

There was an admission in Gregory that Julian did not resort to direct persecutions against Christians, a fact he deplored: "For, besides his other motives, he begrudged the honour of martyrdom to our combatants, and for this reason he contrives now to use compulsion, and yet not to seem to do so. That we might suffer, and yet not gain honour as though suffering for Christ's sake."[181] Gregory was especially thankful to God for the brevity of Julian's life, for, had the emperor lived long enough, he would have been able to establish throughout the empire pagan institutions copied on the Christian model, thus depriving Christianity of any further significant influence.[182] But Gregory saw in Julian a person to be pitied more than hated: "How should I not weep for the unhappy man himself; for the persecutors more than for the persecuted? How not

---

[178]Socrates, HE 3.23 (NPNF-2 II) 92.

[179]King, *Julian the Emperor*, gives the text of the orations and calls them *Gregory Nazianzen's Two Invectives against Julian the Emperor.*

[180]Gregory of Nazianzus, *First Invective* 72; King, *Julian the Emperor*, 41-42.

[181]Ibid., 58. King, *Julian the Emperor*, 33.

[182]Ibid., 111. King, *Julian the Emperor*, 74-75.

He (Julian) also, having the same design, was intending to establish schools in every town, with pulpits and higher and lower rows of benches, for lectures and expositions of the heathen doctrines. . . . He was purposing also to build inns and hospices for pilgrims, monasteries for men, convents for virgins, places for meditation, and to establish a system of charity for the relief of prisoners . . . things which he had especially admired in our institutions.

There is little doubt that Julian's purpose had often been to graft Christian practices on paganism, while attacking Christians themselves.

bewail yet more than those that went over to the side of evil, the man that carried them with him?"[183]

The succession of Julian proved very difficult. Ammianus Marcellinus speaks of the disarray and the tumultuous haste in the choosing of a new emperor. No agreement could be reached among different factions. The fact that Julian had no descendent did not help the situation. After long debates and compromises it was agreed to ask the good friend of Julian, Salutius Secundus, to accept the post. Citing poor health and old age, he declined. After other painful deliberation, a group of hot-headed soldiers chose Jovian as emperor. Jovian immediately rallied the troops and was proclaimed augustus.[184] The fate of the empire again changed radically.

An assessment of the historical meaning of Julian remains difficult. He did not substantially alter paganism. Oracles lost their meaning. Except for some defections of church members, Christianity did not unduly suffer. In some instances, as that of Daphne and Babylas, it received a boost. The genius of Julian was readily acknowledged, though it was often considered by Christian writers as misplaced. Speaking of Julian Augustine noted that his "gifted mind was deceived by a sacrilegious and detestable curiosity, stimulated by the love of power."[185] Some historians, including Gibbon, have taken a dual position in their assessment of Julian's achievements. They praise him for his attempt to restore the Roman empire to its lost glory. But they also express surprise that such a genius would have been so misled by superstition. The world of history, art and literature often considered Julian as a good model for their poems, dramas, novels, and other masterpieces.[186]

The Age of Theodosius

According to Theodoret, Jovian was determined to undo the reforms undertaken by Julian. He fought impiety with a zeal that earned him a rank among the martyrs. The army was revamped so as to eliminate the

---

[183]Ibid., 51. King, *Julian the Emperor*, 29.

[184]Ammianus Marcellinus, ResGest 25.5.1-7.

[185]Augustine, CivDei 5.21. (NPNF-1 II), 103.

[186]In his epilogue to *The Emperor Julian* (Berkeley: University of California Press, 1976) Robert Browning gives us a long, though still incomplete, list of authors who, throughout the centuries, have attempted to vindicate Julian by making him the subject of their masterpieces.

vicious discipline introduced into it by Julian.[187] It appeared that the new Christian emperors would have an easy task. Paganism was disorganized and lacked an official priesthood, a fact Julian had tried to remedy by instituting a high priest for every province. But the achievements of Julian were not as fruitless as Christian writers claimed, and, after his death, paganism enjoyed several decades of relative toleration. Many of its shrines survived in spite of sporadic laws prohibiting them. Jovian's edict of tolerance, praised by the philosopher Themistius, may have included pagans.[188] Valentinian and Valens did not substantially alter Jovian's policies.

Already under Julian, Jovian, Valentinian, and Valens had taken a strong stand as Christians, being ready to resign their commission rather than deny their faith.[189] Ammianus Marcellinus commented on Jovian's Christian stance, praised him for his care in selecting state officials, but gave him poor marks on his education and morals.[190]

Both Socrates and Sozomen reported that when Jovian was considered to be emperor he pronounced himself openly Christian and did not wish to reign over those who had espoused the pagan religion. Being aware of that the whole army pronounced itself Christian, and Jovian could accept the mandate of emperor in earnest.[191] Soon after he proclaimed Christianity the only true religion. His reforms included a search for unity, away from theological dissensions, recalling Christians from exile, closing some of the pagan temples, stopping sacrifices, restoring privileges to churches, enlisting the help of Athanasius in matters of religion.[192]

At the death of Jovian in 364 Valentinian became emperor. He divided the empire and shared it with his younger brother Valens. He kept the West and put Valens in charge of the East. But it soon became obvious that the two brothers did not share the same views on religion.

---

[187]Theodoret, HE 4.1.
[188]Socrates, HE 3.25.
[189]Ibid., 3.13.
[190]Ammianus Marcellinus, ResGest 25.10.15.
[191]Socrates, HE 3.22; Sozomen, HE 6.3.
[192]Socrates, HE 3.24; Sozomen, HE 6.3; Theodoret, HE 4.2.

Under Julian, Valentinian had been dismissed from his command in the army under circumstances reported by Sozomen and confirmed by Theodoret:

> When they [Julian and Valentinian] were about to enter the temple, the priest, in accordance with the pagan custom, sprinkled water upon them with the branch of a tree. A drop fell upon the robe of Valentinian; he scarcely could restrain himself, for he was a Christian, and he rebuked his asperser. It is even said that he cut off, in view of the emperor, the portion of the garment on which the water had fallen, and flung it from him. From that moment Julian entertained inimical feelings against him and soon after banished him.[193]

When Jovian became emperor, he recalled Valentinian from Exile.

Valentinian was known for his religious tolerance. Said Ammianus Marcellinus: "His reign was distinguished by toleration, in that he remained neutral in religious differences neither troubling anyone on that ground nor ordering him to reverence this or that. He did not bend the necks of his subjects to his own belief by threatening edicts, but left such matters undisturbed as he found them."[194]

Quite different was the position of Valens who, after having espoused the Arian heresy, became intolerant of orthodox Christianity. He issued numerous edicts of persecution against Christians of different persuasion, thus giving the concept of persecution a different twist. Under his rule it became Christians against Christians, so as to vindicate what Julian had predicted. His tactics consisted in depriving churches from their leadership, leading to depopulation and dispersion. Socrates reported that in Alexandria "Some [monks] were dragged before the tribunals, others cast into prison, and many tortured in various ways, and in fact all sorts of punishments were inflicted upon persons who aimed only at peace and quiet."[195] While in Antioch, however, Valens came into contact with Themistius, who delivered a clever oration pointing out the difficulties in establishing a theology that would prove one infallibly correct. It is

---

[193]Sozomen, HE 6.6 (NPNF-2 II) 350; Theodoret, HE 3.12. See also Augustine, CivDei 18.52.

[194]Ammianus Marcellinus, ResGest 30.9.5. (LCL III) 371-73. See Socrates, HE 4.1.

[195]Socrates, HE 4.24 (NPNF-2 II) 109.

reported that, after hearing that oration, Valens became more considerate and less severe.[196]

When Valentinian's son Gratian succeeded him as emperor, the relationship between paganism and Christianity became further defined. On the day of his coronation he refused to wear the priestly robe and to be hailed as *pontifex maximus*. He claimed that that part of the ceremony did not become a Christian prince.[197] Under his rule the official and legal relations between paganism and the government were finally abrogated.[198] But enlightened Christians understood that it was not possible or even advisable to try to destroy the old society too rapidly and to replace it with a new order. Gratian left some pagan temples open, but forbade any state funds to be allocated to any of their activities. This setback threatened the splendor of some pagan feasts and ceremonies.[199] Debates continued in the Senate over the value of ancestral heritage. But Gratian's stand was upheld and continued under Theodosius. The argument often shifted to economic necessities. The cash was needed for military success, an argument the Senators could not oppose. Thus the fight against paganism sounded less ominous.

Christian writers have generally applauded Gratian's decisions about the church. He opposed the cruel policies of his uncle Valens, recalling those he had sent into exile. He tried to protect all sects to the exclusion of Eunomians, Photinians, and Manichaeans. He restored buildings to the churches. He also chose Theodosius as his colleague.[200]

Gratian died at the age of twenty-four. He was criticized for his excessive devotion to sports and for adopting some of the barbarian

---

[196]Sozomen, HE 6.36-37.

[197]According to Zosimus, HistNova 4.36, the rejection ot the imperial robe precipitated the early demise of Gratian. Even Constantine would not have committed such a foolish act.

[198]William K. Boyd, *The Ecclesiastical Edicts of the Theodosian Code*, Studies in History, Economics, and Public Law 24/2 (New York: Columbia University Press, 1905) 24-25.

[199]For a description of Gratian's decisions and the pagan reaction to them, see Gaston Boissier, *La Fin du paganisme: Etude sur les dernières luttes religieuses en occident au quatrième siècle*, 2 vols. (Paris: Hachette, 1907) 2:259-62.

[200]Socrates, HE 5.2; Theodoret, HE 5.2.

customs at the end of his life. After praising his energy and ability, Ammianus Marcellinus added:

> He was a young man of splendid character, eloquent, self-restrained, warlike, and merciful, and was already on his way to rivalry with the most distinguished emperors while yet a comely down was creeping over his cheeks, had not his natural inclination for unbecoming conduct, which was given free rein by his intimates, turned him to the frivolous pursuits of the emperor Commodus, although without that prince's thirst for blood.[201]

He was treacherously assassinated in Lyons.

Theodosius, successor of Gratian, is remembered as the emperor who, through the compilation of the voluminous *Codex Theodosianus*, put an official end to paganism. We know more about his rule from the code than from any other sources. His tenure as emperor from 379 to 395 was marked by successes as well as by troubled events which took away some of the luster of his accomplishments. His energies were turned toward the vindication and unification of Christianity as much as toward a final assault on paganism.

At the end of the fourth century, in spite of the numerous dissensions tearing it apart, Christianity was well established as the new religion of the empire. But it did not mean that paganism was totally out, though it was dying as much by the lack of internal organization as through the edicts of Christian emperors. Paganism made itself dependent on the support of the state, and when that support diminished or vanished, it could not find the inner resources to survive.

Less than a year after becoming emperor, Theodosius issued an edict clarifying his intentions concerning Christianity. It is reproduced in Sozomen:

> Reflecting that it would be better to propound his own religious views to his subjects, so as not to appear to be using force by commanding the unwilling subject to worship contrary to his judgment, Theodosius enacted a law in Thessalonica, which he caused to be published at Constantinople, well knowing that the rescript would speedily become public to all the other cities, if issued from that city, which is a citadel of the whole empire. He made known by this law his intention of

---

[201]Ammianus Marcellinus, ResGest 31.10.18 (LCL III) 453-55.

leading all his subjects to the reception of that faith which Peter, the chief of the apostles, had, from the beginning, preached to the Romans, and which was professed by Damasus, bishop of Rome, and by Peter, bishop of Alexandria. He enacted that the title of "Catholic Church" should be exclusively confined to those who rendered equal homage to the Three Persons of the Trinity, and that those individuals who entertained opposite opinions should be treated as heretics, regarded with contempt, and delivered over to punishment.[202]

The enforcement of the edict was elaborated on by Sozomen. Theodosius, at a specially convened council urged the leaders of all different sects to settle their ambiguous points of doctrine. Many contentions arose, and members of different sects did not approve of their leaders to argue their points of view in front of an intolerant emperor. Following the council, Theodosius enacted further laws according to which heretics could not own church buildings, give public instruction in faith, or ordain bishops. Punishments ensued and were justified on the grounds that unity of church was essential.[203]

Augustine praised Theodosius' faith and piety and credited him with miraculous protection on the part of God. He won his battle against usurper and tyrant Eugenius more by prayer than by the sword:

> Some soldiers who were at the battle reported to me that all the missiles they were throwing were snatched from their hands by a vehement wind, which blew from the direction of Theodosius' army upon the enemy; nor did it only drive with greater velocity the darts which were hurled against them, but also turned back upon their own bodies the darts which they themselves were throwing.[204]

Eugenius, who for two years was able to have himself elected illegally emperor of the West, compromised with the pagans while trying not to alienate the church. Theodosius was able to defeat him and to become sole emperor of both East and West.

It is difficult to reconstruct a credible portrait of Theodosius from the records we have. They are fewer than one could expect and often come from polemical writings not entirely trustworthy. The estimate of his life

---

[202]Sozomen, HE 7.4 (NPNF-2 II) 378.
[203]Ibid., 7.12.
[204]Augustine, CivDei 5.26 (NPNF-1 II) 106.

has focused on his edicts more than on his military and civic achievements. He showed a definite antipagan trend and, in his last legislation of 391, proved to be a ruler intent on seeing his wishes fulfilled. He can be regarded as the one who brought to its final realization the Christian revolution initiated by Constantine. Yet no Roman emperor, however determined to impose his will, could totally reject the heritage which brought glory to Rome. Thus Christian emperors veered from side to side, trying to minimize compromise while appearing to be firm in the implementation of their edicts. Conviction had to be mitigated with expediency. The background of people and their leaders could not be legislated away. In fact it never totally died, and Christianity absorbed a great deal of it under diverse guises. In spite of attempts on the part of the church to stifle it, the voice of reason continued to be heard among non-Christian intellectuals. In the first part of his reign Theodosius remained on good terms with pagan philosophers, especially Themistius and Libanius who opposed his policies in his *Pro templis*.

Whereas the major preoccupations of Theodosius were in the area of pagan-Christian relationships, he also took a strong stand on the Jewish question. But his attempt at fairness toward the Jews drew criticism from Christians, especially from Ambrose who had a mesmerizing and sometimes unhealthy influence on the emperor.

In one specific instance the Jewish synagogue at Callinicum was burned down by Christian monks at the order of the bishop. It was a clear act of unprovoked persecution. A meeting place of Valentinian Gnostics was also destroyed as an act of vengeance against heretics. In an attempt at fairness, Theodosius ordered the bishop to rebuild the synagogue at his own expense. As a protest, Ambrose wrote a long and vitriolic letter to the emperor.[205] It was replete with obsequious flattery of Theodosius and with numerous distorted allusions to biblical passages. In essence it condemned Theodosius as an enemy of God if he went ahead with the order. Ambrose threatened him with his own silence which, he thought, would be unbearable for Theodosius.

Drawing on some specious examples of history, Ambrose attempted to convince the emperor that the bishop was right and that the Jews deserved what they got according to divine judgment. Ambrose was

---

[205]Ambrose, Letter 40.

appalled by the idea that Christian money be spent on the rebuilding of a synagogue, something that would most certainly attract God's condemnation. At this point Ambrose reminded the emperor of what happened when Julian attempted the rebuilding of the temple in Jerusalem. The same if not worse punishment would be the lot of Theodosius unless he changed his order concerning a people God has so decidedly rejected: "There is, then, no adequate cause for such a commotion, that the people should be so severely punished for the burning of a building, and much less since it is the burning of a synagogue, a home of unbelief, a house of impiety, a receptacle of folly, which God Himself has condemned."[206]

The argument was extended into all sorts of accusations and rationalizations. It was evident that, at first, Theodosius did not rally to the position of Ambrose who, then, in desperation, delivered a sermon in the presence of the emperor. He also refused to administer the eucharist until Theodosius retracted his order. Caught in a no-win situation Theodosius yielded to Ambrose's pressure.[207]

The conflict between Theodosius and Ambrose signaled the uneasiness created by anti-Jewish legislation as it was formulated in the days of Constantine. It was designed to promote the growth of the church, much too often at the expense of the Jews. A decree issued in 315 prohibited conversion to Judaism. Later laws forbidding intermarriages and Jewish ownership of Gentile slaves were meant to make proselytism very difficult.[208] But most emperors took it as their responsibility to protect Jewish communities, often to the chagrin of zealous Christians. Julian paid no attention to anti-Jewish legislation that had been formulated by his predecessors. Theodosius tried to view the situation at Callinicum from a realistic point of view and exercise fairness. He had to learn than fairness can be overruled by persuasion.

Two events of dangerous magnitude tested the religion of Theodosius and his advisers, namely the sedition of the people of Antioch and the massacre that happened in Thessalonica.

---

[206]Ibid., 40.14 (NPNF-2 X) 442.

[207]The details of the sermon and the confrontation between Ambrose and Theodosius are contained in letter 41 sent to Ambrose's sister Marcellina. The date of the two letters is probably 388.

[208]Meeks and Wilken, *Jews and Christians*, 25.

The heavy taxation of the people of Antioch brought the city to the limits of the acceptable. Around 387 the upper class of citizens tried to negotiate with the authorities and find a compromise to a situation which had been worsening by the day. But other citizens, out of patience, exploded in a revolt, inflicting heavy damage on state property. They then threw down the statues of the emperor Theodosius and of his deceased wife Flaccilla and dragged them through the streets of Antioch. Though they were brought back to order, the damage was irreparable. In his rage Theodosius entertained the plan to destroy Antioch. Fear and terror now ruled in a city that had already suffered severe shortages of food and lived in constant uncertainty. The Bishop Flavian was unable to control the situation.

When the people of Antioch learned that Theodosius planned a massacre of many citizens, they begged Flavian to intercede with the emperor. Theodosius received the Bishop but was unmoved, at least until a group of young men sang litanies at the table of Theodosius, who was overcome by pity to the point of tears. Accounts differ on how the emperor finally yielded and forgave the city.[209]

The sedition in Antioch revealed the preaching mastery of John Chrysostom who delivered twenty one homilies to the citizens of the city, trying to place the episode within a spiritual understanding, consoling the people in their affliction, explaining how their fear was salutary, and finally reflecting on the reconciliation of Theodosius with the city.

In the second homily John Chrysostom depicts the desolation of Antioch:

> When the wrath of the Emperor is expected to come as a fire from above, every one presses to go forth in time, and to save the bare body, before the fire in its progress reaches them. And now our calamity has become an enigma; a flight without enemies; an expulsion of inhabitants without a battle; a captivity without capture! We have not seen the fire of barbarians, nor beheld the face of enemies; and yet we experience the sufferings of captives.[210]

---

[209]For a Christian point of view of those events, see Sozomen, HE 7.23; Theodoret, HE 5.19; and especially the twenty-one homilies of John Chrysostom, Statues.

[210]John Chrysostom, Statues, Hom 2.4 (NPNF-1 IX) 345.

It was not easy to appease the wrath of Theodosius. John Chrysostom suggested that while celebrating the festival of the Passover, Theodosius could be reminded that Christ forgave the whole world, so the emperor could imitate the one he was proclaiming as his Lord.[211]

After Theodosius granted his pardon, when some antiochenes may have already been killed by magistrates, John Chrysostom offered the action of the emperor as a model of what Christianity is capable:

> What could be gentler than such a soul? Let the Gentiles henceforward be ashamed; or rather, instead of being ashamed, let them be instructed; and leaving their native error, let them come back to the strength of Christianity, having learned what our philosophy is, from the example of the Emperor and of the Priest.[212]

The massacre at Thessalonica was a far more serious offense on the part of Theodosius. In the year 390 a sedition took place in Thessalonica over a strange incident. Sozomen and Theodoret report it in some detail as follows. A scoundrel charioteer saw the commanding general of the city, Botheric, shamefully exposed at a tavern, and dared insult him. The charioteer was arrested and jailed. At the next big race a mob tumultuously demanded the release of the prisoner, who was considered important for the contest. When Botheric refused, he and some of his magistrates were killed. In his rage, Theodosius ordered reprisals. Over seven thousand people, most of them innocent, were put to death execution-style, without trial or condemnation. Theodosius's action was severely reprimanded by Ambrose who refused him entry into the church at Milan and demanded a public penance.[213]

Details of the incident reveal the inner conflicts of Christianity and the precarious relationship between state and church as well as the complex interinfluence of the spiritual and the temporal. The action of Ambrose amounted to excommunication. It might be pertinent to quote some of the words of Ambrose to the emperor, as recorded by Theodoret:

---

[211]Ibid., Hom 3.2.

[212]Ibid., Hom 21.19 (NPNF-1 IX) 488. It is from Theodoret, HE 5.19 that we learn that magistrates had already put some citizens of Antioch to death before the tragedy was reported to Theodosius.

[213]Sozomen, HE 7.25; Theodoret, HE 5.17.

You seem Sir, not to know . . . the magnitude of the bloody deed that
has been done. Your rage has subsided, but your reason has not yet
recognised the character of the deed. Peradventure your Imperial power
prevents your recognising the sin, and power stands in the light of
reason. . . . We must not because we are dazzled by the sheen of the
purple fail to see the weakness of the body that it robes. . . . With what
eyes then will you look on the temple of our common Lord—with what
feet will you tread that holy threshold, how will you stretch forth your
hands still dripping with the blood of unjust slaughter? How in such
hands will you receive the all holy Body of the Lord? How will you
who in your rage unrighteously poured forth so much blood lift to your
lips the precious Blood? Begone. Attempt not to add another crime to
that which you have committed. Submit to the restriction to which the
God the Lord of all agrees that you be sentenced.[214]

For eight months, so reports Theodoret, the emperor was dismayed,
shedding tears in his palace. Then Rufinus, a trusted controller of the
imperial household, asked for the emperor's permission to seek mercy
from Ambrose. To that the emperor answered: "He will not yield. . . . I
know the justice of the sentence passed by Ambrose, nor will he ever be
moved by respect for my imperial power to transgress the law of God."[215]

After several attempts by Rufinus, the emperor agreed to let him seek
forgiveness from Ambrose. But upon meeting Rufinus, Ambrose rebuked
him for having been a party to the slaughter in Thessalonica. Seeing how
desperate his cause was, Rufinus sent word to Theodosius not to attempt
to see Ambrose. It was too late, for the emperor was already on his way
to Milan, ready to accept the disgrace he thought he deserved. The
meeting between Theodosius and Ambrose was filled with pathos.
Ambrose unleashed on Theodosius the harshest and most unforgiving
words he was capable of and made the emperor beg for mercy even
more. Finally Ambrose condescended to listen to the emperor, provided
he issued an edict making his passion null and void. When the edict was
issued, Ambrose agreed to loose the bond of punishment he had imposed
on the emperor, who then went through all the acts of penance described
in Theodoret, who then added: "On his return to Constantinople

---

[214]Theodoret, HE 5.17 (NPNF-2 III) 143.
[215]Ibid., 5.17 (NPNF-2 III) 143.

Theodosius kept within the bounds of piety which he had learnt from the great archbishop." He brought the story to its conclusion by having Theodosius declare: "I have learnt after great difficulty the differences between an emperor and a priest. It is not easy to find a man capable of teaching me the truth. Ambrosius alone deserves the title of bishop."[216]

We find further details of the events in Thessalonica in a letter (51) Ambrose sent to Theodosius. Penance and repentance were required from the emperor, but there was also the notion that the devil was acting through him and that the renewal of his faith would also mean the defeat of the Evil One. Augustine praised the contrition of Theodosius as admirable religious humility. His act of penance was presented as a model for Christians, who interceded for him, knowing that his faith was greater than the offence.[217]

Though not directly connected with the conflicts between Christians and pagans, the events at Thessalonica seem to have precipitated the doom of paganism in the face of the new religious zeal Theodosius had gained in the process. Up to that point the emperor's commitment to the eradication of paganism lacked determination, though the decrees had been issued. Whatever the role of Ambrose, it had a deep impact on Theodosius for the few remaining years of his rule. Theodoret pointed out the radical change in the emperor. Up to that point he felt the master of his decisions without consulting religious figures. In fact Ambrose was not consulted, nor even informed, of the massacre at Thessalonica until after it had already happened. All had changed, and the emperor was only too eager to show his unfailing commitment to the Christian cause. There is little doubt that, at this point, Ambrose was not only consulted but was a driving force in Theodosius's decisions. Paganism became its last sacrificial victim.

During his tenure as emperor Theodosius decreed attacks on paganism, forbidding sacrifices and destroying shrines. Some had minor results, others had great consequences. For most of his reign Theodosius was emperor in the East. He did not become sole emperor until 394, just a few months before his death in 395. He was well positioned to remedy the lax policies of his predecessor Valens who allowed all kinds of pagan

---

[216]Ibid., 5.17 (NPNF-2 III) 145.
[217]Augustine, CivDei 5.26.

rituals and festivities to be carried on, including Bacchic frenzies of votaries initiated into the orgies of Dionysus. But it was not to last. "When the right faithful Theodosius found all these evils he pulled them up by the roots, and consigned them to oblivion."[218] The lines separating civil and ecclesiastical authority were no longer clearly discernible.

Christian writers took a certain pleasure in emphasizing the enormous work it took to demolish pagan temples and the need of divine intervention to finish the job. This is how we come across descriptions of the magnificence of some of the temples destroyed.[219] The process of demolition had been going on for some time before the reign of Theodosius, though it had often been sporadic and disorganized, and did not enter its final phase until 391. Pagans still occupied high ranking positions in the empire, often to a larger extent than Christians. Sometimes and ironically, the execution of the new Christian laws was entrusted to pagan officials, thus adding insult to injury. It led to unavoidable compromises on the social as well as the religious levels.

The Theodosian Code contains a collection of the laws passed by the emperors from the time of Constantine on. It is obscure in places and often poorly written. It no longer has the force and the clarity of the former judicial spirit of Rome. Yet it is the major source of our knowledge for the period, however incomplete it may be. Most of the laws on religion have been grouped together.[220] Existing records are insufficient to assess the extent of the implementation of the edicts. We do not know the number of pagan temples destroyed by Christians. At Antioch Libanius decried the freedom that groups of monks have attributed to themselves in order to destroy rural shrines across the countryside. Edicts were not carried out systematically, and the penalty often depended on the zeal of bishops and monks. After the episode at Thessalonica, Theodosius came out of ambivalent policies and showed a much firmer resolve against paganism.

It was in the city of Alexandria that the edicts of Theodosius created the most bloody encounters between pagans and Christians. The story revolves around the fate of three major temples, that of Dionysus, that of

---

[218]Theodoret, HE 5.20 (NPNF-2 III) 146.
[219]See the descriptions provided by Theodoret, HE 5.21.
[220]The important laws on religious reform are grouped in section 16.10 of the code, e. g. 16.10.2; 16.10.5; 16.10.11; 16.10.12; 16.10.22; 16.10.25....

Mithra, and that of Serapis. The records available are conflicting and sometimes contradictory. But they agree in the essential developments which have marked the end of the the reign of Theodosius.

The first reported encounter happened when the bishop of Alexandria obtained permission from Theodosius to convert the temple of Dionysius into a church. Conflicts which ensued are described by Sozomen. Christians were not content to take over the building. They seized the opportunity to ridicule the scandalous practices of Dionysian religion by displaying the temple objects in a procession which enraged many of the citizens. Pagans could not suffer that injury in silence and organized a plan of attack against Christians, many of whom were killed or wounded. Knowing that they would have to pay for their act, the rebellious pagans chose to invade the Serapeum and transform it into a temporary citadel. They dragged many Christians with them and compelled them to offer sacrifices. Those who refused were tortured to death. Efforts on the part of officials to subdue the mob in the Serapeum failed. Instigated by one of their own philosophers, those in the Serapeum vowed to defend the religion and traditions of the gods of their fathers, even if it meant death.

Word of those events came to Theodosius who proclaimed the dead Christians as martyrs. He was also ready to forgive the rebels, hoping that his clemency would lead them to embrace Christianity. He then decreed the destruction of the temples at Alexandria. At that news the Christians began to shout for joy to the point that those who held the Serapeum were sufficiently frightened to flee.[221]

It was probably in 391, in the context of the final blow Theodosius intended to inflict on paganism, that the temples to Mithra and Serapis were destroyed. In any event, it was after the oration of Libanius, *Pro templis*, in which it is assumed that the Serapeum is still in existence. From Socrates we learn that it was at the solicitation of Theophilus, Bishop of Alexandria, that Theodosius ordered the demolition of the two temples.[222] The Mithreum had already been the occasion of bloody conflicts between pagans and Christians during the reign of Constantius. A certain Christian George, wishing to establish a church on the spot ordered it to be cleansed. In the innermost sanctuary, the adytum, they

---

[221]Sozomen, HE 7.15.
[222]Socrates, HE 5.16.

found the skulls of many people believed to have been immolated to the god for purposes of divination. Christians carried the evidence through the city in a triumphant procession. Exasperated by such humiliation, pagans arose against the Christians and killed a number of them. Christians ceased to cleanse the Mithreum, and George was dragged out and burned by the pagans.[223] Again in the final attempt of the Christians to destroy the Mithreum, severe conflicts arose in Alexandria in which many more Christians than pagans perished.[224]

But it was undoubtedly the destruction of the Serapeum which was the crown of Christian successes in Alexandria. Theodoret referred to the magnificence of the temple "excelling in size and beauty all the temples in the world." He then described how the god himself was torn to pieces and how the rest of the edifice came down.[225] Socrates elaborated further on the encounters between pagans and Christians and the cost in blood of those reforms. Finally the disturbances came to an end, and the governor of Alexandria and the commander-in-chief of the troops in Egypt helped Theophilus to complete the work of demolition. Most of the spoils were used for the relief for the poor, according to Theodosius's wish. It was also in the process of the demolition of the Serapeum that hieroglyphics in the form of crosses were found on stones of the temple. Both Christians and pagans interpreted them according to their prophetic insights.[226]

The nature of the sources at our disposal do not allow an objective view of the events reported in Christian historians. The decline of paganism was due as much to its own internal process of desuetude as to the intervention of Christians. Many pagan rituals and sacrifices had already come to an end before the time of Theodosius. Some scholars contend that, in spite of his antipagan zeal at the end of his tenure, Theodosius did not explicitly order the destruction of the Serapeum.[227] It is safe to assume that after 391 the old religion had no further official place in public life, though pagan rituals continued in some form. For all practical

---

[223]Ibid., 3.2.
[224]Ibid., 5.16.
[225]Theodoret, HE 5.22 (NPNF-2 III) 147-48.
[226]Socrates, HE 5.16-17.
[227]N. Q. King, *The Emperor Theodosius and the Establishment of Christianity* (London: SCM Press, 1961) 81.

purposes, paganism in the East was already potentially extinct, and it had clearly entered the process of dying in Rome. Large segments of the army remained under pagan control well into the fifth century, as exemplified by Generidus, a general in Attalus' army. His story is recounted by Zosimus.[228]

Theodosius died in Milan after a short illness on January 17, 395. Before his death he had summoned his two sons to divide the empire among them. He appointed Honorius his successor in the West, and Arcadius his successor in the East. Forty days later, on February 25, Ambrose delivered the funeral oration in which he elaborated on how all the elements of nature had joined the faithful in mourning the departure of the greatest of princes. Theodosius was compared to great personalities of the Old Testament, especially Joseph, Jacob, and the great reformer Josiah.

Estimates of Theodosius's reign vary greatly. Christians praised his virtues. The compilation of the Theodosian Code continued long after his death and probably was never finished. A Christian state was now in the balance. The major antipagan edicts of 391 seemed to have brought to an end the last surviving voices of paganism, of its temples, of its sacrifices, of its oracles, of its priests and representatives. But Theodosius had his severe critics among secular historians, especially Zosimus. They accused him of immorality and scandalous behavior. They viewed him as a ruler given to pleasure and insolence.[229]

Many contend that Theodosius received more credit than his due in the downfall of paganism which would have happened even without his legislation, though it may have taken longer. On the other hand the legislation of the Theodosian code did not mean the total end of paganism. Some of it survived in many subtle forms, sometimes becoming a part of Christian festivals and rituals. But age-old institutions had to bow to the necessities of time. The omphalos lost to the cross, and Apollo could not compete with Christ. His last official oracle was probably pronounced at Didyma, well into the days of Theodosian rule.

---

[228]Zosimus, HistNova 5.46.

[229]Ibid., 4.41: "Thus things went from bad to worse under Theodosius's rule: nothing excellent or exemplary was applauded, but every form of luxury and wantonness day by day increased a cubit in stature, as the saying goes."

In 398, Claudian, the last great Latin poet of a dying heathen world, wrote a panegyric in honor of Theodosius' son, now Emperor Honorius. In it we find the suggestion that, though the Delphic oracle had been dead for some time, it spoke again in honor of Honorius:

> What presages were there not then of future prosperity? What songs of birds, what flights of good omen in the heavens? What was the hurrying to and fro of seers? Horned Ammon and Delphi so long dumb at length broke their silence. . . . The rock of Cumae, shrine of raging Sibyl, thundered once again.[230]

The divine center was again elusive. While Christians celebrated their triumph amid their own disputes and dissensions, paganism searched for its place in the memory of future generations, having been conquered through legislation, but not having totally relinquished its grip on the hearts and imagination of those sensitive to a past which refused to accept its death sentence.

---

[230]Claudian, *Panegyric on the Fourth Consulship of the Emperor Honorius* 8.141-48 (LCL I) 297.

Chapter 9

From Persecution to Religious Freedom

The oftener we are mowed down by you, the more in number we grow; the blood of Christians is seed.
—Tertullian

We gaze up at the same stars, the sky covers us all, the same universe encompasses us. What does it matter what practical system we adopt in our search for truth? Not by one avenue only can we arrive at so tremendous a secret.
—Symmachus

The first three centuries of our era were marked by tensions which often evolved into acts of violence. Empire and church stood in a dialectical relationship difficult to define. No one can even surmise what the development of Christianity would have been apart from the conflicts which forced both pagans and Christians to argue and often to fight each other. The monumental library of documents and writings left behind by church fathers owes a great deal of its content to apologetic activity, to the need to defend the faith against all kinds of attackers. If truth were to survive, paganism could not. Conversely, in times of upheaval, many Romans believed that the *Pax Deorum* could be preserved only through a systematic annihilation of that which threatened the gods of the land.

It became imperative for Roman emperors to assess the powers controlling the universe and to ensure that all obstacles to divine providence be removed. The choice of gods to whom to entrust the fate of the empire remained a burning question to resolve. The lack of consensus could be staggering as exemplified by the radically opposite views adopted by Constantine and Julian. Political destiny depended on a commitment to religious practices and expectations. Fortune or misfortune could not be disconnected from the nature of the gods worshiped.

Christians shared the same concerns and often wondered about the forces at work in the world. Even in a post-Constantine, Christianized empire, the questions of fate, destiny, and necessity were not resolved on the level of faith alone. When Basil addressed his first letter to the philosopher Eustathius he conceded that there is a Necessity (ἀνάγκη) and a Fate (εἱμαρμένη) which rule all the events of our lives, and that human beings have control over nothing. According to him, all human life is driven by a kind of Luck (τύχη).

Romans' hope to create an all-inclusive religious climate was frustrated by Christians who rejected syncretistic modes of thinking, especially in the case of the worship of *Sol Invictus*. It seemed that pagans and Christians could agree on the importance of the sun. But Tertullian chose to refute the argument that Christians were worshipers of the sun because they set aside Sun-day for celebration.[1] Without any philosophical common ground, the coexistence of church and state gravitated between tolerance and persecution.

The rapid progress of Christianity appeared more than a nuisance in the Roman empire. Paganism was challenged and awakened from its lack of commitment to long-standing religious traditions. A new sense of terror and apocalyptic foreboding as expressed in Christian proclamation stirred many pagans into reaction. An obscure sect was bold enough to denounce Roman ancestral religion and to relegate it to the realm of absurdity. New cultic expressions such as Mithraism were born, and attempts at keeping alive expiring oracles produced only limited results. Greek and Roman traditions proved insufficient to answer each and every situation. Egyptian mystery practices and Chaldaean oracles were added to existing rituals. Even Christianity could not remain free of oriental influences infiltrating it through Gnostic and Manichaean esoteric rites and beliefs.

The notion of treason which had been confined mostly to political conduct was now applied to religious stances. The *Pax Deorum* could not survive if its gods were reviled or reduced to the role of demons. Christians sharpened their message. Their unpopularity often provoked brutal responses.

---

[1]Tertullian, Apol 16.

Roman authorities had already learned how to deal with nonpolitical factions. Christians were the object of the same accusations as philosophical groups, especially the Stoics.[2] Seneca chose to withdraw from political life in what amounted to a form of persecution for his contempt for government. Christians waged their battles against the cultural aberrations of pagan society even after they had become part of its aristocracy.

Opponents of Christianity included articulate and persuasive thinkers such as Celsus and Porphyry, and later Libanius and Symmachus. As time went on, the debate became more civil. In the early stages there was no dialogue, just virulent diatribe. By the time of Libanius and Symmachus, great changes had already taken place in the empire, with church officials in positions of leadership. Secular philosophers were forced to defend paganism and disparage Christianity. The roles were much less clearly defined. Church fathers who lived through the radical transformations in the days of Constantine had to alter their outlook on history and divine purpose. For apologists such as Eusebius and Lactantius the concept of "Roman" became equated with that of "Christian." Few developments in history matched the dramatic intensity of those years.

Christians and the Calamities of the Empire

The progressive erosion of Roman dominion and the forecast of its doom were often attributed to the presence of Christians in the empire. In the same way Apollo was silenced by the proximity of Christians, pagan intelligentsia began to see in the new religion the main obstacle to Roman success and the cause of all the calamities befalling the citizens and their government.

Pagans were acquainted with the philosophical outlook which predicted the obsolescence of the world and the unavoidable conflagrations it must suffer. Plato elaborated on the process in his *Timaeus*, reflecting on the errant cause which prevents divine purpose from reaching its creative design. Socrates thought that what we find in the recurring cycles is the propensity toward annihilation of life rather than blessing. From the beginning diverse destructions of the human race have been the result of fire, floods, and other catastrophes. Socrates concluded that for everything

---

[2]Marta Sordi, *The Christians and the Roman Empire*, trans. Annabel Bedini (Norman: University of Oklahoma Press, 1986) 28.

that has come into existence destruction is appointed, and that the fabric of all that is will be dissolved into nothingness.[3] Both pagans and Christians were well acquainted with the available works of Plato.

When Plutarch wrote his *De sera numinis vindicta* (*On the Delays of the Divine Vengeance*), he reminded his contemporaries that only the postponement of divine vengeance could be salutary to a nation in need of undeserved divine providence for its survival. Plutarch rejected the concept of divine punishment in favor of a healing process. To those who were astonished at God's behavior he intimated that "we should become cautious in such matters, and hold the gentleness and magnanimity displayed by God a part of virtue that is divine, which by punishment amends a few, while it profits and admonishes many by the delay."[4] From the beginning of the second century on, Roman intellectuals knew the works of Plutarch.

Equally important, though less contemporary, was the work of Lucretius, *De rerum natura* (*On the Nature of Things*). In it Lucretius wove a poetic view of an aging world, just a small fragment of the whole cosmos which contains many other assemblages. This old machine we know and which we call earth is now the victim of time's ineluctability and will soon come to a ruinous death. He ends his book 2 by portraying a farmer despondent at the thought of the future: "The sorrowful planter too of the exhausted and shrivelled vine impeaches the march of time and wearies heaven, and comprehends not that all things are gradually wasting away and passing to the grave, quite forspent by age and length of days."

Romans accepted their anxieties and fears. But they often could not explain the onslaught of powers which brought discouragement and failure to their endeavors and military ambitions. From tenets of philosophy to the identification of a scapegoat there was only a short

---

[3]Plato, Rep 546A. For the major arguments on the vulnerability of the world and the calamities besetting it see in particular the extensive passages in Tim 27C-30C; 37C; 47C; 48A; 22AC; 23AB; 69C.

[4]Plutarch, SeraNum 551C (LCL. Mor VII) 199. The anthropomorphism of the pagans has been the object of attacks by church fathers. Plutarch's gentle divinity is echoed in some Christian writings: "But the true gods and those who are worthy to have and to wear the dignity of this name, neither conceive anger nor indulge a grudge, nor do they contrive by insidious devices what may be hurtful to another party." Arnobius, AdvGent 1.23 (ANF VI) 418.

step. Christians, through their refusal to comply with the requirements of the gods of the land, were viewed as the cause of all the calamities. By disconnecting themselves from the mainstream of Roman idealism they threatened the consecration of communal self-affirmation so important to the world in which they lived.

Tolerance and logic did not always match. Christians knew the philosophical arguments also. Church fathers were acquainted with the writings of Plato, Lucretius, and Plutarch, and other Greek and Roman authors. They shared a cultural background they often felt compelled to deny, thus sapping the collective authority needed to maintain unity.

We find in the writings of Cyprian a close parallel to Lucretius's ideas. The collapse of the Roman empire will be the result of natural causes, not a punishment of the gods against the Christians. In his fifth treatise he replied to Demetrianus, who contended that all the reversals of fortune suffered by the world were to be imputed to Christians. They were the cause of repeated wars, famines, pestilences, and so on. To the attacks of Demetrianus that Christians were responsible for droughts, Cyprian answered with a Lucretian argument: "And in this behalf, since you are ignorant of divine knowledge, and a stranger to the truth, you must in the first place know this, that the world has now grown old, and does not abide in that strength in which it formerly stood; nor has it that vigour and force which it formerly possessed."[5]

After pursuing the debate on the basis of logic, showing that decay and weakness are unavoidable, until it all leads to death, Cyprian turned the argument around against Demetrianus: "These things [diseases, pestilence, wars, droughts . . . which had been foretold of old] happen not, as your false complaining and ignorant inexperience of the truth asserts and repeats, because your gods are not worshipped by us, but because God is not worshipped by you."[6] Then came the challenge: "If your gods have any deity and power, let them themselves rise to their own vindication, let them defend themselves by their own majesty. But what can they advantage their worshippers, if they cannot avenge themselves on those who worship them not?"[7] If Christians could be proven criminals, condemnation and death would be in oder. If they are

---

[5]Cyprian, Treat 5.3 (ANF V) 458.
[6]Ibid., 5.5 (ANF V) 459.
[7]Ibid., 5.14 (ANF V) 462.

not criminals, the law does not allow the persecution of innocent people. Cyprian wrote at length to praise martyrdom.

By the turn of the third century the habit of calling Christians atheists was well established. Romans did not know how to refute a Christian God, and never really attempted to. The bone of contention remained the stubborn refusal of Christians to worship the pagan gods considered the protectors of the empire and whose displeasure meant ruin. The situation became worse when the gods were demoted to demons or refused any existence at all.

Several decades before Cyprian, Tertullian had already replied to the heathen who viewed Christians as the cause of public calamities. If Christians were to be blamed for the catastrophes of the world, it would have meant giving to such a young movement incredible powers against which all the gods of the land could not prevail. The answer must be somewhere else. Tertullian drew up a long list of past disasters, from the cataclysm which swallowed Atlantis to all the famines, earthquakes and other destructive moves of nature. Where were the Christians in all of those instances?[8]

Natural events were beyond the control of pagan gods. Continents were disrupted from their peace. Geography was altered by conflagrations beyond imagination. Tertullian listed many of them, and then asked: "Where were your gods themselves in those days, when the flood poured its destroying waters all over the world?"[9] Not with a little indignation, he fired back at pagan accusations:

> If the Tiber rises as high as the city walls, if the Nile does not send its waters up over the fields, if the heavens give no rain, if there is an earthquake, if there is famine or pestilence, straightway the cry is: Away with the Christians to the lion [Christianos ad leonem]![10]

Writing on the eve of Diocletian's great persecution, Arnobius entered into long debates that often resembled Platonic arguments, though he rejected most of the tenets of Greek philosophy. There is no justifiable hatred of Christ because the pagans have not suffered from his presence in the world. Pagans retorted that Christ deserved rejection because his

---

[8]Tertullian's argument is developed in AdNat 1.9.
[9]Tertullian, Apol 40 (ANF III) 47.
[10]Ibid.

disciples focused their efforts on driving religion from the world by attacking those who honor the traditional gods. Arnobius conceded that pagans were entitled to their ways of worship when praising Apollo, Jupiter, Mars, or any other divinity. But when compared to the true God, those divinities appeared as lesser and wicked and deserved to be displaced by the creator of the world.[11]

The introduction to *Adversus gentes* sets the tone for the debate between pagans and Christians by identifying the nature of the conflict and by defining the major propositions:

> Since I have found some who deem themselves very wise in their opinions, acting as if they were inspired, and announcing with all the authority of an oracle, that from the time when the Christian people began to exist in the world the universe has gone to ruin, that the human race has been visited with ills of many kinds, that even the very gods, abandoning their accustomed charge . . . have been driven from the regions of earth. . . . For I should not deny that that charge is a most serious one, and that we fully deserve the hatred attaching to public enemies, if it should appear that to us are attributable causes by reason of which the universe has deviated from its laws, the gods have been driven far away, and such swarms of miseries have been inflicted on the generations of men.[12]

The verbal debate between pagans and Christians revealed its ambiguity and inconsistency. If it could be proven that Christians were the cause of floods, droughts, destroyed harvest, and all other calamities, it would equally mean that the pagans would have to blame themselves for allowing such a situation to develop through the neglect of their cults and through the recognition that the weakness of their gods allowed the rapid spread of Christian propaganda. From an early Christian point of view, shared by Arnobius, calamities did not arise because of the presence of Christianity, but because of the sins of the people. Neither pagans nor Christians can change the flow of time, though they might greatly influence its content.

The intrusion of Christianity into Roman life was viewed by pagans as an obstacle to universal well-being and safety. The church, which was

---

[11]Arnobius, AdvGent 2.2.
[12]Ibid., 1.1 (ANF VI) 413.

of recent origin and had no credible history, dared attempt to displace Greek and Roman ancestral religions and their rites. Arnobius argued that length of time is irrelevant and relative: "Four hundred years ago, my opponent says, your religion did not exist. And two thousand years ago, *I reply*, your gods did not exist."[13] The argument continued, and Arnobius conceded that the antiquity of pagan religion constituted a valid inference of its appeal, though wrong. He contended that Christian religion, because of its universality, is not new at all, though Christians have been late in learning what they should revere and follow.[14] No one could successfully argue that the wretchedness of the world belonged to any particular period in history. But pagans kept asserting that the fate of the empire has suffered because of the emergence of Christianity at a time when barbarian invasions began to threaten its stability.

The charge of impiety was levelled at Christians because they did not erect temples, build altars, offer sacrifices, set up statues. . . . Arnobius seemed to agree that Christians did not have any temples.[15] The debate was not new. According to Origen, Celsus had already developed long and persuasive arguments against the Christians who could not tolerate temples, altars, and images and who refused to build them themselves. This was adduced as a proof that they were godless and that they placed themselves in the category of forbidden and secret society.[16] This assertion has often been the cause of contention, for Christians had places of worship, though they may have refrained, up to the time of Constantine, to erect elaborate and pretentious structures such as the pagans had for their gods. For Arnobius, of course, it was a foregone conclusion that pagans have built sumptuous temples to their gods in vain, if not sometimes as an insult to their proclaimed majesty.[17]

---

[13]Ibid., 2.71 (ANF VI) 461.

[14]Ibid., 2.72. Arnobius 2.75 (ANF VI) 462 anticipates the argument of pagans questioning the reasons why God would have sent a savior so late in the process of history. To that he proposes a philosophical answer that within eternity the notion of late or early becomes insignificant: "For where there is no end and no beginning, nothing is too soon, nothing too late."

[15]Ibid., 6.1-3.

[16]Origen, CCel 7.62; 8.17.

[17]Arnobius, AdvGent 6.8.

Arnobius emphasized the temporality of Roman gods, the fallacy of any claim to their presence in human affairs, and mostly the provincial nature of their alleged rule: "What! do the Romans have gods to themselves, who do not help other nations? and how can they be gods, if they do not exercise their divine power impartially towards all nations everywhere?"[18]

The question of Arnobius's Platonism has often been a source of debate. He suggested that some Platonic tenets resembled Christian ideas about God, though Plato belonged to the world of pagans and shared their misguided concept of the divinity. But he also referred to Plato as a man reverent and scrupulous in his wisdom, who could lead pagans to contemplate the true meaning of their calamities:

> Plato, that sublime head and pillar of all philosophers, has declared in his writings, that those cruel floods and those conflagrations of the world are a purification of the earth; nor did that wise man dread to call the overthrow of the human race, its destruction, ruin, and death, a renewal of things.[19]

With Arnobius, whose writings have sometimes been neglected or judged inferior, the apologetic activity of the early church was at a crucial turning point. The persecutions under Diocletian and Galerius, as well as the rise of Constantine to power altered the tone and content of the debates. The responsibility of Christians in the fate of the empire remained an issue.

In the post-Constantine era pagans attributed political and social adversities to Christianity to a degree even higher than in the days of Tertullian, Cyprian, and Arnobius. This time the emperor himself was guilty of sacrilege and added to disasters by issuing antipagan edicts and by threatening heathen religion on all levels. Pagans lost the voice of authority, and their opposition was mostly verbal and literary as in the case of Libanius and Symmachus. Temples were closed, sacrifices prohibited. The number of pagans was dwindling, and even the short attempts at restoration during the reign of Julian did not produce any spectacular revival of paganism. Established customs were uprooted by the triumphal march of Christianity. Yet the empire was collapsing, and

---

[18]Ibid., 4.4 (ANF VI) 477.
[19]Ibid., 1.8 (ANF VI) 416. See also 2.51.

remaining pagans continued to believe that Christians were to blame for the disfavor of the gods. It was a time of nostalgia for past achievements now lost beyond their vanishing points.

Augustine tried to provide a rationale for the state of affairs, sometimes wishing that the "city of God" would not require the total annihilation of the "City of man." He was contemplating the downfall of an empire that, according to him, had always carried within itself the seeds of its own collapse, because it was based on deceit and violence. But could anyone sincerely proclaim that Christianity was the solution? Christians were in a position of superiority, but the church was a movement of dissensions, recriminations, and progressively usurpation. Christian religion won more by legislation than by conviction. The faith of the martyrs was no longer needed nor desired. In many instances greed replaced the simple and ascetic way of life of former generations of Christians.

In their assessment of the fate of Roman society, pagans became obsessed with the need to blame Christians for their setbacks. Augustine could not ignore such an important fact. At one point he quoted a saying that had become a proverb because of the frequency of its use:

> And it is an old proverb, yet one that began from Christian times, "God gives no rain; count it to the Christians!" Although it was those of old who said thus. But these now say also, "That God sends no rain, count it to the Christians! God sends no rain; we sow not. God sends rain; we reap not."[20]

In the introduction to his *De civitate Dei* Augustine rebuked pagans who persisted in blaming the Christian religion for the calamities of the empire and especially for the invasion of Rome by the Goths. It was a time of confusion. Ills and disasters were shared by pagans and Christians alike, and Augustine had to appeal to a sense of universality to convince his contemporaries that all things came from the same God, even for those who mistook religion for their personal luck as they were spared by the barbarians.

According to Augustine, the proverb: "Drought and Christianity go hand in hand"[21] proved nothing but the ignorance of those who used it.

---

[20]Augustine, Psalms 81 (NPNF-1 VIII) 390.
[21]Augustine, CivDei 2.3 (NPNF-1 II) 24.

To insist on the culpability of Christians every time disasters befell the empire was a weak attempt to camouflage a despair for which there was no solution. If the Romans worshiped their gods in order to prevent disasters, mused Augustine, why then were those gods of so little help? Why did so many disasters happen before there was Christianity? Who was responsible then?

Pagans were still coping with the effects of the blows inflicted on their practices by Theodosius. It was obvious to them that the gods who allowed Rome to rise to its position of glory were now silent and had withdrawn their favors from a people who deserved chastisement for their abandonment of traditional worship. Even Augustine had to acknowledge that pagan Rome had prospered and that a great deal of Christian history had been calamitous. But, in the final analysis, there was the *civitate Dei*, the spiritual world that can transcend all of the vicissitudes of temporal time in the city of man.

By the fifth century there was little doubt as to the final religious orientation of the empire. Yet several apologetic voices were still heard to put to rest the idea that Christians had brought demise upon Rome. Sozomen suggested that in some instances the calamities decried by the pagans were the means by which those pagans were brought to Christianity.[22]

Orosius wrote his *Historiarum adversus paganos libri vii (Seven Books of History Against the Pagans)* to emphasize that catastrophes of all magnitudes had visited the human race long before the advent of Christianity, thus refuting the contention that the perils of Rome were connected with its conversion to it. In fact Rome had been spared much of the misery inflicted on other kingdoms, and in some way, was providential in the spreading of Christianity. Barbarian invasions could be viewed as Rome's punishment for the persecution of Christians. But the true mission of Rome was to bring the heathen world to the light of Christ. The role of the church was to mitigate, through prayer, the chastisements deserved by the world.[23]

---

[22]Sozomen, HE 7.20.

[23]Orose (Orosius), *Histoires contre les païens*, Texte établi et traduit par Marie-Pierre Arnaud-Lindet (Paris: Les Belles Lettres, 1990) 6.1, 27: "Quand il n'y avait pas encore d'église pour modérer par ses prières les châtiments mérités par le monde, les malheurs des hommes étaient bien plus graves."

Zosimus, a propagan fifth-century historian of Rome, still attempted to vindicate the elemental proposition that had been believed by so many before him, namely that there was a double equation on which historical truth rested: The loyalty to pagan religious traditions meant the glory of Rome whereas a neglect of those traditions led to decadence and misery.

Finally a word may be said about the writings of Salvian, a fifth-century monk and preacher who, in his *De gubernatione Dei*, argued that the chastisements inflicted by God on Rome were the results of the sinful life of the Romans. God was not indifferent to the fate of Rome but could not leave it unpunished even after it became Christian.

From Verbal Assault to Physical violence

The New Testament did not envisage pagans as the source or cause of persecutions. That role was assigned to Jews. Christ spoke of the tribulations his followers would have to endure because of the displeasure of Jewish leaders and institutions. Persecutions of disciples would go through all the stages allowed by law and, as a last resort, they would be delivered to governors and Roman powers to execute a punishment beyond Jewish legal empowerment.[24] In the days of Jesus the new group of disciples was regarded as an integral part of Judaism, subject to its religious requirements. The concept of an independent church was not even entertained.

The Book of Acts, if we are willing to attribute to it historical accuracy, vindicated the same outlook. Whether in Jerusalem or in the Diaspora, the conflicts confronting the apostles were of Jewish origin, except perhaps for the episode in Acts 19 where the encounter with the pagan Demetrius over the status of the goddess Diana in Ephesus ended up in riots which were silenced by the Roman authorities and which did not lead to persecution.

In Acts 4 Peter and John were arrested on the orders of the priests, the captain of the temple, and the Sadducees, but released for lack of evidence against them. Stephen's case proved more tragic, and the events leading to his death at the hand of Jews marked a decisive turn in the direction of the new movement. The six surviving Hellenists, who left Jerusalem to escape the fate of their colleague, may be regarded as the

---

[24]Matthew 10:17-18; 23:34; Mark 13:9; Luke 12:11, 21:12.

originators of what became later the Christian church. Emboldened and angry Jewish authorities continued to persecute the disciples. In Acts 12 the execution of James on the orders of Herod marked a new turn in Jewish ferocity. Since it pleased the Jewish mobs, he also had Peter arrested and imprisoned, but to no avail since that act of violence ended up in the miraculous escape of the disciple.

As soon as Paul joined the new movement, Jews seemed determined to stop him, from the very moment of his conversion in Damascus (Acts 9:22-23). The same scenes are repeated throughout the Book of Acts, sometimes with the added accusation that Paul and his companions deliberately set themselves up against the decrees of Caesar (Acts 17:7). Such accusations were meant to force Roman authorities to enter the arena of persecution, a fact which did not occur. On the contrary. The end of the Book of Acts spared no details on how Paul was brought by the Jews to the Governor Felix for his prosecution as a pestilence and as the ringleader of the sect of the Nazarenes. Felix, whose wife was a Jewess, listened to Paul's defense, and, just to please the Jews, kept Paul in prison for two years, at which time his successor Festus took over. But when Festus proposed that Paul go to Jerusalem to be tried there, Paul derailed the plot of the Jews by appealing to Caesar, an appeal with which Festus concurred. According to Luke, King Agrippa and Berenice came to Caesarea to welcome Festus. This was the occasion of the long defense of Paul in front of all of them. Soon Paul was on his way to Rome, and the inconclusive end of the Book of Acts leaves us with the impression that he could go about teaching and preaching "quite openly and unhindered."

Up to the year 64 no open hostility on the part of Roman authorities against the new sect can be documented. Tertullian cited Nero as the first Roman emperor to be involved in the persecution of Christians: "Consult your histories; you will there find that Nero was the first who assailed with the imperial sword the Christian sect, making progress then especially at Rome."[25] But it was not until the latter part of his reign that Nero became violent against the Christians.[26]

---

[25]Tertullian, Apol 5 (ANF III) 22. See also Scorp 15.

[26]Eusebius, HE 2.22.8 (NPNF-2 I) 125: "It is probable indeed that as Nero was more disposed to mildness in the beginning, Paul's defense of his doctrine was more easily received; but that when he had advanced to the commission of

Assessments of persecutions under Nero vary greatly. His determination to make a scapegoat of the Christians for the fire in Rome was only partially successful. Tacitus reported the growing suspicion of the citizenry that the emperor himself committed the crime. Suetonius remained silent on that subject. Very often pagans considered Jews and Christians guilty of the same crimes. But in the case of Nero the two groups were disassociated, probably as a result of the influence of Poppaea and Tigellinus on the emperor. The Neronian persecution, though it did not greatly affect the life of the church in Rome, remained memorable because of the number of martyrs, among them probably even Peter and Paul.[27]

The nature and severity of the persecutions under Domitian cannot be firmly established. The conflict originated with the levy of taxes on Jewish people and then on Christians, often regarded as part of Judaism. On the basis of the information collected from Hegesippus, Eusebius referred to an edict of Domitian ordering the slaying of all the descendants of David.[28] This brought hardship on many members of the Roman nobility related to Jews. According to some sources persecutions under Domitian began with high ranked personalities of the empire before they were directed at Christians.[29] There is no consensus on the degree of

---

lawless deeds of daring, he made the apostles as well as others the subjects of his attacks." Tertullian does not concede any virtue to Nero at any time. See especially AdNat 1.7 where the ruthlessness and immorality of Nero are strongly emphasized.

[27]The tradition of the martyrdom of Peter and Paul in Rome was preserved by Eusebius, HE 2.25.5 (NPNF-2 I) 129 "It is, therefore, recorded that Paul was beheaded in Rome itself, and that Peter likewise was crucified under Nero." There are many more questions and debates about Peter's death in Rome than about Paul's.

[28]Eusebius, HE 3.19.

[29]Ibid., 3.17. Eusebius does not mention any names in connection with those "well-born and notable men at Rome." All he says is that it was without cause. But in HE 3.18.5 Eusebius refers to Flavius Clemens, a cousin of Domitian and to his wife Domitilla, a niece of the emperor, as victims of Domitian's brutality. The case of Domitilla is clear for Eusebius. As a Christian she was exiled to the island of Pontia. As for Flavius Clemens the record is far less clear. Suetonius refers to his brutal death at the hand of Domitian: "Finally he executed, suddenly and on some trivial pretext, his own cousin, Flavius Clemens, just before the

hardship brought on the Jews. Suetonius and Epictetus refer to people who acted like Jews without belonging to Judaism to avail themselves of the status of *religio licita*.[30]

The cruelty of Domitian was stressed by the church fathers. They associated him with Nero. Under his reign persecutions were methodical and difficult to escape.[31] Yet he is often portrayed as more humane than Nero and as having himself decreed an end to persecution: "Domitian, too, a man of Nero's type in cruelty, tried his hand at persecution; but as he had something of the human in him, he soon put an end to what he

---

completion of a consulship." Domitian 15.310. The charge mentioned by Suetonius is "despicable idleness." But Dio Cassius, RomHist 67.14.2 (LCL VIII) 349, reports that Domitian accused Flavius Clemens and his wife Flavia Domitilla of atheism (ἀθεότητος). Then he adds: "The charge brought against them both was that of atheism, a charge on which many others who drifted into Jewish ways were condemned." Such charges have also been used against Christians, and some scholars have concluded that Flavius Clemens died as a Christian martyr. But had that been the case, Christian writers would have mentioned such an illustrious martyr so early in the history of the church.

[30]Suetonius, Caesars: Domitian 12.308: "Domitian's agents collected the tax on Jews [a tax which had been imposed already by Vespasian after the fall of the Jerusalem temple] with a peculiar lack of mercy; and took proceedings not only against those who kept their Jewish origins a secret in order to avoid the tax, but against those who lived as Jews without professing Judaism." In Epictetus, Disc 2.20-22 (LCL I), 273, we read:

> Why do you deceive the multitude, why do you act the part of a Jew, when you are a Greek? Do you not see in what sense men are severally called Jew, Syrian, or Egyptian? For example, whenever we see a man halting between two faiths, we are in the habit of saying, "He is not a Jew, he is only acting the part." But when he adopts the attitude of mind of the man who has been baptized and has made his choice, then he both is a Jew in fact and is also called one. So we also are counterfeit "Baptists" (παραβαπτισταί), ostensibly Jews, but in reality something else.

[31]Ignatius, MartIgn 1 (ANF I) 129

had begun, even restoring again those whom he had banished."[32] But most pagan and Christian sources would point against such clemency.

The persecutions under Domitian remained memorable because of the banishment of John to Patmos. Apocryphal New Testament literature gave a long and detailed account of it.[33] Jerome mentioned specifically the liberation of John from Patmos and his return to Ephesus after the death of Domitian. Under Nerva the Senate annulled the policies of Domitian, and Christians were free again.[34] Lactantius elaborated on the tragic fate of Domitian at the hands of his own people: "Having been instigated by evil demons to persecute the righteous people, he was then delivered into the power of his enemies, and suffered due punishment. To be murdered in his own palace was not vengeance ample enough; the very memory of his name was erased. For although he had erected many admirable edifices, and rebuilt the capitol, and left other distinguished marks of his magnificence, yet the senate did so persecute his name, as to leave no remains of his statues, or traces of the inscriptions put up in honour of him; and by most solemn and severe decrees it branded him, even after death, with perpetual infamy."[35]

Sordi summarized the importance of the persecution under Domitian in terms of the relationship between church and empire. Christians were identified once and for all as a distinct religious group no longer

---

[32]Tertullian, Apol 5 (ANF III) 22. Tertullian's information is most probably derived from the remaining fragments of Hegesippus: "Thereupon Domitian passed no condemnation upon them [the relatives of Christ], but treated them with contempt, as too mean for notice, and let them go free. At the same time he issued a command, and put a stop to the persecution against the Church." *Fragments from his Five Books of Commentaries on the Acts of the Church* (ANF VIII) 763. The clemency attributed to Domitian contradicts some of the sources on his reign. In all probability that clemency did not occur until Nerva, who succeeded Domitian and reversed his policies concerning Christians. See also Sordi, *Christians*, 42.

[33]See especially *Acts of the Holy Apostle and Evangelist John the Theologian: About his Exile and Departure* (ANF VIII) 560-64. The exile of John is also mentioned by Christian historians but without elaboration. Eusebius, HE 3.18.

[34]Jerome and Gennadius, Lives 9.

[35]Lactantius, DeMort 3 (ANF VII) 302.

protected by the legitimacy of the Jewish religion. Christianity became a definite *superstitio illicita* accused of atheism.[36]

A rescript of Trajan that became both famous and efficient provided further clarification on the relationship of the church to the empire. It was the outcome of the correspondence between Pliny the Younger and the emperor. In 111 Pliny became governor of Bithynia, a province plagued by numerous problems, especially financial ones. But, in spite of all of his administrative duties, he had not come into contact with many Christians before this assignment. Faced with problems he could not resolve, and full of doubt as to how he was to proceed, he wrote a long letter to Trajan to ask for his guidance. In that communication he exposed what he learned about the Christian movement. He had put the Christians to the test of worshiping the gods and the emperor and of cursing Christ. Those who refused to comply were identified as hard core Christians. But what he knew about the church was not sufficient to warrant any drastic action.

Pliny exposed to Trajan what he decided to do with the Christians while awaiting his answer:

> In the meanwhile, the method I have observed towards those who have been denounced to me as Christians is this: I interrogated them whether they were Christians; if they confessed it I repeated the question twice again, adding the threat of capital punishment; if they still persevered, I ordered them to be executed. For whatever the nature of their creed might be, I could at least feel no doubt that contumacy and inflexible obstinacy deserved chastisement.[37]

But the doubts of Pliny persisted, for he had no personal knowledge of Christian doctrine and relied on hearsay:

> They [possibly renegate Christians] affirmed, however, the whole of their guilt, or their error, was, that they were in the habit of meeting on a certain fixed day before it was light, when they sang in alternate verses a hymn to Christ, as to a god, and bound themselves by a solemn oath, not to any wicked deeds, but never to commit any fraud, theft or

---

[36]Sordi, *Christians*, 52-53.
[37]Pliny, Letters 96 (LCL II) 401-403.

adultery, never to falsify their word, nor deny a trust when they should be called upon to deliver it up.[38]

Thus the strongest accusation Pliny could level at Christians is that they disobeyed his order forbidding political associations. The more esoteric practices of Christian assemblies were unknown to Pliny, though he had heard that Christians were involved in the murdering and eating of children and of drinking the blood, an obviously gross distortion of the Eucharist.

As much as the letter of Pliny was prolix and full of uncertainties, the reply of Trajan was to the point. It might be useful to quote it at length:

> The method you have pursued, my dear Pliny, in sifting the cases of those denounced to you as Christians is extremely proper. It is not possible to lay down any general rule which can be applied as the fixed standard in all cases of this nature. No search should be made for these people; when they are denounced and found guilty they must be punished; with the restriction, however, that when the party denies himself to be a Christian, and shall give proof that he is not (that is by adoring our Gods) he shall be pardoned on the ground of repentance, even though he may have formerly incurred suspicion. Informations without the accuser's name subscribed must not be admitted in evidence against anyone, as it is introducing a very dangerous precedent, and by no means agreeable to the spirit of the age.[39]

The rescript of Trajan remained a model of legal action. Tertullian elaborated on it, seeing in it both the good and the evil, and a great contradiction in that Christians should be left alone, while they also should be punished: "O miserable deliverance,—under the necessity of the case, a self contradiction [*sententiam necessitate confusam*]! It forbids them to be sought after as innocent, and it commands them to be punished as guilty."[40]

It would be difficult to assess the extent of any persecution under Trajan. Patristic literature has focused on the martyrdom of Ignatius. His sentence pronounced by Trajan himself read: "We command that Ignatius,

---

[38]Ibid., (LCL II) 403-405.

[39]Pliny, Letters 97 (LCL II) 407.

[40]Tertullian, Apol 2 (ANF III) 19. Eusebius repeated what he found in Tertullian without offering any further comment. HE 3.33.1-4.

who affirms that he carries about within him Him that was crucified, be bound by soldiers and carried to the great [city] Rome, there to be devoured by the beasts, for the gratification of the people."[41] Jerome preserved the tradition and reproduced for posterity the last words of the saint as he was about to be torn to pieces by the wild beasts: "I am the grain of Christ. I am ground by the teeth of the wild beast that I may be found the bread of the world."[42]

The major religious unrest under the rule of Hadrian, successor of Trajan, did not involve Christians but Jews. Already Trajan witnessed bloody Jewish uprisings in Cyprus, Egypt, and Cyrene, a discouraging omen of what Hadrian had to contend with. In a preempting move he attempted to eradicate Jewish influence by reorganizing Judea. Since Jerusalem was still in ruins after its destruction in 70, the emperor ordered that a new city be built on that spot and be named *Aelia Capitolina*, in honor of the emperor Aelius Hadrian. It was to become a Roman colony with mostly Greek settlers. A temple to Jupiter Capitolinus was erected in the new city, and the emperor was to be worshiped there. It is generally agreed that Hadrian built a temple to Venus on the alleged spot of the crucifixion, a temple which was ordered destroyed by Helena in search of the original cross on which Christ died.

The plan of Hadrian was to transform the old Jerusalem into a new center of Greco-Roman culture. The Jews rebelled against such a scheme, and, in a bloody revolt led by Bar-Kochba, they made their last assault against the Roman empire. In spite of their courageous resistance, the uprising failed. Hadrian was determined to remove the name of Judea from the list of Roman regions. He renamed it *Provincia Syria Palaestina*. Under penalty of death, the remaining Jews were forbidden to enter *Aelia Capitolina*.[43]

The instability created by the Jewish revolt may have affected Hadrian's position regarding Christians in either positive or negative ways. There was an unusual surge in theological writings sent to Hadrian in defense of Christianity. Two of those works were penned by the oldest

---

[41]Ignatius, MartIgn 2 (ANF I) 130.
[42]Jerome and Gennadius, Lives 16 (NPNF-2 III) 367.
[43]Eusebius, HE 4.6.3 (NPNF-2 I) 177: "For the emperor gave orders that they should not even see from a distance the land of their fathers. Such is the account of Aristo of Pella."

apologists known to us: the *Chronicle* of Quadratus, of which only a few lines are preserved in Eusebius[44] and the *Apology* of Aristides.[45] The *First Apology* of Justin was also dedicated to Hadrian.

As in the case of Trajan, local governors sought the advice of the emperor for ways in which to deal with Christians. Serennius Granianus, proconsul of Asia, left behind a correspondence preserved in Eusebius. In it Granianus reminded the emperor that it would not be just to slay Christians without a proper accusation and trial just to satisfy the outcries of the populace. An appeal was made to the rescript of Trajan. In view of this Hadrian issued his own rescript preserved in two Patristic documents by Justin and Eusebius. The version given by Eusebius reads as follows.

> To Minucius Fundanus. I have received an epistle, written to me by Serennius Granianus, a most illustrious man, whom you have succeeded. It does not seem right to me that the matter should be passed by without examination, lest the men be harassed and opportunity be given to the informers for practicing villainy. If, therefore, the inhabitants of the province can clearly sustain this petition against the Christians so as to give answer in a court of law, let them pursue this course alone, but let them not have resort to men's petitions and outcries. For it is far more proper, if anyone wishes to make an accusation, that you should examine into it. If anyone therefore accuses them and shows that they are doing anything contrary to the laws, do pass judgment according to the heinousness of the crime. But, By Hercules! if anyone brings an accusation through mere calumny, decide in regard to his criminality, and see to it that you inflict punishment.[46]

This rescript of Hadrian predates the Jewish revolt by about ten years. To the best of our information the emperor made no attempt to change his position after the Jewish uprising. On the contrary. Referring to the *Historia Augusta*, Sordi suggests that "Hadrian had already thought of

---

[44]Ibid., 4.3.1-3. Aristides and Quadratus are included in the *Lives of Illustrious Men* of Jerome and Gennadius. (NPNF-2 III) 368.

[45]Two versions of the *Apology* of Aristides are preserved. One is a translation from the Greek, the other one a translation from the Syriac. They are both included side by side in ANF X, 263-79.

[46]Eusebius, HE 4.9.1-3 (NPNF-2 I) 182. A slightly different translation is found in Justin Martyr, 1 Apol 68.

giving Christianity official recognition and had had temples prepared without statues, ready to be consecrated to Christ."[47]

Neither the rescript of Trajan, nor that of Hadrian, totally eradicated local persecutions. There was enough room for interpretation in those documents to justify accusations against Christians. But the rescripts had a beneficial influence on the life of the church. Their authority was often invoked. When Marcus Aurelius became emperor, Melito, the bishop of Sardis, took upon himself to remind him of the rescript of Hadrian and of a decree sent by his immediate predecessor, Antoninus Pius, to the cities of Thessalonica, Athens, and Larissa, forbidding them to take any measures against Christians.[48] With Marcus Aurelius, the Antonine rule came to an end. His attitude towards Christians was mentioned earlier in this work.

Though there were no official persecutions under Marcus Aurelius, a number of Christians were put to death, sometimes without his knowledge or consent. Justin Martyr perished during his reign after he settled in Rome as a Christian teacher. His death was as isolated event, probably the result of a plot by Cynic philosophers who succeeded in bringing to an end his Christian teaching by silencing him. Eusebius gave us a detailed account of the martyrdom of Polycarp, which he placed during the reign of Marcus Aurelius in the year 166.[49] But modern scholarship has rejected such chronology and places the death of Polycarp during the reign of Antoninus Pius, around 155.

The martyrdom of Christians in Lyons (Lugdunum) represents the most serious outbreak of violence against the church during the tenure of Marcus Aurelius, though it is likely that he was only marginally involved in it. We owe to Eusebius our information about those events. Names of martyrs were recorded, and we have detailed scenes of courage which preceded their death. Among them were the well-known Blandina, Maturus, Sanctus, Attalus, and the ninety-year-old Bishop Pothinus.[50] Many of those who perished belonged to the nobility of the town. This made the outburst of violence against Christians even more perplexing. According to Eusebius, the trouble started when Christians were excluded

---

[47]Sordi, *Christians*, 67.
[48]Eusebius, HE 4.26.10.
[49]Ibid., 4.15.1-48.
[50]Ibid., 5.1.1-3, 4.

from houses, baths, and markets, and were not tolerated in any place whatsoever, especially the premises of pagan gods. Trials were set up by the governor with the usual accusations against Christians, especially those of Thyestian feasts and Oedipean intercourse. Patristic literature shows how extensively those accusations recurred.[51] Eusebius concluded that it was on the basis of those charges that the populace of Lyons burst into a rage that no authorities could mitigate. The rescript of Trajan was interpreted in many different fashions, allowing Christians to be put to death on the outcries of the people, a turn of events belying former imperial intents. Marcus Aurelius, not especially impressed by the bravado of Christians, was not eager to invoke former rescripts or to intervene in the conflagration. Later, Tertullian complained about the lack of fairness in the application of Roman law to Christians.[52]

The first empire-wide persecution of Jews and Christians took place under Septimius Severus. But the records on those events are very scarce and contradictory. Among church fathers Eusebius stood alone in giving some details of Severus's stance against the church, mostly in Egypt. Surprisingly, Eusebius did not mention the martyrdom of Perpetua and Felicitas, while he informed us that Leonides, Origen's father, perished in those persecutions.[53]

In the early days of the reign of Septimius Severus the church enjoyed peace, and the emperor showed special favors toward Christians. This may be due to the fact that both Christians and Jews supported him in his conflict with Niger. The situation changed when Severus had to fight Albinus in the East. At that time the Jews rebelled against him. It is possible that we have here the background of the edict of Severus forbidding conversion to Judaism and Christianity. But it remains a puzzle for historians who attempt to elucidate the reasons why a problem

---

[51]Justin Martyr, 1 Apol 26; Tatian, OratGr 25; Theophilus, AdAut 3.4; Athenagoras, Leg 3; Tertullian, Apol 7-8; Minucius Felix, Oct 9.

[52]Tertullian, Apol 2 (ANF III) 18-20: "Christians alone are forbidden to say anything in exculpation of themselves, in defense of the truth, to help the judge to a righteous decision." Tertullian continued by comparing how the law was applied to society as a whole, yet in a very different way when dealing with Christians.

[53]Eusebius, HE 6.1.

with the Jews would have produced an edict against Christians. The edict targeted Christians more than Jews.

The shift in Severus's attitude took place at the beginning of the third century. Perpetua and Felicitas died in 202, probably in Carthage. But it is difficult to ascertain whether their death was the result of an empire-wide edict. There is in fact more emphasis placed on the tolerance of Severus than on his anti-Christian sentiments. A comment offered by Tertullian remains perplexing:

> Even Severus himself, the father of Antonine, was graciously mindful of the Christians; for he sought out the Christian Proculus, surnamed Torpacion, the steward of Euhodias, and in gratitude for his having once cured him by anointing, he kept him in his palace till the day of his death [211]. . . . Both women and men of highest rank, whom Severus knew well to be Christians, were not merely permitted by him to remain uninjured; but he even bore distinguished testimony in their favour, and gave them publicly back to us from the hands of a raging populace.[54]

It would be a curious behavior on the part of Severus to defend publicly some Christians while ordering the persecution of others.

The debate on the persecutions under Severus remains ongoing and is unlikely to be satisfactorily settled. Some distinctions have been made in the nature of the persecutions which seem to have been directed to new converts. Examples of wide-ranging acts against Christians have been adduced.[55] At the other end of the spectrum we find Sordi who refutes any possibility of such persecutions, while she too cannot solve the problem of those being mentioned by pagan and Christian writers: "We can thus conclude that Septimius Severus did not issue an edict against either Jews or Christians. The question which remains to be asked is why later pagan and Christian sources should have reported persecution during this period."[56]

---

[54]Tertullian, AdScap 4 (ANF III) 107.

[55]Frend, *Martyrdom*, 240: "The Severan persecution was the first coordinated world-wide move against Christians." Frend gives numerous examples of events connected with that persecution.

[56]Sordi, *Christians*, 82. Charles Guignebert had reached a similar conclusion: "Il n'y a pas eu sous Sévère de persécution générale de l'Eglise: Il y a eu des violences locales, sorties de mouvements populaires, de calomnies, d'initiatives

By the third century the Christian movement had developed into a respectable presence in the empire. Origen had already neutralized the attacks of Celsus. Tertullian pointed out that Christians were to be found on all levels of public life. Christian influence grew to the point that some wondered whether Christianity might become the dominant religion of the empire. This may explain the rise of the first Christian emperor, Philip the Arab, and the strong reaction against him.

Philip became emperor in 244. If indeed he was a christian, church historians and apologists did not put any emphasis on his reign and did not not consider his contribution to church life as worthy of comment. Eusebius reports his succession to Gordianus as a matter of fact. When Philip wanted to enter a paschal vigil, he was not allowed to do so by the person who presided, commonly believed to be Babylas who was martyred under Decius and became the nemesis of Julian. Philip had first to acknowledge that he was in need of penance for the crimes he committed. This seemed to have been a prelude for the way Ambrose treated Theodosius after the massacre at Thessalonica.[57] From Eusebius we know that Philip corresponded with Origen, probably on questions of theology and heresy.[58]

The religious motives of Philip remain a question of debate. His support of Christianity provoked violent reactions in some segments of paganism. Yet he is also considered a loyal believer in the eternal mission of Rome which he may have attempted to link with Christianity:

> The fact that the huge quantity of coins minted for the formal cele-brations marking Rome's thousandth anniversary bore the inscription "Roma aeterna," points to Philip's intention of replacing the various deities of the empire with the political concept of Rome itself. The first Christian emperor was evidently attempting to work towards some kind of common ground on which the political ideal of Rome and the sacredness of its mission, guaranteed by *aeternitas*, would overcome all religious differences and be acceptable to the Christians as well.[59]

privées ou de volontés souveraines de gouverneurs; il n'y a pas eu d'intervention directe du pouvoir central." *Tertullien: Etude sur ses sentiments à l'égard de l'empire et de la société civile* (Paris: Ernest Leroux, 1901) 121.

[57]Eusebius, HE 6.34.

[58]Ibid., 6.36.

[59]Sordi, *Christians*, 98.

Philip's perspective was not out of line with the feeling developing in some apologetic literature that the empire could be a legitimate source of divine authority.

After the death of Philip, in a less-than-honorable conspiracy, Decius came to power in 249. Almost immediately he devised the first systematic plan to enforce an empire-wide worship of the gods. For Christianity it meant inevitable persecutions, which slowly moved from province to province until they became almost universal. A system was put in place to ensure compliance by all citizens. All the inhabitants of the empire, regardless of status or philosophical persuasion, were required to sacrifice in the presence of local authorities. Magistrates would deliver to them official certificates stating their compliance. It became an issue of safety to possess such a certificate (*libellus*). Without it citizens incurred the danger of reprisal.

Patristic literature portrayed Decius as an arch enemy of Philip, and the Decian persecutions were regarded as a direct outcome of the hatred of Philip. Jerome emphasized that point and made Decius the murderer of Philip.[60] Eusebius had taken the same stance, attributing the persecution of Christians to Decius's hatred of Philip.[61] Patristic literature may not be fair to Decius, who did not intend to single out Christianity for destruction. He was faced with a serious decline in Roman discipline and tried to restore order by appealing to long-standing traditions in religious practice.

Decius's edicts of persecution are no longer extant. The exact anti-Christian wording of the documents can no longer be properly assessed. We gather from the writings of Cyprian that those edicts produced more apostates than martyrs, which led him to pen the treatise *De lapsis*. The possession of official certificates meant a formal acknowledgement of the divinities ensuring the safety of the empire and the emperor. Some ancient sources suggest that, beyond the fulfilment of the pagan requirement, Christians could worship in their own way. This seemed to have appealed to many of them who procured for themselves illegal certificates to avoid persecutions.

---

[60]Jerome and Gennadius, Lives 54.
[61]Eusebius, HE 6.39.1.

After praising the courage of the martyrs who invaded the market place eager to sacrifice their lives as a protest against the edict of Decius, Cyprian condemned those who sought a way out of the persecutions by fraudulently obtaining their certificates: "Nor let those persons flatter themselves that they need repent the less, who, although they have not polluted their hands with abominable sacrifices, yet have defiled their conscience with certificates."[62] Eusebius chose equally harsh words against church members who declared that they had never been Christians after being encouraged to defect by influential friends and superiors.[63] It was a vindication for the pagans who had all along complained that there were not enough persecutions against the church. Even Christians sometimes wished for persecutions in order to avoid internal dissensions and troubles.[64] Those who lost their lives as martyrs were deemed more important for the Christian cause than those who survived, especially those who avoided persecution through ruse. But it was also a time for reconciliation, which was very difficult to support even in the name of Christian forgiveness. After expressing his grief for the downfall of so many Christians, Cyprian stated:

> I sympathize with you in your suffering and grief, therefore, for our brethren, who, having lapsed and fallen prostrate under the severity of the persecution, have inflicted a like pain on us by their wounds, inasmuch as they tear away part of our bowels with them,—to these the divine mercy is able to bring healing.[65]

Discord arose among Christians on how to handle the question of apostasy. Novatianists took a strong position against readmitting to the fellowship those who had lapsed, even if they were forgiven by God. They separated themselves from the church in order not to have any contact with such wavering members.[66]

For the church the persecution initiated by Decius evolved into a serious crisis of authority and integrity. For the pagans it was not certain

---

[62]Cyprian, DeLaps 8 and 27 (ANF V) 439, 444. See also Epist 10 (ANF V) 290-92.

[63]Eusebius, HE 6.41.12.

[64]Origen, CCel 3.15.

[65]Cyprian, Epist 11 (ANF V) 292.

[66]Socrates, HE 4.28 and 5.19.

whether Christians had suffered enough of a blow and whether the loyalty to old gods was reestablished. There were too many ways out of sacrificing, and no one was sure as to how many Christians lost their lives in the process. But the empire had to deal with more than rebellious citizens. The time had come when it was necessary to oppose the church as an influential institution.

As expected, the death of Decius in 251 after a short reign of only two years, was viewed by Christian apologists as a curse of God against a beast. Such was the expected view of Lactantius.[67] A similar view was expressed by Eusebius.[68]

Valerian and Gallienus seem to have adopted Decius's approach to persecutions. But Dionysius of Alexandria and Eusebius report that the first years of the reign of Valerian were marked by tolerance toward Christians. After referring to a passage in Revelation prophesying the coming of the persecution for forty-two months, Dionysius and Eusebius say:

> It is wonderful that both of these things occurred under Valerian; and it is the more remarkable in this case when we consider his previous conduct, for he had been mild and friendly toward the men of God, for none of the emperors before him had treated them so kindly and favorably; and not even those who were said openly to be Christians received them with such manifest hospitality and friendliness as he did at the beginning of his reign. For his entire house was filled with pious persons and was a church of God.[69]

Both Dionysius and Eusebius described how the persecutions began when the ruler of the synagogue of the Magi persuaded Valerian to move against the Christians. The reference is obviously to Macrianus, who was an able general of Valerian and may have been devoted to magic art.

---

[67]Lactantius, DeMort 4.
[68]Eusebius, HE 7.1; OratSanct 24.
[69]Dionysius, *Extant Fragments, Epistle* 11 (ANF VI) 106; Eusebius, HE 7.10.3 (NPNF-2 I) 298. I have quoted the text of Eusebius, though both texts are almost identical. The reference to Christian emperors is confusing. Philip was generally regarded as Christian. We do not know whom else Eusebius and Dionysius may have had in mind, perhaps Alexander Severus who is said to have kept an image of Christ with his lares.

By the time of Valerian the empire had suffered some of the worst reversals of its history with disastrous invasions of Goths and Persians. The mood was somber among Christians and pagans alike. It seemed that everybody was expecting the eminent end of the world. Mutual recriminations for those setbacks abounded on both sides, and superstition was at one of its highest points among pagans who still blamed the Christians for the calamities of the empire. Valerian attributed the lack of political stability to the neglect of ancient traditions. Christians were not the only alleged culprits. Many in the Roman intelligentsia refused to sacrifice. Arrests included members of the senatorial and equestrian order, as well as freedmen who were found guilty of disobeying imperial orders. According to Gregory Thaumaturgus, Christians were suspected to have served as spies for the invading Goths.[70] But in spite of the persecution, the church had arisen to a position of influence and even of relative wealth at a time when Roman currency was almost worthless.

We do not know the text of Valerian's edict. We can only surmise its content from some of the writings of Cyprian and Dionysius. Doubts have persisted on how emperors enforced their decrees and on how they viewed persecutions. Changing their position toward Christians could have meant to be unloyal to their own edicts. The distinction between *de jure* legislation and *de facto* tolerance perpetuated confusion among pagans and Christians. We do not know how severe the persecutions under Valerian were. According to Jerome, victims under the rules of Valerian and his son Gallienus included notable persons such as Cyprian, Dionysius, and Methodius,[71] a statement difficult to verify and in contradiction with other sources, especially Eusebius who mentioned Dionysius as a bishop under Gallienus. But there was also a progressive recognition that edicts could be mistaken and had to be revoked, the only way to put an end to persecutions. Gallienus concluded that his father Valerian had been too eager to resort to old traditions and that his well intended persecutions were a mistake.

Gallienus's edict of tolerance marked a turning point which culminated in the Edict of Milan. The church was by then recognized as a power to be reckoned with. Gallienus's edict went directly and personally to bishops, giving them an official recourse against persecution:

---

[70]Frend, *Martyrdom*, 317.
[71]Jerome and Gennadius, Lives 67, 69, 83.

The Emperor Caesar Publius Lucinius Gallienus, Pius, Felix, Augustus, to Dionysius, Pinnas, Demetrius, and the other bishops. I have ordered the bounty of my gift to be declared through all the world, that they may depart from the places of religious worship. And for this purpose you may use this copy of my rescript, that no one may molest you. And this which you are now enabled lawfully to do, has already for a long time been conceded by me.[72]

In a bold exaggeration Sozomen declared: "Almost all the barbarians had professed to hold the Christian doctrine in honor, from the time of the wars between the Romans and foreign tribes, under the government of Gallienus and the emperors who succeeded him."[73] In his *De mortibus persecutorum* Lactantius did not mention Gallienus. To Valerian, however, he assigned a tragic end as the result of his persecutions.[74]

Imperial rescripts such as that of Gallienus were motivated by political as well as religious constraints. Emperors could not foresee the long-range implications of their rescripts and edicts. Gallienus's rescript was a great relief to the church. But it did not mean the capitulation of old traditions. After Gallienus, events developed rapidly and led to two historical moments of crucial importance, though very contradictory in their nature: The great persecution and the official christianization of the empire.

What became known as the last great persecution under Diocletian should, in fact, be attributed mostly to Galerius, the true architect of the reaction against Christians. The last attempt of paganism to bring Christianity back to the fold of the old gods gravitated between nobility and violence. By the fourth century it was no longer a question of eliminating Christianity from the life of the empire. No emperor of that time would have seriously entertained such a possibility. The church had become a power whose threat to old religion had to be curbed and whose influence was often coveted. But popular fury against Christians had not yet abated. One could still hear the chant of the crowds at the popular games of the Circus Maximus: *Christiani tollantur, Christiani non sit* (out with the Christians, let Christians not be any more). It would be tempting

---

[72]Eusebius, HE 7.13.2 (NPNF-2 I) 302.
[73]Sozomen, HE 2.6 (NPNF-2 II) 262.
[74]Lactantius, DeMort 5.

to correlate such chants to imperial decisions against Christians. But that pattern does not fit the mood of Diocletian.

The movement toward the great persecution was slow and often indecisive. Diocletian's commitment to pagan gods and especially the oracle of Apollo is well documented. Lactantius and Eusebius assign as the cause of the persecution the episode in which Diocletian was unable to obtain a response from the oracle because of the presence of Christians in the vicinity.[75] Diocletian could not concede such a power to Christians. When it became evident that mere persuasion would not bring Christians back to the old gods, he opted for persecutions.

Diocletian attached a great deal of importance to omens and soothsayings. He was surrounded by and devoted to holy images, always close to priests who interpreted for him things to come. He sought to find in religion, through sacrifices and dedications, the stability and permanence lacking in his government. His gods were made personal. Soon after becoming emperor he bestowed on himself the name of Jupiter. When he elevated Maximian to the post of Augustus, he named him Hercules. Yet all the while, Christianity was encroaching not only on the affairs of state, but also on his personal life. Following a clue from Lactantius, it has been contended that his wife and daughter were Christian catechumens or at least strongly inclined towards Christianity: "And now Diocletian raged, not only against his own domestics, but indiscriminately against all; and he began by forcing his daughter Valeria and his wife Prisca to be polluted by sacrificing."[76]

The hope of bringing paganism and Christianity together as a power capable of stemming barbarism was not to be realized yet. In fact it never happened. Christianity had suffered rebuke from the pens of Pophyry and Celsus. But it emerged stronger than before. It appeared more detached from and less vulnerable to the absurdities of paganism. Yet it could not be granted the kind of freedom which would prove deleterious to the safety of the empire. Several years before the official persecution, Diocletian already feared the aberrations of some Christian movements. The *Codex Gregorianus* preserved his 297 edict against the Manichaeans, mostly in their attempt to undo what had been established by the antiquity of Roman tradition.

---

[75]Ibid., 11; Eusebius, VConst 2.50, 54.
[76]Lactantius, DeMort 15 (ANF VII) 306.

Attempts at syncretism were still alive, though not always well defined and implemented. When the Romans spoke of what had been fixed and established by tradition, it remained a vague statement which could not be supported in facts. There was no inherent unity in pagan polytheist perspectives. Perhaps the only convincing attempt at universality came from the worship of the sun. In 274 the emperor Aurelian built a magnificent temple to *Sol dominus imperii Romani*. Long before that, Christians had already been accused of worshiping the sun, and they protested the charge:

> In the same way, if we devote Sun-day to rejoicing, from a far different reason than Sun-worship, we have some resemblance to those of you who devote the day of Saturn to ease and luxury, though they too go far away from Jewish ways, of which indeed they are ignorant.[77]

The most persuasive reports of the events which led to the persecutions came from Lactantius, who was considered illustrious enough to be brought by Diocletian to Nicomedia as a teacher of Latin rhetoric, a position he kept after his conversion to Christianity. However slanted or passionate they may be, we have firsthand accounts of the persecutions. The texts in Eusebius appear more suspicious to some scholars who have questioned his behavior during the persecution. It has been adduced that he fled to avoid arrest or that he momentarily renounced the faith to escape persecution. There is, however, little solid evidence to support those charges.

Lactantius emphasized how Diocletian and Galerius disagreed on the means by which to curb Christianity. For many years Diocletian showed a surprising restraint, believing that bloodshed would achieve nothing but upsetting the fragile balance of peace in the empire. From the beginning Galerius was for a massive slaughter of Christians. Father and son-in-law (Galerius having been forced to marry Valeria for political expediency) did not see eye to eye. Galerius had a strong ally in his mother whose passion against Christians equalled that of her son. As for Diocletian, he decreed persecutions only after the defeat of the oracle of his god, a victim to Christian presence and influence. He concluded that nothing short of drastic actions against Christians could restore ancient traditions.

---

[77]Tertullian, Apol 16 (ANF III) 31.

Eusebius mused on the causes of the persecution from a different point of view, saying little about its political reasons. For him the persecution was a divine necessity dictated by the abuse Christians had made of their freedom to justify laxity and open war against each other.[78] He then showed how the persecution began against Christians serving in the army. We may infer from this that the emperor no longer felt secure while surrounded by Christian soldiers and that he could not trust them to obey his orders. The argument finds its complement in Lactantius where Diocletian, before entering the persecution, still tried to convince Galerius that it might be sufficient to exclude Christians from the court and the army and that nothing would be gained through bloodshed but the pride of martyrdom on account of those who would have died.[79]

According to Eusebius, the persecution resulted from five consecutive edicts ordering the destruction of churches and Scriptures, demoting Christians in positions of leadership, and imprisoning those who refused to sacrifice.[80] All of this was meant to deprive Christians of their influence and to convince them of the superiority of pagan ways of life.

There was also a Neronian twist to the causes of persecution, mostly as reported by Lactantius. Once the date was chosen to initiate the persecution, on the festival of the God Terminus (February 23, 303), we see Galerius and Diocletian looking at the Christian church from the palace and debating whether it should be set on fire. Again the wisdom of Diocletian prevailed as he voiced his fear that other buildings might also perish in the blaze. The church was then demolished by the Pretorian guards.[81] Soon after, Galerius sent his emissaries to set the palace on fire so Christians could be blamed and so their name could become odious on

---

[78]Eusebius, HE 8.1.7 (NPNF-2 I) 323:

But when on account of the abundant freedom, we fell into laxity and sloth, and envied and reviled each other, and were almost, as it were, taking up arms against one another, rulers assailing rulers with words like spears, and people forming parties against people, and monstrous hypocrisy and dissimulation rising to the greatest hight of wickedness, the divine judgment with forbearance, as is its pleasure, while the multitudes yet continued to assemble, gently and moderately harassed the episcopacy.

[79]Lactantius, DeMort 11 (ANF VII) 305.

[80]Eusebius, HE 8.2.1-5.

[81]Lactantius, DeMort 12.

account of the fire. Diocletian responded with anger, torturing many in his entourage to secure confessions. Then two weeks later another fire was set but put out before it could cause a great deal of damage. This time the response of Diocletian was fierce and cost the lives of many. It was then that he forced his wife and daughter to sacrifice.[82] There is little basis to doubt those reports of Lactantius, though we may wonder why Diocletian who had proven himself perceptive and wise on many other occasions, would not have detected the stratagem of Galerius, who fled in haste after those events to escape being burned alive.

Edicts continued to be issued both East and West. Lactantius reported how orders of persecution were sent also to Maximian and Constantius as a way to reach agreement among the four rulers. Maximian, the new Hercules, enforced the edicts throughout Italy. In Gaul and Britain, however, Constantius made certain not to hurt Christians but only their property.[83] When Maximin Daia became emperor in the East in 305 he changed the methods of persecution in order to avoid martyrs. Christians were condemned to hard labor. Eusebius gives us the text of the rescript of Maximin Daia as it was inscribed on the pillar of Tyre.[84] The intended impact was clear: Strike at Christianity and restore the pagan gods. It was one more futile attempt of dying paganism to hope for an illusory unity in the name of ancestral traditions.

Persecutions continued until 311, and even beyond in some pockets of the empire. In the last moments of his life Galerius issued his edict of toleration. The impetuous persecutor who was disturbed by the toleration and hesitation of his colleagues, was now in the role of conciliator. It was not a change of heart but circumstances beyond his control that shifted his position. Lactantius gave us a long description of the fated last days of Galerius and the sickness which visited him as a result of persecution. Then he concluded:

> These things happened in the course of a complete year [311]; and at length, overcome by calamities, he was obliged to acknowledge God, and he cried aloud, in the intervals of raging pain, that he would re-

---

[82]Ibid., 14-15.
[83]Ibid., 15.
[84]Eusebius, HE 7.1-14.

edify the church which he had demolished, and make atonement for his misdeeds. And when he was near his end, he published an edict. . . .[85]

This specific view of the end of Galerius reflects more apologetic fervor than historical accuracy. The edict of Galerius itself was preserved by lactantius and Eusebius. It speaks of the wish to bring the Christians back to the religion of their forefathers, of how they were subdued through persecution, how the time has now come for toleration, and finally this: "Wherefore on account of this indulgence of ours, they [the Christians] ought to supplicate their God for our safety, and that of the people, and their own, that the public welfare may be preserved in every place, and that they may live securely in their several homes."[86]

By then the empire was at the edge of revolutionary changes. Persecutions were assessed from many different points of view. Harnack contended that they were doomed to remain ineffective. Christians were destined to rule the world and would have triumphed even without the conversion of Constantine.

---

[85]Lactantius, DeMort 33 (ANF VII) 315.

[86]Eusebius, HE 8.17.10 (NPNF-2. I) 340. See also Lactantius, DeMort 34 (ANF VII) 315 The latin text of Lactantius clearly shows that we are not dealing here with any philosophical statement on religious freedom but solely with the welfare of the public order in the name of tolerance. But there is an enormous gap between tolerance (*indulgentia*) and religious freedom. Christians were reminded that their duty was "in consequence of this our toleration, to pray to their God for our welfare, and for that of the public, and for their own; that the commonweal may continue safe in every quarter, and that they themselves may live securely in their habitations." (*Unde iuxta hanc indulgentiam nostram debebunt deum suum orare pro salute nostra et rei publicae ac sua, ut undique uersum res publica perstet incolumis et securi uiuere in sedibus suis possint.*)

The beginning of the edict is equally revealing in its intent: "Amongst our other regulations for the permanent advantage of the commonweal, we have hitherto studied to reduce all things to a conformity with the ancient laws and public discipline of the Romans. It has been our aim in an especial manner, that the Christians also, who had abandoned the religion of their forefathers, should return to right opinions." (*Inter cetera quae pro rei publicae semper commodis atque utilitate disponimus, nos quidem uolueramus antehac iuxta leges ueteres et publicam disciplinam Romanorum cuncta corrigere atque id prouidere, ut etiam christiani, qui parentum suorum reliquerant sectam, ad bonas mentes redirent.*)

The *pax deorum* crossed over to a new interpretation under Constantine. The search for unity continued amid threats, both external and internal. Neither paganism nor Christianity could propose a unity acceptable to all. The world was in need of religious reorientation. But it was not in the destiny of that world to find peace, either political or religious. There was a certain nobility on the part of emperors who tried to save the "whole race of the Romans." They failed when they resorted to violence. The yearning may have been right, the means toward the end wrong. It was the apologists' view that divine providence would finally shine also on pagans. *Sol Invictus* faded. *Christus Victor* languished amidst all the dissensions tearing the church apart and was less evident in a post-Constantine era than during the persecutions. Yet Christianity had ensured its success through a message that, in spite of the many divergent interpretations, could be articulated more convincingly than the sacrificial practices of paganism. In an age besieged by threatening forces on all sides, the elusive quest for remedy compelled many pagans to search in Christianity for that which no longer could be provided by their ancestral traditions. The recurring crises in the empire contributed greatly to the growth of Christianity, both geographically and socially.

In the Constantine and post-Constantine era the notion of persecution changed radically. It should have disappeared altogether. But neither the church nor the empire enjoyed stability and peace. The rhetoric of apologists such as Lactantius remained vindictive. It was shared by Constantine. As the dominion of the church replaced that of the empire, the societal modus operandi did not exhibit radical changes. Ruling classes tend to oppress the opposition, whatever the claims to nobility. But one transformation clarified the position of the church. Its existence had become a *de jure* as well as a *de facto* reality, a proposition that was never clear before. Edicts of persecution as well as of tolerance left the church in the situation of not knowing the real meaning of any of it. Roman authorities never formulated any long-standing rules or laws governing the existence of Christians.

The short reign of Julian might have provided the stage for new persecutions. But his attacks were verbal. The great leader who, according to the *gratiarum actio* of his panegyrist Mamertinus, had inspired warm affection in all the hearts of the human race, was not inclined to use force to achieve his philosophical ends. The philosopher-king preferred rational argumentation. Yet it was during his tenure as emperor that the death of Saint George in Alexandria shook the religious world.

The story of George, already mentioned in Chapter 8, deserves further comment because it reflects a turn of events that not even Julian would have wished changed in spite of his hatred of Christianity. Socrates stressed the dilemma of Julian who sensed that paganism could not be restored through acts of violence. Masses could not be trusted in their thirst for revenge, and Julian refused to play the game their way.

The incident began when George was given permission by Constantius to build a church on the location of a former temple to Mithra and exposed the absurdities of paganism in ways which appeared sacrilegious. Even Socrates had to concede that the rage of the populace was understandable: "George, however, was at that time, and had for some time previously been, exceedingly obnoxious to all classes, which is sufficient to account for the burning indignation of the multitude against him."[87] But this was not sufficient reason for his brutal death inflicted on him by the mob. Angered by such an action Julian responded by an unusually long edict to the people of Alexandria. It is preserved for us in Socrates (HE 3.3). In it Julian pursued his quest for legal propriety and religious decency. The tone is angry and reproachful: "By Serapis I conjure you to tell me, for what unjust deed were ye so indignant at George?" The crime of the Alexandrians was to have bypassed the law and polluted their city: "Being on all these accounts enraged against George as the adversary of the gods, you have again polluted your sacred city; whereas you ought to have impeached him before the judges." The lack of shame on the part of Alexandrians was beyond the acceptable for Julian: "The people have had the audacity to tear a man to pieces, like dogs; nor have they been subsequently ashamed of this inhuman procedure, nor desirous of purifying their hands from such pollution, that they may stretch them forth in the presence of the gods undefiled by blood."

We may suspect Christian partisanship on the part of Socrates. But the story is also elaborated upon by Ammianus Marcellinus who connected the death of George with that of two other Alexandrian martyrs, Dracontius and Diodorus. Then he concluded: "The emperor, on

---

[87]Socrates, HE 3.3 (NPNF-2 II) 79. The narrative on George is in chaps. 2 and 3.

hearing of this abominable deed, was bent upon taking vengeance, but just as he was on the point of inflicting the extreme penalty upon the guilty parties, he was pacified by his intimates, who counselled leniency. Accordingly, he issued an edict expressing, in the strongest terms, his horror at the outrage that had been committed, and threatened extreme measures in case in the future anything was attempted contrary to justice and the laws."[88] For Julian the voice of reason required the rule of law. Religious persecutions were not acceptable in an empire whose laws were directed to the preservation of order.

As the church grew in authority and power it could not avoid the role of persecutor. Persecuted often turned persecutor in the kind of historical irony that baffles rationality and the Christian spirit. It was again in Alexandria that Christian persecutions cost the life of the erudite Hypathia. She was a philosopher and a member of the prestigious town council. As a professor of philosophy she had become known by her peers as "the stainless star of Wisdom's discipline." She was the daughter of the renowned philosopher Theon and the teacher of the notorious bishop of Ptolemais, Synesius. Perhaps more than anyone else, Synesius embodied the new type of Christianity. His life reflected a syncretistic harmony of Neoplatonic culture and Christian perspectives. Though he became bishop in 410, he openly rejected many Christian dogmas he found unacceptable.

The story of Hypatia is briefly recounted by Socrates.[89] Praise is lavished on her for her culture, knowledge, and exceptional virtue. But having been accused by Christians of subversion, she was attacked by a church mob, dragged through the streets of Alexandria, and then murdered with shards of pottery before being burned in 415. Cyril, the patriarch of Alexandria, was at that time in conflict with the prefect of the city, Orestes, a close friend of Hypatia. It was the contention of Christians that Hypatia may have fueled the dispute. The exact involvement of Cyril in this tragic episode is hard to ascertain, and he remained in Alexandria. Socrates tried to exonerate Cyril: "This affair brought not the least opprobrium, not only upon Cyril, but also upon the whole Alexandrian church. And surely nothing can be farther from the spirit of

---

[88]Ammianus Marcellinus, ResGest 22.11.11 (LCL II) 263.
[89]Socrates, HE 7.15.

Christianity than the allowance of massacres, fights, and transactions of that sort."[90] Socrates chose to speak of the event with indignation and shame, writing a much-belated obituary of Hypathia, praising her stature and dignity as far surpassing those of her Christian murderers.

As such, the death of Hypatia was not the result of an ideological conflict between paganism and Christianity. It was mostly a reminder that the authority of the church could no longer be challenged without severe consequences. The extent of acts of violence on the part of Christians against their opponents is not well known but sufficiently documented to conclude that it was more widespread than reported by church historians of the period.

The triumph of Christianity rested on its persuasive interpretation of martyrdom more than on its power of argumentation. Patristic literature is replete with lists of martyrs, treatises on martyrdom, and eloquent panegyrics to those who lost their lives because of their faith. Direct exhortations to martyrdom abound. Christians were willing to sacrifice their lives as witnesses to the redemptive purpose of Christ. Many would have been disappointed to die a peaceful death. We find such a perspective in Ignatius, who was glad to see the persecution end but was saddened by the fact that he was deprived of martyrdom, which he suffered at a later time.[91] Paganism could also rise to the defense of its religion, but it never became a heroic faith. Its adherents seldom suffered punishment or death for their convictions.

God is sometimes portrayed as ordaining martyrdom and as finding pleasure in it:

> How beautiful is the spectacle to God when a Christian does battle with pain; when he is drawn up against threats, and punishments, and tortures; when mocking the noise of death, he treads under foot the horror of the executioner; when he raises up his liberty against kings and princes, and yields to God alone, whose he is; when, triumphant

---

[90]Ibid., 7.15 (NPNF-2 II) 160.

[91]Ignatius, MartIgn 1 (ANF I) 129:

Wherefore he rejoiced over the tranquil state of the church, when the persecution ceased for a little time, but was grieved as to himself, that he had not yet attained to a true love to Christ, nor reached the perfect rank of a disciple. For he inwardly reflected, that confession which is made by martyrdom, would bring him into a yet more intimate relation to the Lord.

and victorious, he tramples upon the very man who has pronounced sentence against him![92]

The blood of the martyrs was viewed as the most powerful seeds for the growth of the church: "Then the people grew more numerous by being attacked. Then the blood of the martyrs, watering the churches, nourished many more champions of true religion, each generation stripping for the struggle with the zeal of those that had gone before."[93]

Martyrdom enlightened religious and political necessities. Already in New Testament times, external circumstances, often referred to as the world, gave meaning to a concept of suffering in the name of the coming kingdom. It is not by accident that the Greek term μάρτυς came to mean both witness and martyr. It was at first used in the legal sense of a witness, of one who testifies to the truth with a clear conscience. God is often called upon as the ultimate witness (I call upon God as my witness). When one witnesses unto death, one becomes a martyr. For some Christians it was no longer possible to be true witnesses for Christ without paying for it with their life.

Cyprian, a martyr himself, wrote extensively to exhort Christians to martyrdom in order to achieve entrance to heaven and immortality.[94] Tertullian, who wrote treatises and panegyrics on martyrdom, saw the death of God's saints as a triumph over the forces of evil.[95] After describing the agony of martyrdom he concluded: "The sole key to unlock Paradise is your own life's blood."[96] In his view martyrs became the greatest examples for the edification of the church.[97]

But Tertullian's position on martyrdom could be very ambivalent. To a Roman governor he could proudly declare: *Crudelitas vestra gloria est nostra* ("Your cruelty is our glory").[98] At the same time he was willing to acknowledge that Christians often placed Roman authorities in delicate

---

[92]Minucius Felix, Oct 37 (ANF IV) 196.
[93]Basil, Letter 164 (NPNF-2 VIII) 216.
[94]Cyprian, Epist 25.3 (ANF V) 303.
[95]Tertullian, Apol 27 (ANF III) 41. See also his AdMart and *Martyrdom of Perpetua and Felicitas* in (ANF III) 693-706.
[96]Tertullian, DeAnim 55 (ANF III) 231.
[97]Tertullian, *The Passion of the Holy Martyrs Perpetua and Felicitas* In *Martyrdom of Perpetua and Felicitas*. (ANF III) 705.
[98]Tertullian, AdScap 5 (ANF III) 107.

situations by forcing them to apply laws they would have been more than willing to ignore. He recounted how on one occasion the Christian population of a province of Asia provocatively invaded the judgment seat of the governor Arrius Antoninus, forcing him to put some to death. Then the governor exclaimed in exasperation: "O miserable men, if you wish to die, you have precipices or halters."[99] True, Christians wishing death could have thrown themselves from precipices or could have hanged themselves. But it was not death the Christians wished, but the powerful testimony of martyrdom. To make martyrdom forceful, the society inflicting it must be made as cruel as possible. Even in his fanatic approach to martyrdom Tertullian betrays some fallacies inherent in his positions.

The veneration of Martyrs became an axiomatic postulate. They were assured of lasting reputation on earth as in heaven. The church's respect for its saints exceeded that of the pagans for their fallen heroes in battles. It has often been contended that the early church exaggerated the number of martyrs. But whatever the number, it remained a fact that their sacrifice became the cornerstone of faith for several centuries. Yet the veneration of martyrs was not free from legendary accretions years after their death. Miracles have been attributed to them or to the relics they left behind. Eusebius thought that the martyrs, in the company of Christ, could atone for the sins of those who lapsed during the persecutions.[100]

If we trust Augustine, miracles attributed to martyrs were compared to the prodigies performed by heathen demons. The point was to prove martyrs' miracles superior to that of pagan demons. Augustine conceded that heroes such as Hercules and Romulus deserve credit for their marvels, but they should not have been elevated to the rank of god: "But our martyrs are not our gods; for we know that the martyrs and we have both but one God, and that the same. Nor yet are the miracles which they [the demons or gods] maintain to have been done by means of their temples at all comparable to those which are done by the tombs of our martyrs."[101]

By the time of Jerome, the veneration, if not direct worship, of those who suffered death for their faith had become a problem to be opposed

---

[99]Ibid.
[100]Eusebius, HE 6.42.5.
[101]Augustine, CivDei 22.10 (NPNF-1 II) 491.

and refuted. There was the danger that martyrs might come to assume within Christianity what the gods meant for paganism. Jerome did not deny the place of honor reserved for martyrs but he cautioned against abuses which might distort the meaning of their calling. The score must be kept straight: "Madman, who in the world ever adored the martyrs? who ever thought man was God?"[102] Augustine questioned the intent of his mother when, as was the custom in Africa, she brought to the places of the saints cake, and bread, and wine but was forbidden by the doorkeeper to offer them. She thought herself guilty and did not question the prohibition, which was issued by Ambrose. At stake was the fact that a connection could be made between those practices and pagan rituals on behalf of the dead.[103] Later Augustine thought to clarify his position on the honor payed to martyrs:

> But, nevertheless, we do not build temples, or ordain priests, rites, and sacrifices for the same martyrs; for they are not our gods, but their God is our God. Certainly we honor their reliquaries, as the memorials of holy men of God who strove for the truth even to the death of their bodies. . . . But who ever heard a priest of the faithful, standing at an altar built for the honor and worship of God over the holy body of some martyr, say in the prayers, I offer to thee a sacrifice, O Peter, or O Paul, or O Cyprian?[104]

For some church fathers the concept of martyr acquired a broader sense than death for your faith. To live a life of faithfulness in the midst of danger was regarded as heroic a posture as dying for your faith. If death could be a strong statement, so could the right kind of life:

> Many indeed err who say, With our blood we have overcome the wicked one; and if he remains, they are unwilling to overcome. . . . Even now, if thou hast conquered by good deeds, thou art a martyr in Him. Thou, therefore, who seekest to extol martyrdom with thy word, in peace clothe thyself with good deeds, and be secure.[105]

---

[102]Jerome, CVig 5 (NPNF-2 VI) 418.
[103]Augustine, Conf 6.2.
[104]Augustine, CivDei 8.27 (NPNF-1 II) 164.
[105]Commodianus, Instr 62 (ANF IV) 215.

Athanasius voiced a similar belief when he asserted that to make a strong stand for the faith is equivalent to martyrdom in honor and merit.[106]

In Clement of Alexandria we find an unexpected rebuke of those who deliberately provoked their death in order to be counted among martyrs. Some Christians were at fault for refusing to avoid persecution and even more for engineering their own capture. In that case they were guilty of becoming accomplices in the crimes of the persecutors. Provocation which led to persecution could not be regarded as a laudable Christian attitude.[107] Perhaps persecution and martyrdom were not meant for everybody. Even Christ advised his followers when persecuted in one city to flee to another one.[108] Mindful of such an injunction on the part of Christ, Ambrose added: "so that no one, whilst longing for the crown of martyrdom, may put himself in the way of dangers which possibly the weak flesh or a mind indulged could not bear or endure."[109] In many instances Christians came to realize that it was as hard to live for Christ as to die for him.

Caesar and Christ: The Kingdom within the Empire

For the early church the world appeared as a baffling arena of conflicts which left all segments of society apprehensive and frustrated. Divine providence governed the world, though not always in a clear fashion. Christian faith could be interpreted as a call to withdraw from the world as well as an obligation to bring to that world all that the biblical message was enjoining, including respect for and obedience to secular authorities. Christians understood the importance of their

---

[106]Athanasius, AdEpisc 21.

[107]Clement of Alexandria, Strom 4.10.

[108]Matthew 10:23. But see also the strong reaction of Tertullian, DeFuga 9 (ANF IV) 121 against those who found comfort in such a text which according to him could not have been the intention of the apostles:

Where, then, do you show that they renewed the command to flee from city to city. . . . And yet who will flee from persecution, but he who fears? Who will fear, but he who has not loved? Yes; and if you ask counsel of the Spirit, what does He approve more than that utterance of the Spirit? For, indeed, it incites all almost to go and offer themselves in martyrdom, not to flee from it.

[109]Ambrose, OffMin 1.37.187 (NPNF-2 X) 32.

contribution in ensuring the existing world order. They shared with their secular contemporaries the fear that if the Roman empire fell, everything would return to chaos, even for the church. Against their will, and often in spite of all proofs to the contrary, they wished and even prayed for the prosperity and eternity of the Roman people.

A strong sense of common destiny bound Christians and pagans together. Though that kind of solidarity was threatened in times of turmoil and persecutions and though violent attacks against each other underscored the history of the period, many church fathers emphasized, sometimes with a touch of contradiction, the indissoluble unity of all things ordained by God. The welfare of the world depended on the goodness or evilness of emperors as well as on the reactions of Christians to situations beyond their control. On that basis there was more than the desire for martyrdom. We find eloquent pleas for justice which should apply to Christians as well as to pagans. Both should be exonerated of crimes if innocent and punished if guilty.[110] Christians should be treated justly according to the common law. They should not be unlawfully condemned on false accusations through prejudice. There was a tacit, and sometimes clearly expressed, commitment on the part of Christians to obey the laws in civil matters. Their Scriptures taught them that every power is instituted by God and that opposition to it could be detrimental to the welfare of the state. Conflicts arose when they were forced into actions and rites, especially sacrificing to heathen divinities, that would have meant a denial of their God. But even in the midst of hardships Christians remained well disposed toward the Roman government.[111]

On occasion martyrdom was viewed as an inherent necessity within the structure of the Roman empire itself. Glen Warren Bowersock tries to demonstrate that martyrdom belonged to the global outlook of Roman society:

> What emerges strikingly from an examination of this material is that the martyrdoms form a cohesive part of the structure of the Roman empire—both bureaucratic and social—and not simply a disconcerting obstruction to the smooth functioning of the imperial government. To

---

[110]See especially such pleas as found in Justin Martyr, 1 Apol; Athenagoras, Leg; Tertullian, Apol.

[111]Athenagoras, Leg 1.

put this in another way, Christianity owed its martyrs to the *mores* and structure of the Roman empire.[112]

To support his contention further, Bowersock argues that martyrdom never had any connection with Judaism or Palestine. It must be placed totally within Greco-Roman traditions and culture. Such a position tends to ignore the strong patristic reactions against Judaism as the enemy of Christianity, as well as New Testament evidence of Jewish persecutions.

The most eloquent pleas for common justice came from Tertullian, who was well acquainted with the details of Roman law. He often exposed the unlawful conduct of those who distorted the judicial process in order to obtain confessions from Christians.[113] The assumption of guilt against Christians led to less than honorable behavior on the part of those who were entrusted with the enforcement of the law: "Well, you think the Christian a man of every crime, an enemy of the gods, of the emperor, of the laws, of good morals, of all nature; and you compel him to deny, that you may acquit him, which without his denial you could not do."[114]

Whether correctly or not, Tertullian was attempting to define a new and more realistic *modus vivendi* for a society finding itself at the juncture between the secular and the new faith. The balance was hard to keep in view of the many new converts: "The outcry is that the State is filled with Christians—that they are in the fields, in the citadels, in the islands: they make lamentation, as for some calamity, that both sexes, every age and condition, even high rank, are passing over to the profession of the Christian faith."[115] Far from denying such a contention, Tertullian reinforced it: "We are but of yesterday, and we have filled every place among you—cities, islands, fortresses, towns, marketplaces, the very camp, tribes, companies, palace, senate, forum,—we have left nothing to you but the temples of your gods."[116] There is no need to mention the exaggeration and self-serving nature of those statements. It

---

[112]Glen Warren Bowersock, *Martyrdom and Rome* (Cambridge: Cambridge University Press, 1995) 28.

[113]Tertullian, AdNat 1.2.

[114]Tertullian, Apol 2 (ANF III) 19. The argument is continued through many passages in the *Apologeticum* where Tertullian objects to the lack of due process and the way in which Christians were often denied to present their defense.

[115]Ibid., 1 (ANF III) 17.

[116]Ibid., 37 (ANF III) 45.

had become almost a leitmotif for Tertullian to prove that Christians were not as useless as often claimed in the promotion and welfare of Roman causes. Minucius Felix and Origen also grappled with the accusations that Christians did not take sufficient part in Roman life. Distortions and misinterpretations abounded, and Christians themselves were not always certain as to the extent of their participation in society when they were considered enemies of it.

Those who embraced the Christian faith at the price of hardship and often cruelty were faced with the difficult task of obeying the biblical command to honor secular authorities and even to pray for them. Jews and Christians had learned that wishing evil for the empire was also to invite disaster for their existence. Rabbi Hananiah once said: "Do thou pray for the welfare of the empire, because were it not for the fear it inspires, every man would swallow his neighbor alive."[117] Beyond the fear that was deemed necessary to keep any society within the bounds of decency, Christians also believed that God regulates and appoints kingdoms and kings in some kind of eternal decree not always clear to every one. It is because of God's will and not through a deliberate act of reflection that Christians pray for the emperor. All scriptural commands are inspired and must be upheld even when in conflict with religious expectations. Thus Polycarp urged the Philippians to: "Pray for all the saints. Pray also for the Emperors, and for potentates, and princes, . . . and for the enemies of the cross."[118] But the reason given by Polycarp for doing so is the perfecting of the saints, and not a genuine respect for potentates.

Athenagoras argued that Christians were more deserving because of their concern and prayers for the emperor: "For who are more deserving to obtain the things they ask, than those who, like us, pray for your government, that you [the emperor] may, as is most equitable, receive the kingdom, son from father, and that your empire may receive increase and addition, all men become subject to your sway? And this is also for our advantage, that we may lead a peaceable and quiet life, and may

---

[117]Judah Goldin, *The Living Talmud: The Wisdom of the Fathers and Its Classical Commentaries*, selected and translated by Judah Goldin (Chicago: University of Chicago Press, 1957) 119-20.

[118]Polycarp, Phil 12.3 in *Apostolic Fathers*. (LCL I) 299.

ourselves readily perform all that is commanded us."[119] Athenagoras shared the widespread belief that the Roman empire could ensure peace for all. But his last statement was unrealistic. Christians did not perform all that was commanded them, and many payed for it with their lives. Theophilus, who also wished for a quiet and peaceful life for the church, was more cautious in his interpretation of the biblical command: "Moreover, concerning subjection to authorities and powers, and prayer for them, the divine word gives us instructions, in order that we may lead a quiet and peaceful life. And it teaches us to render all things to all, honour to whom honour, fear to whom fear, tribute to whom tribute; to owe no man anything, but to love all."[120]

Tertullian's *Apology* contained the most elaborate arguments on the universality of all things under the leadership of the eternal God. Since all is preordained and nothing can escape the purpose of God, the existence of the Roman empire must be viewed as a an act of divine will. In that context prayers for the safety of emperor and empire are a natural outcome of faith.

More surprising was the contention of Tertullian that emperors are in fact aware of their dependence on the Christian God: "They know from whom they have obtained their power; they know, as they are men, from whom they have received life itself."[121] This seemed to provide a justification for the questionable resolve of Christians to ensure divine blessings for the emperor and his empire: "Without ceasing, for all our emperors we offer prayer. We pray for life prolonged; for security to the empire; for protection of the imperial house; for brave armies, a faithful senate, a virtuous people, the world at rest, whatever, as man or Cæsar, an emperor would wish. These things I cannot ask from any but the God from whom I know I shall obtain them."[122] When statements of this kind came to the ears of pagans, the reaction was that of suspicion that all the Christians desired was escape from persecution and not honest admiration of Roman power and merit. Tertullian foresaw the argument and

---

[119]Athenagoras, Leg 32 (ANF II) 148.
[120]Theophilus, AdAut 3.14 (ANF II) 115.
[121]Tertullian, Apol 30 (ANF III) 42.
[122]Ibid.,

answered it.[123] Then he gave his rationale of why the Christians benefit from their obedience to the command of honoring Rome's greatness:

> There is also another and a greater necessity for our offering prayer in behalf of the emperors, nay, for the complete stability of the empire, and for Roman interests in general. For we know that a mighty shock impending over the whole earth—in fact, the very end of all things threatening dreadful woes—is only retarded by the continued existence of the Roman empire. We have no desire, then, to be overtaken by these dire events; and in praying that their coming may be delayed, we are lending our aid to Rome's duration.[124]

We may have reached here the outside limits of historical interpretation when even Christians endow emperors with the power to alter God's purpose. In the final analysis empire and church are united in the same goal of preserving peace and delaying the final consummation. Divine eschatology can fluctuate according to the fervor of Christian prayers for secular powers.[125]

The search for peace in a troubled world led the church to reevaluate the nature of the empire, even in times of conflicts. The purpose of the Roman rule was beneficial to all, and Christians often agreed to become the allies of the Romans in promoting peace.[126] Irenaeus was willing to disregard the cruelty of persecutions in his hometown in order to lavish praise on the Romans: "Through their instrumentality the world is at peace, and we walk on the highways without fear, and sail where we will."[127] No one wanted to forego participation in the greatness of a society whose efficiency and benefits even Christians had to acknowledge. At points they claimed some credit for it. In an Apology of Melito, reported by Eusebius, we find a description of how, through the philosophy of Christianity made available to barbarians, Rome had grown in splendor and on how things have become glorious in the empire due to the prayers of Christians.[128]

---

[123]Ibid., 31.
[124]Ibid., 32 (ANF III) 42-43.
[125]Ibid., 39.
[126]Justin Martyr, 1 Apol 12.
[127]Irenaeus, AdvHaer 4.30.3 (ANF I) 503.
[128]Eusebius, HE 4.26.5-8.

The admiration for Romans went beyond prayers. In times of prosperity Christians dressed in ways celebrating the "piping times of peace" when the blessings rained from the empire as from heaven.[129] Tertullian reflected on the fact that Christians were more prone to celebrate festivals in honor of emperors and victories than were the pagans: "You will now-a-days find more doors of heathens without lamps and laurel wreaths than of Christians."[130] Hence the warning against idolatry. The theme is repeated in a communication to his wife where he warns of the dangers of taking part in heathen rites.[131] A great deal of what we find in the *Apologeticum* has changed after Tertullian became a Montanist. In the *De corona* and the *De idolatria* he criticized those who were prepared to honor Romans in ways that his new religious commitments no longer permitted.

The early church often found itself in a strange dialectical necessity, continuously reassessing that which it could not live with and at the same time could not live without. The future of the church depended on the welfare of the empire, and at the same time was threatened by it. The pagan world experienced some of the same uneasiness. It could not tolerate the competition of the Christian faith, while surmising the superior moral and spiritual benefits to be derived from it. The journey through patristic writings cannot be freed from surprises, one of which is the honor accorded to emperors and secular institutions. But at one point the line was carefully drawn. Whatever the praise of the emperor, no Christian could worship him. Emperor worship, so dear to many Romans, was the major stumbling block for Christians, and they provided many explanations for their negative reactions:

> Wherefore I will rather honour the king [than your gods], not, indeed, worshipping him, but praying for him. But God, the living and true God, I worship, knowing that the king is made by Him. You will say, then, to me, "Why do you not worship the king?" Because he is not made to be worshipped, but to be reverenced with lawful honour, for he is not a god, but a man appointed by God, not to be worshipped but to judge justly.[132]

---

[129]Tertullian, DePal 1.
[130]Tertullian, DeIdol 15 (ANF III) 70.
[131]Tertullian, AdUxor 2.6.
[132]Theophilus, AdAut 1.11 (ANF II) 92.

On the basis of the Gospel saying that we should render to Caesar the things that are Caesar's and to God the things that are God's, Irenaeus attributed to Christ the final judgment on the honor to be given to the emperor: "naming indeed Caesar as Caesar, but confessing God as God" (*Caesarem quidem Caesarem nominans, Deum vero Deum confitens*).[133] By honoring the emperor, Christians may have unwittingly transferred on him some of the respect due to God alone. Tertullian refrained from calling the emperor Lord, a title even Augustus did not have, while at the same time conceding that such a title belonged to him, provided it is different in meaning from the one reserved for God.[134] In fact, Christians understood the position of the emperor better than the pagans. In a declaration that would have astounded his imagined pagan interlocutors, Tertullian declared:

> So that on valid grounds I might say Cæsar is more ours than yours, for our God has appointed him. Therefore, as having this propriety in him, I do more than you for his welfare . . . in keeping the majesty of Cæsar within due limits, and putting it under the Most High, and making it less than divine, I commend him the more to the favor of Deity.[135]

In the same breath he suggested that to give the emperor the title of God would be to rob him of his true title. For indeed, if emperors were divine and Christians refused to worship them, then Christians should be punished.[136] This was his daring response to the accusations against those who refused to worship the emperor. Yet all the while Christians must have wondered at the praise Tertullian reserved for the emperor whom he considered second only to God and before and above all the pagan gods:

---

[133]Irenaeus, AdvHaer 3.8.1 (ANF I) 421. Around 180 Donata of Sicili coined the formula: "Honor for Caesar as Caesar, but fear for God." (*Honorem Caesari quasi Caesari; timorem autem Deo.*)

[134]Tertullian, Apol 34.

[135]Ibid., 33 (ANF III) 43. Tertullian, AdNat 1.17 (ANF III) 126, accused pagans of mocking the emperor by calling him god: "We do not call the emperor God; For on this point *sannam facimus* [literally: 'we make faces'], as the saying is. But the truth is, that you who call Cæsar God both mock him, by calling him what he is not, and curse him, because he does not want to be what you call him. For he prefers living to being made a god."

[136]Tertullian, Apol 10.

a Deo secundus ante omnes et super omnes deos.[137] For most Christians it remained difficult to set absolute limits within which a reverence of the emperor was not contrary to their faith. It became necessary to determine where the concept of "honoring" stopped and that of "worshiping" began. In the case of sacrifices it was always clear, and Christians knew where they stood in their refusal to perform them. In other areas it was not always that clear.

Even late in his life, as he was writing to Scapula, Proconsul of Carthage, Tertullian had maintained his ambivalent appraisal of Christian attitudes in regard to the respect due to emperors: "A Christian is enemy to none, least of all to the Emperor of Rome, whom he knows to be appointed by his God, and so cannot but love and honour; and whose well-being moreover, he must needs desire, with that of the empire over which he reigns so long as the world shall stand—for so long as that shall Rome continue. To the emperor, therefore, we render such reverential homage as is lawful for us and good for him, regarding him as the human being next to God who from God has received all his power, and is less than God alone."[138]

Tertullian was almost prophetic in his analysis of the position of Roman authority. For him no emperor could have been Christian. Yet a great deal of his writing could be considered as foreshadowing the emergence of the Constantine era and the Christianization of the empire. Would Christian emperors have received more praise from Tertullian than pagan emperors? Would he have agreed with Lactantius and especially Eusebius in their assessment of the role of Christian emperors?

---

[137]Ibid., 30. Tertullian had to oppose the practice of emperor worship while recognizing some divine status to the ruling emperor. He knew that ever since the rule of Augustus the empire was considered under the leadership of a semidivine being in the person of the emperor who became the key to the continuation of the *Pax deorum*. Even in a post-Constantine Christian empire some Christians could not relinquish the belief of the divinity of the emperor, or later still of the divine status accorded to their respective kings. At the turn of the fifth century the Christian writer Vegetius in his *De re militari* still portrays the emperor as God present and corporeal (*tanquam praesens et corporalis deus*). See also the discussion in Michel Meslin, *Le Christianisme dans l'empire romain* (Paris: Presses Universitaires de France, 1970) 112-15.

[138]Tertullian, AdScap 2 (ANF III) 105-106.

In the third century, and even in the first part of the fourth century, Christians were willing to concede that the fate of the church was closely linked with that of the empire and that only their mutual survival could ensure peace and progress. By the end of the fourth century, after the completion of the Theodosian code, one no longer had that feeling. The triumphant church could ensure its own survival unrelated to the fate of the empire. History proved that that was indeed the case, though the collapse of the empire did not systematically mean the end of paganism. There is not a little wonder about the fact that the early church came to regard the existence of the Roman empire as providential while, at the same time, Christians were declared, mostly during persecutions, enemies of Rome.

For the church, existence in a secular world dictated compromises. Civic and cultural syncretism was unavoidable to ensure a life of peace and relative comfort. Christians, as well as their pagan counterpart, needed to borrow money, to hold office, to assume their place in society. A great deal of it required the swearing of an oath, a necessity which placed Christians in delicate situations. Subtle distinctions were made between the emperors and the demons they represented. Oaths had to be qualified:

> Though we decline to swear by the genii of the Cæsars, we swear by their safety, which is worth much more than all your genii. Are you ignorant that these genii are called "Dæmones." . . . We respect in the emperors the ordinance of God, who has set them over the nations. . . . But as for dæmons, that is, your genii, we have been in the habit of exorcizing them, not of swearing by them, and thereby conferring on them divine honour.[139]

We find a much more cautious attitude in Origen who was forced to answer pointed accusations of Celsus: "We have already said that we must not swear by a human king, or by what is called 'the fortune of the king.' It is therefore unnecessary for us again to refute these statements: 'If you are commanded to swear by a human king, there is nothing wrong in that. For to him has been given whatever there is upon earth; and whatever you receive in this life, you receive from him.' We deny, however, that all things which are on the earth have been given to the

---

[139]Tertullian, Apol 32 (ANF III) 43. See also AdNat 1.17.

king."[140] On occasion Christians were aware that their oath may have
meant a contract in the name of idols. They needed to free their
conscience from unnecessary guilt: "In borrowing money from heathens
under pledged securities, *Christians* give a guarantee under oath, and
deny themselves *to have done so*."[141]

Civic obedience meant compliance with government mandates,
including that of paying taxes. Though Christians surmised that their
taxes might be used to promote causes deleterious to their existence and
welfare, they seem to have accepted such arrangements as divinely
ordered, mostly when one took seriously the advice of Christ to render
unto Caesar what belongs to Caesar, a saying that originated in the
context of paying taxes. Such was the position of Justin, who remarked
that all taxes, ordinary and extraordinary, were more readily paid by
Christians than by others.[142]

For Tatian secular commands were valid, provided they did not
require a denial of God. Thus paying taxes, as well as any other kind of
serfdom, were all within a divinely appointed order of society.[143] To that
Tertullian added a twist supposed to glorify the honesty of Christians, for,
indeed, they not only accepted to pay taxes, but their sense of duty
prevented them from resorting to fraud, a claim which could not be
shared by all. For such behavior the empire should be thankful.[144]
Because of that, he was also horrified when Christians were listed as
taxpayers together with dishonorable people.[145]

Service in the imperial army proved the supreme test of loyalty. The
information we possess in that area is unclear, sometimes confusing.
Almost from the beginning of the existence of the church it became a
disturbing issue. As early as the end of the first century Clement of Rome

---

[140]Origen, CCel 8.67 (ANF IV) 665.

[141]Tertullian, DeIdol 23 (ANF III) 75.

[142]Justin Martyr, 1 Apol 17.

[143]Tatian, OratGr 4 (ANF II) 66. To his protest for being treated as a
miscreant, Tatian added: "Does the sovereign order the payment of tribute, I am
ready to render it. Does my master command me to act as a bondsman and to
serve, I acknowledge the serfdom. Man is to be honoured as a fellowman; God
alone is to be feared."

[144]Tertullian, Apol 42.

[145]Tertullian, DeFuga 13.

admonished Christians to serve in the army in readiness and submissiveness to the emperor and his generals.[146] Ignatius warned against desertion.[147] The dilemmas Christians confronted in the army were of a serious nature. Should a Christian kill under any circumstances? On that score, doubts persisted on the part of some generals that Christians could be good soldiers. And should a Christian give an oath to an emperor who may be the enemy of Christ? There are exaggerated, if not spurious, accounts of Christian miracles that gave Roman armies the victory, as in the case of Marcus Aurelius's German campaign. (The episode was already mentioned in the previous chapter.)

Though Tertullian would have us believe in his *Apologeticum* that Christians had filled every place, which also meant that soldiers were found in camps and fortresses, in his later writings he denounced the propriety of Christians serving in the imperial army. Since there can be no agreement between divine and human sacrament, no one can serve both God and Caesar. Furthermore a Christian cannot wage war, for the Gospel forbids the wearing of arms.[148] The argument was more extensively developed in the *De corona* where military service was rejected as contrary to God's will and purpose. He who takes the sword shall perish by the sword, even more so if he happens to carry a flag hostile to Christ. Military life involves offenses against God's law.[149] Again we feel that the Tertullian speaking here is quite different from the one who wrote the *Apologeticum*.

The extent of Christian participation in the imperial army is far from clear. The statement of Eusebius that the persecutions under Diocletian began with the brethren in the army would indicate a substantial contingent of Christians in the imperial forces.[150] Lactantius supported such a position but mentioned that Christian soldiers were compelled to sacrifice and perform other impieties or be dismissed from the army.[151]

---

[146]Clement, 1 Corinthians 37:1-4.

[147]Ignatius, ToPolyc 6.2.

[148]Tertullian, DeIdol 19. The whole section is devoted to a discussion of military service.

[149]Tertullian, DeCor 11. This chapter is devoted to military service.

[150]Eusebius, HE 8.1.8.

[151]Lactantius, DeMort 10.

Caesar *and* Christ or Caesar *or* Christ! The answer to those questions meant harmony or disruption. As the church grew stronger geographically and numerically, it was to the advantage of Christians to seek a life of peace and conciliation through their role as loyal citizens of an empire that had been able to convince them of benefits from which no one wanted to be excluded. The laws of reciprocity did not always work, and pagans and Christians still had to live in suspicion of each other. When reactions turned violent to the point of persecutions, Christians had to renounce the ideal of a harmony between church and state. Though church and empire shared a common destiny, distinctions separating the one from the other persisted unresolved. Two major lines of thought and conduct seemed to run parallel and sometimes to contradict each other. Alternatively, and sometimes concurrently, Christians adopted the more pessimistic and apocalyptic view of eschatology. The world of man would be replaced by the city of God. Not much was redeemable in the present, and the empire was viewed as the forces of the Antichrist. On the other hand we also find a church militant and intent on transforming the present world into a society built on the Gospel principles. To achieve this they had to become a part of the surrounding world and respect its structure as a God-given necessity.

The Quest for Tolerance and Religious Freedom

Troubled times and persecutions produced martyrs and philosophers. The former were willing to sacrifice their lives for absolute ideals. The latter sought a wider context to divine will and purpose. Some church fathers were involved in a quest which at first appeared out of reach, yet in need of vindication. It was the quest for religious freedom.

Two spiritual masters of antiquity left a legacy that even today inspires many orations on religious freedom. They are Tertullian and Lactantius. Tertullian wrote to Scapula:

> It is a fundamental human right, a privilege of nature, that every man should worship according to his own convictions: one man's religion neither harms nor helps another man. It is assuredly no part of religion to compel religion [*non est religionis cogere religionem*]—to which free

will and not force should lead us. . . . Accordingly the true God bestows His blessings alike on wicked men and on His own elect.[152]

Religious freedom, however, implies mutual tolerance, and in this case an implied recognition of the legitimacy of pagan gods, a position that not all Christians of his day were willing to share with Tertullian:

> Let one man worship God, another Jupiter; let one lift suppliant hands to the heavens, another to the altar of Fides . . . let one consecrate his own life to his God, and another that of a goat. For see that you do not give a further ground for the charge of irreligion, by taking away religious liberty, and forbidding free choice of deity, so that I may no longer worship according to my inclination, but am compelled to worship against it.[153]

The argument was continued as a criticism of Roman practices in considering Christians guilty of not worshiping the gods of Rome. In fact Rome had a rather generous approach to religious freedom, and liberty

---

[152]Tertullian, AdScap 2 (ANF III) 105. The beginning of the text restates Tertullian's concept of the universality of the Christian God: "We are worshippers of one God, of whose existence and character Nature teaches all men." It follows closely the Stoic arguments Paul used in Romans 1 and 2.

[153]Tertullian, Apol 24 (ANF III) 39. We find a similar discussion in Clement of Alexandria, Protr 10 (ANF II) 202, but in a larger context than just religious freedom: "Let, then, the Athenian follow the laws of Solon, and the Argive those of Phoroneus, and the Spartan those of Lycurgus: but if thou enrol thyself as one of God's people, heaven is thy country, God thy lawgiver."

But the argument is much more forceful in Tertullian, Apol 24 (ANF III) 39, who persists in pointing out that religious freedom belongs to the very nature of religion and does not depend on human decisions about it: "We give offense to the Romans, we are excluded from the rights and privileges of Romans, because we do not worship the gods of Rome. It is well that there is a God of all, whose we all are, whether we will or no." Already as early as the second century we find Athenagoras in his *Legatio pro Christianis* reminding the Romans that the empire is indeed pluralistic by accepting traditions and laws from everywhere, even if absurd. There is liberty of worship because of the belief that the fear of the gods will prevent injustice and crimes. Why then are Christians treated differently? Thus the plea of Athenagoras, Leg 2 (ANF II) 130: "What, therefore, is conceded as the common right of all, we claim for ourselves, that we shall not be hated and punished because we are called Christians."

was granted to worship any god, save the true God. Tertullian exposed the fallacies of a religious freedom which excludes any aspect of worship. Compulsion and religion cannot coexist. No free person should be compelled to worship any gods, if not voluntarily.

Lactantius chose a more philosophical route, making the very essence of religion the foundation of freedom. Any aspect of force and violence destroys the meaning of religion: "There is no occasion for violence and injury, for religion cannot be imposed by force; the matter must be carried on by words rather than by blows, that the will may be affected. Let them unsheathe the weapon of their intellect; if their system is true, let it be asserted. We are prepared to hear if they teach; while they are silent, we certainly pay no credit to them, as we do not yield to them even in their rage."[154]

Lactantius exposed the absurdity of religious systems in need of violence for their defense: "For religion is to be defended, not by putting to death, but by dying; not by cruelty, but by patient endurance; not by guilt, but by good faith: for the former belong to evils, but the latter to goods; and it is necessary for that which is good to have place in religion, and not that which is evil. For if you wish to defend religion by bloodshed, and by tortures, and by guilt, it will no longer be defended, but will be polluted and profaned. *For nothing is so much a matter of free will as religion;* in which, if the mind of the worshipper is disinclined to it, religion is at once taken away, and ceases to exist."[155]

We have already mentioned in previous chapters how some imperial rescripts from Trajan to Galerius included some form of tolerance for the Christian religion. With the ascension to power of Constantine it seemed that religious freedom had become axiomatic. It may be worth quoting again the end of the edict of Milan, the milestone of the period:

> We have, therefore, determined, with sound and upright purpose, that liberty is to be denied to no one, to choose and to follow the religious observances of the Christians, but that to each one freedom is to be given to devote his mind to that religion which he may think adapted

---

[154]Lactantius, DivInst 5.20 (ANF VII) 156.
[155]Ibid., 5.20 (ANF VII) 157. Italics mine.

to himself, in order that the Deity may exhibit to us in all things his accustomed care and favor.[156]

The Edict of Milan, however, had a pro-Christian slant, and even Constantine could not resist violating its spirit and purpose, as when he ordered the destruction of the temple of Aesculapius at Aegae.[157] There was still a strong suspicion that pagan cults were the province of demons and were not acceptable in a Christianized world. But Theodosius was more direct on that point than Constantine: "We desire that all people governed by our clemency should live in accord with the religion which the Apostle Peter committed to the Romans and which he teaches to this day, as the faith affirms."[158] As might be expected, it was the turn of pagan philosophers to come to the defense of religious freedom from their own perspective.

The pagan apology for their religious traditions followed closely the history and vicissitudes of the Altar of Victory which had adorned the Senate for several centuries. From Dio Cassius we learn that after the victory at Actium, Caesar Augustus showed his gratitude by dedicating the temple of Minerva and the Curia Iulia erected in honor of his father.

> In the latter he set up the statue of Victory which is still in existence, thus signifying probably that it was from her that he had received the empire. It had belonged to the people of Tarentum, whence it was brought to Rome, placed in the senate chamber, and decked with the spoils of Egypt.[159]

For more than three centuries the Altar of Victory had remained the undisputed symbol of imperial grandeur, invoked on every military occasion not only as a plea for victory but also as the sign of the triumph of the Roman spirit. It consisted of the statue of a woman standing on top of a globe, her arms extended, and a wreath of laurel on her head. It was

---

[156]Eusebius, HE 10.5.5 (NPNF-2 I) 379.

[157]Eusebius, VConst 3.56.

[158]CodTheod 16.2.2. Quoted by Hermann Doerris, *Constantine and Religious Liberty* (New Haven CT: Yale University Press, 1960) 51. See also Sozomen, HE 7.4. Doerris adds the interesting comment that the Reformed Church of Zürich in the days of Zwingli adopted this provision of the *Codex Theodosianus* as the basis for the church-state relationship.

[159]Dio Cassius, RomHist 51.22.1-2 (LCL VI) 63.

at its feet that senators took their oaths and made their commitments to unity and peace in the preservation of all that was noble in religious traditions. The Altar of Victory provided the constant hope of success against barbarians and the promise of eternal power for Rome. No one ever considered any criticism against such a magnificent protector of Roman causes and especially its cults. In an uninterrupted way senators had offered incense on the altar ever since the days of Augustus.

The mood in the senate changed drastically with the ascension of Constantius II who, during a visit to Rome in 357, ordered the removal of the Altar of Victory, though he allowed other pagan cults to continue. Neither Constantine nor his sons seem to have been disturbed by the pagan traditions of the senate. They were more concerned with the development of Constantinople. It is with Constantius II that the open war on the Altar of Victory began.

As expected, the attempt at restoring paganism under Julian included the reinstitution of the Altar of Victory. Jovian, the successor of Julian was a Christian, but had a policy of religious tolerance and, during his short reign of eight months, did not attempt to undo all the pagan reforms of Julian, though he reinstituted the privileges of the church. He even received the approbation of the pagan rhetorician Themistius who praised him for his decision that

> what pertains to religion and the cult of the divine will should be according to the judgment of the individual, thus imitating the Deity, who placed in all men a natural appetite for religion, yet desired that the nature and method of propitiating the divine will should be determined by the preference and free choice of each personality.[160]

Valentinian I and Valens preferred to compromise and tolerated some of the changes Julian enacted. They chose to close their eyes on the presence of the Altar of Victory in its prominent position in the Senate.

Toward the end of his rule, Gratian became more focused on Christian reforms. He refused the pagan title of *Pontifex Maximus* and ordered the removal of the Altar of Victory from the Curia. By cutting the funds to maintain the public cult, he inflicted a serious blow on Roman traditions. When a few months later Gratian was murdered, pagans saw in his death a divine vengeance against his desecration of

---

[160]Themistius, *Oratio de Religione*. Quoted in Boyd, *Ecclesiastical Edicts*, 23.

Roman religion. The fate of the Altar of Victory, however, was more precarious than ever. It was briefly restored by Eugenius at a time when Theodosius was no longer in control of the West. The senate had petitioned Eugenius whom they regarded as only a superficial Christian. At first Eugenius refused, but finally yielded. The pagan success was brief. Eugenius was defeated by Theodosius who, in a final imperial act, sealed the fate of the Altar of Victory for ever. It never reappeared in the senate in spite of eloquent appeals from pagans. With it a great deal of the glorious history of Rome vanished. Paganism was struggling for a last endeavor at survival. Theodosian edicts, both for religious and economic reasons, ended state financial support for all rites and sacrifices. Zosimus saw in those edicts not only the defeat of paganism but also the death of noble Rome and the reason for all the barbarian invasions.[161]

Dying paganism produced its defenders. The most influential one was Symmachus, prefect of Rome who, since the 360s, had been the leading figure in the senate and the *Praefectura urbana* with the title of *Praefectus urbi sacra vice iudicans*. The office carried great prestige and power and was coveted as the highest achievement of a senatorial career. The emperor relied heavily on the competence of that office for decisions of importance. The tenure of Symmachus as prefect fluctuated with the whim of emperors and could be greatly influential or unexpectedly threatened. As a rule it was the responsibility of the prefect to oversee the festivals and ensure their regularity. Even after the removal of the Altar of Victory, Symmachus saw to it that the priesthood continue to function and the senate not be totally deprived of its traditions. The position of prefect became more and more tenuous with the growth of Christianity and with the fact that emperors were Christian, at least nominally. For a long time pagans in the senate relied on Symmachus's administrative power and oratory eloquence to extricate them from the conflicts with their Christian counterparts and to restore the Altar of Victory to its proper place in the curia.

Symmachus's trouble came not so much from the senate as from the most powerful bishop of the day, Ambrose, who controlled the destiny of the church of Milan, a frequent refuge of Christian emperors. It was to be expected that, under the influence of Ambrose Symmachus would be

---

[161]Zosimus, HistNova 4.59.

replaced by a Christian prefect before he could lead the pagan reaction to a successful conclusion. At the peak of the controversy between Ambrose and Symmachus, by imperial order, the title of prefect went to Pinianus, a Christian. It was a clear sign to Symmachus that the times had changed and that it would be difficult, if not impossible, to continue to claim that, without the support of the traditional gods, Rome would suffer hardship.

We know of at least four attempts made by pagan senators to try to restore the Altar of Victory in the curia. The first happened in 382 when pagan senators delegated Symmachus to plead their cause with Gratian. He was refused an audience and bitterly complained about it in the name of justice: "In the reign of the late Emperor [Gratian] audience with him was refused to me by unscrupulous officials for the precise reason that justice was likely to prevail, my lords and Emperors."[162] The reason for the denial of the audience was given by Ambrose as he reflected on the second attempt made to Valentinian II in 384:

> For, nearly two years ago, when the same attempt was being made, holy Damasus, bishop of the Roman church, elected by the judgment of God, sent me a memorial, which the Christian senators in great numbers put forth, protesting that they had given no such authority. . . . This memorial I sent to your Clemency's brother [Gratian]. . . .[163]

The intervention of Pope Damasus, with the obvious help of Ambrose, was successful. According to some records Symmachus was temporarily banned from Rome by Gratian as a punishment for his plea on behalf of the pagans.

The second attempt, already mentioned, took place under Valentinian II in 384. It was in the form of a plea presented to the Senate and the Emperor and preserved in the eloquent *Memorial* of Symmachus. When Ambrose heard of it he insisted on receiving a copy of it:

---

[162]Symmachus Relat 3.1.35. *Relationes* 3 was written in 384 during the second plea to Valentinian II. It is also known as the *Memorial* of Symmachus. The text followed is that of R. H. Barrow in *Prefect and Emperor: The Relationes of Symmachus* (Oxford: Clarendon Press, 1973). It is reproduced in Ambrose's Letter 17. At some points the division of the texts differ. In those instances the references in Ambrose are given in parentheses.

[163]Ambrose, Letter 17.10 (NPNF-2 X) 413.

If it were a civil cause the right of reply would be reserved for the opposing party; it is a religious cause, and I the bishop make a claim. Let a copy of the memorial which has been sent be given me, that I may answer more fully, and then let your Clemency's father be consulted on the whole subject, and vouchsafe an answer. Certainly if anything else is decreed, we bishops cannot contentedly suffer it and take no notice; you indeed may come to the church, but will find either no priest there, or one who will resist you.[164]

The threat of excommunication of the emperor if he yielded to the pagan senators and Symmachus was apparently effective. Ambrose received the text of Symmachus's memorial, which he appended to his seventeenth letter. Then he wrote his eighteenth letter to answer the points of Symmachus.

In his seventeenth letter Ambrose posited himself as a great defender of true religion against superstition, an interesting reversal of roles, since up to the time of Constantine it was the Christian religion which was labelled a superstition. Ambrose called the pagan gods "devils." The whole letter was an uninterrupted attack on paganism in a harsh and bullying style not becoming his position as Bishop of Milan. He must have been concerned about the spirit of tolerance of Valentinian, who at one time gave permission to Symmachus to prosecute and punish those who did harm to pagan temples. Thus Ambrose was taking no chances and resorted to menaces which came close to a certain form of blackmail, if not persecution.

The letter also contained exaggerations. His claim that the senate was by then made up of a great majority of Christians is difficult to ascertain. The senate mood as portrayed by Ambrose implied that Christians were continuously insulted by pagans, that they were compelled against their will to offer sacrifices, that they had to swear by the altar. Constant appeal was made to Valentinian II to remember the virtues and merits of his father Valentinian I and his brother Gratian, and not to betray them: "Wherefore, O Emperor, since you see that if you decree anything of that kind, injury will be done, first to God, and then to your father and

---

[164]Ibid., 17.13 (NPNF-2 X) 413.

brother, I implore you to do that which you know will be profitable to your salvation before God."[165]

There is no agreement on the date of the third attempt which probably took place between 388 and 391 in a petition to Theodosius. But even Symmachus must have surmised the futility of the attempt, as it was the time at which the emperor was at the peak of his antipagan legislation which could fill several volumes.

The fourth attempt was temporarily successful in 392 when usurper Eugenius was able to restore the Altar of Victory before being defeated by Theodosius. The conflicts connected with the episode are referred to in the fifty-seventh letter of Ambrose addressed to Eugenius. In it the emperor was rebuked for his conduct in regard to pagan cults. According to Ambrose Eugenius overstepped his authority as emperor to make himself an enemy of God. No further attempts at restoring the Altar of Victory are documented, though some historians have portrayed Symmachus as relentless in his endeavors until his death in 405.

The most important pagan document of the period is *Relationes* 3 also known as the *Memorial* of Symmachus. Though sometimes indignant, the tone of the address was tolerant and conciliatory, always skilfully avoiding direct and unfriendly criticism of Christian emperors. While a devoted pagan, he bore no grudge against his Christian adversaries. He even was on intimate terms with some of those who opposed his actions, including Pope Damasus and Ambrose. He scrupulously refrained from any language that could be construed as an attack on Christianity. The magnanimity of thought and the eloquence of style of Symmachus were viewed by Ambrose as traps into which Christians should not fall.[166] In comparison the address of Ambrose was full of sophistry, intimidation, and what could already have been considered as Christian sloganism. But Ambrose won the day, though the words of Symmachus had a profound impact on Christians as well as on pagans. Other Christian Writers were more willing to concede his undisputed and distinguished eloquence.[167]

The search for peace and conciliation in a religious world full of discord led Symmachus to speak of the divinity in such sublime terms as to place it beyond the absurdities of human quarrels. In the name of tradi-

---

[165]Ibid., 17.17 (NPNF-2 X) 414.
[166]Ibid., 18.2.
[167]Socrates, HE 5.14.

tions which have provided well-being and security for Rome and in honor of the legacy of those who are no more, Symmachus pleaded for respect of the divine essence even if honor cannot be given to specific gods:

> We ask you to give us back our religious institutions as they used to be when for so long they were of value to the state. . . . We are not on such good terms with the barbarians that we can do without an Altar of Victory. . . . If honour is refused to the divinity herself, at any rate let it be duly given to the divine name.[168]

As a background for his appeal for the restoration of the Altar of Victory, Symmachus made two pleas with universal appeal, while relating to specific events. He bemoaned the fact that ornaments have been taken away from the Senate without realizing that they were the elements safeguarding the perpetuity of Roman traditions as well as the good names of the emperors. The second plea was more fervent and related to the loss of moral values. In the absence of the Altar of Victory the whole benefit connected with the taking of an oath had disappeared:

> Where else are we to take an oath of allegiance to your laws and ordinances? What religious sanction is going to deter the treacherous from giving false evidence? . . . That altar holds together the harmony of all as a group and that same altar makes its appeal to the good faith of each separately, and nothing gives more authority to the proceedings of the senate than the feeling that all its measures are passed by a body of men acting, as it were, on oath.[169]

It was not until the removal of the Altar of Victory that the pagan segment of the senate realized its importance in the life of Roman politics.

Then Symmachus turned to his philosophical argumentation for the existence of divinities and the benefits they bestow. The divine mind assigns particular destinies no one should frustrate without doing harm to the soul with which he was endowed at birth. Sometimes the life of reason must be supplemented by religious faith:

> Man's reason moves entirely in the dark; his knowledge of divine influences can be drawn from no better source than from the recollec-

---

[168]Symmachus, Relat 3.2-3. 35-37. (Ambrose 3-4).
[169]Ibid., 3.5. 37. (Ambrose 6).

tion and the evidences of good fortune received from them. If long passage of time lends validity to religious observances, we ought to keep faith with so many centuries, we ought to follow our forefathers who followed their forefathers and were blessed in so doing.[170]

In a style often reminiscent of earlier Christian apologists, especially Tertullian, Symmachus evoked a realm of religious faith encompassing both universality and mystery. No one individual or group can lay claim to a full understanding of the divinity which cannot be reduced to human argument. There are many avenues leading to God, and they all require a spirit of tolerance and awe: "And so we ask for peace for the gods of our fathers, for the gods of our native land. It is reasonable that whatever each of us worships is really to be considered one and the same. We gaze up at the same stars, the sky covers us all, the same universe compasses us. What does it matter what practical system we adopt in our search for the truth? Not by one avenue only can we arrive at so tremendous a secret. But this is the kind of case for men to put with time on their hands; at the moment it is prayers that we present to you, not debating arguments."[171]

This was no doubt the most persuasive part of the oration. It was often conjectured that, if not for the overwhelming influence of Ambrose, Symmachus may have succeeded in his appeal. Ambrose won the day with his reply in his eighteenth letter, a document which does not match the eloquence of the *Relationes*, while displaying a spirit of retaliation for the evils the Roman empire inflicted on Christians in a pre-Constantine era. The request of Symmachus to substitute prayers for debating arguments fell on deaf ears with Ambrose, who paraded Christianity as the only way to truth, while exposing the fallacies of pagan claims, especially that calamities and famines were due to the abandonment of the worship of the gods.

The speech of Symmachus remained well known to Christians as well as to pagans. Some twenty years later Prudentius wrote a reply to Symmachus in which he paraphrased the plea quoted above:

We all draw life from the same atmosphere under the same sun, all living beings share the same air; but we follow different paths when we

---

[170]Ibid., 3.8. 39-41
[171]Ibid., 3.10. 41.

inquire into the being and nature of God, and by ways far apart approach the same secret; every race has its own custom, and that is the line along which it must hasten to reach the great mystery.[172]

Though a fervent Christian, Prudentius wrote more as a literary author than a theologian. The lines of argumentation between pagans and Christians had entered a new phase. Pagans found themselves in the apologetic role as defender of their religion in the same way Christians had to play that role in preceding centuries. Symmachus contributed greatly to that change. In his writings we come face to face with the last eloquent appeal for the official recognition of pagan religion.

Change, as it was happening in the days of Symmachus, seemed to forecast lack of happiness and even disaster. The decisions by Christian emperors to deprive religious institutions of private bequests was viewed by Symmachus as an unforgivable affront to those dying men who made those bequests. The punishment of the gods was inevitable: "Let no one imagine I am pleading the cause only of religion; it is from acts of the kind I have described that all the disasters of the Roman race have arisen."[173] Symmachus then described the reasons for a miserable harvest and the subsequent famine.

The fate of Symmachus in the senate suffered serious setbacks. He was accused of using his position to mistreat Christians. At one point Valentinian ordered him to release from prison those who were put there by him. Angered, Symmachus produced his defense in *Relationes* 21, pointing out that even Pope Damasus agreed that no harm had ever come to Christians from Symmachus. When it was discovered that he had participated in the rebellion of Maximus against Theodosius and that he had written a panegyric on Maximus, he was impeached for high treason. Maximus begged for mercy from Theodosius, but to no avail. He was executed, and Symmachus felt more and more isolated amid formidable hostility. Socrates reports that on one occasion, to avoid capital punishment, Symmachus took refuge in a church.[174]

Another influential pagan voice at the end of the fourth century was that of Libanius. We possess most of his voluminous writings. His

---

[172]Prudentius, COratSymm 2.85-90 (LCL II) 13-15.
[173]Symmachus, Relat 3.15. 43-45. (ambrose 14).
[174]Socrates, HE 5.14.

approach to the defence of pagan religion is contained in his thirtieth oration: *Pro templis*. The tone of the speech is terse and minatory. His compositions show him as a master of oratory, as a man who has carefully practiced the science of words. But he does not exhibit the savvy of Symmachus or the philosophical depth of Themistius. His influence, however, was beyond doubt, both among pagans and Christians. He drew an attractive picture of the religious climate of the times. But it was not always coherent, and sometimes even contradictory. His culture revealed a deep syncretistic tendency, somehow in the way of a sophist who knew classical literature to perfection.

By training and conviction Libanius was a universalist who liked to portray the greatness and eternity of Rome as the product of a long religious development going back for centuries, even millennia. The beginning of his *Pro templis* was devoted to a review of the religious traditions from which the Romans derived their gods, the guardians and protectors of the empire. His greatest hero and friend was Julian in whom he saw the epitome of devotion to Roman religion. He considered Julian the ideal prince worthy of divine apotheosis. He often referred to the true light Julian brought to the world and often said that before Julian all was night and after Julian it will be night again. We cannot ascertain the depth of Libanius' knowledge of Christianity. We know, however, that he had prominent Christians as students: John Chrysostom, Basil and Gregory of Nazianzus. But how much he learned from them about their faith remains a conjecture.

Libanius's pleading for the preservation of pagan temples was motivated as much by his conviction that he must speak out as by his revulsion at the behavior of Christian emperors, which he does not hesitate to label as anti-Roman: "Let temples everywhere remain in being, then, or else let these people agree that you emperors are ill-disposed to Rome since you allow her to act in a manner that will cause her harm."[175]

The fate of the Altar of Victory, already eloquently debated by Symmachus, was more than he could witness without voicing his disgust at Christian arrogance and intolerance. But he also knew that his case was weak, that many temples had already been destroyed, and that Theodosius, to whom he addressed his *Pro templis* was at the peak of his

---

[175]Libanius, ProTemp 34 (LCL II) 131.

antipagan legislation and was not to be swayed by his oratory. He was in poor health and saddened by the fact that many of his students had abandoned the classical training for more lucrative positions. He saw not only pagan religion in the death throes, but he also witnessed the collapse of the foundation on which it was built.

The *Pro templis* cannot be dated with precision. All we know for certain is that it was produced during the rule of Theodosius and before the destruction of the Serapeum in Alexandria in 391. Libanius referred to the continued operation of the Serapeum. The most likely date is 386. By that time the reputation of the Roman gods had already suffered through the Christianization of the empire. Educated people rejected the old Roman religious myths in favor a more culturally acceptable religious perspectives. The verve of Christian critics such as Arnobius and Lactantius had had its impact on many intellectuals. Yet Roman worship was still inextricably linked to the history and fortunes of Rome, still viewed as the queen of the world. Libanius counted on such feelings to prevail. But it was not to be. The old Roman religion failed to adapt to the changing times. It refused to consider itself vulnerable and relentlessly invoked the old virtues it inculcated in its participants. Libanius was no exception as he nostalgically spoke of the greatness of a system he could not conceive as dying. In his *Pro templis* (30.4-5) he voices his indignation at the process of desacralization of Roman religion. He points out that shrines and temples were the first buildings erected after the walls of any city. They provided the utmost protection, and even robbed of their honor, they remain the signs of the greatness and past triumph of a society now threatened by legislation. In fact it was not unusual for Christian churches to be erected in the midst of pagan temples, in spots of importance within cities.

Persecuted pagans, Libanius argued, must be granted toleration and freedom of worship as allowed by law. Any departure from this time-old Roman practice would force pagans to take the law in their own hands, a fact that would be detrimental to all. Furthermore Christian claims to have the monopoly on divine benefits were absurd. Continuing sacrifices at Rome and Alexandria kept the glory of the empire shining. From that perspective the destruction of temples were acts of blind stupidity. They deprived the people of their religious freedom and of all the art and culture connected with those temples. On this last point the verve of Libanius crosses over to exaggeration:

For instance, in the city of Boroea there was a bronze statue of
Asclepius, in the likeness of the handsome son of Cleinias. In it art
matched nature; such was its perfection that even those who could see
it every day still wanted to look at it. . . . Yet this statue, Sire, so
carefully made no doubt with much toil and brilliant genius, has been
broken up and exists no more. The mob's handiwork has been to tear
apart the masterpiece of Pheidias.[176]

At the cost of personal danger Libanius undertook his severe criticism
of Theodosian conduct and requested an immediate halt to the abuse of
temples.[177] The most severe indictment was directed at the monks much
more than at Theodosius, who still allowed some functions at the temples:

You [Theodosius] then have neither ordered the closure of temples nor
banned entrance to them. From the temples and altars you have
banished neither fire nor incense nor the offering of other perfumes. But
this black-robed tribe [monks], who eat more than elephants and, by the
quantity of drink they consume, weary those that accompany their
drinking with the singing of hymns. . . . These people, Sire, while the
law yet remains in force, hasten to attack the temples with sticks and
stones and bars of iron, and in some cases . . . with hands and feet.[178]

Sometimes—so claimed Libanius—those monks have turned the
destruction of temples into a lucrative business.

In the most eloquent section of the oration Libanius recited the long-
standing blessings that had come to people from the gods, especially for
the farming communities, for families and their labors, for the inspiration
that had come with the virtues of religion. He described the beauty of
sacrifices and feasts at the homes of village notables. No one should
deprive the people of those benefits in the name of religious reform and
intolerance.[179]

But far worse than depriving people of what was dear to their
feelings and expectation was the wilful crime against their physical

---

[176]Ibid., 22 (LCL II) 121. The attribution of the statue to Pheidias must be
taken as a rhetorical device. It is doubtful that anybody could have taken
Libanius literally on that point.
[177]Ibid., 2.
[178]Ibid., 8 (LCL II) 107-109.
[179]Ibid., 9, 10, 11, 19.

persons, especially the needy ones. Libanius showed sheer outrage at the destruction of the relief programs of the pagans:

> But your expulsion of people who by their personal care provided relief for poverty among old men and women and fatherless children, the majority of them suffering from severe physical handicaps—is not this murder? Isn't it execution? Isn't this sentencing them to death, and a death worse than ever, by starvation? . . . Then in massacring their protectors, you have been massacring these innocents. . . . This killing without trial is a confession that there are no good grounds to condemn them.[180]

The end of the oration sounded like an admonition to Theodosius. On the one hand he reassured the emperor that pagans have been schooled to obedience and that they will respect imperial decrees. But at the same time there will be vengeance against those who, without the permission of the emperor, arose unlawfully against innocent people whose crime was to worship and to defend the very Roman law.

Thus we come to the end of an age in turmoil. The lines separating Christians and pagans were no longer clear. Roles had been reversed. Persecuted became persecutors. There was ample evidence that, by the end of the fourth century, temples to the Roman gods survived the onslaught of antipaganism. Many of them became public monuments in a Christianized world. The quest for a divine center became less focused, but as necessary as ever. To a great extent Christianity owed its triumph to Roman ways and culture, a phenomenon worthy of special analysis.

---

[180]Ibid., 20 (LCL II) 119-21.

Chapter 10

Classical Culture
and Christian Faith

Idiotae, quorum semper maior pars est.
(The uneducated are always in a majority with us.)
    —Tertullian

But this one thing was inhumane, and ought to be buried in eternal
silence, namely, that he forbade teachers of rhetoric and literature to
practice their profession, if they were followers of the Christian
religion.
    —Ammianus Marcellinus on Julian

By the time Christian faith emerged as a serious contender with pagan-ism, Roman religion had plodded through numerous perspectives in search of a stable foundation. Its gods had to be proven the undisputed protectors of the empire. The impassible Epicurean gods who never inter-fere with human life were not destined to dominate the religious and cultural scene of the Romans. Lucretius's influence was severely curtailed because of his advocacy of a form of enlightenment that led to the rejection of commonly accepted traditions and rituals, most of them dear to imperial Rome. Plato's universalism of perfect geometric forms, behind which all reality was hidden, was even further removed from popular consciousness. Of the major philosophical currents, Stoicism was still vying for recognition, but its destiny was so closely related to the universal logos that it failed to affect the religious outlook of the multitudes. Neoplatonism did not greatly alter popular religion in spite of Porphyry's extensive analysis of oracles. On the whole, the Roman empire at the time of the rise of Christianity was not the scene of innovative and progressive religious thought. Compared to the Greek legacy, Romans could be credited with only meager attempts at pursuing the paths of Hellenistic science. Only Neoplatonism could lay claim to respectable originality, and that only within limited circles.

Into such a world Christians introduced a God who was by nature creator, immutable in his purpose, and in control of historical events. Ironically, Celsus and other pagan philosophers failed to perceive that Christians were often closer to Platonic philosophy and Stoic ethics than most among the Roman intelligentsia. The question of classical culture became important to all, though Christians were divided on the spiritual value of it. Some church fathers pleaded for a disconnection from pagan philosophical tenets, while others chose to defend them. Neither Christians nor pagans had a holistic view of the relationship between culture and religion, a phenomenon which kept both in permanent conflict.

Most early church apologists quoted classical literature for polemical ends. Poets, playwrights, and philosophers had fashioned a worldview that stood in opposition to the new faith. Christians portrayed the heathen world as evil and hoped that some day the kingdom of God would become reality in a world freed from paganism. Such a view, however, did not emerge until the writings of Tertullian and was not seriously considered until after the reign of Constantine. Early Christianity never entertained the thought or the wish of the collapse of the Roman empire as the result of the existence of the church. Christians were a tiny minority, often unnoticed in the giant empire of its day. It was not until the fourth century that the triumph of the church heralded the end of pagan domination. French writers especially liked to reflect on that period in terms of the collapse of paganism.[1]

As the church grew in number and influence, it had to reflect more seriously on its existence in a world it could not accept but without which it could not survive. The Roman empire provided an attractive stage upon which the life of its institutions could thrive. Christians were only too aware of the fact that the professional and cultural life of the empire was in the hands of learned pagans. But they also knew that paganism exhibited the weakness of fragmentation and a lack of solidarity among the mass of its followers. To that, in spite of doctrinal disputes, the church could oppose a strong sense of unity and clearness of purpose. What the church lacked in secular power and recognition was compensated by its zeal and fervor.

---

[1] For example, Boissier, *Fin du paganisme;* Henri-Irénée Marrou, *Saint Augustin et la fin de la culture antique* (Paris: Editions E. de Boccard, 1958).

In the first centuries of the Common Era pagans and Christians had formed their specific perspectives on the cultural dimensions of their worlds. But they both failed to produce the magnetic personalities around whom culture can gravitate for a certain time, especially such giants as Plato, Aristotle, or Cicero. There was no need to enter long arguments to explain what was meant by being Platonic, Aristotelian, or Ciceronian. It was much more difficult to define what was meant by culture at any given moment. Cicero had already connected all learning, especially philosophy, with divine influence and inspiration:

> As to philosophy, the mother of all arts, what else is it except, as Plato held, the gift, or, as I hold, the discovery of the gods? It instructed us first in the worship of gods, then in the justice of mankind at large which is rooted in the social union of the race of men, and next taught us the lessons of temperance and greatness of soul, and thus dispersed the darkness from the eyes as it were of the mind, so that we saw all things above, below, things first and last and in between.[2]

Early Christians viewed such statements with suspicion, though they could not always provide an adequate refutation of them. Most of them were steeped in pagan learning before they became Christians. Their faith demanded a rebuttal of all that was not according to Gospel precepts. Yet their ways of argumentation, their cultural background, and very often their training could not be disconnected from ingrained traditions. As the centuries went by one could no longer assess paganism apart from the inroads of Christianity, nor could one understand Christianity without its indebtedness to pagan influences. The two spiritual and intellectual worlds of paganism and Christianity could not be defined apart from the constant interaction of the one with the other.

Educated pagans resented Christian attacks against them, for those attacks came from people they considered illiterates and outcasts, the dregs of the population and a cause of shame for the glory of Rome. At the early stages of the church most Christians did not belong to the well-taught classes of the society. Tertullian had already acknowledged that the church was composed of mostly uneducated people. Minucius Felix allowed Caecilius to level damaging accusations against Christians. He referred to them as "unskilled in learning, strangers to literature, without

---

[2]Cicero, TuscDisp 1.64 (LCL XVIII) 75.

knowledge even of sordid arts."[3] That such people should make pronouncements on divine majesty called for stern reproach by the non-Christian intellectuals. In their eyes the church gathered from "the lowest dregs" a group of people who have no right to rage against the gods.[4] There was no denial that at first Christianity made but few converts from the aristocracy, or the educated upper classes in general.

Paganism's survival depended on the support of the aristocracy of the empire. Had Christians been able to tap that source from the beginning, paganism would have been weakened much earlier. The conflict between pagans and Christians as to who best represented the ideal spirit of the time led to mutual accusations of all kinds. To the argument that Christianity was polluted with abominable practices, including incest, Minucius Felix replied that in fact pagans are guilty of all of what they accused Christians to practice. Then he added:

> Neither do we at once stand on the level of the lowest of the people, if we refuse your honours and purple robes; and we are not fastidious, if we all have a discernment of one good, but are assembled together with the same quietness with which we live as individuals; and we are not garrulous in corners, although you either blush or are afraid to hear us in public.[5]

Early Christian Perspectives on Classical Culture

The relationship of Christianity to classical culture does not fit any precise pattern. The more the church entered the process of organization and the more it attempted to define its theology, the more it had to define what it meant by the "world" as an entity different from the kingdom of God. Justin refused to reject heathen learning in totality. He maintained that God was the source of inspiration for many pagan writers. Yet he found that inspiration insufficient. Heathen knowledge was not wrong, but it had to be rejected because it was not in total agreement with the teaching of Christ:

---

[3]Minucius Felix, Oct 5 (ANF IV) 175.
[4]Ibid., 8 (ANF IV) 177.
[5]Ibid., 31 (ANF IV) 192.

And I confess that I both boast and with all my strength strive to be found a Christian; not because the teachings of Plato are different from those of Christ, but because they are not in all respects similar, as neither are those of the others, Stoics, and poets, and historians. For each man spoke well in proportion to the share he had of the spermatic word [Logos], seeing what was related to it.[6]

Basic cultural perspectives were formed in the molds of pagan traditions. Though Christians denied the validity of those traditions, they could not escape certain syncretistic influences often subtle and not easily identifiable as pagan. With time the church had to deal not only with the uniqueness of its theology, but also with its assessment of the arts, of music, of painting, of poetry. The most expedient solution was to consider all of it as emanating from the same impure source. Apollo and the Muses became the channels of some corrupted spirit. Poets such as Homer and Virgil could not be totally dismissed, though sometimes condemned without proper trial.

After their conversion, many Christians kept their pagan names. Harnack gives a list of those names connected with mythology and soothsaying and then concludes: "The martyrs perished because they declined to sacrifice to the gods whose names they bore!"[7] Such a phenomenon was indeed striking and not in keeping with some other strong stances adopted by Christians:

Now this is remarkable! Here was the primitive church exterminating every vestige of polytheism in her midst, tabooing pagan mythology as devilish, living with the great personalities of the Bible and upon their words, and yet freely employing the pagan names which had been hitherto in vogue![8]

As the church grew in numbers, it also accepted in its ranks less than worthy proselytes who were not eager to abjure pagan ways of life, mostly when it meant hardship or inconvenience. In his *Pro templis* Libanius exposed the hypocrisy of such wavering Christians.

---

[6]Justin Martyr, 2 Apol 13 (ANF I) 192-93.
[7]Harnack, *Mission and Expansion*, 422.
[8]Ibid., 422-23.

Christian apologists questioned the cultural foundation of Roman religion and the relevance of the gods of the empire. Religion and politics were closely intertwined, and educated pagans did not attempt to disconnect them too radically. The performance of sacrifices was often a mere demonstration of citizens' proper relationship to the ruling powers rather than a compelling urge to fulfill religious duties. Seldom was there any attempt on the part of Roman writers to defend the truth of the legends on which ritual was based. The myths fabricated by poets of old were taught to the young without subjecting them to rigorous analysis. There was no Roman Socrates to challenge unverified propositions. For that reason, secular literature from the pagan past was viewed with suspicion by Christians. They often avoided it. At other times they struggled in their conscience to justify some of it. At any rate they never dealt with more of it than absolutely necessary.

Estimates of the value of classical culture fluctuated within geographical regions. In third-century Alexandria, for instance, spiritual matters and classical culture were often fused together, especially among Christian Platonists. Clement of Alexandria and Origen were quite at home with classical literature. In other parts of Africa Tertullian struggled with the relevance of pagan culture, as did his followers Arnobius and Lactantius. It is also reported that, while in Alexandria, a certain Anatolius founded a school of Aristotelian philosophy before becoming the bishop of Laodicea in 269.

Leaders of the early church never envisioned the formation of a Christian culture that would be independent from the world of Roman dominion. Rather they had to grapple with the limits within which they could live at peace with the education provided for their children. They had to define their own principles according to which social life remained possible without compromising their faith. At points they had to take a stand against elements in pagan traditions which contradicted their faith. But they also analyzed and interpreted pagan tenets in such a way as to prove them compatible with Christian life. The intellectual climate of second and third-century Alexandria proved beneficial in the formulation of syncretistic compromises.

The education of the young posed the most severe problems. Christian children were exposed to pagan traditions in secular schools. Even those firmly anchored in their belief of the uniqueness of Christianity had to acknowledge the need of cultural unity in order to preserve order in society. Faith had to be redefined in a broader context, less antagonistic to pagan traditions. Progressively Christian children were taught how to view heathen learning in a positive light. True, it was not until the Cappadocians that the church reached a vision of global Christian civilization with the epoch-making treatise of Saint Basil: *Ad adolescentes, de legendis libris gentilium* (*Address to Young Men on Reading Greek Literature*). But the trend was already there much earlier. We have no indication that the church, at its early stages, attempted to establish independent Christian schools with antipagan curricula. On the contrary. There seems to be a leitmotiv among church fathers from Origen to Basil or from Tertullian to Jerome encouraging Christians not to neglect learning, however pagan it may be in essence. Even heathen learning can be used to strengthen the faith.

Tertullian who, on some occasions, pleaded for a disconnection between Athens and Jerusalem, between Christian faith and pagan learning, had to admit that it would be greatly detrimental to deprive children of pagan learning. With him we enter a paradoxical argument. On the one hand he condemned the secular culture of his day, forbidding Christian schoolmasters to teach it. On the other hand he encouraged Christian children to attend pagan schools in order not to be deprived of culture:

> If teaching literature is not lawful to God's servants, neither will learning be likewise; and, how could one be trained unto ordinary human intelligence, or unto any sense or action whatever, since literature is the means of training for all life? How do we repudiate secular studies, without which divine studies cannot be pursued? Let us see, then, the necessity of literary erudition; let us reflect that partly it cannot be admitted, partly cannot be avoided. Learning literature is allowable for believers, rather than teaching; for the principle of learning and of teaching is different.[9]

The heathen had been able to create a zeitgeist which reflected universal principles of learning and believing. Christian apologists could no longer dismiss a cultural context without which even faith would be deprived of cogency and persuasion. But Tertullian was only too aware of the traps Christians might fall into if wrongly connected to pagan culture, for literature was also the way to teach idolatry. He found himself

---

[9]Tertullian, DeIdol 10 (ANF III) 66.

compelled to bring the argument to an end, though not in a most convincing fashion. The responsibility falls on the Christian and on his ability to understand the power of idolatry:

> But when a believer *learns* these things, if he is already capable of understanding what idolatry is, he neither receives nor allows them; much more if he is not yet capable. Or, when he *begins* to understand, it behooves him first to understand what he has previously learned, that is, touching God and the faith. Therefore he will reject those things, and will not receive them; and will be as safe as one who from one who knows it not, knowingly *accepts* poison but does not *drink* it.[10]

The difficulties expounded by Tertullian did not lend themselves to simple solutions. Neither schoolmasters nor students could find in his exposé any definite guidelines for Christian conduct. Each Christian had to decide on the limits within which pagan culture was to be commended without being a cause of idolatry. Again, the measuring stick was faith, and not rational thinking. There was no logical way in which pagan culture could be rejected without inflicting some damage on Christian thinking and practice. Tertullian knew the illusion of the claim that one could be totally free from pagan cultural influences. At the bottom of his heart he probably did not even wish that. His intransigence was no longer convincing. He had come to like and respect that which his faith forced him to oppose.

In the *Apologeticum* we find him challenging the assumption that Roman authorities, especially the emperor, were devoted to serve only the pagan outlook. Yet the secular system imposed on Christians a great number of civil disabilities which created a strong sense of injustice. This had to be fought in the name of dignity and respect for all. On that score, Tertullian took the stance that no compromise was desirable between Christianity and secular culture, a stance he modified whenever needed to allow Christian participation in important social developments.

The position of Tertullian on heathen learning is well known. There was no concord between the Academy and the church, between heretics and Christians. Greek logic failed the test of Christian faith:

---

[10]Ibid., 67.

Unhappy Aristotle! who invented for these men dialectics, the art of building up and pulling down; an art so evasive in its propositions, so farfetched in its conjectures, so harsh, in its arguments, so productive of contentions—embarrassing even to itself, retracting everything, and really treating of nothing.[11]

Tertullian opened his *De testimonio animae* with an evaluation of how poets and philosophers attempted to explain the presence of the soul within the body, making it either divine and immortal or temporal and perishable. While he gravitated between respect and rejection, he called on the soul to give its own witness and yearned for a rudimentary simplicity unaffected by the accumulation of theories and perspectives. He searched within himself for a soul that would reveal itself to him free from a training as received in schools and libraries or in Attic academies or porticoes. There was a long road, according to Tertullian, to the rediscovery of the soul in its "simple, rude, uncultured, and untaught" state as a unique possession unstained by human wisdom. Even Christians succumbed to the need to wrest from the soul a testimony which confirmed them in their position, though they may have lost the divine element in them.[12] For Tertullian, wisdom preceded learning as found in books: "Unquestionably the soul existed before letters, and speech before books, and ideas before the writing of them, and man himself before the poet and philosopher."[13]

Greatness and religion were not synonymous for Tertullian. He disputed the fact that Romans became better citizens because of their religion:

The Romans, therefore, were not distinguished for their devotion to the gods before they attained to greatness; and so their greatness was not the result of their religion. Indeed, how could religion make a people great who have owed their greatness to their irreligion.[14]

---

[11]Tertullian, PraescrHaer 7 (ANF III) 246.
[12]Tertullian, TestAnim 1 (ANF III) 175-76.
[13]Ibid., 5 (ANF III) 178.
[14]Tertullian, Apol 25 (ANF III) 40. For a similar argument see also AdNat 2.17.

Tertullian's cultural equation did not fit either the Christian or pagan mold. Pagan culture suffered from criticism under the pens of prominent writers ever since the days of Homer. For that reason, Romans were as guilty of rejecting it as Christians. More than any other church father, Tertullian stressed the inevitability of change in cultural patterns and showed how no one could escape such a necessity:

> Now, first, when you direct against us the general charge of divorcing ourselves from the institutions of our forefathers, consider again and again whether you are not yourselves open to that accusation in common with us. For when I look through your life and customs, lo, what do I discover but the old order of things corrupted, nay, destroyed by you? Of the laws I have already said, that you are daily supplanting them with novel decrees and statutes. As to everything else in your manner of life, how great are the changes you have made from your ancestors—in your style, your dress, your equipage, your very food, and even in your speech; for the old-fashioned you banish, as if it were offensive to you! Everywhere, in your public pursuits and private duties, antiquity is repealed; all the authority of your forefathers your own authority has superseded. To be sure, you are for ever praising old customs; but this is only to your greater discredit, for you nevertheless persistently reject them.[15]

Pagans and Christians shared a wide range of common interests, and Tertullian argued that the man of faith should by no means be excluded from participation in the life of secular society.[16]

---

[15]Tertullian, AdNat 1.10 (ANF III) 118.

[16]This is especially the case in Tertullian, Apol (ANF III) 49, particularly in chapter 42: "We are called to account as harm-doers . . . and are accused of being useless in the affairs of life. How in all the world can that be the case with people who are living among you, eating the same food, wearing the same attire, having the same habits, under the same necessities of existence." And then we find this unexpected confession: "We sojourn with you in the world, abjuring neither forum, nor shambles, nor bath, nor booth, nor workshop, nor inn, nor weekly market, nor any other place of commerce."

Tertullian overstressed the argument to the point of contradiction: "We sail with you, we fight with you, and till the ground with you; and in a like manner we unite with you in your trafficking—even in the various arts we make public property of our works for your benefit." At least in the area of warfare, Tertullian

With Origen, the relationship of Christianity to its secular environment became better focused. Christianity evolved into a small universe of its own and was no longer regarded as an appendage of the classical world. It developed its own intellectual and theological foundation.

In his *Historia ecclesiastica* (6.3) Eusebius reflected on the emerging antagonism between Christian culture and classical tradition. He related how, in Alexandria, Origen was entrusted with the sole authority in the area of elementary education and how he succeeded in gathering a great number of students. Then he decided that teaching literature contradicted his Christian convictions and terminated his lectures as hindrances to the study of sacred Scriptures. He was only seventeen when he became the principal of the elementary school of Alexandria. As a young idealist, he also parted with all the volumes of ancient literature. He was concerned that Christianity be presented in its simple and direct form without the adornment of artistic styles and artifices. The Gospel had to be plain on its own level.

Nevertheless, it is difficult to conceive of Origen as the architect of a Christian culture unrelated to traditional classical tenets. His later works abound with the knowledge and praise of ancient masters. He integrated cultural elements crossing over from Judaism, Greek philosophy, Ciceronian *cultura animi*, and Christian beliefs. Erasmus called him the fountain of theology. Origen's journey from Athens to Jerusalem via Alexandria, with all the religious obstacles he had to overcome, made him one of the best integrated personalities of the Christian church. He never abandoned the postulate that Christianity was not meant to isolate us from culture, but to transform that culture by a greater ideal. But what was that larger ideal?

---

contradicts here what he enjoins in the DeCor 11, where he questions Christian participation in the Roman army. A similar argument appears in Diog 5.2-4 (LCL II) 359. Speaking of Christians we read:

> For they do not dwell in cities in some place of their own, nor do they use any strange variety of dialect, nor practise an extraordinary kind of life. . . . Yet while living in Greek and barbarian cities, according as each obtained his lot, and following the local customs, both in clothing and food and in the rest of life, they show forth the wonderful and confessedly strange character of the constitution of their own citizenship.

Origen attended the lectures of Ammonius Saccas, the Neoplatonic philosopher whose reputation transcended the city of Alexandria. The influence of Neoplatonic philosophy on the mind of Origen is beyond doubt, and the church grappled with his legacy for centuries to come, often relegating his teachings to the realm of heresy. Yet the cultural context of the church was more clearly defined in his writings than by anyone else. Pagans recognized his greatness and were attracted to his teachings.[17] Julia Mammaea, mother of the emperor Alexander Severus, after hearing of the reputation of Origen, sent for him with military escort so that he could stay with her in Antioch and give her instruction.[18] Eusebius also reported how philosophers of his age admired Origen's teaching, submitted their works to him for his judgment, and even dedicated their books to him.[19]

For Origen Christianity was not a late religious development but the only natural and original religion. The teachings of the church are in agreement with universal nature.[20] Christ was the supreme schoolmaster of the human race:

> Christ was the "schoolmaster" of the human race, and Christianity was the peak of His education, the 'true' *paideia*, the "true" culture. Origen and his successors taught the pagan that to become a Christian was to step, at last, from a confused and undeveloped stage of moral and intellectual growth into the heart of civilization.[21]

The *Contra Celsum* clarifies the relationship of Christianity to the wisdom of the times. Though argued from a polemical point of view, it comes across with force and conviction.

But very little was said concerning classical literature. Origen answered Celsus point by point, and Celsus was primarily concerned with

---

[17]Eusebius, HE 6.3, especially 6.3.13 (NPNF-2 I) 252. "By giving such evidences of a philosophic life to those who saw him, he aroused many of his pupils to similar zeal; so that prominent men even of the unbelieving heathen and men that followed learning and philosophy were led to his instruction."

[18]Ibid., 6.21.3-4.

[19]Ibid., 6.19.1-2.

[20]Origen, CCel 3.40.

[21]Peter Brown, *The World of late Antiquity A.D. 150–750* (New York: Hartcourt Brace Jovanovich, 1971) 84.

discrediting Christianity rather than comparing it to the world of ancient masters. Origen refuted charges of foolishness and ignorance directed at Christians. He preferred to view the question on a more universal level:

> This statement [of Celsus] also is untrue, that it is "only foolish and low individuals, and persons devoid of perception, and slaves, and women, and children, of whom the teachers of the divine word wish to make converts." Such indeed does the Gospel invite, in order to make them better; but it invites also others who are very different from these, since Christ is the Saviour of all men, and especially of them that believe, whether they be intelligent or simple.[22]

Origen claimed better judgment than that of Celsus in determining the nature of wisdom:

> Moreover it is an excellent thing for a man to *be* wise, but not to *seem* so, as Celsus says. And it is no hindrance to the knowledge of God, but an assistance, to have been educated, and to have studied the best opinions, and to be wise. And it becomes us rather than Celsus to say this, especially if it be shown that he is an Epicurean.[23]

Origen objected to Celsus's use of epithets such as uninstructed and ignorant to designate Christians. The question revolved around the comparison of one form of learning with another one. According to Origen Celsus failed to grasp the wider context of learning by limiting himself to his Greek heritage.[24] Then he added: "We do *not* maintain, however, that it is impossible for one who has not been trained in earthly wisdom to receive the 'divine,' but we *do* acknowledge that all human wisdom is 'folly' in comparison to the 'divine.' "[25]

Origen did not deny the legacy of Greek learning. But it must lead to a greater knowledge as revealed in the Bible:

> And those among us who are the ambassadors of Christianity sufficiently declare that they are debtors to Greeks and Barbarians, to wise men

---

[22]Origen, CCel 3.49 (ANF IV) 484.
[23]Ibid.,
[24]Ibid., 6.14.
[25]Ibid., (ANF IV) 579. Neither Origen nor other church fathers could free themselves from the discussion on wisdom as expounded by Paul in his correspondence with the Corinthians.

and fools, . . . in order that as far as possible they may lay aside their ignorance, and endeavour to obtain greater prudence, by listening also to the words of Solomon.[26]

At points Origen had to counter the argument of Celsus that Christ knew the works of Plato and deliberately perverted the language of the philosopher.[27]

Origen compelled his contemporaries to raise the question of what was meant by Christian culture and by secular culture. The problem was never solved. Clement of Alexandria and Augustine struggled with the same questions. Christianity could not exist outside of the secular, and the secular was in constant need of being enlightened by the Christian ideal. With Origen began the movement of sorting out what could be integrated into the Christian movement and what had to be rejected. Clement adopted a pattern which led him to reject the poets of old while giving considerable credit to Greek philosophers.[28] He regarded learning and erudition as the powers transforming human nature for the better. He also rejected the claims that faith could be attained without the proper cultural training.[29]

Educated pagans questioned the validity of Christian writings, mostly when church members acknowledged that they were authored by unlearned people. When literary craftsmanship defined credibility,

---

[26]Ibid., 3.54 (ANF IV) 485.

[27]Ibid., 6.16.

[28]Clement objected to the shamelessness connected with the worship of the gods: "Stop. O Homer, the song! It is not beautiful; it teaches adultery, and we are prohibited from polluting our ears with hearing about adultery." Protr 4 (ANF II) 189. In contrast he considers philosophy as the image of truth, as a divine gift to the Greeks. Strom 1.2.5.

[29]Clement of Alexandria, Strom 1.6 (ANF II) 307. Reflecting on the benefits of culture he says: "For it is not by nature, but by learning, that people become noble and good, as people also become physicians and pilots. . . . But as we say that a man can be a believer without learning, so also we assert that it is impossible for a man without learning to comprehend the things which are declared in the faith." Of interest also is his quotation of Anaxarchus: "Erudition benefits greatly and hurts greatly him who possesses it; it helps him who is worthy, and injures him who utters readily every word, and before the whole people. It is necessary to know the measure of time. For this is the end of wisdom."

Christians confronted harsh criticism on the part of sophisticated pagans. Arnobius addressed that question, but not convincingly. To the charge that Christian writings should not be believed because they were crafted by unlearned and ignorant men, he retorted that people of simple minds do not resort to tricks or false ornaments in order to distort the truth: "For truth never seeks deceitful polish, nor in that which is well ascertained and certain does it allow itself to be led away into excessive prolixity."[30] He argued that truth cannot be made dependent on the correct structure of sentences. He did not, however, refute his opponents who qualified Christian narratives as being overrun with barbarisms and solecisms, and disfigured by blunders. One must seek the essence of the truth, in whichever way it is expressed: "For if we allow that it is reasonable, let us cease to use certain kinds of fruit because they grow with prickles on them. . . . Or how is the truth of a statement diminished, if an error is made in number or case, in preposition, participle, or conjunction?"[31]

The stylistic superiority of heathen writers did not ensure the correctness of what they proposed:

> Because you are skilled in declining verbs and nouns by cases and tenses, *and* in avoiding barbarous words and expressions; because you have learned either to express yourselves in harmonious, and orderly, and fitly disposed language, or to know when it is rude or unpolished . . . do you therefore think that you know what is false, what true, what can or cannot be done, what is the nature of the lowest and highest? Have the well-known words never rung in your ears, that the wisdom of man is foolishness with God?[32]

Arnobius wrote for the perplexed pagans of his day. His argumentation lacked theological depth. His approach was polemical. Like many of his contemporary Christian writers he excelled more at exposing the absurdity of pagan beliefs than at justifying the Christian position. His student and disciple Lactantius far surpassed him in rhetoric. But like Arnobius, Lactantius was no great theologian. He never totally overcame his pagan beginnings. In his assessment of him Jerome complained that Lactantius was a master at demolishing his opponents' argument but was

---

[30]Arnobius, AdvGent 1.58 (ANF VI) 429.
[31]Ibid., 1.59 (ANF VI) 430.
[32]Ibid., 2.6 (ANF VI) 435.

not very successful in expounding the Christian point of view: "Lactantius has a flow of eloquence worthy of Tully: Would that he had been as ready to teach our doctrines as he was to pull down those of others!"[33]

The writings of Lactantius revealed his mastery of oratory, which earned him the flattering designation of the Christian Cicero. Though still polemical in purpose, he surpassed many other Christian writers by being persuasive and by trying to bring faith into harmony with reason. His reputation was everywhere well established. Diocletian appointed him professor of rhetoric at Nicomedia. Constantine chose him as a tutor for his son Crispus. Lactantius lived and wrote in the context of revolutionary events that changed the face of the world. But, unlike Eusebius, he refrained from distorting historical events by forcing them into a Christian mold. He addressed himself to learned pagans, debating their points of view on their own grounds to the extent that he appealed to pagan writings often more than to Scriptures. The dominating voice in his *Divinae institutiones* was that of the Sibyl. He witnessed the rise and downfall of emperors and wrote about it with passion in his *De mortibus persecutorum*.

Lactantius praised Plato, Aristotle, and other Greek philosophers for their conception of God. But his admiration went to Roman writers, especially Cicero, Seneca, and most of all to Marcus Varro whom he considered the most learned man of all times.[34] His praise of those authors did not preclude his criticism of their writings and ideas. As to the Greek poets, he was less harsh in his criticism of Homer and Hesiod than Clement of Alexandria. But he gave them little credit in their effort to discover and pursue truth.[35]

Like his master Arnobius, Lactantius contended that truth does not depend on the stylistic way in which it is expressed. While accepting the value of logic and dialectics, he still maintained that: "Divine learning

---

[33] Jerome, Letter 58 (NPNF-2 VI) 122.

[34] Lactantius, DivInst 1.5-6.

[35] Ibid., 1.5 (ANF VII) 14: "Homer was able to give us no information relating to the truth, for he wrote of human rather than divine things. Hesiod was able, for he comprised in the work of one book the generations of the gods; but yet he gave us no information, for he took his commencement not from God the Creator, but from chaos."

does not stand in need of this, because the seat of wisdom is not the tongue but the heart; and it makes no difference what kind of language you employ, for the question is not about words, but facts. And we are not disputing about the grammarian or the orator, whose knowledge is concerned with the proper manner of speaking, but about the wise man, whose learning is concerned with the right manner of living."[36]

Lactantius bemoaned the fact that the literary merits of Christian Scriptures were in no way close to those of pagan literature. This created a hindrance in convincing pagans to espouse the Christian faith: "But a well-composed poem, and a speech beguiling with its sweetness, captivate the minds of men, and impel them in what direction they please. Hence, when learned men have applied themselves to the religion of God, unless they have been instructed by some skilled teacher, they do not believe. For, being accustomed to sweet and polished speeches or poems, they despise the simple and common language of the sacred writings as mean."[37]

Ever since the days of Augustus the unity of the *Pax Romana* remained the frustrated dream of all emperors. Caesar Augustus hoped that his work would remain for ever:

> May I be privileged to build firm and lasting foundations for the Government of the State. May I also achieve the reward to which I aspire: that of being known as the author of the best possible Constitution, and of carrying with me, when I die, the hope that these foundations which I have established for the State will abide secure.[38]

To political ambitions was added the dream of a common body of ideas uniting all the citizens. Education became a passport to acceptance within the community with all the rights and privileges it entailed. But with the advent of Christianity new barriers were erected against cultural integration, and by the time of Constantine there arose the need for a different basis for unity.

Tertullian had already advocated a disconnection from the pleasures of secular society, a call to indifference or perhaps even to contempt: "Let us mourn, then, while the heathen are merry, that in the day of their

---

[36]Ibid., 3.13 (ANF VII) 81.
[37]Ibid., 6.21 (ANF VII) 188.
[38]Suetonius, Caesars: Augustus 28.

sorrow we may rejoice; lest, sharing now in their gladness, we share then also in their grief."[39] With the advent of Constantine and the triumph of Christianity, it seemed axiomatic that the emperor was the servant of God in human history. Eusebius quoted the alleged speech of Constantine in which he praised himself as the new savior of the human race:

> Accordingly, beginning at the remote Britannic Ocean, and the regions where, according to the law of nature, the sun sinks beneath the horizon, through the aid of divine power I banished and utterly removed every form of evil which prevailed, in the hope that the human race, enlightened through my instrumentality, might be recalled to a due observance of the holy laws of God.[40]

From Eusebius we might be led to conclude that Constantine abandoned the gods of Rome to espouse Christianity. In that case the break with former traditions would have been complete. But Constantine was more acquainted with the form of his new religion than with its substance. For some time after his conversion, pagan and Christian elements mingled in ways which led to confusion rather than reassurance. Constantine's adherence to the Christian faith was far from being as spectacular as reported by Eusebius and sometimes by Lactantius. Ambiguities continued to plague a populace ignorant of the fundamentals of Christian tenets. The habits of classical life and thought could not be abrogated overnight. The new wine poured into old bottles did not cause a great deal of breakage, for in fact the wine was not as new as proclaimed. Classicism had already become a tacit way of life for many Christians, and a repudiation of it would not have served the cause of Christianity. Constantine was aware of the pitfalls involved, and he continued in many of the old ways in religion and philosophy. The new world could not totally free itself from old traditions. Confusion and ambiguities resulted in new syncretistic compromises which reshaped both the pagan traditions and the new Christian faith.

The Role of Classical Culture in Julian's Reform

Julian's approach to classical culture was determined by three elements: his profound dislike of Constantine, his firm conviction that

---

[39]Tertullian, DeSpect 28 (ANF III) 90.
[40]Eusebius, VConst 2.28 (NPNF-2 I) 507.

pagan writings were vastly superior to Christian scriptures, and his relentless effort to produce a philosophical picture of a learned person.

The extant portions of Julian's writings picture Constantine as a greedy, irreligious, and ignorant ruler who brought useless turmoil on the empire. Not only did he lack education himself, but he could not communicate any virtue to his sons who were doomed to disaster.[41] In a scenario where the Caesars had to present their own achievement, Julian placed Constantine at the bottom of the list.[42] Later, Hermes asked Constantine what the height of his ambitions was. To that Constantine replied: "To amass great wealth . . . and then to spend it liberally so as to gratify my own desires and the desires of my friends."[43] Constantine's search for lust and his irreverent conduct were blamed on his blind allegiance to Jesus.[44] The hatred Julian entertained for Constantine was also extended to his mother Helena who, even more than her son, was devoted to the Christian cause.[45]

Though there was not yet an officially recognized canon of New Testament scriptures during the reign of Julian, the church had ample biblical and nonbiblical documents serving as the foundation for its faith and practice. On that score it had a substantial edge over paganism. Julian found Christians obsessively committed to their scriptures and could not tolerate the competition. It appeared best to him to undertake a systematic demolition of Christian scriptures and even to make church members witnesses against themselves:

> Accordingly everyone who possessed even a small fraction of innate virtue has speedily abandoned your impiety. It were therefore better for you to keep men from learning rather than from sacrificial meats. But you yourselves know, it seems to me, the very different effect on the intelligence of your writings as compared with ours; and that from studying yours no man could attain to excellence or even to ordinary

---

[41]Julian, Heracl 228AB.

[42]Julian, Caes 328D.

[43]Ibid., 335B (LCL II) 411.

[44]Ibid., 336AB.

[45]Julian, Corinth. The text of this fragment is mutilated and incomplete. The extended meaning comes from Libanius who speaks of Helena as the "Wicked stepmother." See n. 5 to the text *To the Corinthians* in LCL III, 297. There are references to that effect in Zosimus.

goodness, whereas from studying ours every man would become better than before, even though he were altogether without natural fitness. But when a man is naturally well endowed, and moreover receives the education of our literature, he becomes actually a gift of the gods to mankind.[46]

Culture, for Julian, was an integral part of religion. Without participating in pagan rituals, no one could claim virtue or learning. After reviewing the benefits bestowed on the empire by the gods, Julian offered another challenge to Christians: "Consider therefore whether we are not superior to you in every single one of these things, I mean in the arts and in wisdom and intelligence."[47]

Julian left no doubt that those who cut themselves off from Hellenic religion could not be the beneficiaries of classical culture. By denying the existence of pagan gods Christians became outcasts in regard to classical learning. Gregory of Nazianzus objected to Julian's identification of Greek culture and learning with Greek religion. Such a stance was worthy of ridicule, as if Julian had become the sole authority of the way in which Greek words are used. No legislation could exclude people from speaking and writing a language, be it Greek or some other. The words of the Greek language were not Julian's property. Those who did not agree with Hellenistic religion were nonetheless entitled to speak Greek if they so desired without any one single person defining how that language must be spoken. If speaking Greek belongs to the religion, then Julian should show where it is the rule.[48] For Gregory of Nazianzus it was faith, and not the language in which it was expressed, that constituted the true foundation of reasoning.

But Julian was not alone in defending the revival of religion by appealing to the old culture. Militant pagans had done so all along. No religion survives in a vacuum. Christianity began to thrive only when it began to assimilate some of the cultural perspectives of the world in

---

[46]Julian, CGal 229DE (LCL III) 385-87.

[47]Ibid., 235C (LCL III) 387.

[48]Gregory of Nazianzus, *First Invective against Julian*, 103, in King, *Julian the Emperor*, 69. The first Invective here corresponds to Gregory's oration 4. On this subject see also Jaroslav Pelikan, *Christianity and Classical Culture: The Metamorphosis of Natural Theology in the Christian Encounter with Hellenism* (New Haven CT: Yale University Press, 1993) 23.

which it developed. It may have been the irony of the age that pagans and Christians opposed each other on the basis of the same cultural traditions.

The decision of Julian to forbid Christians to teach in public schools was motivated by philosophical as well as religious concern. In his *Rescript on Christian Teachers*[49] he made education dependent on sound moral judgment rather than rhetorical art. The primary qualification for teaching is a sound moral character. That, for Julian, precluded the teaching of what one does not believe. Christians who attributed false opinions to the segment of Hellenic culture considered divinely inspired should not teach it at all. Honesty and professional integrity dictate the limits within which teaching takes place. Julian's *Rescript* is reproduced in appendix 4.

Beyond his philosophical ruminations on the nature of education and the moral character of teachers, Julian took precise legislative steps to ensure his control over pagan culture and what he believed were its benefits for the empire. Though he avoided physical attacks on Christians, he issued decrees that would lead to complaints. On 17 June 362 he decreed that professors and schoolmasters must obtain a licence or stop teaching. Portions of the decree survived in the *Codex Theodosianus*:

> Schoolmasters and teachers should excel in morality in the first place, and next in eloquence. But since I cannot be present myself in each city, I order that whoever wishes to teach should not rush hastily or uncircumspectly into this profession, but should be approved by the judgment of the council and obtain a decree of the curials, by common agreement and consent of the best men. For this decree will be referred to me to deal with, so that they may take up their posts in the city schools with my approval as a kind of higher commendation.[50]

There was in fact no direct reference to Christian teachers. Julian carefully avoided such a specific focus. He knew, however, that they could not obtain such licences. When it became obvious that Christians continued to teach against the letter of the edict, Julian became more pointed in his attacks, especially when it concerned the teaching of the liberal arts and the influence of teachers on the young. Julian's position

---

[49]Julian, ChrTeach 422A-424A.
[50]CodTheod 13.3.5. Quoted in Browning, *The Emperor Julian*, 169.

angered not only Christians who felt excluded from the cultural life of their society, but also enlightened pagans who exposed the excess of the emperor. Among them Ammianus Marcellinus recorded his reaction:

> For after many other things, he also corrected some of the laws, removing ambiguities, so that they showed clearly what they demanded or forbade to be done. But this one thing was inhumane, and ought to be buried in eternal silence, namely, that he forbade teachers of rhetoric and literature to practice their profession, if they were followers of the Christian religion.[51]

Ammianus Marcellinus sensed only too well that, by making classical literature the cornerstone of the existing order, Julian was equating historical heritage with his limited view of Greco-Roman traditions. Such a distortion proved unacceptable. After Julian's death, Libanius, in his *Oration* 18 was much kinder to the memory of the emperor whom he praised for his high regard for learning. Libanius saw no deviousness in Julian's attempt to prove that learning and religion are intimately related and their destinies intertwined. Thus, Christians could not be bona fide cultured citizens.

By the time of Julian the church had already produced Christian intellectuals who appreciated and praised the link between their religion and the classical tradition. Julian was trying to destroy that link. By giving due recognition to classical learning, many Christians had gained prestige and influence in their communities and were highly esteemed by their pagan peers. Christians became masters of rhetoric and could present the apology of their religion quite convincingly. Julian sought to deprive them of the weapon of rhetoric. This was the part of Julian's intentions that Gregory of Nazianzus attacked the most vehemently. Rhetoric could be adapted to a Christian usage as well as to a pagan one. Julian considered rhetoric the best weapon to defeat Christianity. He was not ready to concede to rhetoric a more universal meaning which would also serve the cause of Christians.[52]

---

[51]Ammianus Marcellinus, ResGest 22.10.7 (LCL II) 257.

[52]For a more detailed study on the use of rhetoric in the early church see Averil Cameron, *Christianity and the Rhetoric of Empire: The Development of Christian Discourse* (Berkeley: University of California Press, 1991). For a more focused exposé on rhetoric among the Cappadocians, see Pelikan, *Christianity*

Rhetoric had become an integral part of *paideia*. It was no longer regarded as only a literary device to enhance one's ability to shine in public. Those who could use the gift of persuasive speech could transform that art into a form of self-control. Gregory of Nazianzus acknowledged that fact when he boasted that he could learn how to bridle his anger by utilizing the proper measured words. Julian was aware of how the power of rhetoric in the hands of Christians could undo his attempts at pagan reforms. On that score he was right. Rhetoric had been one of the most powerful weapons in the Christian arsenal:

> To have presented Christianity in this manner was a masterstroke of writers who were, themselves, highly educated men. Christian writers of the fourth and fifth centuries wielded with dazzling effect the rhetoric of paradox. . . . It was an open secret that many Christian bishops owed their prestige in society at large to the fact that they had once been rhetors.[53]

But rhetoric had to be redefined. Pagan philosophers were the masters of logic and rationality. In Christian debates it was faith and not argument which supported truth. Christian masters had learned that persuasion had to be supplemented by practices which kept the faithful constantly alert. Thus liturgy and preaching had to include the power of repetition, the most efficient element in the unity and self-affirmation of religion.

A more serious bone of contention arose after the death of Julian as to whether or not he forbade Christian children from attending pagan schools. There was a hint to that in Ambrose.[54] In Socrates we find a direct reference to that effect. Julian bemoaned the fact that martyrs from the time of Diocletian had attained great honor. Further persecutions

---

and Classical Culture, 15-19 and the way it is refuted.

[53]Peter Brown, *Power and Persuasion in Late Antiquity: Towards a Christian Empire* (Madison: University of Wisconsin Press, 1992) 74-75.

[54]Ambrose, Letter 17.4 (NPNF-2 X) 412. "And they are complaining of their losses, who never spared our blood, who destroyed the very buildings of the churches. And they petition you to grant them privileges, who by the last Julian law denied us the common right of speaking and teaching." Ambrose continued his argument that through such a law the Christians were deceived. One could assume that the law of Julian meant that Christian pupils could no longer in good faith attend schools where paganism was taught with the force of law.

would only enhance the Christian cause. Thus, Julian decided to flex the cultural muscle: "This then was the plan he pursued: he enacted a law by which Christians were excluded from the cultivation of literature; 'lest,' said he, 'when they have sharpened their tongue, they should be able the more readily to meet the arguments of the heathen.' "[55]

It is impossible to identify the specific law referred to by Socrates. Christians were not directly mentioned in the rescripts or decrees of Julian in regard to teaching and learning. Theodoret is even more precise regarding the alleged law of Julian:

> First of all he prohibited the sons of the Galileans . . . from taking part in the study of poetry, rhetoric, and philosophy, for, said he, in the words of the proverb "we are shot with shafts feathered from our own wings," for from our own books they take arms and wage war against us.[56]

Both Socrates and Theodoret produced their histories some eighty years after the death of Julian. They may have quoted from memory or they may have relied on sources no longer available to us. Or they may have given their own interpretation of the intentions of Julian. On that score they may have been right, though their arguments may not have been grounded in existing legislation. Certainly the rescript of Julian was directed at Christian teachers, and certainly he made it difficult for Christians to attend pagan schools. But it is unlikely that Julian would have resorted to legislation to exclude Christians from schools. Had that been the case, we would have heard from it in Gregory of Nazianzus's two invectives against Julian.

Christians were presented with difficult dilemmas, and many parents opted for not sending their children to pagan schools. But they knew that such action would deprive young people from moving up the ladder of liberal professions and of becoming influential in society. The times demanded a good education, and many christians saw no conflict in attending pagan schools. Some church fathers were trained at the feet of pagan masters. Christian intellectuals were aware of the fact that, to exercise power over people, you needed to be able to use the persuasion of words. Preaching relied not only on faith, but also on education. The

---

[55]Socrates, HE 3.12 (NPNF-2 II) 85.
[56]Theodoret, HE 3.4 (NPNF-2 III) 97.

importance of proper speech could not be overlooked in Christian attempts to convert influential Romans. To commend respect one had to be part of the prevalent *paideia*. Eloquence went a long way to ensure respect in Roman society.

It has often been conjectured that when Julian challenged Christian scholars to stick to the interpretation of Matthew and Luke, that he also encouraged them to produce their own literature. To each religion its own culture. Not much is known about Christians having met that challenge. Both Socrates and Sozomen refer to attempts made in that direction. The most extensive exposé is found in Socrates. He speaks of the two Apollinares, father and son, who undertook the composition of Christian literature destined to serve the same purpose as classical works. Here are in a summary form the comments of Socrates:

> The imperial law which forbade Christians to study Greek literature, rendered the two Apollinares . . . much more distinguished than before. For both being skilled in polite learning, the father as a grammarian, and the son as a rhetorician, they made themselves serviceable to the Christians at this crisis. For the former, as a grammarian, composed a grammar consistent with the Christian faith: he also translated the Books of Moses into heroic verse; and paraphrased all the historical books of the Old Testament, putting them partly into dactylic measure, and partly reducing them to the form of dramatic tragedy. . . . The younger Apollinaris, who was well trained in eloquence, expounded the gospels and apostolic doctrines in the way of dialogue, as Plato among the Greeks had done. Thus showing themselves useful to the Christian cause they overcame the subtlety of the emperor through their own labor.[57]

Socrates reflected on how the death of Julian liberated Christians from his edicts, but also rendered the work of the Apollinares of no account. After a long debate on the nature of Greek writings and on the reasons why they were never regarded as inspired by Christians, Socrates praised the coexistence of Greek and Christian culture:

> Should any one imagine that in making these assertions we wrest the Scriptures from their legitimate construction, let it be remembered that the Apostle not only does not forbid our being instructed in Greek

---

[57]Socrates, HE 3.16 (NPNF-2 II) 86-87.

learning, but that he himself seems by no means to have neglected it, inasmuch as he knows many of the sayings of the Greeks.[58]

Sozomen gives a similar account but mentions only one Apolinarius:

> Apolinarius, therefore, employed his great learning and ingenuity in the production of a heroic epic on the antiquities of the Hebrews to the reign of Saul, as a substitute for the poem of Homer. He divided his work into twenty-four parts, to each of which he appended the name of one of the letters of the Greek alphabet, according to their number and order. He also wrote comedies in imitation of Menander, tragedies resembling those of Euripides, and odes on the model of Pindar. In short, taking themes of the entire circle of knowledge from the Scriptures, he produced within a very brief space of time, a set of works which in manner, expression, character, and arrangement are well approved as similar to the Greek literatures and which were equal in number and in force. Were it not for the extreme partiality with which the productions of antiquity are regarded, I doubt not but that the writings of Apolinarius would be held in as much estimation as those of the ancients.[59]

None of the works of the Apollinares have survived, and one can only conjecture on their nature and number. From the accounts of Socrates we may infer that they were inferior in quality to Greek literature. In fact nothing would have changed much if they had never been written. Consequently, Socrates encouraged a return to Greek learning, a position Sozomen opposed. The reform of Julian was too short to tip the scales in favor of the new epic Christian literature. Church members preferred the Scriptures themselves.

Julian's anti-Christian writings lacked focus and persuasion. *Against the Galilaeans*, which was supposed to be his masterpiece of apologetic, petered out in long and diffuse arguments, a fact that may be partially

---

[58]Ibid., (NPNF-2 II) 88. Socrates' generous estimate of Greek learning may also be due to the fact that as a youth he received his education from two pagan grammarians, Helladius and Ammonius, who were Egyptian priests in Alexandria. This would explain the long reports by Socrates on the destruction of the Serapeum in Alexandria. Both of his teachers probably elaborated on those events.

[59]Sozomen, HE 5.18 (NPNF-2 II) 340.

due to the selections of Cyril.[60] His knowledge of Greek was beyond doubt. Sometimes he referred to a Platonic universality which contradicted the rest of his arguments. He spoke of the existence of a higher God that belonged to all peoples, thus sapping the argument of the superiority of the Greeks:

Now that the human race possesses its knowledge of God by nature and not from teaching is proved to us first of all by the universal yearning for the divine that is in all men whether private persons or communities, whether considered as individuals or as races. For all of us, without being taught, have attained to a belief in some sort of divinity, though it is not easy for all men to know the precise truth about it, nor is it possible for those who do know it to tell it to all men.[61]

The writings and decrees of Julian did not alter the landscape of culture and learning to any appreciable extent. But it was an important episode in the continuous search for a divine center. Julian remained a sort of a pagan saint. His lofty spirituality often transcended his narrow fanaticism. His ardent commitment to a pagan revival, though doomed, was marked by intelligence and idealism. The quest for coexistence in a cultural environment that was becoming common to both Christians and pagans had entered a new phase, but not the last one.[62] The reign of

---

[60]For the fate of the text of Julian's CGal, see n. 121 in chap. 8 of this work.

[61]Julian, CGal 52B (LCL III) 321. The last statement quoted is obviously a reference to Plato in Tim 28C: "To discover the Father and Maker of this universe is a task almost beyond our human means. And having discovered Him, to declare Him unto all men remains beyond our power" (author's translation).

[62]One could mention here the negative reaction of Nietzsche against attempts to substitute Christian writings to Greek literature in the early Church:

In the very heart of Graeco-Roman splendor, which was also a splendor of books, in the heart of a literature not yet atrophied and dispersed, when it was still possible to read a few books for which we would now trade half of all that is printed, the simpleminded presumption of the Christian agitators known as the Fathers of the Church dared to decree: "We have our own classical literature. We don't need that of the Greeks." And they pointed proudly to certain collections of legends, apostolic epistles, and apologetic penny tracts—the same kind of literature with which the English Salvation Army wages its war against Shakespeare and other pagans.

Julian revealed a most perplexing phenomenon. The advent of Constantine altered the religious scene, but not the cultural one. Pagans and Christians were fated to share the same cultural traditions and partake of the same process of learning.

After Julian—Towards a Universalization of Culture

The inconclusive attempts of Julian to restore paganism reopened the debate on the distinction between secular and Christian culture. The intrinsic nature of what constituted knowledge and learning did not allow such a dichotomy. Definitions and redefinitions to serve special needs did not end in any acceptable solution. Christianity could not exist outside of the secular, nor could it disconnect itself from external influences that had shaped the stage on which it was to evolve into a world religion. It was in fact the universality of Greek thought that fostered the idea of world religion, either on the pagan or Christian side. Church fathers faced the challenge of deciding what of classical culture should be integrated into the Christian movement and what had to be rejected as detrimental to the faith. The conflict was to become perennial. The lines separating secular from religious were no longer clearly visible. The Theodosian code remained inconclusive. Legislation never solved religious disputes.

Julian presented a biased model of late paganism. Sacrificial excesses, political events, polemical diatribes did not enhance the long-standing quests of paganism. On the contrary. With Julian we witness the collapse of the internal cultic essence of paganism through an exaggerated commitment to superstition and through a narrowly focused attempt to explain every religious element through the eyes of philosophy. Julian's appeal to Platonic and Neoplatonic tenets brought him personal satisfaction but did not generate a lasting influence. Confusion rather than clarity of purpose dominated the thought of intellectuals for generations after Julian, and that on the side of pagans as well as Christians. Paganism did not die in spite of the legislation of Christian emperors, and Christianity lost a great deal of its original enthusiasm in spite of imperial support. Some writers, such as Ammianus Marcellinus, took the middle road while attempting to span bridges between the *cultus deorum* that had been the

---

The Genealogy of Morals, 281. In *The Birth of Tragedy* and *The Genealogy of Morals* (Garden City NY: Doubleday, 1956).

lifeline of paganism and the relentless antipagan legislation of the Theodosian code.[63] Pagan senators continued to rule in Rome, and the cultural basis of the empire did not change as radically as often contended.

The now defunct works of the Apollinares notwithstanding, Christianity could not boast of a classical tradition comparable to that of the Greeks. Due to its ascetic view of life, Christianity often appeared as primitive if not barbaric. The relics of some martyrs in its basilicas could not match the splendor of a Serapeum. On balance, it was Ammianus Marcellinus's contention that "Julian's gifts to Rome were piety and philosophy; those of Theodosius, Christianity and barbarism."[64]

A strong feeling of uneasiness permeated much of the outlook of the Cappadocians, especially Basil, on the relationship between Christian faith and classical learning. The fear subsisted that, in the very spirit of triumph, Christian thought was in danger of impoverishing itself through the neglect of a culture which gave it its impetus. The cultural life of Caesarea, for example, deteriorated so much through its Christianization that Basil exposed the tragic results of it.

> Now we have no more meetings, no more debates, no more gatherings of wise men in the Forum, nothing more of all that made our city famous. In our Forum nowadays it would be stranger for a learned or eloquent man to put in an appearance, than it would for men, shewing a brand of iniquity or unclean hands, to have presented themselves in Athens of old.[65]

Caesarea had indeed become more Christian and more religious, but it was at the cost of its intellectual soul. There was no other way but to raise the question: was the loss of culture an unavoidable consequence of Christianization? For Basil the answer was clear, and he produced his well-known defense of classical education.

It took the early church a long time to come to grips with its mission in a world in which it felt so alien. Despite its fervent claim to divine revelation and to absolute truth of its message, Christianity was altering

---

[63]For a detailed study of Ammianus Marcellinus' view of the status of Christianity, see R. L. Rike, *Apex Omnium: Religion in the Res gestae of Ammianus* (Berkeley: University of California Press, 1987).

[64]Rike, *Apex Omnium*, 129.

[65]Basil, Letter 74.3 (NPNF-2 VIII) 169.

its modus operandi to integrate itself more and more into public opinion. Its credibility as an institution came as early as the second century when it acquired the fundamental rudiments of ecclesiastical organization. To that was added an intellectual and philosophical basis mostly under the leadership of prominent church fathers in the third and fourth centuries. In the post-Constantine era it had to redefine itself both as a religious force and as a world power. Christianity could no longer boast that its strength came from the lowly classes. Jerome and Gennadius undertook to present long lists of illustrious Christians whose work and wisdom had been overlooked though they had been superior in intelligence to acclaimed philosophers of paganism:

> Let Celsus, Porphyry, and Julian learn, rabid as they are against Christ, let their followers, they who think the church has had no philosophers or orators or men of learning, learn how many and what sort of men founded, built and adorned it, and cease to accuse our faith of such rustic simplicity, and recognize rather their own ignorance.[66]

There was, however, little consistency in Jerome's approach to classical culture. He did not formulate a strong argument either in favor of secular learning or of its rejection.[67] But at the same time he pointed out that the illustrious men of the faith did not come from the Academy of Plato or from the Lyceum of Aristotle, but from what was usually considered as the worthless populace of the empire. He found support for that position in the New Testament and agreed with Paul's contention that Christian faith could not be indebted to secular wisdom. We find such arguments in book III of Jerome's *Commentary on Galatians*.

It takes a great deal of sophistication in learning to see the fallacies of that very learning. Many late church fathers denounced the secular nature of classical culture, but only after they themselves had been its beneficiaries. Once it had become part of their educational training, it no longer was credible that they could totally renounce it. Again we find in Jerome an enlightening episode. When a Roman friend, Domnio, informed him that an ignorant monk had chosen to misinterpret his works

---

[66]Jerome and Gennadius, Preface to Lives (NPNF-2 III) 359.

[67]Jerome, Letter 21 and the comment of Marrou. *Saint Augustin*, 397: "St. Jérome par exemple estimera encore que la culture profane avec tout ce qu'elle implique d'inquiétant est, au moins dans le cas général, un mal inévitable."

written against Jovinian, Jerome became enraged and bitterly complained about it. At issue was not the kind of criticism the monk was offering, but the fact that he was illiterate in terms of general culture:

> You [Domnio] inform me, moreover, that this home-grown dialectician . . . has read neither the "Categories" of Aristotle nor his treatise "On Interpretation," nor his "Analytics," nor yet the "Topics" of Cicero, but that, moving as he does in uneducated circles . . . he ventures to construct illogical syllogisms and to unravel by subtle arguments what he is pleased to call my sophisms.[68]

Jerome then raised the rhetorical question as to whether his learning at the feet of great masters or through the works of great philosophers might have been in vain. Perhaps he gained nothing by having Gregory of Nazianzus as his teacher, or for having studied Hebrew, the Law, the Prophets, the Gospels and the Apostles. The point was finally reached when proper credentials in both Christian and secular learning were necessary to become part of the intellectual elite. Classical culture and Christian learning fused together to form the perfect Christian scholar, the accomplished person worthy of trust.

In a letter to Eustochium, Jerome undertook to analyze and criticize the hypocrisy, profligacy, and luxury of Roman society and to appeal to Christians to abandon traditional culture from which so many of the sins have sprung; "For 'what communion hath light with darkness? And what concord hath Christ with Belial?' How can Horace go with the psalter, Virgil with the gospels, Cicero with the apostle?"[69] Then Jerome invited his readers on a journey through his own experience with Classical learning and the struggle he had undergone to place it in the right perspective. Secular learning was such a part of his essence and being that he could not find a logical way to disconnect himself from it. The reading of classical authors was compelling, and their style was superior to biblical writings:

> Many years ago, when for the kingdom of heaven's sake I had cut myself off from home, parents, sister, relations, and—harder still—from the dainty food to which I had been accustomed; and when I was on my way to Jerusalem to wage my warfare, I still could not bring myself to

---

[68]Jerome, Letter 50.1 (NPNF-2 VI) 80.
[69]Jerome, Letter 22.29 (NPNF-2 VI) 35.

forgo the library which I had formed for myself at Rome with great care and toil. And so, miserable man that I was, I would fast only that I might afterwards read Cicero. After many nights spent in vigil, after floods of tears called from my inmost heart, after the recollection of my past sins, I would once more take up Plautus. And when at times I returned to my right mind, and began to read the prophets, their style seemed rude and repellent.[70]

This account became known in Rome and among Christian intellectuals who saw their own dilemmas in Jerome's experience. No learned person could clearly identify the realm of thought which was typically Christian and that which was typically pagan. Like Jerome, they could not totally renounce the charm and influence of their training in their young years. Was Jerome really reproaching himself for what he had studied, or was he concerned and worried that Christianity was becoming much too closely fashioned on pagan culture? It had happened before that Jerome criticized bishops and priests who relied on rhetoric for their sermons and who tried to imitate the learning of the Academy or the Lyceum. But he had to admit that he himself was incorrigible when it came to the charm of classical works of literature. His heart was never at peace with his mind, and very often the yearning of the heart was overpowered by the thirst of the mind.

In a stirring confession, unique in patristic writings, Jerome details a dream of what happened when he arrived in heaven after his death:

> Suddenly I was caught up in the spirit and dragged before the judgment seat of the judge. . . . Asked who and what I was I replied: "I am a Christian." But He who presided said; "Thou liest, thou art a follower of Cicero and not of Christ [*Mentiris, Ciceronianus es, non Christianus*]. For where thy treasure is, there will thy heart be also." Instantly I became dumb, and amid the strokes of the lash—for He had ordered me to be scourged—I was tortured more severely still by the fire of conscience. . . . Yet for all that I began to cry and to bewail myself, saying: "Have mercy upon me, O Lord: have mercy upon me." Amid the sound of scourges this cry still made itself heard. At last the bystanders, falling down before the knees of Him who presided, prayed that He would have pity on my youth, and that He would give me space to repent from my error. He might still, they urged, inflict torture on me, should I ever

---

[70]Jerome Letter 22.30 (NPNF-2 VI) 35.

again read the works of the Gentiles. Under the stress of that awful moment I should have been ready to make even still larger promises than these. Accordingly I made oath and called upon His name, saying: "Lord, if ever again I possess worldly books, or if ever again I read such, I have denied Thee."[71]

What followed was a request from Jerome that he be allowed to go back to the world of the living to discourage them from falling into the same errors. The struggle continued. The issue remained the extent to which Classical learning could be made a part of Christian intellectualism and to what extent it was detrimental to the faith. To those questions there were many possible answers, and none were satisfactory. The world was becoming the arena of global culture, and for generations to come the definitions of secular and Christian, temporal and spiritual were to be blurred beyond recognition. What, then, was the source of the conflict and why was it so intractable?

In spite of the shortcomings and fallacies of his works, credit should be given to Eusebius for having been able to make the new religion he was so ardently defending intelligible to a large segment of the public. To that end he knew how to avail himself of the categories of Greek thought in order to describe with logic and lucidity the matters of the Christian faith. His long quotations of Greek works, some of which would not be know to us outside of his works, testify to his closeness with that form of thinking, even when involved in serious refutations of the passages cited. It becomes clear in a work such as the *Praeparatio evangelica* that Eusebius had a very definite purpose in mind, namely to prove that all historical events of the old world were part of a process leading to the coming of Christ. Greek philosophy, Jewish religion, and Roman political events formed the basis on which Christianity could logically develop.

The success of the Christian movement meant radical changes in global culture. The long and often confusing Theodosian legislation shattered the foundation of a true *Romanitas*. Some, like Gibbon, suggested that the genius of Rome came to an end with Theodosius. Others believed that the final stages of decadence of the Roman world have been ushered in by Augustine.

---

[71]Ibid., 35-36.

The voluminous writings of Augustine almost forbid a coherent approach to classical culture, part of which he rejected, and part of which he felt compelled to praise. Classical traditions relating to the gods had to be denounced not only on the basis of their absurdity, but also because it was a direct command of the Christian God:

> For this reason He [God] hath both foretold and commanded the casting down of the images of the many false gods which are in the world. For nothing so effectually renders men depraved in practice, and unfit to be good members of society, as the imitation of such deities as are described and extolled in pagan writings.
>
> In fact, those most learned men . . . were accustomed to set forth as models for the education of youth the examples of men whom they esteemed eminent and praiseworthy, rather than the example given by their gods.[72]

Augustine could not escape a deeply entrenched fundamentalist current that had been ingrained in Christian thought through the preaching and writing of countless church members and apologists. It regarded pagan religion and culture as basically sinful, in spite of the fact that classical culture dominated the scene and was sometimes promoted by Christians themselves. As a bishop and religious critic Augustine condemned the very literature he had taught to his students while their professor. Yet even later in his life, as he was reflecting back on his journey that led him to God, he had to confess that without the writings of Cicero it would have been difficult for him to espouse the Christian faith:

> In the ordinary course of study, I lighted upon a certain book of Cicero, whose language, though not his heart, almost all admire. This book of his contains an exhortation to philosophy, and is called *Hortensius*. This book, in truth, changed my affections, and turned my prayers to Thyself, O Lord, and made me have other hopes and desires. Worthless suddenly became every vain hope to me; and, with an incredible warmth of heart, I yearned for an immortality of wisdom, and began to arise that I might return to Thee. . . .
>
> In Greek the love of wisdom is called "philosophy," with which that book inflamed me.[73]

---

[72]Augustine, Letter 91.3-4 (NPNF-1 I) 377.
[73]Augustine, Conf 3.4.7-8 (NPNF-1 I) 61-62.

Though Augustine was aware of the biblical admonition against philosophy, it was much too hard for him to deny the influence of so powerful a force in his life. Later, in the same reflections, he came back to an analysis of the impact of Cicero's *Hortensius* on his life. While reading it again, he concluded: "I was roused to a desire for wisdom; and still I was delaying to reject mere worldly happiness. . . . But I, miserable young man, supremely miserable even in the very outset of my youth, had entreated chastity of Thee, and said, 'Grant me chastity and continency, but not yet.' "[74]

The denunciation of classical culture had to be balanced by the creation of a credible Christian program of higher education. Attempts in that direction were already present in the reactions of Ambrose, Jerome, Gregory of Nazianzus, Basil, and others. Now it was Augustine's turn to assess the situation. He could not dismiss the accomplishments of Roman culture. He was a product of it. He had benefited from a system of education that set him apart from the run of his contemporaries. He had many friends who enjoyed successful careers as rhetors, as teachers, as poets. Education determined social mobility, and in a very dramatic way, favored some over against others. There was a tacit, and sometimes visible, link between those who were fortunate enough to be part of the educated world, pagans as well as Christians. Renowned teachers ensured some homogeneity in the way culture was transmitted and sometimes engraved in the memory of students. Yet Augustine undertook to prove that all of this was inadequate, insufficient, and sometimes deleterious. Since the coming of Christ there was a new universal perspective on life, the perspective of redemption. Within such a context there was a new way of knowing that did not depend on any system of Education. Augustine could claim, without giving any explanation of the phenomenon, that now any old woman who had become a Christian knew more about the nature of the invisible world than did Porphyry in all of his learned philosophical sophistication: "We should sympathize with this great philosopher [Porphyry] in the difficulty he experienced in acquainting himself with and confidently assailing the whole fraternity of devils, which any Christian old woman would unhesitatingly describe and most

---

[74]Ibid., 8.7.17 (NPNF-1 I) 123-24.

unreservedly detest."[75] The catholic church owed its universality to its simplicity. Ammianus Marcellinus had already defined Christianity by two derogatory terms as a *religio absoluta et simplex*. (*Christianam religionem absolutam et simplicem anili superstitione confundens*.)[76]

The role of Augustine in the development of Christianity has been assessed from different points of view. Next to Saint Paul who deserves the title of first theologian of the church, Augustine has often been considered as the one who shaped Christian thought into a formal system. He thus provided the link with the Middle Ages. He was remembered as the "dark genius of imperial Christianity." He witnessed a great deal of the collapse of the empire. He must have felt that the battle between paganism and Christianity tended to become secondary at a time when the illustrious culture of Rome was threatened to be engulfed in waves of barbarism inflicted by invading hordes. The times called for historical recreation, and that recreation could not occur in the absence of a well defined piety. The war on pagan religion and culture was becoming a war threatening everybody, whether Christian or heathen. At that crucial junction in history, Augustine was regarded as the one who brought Christianity to its intellectual peak, but also as the one who ushered in its decline.

Some scholars have not been very generous with Augustine. Henri-Irénée Marrou considers him as the one responsible for starting the journey toward the decadence of the Middle Ages. Augustine did not possess what was required for the preservation and survival of culture. He exhibited his lack of knowledge of the Greek language, his total disregard for scientific inquiry, his questionable speculations, and his distorted notion of authority.[77] His knowledge of philosophy was not impressive, and he did not even seem to know the major works of Cicero, whom he often admired. There is, concludes Marrou, something which irretrievably

---

[75] Augustine, CivDei 10.11 (NPNF-1 II) 187.

[76] Ammianus Marcellinus, ResGest 21.16.18 (LCL II) 183. "The plain and simple religion of the Christians he [Constantius] obscured by a dotard's superstition."

[77] Marrou, *Saint Augustin*, 542: "Jusqu'en ses lacunes et ses déformations, l'esprit de Saint Augustin nous a paru annoncer l'intellectual médiéval: oubli du grec, effacement des mathématiques et de l'esprit scientifique, goût de la spéculation aventureuse et les *mirabilia*, confiance excessive dans les constructions de l'esprit et l'autorité de la tradition écrite."

dies with Augustine. In a word he is the perfect "lettré de la décadence."[78]

For Augustine the times created the person. Yet he was not the best critic of Roman culture and religion. Some remarkable documents in that field came from Symmachus, others from Libanius. They created the need and the challenge for Christians to define what they meant by culture. But too many church fathers invested their time debating what culture was not and why pagans were wrong in pursuing the study of their literature and traditions. Augustine could not break that mold. He kept trying to convince Christians that their intellectual life could thrive only in a relentless opposition to the traditional culture of the Roman world. Thus the question of Christian culture remained vague and never emerged into anything coherent.

The spiritual struggle dominating the life of Christian intellectuals was larger than what their faith could resolve. They had to oppose in principle a pagan culture which had shaped their moral, spiritual, and intellectual outlooks and from which they could not free themselves. In fact, up to the time of Constantine the question of a different culture for Christians as opposed to pagans did not even arise. The Roman ethos was not to be rejected in spite of the evils inflicted on the church. Many hoped that the church would eventually become the leading political force. Until then they accepted the world as it was. At best their faith required detachment from pagan ways, not an intellectual revolution. In a post-Constantine era the criticism of paganism became more vocal and sometimes verbally violent. Yet the leading minds of Christianity of the time: Gregory of Nazianzus, Basil, John Chrysostom, Ambrose, Jerome, and others never pushed their criticism to the point of final separation. They remained authentic participants in a culture that had given form and content to the world in which they evolved. At many points they were thankful for it, even when they felt guilty of not being totally true to their faith.

No account of the shifts in social and cultural perspectives in the late Roman empire could be complete without mentioning the enormous increase in authority and prestige granted to the clergy by Constantine and subsequent Christian emperors. Religious leaders had to perform the

---

[78]Marrou, *Saint Augustin*, 663.

increasingly demanding and difficult functions of a rapidly growing Christian society. Bishops became more than religious overseers of their flock. They assumed many roles which until then were purely secular, mostly in the fields of political life, diplomatic responsibilities, economic affairs, and even jurisprudence. Constantine had already allowed the existence of ecclesiastical courts as a substitute for civil courts.[79] The education of the clergy was no longer regarded as a mere divine gift, but also as a necessity. No one knew any more whether the pagan world was being Christianized or the Christian world paganized. By the fourth century it became apparent that the church was remodelling itself on the pattern of Roman society. Its ranks included urban notables who barely remembered the lowly origins of Christianity. Church organization reflected the hierarchy of Roman society, and it became important to be able to move up the ladder of status and authority.

After Constantine the church had become wealthy, at least in some parts of the empire. It owned more and more sumptuous buildings. The rhetoric also changed. Once in a position of dominion, the church was no longer fervently involved in the attempt to convert pagans. It turned its attention to itself, to its doctrines which brought sorrow and divisions. It also generated its own conflicts in areas of organization and authority. The small communities of the faithful which weathered the persecutions had become institutions concerned with their self-centered economic and social status. And yet the Christian masses remained uneducated, rendering the authority of bishops and leaders more authoritarian and perhaps even tyrannical. But the injunctions of the Gospel remained true, and the kingdom of God was assailed not by wisdom, but by faith, even violence.[80] As late as Augustine we hear strange complaints about this state of affairs:

---

[79]Jones, *Later Roman Empire* I:90-91. For a more complete treatment of how church law progressively became universal law in the empire see especially Jean Gaudemet, *L'Eglise dans l'Empire romain: IVe–Ve siècles* (Paris: Sirey, 1958). According to him it was to be expected that Christian emperors would come to regard themselves the supreme authority in both ecclesiastical and secular matters to the point that the difference between the two often vanished.

[80]Matthew 11:12.

In the midst, then, of this great strife of my inner dwelling . . . troubled both in mind and countenance, I seized upon Alypius, and exclaimed: "What is wrong with us? . . . The unlearned start up and 'take' heaven, and we, with our learning, but wanting heart, see where we wallow in flesh and blood!"[81]

The role of bishops and the nature of church leadership required further definition. In the post-Constantine era no one could reach any consensus on anything. In matters of belief and conduct church leaders were torn between the need to remain true to Gospel requirements and injunctions and the new temptations to seek authority and power in a world they sought to dominate. Sectarian quarrels, rivalries, intrigues, and misguided notions of authority led some of the most prominent bishops to resort to reprehensible behavior. Such was the case with Damasus, a renowned bishop of Rome for almost twenty years at the end of the fourth century (366–384). During the election process he was challenged by a rival, Ursinus, who had the support of other bishops. The reaction of the Damasus group was swift and bloody. According to Ammianus Marcellinus 137 citizens lost their lives in a single day.[82] The victory of Damasus was a harbinger of many things to come in the increasing struggle for dominion. In the new Christian world, the question of credentials often replaced the claim of divine vocation.

What, then, were the qualifications for priestly office, and who among secular or Christian critics could establish the norms? To what should anybody owe a priestly office? Gregory of Nazianzus offered the challenge:

If certain men could look upon us naked and consider our suitability for priestly office among themselves, what would one of us have that was superior to what the other has? Birth? Education? Freedom of intercourse with the great and the illustrious? Theological knowledge? All of these qualities are found among us in a more or less equal measure.[83]

Once it had acquired imperial status, Christianity was adapting to meet public opinion in a way quite different from the days of rejection

---

[81]Augustine, Conf 8.8.19 (NPNF-1 I) 124.
[82]Ammianus Marcellinus, ResGest 27.3.12-13. Socrates, HE 4.29.
[83]Gregory of Nazianzus, Epistle 249.32. Quoted in Bregman, *Synesius*, 62-63.

and persecution. It became its responsibility to demonstrate its superiority to paganism. It progressively did it by providing an intellectual, spiritual, and philosophical basis generally absent from paganism which relied mostly on external shows and rituals. That was both the greatness and weakness of paganism. Its loose organization did not evolve into conflicts of authority and rivalry. But it also failed to secure for itself an intellectual foundation that could withstand the growth of Christianity. There were few defenders of Greek and Roman religion of the caliber of Plutarch. Christianity produced its own philosophers who were often trained at secular schools by pagan masters, and who sometimes moved into the office of bishop.

The educational and philosophical background of bishops was often made evident. When Jerome compiled his *Lives of Illustrious Men*, he often referred to the education of bishops and their literary accomplishments. For example, he dismissed all the achievements of Damasus in Rome to retain only one fact, namely that he was talented for making verses and that he published many works in heroic metre.[84] Both Socrates and Sozomen give instances of philosophers become bishops. A certain Sisinnius who, after many contentions, became bishop of Constantinople, had been the student of Maximus of Ephesus at the same time as Julian.[85] Such a background which he shared with the most reputable pagans was not openly questioned. As to his behavior as bishop, he was praised for his eloquence, learning, and skills, but also rebuked for indulging in actions not becoming a servant of the church. He ate sumptuously, bathed twice a day in public baths, and insisted on wearing white garments instead of black. But in any argument with his opponents, he was the winner.[86]

Even more astounding was the story of Theotimus who supervised the church of Tomi and all surrounding churches in Scythia. He was brought up in the practice of philosophy, and as an act of reverence to his learning he kept the long hair which he wore when he first devoted himself to philosophy. The barbarian Huns showed a great deal of

---

[84]Jerome and Gennadius, Lives 103.
[85]Socrates, HE 5.21.
[86]Ibid., 6.22.

admiration for him, and in honor of the many divine deeds he performed, they called him the god of the Romans.[87]

The most prominent example of the philosopher bishop was the student of Hypatia, Synesius of Cyrene. Before becoming the bishop of Ptolemaïs he was a fervent Neoplatonist, which he remained even as a Christian to the end of his life. He was, to say the least, an unconventional bishop, always ready to apply his erudition to criticize many church actions and dogmas. The murder of his teacher Hypatia by a Christian mob just a few months after his death would certainly have enraged him. His Christian loyalties were never disconnected from his pagan upbringing. It has been suggested that he was a baptized Neoplatonist rather than a fervently devoted Christian.[88]

It was no longer clear whether political and social circumstances or spiritual matters determined the role and functions of bishops. At points the distinction faded away. Most bishops enjoyed their status which included reverence by the powerful, who sometimes feared excommunication. The voice of the bishop could affect the affairs of the empire, if one remembers Ambrose and his power over Theodosius. In the episode of the burning of a synagogue on the orders of a bishop (see chapter 8), Ambrose told the emperor: "Let us suppose that that Bishop was too eager in the matter of burning the synagogue, and too timid at the judgment seat, are you not afraid, O Emperor, lest he comply with your sentence, lest he fail in his faith?"[89] We certainly have here an ominous rationalization of violence which surpassed the reasons for persecutions in the pre-Constantine empire. Libanius bitterly complained of this kind of abuse when the beautiful temples of the empire were destroyed on the orders of monks and priests who deserved only contempt for their behavior.[90]

But there were also kinder pagan assessments of church leadership. Speaking of pagans who were seeking wealth and status in the city life, Ammianus Marcellinus suggested that they might be happier if they followed the examples of bishops:

---

[87]Sozomen, HE 7.26.
[88]For a more detailed study of Synesius, see the eloquent and insightful study of Bregman, *Synesius*.
[89]Ambrose, Letter 40.6 (NPNF-2 X) 441.
[90]Libanius, ProTemp 8.

These men might be truly happy, if they would disregard the greatness
of the city behind which they hide their faults, and live after the manner
of some provincial bishops, whose moderation in food and drink, plain
apparel also, and gaze fixed upon the earth, commend them to the
Eternal Deity and to his true servants as pure and reverent men.[91]

To that we should add that church relief programs for the poor were often
the result of bishops' initiative. Sometimes, as in the case Basil, they
served at the tables of the poor and even tended to the needs of the
lepers.

Critics of Christianity, however, pointed out that a great deal of the
power and authority the church had acquired was not legitimate and
bordered on usurpation, sometimes on the weakness of emperors who
feared retribution by bishops. The question of status became an increasingly complex social and cultural obsession. Church members got into the
habit of wanting to be baptized only by notable leaders. Gregory of
Nazianzus condemned such a position. Certainly some priests were not
worthy of their office, but that did not take away their right to perform
church rituals. Gregory's advice was simple, though probably not
convincing:

> Do not say, "A bishop shall baptize me,—and he a Metropolitan,—and
> he of Jerusalem . . . ,—and he of noble birth, for it would be a sad
> thing for my nobility to be insulted by being baptized by a man of no
> family." Do not say, "I do not mind a mere priest, if he is a celibate,
> and a religious, and of angelic life; for it would be a sad thing for me
> to be defiled even in the moment of my cleansing." Do not ask for
> credentials of the preacher or the baptizer.[92]

Friendship with authorities in power was coveted by many church
notables. When a new governor was sent to Neocaesarea, Basil promptly
sent him a letter to reassure him that he would consider him as a close
friend, though they had not met before:

> And so, if, though I had never had the pleasure of meeting your
> excellency in person, I speak of myself as a familiar friend, pray do not
> set this down to mere empty compliment. . . . Accept then, most

---

[91]Ammianus Marcellinus, ResGest 27.3.15 (LCL III) 21.
[92]Gregory of Nazianzus, OratBapt 26 (NPNF-2 VII) 369.

excellent Sir, the greeting which I send you, for it is inspired by true and unfeigned friendship. I abhor all servile compliment. Pray keep me enrolled in the list of your friends.[93]

The subtle and sometimes blatant shift toward worldliness on the part of the clergy elicited strong rebukes from those who felt compelled to vindicate and uphold the life of the gospel. Many priests and bishops succumbed to allurements of secular society, sometimes even copying the conduct of pagans. Jerome spoke indignantly of priests who abused their power and felt quite at home among depraved women whose houses were filled with flatterers and not so reputable guests. Then Jerome voiced his harsh criticism:

> The very clergy, who ought to inspire them with respect by their teaching and authority, kiss these ladies on the forehead, and putting forth their hands . . . take wages for their visits. They, meanwhile, seeing that priests cannot do without them, are lifted up into pride. . . . After an immoderate supper they retire to rest to dream of the apostles.[94]

The search for vain outward appearance at the cost of spiritual discipline vitiated a great deal of the function of the clergy. The need to compete with pagan social ostentatiousness deprived some of the clergy of its specific role in a world in need of renewal and stability. It proved more and more difficult to remain true to the philosophy of life the persecuted church had adopted. Abuse and lack of judgment were everywhere in evidence:

> There are others—I speak of those of my own order—who seek the presbyterate and the diaconate simply that they may be able to see women with less restraint. Such men think of nothing but their dress; they use perfume freely, and see that there are no creases in their leather shoes. Their curling hair shows traces of the tongs; their fingers glisten with rings; they walked on tiptoe across a damp road, not to splash their feet. When you see men acting in this way, think of them rather as bridegrooms than as clergymen.[95]

---

[93]Basil, Letter 63 (NPNF-2 VIII) 162.
[94]Jerome, Letter 22.16 (NPNF-2 VI) 28. The reference to the immoderate supper (Cena dubia) is an allusion to Terence "Phormio," 342.
[95]Ibid., 22.28 (NPNF-2 VI) 34.

Spiritual dominion also meant temporal benefits, and many church leaders made sure that it came their way. Ambrose arose against such practices with indignation: "It is the glory of a bishop to make provision for the wants of the poor; but it is the shame of all priests to amass private fortunes."[96]

Perhaps the most eloquent plea against an emulation of the lifestyle of wealthy noblemen of the late empire and against any compromise with the allurements of Mammon came with the resignation of Gregory of Nazianzus from his bishopric at Constantinople. He was the teacher of Jerome, and both shared many of the same views on the subject. He went too far, according to the ruling clergy, and his appeal to austerities of old fell on deaf ears. His farewell address, delivered in 381 during the ecumenical council held at Constantinople, remains one of the most eloquent and passionate pieces of patristic literature. Through this act of personal sacrifice he hoped to restore peace and unity to a divided church. The emotion of the moment, however, was soon lost, and the church continued its downward slide into worldliness.

Much of the address of Gregory centered on the dissensions within the church and the frustration he experienced in his attempt to be the best pilot possible through those troubled times. The hostility that had marked every aspect of church life had also devastated most of the leadership of the community at large. The church had become the arena of contradictions and sectarianism with little or no toleration for differing points of views. Heresy was rampant, and no one knew who would next be called a heretic and be persecuted for it. Resources were diverted towards horse races and theatres at the expense of spiritual needs. What seemed to be a proof of greatness soon became a sign of weakness. The values of old had vanished with the triumph of ease and material success. The church had finally copied the pagan mode of affluent life and, in the process, lost its raison d'être. Too many had abdicated true investigation of spiritual matters and had been dazzled by the brilliance and the glamor of city life, far beyond what becomes a Christian. Gregory rose up to the challenge and fell amid the throes of church worldliness:

> Perhaps we may be reproached, as we have been before, with the exquisite character of our table, the splendour of our apparel, the officers

---

[96]Jerome, Letter 52.6 (NPNF-2 VI) 92.

who precede us, our haughtiness to those who meet us. I was not aware that we ought to rival the consuls, the governors, the most illustrious generals, who have no opportunities of lavishing their incomes; or that our belly ought to hunger for the enjoyment of the goods of the poor, and to expend their necessaries on superfluities, and belch forth over the altars. I did not know that we ought to ride on splendid horses, and drive in magnificent carriages, and be preceded by a procession and surrounded by applause, and have every one make way for us, as if we were wild beasts, and open out a passage so that our approach might be seen afar. If these sufferings have been endured, they have now passed away: Forgive me this wrong. Elect another who will please the majority: and give me my desert, my country life, and my God, Whom alone I may have to please, and shall please by my simple life.[97]

What followed was a series of farewell salutations to friends, colleagues, his beloved city, his own position within it, and everything that had been dear to him and to those around him who still attempted to vindicate the life of the gospel.

There was no logical conclusion to the intense conflicts between Christianity and paganism in the realm of social traditions and culture. Church fathers tried to work out a new conception of life, time, and history. The realm of redemption took on different aspects according to the status of the church in a rapidly changing world. Christian theologians attempted to formulate the best ways to control the new structure of human thought and behavior without showing contempt for the legacy of the pagan world. It is debatable whether church leaders rose up to the task of providing a satisfactory replacement for classical culture. There is no lack of contention that Christianity precipitated the era of intellectual decadence which ushered in the dark ages. It is interesting to note,

---

[97]Gregory of Nazianzus, *The Last Farewell*, 24 (NPNF-2 VII) 393. There were in fact many complex reasons for the lack of popularity of Gregory. They were due to the uneasy truce Theodosius had tried to achieve in Constantinople, often without success. Arianism was not defeated there, and the East looked quite different religiously from the West. An interesting and insightful summary of the problems and of the difficulties Gregory could not surmount is given by J. H. W. G. Liebeschuetz, *Barbarians and Bishops: Army, Church, and State in the Age of Arcadius and Chrysostom* (Oxford: Oxford University Press, 1990) 157-65.

however, that in 425 Theodosius II, who pursued a life of piety and learning, reorganized the University of Constantinople with the purpose of reviving Roman learning from a Christian point of view. It was to be distinct from the University of Athens which had remained pagan in spirit. But by the end of the fifth century decadence was rampant, and it was served the final blow in the edict of Justinian in 529 according to which all classical learning was banned. But even in such a world which was the product of the Theodosian code, society had to function, and students were still trained in the traditional disciplines of medicine, liberal professions, and technical studies. Nothing died absolutely. In fact a prominent leader of the times, Cassiodorus, encouraged by the learned pope Agapetus, laid the foundation for a Christian university in Rome in 535, six years after the Justinian edict. The nostalgia for a pagan cultural past surfaced again. Cassiodorus remained famous for his major work *Institutiones divinarum et saecularium litterarum* which was a revealing treatise on the correlation between religious and profane education.

Pierre Chuvin points out that the so-called "last pagans" were found among intellectuals, historians, philosophers, and poets. The pagan background persisted as did some of the shrines, especially those of Apollo. Paganism was not eradicated from the masses. There was a pagan spirit that refused to be defeated:

> This kind of paganism could not have survived without the existence of a pagan population large enough to protect the sacred character of those places, and discreet enough not to attract the wrath of the authorities. Although extirpated from the public domain by the laws of Theodosius I, paganism maintained a secret vitality in the hearts and souls of individuals.[98]

---

[98]Pierre Chuvin, *A Chronicle of the Last Pagans* (Cambridge MA: Harvard University Press, 1990) 118. Other scholars who praised the last pagans nonetheless pointed out that they were doomed to defeat because Greek learning had entered a period of sclerosis which also meant the death of the the the old religion.

De quelque côté que l'on se tourne, on contaste parmi cette élite intellectuelle du paganisme que goût du merveilleux, ritualisme formaliste, absence totale de sens critique vis-à-vis des réalités religieuses païennes, absence également flagrante de toute pensée originale et vivante. L'école grecque est sclérosée, comme la religion qu'elle prétend défendre.

Collections of classical works continued to influence the cultural scene in spite of antipagan legislation. Christian biases were replaced by pagan biases, as in the case of the historian Zosimus. More influential were scholars such as Martianus Capella, a contemporary of Augustine. He produced a work in nine books, commonly known as *On the Marriage of Philology and Mercury*, although only the first two books bear that name. The other seven books were the foundation of what is now known as the liberal arts.[99] The impact of the work on the culture of the Middle Ages and the Renaissance remains beyond doubt, though in its own day it was far less influential. It took another century for works that no longer distinguished between Christianity and paganism and gave them equal status to transmit learning in a more universal way. One could mention here *The Consolation of Philosophy* of Boethius, who died just five years before the edict of Justinian.

The fall of Rome proved to the intellectual world that no matter how well founded a culture might be, it cannot totally escape the instability and fragility emerging from catastrophic events and circumstances. The best cultural achievements lack permanence. The process of decay and death is everywhere at work. It was for the church to prove that it could infuse into terrestrial things an eternal principle not subject to that decay. But it was not until the age of Scholasticism and the Renaissance that this eternal principle became more visible, and it owed its strength to the revival of Greek and Roman culture.

Marcel Simon, *La civilisation de l'antiquité et le christianisme* (Paris: Arthaud, 1972) 257.

[99]The work of Martianus Capella remained known under the title *De nuptiis Philologiae et Mercurii*. That title does indeed apply to the two first books. The other seven books which defined the seven liberal arts were entitled *De arte grammatica, De arte dialectica, De arte rhetorica, De geometrica, De arithmetica, De astrologia, De harmonia.*

Chapter 11

Wɧen tɧe Goɒs Are Silent

*When the Roman Empire was decapitated, the whole world perished in
one city.*
—Jerome

*If God exists, it is difficult to believe that He could have completely
forsaken the ancient pagan world which produced so much that is great
and beautiful.*
—Berdyaev

At the turn of the fifth century the great poet and epigrammatist Palladas
captured the somber mood of dying paganism at the hand of what he
considered Christian mediocrity. His fierceness and vigor captivated the
minds of the last generation of educated pagans in his beloved Alexandria. As the ancient world was collapsing around him and as he saw no
hope for the future, he exclaimed: "If we are alive, then life itself is
dead." The gods retreated, victims of imperial legislation. They left
behind no specific teaching, no moral and ethical code to be respected by
their followers. There was no Sermon on the Mount, no beatitudes, no
theological justification for rituals and practices that sprang from the
glory of temples such as the Serapeum or ancient Delphi. No one could
estimate the lasting impact of the death of a culture that had moved the
spiritual and intellectual world for so long but that never coalesced
around a well-defined center. The splendor and magnificence of its visible
monuments could not ensure its permanence. The gods fell silent. Their
abodes disappeared.

The explanation of the demise of paganism by Christian writers was
simple and direct. That which was *extra ecclesiam* could be only idolatry
and was doomed to the principle of *nulla salus*. Augustine, a contemporary of Palladas, did not find a specific reason to rejoice in the troubles
of the empire. He argued that, from the beginning, through all the personalities of the Old Testament and especially the prophets, God had decreed
the coming of Christ and the universality of the church. In a spirit of

triumph he raised the rhetorical question that had baffled the best minds of the times, even of the last dying pagans: "Where are their gods? Where are the vaticinations of their fanatics, and the divinations of their prophets? Where are the auguries, or the auspices, or the soothsayings, or the oracles of demons."[1] But Augustine refused to attribute the collapse of paganism to the rise of Christianity. It was dying because of its own weakness and falsehood. It was exiting the stage of the world because it could no longer be part of the drama, having failed to acknowledge the true creator and master of the universe. The play would proceed without them.

The picture painted by Augustine does not include all the brush strokes. For all practical purposes the spirit of paganism was still thriving in cities such as Alexandria. Cyril, who became bishop of that city in 412, knew it only too well. He could not escape the feeling of a Julian *redivivus*. He feared that Hellenism emerged stronger from Julian's attacks on Christians, and that Christianity was not as persuasive as often contended. He undertook to write his lengthy *Contra Julianum*, a contradiction in terms and spirit if indeed paganism was dead.[2] In Alexandria, especially, Platonic and Neoplatonic philosophy defined the intellectual scene. Theon and then his daughter Hypatia, until her death in 415, dominated the cultural landscape. Hypatia's imprint on intellectual life contrasted ironically with the ferocity of uneducated Christian avengers. In those troubled times in Alexandria, it was not paganism that was dying. It was the very principles on which Christian faith rested that were consigned to dark corners of hatred and vengeance. There was no room for the elegance of philosophical thought and discourse. There was no room for peace and understanding. Christ was dying again, this time not on a cross in Jerusalem, but in the very hearts of those who proclaimed themselves his followers. Faith fell victim to political intrigues. Most Christian writers of the day ignored the event. Socrates spoke of it with indignation and shame.[3] For a moment at least, the God revealed in

---

[1]Augustine, ConsEv 1.32.50 (NPNF-1 VI) 98.

[2]For a text of Cyril's *Contra Julianum*, see especially Paul Burguière and Pierre Evieux, *Cyrille d'Alexandrie: Contre Julien* (Paris: Editions du Cerf, 1985). It is a bilingual edition (Greek and French). The *Contra Julianum* is the major source we have for a rebuilt text of Julian's *Contra Galilaeos*.

[3]Socrates, HE 7.15. It is surprising to find in Socrates, a historian dedicated

Christ was relegated to the realm of silence to make way for a triumphalistic mood totally foreign to the Gospel spirit.

In the post-Constantine era many faithful still dreamt of a time when the rule of Christianity would bring the perfect kingdom on earth. Lactantius tried to portray such a world that could not be achieved as long as vestiges of paganism survived:

> Lay aside every evil thought from your hearts, and the golden age will at once return to you, which you cannot attain by any other means than by beginning to worship the true God. . . . But if God only were worshipped, there would be no dissensions and wars, since men would know that they are the sons of one God. . . . There would be no frauds or plunderings. . . . There would be no adulteries, and debaucheries, and prostitutions of women. . . . There would not, therefore, as I have said, be these evils on earth, if there were by common consent a general observance of the law of God, if those things were done by all which our people alone perform. How happy and how golden would be the condition of human affairs, if throughout the world gentleness, and piety, and peace, and innocence, and equity, and temperance, and faith, took up their abode! In short there would be no need of so many and varying laws to rule men, since the law of God alone would be sufficient for perfect innocence; nor would there be any need of prisons, or the swords of rulers, or the terror of punishments.[4]

Realizing how far from such achievements were both the church and the empire, Lactantius resorted to a rational explanation of the circumstances keeping the dream from becoming reality. Surprisingly, he did not appeal to the Scriptures, but to Cicero detailing how human nature places obstacles on the path to coherence. Confusion permeates all human endeavors at living the life of gods. Lactantius knew that no God, not even the one proclaimed by the church, could bring order out of that much chaos.

---

to the defense of Christianity, such a sense of indignation at the misconduct of the church of Alexandria and such a high praise of Hypatia.

[4] Lactantius, DivInst 5.8 (ANF VII) 143.

Deus Absconditus

It is the destiny of most religions to suffer the fate of all living things, growing to full strength, experiencing the woes of decay and obsolescence, and slowly or brutally moving to their death and possible resurrection. The great epiphanies are not meant to last. The explosion of religious life generated by the birth of new ritual movements must give way to a more rational analysis within which the gods lose their original importance. A nostalgic hope for the continuous presence of gods among mortals proves insufficient to alter the inexorable movement which leads to the death of the best historical impulses. Plato faced the religious predicament of his contemporaries by reminding them, through Socrates, of a process of decadence which keeps us hoping again for that which lies buried in a distant past.[5]

Early Christianity had inherited from its Old Testament background a long tradition of the *Deus absconditus*. The perfection of God precluded any direct contact between the creator and fallen creation. One could not see God face to face and live. Death was the price to pay for any contact between the mortal and the immortal. Even redemption came through channels which ensured the separation of God from his people. The prophet, more than anybody else, knew that God remains inaccessible, the true *Deus absconditus:* "Truly, thou art a God who hidest thyself, O God of Israel, the Savior."[6]

From the inception of Yahwistic religion under the leadership of Moses, the threat of divine absence was meant to create fear in the hearts of the unfaithful. But it was the whole people who were the target of divine anger and vengeance, and it was the whole people who would be deprived of God's presence:

> Then my anger will be kindled against them in that day, and I will forsake them and hide my face from them, and they will be devoured; and many evils and troubles will come upon them, so that they will say in that day, "Have not these evils come upon us because our God is not among us?" And I surely will hide my face in that day. . . .[7]

---

[5]Plato, Phil 16CE.
[6]Isaiah 45:15.
[7]Deuteronomy 31:17-18.

God is portrayed in the text as the one whose hiddenness ensures the ruin of the people: "I will hide my face from them, I will see what their end will be."[8]

In the Old Testament the distance of God gave rise to the prophetic voice. One of the derivations of the term prophet is the "one who speaks for" (God) (πρό φήμι). Prophets took upon themselves to reassure the people that the absence of God cannot be permanent, and that the hope of his presence cannot be continuously defeated.[9] But there was no systematic correlation between the wishes and prayers of a people and the response of their God: "Then they will cry to the LORD, but he will not answer them; he will hide his face from them at that time, because they have made their deeds evil."[10] Even in utter discouragement and against any hope of success, the prophet kept proclaiming a God who was not likely to reveal himself: "If I say, 'I will not mention him, or speak anymore in his name,' there is in my heart as it were a burning fire shut up in my bones."[11]

The Hebrews developed a strong sense of divine hiddenness and felt more reassured with divine absence than with the presence of their God. They remembered how their forefathers in the wilderness begged Moses to make sure that God would never address them directly: "You speak to us, and we will hear; but let not God speak to us, lest we die."[12] The Hebrew language betrayed an obsessive fear of divine presence. The same verb (פקד paqad) meant to visit or to punish. Divine presence brought with it retribution. At points we find a genuine yearning for divine absence, mostly when the proximity of God means tribulation. Job offered to God one of the most unusual prayers: "Let me alone, that I may find a little comfort."[13] The Psalmist echoed the same feeling as he questioned God's persistence to stand far off and refuse his help in times of trouble.[14]

---

[8]Deuteronomy 32:20.
[9]Isaiah 8:17.
[10]Micah 3:4.
[11]Jeremiah 20:9.
[12]Exodus 20:19.
[13]Job 10:20.
[14]Psalm 10:1. See also vv. 10-11 where the absence of God gives hope to the

Elijah's experience on Mount Horeb remains the focal point of any Old Testament debate on the presence and absence of God. It reveals the profound inadequacy of people's expectations of theophanies. God was neither in the wind, nor in the earthquake, nor in the fire, but in a thin silence.[15] What kind of voice does one hear when the forces of evil keep God from revealing himself? The remoteness of God reached its tragic apex in the Gospels when Christ, dying on a cross, cried out to God, "Why hast thou forsaken me?" When God is silent the forces of chaos rule supreme, and no savior can alter such divine decision.

Spiritual disconnection from God can be aggravated by geographical distance from the centers of revelation. It was in the Babylonian exile that Hebrews had to contend not only with the hiddenness, but also with the nature of their God. Ezekiel tried to reconstruct a prophetic outlook that would vindicate God's action while renewing the hope of the people, two propositions which did not allow a simple solution. The notion of God indwelling in his people apart from places of worship took root. God could be manifested in his spirit, and thus Ezekiel could formulate a solution to the plight of his people and proclaim the renewed presence of their God through the agency of the spirit: "I will not hide my face any more from them, when I pour out my spirit upon the house of Israel, says the Lord GOD."[16]

In the New Testament, John the Baptist's offer of the kingdom of God could not be disassociated from divine hiddenness. Nothing short of a total metanoia could alter the decision of God to stay away from his people. Christ reinforced the message. He himself felt the distance from God and would not proclaim his messiahship to a people who had lost the faculty to search for divine immanence. His words and his miracles convinced many. But there was also a fear that the proximity of his God could spell disaster for those around him. All three authors of the Synoptic Gospels report that after a spectacular miracle, the people begged Jesus to leave their neighborhood, for a great fear had taken hold of them.[17]

---

evildoer in his belief that the divinity can be so hidden and so forgetful that evil deeds may go unpunished.

[15]First Kings 19.
[16]Ezekiel 39:29.
[17]Matthew 8:28-34; Mark 5:14-17; Luke 8:26-39.

In the Gospel of John, the eternal logos becomes the principle spanning light and darkness, mortality and eternal life. But, as in the case of the Heraclitean logos, there could be no logical and rational way to understand divine action in the midst of that which is foreign and hostile to it. The equation of Christ and the logos was insufficient to resolve the historical distance of God from his people. It must be superseded by another equation, that of the logos and the divine spirit. Christ could be the redeemer only through his absence, and to the bewilderment of his disciples, he told them so: "Nevertheless I tell you the truth: it is to your advantage that I go away, for if I do not go away, the Counselor will not come to you; but if I go, I will send him to you."[18] The paradoxical proposition of Christ remained open-ended, and the church has forever been involved in explaining why the spiritual presence of God requires his physical distance. The hiddenness of God becomes a *sine qua non* condition of his majesty and redeeming love. Pascal thought that no religion can be true if it does not affirm the hiddenness of God.[19]

Since salvation results from an inscrutable act of divine grace, it does not belong to rational thought to explain God. A proper understanding of *Deus absconditus* leads to the consciousness of *homo absconditus*, to the realization that we shall never solve the puzzle of existence, however much we try to cross from absurdity to logic. Religion remains mystery.

In the Greco-Roman world the question of divine rule among the people fluctuated greatly from period to period and from system to system. On the philosophical side, Platonic dualism kept the divinity apart from physical reality. Thus in Platonic philosophy the stress falls on the quest for the universally existent. There is no pretension to understand or explain the divine mind or ultimate creative purpose.

---

[18]John 16:7.

[19]Pascal, Pensées 598: "Dieu étant ainsi caché, toute religion qui ne dit pas que Dieu est caché n'est pas véritable; et toute religion qui n'en rend pas la raison n'est pas instruisante. La nôtre fait tout cela: *Vere tu es Deus absconditus.*" So also in Thomas Aquinas, who spent his life trying to explain the ways through which we could know God, we find a note of resignation in front of the majesty and greatness of God. For of God we can say only what he is not, and never what he is: "*Non enim de Deo capere possumus quid est, sed quid non est.*" CGent 1.1.30.

In Neoplatonism, God's hiddenness was translated into a high level of mysticism. Any knowledge of God required a specific initiation. True religion was no longer for the masses: "The divine is not expressible, so the initiate is forbidden to speak of it to anyone who has not been fortunate enough to have beheld it himself."[20]

On occasion the remoteness of the gods was attributed to the limitations imposed on human knowledge by the inadequacy of the mind. Christian apologists were eager to espouse such a view concerning the Gentiles, with the presupposition that the Christian God was not subject to the same constraints. Eusebius quoted Xenophon's *Epistle to Aeschines* to support the point:

> That the things of the gods are beyond us is manifest to every one; but it is sufficient to worship them to the best of our power. What their nature is it is neither easy to discover nor lawful to inquire. For it pertains not to slaves to know the nature or conduct of their masters, beyond what their service requires.[21]

Such a statement could be adopted by many Christians.

Much more difficult to resolve was the Epicurean affirmation of the existence of the gods while removing them from any concern about human affairs. Again Eusebius grasped the opportunity to compare the Christian and heathen views of divine providence, showing the inadequacy of the Epicurean system. He chose Atticus, who was sympathetic with the Epicurean point of view, to expose a fallacy that could find no agreement with rational thinking:

> For what difference does it make to us, whether you banish deity from the world and leave us no communion therewith, or shut up the gods in the world and remove them from all share in the affairs of earth? For in both cases the indifference of the gods towards men is equal, and equal also the security of wrongdoers from fear of the gods.[22]

---

[20]Plotinus, *The Good and the One* 11. In *The Esential Plotinus*, 87.

[21]Eusebius, PraepEv 745ab. We find in Plato statements similar to that of Xenophon: "We commonly assert that men ought not to enquire concerning the greatest god and about the universe, nor busy themselves in searching out their causes, since it is actually impious to do so; whereas the right course, in all probability, is exactly the opposite." Laws 821A (LCL XI) 111.

[22]Eusebius, PraepEv 799d.

Oracular religion, either by design or through theological necessity, remained ambiguous. It compelled philosophers of the Roman world to formulate explanations of phenomena which would not naturally belong to the religious mode. The death of gods, the obsolescence of their message, their appearance and disappearance from the human scene could not be explained in terms acceptable to those who found in religion the last refuge against the blows of destiny. Cicero defended the Delphic oracle that, for a long time, found its legitimacy in the great number of people consulting it. Such commitment on the part of so many people must have meant that the oracles communicated truth. The fact that it was stricken by obsolescence and even silence may be explained by the same argument in a negative sense. There came a time when the prophecies were no longer true. Cicero conceded the point, but not without giving his interpretation of the vicissitudes of Delphic religion:

> Possibly too, those subterraneous exhalations which used to kindle the soul of the Pythian priestess with divine inspiration have gradually vanished in the long lapse of time; just as within our own knowledge some rivers have dried up and disappeared, while others, by winding and twisting, have changed their course into other channels. But explain the decadence of the oracle as you wish, since it offers a wide field for discussion, provided you grant what cannot be denied without distorting the entire record of history, that the oracle at Delphi made true prophecies for many hundreds of years.[23]

Thus again, religion draws its strength more from the past than from the present, a motif often repeated by writers of the Greco-Roman world.[24] Plutarch spent a great amount of time analyzing and explaining the woes of Delphic oracular religion. The major aspects of the debate were already mentioned in chapter 4. But he insisted on the fact that there never were any direct messages from the god, only what the Pythia could

---

[23]Cicero, DeDiv 1.38 (LCL XX) 269.

[24]See especially the explanations given by Plutarch: "For we must not show hostility towards the god, nor do away with his providence and divine powers together with his prophetic gifts; but we must seek for explanations of such matters as seem to stand in the way, and not relinquish the reverent faith of our fathers." PythOr 402E (LCL V) 305.

reveal through her inspiration.[25] There is no medium that could communicate the divine message without contaminating it: "For pure design cannot be seen by us, and when it is made manifest in another guise and through another medium, it becomes contaminated with the nature of this medium."[26]

It was the prerogative of the gods to listen or not to listen, to hear or not to hear, to speak or not to speak regardless of the importance of the moment or the intensity of the suffering. It did not escape the attention of Euripides, who liked to point out the futility in expecting divine help in times of sorrow: "Electra the wretched prays; year after year her father's blood cries from the ground; but no god hears."[27]

In Neoplatonism we encounter still a different perspective on the presence and absence of the gods. Mystics in the Egyptian branch of Neoplatonic philosophy changed the name of their god Thoth to that of the three times great Hermes Trismegistus. In a work of hermetic spirituality authored by a devotee of Hermes, the *Perfect Discourse*, we find a moving prophecy on the fate of Egypt when the gods decide to forsake it. It speaks of the world growing old and desolate, of the gods abandoning it and returning to it. Both Lactantius in his *Divinae institutiones* and Augustine in his *De civitate Dei* referred to the work and gave their appraisal of it. Extensive portions of the *Perfect Discourse* survived. Here are some excerpts from it:

> And yet (our prophecy continues) a time will come when it will seem that the Egyptians have in vain honoured God (*divinitatem*) with pious heart and assiduous devotion, and all holy reverence for the gods will become ineffective and be deprived of its fruit. For God will return from earth to heaven, and Egypt will be abandoned.

There follows a description of what that abandonment by the gods will mean. The land of many sanctuaries and temples will be covered with coffins and corpses. Nothing but fables concerning religion will survive, and posterity will not believe even in those. Egypt will be a desert, and there will be more dead than living. Then the prophecy continued:

---

[25]Ibid., 397C.
[26]Ibid., 404C (LCL V) 313.
[27]Euripides, El 198-200. In *Medea and Other Plays*, trans. Philip Wellacott (Baltimore: Penguin Books, 1963) 111.

In that day men will be weary of life, and they will cease to think the World worthy of reverent wonder and of worship. . . . They will no longer love this world around us, this incomparable work of God. . . . Darkness will be preferred to light, and death will be thought more profitable than life; no one will raise his eyes to heaven; the pious will be deemed insane, and the impious wise; The madman will be thought brave, and the wickedest will be regarded as good. . . . Then will the earth no longer stand unshaken, and the sea will no more be navigable; heaven will not support the stars in their orbit. . . . The voice of the gods will of necessity be silenced and dumb; the fruits of the earth will rot; the soil will turn barren, and the very air will sicken in sullen stagnation.[28]

The prophecy also alluded to the return of the gods.

The approach of paganism to the remoteness and silence of the gods was not in fact very different from the perspectives Christians had of a *Deus absconditus*. The fate of the Hebrew nation at the hands of consecutive invaders provided a parallel to the events leading to the collapse of the Roman empire. Several church fathers saw direct correlations. In his preface to the Book of Ezekiel, the prophet during the great exile, Jerome shows both a great dislike of Rome (which at one point he called the evil Babylon) as well as a very emotional reaction to the fate of the city:

I was wavering between hope and despair, and was torturing myself with the misfortunes of other people. But when the bright light of all the world was put out, or, rather, when the Roman empire was decapitated, and, to speak more correctly, the whole world perished in one city, "I became dumb and humbled myself, and kept silence from good words, but my grief broke out afresh, my heart glowed within me, and while I meditated the fire was kindled." . . . Who would believe that Rome, built up by the conquest of the whole world, had collapsed, that the mother of nations had become also their tomb.[29]

---

[28]Quotations from the Perfect discourse are taken from Garth Fowden, *The Egyptian Hermes: A Historical Approach to the Late Pagan Mind* (Princeton NJ: Princeton University Press, 1986) 39, 41. Excerpts of the same work are also given in Chuvin, *Chronicle*, 68.

[29]Jerome, PrefEzek (NPNF-2 VI) 500.

When Jerome had weighed the benefits and the liabilities of the fall of Rome, he chose to remain silent instead of proclaiming victory for the Christians. He accepted what we also find in Prudentius, namely that one can remain a Christian without despising the pagan world that provided the richness of culture into which the church could enter. The history of Rome could be viewed as a preparation for the coming of Christ:

> The change from Paganism to Christianity is not a breach with the past, but only the last stage of a development which reached its ideal completion when the far-off successor of Aeneas bowed the knee to Christ; and for Prudentius, as for Aeneas in virgil, Tiber is still a sacred stream, not, however, because it is associated with a river god, but because it flows through Christ's earthly capital and past the tombs of Christian martyrs.[30]

A survey of Roman religion reveals that the national gods were revered mostly in times of success and their silence deplored in times of need. As a result one could accept the contention of Tertullian and others that it was not their religion that made the Romans great, but their greatness that made them religious. The more successful, the more gods were worshiped. Even when excessive, polytheism did not engender rivalry among gods and did not prevent people from believing in their specific functions. The notion of heresy arose with the Christian movement and did not affect pagan religion.

The antipagan legislation of Christian emperors was meant to silence the gods. But it also evolved in the context of one of the greatest historical ironies which brought together the victory of Christianity and the collapse of Rome. While Christianity was moving into the mainstream of religious life, and eventually also of political life, paganism was becoming a forbidden minority in the empire.

It appeared less and less certain that Christianity could ensure peace and stability. The pagan gods fell silent. But they seem to have taken with them into their oblivion all that was the greatness of Rome. Augustine had to concede the point. However reluctantly, he had to agree with the argument of the pagans that while they were offering their sacrifices and performing their rites, the gods were pleased and Rome

---

[30]Prudentius, COratSymm. From the introduction by H. J. Thomson (LCL I) ix-x.

was standing tall and happy. Now that all of that has been abolished, ruin has followed.[31] It was time for the Christian God to speak. But how forcefully? Neither Augustine, nor Jerome, nor Prudentius could celebrate victory with the collapse of Rome. The fall of Rome took with it a great deal of what the church had become. There was no conclusive victory of Christianity over paganism, but the last convulsions in a fight which left neither fulfilled nor confident. The lines separating Christianity from paganism became blurred. The victory of the church was legal and dogmatic rather than cultural and spiritual.

Tḥe "Cḥristianization" of Paganism and tḥe "Paganization" of Cḥristianity

Christian legislation intended to silence the pagan gods was successful in terms of outward religion. Pagan ritual had depended on state support and was accustomed to legislation in its favor. When imperial funds were discontinued, ceremonies and sacrifices suffered greatly. Paganism no longer had an efficient way to defend itself against what was destroying it.

But to assume that the pagan spirit withered away when no longer connected to specific rites would be to ignore the impact of a long history on its people. Christianity did not replace paganism. It would be more appropriate to speak of mutual influences, though in a very polemical context. A world that produced men of letters such as Symmachus, Themistius, and Libanius could not be decreed dead by legislation.

There was a gradual transformation of paganism which rested on tacit forces not readily identifiable. Well into the fifth century it would have been premature to pronounce final death sentences on any aspect of Roman history. In a post-Constantine era pagans had to adapt to a situation for which they were not prepared. They had never envisioned a radical disconnection between their religion and the state. Now they had to adjust to two equally baffling historical shifts, namely that their rituals were no longer those of the state and, even worse, that they had to

---

[31]Augustine, in Sermo 296 as quoted by Boissier, *Fin du paganisme* 2:308: "Quand nous faisions des sacrifices à nos dieux . . . Rome était debout, Rome était heureuse. Maintenant que nos sacrifices sont interdits, voyez ce que Rome est devenue."

contemplate the survival of a religion deprived of its major ceremonies. They still hoped that ecclesiastical edicts would not be strictly applied. In many cases they were not, for those appointed to enforce the laws were often pagan at heart.

The connection between paganism and Roman life was everywhere evident, even after its gods were dethroned and in spite of Christian claims to the contrary, especially the statement entered in the *Codex Theodosianus* (16.10.22) by Theodosius and Honorius to the effect that there were no pagans left. In fact imperial legislation did not suppress freedom of conscience until, perhaps, the edict of Justinian in 529.

The silence of the gods need not mean the total loss of religiosity. The nation of Israel had already proven that its faith could survive the destruction of its temple, an event which could have meant the end of a whole segment of its religious history. So also the pagans lost most of their temples and shrines. But they exhibited a level of religious commitment which Christianity could not eliminate in spite of its legal and theological weapons. The pagan world was forced to seek for a new modus vivendi in a society which had become hostile to it. But it was far from crippled and from having lost its influence. There is an intellectual and spiritual fortitude which can survive physical blows.

All along emperors and leaders of the empire had been careful to assess the forces affecting the destiny of their world and their people. Christians had a different outlook, but were also deeply involved in an analysis of what was legitimate and what was not in terms of their faith. On both sides it was important to survey the field of religion and to remain alert to all possible misinterpretations of the will of the gods. Pagans had to learn the virtue of theological reflection as a means to protect themselves against the claims of Christianity, which was much more successful in that specific arena. Both movements, in whatever form and shape they appeared, could not relinquish the belief that they were the essential elements in a cosmos in the throes of severe tribulations. Traditions do not die easily, even when new and more powerful ones are formed.

Both Christians and pagans could appeal to their history as proof of their strength and validity. The church sought to reinterpret all events in the light of its specific mission. Paganism, which still remembered the glorious days of its supremacy, could not accept its death sentence at the hands of what, for such a long time, it opposed as illegitimate. But both pagan and Christian intellectuals were forced into a dialectical analysis of arguments favoring their greatness, while also exposing their vulnerability. The fall of Rome became the common ground of fear, for it showed how fragile all terrestrial things and all cultural achievements were. No god, either on the pagan or Christian side, could abrogate circumstances which contained the seeds of their decay and eventual dissolution. Consequently, learned Christians did not find specific reasons to rejoice in the collapse of Rome, which by the time of the late empire began to look more and more as their city.

For several centuries Christianity and empire had coexisted through turbulent times and through idealistic perspectives. They were not meant to become a harmonious unity in the midst of conflicting beliefs and practices. Yet they often surmised the harmony which could have allowed them to live at peace with each other. The silence of pagan gods did not put an end to the strange kind of dialectic that had underscored the slow progress of the church. Christians were destined to defend two conflicting views of their mission. On the one hand they had to keep the distinction between world and kingdom, and on the other hand they could not resist the urge to try to transform the world so that it could live at peace with the kingdom. History shows that the church has never been able to resolve those different trends either theologically or practically.

On the surface it might have appeared that there was a logical law of equilibrium. The more the church rose, the greater the decline of Rome and the silence of its gods. In a more simplistic way one could maintain that there was a clearly defined war between paganism and the Christian faith. Such an approach would ignore that paganism never defined itself theologically or through dogmas. There was no radical elimination of the one by the other, simply historical events favoring one more than the other. The death of paganism must be judged on the scales of relativity. Christianity and Roman religion remained in a process of steady change, and it would have been difficult to define the exact causes of conflict. Neither the Christian God nor the divinities of paganism spoke in an absolute and definite voice. It was, however, the Christian determination of faith which eventually secured the silence of pagan gods, and not vice versa. But that silence has never become final. What Christians fought against, at points became part of their system in the form of new rites. The old pagan deities kept a nostalgic role in the evocation of times of plenty and abundance. They lost their religious significance while securing a permanent place in art and literature. Well into late antiquity Christian patrons kept alive the process of domestication of pagan gods which still dwelt within the walls of their households.

As early as the end of the fourth century, pagan rites and ceremonies were infiltrating the life of the church under guises often difficult to detect as contrary to the teaching of the Scriptures.[32] On the other hand, pagans continued to scorn Christian legislation and assert their right to their mode of living. Augustine reports that, right after Honorius issued an edict in 407 forbidding the pagans to celebrate publicly their festivals and solemnities, groups of heathen outraged Christians by dancing in front of their church: "In defiance of the most recent laws, certain impious rites were celebrated on the Pagan feast day, the calends of June, no one interfering to forbid them, and with such unbounded effrontery that a most insolent multitude passed along the street in which the church is situated, and went on dancing in front of the building,—an outrage which was never committed even in the time of Julian."[33] Augustine recounted how, after leaders of the church tried to stop such behavior, their building was repeatedly pelted with stones.

Progressively, such sharp distinctions between paganism and Christianity disappeared. Either through a persuasive syncretistic spirit or through historical necessities, pagan rituals became part of the Christian calendar. The most obvious example is the celebration of Christmas, which the church owes to the midwinter feast of the Saturnalia and the winter solstice of Brumalia, celebrated on December 25. The pagan origin was soon forgotten, but not to everybody's liking. Christians could not overcome a tacit guilt when aware that pagan holidays had been translated into their religious calendar. Occasionally voices of indignation arose, denouncing practices not in tune with truth. At the end of the sixth century the church had not yet made its peace with certain heathen festivals it had incorporated into its life. Martin of Braga's voice of indignation momentarily shook Christians from their complacency: "You shall not perform the wicked celebration of the Calends and observe the holiday of the Gentiles, nor shall you decorate your houses with laurel and green branches. The whole celebration is Pagan."[34] It was a matter of

---

[32]See for instance Jerome, CVig 4-5.
[33]Augustine, Letter 91.8 (NPNF-1 I) 378.
[34]*Acta Conciliarum*, 5.iii.399. Quoted in Prudence Jones and Nigel Pennick,

time only before the church had its own calendar with rituals which incorporated all kinds of celebrations, religious and civic. Bishops could not always convince their faithful to withdraw from participation in some social aspects of pagan festivals. Too many Christians saw that participation as routine activities rather than support of pagan worship. But it is not the purpose of this work to address in detail the paganization of the church. The process is described at length in other works.[35]

Yet the destiny of Rome and Christianity seems to have been inscribed in some universal and eternal decree within which the distinction between paganism and the church was fated to become irrelevant. In the same way Rome had inherited the rich cultural legacy of Greece and had become the center of its development, mixing it with its own civilization, it was now bound to become the center from which religion would radiate in the Western world. Paganism had provided the stage on which contentions and debates were played out. Roman society was indelibly stamped, and Christianity could not hope to eliminate such a historical force overnight. In fact, if it had succeeded, it might have perished as well. The Roman world remained pagan at heart, a fact that helped Christianity more than if it had turned totally indifferent. Christianity could not resist the allurements of a brilliant civilization within which it grew to become a world religion.

Historical ironies abound, but none as striking as the fact that Rome would become the centre from which Christianity would extend to the rest of the world. It was no longer Jupiter or Apollo which dominated the religious landscape. Even Julian had to acknowledge the death of gods he was trying to resurrect in vain. Gone were the glory of the Augustan cult or the pretensions of emperor worship. By the fifth century the most magnificent pagan temples were history. Christianity and Rome became synonymous. The religion ruling the Western world was now Roman catholicism. The pagan gods could finally be decreed silent, if not dead. The age of Theodosius could be considered one of the most revolutionary

---

A *History of Pagan Europe* (London: Routledge, 1995) 76. The progressive and uneasy way in which Christmas became a Christian festival, despite numerous patristic objections, and the irresistible path that led to the adoption of pagan beliefs is described in summary form by Oscar Cullmann, "The origin of Christmas," *The Early Church* (Philadelphia: Westminster Press, 1966) 21-36.
[35]See especially Jones and Pennick, *History of Pagan Europe.*

periods in the history of religious development, a legislative triumph over what appeared as unassailable religious traditions. In the final analysis, however, what hurt the pagans most was not the silencing of their gods but their exclusion from places of service in the new institutional hierarchy of Christian rulers.

Religion without Revelation

Triumphant Christianity became different in its nature and purpose from what it was at its inception. Many martyrs would not have recognized the arguments adduced nor the weapons used. The realm of faith gave way to the emergence of institutions. No one claimed any longer that the spirit of Christ could propagate itself without buildings, organizations, dogmas, and political presumptions. Doctrinal authority and ecclesiastical hierarchy supplanted the Gospel of Christ. In a post-Constantine era one was fighting for supremacy, not meaning. Theological debates raged, and they tore the church to pieces. Orthodoxy and heresy were the products of definitions issued by ruling Christian authorities, and no one knew exactly which is which under different circumstances. The Council of Nicaea reflected more the love for theological formulation than a commitment to an original faith. Conversion to Christianity from paganism often meant expedient compromises rather than spiritual yearning. The invisible divine world of martyrs which could be penetrated only through faith lost its appeal. Human wisdom and expectations replaced the awe and mystery that New Testament writers proposed as the foundation for piety and worship.

For several centuries Christianity tried to argue with pagans that it was not a religion. Yet it was rapidly becoming one. The age of the martyrs survived only in a nostalgia that no one wanted to become reality again. The life of the spirit was far too risky, and elemental faith could no longer sustain the religious community. The passion for faith which dominated the writings of early church fathers slowly turned to arguments, apologias, and attacks. The life of the spirit was superseded by the birth of the Christian institution. The antireligious literature church fathers aimed at pagans came back to haunt the development of the church. Institutions are fated to share similarities which deny them uniqueness. Few could remember the warnings of Christ against Pharisaic practices, and fewer still could grasp the depth of Christ's proposition that worship no longer requires institutions such as the temple of Jerusalem or that of

Mount Gerizim. No one heeded the warning that all that was needed was the spirit.

With the Council of Nicaea a new religious perspective came into being. Mysticism and revelation were dethroned in favor of commonly accepted formulae as definitions of official religion. The birth of dogmatic theology opened the door to varied interpretations which, when correlated to an affirmation of authority, gave rise to multiple sects, each claiming final authority. According to the *Theodosian Code,* Theodosius II in 423 forbade twenty two sects in one strike. None of that brought unity to the church. It was in the destiny of Christian religion to be fragmented into countless sects, movements, denominations, and churches, with no resolution in sight in spite of all efforts at ecumenical dialogue. Somewhere in all of that there is hidden the God of Jesus Christ, nowhere fully absent, nowhere fully present. One is tempted to agree with Harnack that the Gospel of Jesus Christ has very little, if anything, in common with doctrinal authority or ecclesiastical hierarchy. The era of the martyrs has been replaced by the rule of church officials, often with an open praise for its own efficient way to avoid further conflict for its faithful. All it required was conformity to prevalent dogmas. The lines separating the temporal from the spiritual became political more than religious, and have now almost completely disappeared. The disintegration of Rome could not stop the disintegration of the church. In all of that God chose to remain silent.

If paganism was retreating under the blows of triumphant Christianity, it certainly did not mean that the church was exhibiting an acceptable level of unity. The dreams of catholicity expressed by Ambrose and mostly Augustine remained in the area of dreams. At best Christianity could build something that resembled unity in its monastic cells, far from the vicissitudes of the real world. In fact, Roman paganism which was nothing but an amalgamation of diverse myths and rituals, exhibited a far greater sense of unity, mostly because it had never developed the idea of heresy, and consequently avoided internal strife. Not that the gods were at peace with each other. One need only read Hesiod, Homer, the playwrights, or the works of Cicero and Plutarch to be aware of the severity of the conflicts between gods. But there was no secular legislation eliminating some in favor of others. Polytheism was part of the global mentality. Persecutions did not arise until Christians waged an open war against polytheism which was the core of pagan religion.

With the triumph of Christianity came the conviction that the church must become the ruling force in the world. Mass conversion was the easiest way to achieve such a goal, and it could be realized more rapidly through the destruction of pagan temples. Thus Christians became avengers in the name of a faith which had become more and more questionable. The church's intelligentsia was not unaware of the dangers involved in such attitudes, and very often, as under Gratian, there were favors accorded to pagans by allowing them to keep their temples open, though without financial support. Thus deprived of their sumptuous ceremonies, pagan temples no longer reflected their former vitality. The process of dying was not eliminated, just made slower. Conforming Christianity was replacing conforming paganism. At points there was very little change from the past, just a difference of emphasis. Some Christian emperors could not disconnect themselves from a pagan past and its cultural seduction. The coinage of Constantius II was still rooted in the pagan ideal and tried to proclaim the restoration of more prosperous times (*felicitas temporum reparatio*). Not everyone in the church wished the annihilation of pagan culture.

After Constantine, the Christianization of the empire relied heavily on the power the emperor could exercise with the Senate. Thus decisions could be made in the context of impeccable legality. Prudentius reported such an instance during the rule of Theodosius. By a vote of the Senate, which left the body divided, Jupiter was defeated by Christ: "See in how full a house our benches decide that Jupiter's infamous couch and all the worship of idols must be banished far from our purified city! To the side to which our noble emperor's motion calls, great numbers cross, as free in mind as in foot."[36] Roman law became a powerful ally of Christianity.

No matter how much the gods are silenced or withdraw on their own, religion survives, though the spirit may die. It was a powerful insight of Christ that his followers may be bogged down in outward religious forms devoid of transcendence and spirituality. He raised the rhetorical question, which nonetheless was meant seriously: "When the Son of man comes, will he find faith on earth?"[37]

Pagan religious traditions had reshaped the mentality of Roman society. Sacrifices, rites, and ceremonies had established traditions that

---

[36]Prudentius, COratSymm 1.608-12 (LCL I) 397.
[37]Luke 18:8.

seemed to be beyond question. Christianity began without definite traditions, though it often referred to the Old Testament as its background, while rejecting Judaism. From the beginning it claimed absolute authority for its convictions. At that point it was small enough to maintain a sense of unity, though dissensions had been present in its midst from the beginning. When traditions grew to the position of control, the church claimed supremacy through the power of dogma. Christian religion became reflective, that is preoccupied with the picture it had of itself to the exclusion of other possibilities. Persecutions turned inward, opposing Christians to Christians, a historical phenomenon which never ceased to grow. Soon you could speak of Marcionite Christianity, Docetist Christianity, Gnostic Christianity, Montanist Christianity, Manichaean Christianity, Arian Christianity, and so on, almost an infinitum. It may have all originated in a form of dualism which made it impossible to realize the ideal the church had formulated for itself while in the grips of secular forces. Ironically, it was the obsessive need for unity that created the most violent dissensions.

In paganism, the gods were forced out of their functions through well organized Christian legislation. In Christianity, God chose to remain the inaccessible, the mysterious, never to be known in his true nature, never to be totally freed from the myths surrounding his presence among mortals. John Chrysostom wrote persuasively about our inability to comprehend God. In his Περὶ Ἀκαταλήπτου (*De incomprehensibili*) he stated: "But that is an impertinence to say that He who is beyond the apprehension of even the higher Powers can be comprehended by us earthworms, or compassed and comprised by the weak forces of our understanding."[38] The mysterious God remained inaccessible. Piety became a civic virtue, religion a collective response. The church adopted the Roman political hierarchy and, to a great extent, its traditional mentality. It was in the true sense of the term a Roman Catholic church with countless interpretations of what that should mean.

---

[38]Quoted by Rudolf Otto, *The Idea of the Holy*, trans. John W. Harvey (Oxford: Oxford University Press, 1967) 179.

The Transfiguration of the Gods

"Fifteen centuries after the church fathers had valiantly routed the pagan deities and their philosophical apologists, Jupiter had returned in triumph to the realm of the most Christian kings of Europe. The château de Versailles was adorned with gracious images of the gods of Greece and Rome, while Christ and the saints were severely restricted to the chapel."[39] Thus begins the work of Frank E. Manuel analyzing eighteenth-century religion.

Pagan religion, which was often lacking in theological and philosophical depth while its adherents went to temples for no other reason than securing some temporal goods, became more venerable after its death than during the days of its glory. The fate of paganism was closely related to the destiny of the empire, and the gods were invoked in order to secure the well-being of the world, the Roman world. But the more enlightened Romans had already surmised that there is no *imperium sine fine*, and that the eventual collapse of Rome might mean the death of its gods. Some intellectuals sought to ensure universality for Roman religion by including all the gods into a pattern of worship that would satisfy everybody. Such was the position of the Platonist Proclus as late as the fifth century: "It befits the philosopher not to observe the rites of any one city or of only a few nations, but to be the hierophant of the whole world in common."[40]

Generally speaking, however, paganism failed to create a substantial interest on the part of philosophers or writers at large. When Greek and Roman philosophers devoted their efforts to an analysis of religion, it was the metaphysical aspect of it which captured their attention, and very seldom the specific practices. In its rituals paganism appeared as a rather trivial affair, without any orientation toward ethical or moral conduct, devoid of distinct dogmas or tenets which could become the matter for further study, and without a body of writings which would lend itself to exegesis. According to some accepted definitions, it could hardly be called a religion. What rescued it from absurdity was the powerful and

---

[39]Frank E. Manuel, *The Eighteenth Century Confronts the Gods* (New York: Atheneum, 1967) 3.
[40]Quoted in Fowden, *Empire to Commonwealth*, 57.

attractive field it provided for mythological images progressively becoming a part of the human imagination. It could also draw strength from its ability to personify natural forces, especially those which could affect human destiny and that of their society. The distinction between legend and reality was a matter of interpretation or belief. Social forces dictated that even the intelligentsia be part of a religious system that, under rational scrutiny, would baffle the mind of any perceptive person.

Yet paganism survived its own decadence in a process of sublimation which made its gods more real after their death than before. They dominated the artistic and cultural scene many centuries after the religions with which they were connected were hardly remembered in a distant past that failed to be affected by their supposed existence. Without acknowledging it or even knowing it, the church perpetuates a voice of paganism in its midst. On the level of the arts, those voices are much more vibrant. The sibyls in the form of goddesses will continue to grace the ceiling of the Sistine Chapel. Paintings such as the one by Claude Lorrain (Claude Gellée) depicting the Muses with Apollo on Mount Helicon still translate the unending search for inspiration in a vanished world of mythological nostalgia. Poems such as the *Ode to Apollo* and the *Hymn to Apollo* of Keats, the *Hymn of Apollo* of Shelley, Browning's *Apollo and the Fates*, *The Gods of Greece* of Schiller, or some poems of Hölderlin such as *Hyperion* remain the voices of indebtedness for that which has inscribed itself in human memory beyond its original meaning. None of that was meant to celebrate the actual rituals of pagan religion, but it ensured the survival of images supporting the dreams and aspirations of those who still feel connected with the flow of history. If, as Christians believed and proclaimed, the things of this world would pass as mere shadows, then the things that paganism had to offer were more than those mere shadows. They belonged to a universal consciousness worth preserving and celebrating.

The essence of religion expresses itself in transfiguration. The gods must appear freed from the limitations of mortals in mind, soul, body, weakness, or condition. Their human origin must be transcended and transformed by the act of worship. In defense of the humanity of Christ, Arnobius reminded his pagan readers of the way they had deified their own gods who everywhere exhibited human origins and qualities: "Have you not taken from the number of mortals all those whom you now have in your temples; and have you not set them in heaven, and among the constellations?"[41] He then gave a long list of all the honors bestowed upon pagan gods and heroes and begged them to consider that Christ deserved a much greater place of distinction: "With how great distinctions is He to be honoured by us, who, by instilling His truth into our hearts, has freed us from great errors."[42]

Beginning with the fourth century Christianity displaced the gods of Greece and Rome and could boast of a deserved victory. Christ had won over Apollo and the other gods. But even in that case physical death did not mean spiritual extinction. Many gods survived as archetypes of both human frailty and greatness. They no longer lived in their splendid temples. They were freed of human absurdities attributed to them. They found their place in the magnificent art of a splendid Western culture. There they joined Christ, or were joined by him, by a Christ who was transfigured on the mountain and then in the history of a culture that could no longer express its beauty without his participation in it. Through that transfiguration Christ now belongs to the whole of humankind, well beyond the praise of an institutionalized church and well beyond what ecclesiastical theology could have said of him:

> For the unity and variety of the portraits of "Jesus through the centu-
> ries" has demonstrated that there is more in him than is dreamt of in the
> philosophy and christology of the theologians. Within the church, but
> also far beyond its walls, his person and message are, in the phrase of
> Augustine, a "beauty ever ancient, ever new," and now he belongs to
> the world.[43]

The biblical injunction against any representation of the divinity never applied to Christ in the history of Western art.

As the work of the gods among their faithful tends to become too ritualistic, or even boring, it is no longer their physical presence that determines the level of commitment. Essential religion never rested on rational explanations, not even on miraculous and verbal proofs of the power of the gods. As time elapses a religion survives only in its genius

---

[41]Arnobius, AdvGent 1.37 (ANF VI) 422.

[42]Ibid., 1.38 (ANF VI) 423. Similar arguments, but in a different context can be found in Origen, CCel 7.65-67.

[43]Jaroslav Pelikan, *Jesus through the Centuries: His Place in the History of Culture* (New Haven CT: Yale University Press, 1985) 232-33.

to create its own immortality within the religious consciousness of its participants. The writer of the Gospel of John felt it necessary to identify Christ with the logos, that is with the fundamental divine quality which did not begin with the birth of Jesus and did not end with his death on the cross. It was destined to remain the power which could shape and reshape all spiritual aspirations, well beyond any meaning Christians could attribute to it. The perennial element of a divine transfiguration of Christ could never fit the patterns the church would have liked to assign to him. Pagans did not create gospels, nor did they appeal to a logos to immortalize their beliefs and their gods. That was the task of philosophers such as Heraclitus, but not that of pagan theologians, if indeed such ever existed. Even Plutarch could not achieve the transfiguration of Apollo, being much too aware of the liabilities of Delphic religion and the constant annihilation of the good by the unacceptable. Long before that Xenophanes had already warned that the physical nature of the gods could support only an anthropomorphic religion incapable of elevating itself to a more universal monotheism.

The New testament never dealt with pagan gods as such, with either their mortality or immortality. During a missionary journey at Lystra, Paul and Barnabas were mistaken for Zeus and Hermes respectively. They could hardly convince the crowds not to sacrifice to them.[44] The incident is revealing. The crowds are represented as believing in the invisible rule of their gods and to have proclaimed, "The gods have come down to us in the likeness of men!"[45] Except for instances when a divinity needed to appear in a disguised form, as when Athena became the mentor of Telemachus, the notion of divine incarnation was unknown to pagans. Paul and Barnabas did not seize the occasion to preach against heathen divinities, but used the argument that they were not gods themselves, only men. The other known encounter Paul had with pagan cults was in Ephesus in the uproar he created concerning the worship of Artemis.[46] There too the story is inconclusive and may have precipitated the departure of Paul from the city. On another occasion Paul encouraged Christians not to abstain from meats offered to gods, for that would be giving those gods undue power over their lives in the decision of what

---

[44]Acts 14:8-18.
[45]Acts 14:11.
[46]Acts 19:23-41.

they eat or do not eat. In that context Paul voiced an ambivalent assessment of the existence of pagan divinities : "As to the eating of food offered to idols, we know that 'an idol has no real existence,' and that 'there is no God but one.' For although there may be so-called gods in heaven or on earth—as indeed there are many 'gods' and many 'lords'— yet for us there is one God."[47]

The transfiguration of the gods implies their death and a certain fascination with their burial spots. Pagans have put less emphasis on the phenomenon than Christians. Their gods came alive in the arts long after their rule among their faithful and long after their death had been proclaimed. Starting with Helena the church developed a strong fascination for the rediscovery of the cross of Christ. In the modern age, the battle still rages over the authenticity of the Shroud of Turin. What pertains to the death of the divinity never loses its importance. This is perhaps why Paul centered his message on exactly that element: "For I decided to know nothing among you except Jesus Christ and him crucified."[48]

In Christian circles the transfiguration of Christ had to be exclusive and led to the intolerance of any other religious expression. Nietzsche once remarked that the raising of one altar requires the destruction of another. For Christians the principle became absolute to the point of radical separation. Among church fathers who converted to Christianity from paganism we find occasionally, as in the case of Arnobius, an acknowledgment of how they were moved by the pagan ceremonies before becoming Christians. But the two could no longer coexist. The glorified Christ was the sole and supreme ruler of the new kingdom.

Paganism could not maintain its competition with Christianity. In a way it was a more joyous religion, putting the emphasis on the present, though constantly tormented by the social and natural forces which it may have failed to control or assuage. Christianity appeared often more gloomy in its dualistic approach that put the emphasis on future life through a denial of the present one. In a way the church lived in the expectation of its own transfiguration, of that which could rescue it from the evil of the age and take it directly into the eternal presence of its God.

---

[47]First Corinthians 8:4-6a; and see 8:1-13.
[48]First Corinthians 2:2.

    In the Enlightenment, Christianity was opposed to the classical literature it failed to appreciate. Rational explanations greatly diminished the need for transfiguration. In that respect the unpretentious gods of paganism were more appealing. It became fashionable to lament the fact that Christianity was victorious over the empire of Rome, as if that represented one of the greatest catastrophes of history. From Montesquieu to Voltaire, to Gibbon, to Nietszche one finds this leitmotif. The triumph of the Western spirit, even as expressed in its art, and especially in Wagner, over the Greek gods led Nietzsche to qualify such an event as *The Birth of Tragedy*.[49]

    At the beginning of the twentieth century there developed a belief that the ancient gods will return in whatever different form, that there would be a revival of paganism in its true essence. Poets and philosophers have tried to rebuild neopagan movements. It was the most successful under the leadership of Francis Crofts Cornford (1886–1960), a disciple of Jane Ellen Harrison (1850–1928). But it did not last. Much of it was hidden in a silent fog, and the world was not ready for a new Olympian or Delphic religion. There was more appeal in what had happened in a distant past than in what it could mean for the present. It was more appropriate for the gods to remain mute, voiceless, and distant. No human decision can in fact decree the silence of the gods. It is a divine quality directly connected with the mystical nature of gods who have transcended human decisions about them. God's distance and silence mark religion the most profoundly in the Christian system. It is less clear in paganism: "Paganism with its numinous figures is always present; it is constantly coming to the surface as an 'archetype' from the unconscious. . . . And in one way or another we affirm it, and we do not know what we are doing."[50]

    Mystery transcends our ability to verbalize it.

---

[49]The third edition of Nietzsche's *The Birth of Tragedy* (1870–1872) had a new subtitle: *Or, Hellenism and Pessimism* (1886).
    [50]Kornelis H. Miskotte, *When the Gods are Silent*, trans. John W. Doberstein (New York: Harper & Row, 1967) 226.

Epilogue

The omphalos has finally found a permanent abode in the Delphi muse-um, the object of admiration and the symbol of an intriguing past. The museum is where real life has withdrawn to make room for the endless intuition and interpretation of inquiring minds. The artifacts and the gods are frozen there in a silence which proclaims truth no longer as an objective realm of knowledge but as poetry and imagination. The ambiguity of the oracle persists. It is not the task of archaeology to resurrect the voices of the past, just the surroundings in which those voices were possible. There is no language of the stones apart from human spiritual and intellectual participation in distant dreams and sorrows.

There is no original cross in any museum. It was destined to live only in the hearts of the faithful. Its perennial symbolism invades every aspect of Christianity by towering on steeples or hanging over altars. It creates its own ambiguities and forces the Christian world into countless islands of interpretation, often leading to intransigence or even violence.

One can stand on the ruins of Greek and Roman temples or wander amid Christian churches and cathedrals and hope to hear again the voices of old days. There must be somewhere a message that has inscribed itself in the universal consciousness of humankind. As long as the gods are silent the message remains inaudible, and we are left with our doctrines, dogmas, tenets, and systems devoid of revelation and genuine faith.

If one stopped long enough at the Delphic Tholos or at the Church of the Beatitudes, one could hear remnants of messages which refuse to die. But those messages never come back to us in their totality or original impact. If they did, we would probably not understand them. We cannot recreate that which could not survive in its own time. We have now created other worlds, the products of our own cultures. Yet we cannot dismiss the impact of former worlds which allowed us to proceed to the one we now inhabit and cherish. Even in our modern sophistication, we need to be restored and brought back to certain forms of life. A silent past can never be totally dead. It contains too much of our common destiny, of the universal bond of humanity, of our collective meaning.

We have absorbed many of the old rites and superstitions, whether of pagan or Christian origin, and we still search for sacred objects to confirm our faith, and in our better moments still wonder about the prophetic dreams that seemed so important in their own times, but which have lost their meaning in our modern cultures. The survival of Christianity required the removal of pagan divinities. They faded from their place of prominence, but in an indirect and subtle way have been baptized into the new religion. Their temples were in vain. Ours can claim divine favor and permanence. Yet Christianity was more vibrant when it had no history, no great buildings, and no official theologians. Martyrs of early Christianity would not understand the modern church. Every age has to rewrite its history and preserve its traditions. In every age a different Christ dies on a cross and resurrects to a different end. Sometimes many different Christs have to die and resurrect simultaneously in order to satisfy our multiple perspectives. The Christ who walked the roads of Galilee would not be at home in our religious world either. We have vindicated with a vengeance that which he fought against. He has been made into all of what he was not, the battleground of ecumenical councils, of theological and philosophical debates, of fights for supremacy. We can recover his message now only in silence.

For the Greeks it was tragedy, not religion, which defined life. Freedom was never free from fate and destiny. For ordinary mortals Tyche was more powerful than Olympian divinities. The Romans sought to assuage the gods through the proliferation of rites and rituals, hoping thus to avoid what the Greeks could not, seeing the infernal machine grind to its bitter end. It was not successful. The empire collapsed, and so did its gods. Christians sharpened the notion that history must equal truth, though final redemption lies beyond history. God speaks or remains silent, depending on how closely his will is implemented. That too remains ambiguous.

While the search for an elusive center continues, the omphalos and the cross will remain symbols challenging the heart and mind, translating to us neither God's total absence nor his full presence in a world in turmoil. The voice of Apollo was lost in the ruins of Delphi and other shrines of the Roman empire. The message of Christ still stirs the faith of multitudes of Christians, though they are unable to agree on its meaning. For several centuries in the early church the question remained very pertinent: Christ *or* Apollo. Church fathers tried to give a clear answer to that. Yet more and more there emerged a tacit recognition that the right approach could have been: Christ *and* Apollo, the omphalos *and* the cross.

There is room for both in the universal religious consciousness. There are sacred dimensions thay survive the onslaught of time and find expression in that which, at first, appeared totally alien to it. The divine center is everywhere and nowhere, and to its quest there shall be no end.

Appendixes

Justin Martyr on the Sibyl.
From *Cohortatio ad Gentiles* 37. ANF I.288-89.

And you may in part easily learn the right religion from the ancient Sibyl, who by some kind of potent inspiration teaches you, through her oracular predictions, truths which seem to be much akin to the teaching of the prophets. She, they say, was of Babylonian extraction, being the daughter of Berosus, who wrote the Chaldæan history. And when she had crossed over (how, I know not) into the region of Campania, she there uttered her oracular sayings in a city called Cumæ, six miles from Baiæ, where the hot springs of Campania are found. And being in that city, we saw also a certain place, in which we were shown a very large basilica cut out of one stone; a vast affair, and worthy of all admiration. And they who had heard it from their fathers as part of their country's tradition, told us that it was here she used to publish her oracles. And in the middle of the basilica they showed us three receptacles cut out of one stone, in which, when filled with water, they said that she washed, and having put on her robe again, retires into the inmost chamber of the basilica, which is still a part of the one stone; and sitting in the middle of the chamber on a high rostrum and throne, thus proclaims her oracles. And both by many other writers has the Sibyl been mentioned as a prophetess, and also by Plato in his *Phædrus*. And plato seems to me to have counted prophets divinely inspired when he read her prophecies. For he saw that what she had long ago predicted was accomplished; and on this account he expresses in the Dialogue with Meno his wonder at and admiration of prophets in the following terms: "Those whom we call prophetic persons we should rightly name divine. And not least would we say that they are divine, and are raised to the prophetic ecstasy by the inspiration and possession of God, when they correctly speak of many and important matters, and yet know nothing of what they are saying."—plainly and manifestly referring to the prophecies of the Sibyl. For, while the poets who, after their poems are penned, have power to correct and polish, specially in the way of increasing the accuracy of their verse, she was filled indeed with prophecy at the time of the inspiration, but as soon as the inspiration ceased, there ceased also the remembrance of all she had said. And this indeed was the cause why some only, and not all, the meters of the verses of the Sibyl were preserved. For we ourselves, when in that city, ascertained from our *cicerone*, who showed us the places in which she used to prophesy, that there was a certain coffer made of brass in which they said that her remains were preserved. And besides all else which they told us as they had heard it from their fathers, they said also that they who then took down her prophecies, being illiterate persons, often went quite astray from the accuracy of the metres; and this, they said, was the cause of the want of the meter in some of the verses, the prophetess having no remembrance of what she had said, after the possession and inspiration ceased, and the reporters having, through their lack of education, failed to record the metres with accuracy. And on this account, it is manifest that Plato had an eye to the prophecies of the Sibyl when he said this about prophets, for he said, "When they correctly speak of many and important matters, and yet know nothing of what they are saying."

[The passage to which Justin refers is in the *Meno* 99 D.]

Appendix 2

Justin: *Epistle of Marcus Aurelius to the Senate. First Apology.* ANF I.187.

The Emperor Cæsar Marcus Aurelius Antoninus, Germanicus, Parthicus, Sarmaticus, to the People of Rome, and to the sacred Senate, greeting: I explained to you my grand design, and what advantages I gained on the confines of Germany, with much labour and suffering, in consequence of the circumstance that I was surrounded by the enemy; I myself being shut up in Carnuntum by seventy-four cohorts, nine miles off. And the enemy being at hand, the scouts pointed out to us, and our general Pompeianus showed us that there was close on us a mass of a mixed multitude of 977,000 men, which indeed we saw; and I was shut up by this vast host, having with me only a battalion composed of the first, tenth, double and marine legions. Having then examined my own position, and my host, with respect to the vast mass of barbarians and of the enemy, I quickly betook myself to prayer to the gods of my country. But being disregarded by them, I summoned those who among us go by the name of Christians. And having made inquiry, I discovered a great number and vast host of them, and raged against them, which was by no means becoming; for afterwards I learned their power. Wherefore they began the battle, not by preparing weapons, nor arms, nor bugles; for such preparation is hateful to them, on account of the God they bear about in their conscience. Therefore it is probable that those whom we suppose to be atheists, have God as their ruling power entrenched in their conscience. For having cast themselves on the ground, they prayed not only for me, but also for the whole army as it stood, that they might be delivered from the present thirst and famine. For during five days we had got no water, because there was none; for we were in the heart of Germany, and in the enemy's territory. And simultaneously with their casting themselves on the ground, and praying to God (a God of whom I am ignorant), water poured from heaven, upon us most refreshingly cool, but upon the enemies of Rome a withering hail. And immediately we recognised the presence of God following on the prayer—a God unconquerable and indestructible. Founding upon this, then, let us pardon such as are Christians, lest they pray for and obtain such a weapon against ourselves. And I counsel that no such person be accused on the ground of his being a Christian. But if any one be found laying to the charge of a Christian that he is a Christian, I desire that it be made manifest that he who is accused as a Christian, and acknowledges that he is one, is accused of nothing else than only this, that he is a Christian; but that he who arraigns him be burned alive. And I further desire, that he who is entrusted with the government of the province shall not compel the Christian, who confesses and certifies such a matter, to retract; neither shall he commit him. And I desire that these things be confirmed by a decree of the Senate. And I command this my edict to be published in the Forum of Trajan, in order that it may be read. The prefect Vitrasius Pollio will see that it be transmitted to all the provinces round about, and that no one who wishes to make use of or to possess it be hindered from obtaining a copy from the document I now publish.

Appenϑix 3
The Edict of Milan

Text of Lactantius
From *De mortibus persecutorum* 48. ANF VII.320.

And therefore we judged it a salutary measure, and one highly consonant to right reason, that no man should be denied leave of attaching himself to the rites of the Christians, or to whatever other religion his mind
directed him, that thus the supreme Divinity, to whose worship we freely
devote ourselves, might continue to vouchsafe His favour and beneficence
to us. And accordingly we give you to know that, without regard to any
provisos in our former orders to you concerning the Christians, all who
choose that religion are to be permitted, freely and absolutely, to remain
in it, and not to be disturbed any ways, or molested. And we thought fit
to be thus special in the things committed to your charge, that you might
understand that the indulgence which we have granted in matters of
religion to the Christians is ample and unconditional; and perceive at the
same time that the open and free exercise of their respective religions is
granted to all others, as well as to the Christians. For it befits the well-
ordered state and the tranquility of our times that each individual be
allowed, according to his own choice, to worship the Divinity.

Text of Eusebius
From *Historia ecclesiastica* 10.5.2-5. NPNF-2 I.379.

Perceiving long ago that religious liberty ought not to be denied, but
that it ought to be granted to the judgment and desire of each individual
to perform his religious duties according to his own choice, we had given
orders that every man, Christians as well as others, should preserve the
faith of his own sect and religion. . . . We resolved, that is, to grant both
to the Christians and to all men freedom to follow the religion which they
choose, that whatever heavenly divinity exists may be propitious to us
and to all that live under our government. We have, therefore, determined, with sound and upright purpose, that liberty is to be denied to no
one, to choose and to follow the religious observances of the Christians,
but that to each one freedom is to be given to devote his mind to that

religion which he may think adapted to himself, in order that the Deity may exhibit to us in all things his accustomed care and favor.

Appendix 4

Julian's Rescript on Christian Teachers
From *The Works of the Emperor Julian*. LCL III.117-23.

I hold that a proper education results, not in laboriously acquired symmetry of phrases and language, but in a healthy condition of mind, I mean a mind that has understanding and true opinions about things good and evil, honourable and base. Therefore, when a man thinks one thing and teaches his pupils another, in my opinion he fails to educate exactly in proportion as he fails to be an honest man. And if the divergence between a man's convictions and his utterances is merely in trivial matters, that can be tolerated somehow, though it is wrong. But if in matters of the greatest importance a man has certain opinions and teaches the contrary, what is that but the conduct of hucksters, and not honest but thoroughly dissolute men in that they praise most highly the things that they believe to be most worthless, thus cheating and enticing by their praises those to whom they desire to transfer their worthless wares. Now all who profess to teach anything whatever ought to be men of upright character, and ought not to harbour in their souls opinions irreconcilable with what they publicly profess; and, above all, I believe it is necessary that those who associate with the young and teach them rhetoric should be of that upright character; for they expound the writings of the ancients, whether they be rhetoricians or grammarians, and still more if they are sophists. For these claim to teach, in addition to other things, not only the use of words, but morals also, and they assert that political philosophy is their peculiar field. Let us leave aside, for the moment, the question whether this is true or not. But while I applaud them for aspiring to such high pretensions, I should applaud them still more if they did not utter falsehoods and convict themselves of thinking one thing and teaching their pupils another. What! Was it not the gods who revealed all their learning to Homer, Hesiod, Demosthenes, Herodotus, Thucydides, Isocrates, and Lysias? Did not these men think that they were consecrated, some to Hermes, others to the Muses? I think it absurd that men who expound the works of these writers should dishonour the gods whom they used to honour. Yet, though I think this absurd, I do not say that they ought to change their opinions and then instruct the young. But I give them this choice; either not to teach what they do not think admirable, or, if they wish to teach, let them first really persuade their pupils that neither Homer nor Hesiod nor any of these writers whom they expound and have declared to be guilty of impiety, folly and error in regard to the gods, is such as they declare. For since they make a livelihood and receive pay from the works of those writers, they thereby confess that they are most shamefully greedy of gain, and that, for the sake of a few drachmae, they would put up with anything. It is true that, until now, there were many excuses for not attending the temples, and the terror that threatened on all sides absolved men for concealing the truest beliefs about the gods. But since the gods have granted us liberty, it seems to me absurd that men should teach what they do not believe to be sound. But if they believe that those whose interpreters they are and for whom they sit, so to speak, in the seat of the prophets, were wise men, let them be the first to emulate their piety towards the gods. If, however, they think that those writers were in error with respect to the most honoured gods, then let them betake themselves to the churches of the Galilaeans to expound Matthew and Luke, since you Galilaeans are obeying them when you ordain that men shall refrain from temple worship. For my part, I wish that your ears and your tongues might be "born anew," as you would say, as regards these things in which may I ever have part, and all who think and act as is pleasing to me.

For religious and secular teachers let there be a general ordinance to this effect: Any youth who wishes to attend the schools is not excluded; nor indeed would it be reasonable to shut out from the best way boys who are still too ignorant to know which way to turn, and to overawe them into being led against their will to the beliefs of their ancestors. Though indeed it might be proper to cure these, even against their will, as one cures the insane, except that we concede indulgence to all for this sort of disease. For we ought, I think, to teach, but not punish, the demented.

Bibliography

Acts of the Holy Apostle and Evangelist John the Theologian. Translated by Alexander Walker. ANF VIII. 1981.

Aeschylus. *Agamemnon*. Translated by Herbert Weir Smyth. LCL II. 1971.

_____. *The Libation Bearers (The Choephori)*. Translated by Herbert Weir Smyth. LCL II. 1971.

_____. *Eumenides*. Translated by Herbert Weir Smyth. LCL II. 1971.

Amandry, Pierre. *La Mantique apollonienne à Delphes: Essai sur le fonctionnement de l'Oracle*. Paris: Boccard, 1950.

Ambrose. *Concerning Virgins, to Marcellina, His Sister (De virginitate)*. Translated by H. de Romestin. NPNF-2 X. 1979.

_____. *Duties of the Clergy (De officiis ministrorum)*. Translated by H. de Romestin. NPNF-2 X. 1979.

_____. *Letters*. Translated by H. de Romestin. NPNF-2 X. 1979.

_____. *Selections from the Letters of Ambrose and Memorial of Symmachus*. Translated by H. de Romestin. NPNF-2 X. 1979.

Ammianus Marcellinus. *Res gestae, Ammiani Marcelleni rerum gestarum libri qui supersunt*. Three volumes. Translated by John C. Rolfe. LCL. 1963–1964.

Apollodorus. *The Library*. Two volumes. Translated by Sir James George Frazer. LCL. 1918.

Aristides. *The Apology of Aristides the Philosopher*. Translated by D. M. Kay. ANF X. 1980.

Aristophanes. *The Peace*. Translated by Benjamin Bickley Rogers. LCL II. 1924.

Arnobius. *The Seven Books of Arnobius Against the Heathen (Adversus gentes)*. Translated by Hamilton Bryce. ANF VI. 1982.

Athanasius. *Against the Heathen (Contra gentes)*. Edited by Archibald Robertson. NPNF-2 IV. 1980.

_____. *On the Incarnation of the Word (De incarnatione verbi Dei)*. Edited by Archibald Robertson. NPNF-2 IV. 1980.

_____. *To the Bishops of Egypt (Ad episcopos Aegypti)*. Edited by Archibald Robertson. NPNF-2 IV. 1980.

Athenagoras. *A Plea for the Christians (Legatio pro christianis)*. Translated by B. P. Pratten. ANF II. 1983.

Aubertin, Charles. *Étude critique sur les rapports supposés entre Sénèque et Saint Paul*. Paris, 1857. Reissued as *Études sur les rapports entre le philosophe et l'apôtre*. Paris: Didier, 1972.

Augustine. *Against the Epistle of Manichaeus Called Fundamental (Contra epistolam Manichaei quam vocant fundamenti)*. Translated by Richard Stothert. NPNF-1 IV. 1983.

_____. *The City of God (De civitate Dei)*. Translated by Marcus Dods. NPNF-1 II. 1979.

_____. *Confessions*. Translated by J. G. Pilkington. NPNF-1 I. 1979.

_____. *Expositions on the Book of Psalms*. Edited by A. Cleveland Coxe. NPNF-1 VIII. 1983.

_____. *The Harmony of the Gospels (De consensu evangelistarum)*. Translated by S. D. F. Salmond. NPNF-1 VI. 1979.

_____. *Lectures or Tractates on the Gospel according to St. John (In Joannis evangelium tractatus)*. Translated by John Gibb and James Innes. NPNF-1 VII. 1983.

_____. *On Christian Doctrine (De doctrina christiana)*. Translated by J. F. Shaw. NPNF-1 II. 1979.

_____. *Our Lord's Sermon on the Mount According to Matthew (De sermone domini in monte secundum Matthaeum)*. Translated by William Findlay. NPNF-1 VI. 1979.

_____. *Reply to Faustus the Manichaean (Contra Faustum Manichaeum)*. Translated by Richard Stothert. NPNF-1 IV. 1983.

Barnabas. *The Epistle of Barnabas*. Translated by Kirsopp Lake. In *Apostolic Fathers*. LCL I. 1970.

Barnes, Timothy, D. *Constantine and Eusebius*. Cambridge: Harvard University Press, 1981.

Barrow, R. H. *Prefect and Emperor: The Relationes of Symmachus*. Oxford: Clarendon Press, 1973.

Bartlett, John, R. *Jews in the Hellenistic World: Josephus, Aristeas, the Sibylline Oracles, Eupolemus*. Cambridge: Cambridge University Press, 1985.

Basil, *Address to Young Men on Reading Greek Literature*. Translated by Roy Joseph Deferrari and Martin R. P. McGuire. LCL IV. 1939.

_____. *Letters*. Translated by Bloomfield Jackson. NPNF-2 VIII. 1978.

Bidez, Joseph. *Vie de Porphyre le philosophe néoplatonicien avec les fragments des traités ΠΕΡΙ ΑΓΑΛΜΑΤΩΝ et DE REGRESSU ANIMAE*. Hildesheim: Georg Olms Verlagsbuchhandlung, 1964.

Boethius. *The Consolation of Philosophy*. Translated by V. E. Watts. New York: Penguin Books, 1969.

Boissier, Gaston. *La Fin du paganisme: Etude sur les dernières luttes religieuses en occident au quatrième siècle*. Two volumes. Paris: Hachette, 1907.

————. *La Religion Romaine d'Auguste aux Antonins.* Two volumes. Paris: Hachette, 1892.

Bousset, Wilhelm. *Kyrios Christos. A History of Belief in Christ from the Beginnings of Christianity to Irenaeus.* Translated by John E. Steely. Nashville: Abingdon Press, 1970.

Bowersock, Glen Warren. *Martyrdom and Rome.* Cambridge: Cambridge University Press, 1995.

Boyd, William K. *The Ecclesiastical Edicts of the Theodosian Code.* Studies in History, Economics, and Public Law 24/2. New York: Columbia University Press, 1905.

Bregman, Jay. *Synesius of Cyrene: Philosopher-Bishop.* Berkeley: University of California Press, 1982.

Brown, Peter. *The Making of Late Antiquity.* Cambridge: Harvard University Press, 1978.

————. *Power and Persuasion In Late Antiquity: Towards a Christian Empire.* Madison: University of Wisconsin, 1992.

————. *The World of Late Antiquity A.D. 150–750.* New York: Hartcourt Brace Jovanovich, 1971.

Browning, Robert. *The Emperor Julian.* Berkeley: University of California Press, 1976.

Bultmann, Rudolf. *Jesus and the Word.* Translated by Louise Pettibone Smith and Erminie Huntress Lantero. New York: Charles Scribner's Sons, 1958.

Burckhardt, Jacob. *The Age of Constantine the Great.* Translated by Moses Hadas. Berkeley: University of California Press, 1983.

Burkert, Walter. *Greek Religion.* Translated by John Raffan. Cambridge: Harvard University Press, 1985.

Burguière, Paul et Évieux, Pierre. *Cyrille d'Alexandrie: Contre Julien.* Tome 1. Livre 1 et 2. Paris: Les Éditions du Cerf, 1985.

Burney, Charles F. *The Book of Judges.* London: Rivingtons, 1918.

Cameron, Averil. *Christianity and the Rhetoric of Empire: The Development of Christian Discourse.* Berkeley: University of California Press, 1991.

Campbell, Joseph. *The Masks of God: Primitive Mythology.* New York: The Viking Press, 1970.

Chrysostom, John. *The Homilies on the Statues.* Translated by W. R. W. Stephens. NPNF-1 IX. 1983.

————. *Homilies on First Corinthians.* Oxford Translation. NPNF-1 XII. 1983.

————. *Homilies on S. Ignatius and S. Babylas.* Translated by W. R. W. Stephens. NPNF-1 IX. 1983.

————. *Homilies on the Gospel of St. Matthew.* Translated by Sir George Prevost. NPNF-1 X. 1983.

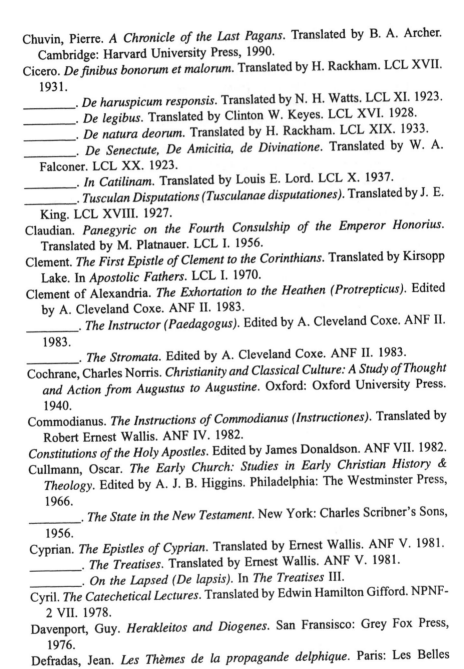

Chuvin, Pierre. *A Chronicle of the Last Pagans.* Translated by B. A. Archer. Cambridge: Harvard University Press, 1990.

Cicero. *De finibus bonorum et malorum.* Translated by H. Rackham. LCL XVII. 1931.

_____. *De haruspicum responsis.* Translated by N. H. Watts. LCL XI. 1923.

_____. *De legibus.* Translated by Clinton W. Keyes. LCL XVI. 1928.

_____. *De natura deorum.* Translated by H. Rackham. LCL XIX. 1933.

_____. *De Senectute, De Amicitia, de Divinatione.* Translated by W. A. Falconer. LCL XX. 1923.

_____. *In Catilinam.* Translated by Louis E. Lord. LCL X. 1937.

_____. *Tusculan Disputations (Tusculanae disputationes).* Translated by J. E. King. LCL XVIII. 1927.

Claudian. *Panegyric on the Fourth Consulship of the Emperor Honorius.* Translated by M. Platnauer. LCL I. 1956.

Clement. *The First Epistle of Clement to the Corinthians.* Translated by Kirsopp Lake. In *Apostolic Fathers.* LCL I. 1970.

Clement of Alexandria. *The Exhortation to the Heathen (Protrepticus).* Edited by A. Cleveland Coxe. ANF II. 1983.

_____. *The Instructor (Paedagogus).* Edited by A. Cleveland Coxe. ANF II. 1983.

_____. *The Stromata.* Edited by A. Cleveland Coxe. ANF II. 1983.

Cochrane, Charles Norris. *Christianity and Classical Culture: A Study of Thought and Action from Augustus to Augustine.* Oxford: Oxford University Press. 1940.

Commodianus. *The Instructions of Commodianus (Instructiones).* Translated by Robert Ernest Wallis. ANF IV. 1982.

Constitutions of the Holy Apostles. Edited by James Donaldson. ANF VII. 1982.

Cullmann, Oscar. *The Early Church: Studies in Early Christian History & Theology.* Edited by A. J. B. Higgins. Philadelphia: The Westminster Press, 1966.

_____. *The State in the New Testament.* New York: Charles Scribner's Sons, 1956.

Cyprian. *The Epistles of Cyprian.* Translated by Ernest Wallis. ANF V. 1981.

_____. *The Treatises.* Translated by Ernest Wallis. ANF V. 1981.

_____. *On the Lapsed (De lapsis).* In *The Treatises* III.

Cyril. *The Catechetical Lectures.* Translated by Edwin Hamilton Gifford. NPNF-2 VII. 1978.

Davenport, Guy. *Herakleitos and Diogenes.* San Fransisco: Grey Fox Press, 1976.

Defradas, Jean. *Les Thèmes de la propagande delphique.* Paris: Les Belles Lettres, 1972.

Deissmann, Adolf. *Paul: A Study in Social and Religious History*. Translated by William E. Wilson. New York: Harper & Row, 1957.

Delcourt, Marie. *L'Oracle à Delphes*. Paris: Payot, 1955.

Dempsey, T. *The Delphic Oracle: Its Early History Influence and Fall*. New York: Benjamin Blom, 1972.

des Places, Édouard. *Oracles Chaldaïques: Avec un choix de commentaires ancients*. Paris: Les Belles Lettres, 1971.

Detienne, Marcel. *Apollon le couteau à la main: Une approche expérimentale du polythéisme grec*. Paris: Gallimard, 1998.

De Tolnay, Charles. *The Sistine Ceiling*. Princeton NJ: Princeton University Press, 1949.

Dio Cassius. *Roman History*. Nine volumes. Translated by Ernest Cary. LCL. 1914–1927.

Diodorus Siculus. *Library of History*. Twelve volumes. Translated by C. H. Oldfather, C. L. Sherman, C. Bradford, Russel M. Geer, and Francis R. Walton. LCL. 1933–1963.

Diogenes Laertius. *Lives of Eminent Philosophers*. Two volumes. Translated by R. D. Hicks. LCL. 1972.

Diognetus. *The Epistle to Diognetus*. Translated by Kirsopp Lake. In *Apostolic Fathers*. LCL II. 1970.

Dionysius. *Extant Fragments*. Translated by S. D. F. Salmond. ANF VI. 1982.

Dionysius of Halicarnassus. *Roman Antiquities*. Seven volumes. Translated by Ernest Cary. LCL. 1937–1950.

Dodd. C. H. *Historical Tradition in the Fourth Gospel*. Cambridge: Cambridge University Press, 1963.

Dodds, E. R. *The Greeks and the Irrational*. Berkeley: University of California Press, 1951.

_____. *Pagan and Christian in an Age of Anxiety: Some Aspects of Religious Experience from Marcus Aurelius to Constantine*. New York: W. W. Norton, 1965.

Doerris, Hermann. *Constantine and Religious liberty*. Translated by Roland A. Bainton. New Haven CT: Yale University Press, 1960.

Drachmann, Anders Bjørn. *Atheism in Antiquity*. Translated by Ingeborg Andersen. Copenhagen: Gyldendal, 1922.

Easton, B. S. "The Purpose of Acts." *Theology*. Occasional Papers 6. London, 1936.

Edwards, Douglas R. *Religion and Power: Pagans, Jews, and Christians in the Greek East*. New York: Oxford University Press, 1996.

Eliade, Mircea. *The Myth of the Eternal Return or, Cosmos and History*. Translated by Willard R. Trask. Princeton NJ: Princeton University Press, 1954.

Empedocles. *Katharmoi.* In Freeman, Kathleen. *Ancilla to the Pre-Socratic Philosophers.* Cambridge MA: Harvard University Press, 1948.

Epictetus. *The Discourses as Reported by Arrian.* Two volumes. Translated by W. A. Oldfather. LCL. 1964.

_____. *Fragments.* Translated by W. A. Oldfather. LCL II. 1964.

Euripides. *Alcestis.* Translated by Arthur S. Way. LCL IV. 1971.

_____. *Electra.* Translated by Philip Vellacott. In *Medea and Other Plays.* Baltimore: Penguin Books, 1963.

_____. *Ion.* Translated by Arthur S. Way. LCL IV. 1971.

_____. *Iphigeneia in Taurica.* Translated by Arthur S. Way. LCL II. 1965.

_____. *The Phoenician Maidens.* Translated by Arthur S. Way. LCL III. 1971.

Eusebius. *Church History (Historia ecclesiastica).* Translated by Arthur Cushman McGiffert. NPNF-2 I. 1982.

_____. *The Life of Constantine (Vita Constantini).* Translated by Ernest Cushing Richardson. NPNF-2 I. 1982.

_____. *The Oration of the Emperor Constantine to the Assembly of the Saints (Oratio ad sanctum coetum).* Translated by Ernest Cushing Richardson. NPNF-2 I. 1982.

_____. *Preparation for the Gospel (Praeparatio evangelica).* Two volumes. Translated by Edwin Hamilton Gifford. Grand Rapids MI: Baker Book House, 1981.

_____. *The Proof of the Gospel Being the Demonstratio Evangelica.* Two volumes. Translated by W. J. Ferrar. London: S.P.C.K., 1920.

Farnell, Lewis Richard. *The Cults of the Greek Cities.* Five volumes. Oxford: Clarendon Press, 1907.

Firmicus Maternus. *The Error of the Pagan Religions (De errore profanarum religionum).* Translated by Clarence A. Forbes. New York: Newman Press, 1970.

Flacelière, Robert. *Greek Oracles.* Translated by Douglas Garman. New York: W. W. Norton, 1965.

Fleury, Amédée. *Saint Paul et Sénèque: Recherches sur les rapports du philosophe avec l'apôtre et sur l'infiltration du christianisme naissant à travers le paganisme.* Two volumes. Paris: Librairie Philosophique de Ladrange, 1853.

Fontenrose, Joseph. *The Delphic Oracle: Its Responses and Operations with a Catalogue of Responses.* Berkeley: University of California Press, 1978.

_____. *PYTHON: A Study of Delphic Myth and its Origins.* Berkeley: University of California Press, 1959.

Fowden, Garth. *The Egyptian Hermes: A Historical Approach to the Late Pagan Mind.* Princeton NJ: Princeton University Press, 1986.

————. *Empire to Commonwealth: Consequences of Monotheism in Late Antiquity*. Princeton NJ: Princeton University Press, 1993.

Fox, Robin Lane. *Pagans and Christians*. New York: Harper & Row, 1986.

Frazer, Sir James George. *The Golden Bough: A Study in Magic and Religion*. New York: Macmillan, 1922.

————. *Pausanias's Description of Greece*. Six volumes. New York: Macmillan, 1913.

Freeman, Kathleen. *Ancilla to the Pre-Socratic Philosophers*. Cambridge: Harvard University Press, 1948.

Frend, W. H. C. *The Early Church*. Philadelphia: J. B. Lippincott, 1966.

————. *Martyrdom and Persecution in the Early Church: A Study of a Conflict from the Maccabees to Donatus*. Garden City NY: Doubleday, 1967.

Galletier, Édouard. *Panegyrici Latini. Panégyriques Latins. Texte établi et traduit par Édouard Galletier*. Paris: Les Belles Lettres, 1949–1952.

Gaudemet, Jean. *L'Eglise dans l'Empire romain: IVe–Ve siècles*. Histoire du droit et des institutions de l'Eglise en Occident. Paris: Sirey, 1958; 1990.

Gibbon, Edward. *The History of the Decline and Fall of the Roman Empire*. Five volumes. New edition ed. Henry Hart Milman. Repr.: Philadelphia: Henry T. Coates, 1880 (after edition of 1848ff.); orig., 1776–1788.

Gilson, Etienne. *The Spirit of Mediaeval Philosophy*. Translated by A. H. C. Downes. New York: Charles Scribner's Sons, 1940.

Goguel, Maurice. *Au seuil de l'Evangile, Jean-Baptiste*. Paris: Payot, 1928.

————. *Les premiers temps de l'Eglise*. Neuchatel: Delachaux et Niestlé, 1949.

Goldin, Judah. *The Living Talmud: The Wisdom of the Fathers and Its Classical Commentaries*. Chicago: University of Chicago Press, 1957.

The Gospel of Thomas. Edited by James M. Robinson. In *The Nag Hammadi Library*. San Francisco: Harper & Row, 1978.

Gregory of Nazianzus. "The Last Farewell." *Oration* 42. Translated by Charles Gordon Browne and James Edward Swallow. NPNF-2 VII. 1978.

————. *Oration 40 On Holy Baptism*. Translated by Charles Gordon Browne and James Edward Swallow. NPNF-2 VII. 1978.

————. *Oration 39 On the Holy Lights*. Translated by Charles Gordon Browne and James Edward Swallow. NPNF-2 VII. 1978.

Gregory of Nyssa. *Against Eunomius (Contra Eunomium)*. Translated by William Moore. NPNF-2 V. 1979

————. *The Great Catechism*. Translated by William Moore. NPNF-2 V. 1979.

Guignebert, Charles. *Jesus*. Translated by S. H. Hooke. New York: University Books, 1956.

_____. *Tertullien: Etude sur ses sentiments à l'égard de l'empire et de la société civile*. Paris: Ernest Leroux, 1901.

Hadot, Pierre. *Porphyre et Victorinus*. Two volumes. Paris: Études Augustiniennes, 1968.

Harnack, Adolf. *The Mission and Expansion of Christianity in the first Three Centuries*. Translated by James Moffatt. New York: Harper & Brothers, 1961.

Harrison, Jane Ellen. *Prolegomena to the Study of Greek Religion*. Cleveland: World Publishing Company, 1959.

Hegel, Georg Wilhelm Friedrich. *On Tragedy*. Edited by Anne and Henry Paolucci. New York: Harper & Row, 1962.

Heraclitus. *On the Universe*. Translated by W. H. S. Jones. In *Hippocrates*. LCL IV. 1931.

Herodotus. *The Histories*. Translated by Aubrey de Sélincourt. New York: Penguin Books, 1954.

Hesiod. *The Homeric Hymns and Homerica*. Translated by Hugh G. Evelyn-White. LCL. 1914.

_____. *Works and Days*. Translated by Dorothea Wender. In *Hesiod and Theognis*. New York: Penguin Books, 1973.

Hoffmann, R. Joseph. *Porphyry's Against the Christians: The Literary Remains*. Amherst: Prometheus Books, 1994.

Homer. *The Iliad*. Translated by A. T. Murray. Two volumes. LCL. 1924–1925.

Homer. *The Odyssey*. Translated by A. T. Murray. Two volumes. LCL. 1919.

Hyginus. *The Myths of Hyginus*. Translated and edited by Mary Grant. Lawrence: University of Kansas Press, 1960.

Ignatius. *Epistle to the Ephesians*. Translated by Kirsopp Lake. In *Apostolic Fathers*. LCL I. 1970.

_____. *Martyrdom of Ignatius*. Author and translator unknown. ANF I. 1981.

_____. *To Polycarp*. Translated by Kirsopp Lake. In *Apostolic Fathers*. LCL I. 1970.

Irenaeus. *Against Heresies (Adversus haereses)*. Edited by A. Cleveland Coxe. ANF I. 1981.

Jeanmaire, Henri. *Dionysos: Histoire du culte de Bacchus*. Paris: Payot, 1978.

Jerome. *Against Jovinianus (Adversus Jovinianum)*. Translated by William Henry Fremantle. NPNF-2 VI. 1979.

_____. *Against Vigilantius (Contra Vigilantium)*. Translated by William Henry Fremantle. NPNF-2 VI. 1979.

_____. *Letters*. Translated by William Henry Fremantle. NPNF-2 VI. 1979.

_____. *Prefaces*. Translated by William Henry Fremantle. NPNF-2 VI. 1979.

Jerome and Gennadius. *Lives of Illustrious Men*. Translated by Ernest Cushing Richardson. NPNF-2 III. 1979.

Johnson, Paul. *A History of Christianity*. New York: Atheneum. 1976.

Jones, Arnold Hugh Martin. *Constantine and the Conversion of Europe.* Baltimore: Penguin, 1972.

————. *The Later Roman Empire 284–602: A Social Economic and Administrative Survey.* Two volumes. Norman: University of Oklahoma Press, 1964.

Jones, Prudence and Pennick, Nigel. *A History of Pagan Europe.* London: Routledge, 1995.

Josephus, Flavius. *The Works of Flavius Josephus.* Four volumes. Translated by William Whiston. Grand Rapids MI: Baker Book House, 1984.

Julian. *The Works of the Emperor Julian.* Three volumes. Translated by Wilmer Cave Wright. LCL. 1913–1923.

Justin Martyr. *Dialogue with Trypho.* Translator unknown. ANF I. 1981.

————. *First and Second Apology,* Translator unknown. ANF I. 1981.

————. *Hortatory Address to the Greeks (Cohortatio ad gentiles).* Translated by Marcus Dods. ANF I. 1981.

————. *On the Sole Government of God.* Translated by G. Reith. ANF I. 1981.

Juvenal. *Satires.* Translated by G. G. Ramsay. LCL. 1918.

Kerényi, C. *The Gods of the Greeks.* Translated by Norman Cameron. New York: Thames and Hudson, 1988.

King, Charles William. *Julian the Emperor.* London: George Bell and Sons, 1888.

King, N. Q. *The Emperor Theodosius and the Establishment of Christianity.* London: SCM Press, 1961.

Klausner, Joseph. *The Messianic Idea in Israel: From its Beginning to the Completion of the Mishnah.* Translated by W. F. Stinespring. New York: Macmillan, 1955.

————. *From Jesus to Paul.* Translated by W. F. Stinespring. New York: Macmillan, 1943.

Labriolle, Pierre de. *La Réaction païenne: Etude sur la polémique antichrétienne du Ier au VIe siècle.* Paris: Artisan du Livre. 1948.

Lactantius. *The Divine Institutes (Divinae institutiones).* Translated by William Fletcher. ANF VII. 1982.

————. *The Epitome of the Divine Institutes (Epitoma divinae institutiones).* Translated by William Fletcher. ANF VII. 1982.

————. *Of the Manner in which the Persecutors Died (De mortibus persecutorum).* Translated by William Fletcher. ANF VII. 1982.

————. *A Treatise on the Anger of God, (De ira Dei).* Translated by William Fletcher. ANF VII. 1982.

Latte, Kurt. "The Coming of the Pythia." *Harvard Theological Review* 33 (1940): 9-18.

Libanius. *Pro templis. Oration 30 to the Emperor Theodosius, for the Temples.* Translated by A. F. Norman, LCL II. 1977.

_____. *Selected Orations and letters.* Three volumes. Translated by A. F. Norman. LCL. 1969.

Liebeschuetz, John Hugo Wolfgang Gideon. *Barbarians and Bishops: Army, Church, and State in the Age of Arcadius and Chrysostom.* Oxford: Oxford University Press, 1990.

Lieu, Samuel N. C., editor. *The Emperor Julian: Panegyric and Polemic.* Liverpool: Liverpool University Press, 1986.

Lightfoot, J. B. *Saint Paul's Epistle to the Philippians.* Grand Rapids MI: Zondervan Publishing House, 1967.

Livy. Fourteen volumes. Translated by B. O. Foster, F. G. Moore, Evan T. Sage, and E. T. Schlesinger. LCL. 1919–1959.

Loisy, Alfred Firmin. *The Origins of the New Testament.* Translated by L. P. Jacks. New York: Collier Books, 1962.

Lucretius. *On the Nature of Things. (De rerum natura).* Translated by H. A. J. Munro. New York: Washingron Square Press, 1965.

Manuel, Frank E. *The Eighteenth Century Confronts the Gods.* New York: Atheneum, 1967.

Marcus Aurelius. *The Meditations.* Translated by G. M. A. Grube. New York: Bobbs-Merrill, 1963.

Marrou, Henri-Irénée. *Saint Augustin et la fin de la culture antique.* Paris: Editions E. de Boccard, 1958.

Meeks, Wayne A., and Wilken, Robert L. *Jews and Christians in Antioch in the First Four Centuries of the Common Era.* Missoula MT: Scholars Press for the Society of Biblical Literature, 1978.

Meslin, Pierre. *Le Christianisme dans l'empire romain.* Paris: Presses Universitaires de France, 1970.

Methodius. *Fragments.* Translated by William R. Clark. ANF VI. 1982.

Minnerath, Roland. *De Jérusalem à Rome: Pierre et l'unité de l'église apostolique.* Paris: Beauchesne, 1994.

_____. *Les Chrétiens et le monde.* Paris: Gabalda, 1973.

Minucius Felix. *The Octavius.* Translated by Robert Ernest Wallis. ANF IV. 1982.

Miskotte, Kornelis H. *When the Gods are Silent.* Translated by John W. Doberstein. New York: Harper & Row, 1967.

Momigliano, Arnoldo. *On Pagans, Jews, and Christians.* Middletown CT: Wesleyan University Press, 1987.

Montefiore, Claude Goldsmid. *Judaism and St. Paul: Two Essays.* New York: E. P. Dutton, 1915.

Munck, Johannes. "Sephen's Samaritan Background." In *The Acts of the Apostles*, 285-300. The Anchor Bible 31. Garden City NY: Doubleday, 1967.

The Nag Hammadi Library. Edited by James M. Robinson. San Francisco: Harper & Row, 1978.

Nietzsche, Friedrich. *The Birth of Tragedy* and *The Genealogy of Morals*. Translated by Francis Golffing. Garden City NY: Doubleday, 1956.

Nilsson, Martin P. *Greek Folk Religion*. Philadelphia: University of Pennsylnania Press, 1972.

_____. *Greek Piety*. Translated by Herbert Jennings Rose. Oxford: Clarendon Press, 1948.

_____. *A History of Greek Religion*. Translated by F. J. Fielden. Oxford: Clarendon Press, 1949.

Nussbaum, Martha C. *The Fragility of Goodness: Luck and Ethics in Greek Tragedy and Philosophy*. Cambridge: Cambridge University Press, 1986.

O'Meara, John Joseph. *Porphyry's Philosophy from Oracles in Augustine*. Paris: Études Augustiniennes, 1959.

_____. *Porphyry's Philosophy from Oracles in Eusebius's Praeparatio Evangelica and Augustine's Dialogues of Cassiciacum*. Paris: Études Augustiniennes, 1969.

Origen. *Against Celsus (Contra Celsum)*. Translated by Frederick Crombie. ANF IV. 1982.

_____. *Commentary on the Gospel of John*. Translated by Allan Menzies. ANF X. 1980.

_____. *De principiis*. Translated by Frederick Crombie. ANF IV. 1982.

Orose (Orosius). *Histoires (contre les païens)*. Texte établi et traduit par Marie-Pierre Arnaud-lindet. Paris: Les Belles Lettres, 1990.

Orosius. *Historiarum adversus paganos libri vii*. See Orose.

Otto, Rudolf. *The Idea of the Holy*. Translated by John W. Harvey. Oxford: Oxford University Press, 1967.

Ovid. *The Art of Love (Ars amatoria)*. Translated by J. H. Mozley. LCL II. 1969.

_____. *Metamorphoses*. Two volumes. Translated by Frank Justus Miller. LCL III-IV. 1946.

Parke, Herbert William. *Greek Oracles*. London: Hutchinson University Library, 1967.

_____. *Sibyls and Sibylline Prophecy in Classical Antiquity*. London: Routledge, 1988.

Parke, Herbert William, and D. E. W. Wormell. *The Delphic Oracle*. Two volumes. Oxford: Basil Blackwell, 1954.

Parker, Robert. *Miasma: Pollution and Purification in Early Greek Religion*. Oxford: Clarendon Press, 1983.

The Pastor of Hermas. Translated by Frederick Crombie. ANF II. 1983.

Pausanias. *Guide to Greece*. Two volumes. Translated by Peter Levi. London: Penguin Books, 1971.

_____. *Description of Greece*. Five volumes. Translated by W. H. S. Jones. LCL. 1969.

Pelikan, Jaroslav. *Christianity and Classical culture: The Metamorphosis of Natural Theology in the Christian Encounter with Hellenism*. New Haven CT: Yale University Press, 1993.

_____. *Jesus Through the Centuries: His Place in the History of Culture*. New Haven CT: Yale University Press, 1985.

Perowne, Stewart. *Caesars and Saints: The Rise of the Christian State, AD 180–313*. New York: Barnes and Noble, 1962.

Pfeiffer, Robert H. *History of New Testament Times*. New York: Harper & Row, 1949.

Philo. *On Rewards and Punishments (De praemiis et poenis)*. Translated by F. H. Colson. LCL VIII. 1968.

_____. *On the Cherubim (De cherubim)*. Translated by F. H. Colson and G. H. Whitaker. LCL II. 1968.

_____. *On the Special Laws (De specialibus legibus)*. Translated by F. H. Colson. LCL VII. 1968.

_____. *Who is the Heir of Divine Things (Quis rerum divinarum heres)*. Translated by F. H. Colson and G. H. Whitaker. LCL IV. 1968.

Pindar. *Pythian Odes*. Translated by J. E. Sandys. LCL. 1961.

Plato. *Dialogues*. Twelve volumes. Translated by R. G. Bury, H. N. Fowler, W. R. M. Lamb, and Paul Shorey. LCL. 1924–1927.

Pliny the Younger. *Letters*. Translated by Betty Radice. LCL II. 1975.

Plotinus. *The Essential Plotinus*. Translated by Elmer O'Brien. New York: Mentor Books, 1964.

Plutarch. *The E at Delphi (De E apud Delphos)*. Translated by Frank Cole Babbitt. *Moralia* V. LCL. 1984.

_____. *Isis and Osiris (De Iside et Osiride)*. Translated by Frank Cole Babbitt. *Moralia* V. LCL. 1984.

_____. *Lygurgus* and *Solon*. Translated by B. Perrin. In *Parallel Lives*. LCL I. 1914.

_____. *The Obsolescence of Oracles (De defectu oraculorum)*. Translated by Frank Cole Babbitt. *Moralia* V. LCL. 1984.

_____. *On the Delays of the Divine Vengeance (De sera numinis vindicta)*. Translated by Phillip H. De Lacy and Benedict Einarson. *Moralia* VII. LCL. 1984.

_____. *On the Sign of Socrates (De genio Socratis)*. Translated by Phillip H. De Lacy and Benedict Einarson. *Moralia* VII. LCL. 1984.

————. *The Oracles at Delphi no Longer Given in Verse (De pythiae oraculis)*. Translated by Frank Cole Babbitt. *Moralia*. V. LCL. 1984.

————. *Superstition (De superstitione)*. Translated by Frank Cole Babbitt. *Moralia* II. LCL. 1928.

Polybius. *The Histories*. Six volumes. Translated by W. R. Paton. LCL. 1922–1927.

Polycarp. *The Epistle to the Philippians*. Translated by Kirsopp Lake. In *Apostolic Fathers*. LCL I. 1970.

Porphyre. *Vie de Pythagore—Lettre à Marcella*. Texte établi et traduit par Édouard des Places. Paris: Les Belles Lettres, 1982.

Potter, David Stone. *Prophecy and History in the Crisis of the Roman Empire: A Historical Commentary on the Thirteenth Sibylline Oracle*. Oxford: Clarendon Press, 1990.

————. *Prophets and Emperors: Human and Divine Authority from Augustus to Theodosius*. Cambridge: Harvard University Press, 1994.

Prudentius. *A Reply to the Address of Symmachus (Contra orationem Symmachi)*. Two volumes. Translated by H. J. Thomson. LCL. 1949, 1953.

Pseudo-Clementine Literature. *The Recognitions of Clement* and *The Clementine Homilies*. Translated by Thomas Smith. ANF VIII. 1981.

Renan, Ernest. *Oeuvres complètes—Histoire des origines du christianisme—L'Église Chrétienne*. Paris: Calmann-Lévy, 1879.

Reverdin, Olivier. *La religion de la cité platonicienne*. Paris: E. de Boccard, 1945.

Ricciotti, Giuseppe. *The Age of Martyrs: Christianity from Diocletian to Constantine*. Translated by Anthony Bull. New York: Barnes and Noble, 1992.

Rike, R. L. *Apex Omnium: Religion in the Res Gestae of Ammianus*. Berkeley: University of California Press, 1987.

Robin, Leon. *Greek Thought and the Origin of the Scientific Spirit*. Translated by M. R. Dobie. London: Alfred Knopf, 1928.

Robinson, John A. T. "The Baptism of John and the Qumran Community." *Harvard Theological Review* 50 (1957). Also in *Twelve New Testament Studies*. Studies in Biblical Theology 34. London: SCM Press, 1962.

Rohde, Erwin. *Psyche: The Cult of Souls and Belief in Immortality among the Greeks*. Two volumes. Translated by W. B. Hillis. New York: Harper & Row, 1966.

Sandmel, Samuel. *The Genius of Paul: A Study in History*. New York: Schocken Books, 1970.

Schweitzer, Albert. *The Mysticism of Paul the Apostle*. Translated by William Montgomery. New York: Henry Holt and Company, 1931.

_____. The Quest of the Historical Jesus: A Critical Study of Its Progress from Reimarus to Wrede. Translated by William Montgomery. New York: Macmillan, 1968.

Scobie, Charles H. H. John the Baptist. Philadelphia: Fortress Press, 1964.

Scriptores Historiae Augustae. Three volumes. Translated by D. Magie. LCL. 1921–1932.

Sevenster, Jan Nicolaas. Paul and Seneca. Leiden: E. J. Brill, 1961.

Simon, Marcel. La Civilisation de l'antiquité et le christianisme. Paris: Arthaud, 1972.

_____. St. Stephen and the Hellenists in the Primitive Church. London: Longmans, Green, 1958.

Socrates Scholasticus. The Ecclesiastical History (Historia ecclesiastica). Editorial translations and revisions. NPNF-2 II. 1979.

Sordi, Marta. The Christians and the Roman Empire. Norman: University of Oklahoma Press, 1986.

Sozomen. The Ecclesiastical History (Historia ecclesiastica). Editorial translations and revisions. NPNF-2 II. 1979.

Strabo. Geography. Eight volumes. Translated by Horace L. Jones. LCL. 1927–1932.

Strauss, David Frederick. The Life of Jesus Critically Examined. Edited by Peter C. Hodgson. Translated by George Eliot. Philadelphia: Fortress Press, 1972.

Suetonius. The Twelve Caesars. Translated by Robert Graves. London: Penguin Books, 1957.

Sulpitius Severus. The Sacred History (Historia sacra). Translated by Alexander Roberts. NPNF-2 XI. 1982.

Symmachus. See R. H. Barrow.

Tacitus. The Complete Works of Tacitus. Translated by Alfred John Church and William Jackson Brodribb. New York: Modern Library, 1942.

Tatian. Address to the Greeks (Oratio ad Graecos). Translated by J. E. Ryland. ANF II. 1983.

Terry, Milton S. The Sibylline Oracles. Translated by Milton S. Terry. New York: AMS Press, 1973.

Tertullian. Ad nationes. Translated by Peter Holmes. ANF III. 1980.

_____. The Five Books Against Marcion (Adversus Marcionem). Translated by Peter Holmes. ANF III. 1980.

_____. Against Praxeas (Adversus Praxeam). Translated by Peter Holmes. ANF III. 1980.

_____. An Answer to the Jews (Adversus judaeos). Translated By S. Thelwall. ANF III. 1980.

_____. The Apology (Apologeticum). Translated by S. Thelwall. ANF III. 1980.

————. *The Chaplet (De corona).* Translated by S. Thelwall. ANF III. 1980.

————. *De fuga in persecutione.* Translated by S. Thelwall. ANF IV. 1982.

————. *The Martyrdom of Perpetua and Felicitas.* Translated by Robert Ernest Wallis. ANF III. 1980.

————. *On Idolatry (De idolatria).* Translated by S. Thelwall. ANF III. 1980.

————. *On Modesty (De pudicitia).* Translated by S. Thelwall. ANF IV. 1982.

————. *On Patience (De patientia).* Translated by S. Thelwall. ANF III. 1980.

————. *On Repentance (De poenitentia).* Translated by S. Thelwall. ANF III. 1980.

————. *On the Pallium (De pallio).* Translated by S. Thelwall. ANF IV. 1982.

————. *The Prescription against Heretics (De praescriptione haereticorum).* Translated by Peter Holmes. ANF III. 1980.

————. *Scorpiace.* Translated by S. Thelwall. ANF III. 1980.

————. *The Shows (De spectaculis).* Translated by S. Thelwall. ANF III. 1980.

————. *The Soul's Testimony (De testimonio animae).* Translated by S. Thelwall. ANF III. 1980.

————. *To his Wife (Ad uxorem).* Translated by S. Thelwall. ANF IV. 1982.

————. *To Scapula (Ad Scapulam).* Translated by S. Thelwall. ANF III. 1980.

————. *A Treatise on the Soul (De anima).* Translated by Peter Holmes. ANF III. 1980.

Theodoret. *The Ecclesiastical History (Historia ecclesiastica).* Translated by Blomfield Jackson. NPNF-2 III. 1979.

Theognis. *Elegies.* In *Greek Elegy and Iambus.* Translated by J. M. Edmonds. 2 volumes. LCL I. 1931.

Theophilus. *To Autolycus (Ad Autolycos).* Translated by Marcus Dods. ANF II. 1983.

Thucydides. *History of the Peloponnesian War.* Translated by Rex Warner. New York: Penguin Books, 1983.

Ulansey, David. *The Origins of the Mithraic Mysteries: Cosmology and Salvation in the Ancient World.* Oxford: Oxford University Press, 1989.

van der Loos, H. *The Miracles of Jesus.* Leiden: E. J. Brill, 1968.

Varro. *De Lingua Latina.* Two volumes. Translated by Roland G. Kent. LCL. 1951.

Virgil. *Aeneid.* Two volumes. Translated by H. R. Fairclough. LCL. 1935, 1934.

Weiss, Johannes. *Earliest Christianity: A History of the period A.D. 30–150.* Two volumes. Translated by the faculty of Seabury-Western Theological Seminary. New York: Harper Torchbooks, 1959.

Whitehead, Alfred North. *Dialogues of Alfred North Whitehead as Recorded by Lucien Price.* Boston: Little, Brown and Company, 1954.

Wilamowitz-Moellendorff, Ulrich von. *Greek Historical Writing and Apollo*. Translated by Gilbert Murray. Chicago: Ares, 1979.

Wilckens, Ulrich, and Georg Fohrer. Σοφία κτλ.. *Theological Dictionary of the New Testament* 7:465-528. Grand Rapids MI: Eerdmans, 1971.

Wilken, Robert L. "Pagan Criticism of Christianity: Greek Religion and Christian Faith." In *Early Christian Literature and the Classical Intellectual Tradition, in Honorem Robert M. Grant*. Edited by William R. Schoedel and Robert L. Wilken. *Théologie historique* 54. Paris: Beauchesne, 1979.

Wink, Walter. *John the Baptist in the Gospel Tradition*. Cambridge: Cambridge University Press, 1968.

Wrede, William (Wilhelm). *The messianic secret*. Translated by J. C. G. Greig. Greenwood SC: Attic Press, 1971.

Xenophon. *Anabasis*. Translated by Carleton L. Brownson. LCL III. 1968.

_____. *Memorabilia*. Translated by E. C. Marchant. LCL IV. 1968.

_____. *Socrates' Defence (Apology)*. Translated by O. J. Todd. LCL IV. 1968.

Zeller, Eduard. *Outlines of the History of Greek Philosophy*. Translated by L. R. Palmer. Cleveland: World Publishing Co., 1955.

Zosimus. *Historia Nova: The Decline of Rome*. Translated by James J. Buchanan and Harold T. Davis. San Antonio TX: Trinity University Press, 1967.

Index